D0061808

A New Model of the Universe

A
NEW MODEL
OF THE UNIVERSE

 PRINCIPLES OF THE PSYCHOLOGICAL
METHOD IN ITS APPLICATION TO PROB-
LEMS OF SCIENCE, RELIGION, AND ART

P. D. Ouspensky

*Translated from the Russian
under the supervision of the author*

VINTAGE BOOKS

A DIVISION OF RANDOM HOUSE

NEW YORK

VINTAGE BOOKS EDITION, October 1971

All rights reserved under International and Pan-American Copyright
Conventions. Published in the United States by Random House, Inc.,
New York. Originally published by Alfred A. Knopf, Inc., in 1931.

ISBN: 0-394-71524-1

Manufactured in the United States of America

PREFACE TO SECOND EDITION

❀

O NE of the American reviewers of the first edition of the " New Model of the Universe " remarks that two ideas in this book presented particular difficulties for him: the idea of esotericism and the idea of the psychological method.

It cannot be denied that, in general, these ideas are very far from modern thought.

But as there is no sense in reading my book without having some conception of the meaning of these two ideas I will try here to show ways of approach to them.

First of all both ideas need the recognition of the fact that human thought can work on very different levels.

The idea of esotericism is chiefly the idea of *higher mind*. To see clearly what this means we must first of all realise that our ordinary mind (including the mind of a genius) is not the highest possible order of human mind. The human mind can rise to a level almost inconceivable for us, and we can see the results of the work of higher mind, those most accessible to us in the Gospels, and then in Eastern Scriptures: in the Upanishads, in the Mahabharata; in works of art such as the Great Sphinx at Gizeh, and in other memorials though they are few in literature and art. The true valuation of the meaning of these and similar memorials and the realisation of the difference between them and others which have been created by ordinary man, or even by a genius, needs experience, knowledge and a special training of the mind and perception and, perhaps, special faculties not possessed by everyone. In any case nothing can be proven.

So that the first step towards understanding the idea of esotericism is the realisation of the existence of a higher mind, that is, a *human* mind, but one which differs from the ordinary mind as much as, let us say, the mind of an intelligent and educated grown up man differs from the mind of a child of six. A genius is only a " Wunderkind." A man of higher mind possesses a *new knowledge* which ordinary man, however clever and intelligent, cannot possess. This is *esoteric knowledge*.

Whether people of higher mind exist now and have existed always, or whether they appear on earth only at long intervals, is immaterial. The important point is that they exist and that we can come into contact with their ideas and, through these ideas, with esoteric knowledge. This is the essence of the idea of esotericism.

In order to understand what I mean by the " psychological method " it is necessary to realise first that the ordinary human mind, the one we know, can also work on very different levels, and then to find the relation of the " psychological method " to the " esoteric method."

We can see different levels of thought in ordinary life. The most ordinary mind, let us call it the *logical* mind, is sufficient for all the simple problems of life. We can build a house with this mind, obtain food, know that two and two make four, that the " Volga falls into the Caspian Sea " and that " horses eat oats and hay." So that in its proper place the logical mind is quite right and quite useful. But when the logical mind meets with problems which are too big, and when it does not stop before them but starts out to solve them, it inevitably falls down, loses touch with reality and becomes in fact " defective." To this " defective mind " and " defective method " of observation and reasoning humanity owes all superstitions and false theories beginning with the " devil with a goose's foot " and ending with marxism and psychoanalysis.

But a logical mind which knows its limitedness and is strong enough to withstand the temptation to venture into problems beyond its powers and capacities becomes a " psychological mind." The method used by this mind, that is, the psychological method, is first of all a method of distinguishing between different levels of thinking and of realising the fact that perceptions change according to the powers and properties of the perceiving apparatus. The psychological mind can see the limitations of the " logical mind " and the absurdities of the " defective mind " — it can understand the reality of the existence of a higher mind and of esoteric knowledge, and see it in its manifestations. This is impossible for a merely logical mind.

If a man of logical mind hears about esotericism he will at once want to know where the people are who belong to the esoteric circle, who has seen them, and when and how he can see them himself. And if he hears that *for him* this is not possible he will then say that it is all nonsense and that no esoteric circle exists at all. Logically he will be quite right. But psychologically it is clear that with such demands he will not go far in his acquaintance with esotericism. A man has to be prepared, that is, he must realise the limitedness of his own mind and the possibility of the existence of another, better, mind.

Nor will esoteric ideas, that is, ideas coming from higher mind, say much to a logical man. He will ask, for instance: where are the proofs that the Gospels were written by people of higher mind?

Where indeed are the proofs? They are there, everywhere, in every line and in every word, but only for those who have eyes to see and ears to hear. But the logical mind can neither see nor hear beyond a very small radius or the most elementary things.

This limitedness of the logical mind renders it powerless even before quite simple problems of ordinary life once they go beyond the limits of its accustomed scale.

The man of logical mind who demands proofs for everything, at the present time, for instance, looks for the cause of the world economic and political crisis everywhere except where it actually lies.

And even if he were told that the causes of the crisis lie in the existence of the Soviet government in Russia, and in the recognition and *support* of this government by other governments, he would never understand it. He is accustomed to think in a certain way and he is unable to think differently. For him the bolsheviks are a " political party " like any other party, and the Soviet Government is a " government " like any other government. He is unable to see that this is a new phenomenon different from anything he knew before.

Where are the proofs of this? he would ask.

And he will never see that this needs no proofs. Just as no proofs are needed of the inevitable appearance of the plague in his house when there is plague in the house opposite against which no steps whatever have been taken on the spot. But a man of logical mind cannot see that Soviet Russia is a plague-house. He prefers to believe in the " biggest social experiment in history," or in the " evolution of bolshevism," or in " bolsheviks giving up propaganda "; as though plague can " give up " propaganda and as though negotiations and treaties and " pacts " with plague were possible. In this particular case, of course, the man of logical mind errs almost consciously because he cannot resist the temptation to take advantage of the opportunity of snatching a profit out of the plague-house. The inevitable result is that the plague appears in his house. But even when it appears the man of logical mind still does not want to understand *where* it has come from and demands " proofs."

But " proofs " are by no means always necessary in order to accept or to deny a given proposition. There are " psychological proofs " which mean much more than facts because facts can lie and psychological proofs cannot lie. But one must be able to feel them.

The term " psychological method " comes from " psychological proofs." On the basis of these proofs it is possible to see the defects of logical think-ing in regions inaccessible to it or in questions too big for it, and, in exactly the same way, it is often possible to see the direction in which lie probable solutions to problems which seem, or appear to be, insoluble. But this does not mean that with the help of the psychological method it will always be possible to find solutions to problems too difficult or too big for the logical mind. Real solutions can come only from higher mind possessing higher knowledge, that is, from esotericism. This is the difference between the psy-chological method and the esoteric method.

Let us try to imagine the four methods of observation and reasoning in relation to the room in which I am writing this. The defective method is based upon a glance at the room through the keyhole or through a narrow slit and its characteristic feature is the certainty that what is seen through the keyhole or the slit represents all there is and that there is and can be nothing else in it except what is visible in this way. Given a certain imagination and a tendency towards superstition the defective method can make something very strange or monstrous out of an ordinary room.

The logical method is based upon a glance at the room from one definite spot, at one definite angle, and usually without enough light. Too big a confidence in it and the defence of this angle of vision makes the logical method defective.

The psychological method compared with the two first would be like a view of the room in daylight, moving about in it in various directions, knowing the objects in it and so on. It is quite clear that it is possible to learn more about the room in this way than by the logical method, and that it is possible to find many mistakes and wrong conclusions of the defective method.

The esoteric method of approach to the study of the room would include not only the whole room with everything it contains but the whole house, all the people in it with all their relationships and their occupations; and further, the position of the house in the street, of the street in the town, of the town in the country, of the country on the earth, of the earth in the solar system and so on. The esoteric method is limited by nothing and always connects every given thing, however small it may be, with the whole.

Examples of " psychological," " logical " and " defective " thinking abound around us. Occasionally we meet with the psychological method in science. In psychology itself the " psychological method " leads inevitably to the recognition of the fact that human consciousness is merely a particular instance of consciousness and that an intelligence exists which is many times superior to the ordinary human intelligence. And only a psychology which starts from this proposition and has this proposition as its foundation can be called scientific. In other spheres of knowledge psychological thinking lies at the root of all real discoveries, but it usually does not keep long. I mean that as soon as ideas which have been found and established by the psychological method become everybody's property and begin to be looked upon as permanent and accepted they become logical and, in their application to phenomena of a greater size, *defective*. For instance, Darwin — his discoveries and his ideas were the product of psychological thinking of the very highest quality. But they had already become logical with his followers and, later on, they became undoubtedly defective, because they stood in the way of the free development of thought.

This is exactly what Ibsen's Dr. Stockmann meant when he spoke about *ageing truths*.

There are truths, he says, which have attained such an age that they have really outlived themselves. And when a truth becomes as old as this it is on the best way to become a lie. . . . Yes, yes, you may believe me or not, but truths are not such long lived Methuselahs as people imagine them to be. A normally constructed truth lives as a rule, let us say, fifteen, sixteen, at the most twenty, years, seldom longer. But such ageing truths become terribly lean and tough. And the majority, having first of all been created by them, later recommends them to humanity as healthy spiritual food. But I can assure you there is not much nourishment in such food. I must speak about this as a doctor. All the truths belonging to the majority are like ancient rancid bacon or like rotten green ham; and from them comes all the moral scurvy which is eating itself into the life of the people around us.

The idea of the degeneration of accepted truths cannot be expressed better. Truths that become old become decrepit and unreliable; sometimes they may be kept going artificially for a certain time, but there is no life in them. This explains why reverting to old ideas, when people become disappointed in new ideas, does not help much. Ideas can be too old.

But in other cases old ideas may be more psychological than the new. New ideas can just as easily be too logical and therefore defective.

We can see many curious examples of the conflict between psychological and logical thinking, which then of necessity becomes defective, in various "intellectual" reforms of old habits and customs. Take, for instance, reforms in weights and measures. Weights and measures which have been created through the centuries, and which are different in different countries, appear at the first glance to have taken one or another form by chance and to be too complicated. But in reality they are always based on one definite principle. In each separate class of things or material to be measured a different divisor (or multiplier) is used, sometimes very complicated as in the English system of weights — 16 ounces to a pound, 14 pounds to a stone for comparatively small weights, and for larger weights 28 pounds to a quarter, 112 pounds to a hundredweight, 20 hundredweight to a ton; or, for instance, a simple multiplier like 8 in the Russian measurement of grain which is never repeated in relation to anything else. This is real psychological method created by life and experience because, thanks to different coefficients in different cases a man making mental calculations involving the measurements of several different materials cannot confuse either objects of different denominations or the measures of different countries (should he have to deal with the measures of different countries) because each order of multiplier itself tells him *what* is being measured and with what measure. Those who do not like these old complicated systems are the school-teachers, as is well known, the most logical people in the world. Different weights and measures seem to them unnecessarily confusing.

In 1793 the Convention decided to replace the existing French measures by one " natural " measure. After lengthy and complicated " scientific " activity and research such a measure was acknowledged as being one tenmillionth of one fourth part of the earth's meridian, which was called a metre.

There is no direct proof of it, but I am sure that the idea of a " natural " measure and the metric system was born in the minds of teachers of arithmetic, because it is so much easier to divide and multiply everything by ten, having done away with all other divisors and multipliers. But for all ordinary necessities of life the metric system of weights and measures is far less practical than the old systems, and it weakens to a considerable degree a man's ability to make simple mental calculations, which is very marked in countries where the metric system has been adopted. Everyone who has ever been in France remembers the French shopkeepers' pencil and paper on which is often written $\frac{5}{10}$, but there are very few who know that this is one of the conquests of the Great French Revolution.

Exactly the same thing takes place in attempts to change the old orthography. All orthographies must certainly be adapted to new requirements, let us say, once in a hundred years, and this takes place of itself, in a natural way. But violent reforms and the introduction of so-called "phonetic" spelling (only so-called because real phonetic spelling is impossible in any language) generally upsets the entire trend of the normal development of a language, and very soon people begin to write in different ways and then to pronounce in different ways, that is, to adapt pronunciation to the new spelling. This is the result of the application of the logical method to a problem which goes beyond the limits of its possible action. And it is quite clear why: the process of reading and writing is not a process of reading and writing *letters*. It is a process of reading and writing *words and sentences*. Consequently, the more words differ from one another in their form and appearance the easier does the process of reading and writing proceed, and the more they resemble one another (as is inevitable in " phonetic " spelling) the slower and the more difficult is the process of reading and writing. It is quite possible that it is easier *to teach* " phonetic " spelling than the normal spelling, but for the rest of his life the man who has been taught in this way is left with a most unsatisfactory instrument for learning other peoples' ideas and for expressing his own.

This is exactly what is happening now in Russia. Just before the revolution a *commission of teachers* (there is no doubt of it in this case) under the presidency of the Rector of Moscow University, was formed for the investigation of ways of reforming spelling. This commission worked out a very absurd " new spelling " absolutely unsuitable for the Russian language, breaking all principles of grammar and contradicting all the laws of the natural development of the language. This " spelling " would never have been accepted if the Academy and the literary circles had had time to express their opinion on it, that is, if the revolution had not occurred just at that time. But having got into power the bolsheviks introduced this new " spelling." And under its influence the language at once began to deteriorate and to lose its strength and clarity. If " phonetic " spelling were to be introduced into English speaking countries the English language would very quickly disappear and twenty or thirty varieties of " pidgin-English " would take its place.

Another interesting example of the logical method as opposed to the psychological, one which is now almost generally accepted in several countries, is the co-education of boys and girls. Logically co-education seems to be quite right, but psychologically it is absolutely wrong, because by this system both boys and girls alike lose many of their characteristic features, particularly those which should be developed in them, and they both acquire other features which they never should have. And besides, both of them learn to lie immeasurably more than they could learn even in the best of the old kind of schools.

Let us take other examples. What could be more logical than the Holy Inquisition with its tortures and burning of heretics; or bolshevism, which began by destroying schools, universities and technical institutes, in this way cutting off its own supply of trained specialists necessary for the new industrialisation which has been so much advertised? If this is not so then why do the bolsheviks need foreign engineers? In this respect Russia for a long time lived on its own resources. And further, what can be more logical and, at the same time, more unsuccessful than all possible prohibitions, like the American experiment in prohibiting alcoholic drinks? And what can be easier? Any fool, if he has the power in his hands, can find something to prohibit and in this way show his vigilance and his good intentions. All this is the result of the logical method. The danger of the logical method in all possible spheres of life lies in the fact that at the first glance it is the easiest and the most effective way.

The psychological method is much more difficult and, in addition, it is often very disappointing because, by following the psychological method a man often sees that he does not understand anything and does not know what to do. Whereas by following the logical method he always understands everything and always knows what to do.

1934

PREFATORY NOTE

❈

WHAT the author found in the course of the travels referred to in the "Introduction," and later, particularly during the time from 1915 *to* 1919, will be described in another book. The present book was begun and practically completed before 1914. But all, even what has already been published separately (*The Fourth Dimension, Superman, The Symbolism of the Tarot* and *What is Yoga?*), has since been revised and more closely connected together. The author could add but very little to the second part of chapter X (*A New Model of the Universe*) in spite of all that has appeared during the last years in the way of "new physics." But in the present book the chapter begins with a general outline of the development of the new ideas in physics, constituting the first part of the chapter. Of course this outline does not pursue the independent aim of acquainting the readers with all existing theories and with all existing literature on the subjects mentioned. Similarly, in other chapters in which the author has had to refer to literature on the questions he touched, it has never been his intention to exhaust all this literature or to indicate its main currents or the principal works or the latest ideas. All he has wished to do in these cases has been to show examples of one trend of thought or another.

The order of the chapters in the present book does not always correspond to the order in which they were originally written, because many things were written simultaneously and serve as an explanation for one another. But each chapter is dated with the year in which it was begun and with the year in which it was revised or finished.

London, 1930

Contents

CHAPTER III : SUPERMAN

CHAPTER IV : CHRISTIANITY AND THE NEW TESTAMENT

CHAPTER V: THE SYMBOLISM OF THE TAROT   186

I

II

ACKNOWLEDGMENTS

THE PUBLISHERS *wish to acknowledge the following permissions that have been granted to them for quotations in this work, and owe their thanks*

To THE CAMBRIDGE UNIVERSITY PRESS *for permission to use extracts from Professor A. S. Eddington's book* Space, Time and Gravitation;

To Messrs. ALLEN & UNWIN, LTD., *for extracts from their translation of Maeterlinck's* The Life of the White Ant;

To THE OXFORD UNIVERSITY PRESS *for an extract from Alexis Tolstoy appearing in* The Oxford Book of Russian Verse, *and permission to use their text for the Rossetti quotation; and*

To Messrs. METHUEN & Co., LTD., *for permission to quote from the translation of Dr. Einstein's* Relativity.

A New Model of the Universe

INTRODUCTION

❋

THERE exist moments in life, separated by long intervals of time, but linked together by their inner content and by a certain singular sensation peculiar to them. Several such moments always recur to my mind together, and I feel then that it is these that have determined the chief trend of my life.

The year 1890 or 1891. An evening preparation class in the Second Moscow "Gymnasium." [1] A large class-room lit by kerosene lamps with large shades. Yellow cupboards along the walls. Boarders in holland blouses, stained with ink, are bending over their desks. Some are immersed in their lessons, some are reading under their desks a forbidden novel by Dumas or Gaboriau, some are whispering to their neighbours. But outwardly they all look alike. At the master's desk sits the master on duty, a tall lanky German, "Giant Stride," in his uniform — a blue tailcoat with gold buttons. Through an open door another such preparation class is seen in the adjoining class-room.

I am a schoolboy in the second or third "class." But instead of Zeifert's Latin grammar, entirely consisting of exceptions which I sometimes see in my dreams to this day, or Evtushevsky's "Problems," with the peasant who went to town to sell hay, and the cistern to which three pipes lead, I have before me Malinin and Bourenin's "Physics." I have borrowed this book from one of the older boys and am reading it greedily and enthusiastically, overcome now by rapture, now by terror, at the mysteries which are opening before me. All round me walls are crumbling, and horizons infinitely remote and incredibly beautiful stand revealed. It is as though threads, previously unknown and unsuspected, begin to reach out and bind things together. For the first time in my life my world emerges from chaos. Everything becomes connected, forming an orderly and harmonious whole. I understand, I link together, a series of phenomena which were disconnected and appeared to have nothing in common.

But what am I reading?

I am reading the chapter on levers. And all at once a multitude of simple things which I knew as independent and having nothing in common

---

[1] "Gymnasiums" were government "classical" schools containing eight classes, i.e., forms, for boys from ten to eighteen.

become connected and united into a great whole. A stick pushed under a stone, a penknife, a shovel, a see-saw, all these things are one and the same, they are all " levers." In this idea there is something both terrifying and alluring. How is it that I did not know it? Why has nobody spoken to me about it? Why am I made to learn a thousand useless things and am not told about " this "? All that I am discovering is so wonderful and so miraculous that I become more and more enraptured, and am gripped by a certain presentiment of further revelations awaiting me. It is as though I already feel the *unity of all* and am overcome with awe at the sensation.

I can no longer keep to myself all the emotions which thrill me. I want to try to share them with my neighbour at the desk, a great friend of mine with whom I often have breathless talks. In a whisper I begin to tell him of my discoveries. But I feel that my words do not convey anything to him and that I cannot express what I feel. My friend listens to me absent-mindedly, evidently not hearing half of what I say. I see this and feel hurt and want to stop talking to him. But the tall German at the master's desk has already noticed that we are " talking " and that I am showing something to my friend under the desk. He hurries over to us and the next moment my beloved " Physics " is in his stupid and unsympathetic hands.

·" Who gave you this book? You can understand nothing in it anyway. And I am sure you have not prepared your lessons."

My " Physics " is on the master's desk.

I hear round me ironical whispers and comments that Ouspensky reads physics. But I don't care. I shall have the " Physics " again to-morrow; and the tall German is all made up of large and small levers!

Year after year passes by.

It is the year 1906 or 1907. The editorial office of the Moscow daily paper *The Morning*. I have just received the foreign papers, and I have to write an article on the forthcoming Hague Conference. French, German, English, Italian papers. Phrases, phrases, sympathetic, critical, ironical, blatant, pompous, lying and, worst of all, utterly automatic, phrases which have been used a thousand times and will be used again on entirely different, perhaps contradictory, occasions. I have to make a survey of all these words and opinions, pretending to take them seriously, and then, just as seriously, to write something on my own account. But what can I say? It is all so tedious. Diplomats and all kinds of statesmen will gather together and talk, papers will approve or disapprove, sympathise or not sympathise. Then everything will be as it was, or even worse.

It is still early, I say to myself: perhaps something will come into my head later.

Pushing aside the papers I open a drawer in my desk. The whole desk is crammed with books with strange titles, *The Occult World, Life after Death, Atlantis and Lemuria, Dogme et Rituel de la Haute Magie, Le Temple de Satan, The Sincere Narrations of a Pilgrim*, and the like. These books and I have been inseparable for a whole month, and the world of Hague

Conferences and leading articles becomes more and more vague, foreign and unreal to me.

I open one of the books at random, feeling that my article will not be written to-day. Well, it can go to the devil! Humanity will lose nothing if there is one article the less on the Hague Conference.

All these talks about a universal peace are only Maniloff's dreams about building a bridge across the pond.[2] Nothing can ever come out of it, first of all because the people who start conferences and those who are going to debate on peace will sooner or later start a war. Wars do not begin by themselves, neither do " peoples " begin them, however much they are accused of it. It is just those men with their good intentions who are the obstacle to peace. But is it possible to expect that they will ever understand this? Has anybody ever understood his own worthlessness?

A great many wicked thoughts occur to me about the Hague Conference, but I realise that none of them are printable. The idea of the Hague Conference comes from very high sources; therefore if one is to write about it at all, one must write sympathetically, especially as even those of our papers which are generally the most suspicious and critical of all that comes from the government disapprove only of the attitude of Germany to the conference. The editor would therefore never pass what I might write if I say all that I think. And if by some miracle he were to pass it, it would never be read by anybody. The paper would be seized in the streets by the police, and both the editor and I would have to make a very long journey. This prospect does not appeal to me in the least. What is the use of attempting to expose lies when people like them and live in them? It is their own affair. But I am tired of lying. There are enough lies without mine.

But here, in these books, there is a strange flavour of truth. I feel it particularly strongly now, because for so long I have held myself in, have kept myself within artificial " materialistic " bounds, have denied myself all dreams about things that could not be held within these bounds. I had been living in a desiccated and sterilised world, with an infinite number of taboos imposed on my thought. And suddenly these strange books broke down all the walls round me, and made me think and dream about things of which for a long time I had feared to think and dream. Suddenly I began to find a strange meaning in old fairy-tales; woods, rivers, mountains, became living beings; mysterious life filled the night; with new interests and new expectations I began to dream again of distant travels; and I remembered many extraordinary things that I had heard about old monasteries. Ideas and feelings which had long since ceased to interest me suddenly began to assume significance and interest. A deep meaning and many subtle allegories appeared in what only yesterday seemed to be naïve popular fantasy or crude superstition. And the greatest mystery and the greatest miracle was that the thought became possible that death may not exist, that those who have gone may not have vanished altogether, but exist somewhere and somehow, and that per-

---

[2] Maniloff, a sentimental landowner in Gogol's *Dead Souls*.

haps I may see them again. I have become so accustomed to think " scientifically " that I am afraid even to imagine that there may be something else beyond the outer covering of life. I feel like a man condemned to death, whose companions have been hanged and who has already become reconciled to the thought that the same fate awaits him; and suddenly he hears that his companions are alive, that they have escaped and that there is hope also for him. And he fears to believe this, because it would be so terrible if it proved to be false, and nothing would remain but prison and the expectation of execution.

Yes, I know that all these books about " life after death " are very naïve. But they lead somewhere; there is something behind them, something I had approached before; but it frightened me then, and I fled from it to the bare and arid desert of " materialism."

The " Fourth Dimension! "

This is the reality which I dimly felt long ago, but which escaped me then. Now I see my way; I see my work, and I see where it may lead.

The Hague Conference, the newspapers, it is all so far from me. Why is it that people do not understand that they are only shadows, only silhouettes, of themselves, and that the whole of life is only a shadow, only a silhouette, of some other life?

Years go by.

Books, books, books. I read, I find, I lose, I find again, again I lose. At last a certain whole becomes formed in my mind. I see the unbroken line of thought and knowledge which passes from century to century, from age to age, from country to country, from one race to another; a line deeply hidden beneath layers of religions and philosophies which are, in fact, only distortions and perversions of the ideas belonging to the line. I see an extensive literature full of significance which was quite unknown to me until recently, but which, as now becomes quite clear to me, feeds the philosophy we know, although it is scarcely mentioned in the text-books on the history of philosophy. And I am amazed now that I did not know it before, that there are so few who have even heard about it. Who knows, for instance, that an ordinary pack of playing-cards contains a profound and harmonious philosophical system? This is so entirely forgotten that it seems almost new.

I decide to write, to tell of all I have found. And at the same time I see that it is perfectly possible to make the ideas of this hidden thought agree with the data of exact knowledge, and I realise that the " fourth dimension " is the bridge that can be thrown across between the old and the new knowledge. And I see and find ideas of the fourth dimension in ancient symbolism, in the Tarot cards, in the images of Indian gods, in the branches of a tree, and in the lines of the human body.

I collect material, select quotations, prepare summaries, with the idea of showing the peculiar inner connection which I now see between methods of thinking that ordinarily appear separate and independent. But in the midst of this work, when everything is made ready, everything takes shape, I suddenly begin to feel a chill of doubt and weariness creeping over me. Well, one more book will be written, but even now, when I am only beginning to write it, I know how it will end. I know the limit beyond which it is impossible to go. The work stands still. I cannot make myself write about the limitless possibilities of knowledge when for myself I already see the limit. The old methods are no good; some other methods are necessary. People who think that something can be attained by their own efforts are as blind as those who are utterly ignorant of the possibilities of the new knowledge.

Work on the book is abandoned.

Months go by, and I become completely absorbed in strange experiments which carry me far beyond the limits of the known and possible.

Frightening and fascinating sensations. Everything becomes alive! There is nothing dead or inanimate. I feel the beating of the pulse of life. I " see " Infinity. Then everything vanishes. But each time I say to myself afterwards that this *has been* and, therefore, things exist that are different from the ordinary. But so little remains; I remember so vaguely what I have experienced; I can tell myself only an infinitesimal part of what has been. And I can control nothing, direct nothing. Sometimes *this* comes, sometimes it does not. Sometimes only horror comes, sometimes a blinding light. Sometimes a little remains in the memory, sometimes nothing at all. Sometimes much is understood, new horizons are disclosed, but only for a moment. And these moments are so short that I can never be certain whether I have seen anything or not. Light flares up and dies before I have time to tell myself what I have seen. And each day, each time, it becomes more and more difficult to kindle this light. It often seems that the first experiment gave me everything, that afterwards there has been nothing but a repetition of the same things in my consciousness, only a reflection. I know that this is not true and that each time I receive something new. But it is difficult to get rid of this thought. And it increases the sensation of helplessness that I feel in the face of the wall behind which I can look for a moment, but never long enough to account to myself for what I see. Further experiments only emphasise my powerlessness to get hold of the mystery. Thought does not grasp, does not convey, what is at times clearly felt. Thought is too slow, too short. There are no words and no forms to convey what one sees and knows in such moments. And it is impossible to fix these moments, to arrest them, to make them longer, more obedient to the will. There is no possibility of remembering what has been found and understood, and later repeating it to oneself. It disappears as dreams disappear. Perhaps it is all nothing but a dream.

Yet at the same time this is not so. I know it is not a dream. In these experiments and experiences there is a taste of reality which cannot be imitated and about which one cannot make a mistake. I know that *all this is there*. I have become convinced of it. *Unity exists*. And I know already that it is infinite, orderly, animated and conscious. But how to link " what is above " with " what is below "?

I feel that a method is necessary. There is something which one must know before starting on experiments. And more and more often I begin to think that this method can be given only by those Eastern schools of Yogis and Sufis about which one reads and hears, *if such schools exist* and if they can be penetrated. My thought concentrates on this. The question of *school* and of a method acquires for me a predominant significance, though it is still not clear and is connected with too many fantasies and ideas based on very doubtful theories. But one thing I see clearly, that alone, by myself, I can do nothing.

And I decide to start on a long journey with the idea of searching for those schools or for the people who may show me the way to them.

1912

*   *

*

My way lay to the East. My previous journeys had convinced me that there still remained much in the East that had long ceased to exist in Europe. At the same time I was not at all sure that I should find precisely what I wanted to find. And above all I could not say with certainty *what* exactly I should search for. The question of " schools " (I am speaking, of course, of " esoteric " or " occult " schools) still contained much that was not clear. I did not doubt that schools existed. But I could not say whether it was necessary to assume the *physical* existence of such schools on earth. Sometimes it seemed to me that true schools could only exist on another plane and that we could approach them only when in special states of consciousness, without actual change of place or conditions. In that case my journey became purposeless. Yet it seemed to me that there might be traditional methods of approach to esotericism still preserved in the East.

The question of schools coincided with the question of esoteric succession. Sometimes it seemed to me possible to admit an uninterrupted historical succession. At other times it seemed to me that only " mystical " succession was possible, that is, that the line of succession on earth breaks, goes out of our field of vision. There remain only traces of it: works of art, literary memorials, myths, religions. Then, perhaps only after a long interval of time, the same causes which once created esoteric thought begin to work once more, and once more there begins the process of " collecting knowledge," *schools* are created and the ancient teaching emerges from its hidden form. This would mean that during the intermediary period there could be no full or rightly organised schools, but only imitation schools or schools that preserve the letter of the old law, petrified in fixed forms.

However, this did not deter me. I was ready to accept whatever the facts which I hoped to find should show me.

There was yet another question which occupied me before my journey and during the first part of it.

Should one and can one try to do something here and now with an obviously insufficient knowledge of methods, ways and possible results?

In asking this I had in mind various methods of breathing, dieting, fasting, exercises of the attention and imagination and, above all, of overcoming oneself at moments of passivity or lassitude.

In answering this question voices in me were divided:

" It does not matter what one does, only one has to do something," said one voice; " but one should not sit and wait for something to come to one of itself."

" The whole point is precisely to do nothing," said another voice, " until one knows surely and definitely what should be done to attain a definite aim. If one begins to do something without knowing exactly what is necessary for what object, this knowledge will never come. The result will be the ' work on oneself ' of various ' occult ' and ' theosophical ' books, that is, make-believe."

And listening to these two voices within me I was unable to decide which of them was right.

Ought I to try or ought I to wait? I understood that in many cases it was useless *to try*. How can one *try* to paint a picture? How can one *try* to read Chinese? One must first study and know, that is, be able to do it. At the same time I realised that in these last arguments there was much desire to evade difficulties or at least to postpone them. However, the fear of amateurish attempts at "work on oneself" outweighed the rest. I said to myself that in the direction I wanted to go it was impossible to go blindly, that one must see or know where one was going. Besides, I did not even wish for any changes in myself. I was going in search of something. If in the midst of this process of search I myself began to change, I should perhaps be satisfied with something quite different from what I wanted to search for. It seemed to me then that this is precisely what often happens to people on the road of "occult" search. They begin to try various methods on themselves and put so much expectation, so much labour and effort, into these attempts that in the end they take the subjective results of their efforts for the results of their search. I wanted to avoid this at all costs.

But a quite different and almost unexpected aim to my journey began to outline itself from the very first months of my travels.

In almost every place I came to, and even during the journey, I met people who were interested in the same ideas that interested me, who spoke the same language as I spoke, people between whom and myself there was instantly set up an entirely distinctive understanding. How far this special understanding would lead, of course I was unable to say at that time, but in the conditions and with the material of ideas I then possessed, even such understanding seemed almost miraculous. Some of these people knew one another, others did not. And I felt that I was establishing a link between them, was, as it were, stretching out a thread which, according to the original plan of my journey, should go round the world. There was something which drew me and which was full of significance in these encounters. To every new man I met I spoke of others I had met earlier, and sometimes I knew beforehand people I was to meet later.

St. Petersburg, London, Paris, Genoa, Cairo, Colombo, Galle, Madras, Benares, Calcutta, were connected by invisible threads of common hopes and common expectation. And the more people I met, the more this side of my journey took hold of me. It was as though there grew out of it some secret society, having no name, no form, no conventional laws, but closely connected by community of ideas and language. I often thought of what I myself had written in *Tertium Organum* about people of a " new race." And it seemed to me that I had not been far from the truth, and that there is actually carried on the process of the formation, if not of a new race, at least of some new category of men, for whom there exist different values than for other people.

In connection with these thoughts I again came to the necessity of putting in order and arranging systematically that which among the whole of our knowledge leads to " new facts." And I decided that after my return I would resume the abandoned work on my book, but with new aims and with new intentions.

At the same time I began to make certain connections in India and in Ceylon, and it seemed to me that in a short time I should be able to say that I had found concrete facts.

But there came one brilliant sunny morning when, on my way back from India, I stood on the deck of the steamer going from Madras to Colombo and rounding Ceylon from the south. This was the third time I had approached Ceylon, during this period, on every occasion from a different direction. The flat shore with blue hills in the distance revealed simultaneously what could never be seen when one was there on the spot. Through my glasses I could see the toy railway going south and all at once several toy stations, which appeared to be almost side by side. I even knew their names: Kollupitiya, Bambalapitiya, Wellawatta, and others.

The approach to Colombo stirred me. I was to know there: first, whether I should again find the man I had met before my last trip to India and whether he would repeat the proposal he had made me regarding my meeting certain Yogis, and secondly where I should go next: should it be back to Russia, or further on to Burma, Siam, Japan and America.

But I was not expecting what actually met me.

The first word I heard on landing was: *war*.

There began then strange muddled days. Everything was thrown into confusion. But I already felt that my search in one sense was ended and I understood then why I had all the time felt that it was necessary to hurry.

A new cycle was beginning. And it was as yet impossible to say what it would be like and to what it would lead. One thing only was clear from the first, that what was possible yesterday became impossible to-day. All the mud was rising from the bottom of life. All the cards became mixed. All the threads were broken.

There remained only what I had established for myself. Nobody could take that from me. And it alone could lead me further.

1914–1930

Chapter I

ESOTERICISM AND MODERN THOUGHT

❊

THE IDEA of a knowledge which surpasses all ordinary human knowledge, and is inaccessible to ordinary people, but which exists somewhere and belongs to somebody, permeates the whole history of the thought of mankind from the most remote periods. And according to certain memorials of the past a knowledge quite different from ours formed the essence and content of human thought at those times when, according to other opinions, man differed very little, or did not differ at all, from animals.

"Hidden knowledge" is therefore sometimes called "ancient knowledge." But of course this does not explain anything. It must, however, be noted that all religions, all myths, all beliefs, all popular heroic legends of all peoples and all countries are based on the recognition of the existence sometime and somewhere of a knowledge far superior to the knowledge which we possess or can possess. And to a considerable degree the content of all religions and myths consists of symbolic forms which represent attempts to transmit the idea of this hidden knowledge.

On the other hand, nothing demonstrates so clearly the weakness of human thought or human imagination as existing ideas as to the content of hidden knowledge. The word, the concept, the idea, the expectation, exist, but there are no definite concrete forms of percept connected with this idea. And the idea itself has very often to be dug out with great difficulty from beneath mountains of lies, both intentional and unintentional, from deception and self-deception and from naïve attempts to present in intelligible forms adopted from ordinary life that which in its very nature can have no resemblance to them.

The work of finding traces of ancient or hidden knowledge, or even hints of its existence, resembles the work of archæologists looking for traces of some ancient forgotten civilisation and finding them buried beneath several strata of cemeteries left by peoples who have since lived in that place, separated possibly by thousands of years and unaware of one another's existence.

But on every occasion that an investigator comes upon the attempts to express in one way or another the content of hidden knowledge he invariably sees the same thing, namely, the striking poverty of human imagination in the face of this idea.

Humanity in the face of the idea of hidden knowledge reminds one of the people in fairy-tales who are promised by some goddess, fairy or magician that they will be given whatever they want on condition that they say *exactly* what they want. And usually in fairy-tales people do not know what to ask for. In some cases the fairy or magician offers to grant as many as three wishes, but even this is of no use. In all fairy-tales of all periods and peoples, men get hopelessly lost when confronted with the question of what they want, and what they would like to have. They are quite unable to determine and formulate their wish. Either at that minute they remember only some small unimportant desire, or they express several contradictory wishes, which cancel one another; or else, as in the fairy-tale of " The Fisherman and the Fish," [1] they are not able to keep within the bounds of possible things and, always wishing for more and more, they end by attempting to subjugate higher forces, not being conscious of the poverty of their own powers and capacities. And so again they fall, again they lose all that they have acquired, because they themselves do not clearly know what they want.

In a jocular form this idea of the difficulty of formulating desires and of men's rare success in it is set forth in an Indian tale:

A beggar, who was born blind, led a single life, and lived upon the charity of his neighbours, was long and incessantly assailing a particular deity with his prayers. The latter was at last moved by this continual devotion, but fearing that his votary might not be easily satisfied, took care to bind him by an oath to ask for no more than a single blessing.

It puzzled the beggar for a long while, but his professional ingenuity at last came to his aid.

" I hasten to obey the behest, generous Lord! " quoth he, " and this solitary boon is all I ask at thy hands, namely, that I should live to see the grand-child of my grand-child playing in a seven-storied palace and helped by a train of attendants to his meal of milk and rice, out of a golden cup." And he concluded by expressing his hope that he had not exceeded the limit of a single wish vouchsafed to him.

The deity saw that he had been fairly done, for though single in form, the boon asked for comprised the manifold blessings of health, wealth, long life, restoration of sight, marriage and progeny. For very admiration of his devotee's astuteness and consummate tact, if not in fulfilment of his plighted word, the deity felt bound to grant him all he asked for.[2]

In the legend of Solomon (1 Kings, 3. 5–15) we find an explanation of these tales, an explanation of what it is that men can receive if they only know what to wish for.

---

[1] A fairy-tale in verse by Pushkin, very popular in Russia and based upon an old fairy story.
[2] 184 *Indian Tales*, published by G. A. Natesan and Co. (Madras, 1920), p. 134.

In Gibeon the Lord appeared to Solomon in a dream by night; and God said, Ask what I shall give thee.

And Solomon said . . . I am but a little child: I know not how to go out or how to come in.

And thy servant is in the midst of thy people . . .

Give therefore thy servant an understanding heart to judge thy people, that I may discern between good and bad . . .

And the speech pleased the Lord that Solomon had asked this thing.

And God said unto him, Because thou hast asked this thing and hast not asked for thyself long life; neither hast asked riches for thyself, nor hast asked the life of thine enemies; but hast asked for thyself understanding . . .

Behold, I have done according to thy words; lo, I have given thee a wise and understanding heart; so that there was none like thee before thee, neither after thee shall any arise like unto thee.

And I have also given thee that which thou hast not asked, both riches and honour . . . and I will lengthen thy days.

The idea of hidden knowledge and the possibility of finding it after a long and arduous search is the content of the legend of the Holy Grail.

The Holy Grail, the cup from which Christ drank (or the platter from which Christ ate) at the Last Supper and in which Joseph of Arimathea collected Christ's blood, was according to a mediæval legend brought to England. To those who saw it the Grail gave immortality and eternal youth. But it had to be guarded only by people perfectly pure in heart. If anyone approached it who was not pure enough, the Grail disappeared. On this followed the legend of the quest of the Holy Grail by chaste knights. Only the three knights of King Arthur succeeded in seeing the Grail.

Many tales and myths, those of the Golden Fleece, the Fire-Bird (of Russian folklore), Aladdin's lamp, and those about secret riches and treasures guarded by dragons or other monsters, serve to express the relation of man to hidden knowledge.

The " philosopher's stone " of alchemists also symbolised hidden knowledge.

All views on life are divided into two categories on this point. There are conceptions of the world which are entirely based on the idea that we live in a house in which there is some secret, some buried treasure, some hidden store of precious things, which somebody at some time may find and which occasionally has in fact been found. And then from this point of view, the whole aim and the whole meaning of life consist in the search for this treasure, because without it all the rest has no value. And there are other theories and systems in which there is no idea of " treasure-trove," for which all alike is visible and clear, or all alike invisible and obscure.

If in our time theories of the latter kind, that is, those which deny the possibility of hidden knowledge, have become predominant, we must not forget that they have become so only very recently and only among a small, although a very noisy, part of humanity. The very great majority of people still believe in " fairy-tales " and believe that there are moments when fairy-tales become reality.

But it is man's misfortune that at those moments when something new and unknown becomes possible he does not know what he wants, and the opportunity which suddenly appeared as suddenly disappears.

Man is conscious of being surrounded by the wall of the Unknown, and at the same time he believes that he can get through the wall and that others have got through it; but he cannot imagine, or imagines very vaguely, what there may be behind this wall. He does not know what he would like to find there or what it means to possess *knowledge*. It does not even occur to him that a man can be in different relations to the Unknown.

The Unknown is not known. But *the Unknown* may be of different kinds, just as it is in ordinary life. A man may not have *precise* knowledge of a particular thing, but he may think and make judgements and suppositions about it, he may conjecture and foresee it to such a degree of correctness and accuracy that his actions and expectations in relation to what is unknown in the particular case may be almost right. In exactly the same way, in regard to the Great Unknown, a man may be in different relations to it; he may make more correct or less correct suppositions about it, or he may make no suppositions at all, or he may even altogether forget about the very existence of the Unknown. In the latter cases, when he makes no suppositions or forgets about the existence of the Unknown, then even what was possible in other cases, that is, the accidental coincidence of conjectures or speculations with the unknown reality, becomes impossible.

In this incapacity of man to imagine what exists beyond the wall of the known and the possible lies his chief tragedy, and in this, as has already been said, lies the reason why so much remains hidden from him and why there are so many questions to which he can never find the answer.

In the history of human thought there are many attempts to define the limits of possible knowledge. But there are no interesting attempts to conceive what the extension of these limits would mean and where it would necessarily lead.

Such an assertion may seem an intentional paradox. People clamour so loudly and so often about the unlimited possibilities of knowledge, about the immense horizons opening before science, and so forth, but in actual fact all these " unlimited possibilities " are limited by the five senses — sight, hearing, smell, touch and taste — plus the capacity of reasoning and comparing — beyond which a man can never go.

We do not take sufficient account of this circumstance or forget about it, and this explains why we are at a loss when we want to define " ordinary knowledge," " possible knowledge " and " hidden knowledge," or the differences between them.

In all myths and fairy-tales of all times we find the idea of " magic," " witchcraft " and " sorcery," which, as we come nearer to our own period, take the form of " spiritualism," " occultism " and the like. But even people who believe in these words understand very imperfectly what they really mean and in what respect the knowledge of a " magician " or an " occultist " differs from the knowledge of an ordinary man; and therefore all attempts to create a theory of magical knowledge end in failure. The result is always something indefinite but, though impossible, not fantastic, because the " magician " usually appears as an ordinary man endowed with some exaggerated faculties in one direction. And the exaggeration of anything on already long-known lines cannot create anything fantastic.

Even if " miraculous " knowledge is an approach to knowledge of the Unknown, people do not know how to approach the miraculous. In this they are greatly hindered by the interference of " pseudo-occult " literature, which often strives to abolish the divisions mentioned above and prove the unity of scientific and " occult " knowledge. Thus in such literature one often finds assertions that " magic " or " magical " knowledge is nothing but knowledge which is in advance of its time. For instance, it is said that some mediæval monks may have had some knowledge of electricity. For their times this was " magic." For us it has ceased to be magic. And what may appear magic for us would cease to be magic for future generations.

Such an assertion is quite arbitrary, and, by destroying the necessary divisions, it prevents us finding and establishing a right attitude towards facts. Magical or occult knowledge is knowledge based upon senses which surpass our five senses and upon a capacity for thinking which surpasses ordinary thinking, *but it is knowledge translated into ordinary logical language, if that is possible or in so far as it is possible.*

In speaking of ordinary knowledge, it is necessary to repeat once more that, though the content of knowledge is not constant, that is, though it changes and grows, it always grows along definite and strictly fixed lines. All scientific methods, all apparatus, all instruments and appliances, are nothing but an improvement upon and a broadening of the " five senses," while mathematics and all possible calculations are nothing but the broadening of the ordinary capacity of comparison, reasoning and the drawing of conclusions. But at the same time some mathematical constructions go so far beyond the realm of ordinary knowledge as to lose any connection with it. Mathematics finds such relations of magnitudes or relations of relations as have no equivalents in the physical world we observe. But we are unable to make use of these mathematical attainments, because in all our observations and reasonings we are bound by the " five senses " and the laws of logic.

In every historical period human knowledge, that is to say, " ordinary knowledge " or the " known," the " accepted " knowledge, embraced a definite cycle of observations and the deductions made from them. As time went on this cycle grew larger but, if it may be so expressed, it always remained on the same plane. It has *never* risen above it.

Believing in the possibility and existence of " hidden knowledge," people always ascribed new properties to it, always regarded it as rising above the plane of ordinary knowledge and stretching beyond the limits of the " five senses." This is the true meaning of " hidden knowledge," of magic, of miraculous knowledge and so on. If we take away from hidden knowledge the idea that it goes beyond the five senses, it will lose all meaning and importance.

If, taking all this into consideration, we make a survey of the history of human thought in its relation to the Miraculous, we may find material for ascertaining the possible content of the Unknown. This should be possible because, in spite of all the poverty of its imagination and the divergence of its attempts, humanity has guessed some things correctly.

Such a summary of the aspirations of humanity to penetrate into the realm of the incomprehensible and the mysterious is especially interesting at the present time, when the psychological study of man has recognised the reality of states of consciousness which were long considered pathological, and has admitted their cognitive value, that is to say, the fact that in these states of consciousness man is able to know what he cannot know in ordinary states. But this study has come to a standstill and has gone no further.

It had been recognised that, remaining on scientific ground, it is impossible to regard the ordinary state of consciousness, in which we are capable of logical thinking, as the only one possible and the clearest. On the contrary it had been established that in other states of consciousness, which are rare and have been studied very little, we can learn and understand what we cannot understand in our ordinary state of consciousness. This in its turn served to establish the fact that the " ordinary " state of consciousness is only a *particular* instance of consciousness, and that our " ordinary " conception of the world is only a *particular* instance of conception of the world.

The study of these unusual, rare and exceptional states of man had established, moreover, a certain unity, a certain connectedness and consecutiveness, and an entirely illogical " logicalness," in the content of the so-called " mystical " states of consciousness.

At this point, however, the study of " mystical states of consciousness " has come to a standstill and has never progressed any further.

It is rather difficult to define a mystical state of consciousness by means of ordinary psychological terminology. Judging by outward signs such a state has much in common with somnambulistic and psycho-pathological states. There is nothing new about the establishing of the cognitive value of " mystical " states of consciousness. This fact is new only to " science." The reality and value of mystical states of consciousness have been and are acknowledged by every religion without exception which exists or has ever existed. According to the definition of the theologians of the Orthodox Church, mystical states of consciousness cannot disclose or add new dogmas, but they disclose and explain the content of dogmas which are already known by revelation. It is evident from this that mystical states of consciousness are not opposed to basic revelation, but are, as it were, regarded as phenomena of the same nature, but of less power. They can explain dogmas given by revelation, but cannot add new dogmas. Unfortunately, theological interpretations always keep within the bounds of the dogmas and canonical rules of a particular religion; they cannot overstep these bounds because of their very nature.

As regards science I have already said that it has shown little interest in mysticism, assigning it to the sphere of pathology, or at best to the sphere of imagination.

The word "mysticism" is used in very different senses, for instance, in the sense of a certain kind of theory or teaching. According to a not uncommon dictionary interpretation the word "mysticism" includes all those teachings and beliefs concerning life beyond the grave, the soul, spirits, hidden forces in man, Divinity, which do not enter into the ordinary and recognised religious teachings.

But the use of this word in such a sense is quite wrong, since its fundamental meaning is thus destroyed. Consequently, in this book the word "mysticism" will from now on be used only in its psychological sense, that is, in the sense of special states of consciousness, and ideas and conceptions of the world *directly* resulting from these states. And if it is mentioned in another sense, i.e. in the sense of certain theories, the fact will be specially noted.

An examination of what is known of mysticism and mystical states of consciousness is of great interest in connection with the idea of hidden knowledge. If we follow neither the religious nor the scientific view but try to compare descriptions of the mystical experiences of people of entirely different races, different periods and different religions, we shall find a striking resemblance among these descriptions, which can in no case be explained by similarity of preparation or by resemblance in ways of thinking and feeling. In mystical states utterly different people in utterly different conditions *learn* one and the same thing and, what is still more striking, in mystical states there is no difference of religions. All the experiences are absolutely identical; the difference can be only in the language and form of the description. In the mysticism of different countries and different peoples the same images, the same discoveries, are invariably repeated. As a matter of fact there may be enough of this material upon which to build a new synthetic religion. But religions are not built by reason. Mystical experiences are intelligible only in mystical states. All that we can get from an intellectual study of mystical states will be merely an approximation to, a hint of, a certain understanding. Mysticism is entirely emotional, entirely made up of subtle, incommunicable sensations, which are even more incapable of verbal expression and logical definition than are such things as sound and colour and line.

In relation to the idea of hidden knowledge mysticism can be regarded as a breaking through of hidden knowledge into our consciousness. This does not however mean that all mystics invariably recognise the existence of hidden knowledge and the possibility of acquiring it through study and work. For many mystics their experiences are an act of grace, a gift of God, and from their point of view no knowledge can ever lead people to this grace or make the acquisition of it easier.

Thus, from one point of view, mysticism could not exist without hidden knowledge, and the idea of hidden knowledge could not be known without mysticism. From the other point of view, the idea of hidden knowledge which is possessed by somebody or other and can be found by intellectual means is unnecessary for mysticism, for the whole of knowledge is contained in the soul of man, and mysticism is the way to this knowledge and the way to God.

In view of this dual attitude of mysticism towards hidden knowledge it is necessary to make a distinction between these two ideas.

Hidden knowledge is an idea which does not fit into any other idea. If the existence of hidden knowledge is admitted, it is admitted as belonging to certain people, but to people whom we do not know, to an inner circle of humanity.

According to this idea, humanity is regarded as two concentric circles. All humanity which we know and to which we belong forms the outer circle. All the history of humanity that we know is the history of the outer circle. But within this circle there is another, of which men of the outer circle know nothing, and the existence of which they only sometimes dimly suspect, although the life of the outer circle in its most important manifestations, and particularly in its *evolution*, is actually guided by the inner circle. The inner or the esoteric circle forms, as it were, a life within life, a mystery, a secret in the life of humanity.

The outer or exoteric humanity, to which we belong, is like the leaves on a tree that change every year. In spite of this they consider themselves the centre of life, not understanding that the tree has a trunk and roots, and that besides leaves it bears flowers and fruit.

The esoteric circle is, as it were, humanity, within humanity, and is the brain, or rather the immortal soul, of humanity, where all the attainments, all the results, all the achievements, of all cultures and all civilisations are preserved.

One can look at the question from another angle and try to find in man himself an analogy with the relation between the esoteric and the exoteric circles of humanity.

Such an analogy can be found in man; it consists in the relation of the " brain " to the rest of the human body. If we take the human organism and examine the relation of the " higher " or the " nobler " tissues, that is to say, mainly the *nerve and brain matter*, to other tissues of the organism, such as muscle tissue, connective tissue, the cells of the skin and so on, we shall find an almost complete analogy with the relation of the inner circle to the outer.

One of the most mysterious phenomena in the life of the human organism is the life-history of brain-cells. It is more or less definitely established by science and can be accepted as a fact that brain-cells do not multiply like the cells of other tissues. According to one theory, brain-cells all appear at a very early age; according to another, they grow in numbers until the organism has reached the age of about twelve. But how they grow and *out of what* they grow remains unknown.

Reasoning logically, science ought to have recognised brain-cells as immortal in comparison with other cells.

This is almost all that can be said about brain-cells, if we remain on recognised scientific ground. But what is accepted is far from being sufficient for the understanding of the nature of the life of brain-cells. Too many facts have to be ignored before it becomes possible to accept the theory of a permanent stock of brain-cells which only diminishes and diminishes. This theory of a permanent stock completely disagrees with the other theory, according to which brain-cells perish or are burnt up in great numbers at every thought process, especially during intense mental work. If it were so, no matter how many they are they would not have lasted long! And bearing this in mind we are forced to admit that the life of brain-cells still remains unexplained and very mysterious.

Indeed, though it is not recognised by science, the life of cells is very short and the replacement of old cells by new ones in a normal organism proceeds continually and may even be increased. It does not enter the scope of the present book to show how this proposition can be proved. For existing scientific methods any observation of the life of individual cells in the human organism presents almost insurmountable difficulties. However, if, reasoning purely by analogy, we suppose that brain-cells must be born from something similar to them, and if at the same time we take it as proved that brain-cells do not multiply, then we must presume that they *evolve* from some other cells.

The possibility of the regeneration or evolution or transformation of one kind of cell into another kind is definitely established, for, after all, *all* the cells of the organism develop from one parent cell. The only question is, from what kind of cells can brain-cells evolve? Science cannot answer this question.

One can only say that if cells of a certain kind regenerate into brain-cells, by this very fact they *disappear* from their former plane, leave the world of their kin, *die* on one plane and are born on another, just as the egg of a butterfly, becoming a caterpillar, dies as an egg, ceases to be an egg; as a caterpillar, becoming a chrysalis, dies as a caterpillar, ceases to be a caterpillar; and as a chrysalis, becoming a butterfly, dies as a chrysalis, ceases to be a chrysalis, that is, leaves the world of its own kin and passes to another plane of being. Similarly, future brain-cells, in passing to another plane of being, cease to be what they were before, die on their former plane of being and begin to live on a new plane of being. On this new plane, while remaining invisible and unknown, they govern the life of other cells, either in their own interests or in the interests of the whole organism. And part of their activity consists in finding among the more evolved tissues cells which are capable of evolving into brain-cells, because brain-cells do not multiply by themselves.

Thus we find in the human organism in the relation of brain-cells to other cells an analogy with the relation of the inner circle to the outer circles of humanity.

Before proceeding further it is necessary to establish the exact meaning of certain concepts which will constantly be met with later.

The first of these is " evolution."

The idea of evolution has occupied a predominant place in Western thought. To doubt evolution has long been regarded as the final sign of retrogression. Evolution has become a kind of universal key which opens all locks.

This general acceptance of a very hypothetical idea in itself arouses doubt. The idea of evolution is comparatively new. Darwin regarded " natural selection " as a proof of evolution in the biological sense. But the popularisation of the idea of evolution in a general sense is chiefly due to Herbert Spencer, who was the first to explain cosmic, biological, psychological, moral and sociological processes from the point of view of one general principle. But individual attempts to regard the world-process as the result of mechanical evolution existed long before Spencer. Astronomical philosophy on the one hand and the biological sciences on the other hand created the modern conception of evolution, which is now applied literally to everything in the world from social forms to marks of punctuation, on the basis of the general principle accepted in advance, that *everything* evolves. " Facts " are selected to support this principle. That which does not fit the principle of evolution is rejected.

According to the ordinary dictionary definition, the word " evolution " means " an orderly and progressive development " governed by certain exact but unknown laws.

In order to understand the idea it must be noted that in the concept of evolution not only what is included in this word is important but also what is excluded by it. The idea of evolution first of all excludes the idea of a " plan " and of a guiding mind. Evolution is an independent and a mechanical process. Further, evolution excludes " accident," that is the entering of new facts into mechanical processes, which incessantly changes their direction. According to the idea of evolution everything always proceeds in the same direction. One " accident " corresponds to another. And moreover the word " evolution " has no antithesis, although, for instance, dissolution and degeneration cannot be called evolution.

The dogmatic meaning which is attached to the word evolution constitutes its most characteristic feature. But this dogmatism has no foundation whatever. On the contrary, there exists no more artificial and feeble idea than that of the general evolution of everything that exists.

The scientific foundations of evolution are: nebular theories of the origin of worlds, with all additions, restrictions and alterations, which really change nothing in the original misconception of the *mechanical process* of construction, and, second, Darwin's theory of the origin of species, also with all the later additions and alterations.

But nebular theories, no matter what names are connected with them, belong to the domain of pure speculation. In fact it is only a *classification* of supposed phenomena, which, through misunderstanding and for lack of anything better, is regarded as a theory of the world-process. As a theory it is not based on any facts or observable laws.

The evolution of organic forms in the sense of the development of new species and classes in all the kingdoms of Nature is " scientifically " based on a whole series of facts, which are supposed to confirm it, from comparative anatomy, morphology, embryology, palæontology, etc.; but in reality all these " facts " have been artificially selected to prove the theory. Every decade denies the facts of the preceding decade and replaces them by new facts, but the theory remains unshakable.

In the very beginning, in introducing the idea of evolution into biological conceptions, a bold assumption was made, because without it no theory could be formed. Later it was forgotten that it was only an assumption. I refer to the famous " origin of species."

The point is that, keeping strictly to facts, it is possible to accept evolution based on selection, adaptation and elimination only in the sense of " preservation of species," because only this can be observed. In reality the appearance of new species, their formation and transition from lower forms to higher, have never been observed anywhere. Evolution in the sense of " development " of species has always been only a hypothesis, which became a theory simply through misunderstanding. The only fact here is the " preservation of species." How they appear we do not know and we must not deceive ourselves on this point.

At this point science by a trick has substituted one card for another. That is, having established the evolution of *varieties* or breeds, it has applied the same evolution to *species*, using the method of analogy. This analogy is quite illegitimate, and in calling it substitution by a trick I do not exaggerate in the least.

The evolution of varieties is an established fact, but varieties all remain within the limits of the particular species *and are very unstable*, that is, with the alteration of conditions they change after several generations or revert to the original type. Species is a firmly established type and, as I have already said, a change of species has never been observed.

This of course does not mean that *everything* that is called species is a firmly established type. Species is a firmly established type only in comparison with variety or breed, which is a type changing almost before our eyes.

In view of the enormous difference between varieties and species, to apply to species what has been established only in relation to varieties is at least a " deliberate mistake." But the magnitude of this deliberate mistake and the almost general acceptance of it as a truth in no way oblige us to take it into account or to presume behind it a hidden possibility.

Moreover, the data of palæontology, far from confirming the idea of an orderly change of species, completely overthrow the idea of species itself as something definite and establish the facts of jumps, retardations, reversions, the sudden appearance of entirely new forms, etc., which are inexplicable from the point of view of an orderly evolution. Also the data of comparative anatomy, to which " evolutionists " are much inclined to refer, begin to turn against them; for instance, it has been found quite impossible to establish any evolution in the case of separate organs such as the eye or organs of smell and the like.

To this it must be added that the concept of evolution in its strictly scientific meaning has already undergone considerable change. And there is now a great difference between the popular meaning of the word in imitatively scientific " essays " and " outlines," and its really scientific meaning.

Evolution is not as yet denied by science. But the word itself is already admitted to have been unsuccessful, and attempts are being made to find another word that would express a less artificial idea and would include not only the process of " integration," but also the process of dissolution.

This last idea will become clear if we understand the fact pointed out before that the word evolution has no antithesis. The meaning of this emerges with particular distinctness in attempts to apply the word evolution to the description of social or political phenomena, where the results of degeneration or disintegration are constantly taken for evolution, and where evolution, which, by the meaning of the word, cannot be dependent on anyone's will, is constantly confused with the results of voluntary processes, which are also recognised as possible. In reality the appearance of new social or political forms does not depend either on will or on evolution, and in most cases they are only an unsuccessful, incomplete and contradictory realisation, or, to put it better, non-realisation, of theoretical programmes, behind which lie personal interests.

The confusion of ideas in relation to evolution is largely dependent on the comprehension, which cannot be altogether obliterated from men's minds, of the fact that in life there is not only one process but many processes, which cross one another, break into one another and bring into one another *new facts*.

Very roughly, these processes can be divided into two categories: creative processes and destructive processes. Both kinds are equally important, because if there were no destructive processes there would be no creative processes. Destructive processes give material for creative. And all creative processes without exception pass sooner or later into destructive processes. But this does not mean that creative processes and destructive processes together constitute what can be called evolution.

Western thought, in creating the theory of evolution, has overlooked the destructive processes. The reason for this lies in the artificially narrowed field of view of the last few centuries of European culture. Owing to this, theories are built upon an insufficient number of facts, none of the observed processes is taken in its entirety; and, in observing only part of the process, men say that this process consists in progressive change or in evolution. It is curious that the inverse process on a large scale cannot be conceived by people of our time. Destruction or degeneration or dissolution proceeding on a large scale will inevitably appear to them as progressive change or evolution.

In spite of all that has been stated, the term " evolution " can be very useful and, applied to facts that really exist, it helps to elucidate their content and their inner dependence upon other facts.

For instance, the development of all the cells of an organism from one parent cell can be called the evolution of the parent cell. The continuous development of cells of higher tissues from cells of lower tissues can be called evolution of cells.

Strictly speaking, all transforming processes can be called evolutionary. The development of a chicken from an egg, the development of an oak from an acorn, the development of wheat from a grain, the development of a butterfly from an egg, a caterpillar and a chrysalis; all these are examples of evolution actually existing in the world.

The idea of evolution (in the sense of transformation) in ordinary thought differs from the idea of evolution in esoteric thought in this respect, that esoteric thought recognises the possibility of transformation or evolution where scientific thought does not see or recognise such a possibility. Namely, esoteric thought recognises the possibility of the transformation of man into superman which is the highest meaning of the word " evolution."

Apart from this meaning, the word " evolution " can be used for the designation of processes favouring improvement of the breed and preservation of the species, as opposed to processes impairing the breed and leading to degeneration of the species.

To return to the idea of esotericism itself, it should be understood that in many ancient countries, Egypt and Greece, for example, there existed side by side two religions, one dogmatic and ceremonial, the other mystical and esoteric. The one consisted of popular cults, representing the half-forgotten forms of ancient mystical and esoteric myths, while the other was *the religion of Mysteries*. The latter religion went far beyond popular cults, explaining the allegorical and symbolic meaning of myths and uniting those who were connected with the esoteric circle or were striving towards it.

Comparatively very little is known about the Mysteries. Their rôle in the life of ancient communities, the part they played in the creation of ancient cultures, is completely unknown to us. Yet it is precisely the " Mysteries " which explain many historical enigmas and, among others, perhaps the greatest historical enigma of all — the sudden appearance of Greek culture in the 7th century, following upon the completely dark 8th and 9th centuries.

In historical Greece the Mysteries appertained to secret societies of a special kind. These secret societies of priests and initiates arranged every year, or at definite intervals, special festivals, which were accompanied by allegorical theatrical performances. These theatrical performances, to which in particular the name of Mysteries was given, were held in different places — the best known were held at Delphi and Eleusis in Greece and on the island of Philæ in Egypt. The character of the theatrical performances and allegorical dramas played there was fairly constant. Both in Greece and in Egypt the idea was always one and the same, namely, the death of the god and his resurrection. The thread of this idea ran through all the Mysteries. Its meaning may be interpreted in several ways. Probably the most correct is to think that the Mysteries represented the journey of the worlds or the journey of the soul, the birth of the soul in matter, its death and resurrection, that is, its return into the former life. But the theatrical representations, which for the people formed the whole content of the Mysteries, were actually of secondary importance. Behind these representations stood *schools*, which were the essence of the whole thing. The purpose of these schools was the preparation of men for initiation. Only those who were initiated into certain secrets might take part in the Mysteries. Initiation was accompanied by complicated ceremonies, some of which were public, and by various tests which the candidate for initiation had to pass. For the crowd, for the masses, *this* constituted the content of initiation, but the ceremonies of initiation were really nothing but ceremonies. The actual tests took place not at the moment immediately before formal initiation, but over a whole course, in some cases a very long one, of study and preparation. And initiation was of course not an instantaneous miracle, but rather a consecutive and gradual introduction to a new cycle of thought and feeling, as is initiation into any science, into any branch of knowledge.

Several suppositions exist as to what ideas prevailed among the peoples at the period immediately connected with the Mysteries, about that which initiation gave or could give.

And one of these suppositions was that initiation gave *immortality*. The Greeks, and also the Egyptians, had a very gloomy idea of life beyond the grave — such was the Hades of Homer, such were the Egyptian ideas of the life beyond. *Initiation* gave freedom from this gloom, gave a way of escape from the never-ending anguish of the " abodes of the dead," gave a kind of *life in death*.

This idea is expressed more clearly than anywhere else in the Easter Hymn of the Orthodox Church, which undoubtedly comes from very remote pre-Christian antiquity and links the Christian idea with the idea of the Mysteries.

> Christ is risen from the dead;
> He has conquered death with death,
> And given life to those who were in tombs.

There is a remarkable analogy between the content of the Mysteries and the earthly life of Christ. The life of Christ, taken as we know it from the Gospels, represents the same Mystery as those which were performed in Egypt on the island of Philæ, in Greece at Eleusis, and in other places. The idea was the same, namely the death of the god and his resurrection. The only difference between the Mysteries as they were performed in Egypt and Greece and the Mystery which was played in Palestine lies in the fact that the latter was played in real life, not on the stage but amidst real nature, in the streets and public places of real towns, in real country, with the sky, mountains, lakes and trees for scenery, with a real crowd, with real emotions of love, malice and hatred, with real nails, with real sufferings. All the actors in this drama knew their parts and acted them in accordance with a general plan, according to the aim and purpose of the play. In this drama there was nothing spontaneous, unconscious or accidental. Every actor knew what words he had to say and at what moment; and he did in fact say exactly what he had to say and in the exact way in which he had to say it. This was a drama with the whole world as an audience for hundreds and thousands of years. And the drama was played without the smallest mistake, without the smallest inexactness, in accordance with the design of the author and the plan of the producer, for in compliance with the idea of esotericism there must certainly have been both an author and a producer.

The idea and the aim of the Mysteries were hidden as well as the substance of initiation. For those who knew of the existence of the hidden knowledge the Mysteries opened the door to that knowledge. This was the aim of Mysteries, this was their idea.

Note. I found a certain coincidence with this idea in John M. Robertson's book, *Pagan Christs* (issued for the Rationalist Press Association, limited) in the chapter "The Gospel Mystery-Play."

The author comes very near to the idea of the "drama of Christ" being a theatrical performance similar to the Mysteries. And the first impression which this chapter gives is that the author says exactly the same thing as has been set forth above. In reality, however, the coincidence is not complete, though it is very curious. The author of *Pagan Christs*, through studying the ancient Mysteries on the one hand and the Gospel text on the other, came to the conclusion that the Gospels do not describe historical events, but a play which was performed for a special purpose and which in its idea is similar to the ancient Mysteries, whereas in its form it is analogous to the later mediæval Mysteries. He brings together the idea of the ancient Mysteries and the idea of the mediæval Mysteries, which consisted of episodes of the life of Christ, and asserts that the legend of the historical Christ was based on precisely such a mystery-play, composed of five acts — The Last Supper, Prayer in the Garden of Gethsemane, the Passion, Trial and Crucifixion, to which later was added the Resurrection from the Dead, a play that had been performed no one knows where and when, and that was described in the Gospels as a real event taking place in Jerusalem.

When the Mysteries disappeared from the life of peoples the link which existed between terrestrial mankind and the hidden knowledge was broken. The very idea of this knowledge gradually became more and more fantastic, and diverged more and more from the accepted realistic view of life. In our days the idea of esotericism is opposed to all the usual views of life.

From the point of view of modern scientific psychological and historical opinions the idea of the inner circle is obviously quite absurd, fantastic and without foundation. It also appears equally fantastic from the point of view of idealistic philosophy, since the latter admits the hidden and incomprehensible as existing only outside physical life, outside the world of phenomena.

From the point of view of the less intellectual doctrines, such as dogmatic Church Christianity or spiritualism and the like, the idea of esotericism in its pure form is equally inadmissible, because, on the one hand, it contradicts the authority of the Church and many of the accepted dogmas and, on the other hand, it exposes cheap animistic theories going under the general name of spiritualism or spiritism, and " miracles " with tables and chairs. And at the same time the idea of esotericism brings the mysterious and miraculous into real, everyday life, and makes one realise that life is not what it appears on the surface on which most men see themselves.

In order to understand the substance of the *idea* of esotericism it must first be realised that the history of humanity is much longer than is usually supposed. But it should be observed that the usual view of text-books and popular " outlines of history," which contain a very short historical period and a more or less dark age before that, is in reality very far from the most recent *scientific* views. Present day historical science is beginning to regard the " prehistoric " period and the " stone age " quite differently from the way in which they were regarded fifty or sixty years ago. It cannot regard the prehistoric period as a period of barbarism, because against this view there speaks the study of the remains of *prehistoric* cultures, memorials of ancient art and literature, the study of the religious customs and rites of different peoples, the comparative study of religions, and particularly the study of language, that is, the data of comparative philology, which show the astonishing psychological richness of old languages. On the contrary, in opposition to the old view there already exist many theories and there appear many new theories on the possibility of ancient prehistoric civilisations. Thus the " stone age " is regarded with more probability as a period not of the beginning, but of the fall and degeneration of previously existing civilisations.

In this respect it is very characteristic that all present-day " savages " without exception, that is to say, peoples whom our culture has found in a savage or semi-savage state, are degenerate descendants of more cultured peoples. This most interesting fact is usually passed over in silence. But not a single savage race that we know of, i.e. no isolated savage or semi-savage people met so far by our culture, has shown any sign of *evolution* in process, in any respect whatever. On the contrary, in every case without exception, signs of degeneration have been observed. I do not speak of degeneration consequent upon contact with our culture, but of degeneration which has been in process for centuries before contact with our culture, and is in many cases perfectly clear and evident. All savage or semi-savage peoples have tales and traditions of a golden age, or of a heroic period; but in reality these tales and traditions speak of their own past, of their own ancient civilisation. The languages of all peoples contain words and ideas for which there is no longer any place in actual life. All peoples had *before* better weapons, better boats, better towns, and higher forms of religion. The same fact explains the superiority of the palæolithic, that is, more ancient drawings, found in caves, to the neolithic, that is, more recent drawings. This also is a fact that is usually passed over altogether or left without explanation.

According to esoteric ideas many civilisations unknown to our historical science have succeeded one another on the earth, and some of these civilisations reached a far higher point than our civilisation, which we regard as the highest ever reached by the human race. Of many of these ancient civilisations no visible traces remain, but the attainments of the science of these remote periods have never been utterly lost. The knowledge attained has been preserved from century to century, from age to age, and has been handed on from one civilisation to another. Schools of a particular kind were guardians of the knowledge, and it was protected in them against non-initiated persons who might mutilate and distort it, and was handed on only from a teacher to a pupil who had undergone a prolonged and difficult preparation.

The term " occultism," which is often used in relation to the content of " esoteric " teachings, has a two-fold meaning. It is either secret knowledge in the sense of knowledge held in secret, or knowledge of the secret, i.e. of secrets concealed from mankind by nature.

This definition is the definition of " Divine Wisdom," or, if we take the words of the Alexandrine philosophers of the 3rd century, it is the definition of the " Wisdom of the Gods," or " Theosophy " in the widest sense of the word, or of the Brahma Vidya of Indian philosophy.

The idea of the inner circle of humanity or the idea of esotericism has many different sides:

(*a*) The historical existence of esotericism, i.e. of the inner circle of humanity itself, and the history and origin of the knowledge it possesses.

(*b*) The idea of the acquisition of this knowledge by men, that is, initiation and " schools."

(*c*) The psychological possibility connected with this idea, that is, the possibility of changing the forms of perception, of broadening the capacity of knowledge and understanding, for ordinary intellectual means are considered to be inadequate for the acquisition of esoteric knowledge.

First of all the idea of esotericism tells us of the knowledge which has been accumulated for tens of thousands of years and has been handed down from generation to generation within small circles of initiates; this knowledge often relates to spheres which have not even been touched upon by science. In order to acquire this knowledge, and also the power which it gives, a man must go through difficult preliminary preparations and tests and prolonged work, without which it is impossible to assimilate this knowledge and to learn how to use it. This work for the mastery of esoteric knowledge, and the methods belonging to it, constitute by themselves a separate cycle of knowledge unknown to us.

It is necessary further to understand that according to the idea of esotericism people are not born in the esoteric circle, and one of the tasks of the members of the esoteric circle is the preparation of their successors, to whom they may hand on their knowledge and all that is connected with it.

For this purpose people belonging to esoteric schools appear at indefinite intervals in our life as leaders and teachers of men. They create and leave behind them either a new religion, or a new type of philosophical school, or a new system of thought, which indicates to people of the given period and country, in a form intelligible to them, the way which they must follow in order to approach the inner circle. One and the same idea invariably runs through the teachings originated by these people, namely, the idea that only a very few can enter the esoteric circle, though many may desire to do so and may even make the attempt.

The esoteric schools which preserve ancient knowledge, handing it over from one to another in succession, and the people who belong to these schools stand apart, as it were, from ordinary mankind, to which we belong. At the same time these schools play a very important part in the life of humanity; but we know nothing of this part and, if we hear about it, we understand imperfectly of what it consists, and we are reluctant to believe in the possibility of anything of the kind.

This is due to the fact that in order to understand the possibility of the existence of the inner circle and the part played by the esoteric schools in the life of humanity, it is necessary to be in possession of such knowledge concerning the essential nature of man and his destiny in the world as is not possessed by modern science, nor, consequently, by ordinary man.

Certain races have very significant traditions and legends built upon the idea of the inner circle. Such, for instance, are the Tibeto-Mongolian legends of the " Subterranean Kingdom," of the " King of the World," the Mystery City of *Agharta* and so on, provided that these ideas actually exist in Mongolia and Tibet and are not the invention of European travellers or " occultists."

According to the idea of esotericism, as applied to the history of mankind, no civilisation ever begins of itself. There exists no evolution which begins accidentally and proceeds mechanically. Only degeneration and decay can proceed mechanically. Civilisation never starts by natural growth, but only through artificial cultivation.

Esoteric schools are hidden from the eyes of ordinary humanity; but the influence of schools persists uninterruptedly in history, and has the aim, so far as we can understand this aim, of helping, when that appears possible, races which have lapsed into a barbarous state of one kind or another to emerge from that state and to enter upon a new civilisation, or a new life.

A savage or semi-savage people or an entire country is taken in hand by a man possessing power and knowledge. He begins to educate and instruct the people. He gives them a religion, he makes laws, builds temples, introduces writing, creates the beginning of art and the sciences, makes the people migrate to another country if necessary, and so on. Theocratic government is a form of such artificial cultivation. Biblical history from Abraham, and possibly even earlier, to Solomon, is an example of the civilising of a savage people by members of the inner circle.

According to tradition, the following historical personages belonged to esoteric schools: Moses, Gautama the Buddha, John the Baptist, Jesus Christ, Pythagoras, Socrates and Plato; also the more mythical — Orpheus, Hermes Trismegistus, Krishna, Rama and certain other prophets and teachers of mankind. To esoteric schools belonged also the builders of the Pyramids and the Sphinx; the priests of the Mysteries in Egypt and Greece, many artists in Egypt and other ancient countries; alchemists; the architects who built the mediæval " Gothic " cathedrals; the founders of certain schools and orders of Sufis and dervishes; and also certain persons who appeared in history for brief moments and remain historical riddles.

It is said that at the present time some members of esoteric schools live in remote and inaccessible parts of the globe, such as the Himalayas or Tibet, or some mountainous regions of Africa. While others, according to similar stories, live among ordinary people, without differing from them at all externally, often belonging even to the uncultured classes and engaged in insignificant and perhaps, from the ordinary point of view, even vulgar professions. Thus a French occultist author stated that he had learned much from an Oriental who sold parrots at Bordeaux. And it has always been so from the earliest times. Men belonging to the esoteric circle, when they appear among ordinary humanity, always wear a mask through which very few succeed in penetrating.

Esotericism is remote and inaccessible, but every man who learns of or guesses at the existence of esotericism has the chance of approaching a school or may hope to meet people who will help him and show the way. Esoteric knowledge is based on direct oral tuition, but before a man can attain the possibility of direct study of the ideas of esotericism, he must learn all that is possible about esotericism in the ordinary way, that is, through the study of history, philosophy and religion. And he must seek. For the gates of the world of the miraculous may be opened only to him who seeks:

Knock, and it shall be opened unto you; ask, and it shall be given unto you.

The question very often arises: why, if the esoteric circle really exists, does it do nothing to help ordinary man to emerge from the chaos of contradictions in which he lives and come to true knowledge and understanding? Why does the esoteric circle not help men to regulate their life on earth, and why does it allow violence, injustice, cruelty, wars, and so on?

The answer to all these questions lies in what has just been said. Esoteric knowledge can be given only to those who seek, only to those who have been seeking it with a certain amount of consciousness, that is, with an understanding of how it differs from ordinary knowledge and how it can be found. This preliminary knowledge can be gained by ordinary means, from existing and known literature, easily accessible to all. And the acquisition of this preliminary knowledge may be regarded as the first test. Only those who pass this first test, those, that is, who acquire the necessary knowledge from the material accessible to all, may hope to take the next step, at which point direct individual help will be accorded them. A man may hope to approach esotericism if he has acquired a right understanding from ordinary knowledge, that is, if he can find his way through the labyrinth of contradictory systems, theories and hypotheses, and understand their general meaning and general significance. This test is something like a competitive examination open to the whole human race, and the idea of a competitive examination alone explains why the esoteric circle appears reluctant to help humanity. It is not reluctant. All that is possible is done to help men, but men will not or cannot make the necessary efforts themselves. And they cannot be helped by force.

The Biblical story of the Golden Calf is an illustration of the attitude of the people of the outer circle towards the endeavours of the inner circle and an illustration of how the people of the outer circle behave at the very time when the people of the inner circle are striving to help them.

Thus, from the standpoint of the idea of esotericism, the first step towards hidden knowledge has to be made in a province open to everybody. In other words, the first indications of the way to true knowledge can be found by everybody in the ordinary knowledge accessible to all. Religion, philosophy, legends, fairy-tales, abound with information about esotericism. But one must have eyes to see and ears to hear.

People of our time possess four ways that lead to the Unknown, four forms of conception of the world — religion, philosophy, science and art. These ways diverged long ago. And the very fact of their divergence shows their remoteness from the source of their origin, that is, from esotericism. In ancient Egypt, in Greece, in India, there were periods when the four ways constituted one whole.

If we apply the principle of Avva Dorotheos, which I quoted in *Tertium Organum* (page 286), to the general examination of religion, philosophy, science and art, we shall see clearly why our forms of conception of the world cannot serve as a way to truth. They are for ever being broken up, for ever being divided, and they for ever contradict both themselves and each other. Obviously, the more they are broken up and separated from one another, the farther they depart from truth. Truth is at the centre, where the four ways converge. Consequently the nearer they are to one another, the nearer they are to truth, the farther from one another, the farther from truth. Moreover, the division of each of these ways within itself, that is to say, the sub-division into systems, schools, churches and doctrines, denotes great remoteness from the truth; and we see in fact that the number of divisions, far from diminishing, increases in every domain and every sphere of human activity. This in its turn may show us, provided we are able to perceive it, that the general trend of human activity leads, not to truth, but in the very opposite direction.

If we try to define the significance of the four ways of the spiritual life of humanity, we see, first of all, that they fall into two categories. Philosophy and science are intellectual ways; religion and art, emotional ways. Moreover each of these ways corresponds to a definite intellectual or emotional type of human being. But this division does not explain everything that may seem to us unintelligible or enigmatic in the sphere of religion, art or knowledge, since in each of these spheres of human activity there are phenomena and aspects which are entirely incommensurable and which do not merge into one another. And yet it is only when they are combined into one whole that they will cease to distort truth and to lead men away from the right path.

Many people will of course protest vehemently and even revolt at the suggestion that religion, philosophy, science and art represent similar, equivalent, and equally imperfect ways of seeking truth.

To a religious man, the idea will appear disrespectful to religion. To a man of science it will appear insulting to science. To an artist it will appear a mockery of art. And to a philosopher it will appear to be a *naïveté* based on a lack of understanding of what philosophy is.

Let us now try to define the basis of the division of the " four ways " at the present time.

Religion is founded on revelation.

Revelation is something proceeding immediately from the higher consciousness or higher powers. If there is no idea of revelation, there is no religion. And in religion there is always something unknowable by the ordinary mind and ordinary thinking. For this reason, no attempts to create an artificial synthetic religion by intellectual methods have ever led or can ever lead anywhere. The result is not religion, but only bad philosophy. All reformations and attempts at simplifying or rationalising a religion bring about equally negative results. On the other hand, " revelation," or what is given by revelation, must surpass all other knowledge. And when we find, on the contrary, that religion is centuries, or even, as happens in many cases, thousands of years behind science and philosophy, the main inference is that it is not religion, but only pseudo-religion, the withered corpse of what once was or may have been religion. Unfortunately, all religions that are known to us in their church form are only " pseudo-religions."

Philosophy is based on speculation, on logic, on thought, on the synthesis of what we know and on the analysis of what we do not know. Philosophy must include within its confines the whole content of science, religion and art. But where can such a philosophy be found? All that we know in our times by the name of philosophy is not philosophy, but merely " critical literature " or the expression of personal opinions, mainly with the aim of overthrowing and destroying other personal opinions. Or, which is still worse, philosophy is nothing but self-satisfied dialectic surrounding itself with an impenetrable barrier of terminology unintelligible to the uninitiated and solving for itself all the problems of the universe without any possibility of proving these explanations or making them intelligible to ordinary mortals.

Science is based on experiment and observation. It must know no fear, must have no dogmas, must create no " taboo " for itself. But contemporary science, by the mere fact of having cut itself sharply off from religion and " mysticism," i.e. by having set up for itself a definite " taboo," has become an accidental and unreliable instrument of thought. The constant feeling of this " taboo " compels it to shut its eyes to a whole series of inexplicable and unintelligible phenomena, deprives it of wholeness and unity, and as a result brings it about that " we have no science but have sciences." [3]

Art is based on emotional understanding, on the feeling of the Unknown which lies behind the visible and the tangible, and on creative power, the power, that is, to reconstruct in visible or audible forms the artist's sensations, feelings, visions and moods, and especially a certain fugitive sensation, which is in fact the feeling of the harmonious interconnection and oneness of *everything* and the feeling of the " soul " of things and phenomena. Like science and philosophy, art is a definite *way of knowledge*. The artist, in creating, learns much that he did not know before. But an art which does not reveal mysteries, which does not lead to the sphere of the Unknown, does not yield new knowledge, is a parody of art, and still more often it is not even a parody, but simply a commerce or an industry.

Pseudo-religion, pseudo-philosophy, pseudo-science and pseudo-art are practically all that we know. We are fed on substitutes, on " margarine " in all aspects and forms. Very few of us know the taste of genuine things.

But between *genuine* religion, *genuine* art, *genuine* science, on the one hand, and the " substitutes " which we call religion, art, and science, on the other, there exist many intermediate stages, corresponding to the different levels of man's development, with different understanding pertaining to each level. The cause of the existence of these different levels lies in the existence of the deep radical inequality which exists between men. It is very

---

[3] The words of Bazaroff, the hero of Turgenieff's novel, *Fathers and Sons*.

difficult to define this difference between men, but it exists, and religions as well as everything else are divided in accordance with it.

It cannot be said, for instance, that paganism exists and that Christianity exists. But it can be said that there are pagans and that there are Christians. A Christianity can be paganism, and a paganism can be Christianity. In other words, there are many people to whom Christianity is paganism, that is to say, those people who turn Christianity into paganism, just as they would turn any religion into paganism. In every religion there are different levels of understanding; every religion may be understood in one way or in another way. Literal understanding, deification of the word, of the form, of the ritual, makes paganism of the most exalted, the most subtle, religion. Capacity for emotional discrimination, for the understanding of the essence, of spirit, of symbolism, the manifestation of mystical feelings, can make an exalted religion out of what may externally seem to be a primitive cult of savages or semi-savages.

The difference lies not in the ideas, but in the men who receive and reproduce the ideas, and so it is in art, in philosophy and in science. One and the same idea is understood in different ways by men of different levels, and it often happens that their understanding differs completely. If we realise this it will become clear to us that we cannot speak of religion, art or science, etc. Different people have different sciences, different arts, and so on. If we knew how and in what respect men differ from one another, we should understand how and in what respect various religions, arts and sciences differ one from another.

This idea can be expressed more precisely (taking the example of religion) by saying that all ordinary divisions such as Christianity, Buddhism, Mahomedanism, Judaism, as well as divisions within Christianity like the Orthodox Church, Catholicism, Protestantism, and further sub-divisions within each creed, such as sects and so on, are so to speak divisions on one plane. It must be understood that besides these divisions there exist divisions of levels, that is to say, there is the Christianity of one level of understanding and feeling, and there is the Christianity of another level of understanding and feeling, beginning from a very low outward ritual or hypocritical level, which passes into the persecution of all heterodox thinking, up to the very high level of Jesus Christ himself. Now these divisions, these levels, are unknown to us and we can understand their idea and principle only through the ideas of the inner circle. This means that if we admit that there is truth at the origin of everything and that there are different degrees of distortion of the truth, we shall see that in this way truth is gradually brought down to our level, though of course in a completely unrecognisable form.

The idea of esotericism also reaches people in the form of pseudo-esotericism, pseudo-occultism. The cause of this lies again in the above-mentioned difference in the levels of men themselves. Most people can accept truth only in the form of a lie. But while some of them are satisfied with a lie, others begin to seek further and may in the end come to truth. Church Christianity has completely distorted the ideas of Christ, but, starting from the Church form, some people who are " pure in heart " may by the way of feeling come to a right understanding of the original truth. It is difficult for us to realise that we are surrounded by distortions and perversions and that apart from these distortions and perversions we can receive nothing *from outside*.

We have difficulty in understanding this, because the fundamental tendency of contemporary thought consists precisely in examining phenomena in the order opposite to that just mentioned. We are accustomed to conceive every idea, every phenomenon, whether in the domain of religion, art or public life, as appearing first in a rude primitive form, in the form of a mere adaptation to organic conditions and of rude savage instincts, of fear, of desire, or memory of something still more elementary, still more primitive, animal, vegetable, embryonic, and gradually evolving and becoming more refined and more complicated, affecting more and more sides of life, and thus approaching the ideal form.

Of course such a tendency of thought is directly opposed to the idea of esotericism, which holds that the very great majority of our ideas are not the product of evolution but the product of the degeneration of ideas which existed at some time or are still existing somewhere in much higher, purer and more complete forms.

This to the modern way of thinking is a mere absurdity. We are so certain that *we* are the highest product of evolution, that we know everything, so sure that there cannot be on this earth any significant phenomena such as schools or groups or systems which have not hitherto been known or acknowledged or discovered, that we have difficulty even in admitting the logical possibility of such an idea.

If we want to master even the elements of the idea, we must understand that they are incompatible with the idea of evolution in the ordinary sense of this word. It is impossible to regard our civilisation, our culture, as unique or the highest; it must be regarded as one of the many cultures which have succeeded one another on the earth. Moreover these cultures, each in its own way, distorted the idea of esotericism which lay at their foundation, and not one of them ever rose, even approximately, to the level of its source.

But such a view would be far too revolutionary, for it would shake the foundations of all modern thought, would involve a revision of all scientific philosophies of the world, and would make perfectly useless, even ridiculous, whole libraries of books written on the basis of the theory of evolution. And above all it would necessitate the withdrawal from the scene of a whole series of " great men " of the past, present and future. This view, therefore, can never become popular and is not likely to take its place side by side with other views.

But if we try to continue with this idea of successive civilisations, we shall see that every great culture of the great cycle of the whole of humanity consists of a whole series of separate cultures, belonging to separate races and peoples. All these separate cultures proceed in waves; they rise, reach the point of their highest development and fall. A race or a people which has reached a very high level of culture may begin to lose its culture and gradually pass to a state of absolute barbarism. The savages of our time, as has been said before, may be the descendants of once highly cultured races. A whole series of these racial and national cultures, taken over a very long period of time, makes up what may be called a great culture or the culture of a great cycle. The culture of a great cycle is also a wave which is made up, like every wave, of a number of smaller waves; and this culture, like the separate cultures, racial or national, rises, reaches its highest point and finally sinks into barbarism.

Of course the division of periods of barbarism and periods of culture must not be understood literally. Culture may entirely disappear in one continent and be partly preserved in another which holds no communication with the first. We may think in precisely this way of our own culture, as times of indubitable, profound barbarism in Europe may have been times of a certain culture in parts of Central or South America, perhaps in some countries of Africa, Asia and Polynesia. The possibility of a culture being preserved in some parts of the world in a period of general decadence does not affect the main principle that culture proceeds in great waves, separated by long periods of more or less complete barbarism. And it is very possible that periods occur, particularly if they coincide with geological cataclysms, with changes in the state of the earth's crust, when every semblance of culture disappears and the remnants of all the earlier humanity start a new culture from the beginning, from the stone-age.

According to the idea of esotericism, not all the valuable things gained by humanity during periods of culture are lost in periods of barbarism. The main substance of what has been gained by humanity in a period of culture is preserved in esoteric centres during a period of barbarism, and afterwards serves for the beginning of a new culture.

Every culture rises and falls. The reason is that in every culture, as we can observe, for example in our own, completely opposed principles, the principle of barbarism and the principle of civilisation, are developed and evolved at the same time.

The beginning of culture comes from the inner circle of humanity, and often it comes by means that are violent. Missionaries of the inner circle civilise savage races sometimes by fire and sword, because there can be no other means but violence to deal with a savage people. Later, the principles of civilisation develop and gradually create those forms of man's spiritual manifestation which are called religion, philosophy, science and art, and also those forms of social life which create for the individual a certain freedom, leisure, security and the possibility of self-manifestation in higher spheres of activity.

This is civilisation. As has been pointed out, its beginning, that is the beginning of all its ideas and principles and of all its knowledge, comes from the esoteric circle.

But, simultaneously with the beginning of civilisation, violence was admitted, and the result is that side by side with civilisation barbarism grows too. This means that parallel with the growth of the ideas which come from the esoteric circle there evolve other sides of life which originated in humanity in the barbarous state. Barbarism bears within itself the principles of violence and destruction. These principles do not and cannot exist in civilisation.

In our culture it is very easy to trace these two lines, the line of civilisation and the line of barbarism.

The savage killed his enemy with a club. Cultured man has at his disposal every sort of technical appliance, explosives of terrible power, electricity, aeroplanes, submarines, poisonous gases, and so on. All these means and contrivances for destruction and extermination are nothing but evolved forms of the club. And they differ from it only in the power of their action. The culture of the means of destruction and the culture of the means and methods of violence are the culture of barbarism.

Further, an essential part of our culture consists in slavery and in all possible forms of violence in the name of the state, in the name of religion, in the name of ideas, in the name of morals, in the name of everything imaginable.

The inner life of modern society, its tastes and interests, are also full of barbarous traits. Passion for shows and amusements, passion for competitions, sport, gambling, great suggestibility, a propensity to submit to all kinds of influences, to panic, to fear, to suspicions. All these are features of barbarism. And they all flourish in our life, making use of all the means and contrivances of technical culture, such as printing, telegraph, wireless telegraphy, quick means of communication, and so on.

Culture strives to establish a boundary between itself and barbarism. The manifestations of barbarism are called "crimes." But existing criminology is insufficient to isolate barbarism. It is insufficient because the idea of "crime" in existing criminology is artificial, for what is called crime is really an infringement of "existing laws," whereas "laws" are very often a manifestation of barbarism and violence. Such are the prohibiting laws of different kinds which abound in modern life. The number of these laws is constantly growing in all countries and, owing to this, what is called crime is very often not a crime at all, for it contains no element of violence or harm. On the other hand, unquestionable crimes escape the field of vision of criminology, either because they have not the recognised form of crime or because they surpass a certain scale. In existing criminology there are concepts: a criminal man, a criminal profession, a criminal society, a criminal sect, a criminal caste, and a criminal tribe, but there is no concept of a criminal *state*, or a criminal *government*, or criminal *legislation*. Consequently the biggest crimes actually escape being called crimes.

This limitation of the field of vision of criminology together with the absence of exact and permanent definition of the concept of crime is one of the chief characteristics of our culture.

The culture of barbarism grows simultaneously with the culture of civilisation. But the important point is the fact that the two cannot develop on parallel lines indefinitely. The moment must inevitably arrive when the culture of barbarism arrests the development of civilisation and gradually, or possibly very swiftly, completely destroys it.

It may be asked why barbarism must inevitably destroy civilisation, why civilisation cannot destroy barbarism.

It is easy to answer this question. First of all such a thing has never been known to happen in all the history we know, whereas the opposite phenomenon, that is, the destruction of civilisation by barbarism, the victory of barbarism over civilisation, has occurred continually and is occurring now. And, as has been mentioned before, we may judge of the fate ot a great wave of culture by the fate of the smaller waves of culture of individual races and peoples.

The root-cause of the evolution of barbarism lies in man himself; in him are innate the principles which promote the growth of barbarism. In order to destroy barbarism it is necessary to destroy these principles. But we can see that never since the beginning of history as we know it has civilisation been able to destroy these principles of barbarism in man's soul; and therefore barbarism always evolves parallel with civilisation. Moreover barbarism usually evolves more quickly than civilisation, and in many cases barbarism stops the development of civilisation at the very beginning. It is possible to find many historical examples of the civilisation of a nation being arrested by the development of barbarism in that very nation.

It is quite possible that in separate cases of small or even fairly large but isolated cultures, civilisation temporarily conquered barbarism. But in other cultures existing at the same time it was barbarism that overcame civilisation, and in time it invaded and overcame the civilisation of those separate cultures which in their own countries had overcome barbarism.

The second reason for the victory of barbarism over civilisation, which can always be seen, lies in the fact that the original forms of civilisation cultivated certain forms of barbarism for the protection of their own existence, their own defence, their own isolation, such as the organisation of military force, an army, the encouragement of military technique and military psychology, the encouragement and legalisation of various forms of slavery, the codification of barbarous customs and so on.

These forms of barbarism very soon outgrow civilisation. Very soon they begin to see the aim of their existence in themselves. Their strength lies in the fact that they can exist by themselves, without help from outside. Civilisation, on the contrary, having come from outside can only exist and develop by receiving outside help, that is, the help of the esoteric circle. But the evolving forms of barbarism very soon cut off civilisation from its source, and then civilisation, losing confidence in the reason for its separate existence, begins to serve the developed forms of barbarism, in the belief that here lie its aim and destiny. All forms created by civilisation undergo a process of change and adapt themselves to the new order of things, that is to say, become subservient to barbarism.

Theocratic government is transformed into despotism. Castes, if they have been recognised, become hereditary. Religion, taking the form of "church," becomes an instrument in the hands of despotism or hereditary castes. Science, transformed into technique, subserves the aims of destruction and extermination. Art degenerates and becomes a means for keeping the masses on the level of imbecility.

This is civilisation in the service of barbarism, in the captivity of barbarism. Such a relation between civilisation and barbarism can be observed throughout the whole of historical life. But such a relation cannot exist indefinitely. The growth of civilisation becomes arrested. Civilisation is, as it were, recast in the culture of barbarism. Finally it must stop altogether. Thereupon barbarism, without receiving an inflow of strength from civilisation, begins to descend to more and more elementary forms, returning gradually to its primitive state, until it becomes what it really is and has been during the whole period in which it was disguised in gorgeous trappings borrowed from civilisation.

Barbarism and civilisation can co-exist in this mutual relationship, which we observe in our historical life, for only a comparatively short period of time. There must come a period when the growth of the technique of destruction will begin to proceed so swiftly that it will destroy the source of its origin, namely, civilisation.

When we examine modern life, we see how small and unimportant a place is occupied in it by the principles of civilisation which are not in servitude to barbarism. How small a place, indeed, in the life of the average man is occupied by thought or the quest of truth! But the principles of civilisation in falsified forms are already used for the aims of barbarism as a means for subjugating the masses and holding them in subjection, and in these forms they flourish.

And it is only these falsified forms which are tolerated in life. Religion, philosophy, science and art, which are not in immediate servitude to barbarism, are not acknowledged in life except in feeble limited forms. Any attempt on their part to grow beyond the very small limits assigned to them is immediately arrested.

The interest of everyday humanity in this direction is exceedingly weak and helpless.

Man lives in the satisfaction of his appetites, in fears, in struggle, in vanity, in distraction and amusements, in stupid sports, in games of skill and chance, in greed of gain, in sensuality, in dull daily work, in cares and anxieties of the day, and more than anything else in obedience and in the enjoyment of obedience, because there is nothing that the average man likes better than to obey; if he ceases to obey one force he immediately begins to obey another. He is infinitely remote from anything that is not connected directly with the interests of the day or with the worries of the day, from anything which is a little above the material level of his life. If we do not shut our eyes to all this, we shall realise that we cannot, at the best, call ourselves anything but civilised barbarians, that is barbarians possessed of a certain degree of culture.

The civilisation of our time is a pale, sickly growth, which can hardly keep itself alive in the darkness of profound barbarism. Technical inventions, improved means of communication and methods of production, increasing powers in the struggle with nature, all take away from civilisation probably more than they give.

True civilisation exists only in esotericism. It is the inner circle which is in fact the truly civilised portion of humanity, and the members of the inner circle are civilised men living in a country of barbarians, among savages.

This throws light from another point of view on the question which is often put and to which I have already alluded: why is it that members of the inner circle do not help men in their life, why do they not take their stand on the side of truth, why are they not eager to uphold justice, to help the weak, to remove the causes of violence and evil?

But if we imagine a small number of civilised men living in a large country peopled by savage and barbarous tribes in perpetual hostility and war with one another; even if we imagine that these civilised people live there as missionaries with full desire to bring enlightenment to the savage masses, we shall see that they will certainly not interfere in the struggle of different tribes or take one side or another in conflicts that may arise. Let us suppose that slaves raise a revolt in this country; that does not mean that civilised men must help the slaves, because the whole object of the slaves is to subjugate their masters and to make them their slaves, while they become masters. Slavery in its most varied forms is one of the characteristic features of this savage country, and the missionaries can do nothing against it; they can only offer, to any who may wish, that they should enter schools and study in them, and so become free. For those who do not enter schools the conditions of life cannot be altered.

This is an accurate picture of our life and of our relation to esotericism, if esotericism exists.

If we now regard the life of the human race as a series of rising and falling waves we are brought to the question of the beginning and the origin of man, the beginning and the origin of rising and falling cultures, the beginning and the origin of the human race. As has been said already, what is ordinarily called the " theory of evolution " in relation to man, that is, all the-

ories of naïve Darwinism, appear to be improbable and completely unfounded as they are now put forward. Still less real are various sociological
theories, that is, attempts to explain certain individual qualities and traits in
a man by the influence of his surroundings or by the demands of the society
in the midst of which he lives.

If we now take the biological side, then in the origin and variation of
species there appear, even for a scientific mind, many circumstances utterly
unexplainable by accident or adaptation. These circumstances compel us to
suppose the existence of a plan in the workings of what we call Nature. And
once we suppose or admit the existence of the *plan* we have to admit the
existence of some kind of mind, of some kind of intelligence, that is to say,
the existence of certain beings who work upon this plan and watch over
the realisation of it.

In order to understand the laws of the possible evolution or transformation of man, it is necessary to understand the laws of Nature's activity and
the methods of the Great Laboratory which controls the whole of life and
which scientific thought endeavours to replace by "accident" occurring always in the same direction.

Sometimes in order to understand bigger phenomena it is useful to find
smaller phenomena in which are manifested the same causes that operate
in the bigger phenomena. Sometimes in order to understand the complexity
of the principles lying at the base of big phenomena it is necessary to realise
the complexity of phenomena which look small and insignificant.

There are many phenomena of Nature which have never been fully
analysed and which, being represented in a wrong light, form a basis for various false theories and hypotheses. At the same time, when seen in the right
light and rightly understood, these phenomena explain many things in the
principles and methods of the activity of Nature.

As an illustration of the above propositions I will take the so-called phenomena of mimicry and, generally, of likeness and resemblance in the vegetable and animal worlds. According to the most recent scientific definitions
the word "mimicry" refers only to the phenomena of imitation by living
forms of other living forms; further, certain utilitarian aims and certain limitations are ascribed to it. In other words only phenomena of a certain definite class and character are referred to mimicry, as distinct from the larger
class of "protective resemblance."

In reality the two phenomena belong to the same order and it is impossible to separate them. Moreover, the term "*protective* resemblance" is
entirely unscientific, because it presupposes a ready-made explanation of the
phenomena of resemblance, which in reality is entirely unexplained and contains many features which contradict the definition *protective*.

In view of this, the word "mimicry" is taken from now on in its full
meaning, that is, in the sense of *any* imitation or copying by living forms either of other living forms or of the natural conditions surrounding them.

The phenomena of mimicry are most clearly manifested in the world of insects.

Certain countries are especially rich in insects which embody in their structure or colouring the various conditions of their surroundings, or the plants on which they live, or other insects. There are insect-leaves, insect-twigs, insect-stones, insect-mosses and insect-stars — fireflies. Even a general and casual study of these insects reveals a whole world of miracles. Butter-flies, whose folded wings represent a large, dry leaf, with serrated edges, with symmetrical spots, veins and an intricate design, stuck to the tree or whirling in the wind. Beetles which imitate grey moss. Wonderful insects, the bodies of which are exact copies of small green twigs, sometimes with a broad leaf at the end. These latter insects are found, for instance, on the Black Sea shore of the Caucasus. In Ceylon there is a large green insect which lives on a certain kind of bush and copies the exact form, colour and dimensions of the leaves of this plant (*Phyllium siccifolium*).

At a distance of about a yard it is quite impossible to distinguish the insect among the leaves from a genuine leaf. The leaves are almost round in shape, an inch and a half or two inches in diameter, with a pointed end, fairly thick, with veins and serrated edges and with a red peduncle below. And precisely the same veins and serrations are faithfully reproduced on the upper part of the insect. Underneath, where the peduncle begins on the real leaf, is a small red body with thin legs and a head with feelers. It is quite invisible from above. The "leaf" covers it and protects it from curious eyes.

Mimicry was for a long time "scientifically" explained as the result of the survival of the fittest, which possess better protective appliances. Thus, for instance, it was said: one of the insects may have been "accidentally" born a greenish colour. Thanks to this greenish colour, it was successful in concealing itself among green leaves, was more able to elude its enemies and had a greater chance of leaving progeny. In this progeny the specimens of a greenish colour survived more easily and had a greater chance of continuing their kind. Gradually, after thousands of generations, there resulted an insect which was entirely green in colour. One of these happened "accidentally" to be flatter than the others and, thanks to this, was less noticeable among the leaves. It could hide better from its enemies and had a greater chance of leaving progeny. Gradually, again after thousands of generations, there resulted a green and *flat* variety. One of these green insects of the flat variety resembled a leaf in shape; thanks to this it was more successful in hiding among leaves, had a greater chance of leaving progeny, and so on.

This theory was repeated so many times in various forms by scientists that it became almost universally accepted, though in reality it is, of course, the most naïve of explanations.

If you examine an insect which resembles a green leaf, or a butterfly whose folded wings are like a withered leaf, or the insect which imitates a green twig with a leaf, you see in each of them not one feature which makes it similar to a plant, not two or three such features, but thousands of features, each of which, according to the old " scientific " theory, must have been formed *separately*, independently of others, for it is utterly impossible to suppose that one insect suddenly, " accidentally," became similar to a green leaf in all its details. " Accident " may be admitted in one direction, but it is quite impossible to admit it in a thousand directions at once. We must either presume that all the most minute details were formed independently of one another, or that some kind of " plan " existed. Science could not admit a " plan." " Plan " is not a scientific idea at all. There remained only " accident." In that case every vein on the insect's back, every green leg, the red neck, the green head with the feelers, all these, every minutest detail, every tiniest feature, must have been formed independently of all the others. In order to form an insect exactly like a leaf of the plant on which it lives, not one, but thousands, perhaps even tens of thousands, of repeated accidents would have been necessary.

Those who invented " scientific " explanations of mimicry did not take into consideration the mathematical impossibility of this kind of " accidental " series of combinations and repetitions.

If we trace the amount of intentional and, to a certain degree, conscious work which is necessary to obtain an ordinary knife-blade from a lump of iron ore, we shall never think that a knife-blade could come into being " accidentally."

It would be an entirely unscientific idea to expect to find in the earth ready-made blades with the trade-mark of Sheffield or Solingen on them. But the theory of mimicry expects much more. On the basis of this or a similar theory one might expect to find in some stratum of rock a typewriter, which has been formed naturally and is perfectly ready for use.

The impossibility of combined accidents is precisely what was for a long time not taken into consideration in " scientific " thinking.

When one trait makes an animal invisible in its surroundings, as a white hare is invisible in the snow or a green frog in the grass, it may at a stretch be explained " scientifically." But when the number of these traits becomes almost incalculable, such an explanation loses all logical possibility.

In addition to what has been stated, the insect-leaf possesses another feature which attracts attention. If you find such an insect dead, you will see that it resembles a faded and half-withered curled leaf.

The question arises: why is it that if a live insect resembles a live leaf a dead insect resembles a dead leaf? The one does not follow from the other. In spite of the outward resemblance, the histological structure of the one and of the other must be quite different. Thus the resemblance of the dead insect to the dead leaf is also a trait which had to be formed quite separately and independently. How did science explain it?

What was it able to say? That at first one dead insect slightly resembled a faded leaf. Owing to this it had a greater chance of concealing itself from its enemies, of begetting more numerous progeny and so on. Science could not say anything else, because this is a necessary deduction from the principle of protective or utilitarian resemblances.

Modern science cannot altogether follow these lines, and though it still retains the Darwinian and post-Darwinian terminology of " protectiveness," of " friends " and " enemies," it cannot now regard the phenomena of resemblance and mimicry from the utilitarian point of view alone.

Many strange facts have been established; for instance, many cases are known in which a change of colouring and form makes an insect or animal *more* conspicuous, subjects it to *greater* danger, makes it more attractive and more inviting *to its enemies*.

The principle of utilitarianism had to be abandoned. And in modern scientific works one may now meet with meaningless and diffuse explanations that the phenomena of mimicry owe their origin to the " influence of the environment acting similarly on different species " or to a " physiological response to constant mental experiences, such as colour sensation." [4]

It is clear that this also is no explanation at all.

In order to understand the phenomena of mimicry and resemblance in general in the animal and vegetable worlds, it is necessary to take a much broader view, and only then will it be possible to succeed in finding their leading principle.

Scientific thought, owing to its definite limitations, cannot see this principle.

This principle is the general tendency of Nature towards decorativeness, " theatricalness," the tendency to be or to appear different from what she really is at a given time and place.

Nature tries always to adorn herself and *not to be herself*. This is the fundamental law of her life. All the time she is dressing herself up, all the time changing her costumes, all the time turning before a mirror, looking at herself from all sides, admiring herself — then again undressing and dressing.

Her actions often appear to us as accidental and aimless, because we always try to attribute to them some utilitarian meaning. In reality, however, nothing can be farther from Nature's intentions than a working towards " utility." Utility is attained only by the way, only casually. What can be regarded as permanent and intentional is the tendency towards decorativeness, the endless disguise, the endless masquerade, by which Nature lives.

Indeed, all these small insects of which I have spoken are dressed up and disguised; they all wear masks and fancy dresses. Their whole life is passed on the stage. The tendency of their life is not to be themselves, but to resemble something else, a green leaf, a bit of moss, a shiny stone.

At the same time one can only imitate what one actually sees. Even man is unable to devise or invent new forms. An insect or an animal is forced

4 *Enc. Brit.*, 14th ed., vol. 15, Mimicry.

to borrow them from its surroundings, to imitate something in the conditions among which it is born. A peacock dresses itself in round sun-flecks, which fall on the ground from the rays passing through the foliage. A zebra covers itself with shadows from the branches of the trees. A fish living on a sandy sea-bottom copies the sand in its colouring. The same fish living on a black slimy bottom will imitate slime in its colouring. An insect living among the green leaves of one particular bush in Ceylon will disguise itself as a leaf of this bush. It cannot disguise itself as anything else. Should it feel a tendency to decorativeness and to theatricalness, a tendency to wearing strange apparel and to masquerading, it will be forced to imitate the green leaves among which it lives. These leaves are all that it knows and sees, and it can invent nothing else. It is surrounded by green leaves, and it dresses up in a green leaf, pretends to be a green leaf, plays the part of a green leaf. We can see in this only one thing, — a tendency not to be oneself, to appear something one is not.[5]

Of course it is a miracle, and a miracle which contains not one, but many enigmas.

First of all, who or what dresses up, who or what strives to be or to appear something he is not?

Obviously not the individual insects or animals. An individual insect is only a costume.

There is somebody or something behind it.

In the phenomena of decorativeness, in the shapes and colouring of living creatures, in the phenomena of mimicry, even in " protectiveness," there can be seen a definite plan, intention and aim; and very often this plan is not utilitarian at all. On the contrary, the disguise often contains much that is dangerous, unnecessary and inexpedient.

What then can it be?

It is *fashion*, fashion in Nature!

Now what is " fashion " in the human world? Who creates it, who governs it, what are its leading principles, and in what lies the secret of its being imperative? It contains an element of decorativeness, though this is often wrongly understood, an element of protectiveness, an element of the emphasising of secondary traits, an element of desire not to appear or not to be what one is, and also an element of imitating what most strikes the imagination.

Why was it that in the 19th century, with the beginning of the reign of machines, cultured Europeans, with their top hats, black trousers and black frock-coats, were transformed into stylised smoke-funnels?

What was it? " Protective resemblance? "

Mimicry is a manifestation of this same " fashion " in the animal world. All imitation, all copying, all concealment, is " fashion." Frogs which are

---

[5] This tendency not to be oneself and the tendency to theatricalness (in human life) are interestingly described in N. N. Evreinov's book, *The Theatre in Life* (St. Petersburg, 1915. G. G. Harrap & Co., London).

green among greenery, yellow in the sand, almost black on black earth — this is not merely " protectiveness." We can trace here an element of what is " done," what is respectable, what everybody does. In the sand a green frog would attract too much attention, would stand out too much, would be a " blot." Evidently, for some reason this is not permitted, is considered contrary to the good taste of Nature.

The phenomena of mimicry establish two principles for understanding the working of Nature: the principle of the existence of a plan in every-thing Nature does, and the principle of the absence of simple utilitarianism in this plan.

This brings us to the question of methods, to the question of how it is done. And this question in its turn immediately leads to another: — how is not only this, but everything in general done?

Scientific thought is forced to admit the possibility of strange " jumps " in the formation of new biological types. The quiet and well-balanced theory of the origin of species of the good old days was long ago abandoned, and there is now no possibility of defending it. " Jumps " are evident and over-throw the entire theory. According to biological theories which became " classical " in the second half of the 19th century, acquired traits become permanent only after *accidental* repetitions in many generations. In actual fact, however, new traits are very often transmitted at once and *in an inten-sified degree.* This fact alone destroys the whole of the old system and obliges us to presume the existence of some kind of powers which direct the appear-ance and stabilising of new traits.

From this point of view it is possible to suppose that what are called the animal and vegetable kingdoms are the result of complicated work done by a Great Laboratory. In looking at the vegetable and animal worlds we may think that in some immense and incomprehensible laboratory of Nature there are produced one after another a series of experiments. The result of each experiment is put into a separate glass tube, is sealed and labelled, and so enters our world. We see it and say " *fly.*" Next experiment, next tube — we say " *bee* "; next — " *snake,*" " *elephant,*" " *horse,*" and so on. All these are experiments of the Great Laboratory. Last of all comes the most difficult and complicated experiment, " man."

In the beginning we see no order and no aim in these experiments. And certain experiments, like noxious insects or poisonous snakes, appear to us as a malicious joke of Nature's at the expense of man.

But gradually we begin to see a system and a definite direction in the work of the Great Laboratory. We begin to understand that the Laboratory experiments *only* with man. The task of the Laboratory is to create a " form " evolving by itself, that is, on the condition of help and support, but with its own forces. This self-evolving form is man.

All other forms are either preliminary experiments for working out material to feed more complicated forms, or experiments for working out definite properties or parts of the machine; or unsuccessful experiments, or the refuse of production, or used material.

The result of all this complicated work is the first humanity — *Adam and Eve.*

But the Laboratory began to work long before the appearance of man. A multitude of forms was created, each of them for perfecting one or another trait, one or another appliance. And each of these forms, in order to be alive, included in itself and expressed some of the fundamental cosmic laws, appearing as their symbol or hieroglyph. Owing to this, the once created forms did not disappear after having served their purpose, but continued to live so long as favourable conditions lasted or so long as they were not destroyed by similar but more perfect forms. The " experiments," so to say, ran away from the Laboratory and began to live by themselves. Later on, the theory of evolution was invented for them. Nature, of course, had in view no evolution for these " experiments " that ran away. Sometimes in creating these experimental forms Nature employed material which had been already used up in man, which was useless for him and which was incapable of transformation in him.

In this way *all* the work of the Great Laboratory had in view one aim — the creation of *Man*. Out of the preliminary experiments and the refuse of the production there were formed animals.

Animals, which are our " ancestors " according to Darwin, are in reality not our ancestors, but very often as much the " descendants " of long-vanished *human* races as we are. We are their descendants, and animals are also their descendants. In us are embodied their properties of one kind, in animals are embodied their properties of another kind. Animals are our cousins. The difference between us and animals is that we, successfully or unsuccessfully, adapt ourselves to changing conditions, or in any case have the faculty of adaptation. Animals, however, have stopped at some one trait, one property which they express, and they go no farther. If conditions change, animals die out. They are incapable of adapting themselves. In them are embodied properties which cannot change. Animals are the embodiment of those human properties which became useless and impossible in man.

This is why animals so often seem to be caricatures of men.

The whole of the animal world is a continuous caricature of human life. There is much in men that has to be cast away before they can become real men. And people are afraid of this because they do not know what they will have left. Perhaps something will remain, but very little. And would anybody have the courage to make such an experiment? Perhaps some people will dare. But where are they?

The properties which are destined sooner or later for the zoological garden still govern our life, and people are afraid to give them up even in their thoughts because they feel that if they lose them there will be nothing left.

And the worst of it is that in the majority of cases they are perfectly right.

But let us go back to the moment when the first man, " Adam and Eve," was issued from the Laboratory and appeared on Earth. The first humanity could not begin any culture. There was as yet no inner circle to help them, to guide their first steps. And man had to receive help from the powers which created him. These powers had to fill the part afterwards played by the inner circle.

Culture began and, as the first man had not yet the habit of mistakes, nor the practice of misdeeds, nor the memory of barbarism, the culture developed with extraordinary speed. Moreover, this culture did not develop negative sides, but only positive sides. Man was living in full unity with Nature, he saw the inner properties in all things, in all beings, he understood these properties and he gave names to all things according to their properties. Animals obeyed him; he was in constant converse with the higher powers which had created him. And man rose to great heights and rose with great rapidity because he made no mistakes in his ascent. But this incapacity to make mistakes and the absence of the practice of mistakes while on the one hand hastening his progress, on the other hand exposed him to great danger because it carried with it the incapacity to avoid the results of mistakes, which nevertheless remained possible.

Eventually man did make a mistake. And he made this mistake when he had already risen to a great height.

This mistake consisted in his beginning to regard himself as being still higher than he actually was. He thought that he already knew what was good and what was evil; he thought that *by himself* he could guide and direct his life *without help from the outside*.

This mistake might possibly not have been so great, its results might have been corrected or altered, if man had known how to deal with the results of his mistakes. But having had no experience of mistakes he did not know how to combat the results of his mistakes. The mistake began to grow, began to assume gigantic proportions, until it began to manifest itself in all sides of man's life. Man began to fall. The wave went down. Man rapidly descended to the level from which he started, *plus the acquired sin*.

And after a more or less long stationary period, the arduous ascent with the help of higher powers began again. The only difference was that this time man had the capacity for making mistakes, *had a sin*. And the second wave of culture began with fratricide, with the crime of Cain, which was placed as the corner-stone of the new culture.

But apart from the " karma " of sin, man had acquired a certain experience through his former mistakes and when, therefore, the moment for the fatal mistake recurred, it was not the whole of humanity which made it. There happened to be a certain number of people who did not commit the crime of Cain, who did not associate with it in any way or profit by it in any respect.

From that moment the paths of humanity diverged. Those who made the mistake began to fall until they again reached the lowest level. But the moment they began to need help, those who did not fall, that is, those who did not make the mistake, were now able to give this help.

Such in short is the scheme of the earliest cultures. The myth of Adam and Eve is the history of the first culture. Life in the Garden of Eden was the form of civilisation which was reached by the first culture. The Fall of Man was the result of his attempt to rid himself of the higher powers who guided his evolution and start a life on his own, relying only on his own judgement. Every culture commits this fundamental mistake in its own way. Every new culture develops some new features, arrives at new results and then loses all. But everything that is really valuable is preserved by those who do not make mistakes, and it serves as material for the beginning of the succeeding culture.

In the first culture man had no experience of mistakes. His rise was very rapid, but it was not sufficiently complex, not sufficiently varied. Man did not develop in himself all the possibilities that were in him, because many things were attained by him too easily. But after a series of falls, with all his luggage of errors and crimes, man had to develop other possibilities inherent in him in order to counterbalance the result of those errors. Further on it will be shown that the development of all possibilities inherent in each point of creation forms the object of the progress of the Universe, and the life of mankind must be studied also in connection with this principle.

In the later life of the human race and in its later cultures the development of these possibilities is effected with the help of the inner circle. From this point of view all the evolution possible to mankind consists in the evolution of a small number of individuals, spread possibly over a long period of time. The mass of humanity itself does not evolve; it merely varies a little, adapting itself to the change of surrounding conditions. Mankind, like an organism, evolves by means of the evolution of a certain very small number of the cells of which it consists. The evolving cells pass, as it were, into the higher tissues in the organism, and thus these higher tissues receive nourishment by absorbing the evolving cells.

The idea of the higher tissues is the idea of the inner circle.

As I mentioned before, the idea of the inner circle contradicts all recognised sociological theories concerning the structure of human society, but this idea brings us to other theories which are forgotten now and which did not receive due attention in their time.

Thus from time to time there arose in sociology the question as to whether humanity could be regarded as an organism and human communities as smaller organisms; that is, is a biological view of social phenomena possible? Contemporary sociological thought adopts a negative attitude in relation to this idea, and it has long been considered unscientific to regard a community as an organism. The mistake lies however in the way the problem itself is formulated. The concept " organism " is taken in too narrow a sense and only in one preconceived idea. Namely, if a human community, nation, people, race, is taken as an organism, it is regarded as an organism either analogous to the *human organism* or higher than the human organism. Actually, however, this idea can be correct only in relation to the whole of *mankind*. Separate human groups, no matter how large they may be, can never be analogous to man, and still less can they ever be superior to him. Biology knows of and has established the existence of entirely different orders of organisms. And if in examining the phenomena of social life we bear in mind the difference between organisms on the different rungs of the biological ladder, the biological view of social phenomena becomes much more possible. But this only on condition that we realise that every human community, such as a race, a people, a tribe, is a lower organism as compared to an individual man.

A race or a nation regarded as an organism has nothing in common with the highly developed and complex organism of individual man, which for every function has a special organ and has very great capacity for adaptation, possesses free movement, etc. In comparison with an individual man, a race or nation as an organism stands on a very low level, that of " animal plants." These organisms are amorphous, for the most part immobile, masses, beings which have no special organs for any of their functions and do not possess the capacity for free movement, but are fixed to a definite place. They put out something like feelers in different directions, and by means of these they seize other beings like themselves and eat them. The whole life of these organisms consists in their eating one another. There are some organisms which possess the capacity for absorbing a quantity of smaller organisms, and so temporarily become very large and strong. Then two of these large organisms meet one another, and a struggle begins between them in which either one or both are destroyed or weakened. The whole external history of humanity, the history of the struggles between peoples and races, consists of nothing but the process, which has just been described, of " animal plants " eating one another.

But in the midst of all this, underneath it all, as it were, proceed the life and activity of the individual man, that is, of the individual cells which form these organisms. The activity of these individual men produces what we call culture or civilisation. The activity of the masses is always hostile to this culture, it always destroys it. Peoples create nothing. They only destroy. It is individual men who create. All inventions, discoveries, improvements, all technical progress, the progress of science, art, architecture and engineering, all philosophical systems, all religious teachings, all these are results of the activity of individual men. The destruction of the results of this activity, their distortion, annihilation, obliteration from the face of the earth — this is the activity of the human masses.

This does not mean that individual men do not serve destruction. On the contrary, the initiative of destruction on a large scale always belongs to individual men, and the masses are merely the executive agency. But masses can never create anything, although they can destroy on their own account.

If we understand that the masses of humanity, that is, peoples and races, are lower beings as compared with individual man, we shall understand that peoples and races cannot evolve in the same measure as individual man.

We have even no idea of the evolution possible to a people or to a race, though we often speak of such an evolution. As a matter of fact, all peoples and nations within the limits of our historical observation follow one and the same course. They grow, develop, reach a certain degree of size and power, and then begin to be divided up, decline and fall. Finally they disappear entirely and become component parts of some other being like themselves. Races and nations die in the same way as individual man. But individuals have certain other possibilities besides death, which the great organisms of the human masses have not, for the souls of these are as amorphous as their bodies.

The tragedy of individual man lies in the fact that he lives, as it were, within the dense mass of such a lower being, and all his activity is in the service of the purely vegetable functions of this blind jelly-like organism. At the same time the conscious individual activity of man, his efforts in the domain of thought and creative work, run *contrary to* these big organisms, *in spite* of them and *in defiance* of them. But of course it would not be true to say that *all* the individual activity of man consists in a *conscious* struggle against these big organisms. Man is conquered and made a slave. And it often happens that man thinks he is serving and must serve these big beings by his individual activity. But the higher manifestations of the human spirit, the higher activities of man, are entirely unnecessary to the big organisms; in most cases, indeed, they are unpleasant to them, hostile and even dangerous, since they divert to individual work forces which might otherwise have been absorbed into the vortex of the life of the big organism. In an unconscious, merely physiological way, the big organism endeavours to appropriate all the powers of the individual cells which are its components, using them in its own interests, that is to say, mainly for fighting other similar organisms. But when we remember that individual cells, that is, men, are far more highly organised beings than big organisms, and that the activities of the former go far beyond the activities possible to the latter, we shall understand this perpetual conflict between man and human aggregates, we shall understand that what is called progress or evolution is that which is left over of individual activities after all the struggle between the amorphous masses and this individual activity has taken place. The blind organisms of the masses struggle with the manifestation of the evolutionary spirit, annihilate and stifle it and destroy what has been created by it. But even so they cannot entirely annihilate it. Something remains, and this is what we call progress or civilisation.

The idea of evolution in the life both of individual man and of human communities, the idea of esotericism, the birth and growth of cultures and civilisations, the possibilities of individual man connected with periods of rise and fall — all these and many other things are expressed in three Biblical myths.

These three myths are not connected in the Bible and stand separately, but in reality they express one and the same idea and mutually complete one another.

The first myth is the story of the Great Flood and of Noah's Ark; the second is the story of the Tower of Babel, of its destruction and the confusion of tongues; and the third is the story of the destruction of Sodom and Gomorrah, of Abraham's vision and of the ten righteous men, for whose sake God agreed to spare Sodom and Gomorrah, but who could not be found there.

The Great Flood is an allegory of the fall of civilisation, of the destruction of culture. Such a fall must be accompanied by the annihilation of the greater part of the human race as a consequence of geological upheavals, or of wars, of the migration of human masses, epidemics, revolutions, and similar causes. Very often all these causes coincide. The idea of the allegory is that, at the moment of the apparent destruction of everything, that which is really valuable is saved according to a plan previously prepared and thought out. A small group of men escapes from the general law and saves all the most important ideas and attainments of the given culture.

The legend of Noah's Ark is a myth referring to esotericism. The building of the " Ark " is the " School," the preparation of men for initiation, for transition to a new life, for new birth. " Noah's Ark," which is saved from the Flood, is the inner circle of humanity.

The second meaning of the allegory refers to individual man. The flood is death, unavoidable, inexorable. But man can build within himself an " Ark " and assemble in it *specimens* of everything that is valuable in him. In such a case these specimens will not perish. They will survive death and be born again. Just as mankind can be saved only through its connection with the inner circle, so an individual man can attain personal " salvation " only by means of a link with the inner circle in himself, that is, by connecting himself with the higher forms of consciousness. And this cannot be done without outside help, that is, without the help of the " inner circle."

The second myth, that of the Tower of Babel, is another version of the first; but the first speaks of salvation, that is, of those who are saved, while the second speaks only of destruction, that is, of those who shall perish.

The Tower of Babel represents culture. Men dream of building a tower of stone " whose top may reach unto heaven," of creating an ideal life on earth. They believe in intellectual methods, in technical means, in formal institutions. For a long time the tower rises higher and higher above the earth. But the moment infallibly arrives when men cease to understand each other, or rather, realise that they have never done so. Each of them understands in his own way the ideal life on earth. Each of them wants to carry out his own ideas. Each of them wants to fulfil his own ideal. This is the moment when the confusion of tongues begins. Men cease to understand one another even in the simplest things; lack of understanding provokes discord, hostility, struggle. The men who built the tower start killing one another and destroying what they have built. The tower falls in ruins.

Precisely the same thing occurs in the life of the whole of humanity, in the life of peoples and nations, and in the life of individual man. Each man builds a Tower of Babel in his own life. His strivings, his aims in life, his attainments, these are his Tower of Babel.

But the moment is inevitable when the tower will fall. A slight shock, an unfortunate accident, an illness, a small miscalculation, and of his tower nothing remains. Man sees it, but it is already too late to correct or alter it.

Or a moment may come in the building of the tower when the different " I "s of a man's personality lose confidence in one another, see all the contradictions of their aims and desires, see that they have no common aim, cease to understand one another, or more exactly, cease to think that they understand. Then the tower must fall, the illusory aim must disappear, and the man must feel that everything that he has done was fruitless, that it has led to nothing and could lead to nothing, and that before him there is only one real fact — death.

The whole life of man, the accumulation of riches, or power, or learning, is the building of a Tower of Babel, because it must end in catastrophe, namely, in death, which is the fate of everything that cannot pass to a new plane of being.

The third myth — that of the destruction of Sodom and Gomorrah — shows still more clearly than the first two the moment of the interference of the higher forces and the causes of this interference. God agreed to spare Sodom and Gomorrah for the sake of fifty righteous men, for the sake of forty-five, for the sake of thirty, for the sake of twenty, at last for the sake of ten. But ten righteous men could not be found and the two cities were destroyed. The possibility of evolution had been lost. The " Great Laboratory " put an end to the unsuccessful experiment. *But Lot and his family were saved.* The idea is the same as in the other two myths, but it particularly emphasises the readiness of the guiding will to make all possible concessions so long as there is any hope of the realisation of the aim set for human beings. When this hope disappears, the guiding will must inevitably interfere, save what deserves salvation and destroy the rest.

The expulsion of Adam and Eve from the Garden of Eden, the fall of the Tower of Babel, the Great Flood, the destruction of Sodom and Gomorrah, are all legends and allegories relating to the history of mankind, to human evolution. Besides these legends and many others similar to them, almost all races have legends, tales and myths of strange *non-human* beings, who passed along the same road before man. The fall of the angels, of Titans, of gods who attempted to defy other more powerful gods, the fall of Lucifer, the demon or Satan, are all falls which preceded the fall of man. And it is an undoubted fact that the meaning of all these myths is deeply hidden from us. It is perfectly clear that the usual theological and theosophical interpretations do not explain anything, because they introduce the necessity of recognising the existence of invisible races or *spirits*, which at the same time are similar to man in their relation to higher forces. The inadequacy of such an explanation " by means of introducing five new unknown quantities for the definition of one unknown quantity " is evident. But at the same time it would be wrong to leave all these myths without any attempt at explanation, because by their very persistency and repetition among different peoples and races they seem to draw our attention to certain phenomena which we do not know but which we should know.

The legends and epics of all countries contain much material relating to non-human beings who preceded man, or even existed at the same time as man, but differed from man in many ways. This material is so abundant and significant that not to make an attempt to explain these myths would mean shutting our eyes intentionally to something we ought to see. Such, for instance, are the legends of giants and the so-called " Cyclopean " structures which one involuntarily associates with these legends.

Unless we wish to ignore many facts or believe in three-dimensional " spirits " capable of building stone edifices, we must suppose that pre-human races were as physical as man and came, just as man did, from the Great Laboratory of Nature, that Nature had made attempts at creating self-evolving beings before man. And further we must suppose that such beings were let out of the Great Laboratory into life, but that they failed to satisfy Nature in their further development and, instead of carrying out Nature's designs, turned against her. And then Nature abandoned her experiment with them and began a new experiment.

Strictly speaking, we have no grounds for considering man as the first or the only experiment of a self-evolving being. On the contrary, the myths mentioned above give us the possibility of presuming the existence of such beings before man.

If this is so, if we have grounds for supposing the existence of *physical races* of pre-human self-evolving beings, where then should we look for the descendants of these races, and are we in any way justified in supposing the existence of such descendants?

We must start from the idea that in all her activity Nature aims at the creation of a self-evolving being.

But can it be supposed that the *whole* of the animal kingdom is the by-product of one line of work — *the creation of man?*

This may be admitted in relation to mammals, we may even include in it all vertebrates, we may consider many lower forms as preparatory forms, and so on. But what place shall we give in this system to *insects*, which represent a world in themselves and a world not less complex than the world of vertebrates?

May it not be supposed that insects represent another line in the work of Nature, a line not connected with the one which resulted in the creation of man, but perhaps preceding it?

Passing to facts, we must admit that insects are in no way a stage preparatory to the formation of man. Nor could they be regarded as the by-product of human evolution. On the contrary, insects reveal, in their structure and in the structure of their separate parts and organs, forms which are often more perfect than those of man or animals. And we cannot help seeing that for certain forms of insect life which we observe there is no explanation without very complicated hypotheses, which necessitate the recognition of a very rich past behind them and compel us to regard the present forms we observe as degenerated forms.

This last consideration relates mainly to the organised communities of ants and bees. It is impossible to become acquainted with their life without giving oneself up to emotional impressions of astonishment and bewilderment. Ants and bees alike both call for our admiration by the wonderful completeness of their organisation, and at the same time repel and frighten us, and provoke a feeling of undefinable aversion by the invariably cold reasoning which dominates their life and by the absolute impossibility for an individual to escape from the wheel of life of the ant-hill or the beehive. We are terrified at the thought that we may resemble them.

Indeed what place do the communities of ants and bees occupy in the general scheme of things on our earth? How could they come into being such as we observe them? All observations of their life and their organisation inevitably lead us to one conclusion. The original organisation of the " beehive " and the " ant-hill " in the remote past undoubtedly required reasoning and logical intelligence of great power, although at the same time the further existence of both the beehive and the ant-hill did not require any intelligence or reasoning at all.

How could this have happened?

It could only have happened in one way. If ants or bees, or both, of course at different periods, had been intelligent and evolving beings and then lost their intelligence and their ability to evolve, this could have happened only because their " intelligence " went against their " evolution," in other words, because in thinking that they were helping their evolution they managed somehow to arrest it.

One may suppose that both ants and bees came from the Great Laboratory and were sent to earth with the privilege and the possibility of evolving. But after a long period of struggle and efforts both the one and the other renounced their privilege and ceased to evolve, or, to be more exact, ceased to send forth an evolving current. After this Nature had to take her own measures and, after isolating them in a certain way, to begin a new experiment.

If we admit the possibility of this, may we not suppose that the old legends of falls which preceded the fall of man relate to ants and bees? We may find ourselves disconcerted by their small size as compared to our own. But the size of living beings is, first of all, a relative thing, and secondly it changes very easily in certain cases. In the case of certain classes of beings, for instance fishes, amphibious animals and insects, Nature holds in her hands the threads that regulate their size and never lets these threads go. In other words Nature possesses the power of changing the size of these living beings *without altering anything in them*, and can effect this change in one generation, that is, at once, simply by arresting their development at a certain stage. Everyone has seen small fishes exactly like large fishes, small frogs, etc. This is still more evident in the vegetable world. But of course it is not a universal rule, and some beings such as man and most of the higher mammals reach almost the largest size possible for them. As regards the insects, ants and bees most probably could be much larger than they are now, although this point may be argued; and it is possible that the change of size of the ant or the bee would necessitate a considerable alteration in their inner organisation.

It is interesting to note here the legends of gigantic ants in Tibet recorded by *Herodotus and Pliny (Herodotus, History, Bk. XI; Pliny, Natural History, Bk. III)*.

Of course it will be difficult at first to imagine Lucifer as a bee, or the Titans as ants. But if we renounce for the moment the idea of the necessity of a human form, the greater part of the difficulty disappears.

The mistake of these non-human beings, that is, the cause of their downfall, must inevitably have been of the same nature as the mistake made by Adam. They must have become convinced *that they knew what was good and what was evil*, and must have believed that *they themselves* could act according to their understanding. They renounced the idea of higher knowledge and the inner circle of life and placed their faith in their own knowledge, their own powers and their own understanding of the aims and purposes of their existence. But their understanding was probably much more wrong and their mistake much less naïve than the mistake of Adam, and the results of this mistake were probably so much more serious that ants and bees not only arrested their evolution in one cycle, but made it altogether impossible by altering their very being.

The ordering of the life of both bees and ants, their ideal communistic organisation, indicate the character and the form of their downfall. It may be imagined that at different times both bees and ants had reached a very high, although a very one-sided culture, based entirely on intellectual considerations of profit and utility, without any scope for imagination, without any esotericism or mysticism. They organised the whole of their life on the principles of a kind of " marxism " which seemed to them very exact and scientific. They realised the socialistic order of things, entirely subjugating the individual to the interests of the community according to their understanding of those interests. And thus they destroyed every possibility for an individual to develop and separate himself from the general masses.

And yet it was precisely this development of individuals and their separation from the general masses which constituted the aim of Nature and on which the possibility of evolution was based. Neither the bees nor the ants wished to acknowledge this. They saw their aim in something else, they strove to subjugate Nature. And in some way or other they altered Nature's plan, made the execution of this plan impossible.

We must bear in mind that, as has been said before, every " experiment " of Nature, that is, every living being, every living organism, represents the expression of cosmic laws, a complex symbol or a complex hieroglyph. Having begun to alter their being, their life and their form, bees and ants, taken as individuals, severed their connection with the laws of Nature, ceased to express these laws individually and began to express them only collectively. And then Nature raised her magic wand, and they became small insects, incapable of doing Nature any harm.

In the course of time their thinking capacities, absolutely unnecessary in a well-organised ant-hill or beehive, became atrophied, automatic habits began to be handed down automatically from generation to generation, and ants became " insects " as we know them; bees even became useful.[6]

Indeed, when observing an ant-hill or a beehive, we are always struck by two things, first by the amount of intelligence and calculation put into their primary organisation and, secondly, by the complete absence of intelligence in their activities. The intelligence put into this organisation was very narrow and rigidly utilitarian, it calculated correctly within the given conditions and it saw nothing outside these conditions. Yet even this intelligence was necessary only for the original calculation and estimation. Once started, the mechanism of a beehive or of an ant-hill did not require any intelligence; automatic habits and customs were automatically learned and handed down, and this ensured their being preserved unchanged. " Intelligence " is not only useless in a beehive or an ant-hill, it would even be dangerous and harmful. Intelligence could not hand down all the laws, rules and methods of work with the same exactness from generation to generation. Intelligence could forget, could distort, could add something new. Intelligence could again lead to " mysticism," to the idea of a higher intelligence, to the idea of esotericism. It was therefore necessary to banish intelligence from an ideal socialistic beehive or ant-hill, as an element harmful to the community — which in fact it is.

Of course there may have been a struggle, a period when the ancestors of ants or bees who had not yet lost the power of thinking saw the situation clearly, saw the inevitable beginning of degeneration and strove to fight against it, trying to free the individual from its unconditional submission to the community. But the struggle was hopeless and could have no result. The iron laws of the ant-hill and beehive very soon dealt with the restless element and after a few generations such recalcitrants probably ceased to be born, and both the beehive and the ant-hill gradually became ideal communistic states.

---

[6] The nature of the *automatism* that governs the life of a beehive or an ant-hill cannot be explained with the psychological conceptions existent in European literature. And I will speak of it in another book in connection with the exposition of the principles of the teaching which was mentioned in the introduction.

In his book *The Life of the White Ant*, Maurice Maeterlinck has collected much interesting material about the life of these insects, which are still more striking than ants and bees.

At the very first attempts to study the life of white ants Maeterlinck experiences the same strange emotional feeling of which I spoke earlier.

. . . it makes them almost our brothers, and from certain points of view, causes these wretched insects, more than the bee or any other living creature on earth, to become the heralds, perhaps the precursors, of our own destiny.

Further, Maeterlinck dwells upon the antiquity of the termites, which are much more ancient than man, and upon the number and great variety of their species.

After this Maeterlinck passes to what he calls the " civilisation of the termites."

Their civilisation which is the earliest of any is the most curious, the most complex, the most intelligent, and in a sense, the most logical and best fitted to the difficulties of existence, which has ever appeared before our own on this globe. From several points of view this civilisation, although fierce, sinister and often repulsive, is superior to that of the bee, of the ant, and even of man himself.

In the termitary the gods of communism become insatiable Molochs. The more they are given, the more they require; and they persist in their demands until the individual is annihilated and his misery complete. This appalling tyranny is unexampled among mankind; for while with us it at least benefits the few, in the termitary no one profits.

The discipline is more ferocious than that of the Carmelites or Trappists; and the voluntary submission to laws or regulations proceeding one knows not whence is unparalleled in any human society. A new form of fatality, perhaps the cruellest of all, the social fatality to which we ourselves are drifting, has been added to those we have met already and thought quite enough. There is no rest except in the last sleep of all: illness is not tolerated, and feebleness carries with it its own sentence of death. Communism is pushed to the limits of cannibalism and coprophagy.

. . . compelling the sacrifice and misery of the many for the advantage or happiness of none — and all this in order that a kind of universal despair may be continued, renewed and multiplied so long as the world shall last. These cities of insects, that appeared before we did, might almost serve as a caricature of ourselves, as a travesty of the earthly paradise to which most civilised people are tending.

Maeterlinck shows by what sacrifices this ideal régime is bought.

They used to have wings, they have them no more. They had eyes which they surrendered. They had a sex; they have sacrificed it.[7]

---

[7] *The Life of the White Ant*, by Maurice Maeterlinck, translated by Alfred Sutro (George Allen and Unwin, London, 1927, pp. 17, 152, 163).

The only thing he omits to say is that before sacrificing wings, sight, and sex, the termites had to sacrifice their intelligence.

In spite of this the process through which the termites passed is called by Maeterlinck evolution. This comes about because, as I have said before, *every* change of form taking place over a long period of time is called evolution by modern thought. The power of this compulsory stereotype of pseudo-scientific thinking is truly astounding. In the Middle Ages philosophers and scientists had to make all their theories and discussions agree with the dogmas of the Church, and in our day the rôle of those dogmas is played by " evolution." It is quite clear that thought cannot develop freely in these conditions.

The idea of esotericism has a particularly important significance at the present stage of the development of the thought of humanity, because it makes quite unnecessary the idea of evolution in the ordinary sense' of this word. It has been said earlier what the word " evolution " may mean in the esoteric sense, namely, the transformation of individuals. And in this meaning alone evolution cannot be confused with degeneration as is constantly done by " scientific " thought, which regards even its own degeneration as evolution.

The only way out of all the blind alleys created by both " materialistic " and metaphysical thought lies in the psychological method. The psychological method is nothing other than the revaluation of all values from the point of view of their *own* psychological meaning and independently of the outer or accompanying facts on the basis of which they are generally judged. Facts may lie. The psychological meaning of a thing, or of an idea, cannot lie. Of course it also can be understood wrongly. But this can be struggled against by studying and observing the mind, that is, our apparatus of cognition. Generally the mind is regarded much too simply, without taking into account that the limits of useful action of the mind, first, are very well known, and, second, are very restricted. The psychological method takes into consideration these limitations in the same way as we take into consideration, in all ordinary circumstances of life, limitations of machines or instruments with which we have to work. If we examine something under a microscope, we take into consideration the power of the microscope; if we do some work with a particular instrument, we take into consideration properties and qualities of the instrument — weight, sharpness, etc. The psychological method aims at doing the same in relation to our mind, that is, it aims at keeping the mind itself constantly in its field of view, and at regarding all conclusions and discoveries *relatively to the state or kind of mind*. From the point of view of the psychological method there are no grounds for thinking that our mind, that is, our apparatus of cognition, is the only possible one or the best in existence. Equally there are no grounds for thinking that all discovered and established truths will always remain truths. On the contrary, from the point of view of the psychological method there can be no doubt that we shall have to discover many new truths, either entirely in-comprehensible truths, the very existence of which we never suspected, or truths fundamentally contradicting those which we have recognised until now. Of course nothing is more terrifying and nothing is more inadmissible for all kinds of dogmatism. The psychological method destroys all old and new prejudices and superstitions; it does not allow thought to stop and re-main contented with the attained results, no matter how tempting and pleasant these results may appear, and no matter how symmetrical and smooth all deductions made from them may be. The psychological method gives the possibility of re-examining many principles which have been con-sidered as finally and firmly established, and it finds in them entirely new and unexpected meaning. The psychological method makes it possible in many cases to disregard facts or what are taken for facts, and allows us to see beyond facts. Although it is only a method, the psychological method nevertheless leads us in a very definite direction, namely towards the *esoteric* method, which is in reality an enlarged psychological method, though en-larged in that sense in which we cannot enlarge it by our own efforts.

1912–1929

Chapter II

THE FOURTH DIMENSION

❈

THE IDEA of the existence of a hidden knowledge, surpassing all the knowledge a man can attain by his own efforts, must grow and strengthen in people's minds from the realisation of the insolubility of many questions and problems which confront them.

Man may deceive himself, may think that his knowledge grows and increases, that he knows and understands more than he knew and understood before, but sometimes he may be sincere with himself and see that in relation to the fundamental problems of existence he is as helpless as a savage or a little child, although he has invented many clever machines and instruments which have complicated his life but have not rendered it any more comprehensible.

Speaking still more sincerely with himself man may recognise that all his scientific and philosophical systems and theories are similar to these machines and implements, for they only serve to complicate the problems without explaining anything.

Among the insoluble problems with which man is surrounded, two occupy a special position — the problem of the invisible world and the problem of death.

In all the history of human thought, in all the forms, without exception, which this thought has ever taken, people have always divided the world into the *visible* and the *invisible*; and they have always understood that the visible world accessible to their direct observation and study represents something very small, perhaps even something non-existent, in comparison with the enormous existent invisible world.

Such an assertion, that is, that the division of the world into the visible and the invisible has existed always and everywhere, may appear strange at first, but in reality all existing general schemes of the world, from the most primitive to the most subtle and elaborate, divide the world into the visible and the invisible and can never free themselves from this division. This division of the world into the visible and the invisible is the foundation of man's thinking about the world, no matter how he names or defines this division.

The fact of such a division becomes evident if we try to enumerate the various systems of thinking about the world.

First of all let us divide all the systems of thinking about the world into three categories:

1. Religious systems.
2. Philosophical systems.
3. Scientific systems.

All religious systems without exception, from those theologically elaborated down to the smallest details, such as Christianity, Buddhism, Judaism, to the completely degenerated religions of "savages," appearing as "primitive" to modern knowledge, invariably divide the world into visible and invisible. In Christianity: God, angels, devils, demons, souls of living and dead people, heaven or hell. In paganism: gods personifying forces of nature, thunder, sun, fire, spirits of mountains, woods, lakes, water-spirits, house spirits — all this is the invisible world.

In philosophy there is the world of events and the world of causes, the world of things and the world of ideas, the world of phenomena and the world of noumena. In Indian philosophy, especially in certain schools of it, the visible or phenomenal world, that is, Maya or illusion, which means a wrong conception of the invisible world, does not exist at all.

In science, the invisible world is the world of small quantities and, strange though it is, also the world of large quantities. The visibility of the world is determined by the scale. The invisible world is on the one hand the world of micro-organisms, cells, the microscopic and the ultra-microscopic world; still further it is the world of molecules, atoms, electrons, "vibrations," and, on the other hand, the world of invisible stars, other solar systems, unknown universes. The microscope expands the limits of our vision in one direction, the telescope in the other. But both increase visibility very little in comparison with what remains invisible. Physics and chemistry show us the possibility of investigating phenomena in such small quantities or in such distant worlds as will never be visible to us. But this only strengthens the fundamental idea of the existence of an enormous, invisible world round the small, visible world.

Mathematics goes even farther. As was pointed out before, it calculates such relations of magnitudes and such relations between these relations as have nothing similar in the visible world surrounding us. And we are forced to admit that the *invisible* world differs from the visible not only in size, but in some other properties which we can neither define nor understand and which only show us that laws, inferred by us for the visible world, cannot refer to the invisible world.

In this way invisible worlds, the religious, the philosophical, and the scientific, are, after all, more closely related to one another than they would at first appear. And these invisible worlds of different categories possess identical properties common to all. These properties are, first: incomprehensibility for us, that is, incomprehensibility from the ordinary point of view, or for ordinary means of cognition; and, second: the fact that they contain the causes of the phenomena of the visible world.

This idea of causes is always associated with the invisible world. In the invisible world of the religious systems, invisible forces govern people and visible phenomena. In the scientific invisible world the causes of visible phenomena always come from the invisible world of small quantities and " vibrations." In philosophical systems the phenomenon is only our conception of the noumenon, that is, an illusion, the real cause of which remains hidden and inaccessible to us.

This shows that on all levels of his development man has always understood that the causes of visible and observable phenomena lie beyond the sphere of his observation. He has found that among observable phenomena certain facts could be regarded as causes of other facts, but these deductions were insufficient for the explanation of *everything* that occurred in himself and around him. Therefore in order to be able to explain the causes it was necessary for him to have an invisible world consisting either of " spirits," or " ideas," or " vibrations."

The other problem which attracted the attention of men by its insolubility and which by the form of its approximate solution determined the direction and development of human thought, was the problem of death, that is, the explanation of death, the idea of future life, of the immortal soul, or the absence of the immortal soul, and so on.

Man could never reconcile himself to the idea of death as disappearance. Too many things contradicted it. There were in himself too many traces of the dead, their faces, words, gestures, opinions, promises, threats, the feelings which they roused, fear, jealousy, desire. All these continued to live in him, and the fact of their death was more and more forgotten. A man saw his dead friend or enemy in his dreams. He appeared exactly as he was before. Evidently he was living *somewhere*, and could come *from somewhere* by night.

So it was very difficult to believe in death and man always needed theories for the explanation of existence after death.

On the other hand, echoes of esoteric teachings on life and death sometimes reached man. He could hear that the visible, earthly, observable, life of man is only a small part of the life belonging to him. And man of course understood in his own way these fragments which reached him, changed them in his own fashion, adapted them to his own level and understanding, and built out of them some theory of future existence, similar to existence on the earth.

The greater part of religious teachings on the future life connect it with the idea of reward or punishment, sometimes in an undisguised, sometimes in a veiled, form. Heaven and hell, transmigration of souls, reincarnation, the wheel of lives — all these theories contain the idea of reward or punishment. But religious theories often do not satisfy man, and in addition to the recognised, orthodox, ideas of life after death there usually exist other, as it were illegitimate, ideas of the world beyond the grave or of the spirit-world, which allow a greater freedom of imagination.

No religious teaching, no religious system, can by itself satisfy people. There is always some other, more ancient system of popular belief underlying it or hiding behind it. Behind external Christianity, behind external Buddhism, there stand the remains of ancient pagan creeds (in Christianity the remains of pagan beliefs and customs, in Buddhism " the cult of the devil "), which sometimes make a deep mark on the external religion. In modern Protestant countries, for instance, where the remains of ancient paganism are already completely extinct, there have come into existence, under the outward mask of logical and moral Christianity, systems of primitive thinking of the world beyond the grave, such as spiritualism and kindred teachings.

And theories of existence beyond the grave are always connected with theories of the invisible world; the former are always based upon the latter.

This all relates to religion and " pseudo-religion." There are no philosophical theories of existence beyond the grave. All theories of life after death can be called religious or, more correctly, pseudo-religious.

Moreover, it is difficult to take philosophy as a whole, so diverse and contradictory are the various speculative systems. Still, to a certain extent, it is possible to accept as a standard of philosophical thinking the view which can see the unreality of the phenomenal world and the unreality of man's existence in the world of things and events, the unreality of the separate existence of man and the incomprehensibility for us of the forms of real existence, although this view can be based on very different foundations, either materialistic or idealistic. In both cases the question of life and death acquires a new character and cannot be reduced to the naïve categories of ordinary thinking. For such a view there is no particular difference between life and death, because, strictly speaking, for it there are no proofs of a separate existence, of separate lives.

There are not and there cannot be any *scientific* theories of existence after death because there are no facts in favour of the reality of such an existence, while science, successfully or unsuccessfully, wishes to deal with facts. In the fact of death the most important point for science is a certain change in the state of the organism, which stops all vital functions, and the decomposition of the body following upon it. Science sees in man no psychic life independent of the vital functions, and all theories of life after death, from the scientific point of view, are pure fiction.

Modern attempts at " scientific " investigation of spiritualistic phenomena and similar things lead nowhere and can lead nowhere, for there is a mistake here in the very setting of the problem.

In spite of the difference between the various theories of the future life, they all have one common feature. They either picture the life beyond the grave as similar to the earthly life, or deny it altogether. They do not and cannot attempt to conceive life after death in new forms or new categories. And this is precisely what makes all usual theories of life after death unsatisfactory. Philosophical and strictly scientific thought shows us the necessity of reconsidering the problem from completely new points of view. A few hints coming from the esoteric teaching partly known to us indicate the same.

It already becomes evident that if the problem of death and life after death can be approached in any way, it must be approached from quite a new angle. In the same way, the question of the invisible world must also be approached from a new angle. All we know, all we have thought till now, shows us the reality and the vital importance of these problems. Until he has answered in one way or another the questions of the invisible world and of life after death, man cannot think of anything else without creating a whole series of contradictions. Right or wrong, man must construct for himself some kind of explanation. And he must base his treatment of the problem of death either upon science, or upon religion, or upon philosophy.

But to a thinking man both the " scientific " denial of the possibility of life after death and the pseudo-religious admission of it, (for we know nothing but pseudo-religion), as well as different spiritualistic, theosophical and similar theories, quite justly appear equally naïve.

Nor can the abstract philosophical view satisfy man. Such a view is too remote from life, too remote from direct, real sensations. One cannot live by it. In relation to the phenomena of life and their possible causes, unknown to us, philosophy is very like astronomy in its relation to the distant stars. Astronomy calculates the movement of stars which are at colossal distances from us. But all celestial bodies are alike for it. They are nothing but moving dots.

Thus, philosophy is too remote from concrete problems such as the problem of future life. Science does not know the world beyond the grave; pseudo-religion creates the other world in the image of the earthly world.

This helplessness of man in the face of the problems of the invisible world and of death becomes particularly obvious when we begin to realise that the world is far bigger and far more complex than we have hitherto thought, and that what we think we know occupies only a very insignificant place amidst that which we do not know.

Our basic conception of the world must be broadened. Already we feel and know that we can no longer trust the eyes with which we see, or the hands with which we touch. The real world eludes us at such attempts to ascertain its existence. A more subtle method, a more efficient means, are needed.

The ideas of the " fourth dimension," ideas of " many dimensional space," show the way by which we may arrive at the broadening of our conception of the world.

The expression " fourth dimension " is often met with in conversational language and in literature, but it is very seldom that anybody has a clear idea of what it really means. Generally the fourth dimension is used as the synonym of the mysterious, miraculous, " super-natural," incomprehensible and incognisable, as a kind of general definition of the phenomena of the " super-physical " world.

" Spiritualists " and " occultists " of various schools often make use of this expression in their literature, assigning to the sphere of the fourth dimension all the phenomena of the " world beyond " or the " astral sphere." But they do not explain what it means, and from what they say one can understand only that the chief property which they ascribe to the fourth dimension is " unknowableness."

The connecting of the idea of the fourth dimension with existing theories of the invisible world or the world beyond is certainly quite fantastic, for, as has already been said, all religious, spiritualistic, theosophical and other theories of the invisible world first of all make it exactly similar to the visible and consequently " three dimensional " world.

Therefore mathematics quite justly objects to the established view of the fourth dimension as something belonging to the " beyond."

The very idea of the fourth dimension must have arisen in close connection with mathematics, or, to put it better, in close connection with the idea of measuring the world. It must have arisen from the supposition that, besides the three known dimensions of space — length, breadth and height — there might also exist a fourth dimension, inaccessible to our perception.

Logically, the supposition of the existence of the fourth dimension can be based on the observation of those things and events in the world surrounding us for which the measurement in length, breadth and height is not sufficient, or which elude all measurement; because there are things and events the existence of which calls for no doubt, but which cannot be expressed in any terms of measurement. Such are, for instance, various effects of vital and psychic processes; such are all ideas, mental images and memories; such are dreams. If we consider them as existing in a real, objective sense, we can suppose that they have some other dimension besides those accessible for us, that is, some extension immeasurable for us.

There exist attempts at a purely mathematical definition of the fourth dimension. It is said for instance: " In many problems of pure and applied mathematics formulæ and mathematical expressions are met with containing four or more variable quantities, each of which, independently of the others, may be positive or negative and lie between $+ \infty$ and $- \infty$. And as every mathematical formula, every equation, can have a dimensional expression, so from this is deduced an idea of space which has four or more dimensions." [1]

The weak point of this definition is the proposition accepted as unquestionable that every mathematical formula, every equation, can have a di-

---

[1] The article " Four-dimensional space " in the Russian Encyclopedia of Brockhaus and Efron.

mensional expression. In reality such a proposition is entirely without ground, and this deprives the definition of all meaning.

Reasoning by analogy with the existing dimensions, it must be supposed that if the fourth dimension existed it would mean that side by side with us lies some other space which we do not know, do not see, and into which we are unable to pass. It would then be possible to draw a line from any point of our space into this " domain of the fourth dimension " in a direction unknown to us and impossible either to define or to comprehend. If we could visualise the direction of this line going out of our space then we should see the " domain of the fourth dimension."

Geometrically this proposition has the following meaning. We can conceive simultaneously three lines perpendicular and not parallel to one another. These three lines are used by us to measure the whole of our space, which is therefore called three-dimensional. If the " domain of the fourth dimension " lying outside our space exists, this means that besides the three perpendiculars known to us, determining the length, the breadth and the height of solids, there must also exist a fourth perpendicular, determining some new extension unknowable to us. Then the space measurable by these four perpendiculars could be called four-dimensional.

We are unable to define geometrically, or to conceive, this fourth perpendicular, and the fourth dimension still remains extremely enigmatic. The opinion is sometimes met with that mathematicians know something about the fourth dimension which is inaccessible to ordinary mortals. Sometimes it is said, and one can even find such assertions in literature, that Lobatchevsky " discovered " the fourth dimension. During the last twenty years the discovery of the " fourth dimension " has often been ascribed to Einstein or Minkovsky.

In reality mathematics can say very little about the fourth dimension. There is nothing in the hypothesis of the fourth dimension that would make it inadmissible from a mathematical point of view. This hypothesis does not contradict any of the accepted axioms and, because of this, does not meet with particular opposition on the part of mathematics. Mathematicians even admit the possibility of establishing the relationship that should exist between four-dimensional and three-dimensional space, i.e. certain properties of the fourth dimension. But they do all this in a very general and rather indefinite form. No exact definition of the fourth dimension exists in mathematics.

Lobatchevsky actually treated the geometry of Euclid, i.e. geometry of three-dimensional space, as a particular case of geometry, which ought to be applicable to a space of any number of dimensions. But this is not mathematics in the strict sense of the word, it is only metaphysics on mathematical themes; and the deductions from it cannot be formulated mathematically or can be formulated only in specially constructed conditional expressions.

Other mathematicians regarded axioms accepted in the geometry of Euclid as artificial and incorrect, and attempted to disprove them on the strength, chiefly, of certain deductions from Lobatchevsky's spherical geometry, and to prove, for instance, that parallel lines meet. They contended that the accepted axioms are correct only for three-dimensional space, and on the basis of their arguments, which disproved these axioms, they built up a new geometry of many dimensions.

But all this is not geometry of four dimensions.

The fourth dimension could only be considered as geometrically proved when the direction of the unknown line starting from any point of our space and going into the region of the fourth dimension could be determined, i.e. when a means of constructing a fourth perpendicular is found.

It is difficult to describe even approximately the significance which the discovery of the fourth perpendicular in our universe would have for our knowledge. The conquest of the air; hearing and seeing at a distance; establishing connections with other planets or with other solar systems; all this is nothing in comparison with the discovery of a new dimension. But so far it has not been made. We must recognise that we are helpless before the riddle of the fourth dimension, and we must try to examine the problem within the limits accessible to us.

After a closer and more exact investigation of the problem itself we come to the conclusion that it cannot be solved in existing conditions. The problem of the fourth dimension, though purely geometrical at the first glance, cannot be solved by geometrical means. Our geometry of three dimensions is as insufficient for the investigation of the question of the fourth dimension as planimetry alone is insufficient for the investigation of questions of stereometry. We must find the fourth dimension, if it exists, in a purely experimental way, and also find a means for a projective representation of it in three-dimensional space. Only then shall we be able to create a geometry of four dimensions.

Even slight acquaintance with the problem of the fourth dimension shows the necessity for studying it from the psychological and physical sides.

The fourth dimension is unknowable. If it exists and if at the same time we cannot know it, it evidently means that something is lacking in our psychic apparatus, in our faculties of perception; in other words, phenomena of the region of the fourth dimension are not reflected in our organs of sense. We must examine why this should be so, what are our defects on which this non-receptivity depends, and must find the conditions (even if only theoretically) which would make the fourth dimension comprehensible and accessible to us. These are all questions relating to psychology or, possibly, to the theory of knowledge.

Further, we know that the region of the fourth dimension (again, if it exists) is not only unknowable for our psychic apparatus, but is *inaccessible* in a purely physical sense. This must depend not on our defects, but on the particular properties and conditions of the region of the fourth dimension itself. It is necessary to examine what these conditions are, which make the region of the fourth dimension inaccessible to us, and to find the relation between the physical conditions of the region of the fourth dimension and the physical condition of our world. And having established this, it is necessary to see whether in the world surrounding us there is anything similar to these conditions, that is, whether there are any relations analogous to relations between the region of three dimensions and that of four dimensions.

Speaking in general, before attempting to build up a geometry of four dimensions it is necessary to create a physics of four dimensions, that is, to find and to define physical laws and conditions which may exist in the space of four dimensions.

Many people have worked at the problem of the fourth dimension.

Fechner wrote a great deal about the fourth dimension. From his discussions about worlds of one, two, three and four dimensions there follows a very interesting method of investigating the fourth dimension by means of building up analogies between worlds of different dimensions, i.e. between an imaginary world on a plane and the three-dimensional world, and between the three-dimensional world and the world of four dimensions. This method is used by nearly all those who have ever studied the problem of higher dimensions, and we shall have occasion to meet with it further on.

Professor Zöllner evolved the theory of the fourth dimension from observations of " mediumistic " phenomena, chiefly of phenomena of so-called " materialisation." But his observations have long been considered doubtful because of the established fact of the insufficiently strict arrangement of his experiments (Podmore and Hislop).

A very interesting summary of almost all that has ever been written about the fourth dimension up to the nineties of last century is to be found in the books of C. H. Hinton. These books contain also many of Hinton's own ideas; but, unfortunately, side by side with the valuable ideas there is a great deal of unnecessary dialectic such as always accumulates round the question of the fourth dimension.

Hinton makes several attempts at a definition of the fourth dimension from the physical side, as well as from the psychological. Considerable space is occupied in his books by the description of a method, invented by him, of accustoming the mind to cognition of the fourth dimension. It consists of a long series of exercises for the perceiving and the visualising apparatus, with sets of differently coloured cubes, which are meant to be memorised, first in one position, then in another, then in a third, and after that to be visualised in different combinations.

The fundamental idea which guided Hinton in the creation of this method of exercises is that the awakening of " higher consciousness " requires the " casting out of the self " in the visualisation and cognition of the world, i.e. the accustoming of oneself to know and conceive the world, not from a personal point of view (as we generally know and conceive it), but as it is. For this it is necessary, first of all, to learn to visualise things not as they appear to us, but as they are, even if only in a geometrical sense; from this there must develop the capacity to know them, i.e. to see them, as they are, also from other points of view besides the geometrical.

The first exercise suggested by Hinton consists in the study of a cube composed of 27 smaller cubes coloured differently and bearing definite names. After having thoroughly learned the cube made up of smaller cubes, it has to be turned over and learned and memorised in the reverse order. Then the position of the smaller cubes has to be changed and memorised in that order, and so on. As a result, according to Hinton, it is possible to cast out in the cube studied the concepts " up and down," " right and left," and so on, and to know it independently of the position with regard to one another of the smaller cubes composing it, i.e. probably to visualise it simultaneously in different combinations. This would be the first step towards casting out the self-elements in the conception of the cube. Further on, there is described an elaborate system of exercises with series of differently coloured and differently named cubes, out of which various figures are composed. All this has the same purpose, to cast out the self-elements in the percepts and in this way to develop higher consciousness.

Casting out the self-elements in percepts, according to Hinton's idea, is the first step towards the development of higher consciousness and towards the cognition of the fourth dimension.

He says that if there exists the capacity of vision in the fourth dimension, that is, if we are able to see objects of our world as if from the fourth dimension, then we shall see them, not as we see them in the ordinary way, but quite differently.

We usually see objects as either above or below us, or on the same level with us, to the right or to the left, behind us or in front of us, and always from one side only — the one facing us — and in perspective. Our eye is an extremely imperfect instrument; it gives us an utterly incorrect picture of the world. What we call perspective is in reality a distortion of visible objects which is produced by a badly constructed optical instrument — the eye. We see all objects distorted. And we visualise them in the same way. But we visualise them in this way entirely owing to the habit of seeing them distorted, that is, owing to the habit created by our defective vision, which has weakened the capacity of visualisation.

But, according to Hinton, there is no necessity to visualise objects of the external world in a distorted form. The power of visualisation is not limited by the power of vision. We see objects distorted, but we know them as they are. And we can free ourselves from the habit of visualising objects as we see them, and we can learn to visualise them as we know they really are. Hinton's idea is precisely that before thinking of developing the capacity of seeing in the fourth dimension, we must learn to visualise objects as they would be seen from the fourth dimension, i.e. first of all, not in perspective, but from all sides at once, as they are known to our " consciousness." It is just this power that should be developed by Hinton's exercises. The development of this power to visualise objects from all sides at once will be the casting out of the self-elements in mental images. According to Hinton, " casting out the self-elements in mental images must lead to casting out the self-elements in perceptions." In this way, the development of the power of visualising objects from all sides will be the first step towards the development of the power of seeing objects as they are in a geometrical sense, i.e. the development of what Hinton calls a " higher consciousness."

In all this there is a great deal that is right, but also a great deal that is arbitrary and artificial. First of all, Hinton does not take into consideration the difference between the various psychic types of men. A method that may prove satisfactory for himself may produce no results or even contrary results for other people. Second, the very psychological foundation of his system of exercises is too unstable. Usually he does not know when to stop, carries his analogies too far and in that way deprives many of his conclusions of all value.

From the point of view of geometry, according to Hinton, the question of the fourth dimension may be examined in the following way.

We know geometrical figures of three kinds:

Figures of one dimension — lines.

Figures of two dimensions — planes.

Figures of three dimensions — solids.

A line is regarded here as the trace of a point moving in space. A plane — as the trace of a line moving in space. A solid — as the trace of a plane moving in space.

Let us imagine a straight line limited by two points, and let us designate this line by the letter a. Let us imagine this line a moving in space in a direction perpendicular to itself and leaving a trace of its movement. When it has traversed a distance equal to its length, the trace left by it will have the form of a square, the sides of which are equal to a line a, i.e. a^2.

Let us imagine this square moving in space in a direction perpendicular to two of its adjoining sides and leaving a trace of its movement. When it has traversed a distance equal to the length of one of the sides of the square, its trace will have the form of a cube, i.e. a^3.

Now if we imagine the movement of a cube in space, what form will the trace left by such a movement, i.e. figure a^4, assume?

Examining the correlations of figures of one, two and three dimensions, i.e. lines, planes and solids, we can deduce the rule that a figure of a higher dimension can be regarded as the trace of the movement of a lower dimension.

On the basis of this rule we may regard figure a^4 as the trace of the movement of a cube in space.

But what is this movement of a cube in space, the trace of which becomes a figure of four dimensions?

If we examine the way in which figures of higher dimensions are constructed by the movement of figures of lower dimensions, we shall discover several common properties and several common laws in these formations.

In fact, when we consider a square as the trace of the movement of a line, we know that all the points of this line have moved in space; when we consider a cube as the trace of the movement of a square, we know that all the points of the square have moved. Moreover, the line moves in a direction perpendicular to itself; the square in a direction perpendicular to two of its dimensions.

Consequently, if we consider the figure a^4 as the trace of the movement of a cube in space, we must remember that all the points of the given cube have moved in space. Moreover, we may deduce from analogy with the above that the cube was moving in space in a direction which is not contained in the cube itself, i.e. a direction perpendicular to its three dimensions. This direction, then, would be the fourth perpendicular unknown to us in our space and in our geometry of three dimensions.

Further, we may determine a line as an infinite number of points; a square as an infinite number of lines; a cube as an infinite number of squares. By analogy with this we may determine the figure a^4 as an infinite number of cubes.

Further, looking at the square we see nothing but lines; looking at the cube we see its surfaces, or possibly even only one of its surfaces.

It is quite possible that the figure a^4 would appear to us as a cube. To put it in a different way, the cube is what we see of the figure a^4.

Further, a point may be determined as a cross-section of a line; a line as a cross-section of a surface; a surface as a cross-section of a solid; a three-dimensional body can therefore be determined as a cross-section of a four-dimensional body.

Generally speaking, in every four-dimensional body we shall see its three-dimensional projection or section. A cube, a sphere, a pyramid, a cone, a cylinder, may be projections or cross-sections of four-dimensional bodies unknown to us.

In 1908 I came across a curious article on the fourth dimension (in Russian) published in the review *Sovremenny Mir.*

It was a letter written by N. A. Morosoff [2] in 1891 to his fellow-prisoners

---

[2] N. A. Morosoff, a scientist by education, belonged to the revolutionary parties of the seventies and eighties. He was arrested in connection with the murder of the Emperor Alexander II and spent twenty-three years in prisons, chiefly in the fortress of Schlüsselburg. Liberated in 1905 he wrote several books, one on the Revelation of St. John, another on Alchemy, on Magic, etc., which found fairly numerous readers in the period before the War. It was rather curious that the public liked in Morosoff's books not what he actually wrote, but what he wrote about. His real intentions were very limited and in strict accordance with the scientific ideas of the seventies. He tried to present "mystical subjects" rationally; for instance, he explained the Revelation as nothing but a description of a thunderstorm. But being a good writer, Morosoff gave a very vivid exposition of his themes, and sometimes he added little-known material. So his books produced a quite unexpected result, and many people became interested in mystical subjects and in mystical literature after reading Morosoff's books. After the revolution, Morosoff joined the Bolsheviks and remained in Russia. Although, as far as

in the fortress of Schlüsselburg. It is of interest chiefly because it contains, in a very picturesque form, an exposition of the fundamental proposition of the method of reasoning about the fourth dimension by means of analogies, which was mentioned above.

The first part of Morosoff's article is very interesting, but in his final conclusions as to what may exist in the domain of the fourth dimension he deviates from the method of analogies and assigns to the fourth dimension the "spirits" which spiritualists evoke in their séances. And then, having denied the existence of spirits, he denies also the objective meaning of the fourth dimension.

It is generally supposed that fortress walls do not exist in the fourth dimension, and that was probably the reason why the fourth dimension was one of the favourite subjects of the conversations held at Schlüsselburg by means of tapping.

N. A. Morosoff's letter is an answer to the questions put to him in one of these conversations. He writes:

My dear friends, our short Schlüsselburg summer is nearing its end, and the dark mysterious autumn nights are coming. In these nights, spreading like a black cloak over the roof of our prison and enveloping with impenetrable darkness our little island with its old towers and bastions, it would seem that the shadows of our friends and predecessors who perished here flit invisibly round about these walls, look at us through the windows and enter into mysterious communication with us who still live. And we ourselves, are we not but shadows of what we used to be? Are we not transformed into some kind of tapping spirits, conversing unseen with one another through the stone walls which divide us, like those that perform at spiritualistic séances.

All day long I have thought of your discussion of to-day about the fourth, the fifth and other dimensions of the space of the universe which are inaccessible to us. With all my power I have tried to imagine at least the fourth dimension of the world, the one in which, as metaphysicians affirm, everything that is under lock and key may suddenly appear open, and in which all confined spaces can be entered by beings able to move not only along our three dimensions, but also along the fourth, to which we are unaccustomed.

You ask me for a scientific examination of the problem. Let us speak first of the world of only two dimensions; and later we will see whether it will give us the possibility of drawing certain conclusions about different worlds.

Let us take a certain plane — for instance, that which separates the surface of Lake Ladoga which surrounds us, from the atmosphere above it, in this quiet autumn evening. Let us suppose that this plane is a separate world of two dimensions, peopled with its own beings, which can move only on this plane, like the shadows of swallows and sea-gulls flitting in all directions over the smooth surface of the water which surrounds us, but remains for ever hidden from us behind these battlements.

---

is known, he has not taken part in destructive work himself, he has written nothing more and on solemn occasions expresses his official admiration of the Bolshevik régime. (Note to the translation.) P. O.

Let us suppose that, having escaped from behind our Schlüsselburg bastions, you went for a bathe in the lake.

As beings of three dimensions you also have the two dimensions which lie on the surface of the water. You will occupy a definite place in the world of shadow beings. All the parts of your body above and below the level of the water will be imperceptible to them, and they will be aware of nothing but your contour, which is outlined by the surface of the lake. Your contour must appear to them as an object of their own world, only very astonishing and miraculous. The first miracle from their point of view will be your sudden appearance in their midst. It can be said with full conviction that the effect you would create would be in no way inferior to the unexpected appearance among ourselves of some ghost from the unknown world. The second miracle would be the surprising changeability of your external form. When you are immersed up to your waist your form will be for them almost elliptical, because only the line on the surface surrounding your waist and impenetrable for them will be perceptible to them. When you begin to swim you will assume in their eyes the outline of a man. When you wade into a shallow place so that the surface on which they live will encircle your legs, you will appear to them transformed into two ring-shaped beings. If, desirous of keeping you in one place, they surround you on all sides, you can step over them and find yourselves free from them in a way quite inconceivable to them. In their eyes you would be all-powerful beings — inhabitants of a higher world, similar to those supernatural beings about whom theologians and metaphysicians tell us.

Now if we suppose that apart from these two worlds, the plane world and the world we live in, there exists a world of four dimensions, superior to ours, it will become clear that in relation to us its inhabitants would be exactly the same as we are in relation to the inhabitants of a plane. They must appear in our midst in the same unexpected way and disappear from our world at their will, moving along the fourth or some other higher dimension.

In a word the analogy, so far, is complete. Further we shall find in the same analogy a complete refutation of all our hypotheses.

If indeed the beings of the four-dimensional world were not purely our invention, their appearance in our midst would be an ordinary, everyday occurrence.

Further Morosoff discusses whether we have any reason to suppose that "supernatural beings" really exist, and he comes to the conclusion that we have no grounds for such a hypothesis unless we are prepared to believe in fairy-tales.

The only indication, worthy of our attention, of the existence of such beings can be found, according to Morosoff, in the teachings of spiritualism. But his own experience in "spiritualism" convinced him that in spite of the strange phenomena that undoubtedly occur at spiritualistic séances, "spirits" take no part in them. So-called "automatic writing," usually cited as a proof of the co-operation of intelligent forces of another world at these séances, is, according to his observations, a result of thought-reading. Consciously or unconsciously a "medium" "reads" the thoughts of those present and from these thoughts obtains the answers to their questions. Morosoff attended many séances, but never met with a case where there was anything in the answers received which was not known to any of the people present, or where answers were in a language unknown to any present. Therefore, though not doubting the sincerity of the majority of spiritualists, Morosoff concludes that " spirits " have nothing to do with phenomena at séances.

His experience of spiritualism, he says, had finally convinced him many years previously that the phenomena which he assigned to the fourth dimension do not really exist. He says that at such spiritualistic séances answers are given unconsciously by the actual people present and that therefore all suppositions concerning the existence of the fourth dimension are pure imagination.

These conclusions of Morosoff are quite unexpected, and it is difficult to understand how they were arrived at. Nothing can be said against his opinion of spiritualism. The psychic side of spiritualistic phenomena is undoubtedly quite " subjective." But it is quite incomprehensible why Morosoff sees the " fourth dimension " in spiritualistic phenomena alone, and why, denying the " spirits," he denies the fourth dimension. This looks like a ready-made solution offered by that official " positivism " to which Morosoff adhered and from which he was unable to depart. His previous arguments led in quite another direction. Besides " spirits " there exist a number of phenomena quite real to us, i.e. of usual and everyday occurrence, but absolutely inexplicable without the help of hypotheses which would relate these phenomena to the world of the fourth dimension. But we are too accustomed to these phenomena and do not notice their " miraculous character," do not notice that we live in a world of perpetual miracle, in a world of the mysterious, the inexplicable and, above all, the unmeasurable.

Morosoff describes how miraculous our three-dimensional bodies would seem to the plane-beings, how these beings would not know whence our bodies come and whither they disappear like spirits appearing from an unknown world.

But in reality are we not beings just as fantastic and as changeable in our appearance for any stationary object, a stone or a tree? Further, do we not possess the properties of " higher beings " for animals? And are there no phenomena for us, for instance, all the manifestations of *life*, about which we do not know whence they come nor whither they go; phenomena such as the appearance of a plant from a seed, the birth of living things, and the like; and further, the phenomena of nature, thunderstorms, rain, spring, autumn, which we can neither explain nor interpret? Is not each of these phenomena of nature taken separately something of which we can feel only a little, touch only a part, like the blind men in the old Eastern fable who defined an elephant each in his own way: one by its legs, another by its ears, a third by its tail?

Continuing Morosoff's reasonings concerning the relations between the world of three dimensions and the world of four dimensions, we have no grounds for looking for the latter only in the domain of " spiritualism."

Let us take a living cell. It may be exactly equal in length, breadth and height to another, a dead cell. And still there is something in the living cell which is lacking in the dead one, something we are unable to measure.

We say that it is " vital force," try to explain the vital force as a kind of motion. But in reality we do not explain anything by this, but only give a name to a phenomenon which remains inexplicable.

According to some scientific theories vital force must be resolvable into physico-chemical elements, into simpler forces. But not one of these theories can explain how the one passes into the other and in what relation the one stands to the other. We are unable to express in a physico-chemical formula the simplest manifestations of life energy. And as long as we are unable to do so, we have no right, in a strictly logical sense, to regard vital processes as identical with physico-chemical processes.

We may accept philosophical " monism," but we have no reasons for accepting the physico-chemical monism imposed on us from time to time, which identifies vital and psychic processes with physico-chemical processes. Our mind may come in an abstract way to the conclusion of the unity of physico-chemical, vital, and psychic processes, but for science, for exact and concrete knowledge, these three classes of phenomena stand quite separate from one another.

For science, three classes of phenomena: mechanical force, vital force and psychic force, pass one into another only partially, and apparently without any fixed or calculable proportions. Therefore, scientists will be justified in explaining vital and psychic processes as a kind of motion only when they have found means of transforming motion into vital and psychic energy and vice versa, and of calculating such a transformation. This means that such an affirmation will be possible only when it is known what number of calories contained in a definite quantity of coal is necessary for starting the life of one cell, or how many atmospheres of pressure are necessary for the formation of one thought or one logical deduction. As long as these are not known, physical, biological and psychic phenomena, as studied by science, take place on different planes. Their unity can be surmised, but nothing can be affirmed positively.

If one and the same force acts in physico-chemical, vital and psychic processes, it may be supposed that it acts in different spheres only partly contiguous to one another.

If science really possessed knowledge of the unity of at least vital and physico-chemical phenomena, it would be able to create living organisms. In this expectation there is nothing extravagant. People construct machines and apparatus which are much more complicated externally than a simple one-cell organism. And yet they are unable to construct such an organism. This means that there is something in a living organism which does not exist in a lifeless machine. A living cell contains something which is lacking in a dead one. And we have every right to call this something equally inexplicable and unmeasurable. And in examining man we have good reasons for putting to ourselves the question: which part is bigger in him, the measurable or the unmeasurable?

"How can I answer your question" (about the fourth dimension), writes Morosoff in his letter to his fellow prisoners, "when I myself have no dimension in the direction indicated by you?"

But what real grounds has Morosoff for affirming so definitely that he has not this dimension?

Can he measure everything in himself? Two principal functions of man, *life* and *thought*, are in the domain of the unmeasurable.

We know so vaguely and so imperfectly what man really is, and we have in ourselves so much that is enigmatic and incomprehensible from the point of view of the geometry of three dimensions, that we have no reason to deny the fourth dimension in denying "spirits." On the contrary, we have ample grounds for looking for the fourth dimension precisely in ourselves.

And we have to confess to ourselves clearly and definitely that we do not know in the least what man really is. For us he is an enigma, and we must accept this enigma as such.

The "fourth dimension" promises to explain something in this enigma. Let us try to see what the "fourth dimension" can give us if we approach it with the old methods but without the old prejudices for or against spiritualism. Let us again imagine a world of plane-beings possessing only two dimensions, length and breadth, and inhabiting a flat surface.[3]

Let us imagine, on this surface, living beings having the shape of geometrical figures and capable of moving in two directions.

At the very beginning of the examination of the conditions of life of these flat beings we come at once face to face with a very interesting fact.

These beings will be able to move only in two directions on their plane. They will be unable to rise above this plane or to leave it. In the same way they will be unable to see or feel anything lying outside their plane. If one of these beings rises above the plane, he will completely pass away from the world of other beings similar to him, will vanish, disappear — no one knows whither.

If we suppose that the organs of vision of these beings are situated on their edges, on their outer lines, then they will not be able to see the world lying outside their plane at all. They will see only lines lying on their plane. They will see each other not as they really are, i.e. in the shape of geometrical figures, but only in the form of lines. In the same way all the objects of their world will also appear to them as lines. And, what is very important, all lines, whether straight, curved, or with angles, or lying at different angles to

---

[3] In these reasonings about imaginary worlds I shall partly follow Hinton's plan, but this does not mean that I share *all* Hinton's opinions.

the line of their edge, will appear to them alike; they will not be able to see any difference in the lines themselves. But at the same time, the lines will differ for them by strange properties which they will probably call the motion or the vibration of lines.

The centre of a circle will be entirely inaccessible to them. They will be quite unable to see it. In order to reach the centre of a circle a two-dimensional being will have to dig or cut his way through the mass of the flat figure having the thickness of one atom. The process of digging will appear to him as an altering of the line of the circumference.

If a cube is placed on his plane, then this cube will appear to him in the form of the four lines bounding the square touching his plane. Of the whole cube only this square will exist for him. He will be unable even to imagine the rest of the cube. The *cube* will not exist for him.

If several bodies come into contact with his plane, for a plane-being there will exist in each of them only one surface which has come into contact with his plane. This surface, that is, the lines bounding it, will appear to him as an object of his own world.

If through his space, that is, through his plane, there passes a multi-coloured cube, the passage of the cube will appear to him as a gradual change in the colour of the lines bounding the square which lies on his plane.

If we suppose that the plane-being is made able to see with his flat side, the one facing our world, it is easy to imagine what a wrong conception of our world he will receive.

The whole universe will appear to him in the form of a plane. It is very probable that he will call this plane æther. Consequently, he will either completely deny all phenomena which take place outside his plane, or regard them as happening on his own plane, in his æther. Unable to explain on his plane all the phenomena observed by him, he may call them miraculous, lying above his understanding, beyond his space, in the " third dimension."

Having observed that the inexplicable events occur in a certain consecutiveness, in a certain dependence one upon another, and also probably in a dependence on some laws, the plane-being will cease to consider them miraculous and will attempt to explain them by means of more or less complicated hypotheses.

The appearance of the dim idea of another parallel plane will be for a plane-being the first steps towards the right understanding of the universe. He will then imagine all the phenomena he is unable to explain on his own plane as occurring on that parallel plane. At this stage of development the whole of our world will appear to him as a plane parallel to his own plane. Neither relief nor perspective will exist for him as yet. A mountain landscape will appear to him as a flat photograph. His conception of the world will certainly be very poor, and full of errors. The big things will be taken for the small, and the small things for the big, and all together, whether near or far, will appear to him equally remote and inaccessible.

Having recognised that there is a world parallel to his plane world, the two-dimensional being will say that of the true nature of the relations between these two worlds he knows nothing.

In the parallel world there will be much that will appear inexplicable for a two-dimensional being. For instance a lever or a couple of wheels on an axle. Their action will appear quite inconceivable to the plane-being, whose conception of laws of motion is limited by motion on a plane. It is quite possible that this phenomenon will be considered supernatural and later will be called, in a more scientific way, " superphysical."

In studying these superphysical phenomena the plane-being may stumble upon the idea that a lever, or wheels, contain something unmeasurable, but nevertheless existing.

From this there is only one step to the hypothesis of the third dimension. The plane-being will base this hypothesis precisely on inexplicable facts, such as the rotation of wheels. He may ask himself whether the inexplicable may not really be the unmeasurable, and then begin gradually to elucidate for himself the physical laws of three-dimensional space. But he will never be able to prove mathematically the existence of this third dimension, because all his geometrical speculations will proceed only on a plane, on two dimensions, and therefore he will project on a plane the results of his mathematical conclusions, in this way destroying all their meaning.

The plane-being will be able to obtain his first notion of the nature of the third dimension merely by means of logical reasonings and comparisons. This means that in examining the inexplicable that lies in the flat photograph (representing for him our world) the plane-being may arrive at the conclusion that many phenomena are inexplicable for him, because in the objects causing these phenomena there may be a certain *difference* which he does not understand and cannot measure.

Further, he may conclude that a real body must differ in some way from an imaginary one. And having once admitted the hypothesis of the third dimension, he will have to say that the real body, unlike the imaginary body, must possess at least a small third dimension.

In the same way the plane-being may come to the recognition that he must necessarily possess the third dimension.

After arriving at the conclusion that a real body of two dimensions cannot exist, that this is but an imaginary figure, the plane-being will have to say to himself that, since the third dimension exists, he must himself possess this third dimension, because otherwise, having only two dimensions, he would be but an imaginary figure, that is, exist only in somebody's mind.

The plane-being will reason in the following way: " If the third dimension exists, I am either a being of three dimensions or I do not exist in reality but exist only in somebody's imagination."

In reflecting why he does not see his third dimension the plane-being may come upon the thought that his extension along the third dimension, just like the extension of other bodies along the third dimension, is very small. These reflections may bring the plane-being to the conclusion that for him the question of the third dimension is connected with the problem of small magnitudes.

In investigating the world in a philosophical way the plane-being will from time to time doubt the reality of everything surrounding him and the reality of himself.

He may then think that his conception of the world is wrong and that he does not even see it as it really is. Reasonings about things as they appear and about things as they are may follow from this. The plane-being may think that in the third dimension things must appear as they are, i.e. that he will see in the same things more than he saw in two dimensions.

Verifying all these reasonings from our point of view, that is, from the point of view of beings of three dimensions, we must recognise that all the conclusions of the plane-being are perfectly right and lead him to a right understanding of the world and to the cognition, though theoretical in the beginning, of the third dimension.

We may profit by the experience of the plane-being and try to find whether there is anything in the world towards which we are in the same relation as the plane-being is towards the third dimension.

In examining the physical conditions of the life of man we find in them an almost complete analogy with the conditions of life of the plane-being who begins to be aware of the third dimension.

We shall start by analysing our relation towards the " invisible."

At first man considers the invisible as miraculous and supernatural. Gradually, with the evolution of knowledge, the idea of the miraculous becomes less and less necessary. Everything within the sphere accessible to observation (and unfortunately far beyond it) is regarded as existing according to certain definite laws, as the result of certain definite causes. But the causes of many phenomena remain hidden, and science is forced to limit itself to a classification of these inexplicable phenomena.

In studying the character and properties of the " inexplicable " in different branches of our knowledge, in physics and chemistry, in biology and in psychology, we can arrive at certain general conclusions concerning the character of the inexplicable. This means that we can formulate the problem as follows: is not the inexplicable a result of something " unmeasurable " for us which exists, first, in those things which, as it appears to us, we can measure fully, and second, in things which, as it appears to us, can have no measurement?

We can think that this very inexplicability may be the result of the fact that we examine and attempt to explain, within the limits of three dimensions, phenomena that pass into the domain of a higher dimension. To put it differently, are we not in the position of the plane-being trying to explain as happening on a plane phenomena that take place in three-dimensional space?

There is a great deal that confirms the probability of such a supposition. It is quite possible that many inexplicable phenomena are inexplicable only because we wish to explain them on our plane, i.e. within our three-dimensional space, while really they occur outside our plane, in the domain of higher dimensions.

Having come to the conclusion that we are surrounded by the world of the unmeasurable, we must admit that, until now, we have had an entirely wrong conception of the objects of our world.

We knew before that we see things and represent them to ourselves not as they really are. Now we may say more definitely that we do not see in things that part of them which is unmeasurable for us, lying in the fourth dimension.

This last conclusion brings us to the idea of the difference between the imaginary and the real.

We saw that the plane-being, having arrived at the idea of the third dimension, must conclude that, if there are three dimensions, a real body of two dimensions cannot exist. A two-dimensional body would be only an imaginary figure, a section of a body of three dimensions or its projection in two-dimensional space.

Admitting the existence of the fourth dimension, we must recognise in the same way that if there are four dimensions, a real body of three dimensions cannot exist. A real body must possess a least a very small extension along the fourth dimension, otherwise it will be only an imaginary figure, the projection of a body of four dimensions in three-dimensional space, like a " cube " drawn on paper.

In this way we must come to the conclusion that there may exist a cube of three dimensions and a cube of four dimensions, and that only the cube of four dimensions will really, actually, exist.

Examining man from this point of view we come to very interesting deductions.

If the fourth dimension exists, one of two things is possible. Either we ourselves possess the fourth dimension, i.e. are beings of four dimensions, or we possess only three dimensions and in that case do not exist at all.

If the fourth dimension exists while we possess only three, it means that we have no real existence, that we exist only in somebody's imagination, and that all our thoughts, feelings and experiences take place in the mind of some other higher being, who visualises us. We are but products of his mind and the whole of our universe is but an artificial world created by his fantasy.

If we do not want to agree with this we must recognise ourselves as beings of four dimensions.

At the same time we must recognise that our own fourth dimension, as well as the fourth dimension of the bodies surrounding us, is known and felt by us only very little and that we only guess its existence from observations of inexplicable phenomena.

Such blindness in relation to the fourth dimension may be caused by the fact that the fourth dimension of our own bodies and other objects of our world is too small and inaccessible to our organs of sense, or to the apparatus which widens the sphere of our observation, exactly in the same way as the molecules of our bodies and many other things are inaccessible to immediate observation. As regards objects possessing a greater extension in the fourth dimension, we feel them at times in certain circumstances, but refuse to recognise them as really existing.

These last considerations give us sufficient grounds for believing that, at least in our physical world, the fourth dimension must refer to the domain of small magnitudes.

The fact that we do not see in things their fourth dimension brings us again to the problem of the imperfection of our perceptions in general.

Even if we leave aside other defects of our perception and regard its activity only in relation to geometry, we shall have to admit that we see everything as very unlike what it really is.

We do not see bodies, we see nothing but surfaces, sides and lines. We never see a cube; we see only a small part of it, never see it from all sides at once.

From the fourth dimension it must be possible to see the cube from all its sides at once and from within, as though from its centre.

The centre of a sphere is inaccessible to us. To reach it we must cut or dig our way through the mass of the sphere, i.e. act in exactly the same way as the plane-being with regard to the circle. The process of cutting through will in that case appear to us as a gradual change in the surface of the sphere.

The complete analogy of our relation to the sphere with the relation of the plane-being to the circle gives us grounds for thinking that in the fourth dimension, or along the fourth dimension, the centre of the sphere is as easily accessible as is the centre of the circle in the third dimension. In other words, we have a right to suppose that in the fourth dimension it is possible to reach the centre of the sphere from some region unknown to us, along some incomprehensible direction, the sphere itself remaining intact. The latter circumstance would appear to us a kind of miracle, but just as miraculous, to the plane-being, must appear the possibility of reaching the centre of the circle without disturbing the line of its circumference, without breaking up the circle.

Continuing to imagine further the properties of vision or perception in the fourth dimension, we shall have to recognise that not only in a geometrical sense, but also in many other senses, it is possible from the fourth dimension to see in objects of our world much more than we do see.

Prof. Helmholtz once said about our eye that if an optician sent him so badly made an instrument, he would never accept it.

Undoubtedly our eye does not see a great many things which exist. But if in the fourth dimension we see without the aid of such an imperfect instrument, we should be bound to see much more, that is, to see what is invisible for us now and to see everything without that net of illusions which veils the whole world from us and makes its outward aspect very unlike what it really is.

The question may arise why we should see in the fourth dimension without the aid of eyes, and what this means.

It will be possible to answer these questions definitely only when it is definitely known that the fourth dimension exists and when it is known what it really is. But so far it is possible to consider only what *might* be in the fourth dimension, and therefore there cannot be any final answers to these questions. Vision in the fourth dimension must be effected without the help of eyes. The limits of eyesight are known, and it is known that the human eye can never attain the perfection even of the microscope or telescope. But these instruments with all the increase of the power of vision which they afford do not bring us in the least nearer to the fourth dimension. So it may be concluded that vision in the fourth dimension must be something quite different from ordinary vision. But what can it actually be? Probably it will be something analogous to the "vision" by which a bird flying over Northern Russia "sees" Egypt, whither it migrates for the winter; or to the vision of a carrier pigeon which "sees," hundreds of miles away, its loft, from which it has been taken in a closed basket; or to the vision of an engineer making the first calculations and first rough drawings of a bridge, who "sees" the bridge and the trains passing over it; or to the vision of a man who, consulting a time-table, "sees" himself arriving at the station of departure and his train arriving at its destination.

Now, having outlined certain features of the properties which vision in the fourth dimension should possess, we must endeavour to define more exactly what we know of the phenomena of that world.

Again making use of the experience of the two-dimensional being, we must put to ourselves the following question: are all the "phenomena" of our world explicable from the point of view of physical laws?

There are so many inexplicable phenomena around us that merely by being too familiar with them we cease to notice their inexplicability, and, forgetting it, we begin to classify these phenomena, give them names, include them within different systems and, finally, even begin to deny their inexplicability.

Strictly speaking, all is equally inexplicable. But we are accustomed to regard some orders of phenomena as more explicable and other orders as less explicable. We put the less explicable into a special group, and create out of them a separate world, which is regarded as parallel to the "explicable."

This refers first of all to the so-called "psychic world," that is to the world of ideas, images and conceptions, which we regard as parallel to the physical world.

Our relation to the psychic, the difference which exists for us between the physical and the psychic, shows that psychic phenomena should be assigned to the domain of the fourth dimension.[4] In the history of human thought the relation to the psychic is very similar to the relation of the plane-being to the third dimension. Psychic phenomena are inexplicable on the "physical plane," therefore they are regarded as opposite to the physical. But their unity is vaguely felt, and attempts are constantly made to interpret psychic phenomena as a kind of physical phenomena, or physical phenomena as a kind of psychic phenomena. The division of concepts is recognised to be unsuccessful, but there are no means for their unification.

In the first place the psychic is regarded as quite separate from the body, as a function of the "soul," unsubjected to any physical laws. The soul lives by itself, and the body by itself, and the one is incommensurable with the other. This is the theory of naïve dualism or spiritualism. The first attempt at an equally naïve monism regards the soul as a direct function of the body. It is then said that "thought is a motion of matter." Such was the famous formula of Moleschott.

Both views lead into blind alleys. The first, because the obvious interdependence of physiological and psychic processes cannot be disregarded; the second, because motion still remains motion and thought remains thought.

The first view is analogous to the denial by the two-dimensional being of any physical reality in phenomena which happen outside his plane. The second view is analogous to the attempt to consider as happening on a plane phenomena which happen above it or outside it.

The next step is the hypothesis of a parallel plane on which all the inexplicable phenomena take place. But the theory of parallelism is a very dangerous thing.

The plane-being begins to understand the third dimension when he begins to see that what he considered parallel to his plane may actually be at different distances from it. The idea of relief and perspective will then appear in his mind, and the world and things will take for him the same form as they have for us.

We shall understand more correctly the relation between physical and psychic phenomena when we clearly understand that the psychic is not always parallel to the physical and may be quite independent of it. And parallels which are not always parallel are evidently subject to laws that are incomprehensible to us, to laws of the world of four dimensions.

At the present day it is often said: we know nothing about the exact nature of the relations between physical and psychic phenomena; the only thing we can affirm and which is more or less established is that, for every psychic process, thought or sensation there is a corresponding physiological process, which manifests itself in at least a feeble vibration in nerves and

---

[4] The expression "psychic" phenomena is used here in its only possible sense of psychological or mental phenomena, that is, those which constitute the subject of psychology. I mention this because in spiritualistic and theosophical literature the word "psychic" is used for the designation of supernormal or superphysical phenomena.

brain fibre and in chemical changes in different tissues. Sensation is defined as the consciousness of a change in the organs of sense. This change is a certain motion which is transmitted into brain centres, but in what way the motion is transformed into a feeling or a thought is not known.

The question arises: is it not possible to suppose that the physical is separated from the psychic by four-dimensional space, i.e. that a physiological process, passing into the domain of the fourth dimension, produces there effects which we call feeling or thought?

On our plane, i.e. in the world of motion and vibrations accessible to our observations, we are unable to understand or to determine thought, exactly in the same way as the two-dimensional being on his plane is unable to understand or to determine the action of a lever or the motion of a pair of wheels on an axle.

At one time the ideas of E. Mach, expounded chiefly in his book *Analysis of Sensations and Relations of the Physical to the Psychic*, were in great vogue. Mach absolutely denies any difference between the physical and the psychic. In his opinion all the dualism of the usual view of the world resulted from the metaphysical conception of the " thing in itself " and from the conception (an erroneous one according to Mach) of the illusory character of our cognition of things. In Mach's opinion we can perceive nothing wrongly. Things are always exactly what they appear to be. The concept of illusion must disappear entirely. Elements of sensations are physical elements. What are called " bodies " are only complexes of elements of sensations: light sensations, sound sensations, sensations of pressure, etc. Mental images are similar complexes of sensations. There exists no difference between the physical and the psychic; both the one and the other are built up of the same elements (of sensations). The molecular structure of bodies and the atomic theory are accepted by Mach only as symbols, and he denies them all reality.

In this way, according to Mach's theory, our psychic apparatus builds the physical world. A " thing " is only a complex of sensations.

But in speaking of the theories of Mach it is necessary to remember that the psychic apparatus builds only the " forms " of the world (i.e. makes the world such as we perceive it) out of something else which we shall never attain. The blue of the sky is unreal, the green of the meadows is also unreal; these " colours " belong to the reflected rays. But evidently there is something in the " sky," i.e. in the air of our atmosphere, which makes it appear blue, just as there is something in the grass of the meadow which makes it appear green.

Without this last addition a man might easily have said, on the basis of Mach's ideas: this apple is a complex of my sensations, therefore it only seems to exist, but does not exist in reality.

This would be wrong. The apple exists. And a man can, in a most real way, become convinced of it. But it is not what it appears to be in the three-dimensional world.

The psychic, as opposed to the physical or the three-dimensional, is very similar to what should exist in the fourth dimension, and we have every right to say that thought moves along the fourth dimension.

No obstacles or distances exist for it. It penetrates impenetrable objects, visualises the structure of atoms, calculates the chemical composition of stars, studies life on the bottom of the ocean, the customs and institutions of a race that disappeared tens of thousands of years ago. . . .

No walls, no physical conditions, restrain our fantasy, our imagination. Did not Morosoff and his comrades fly in their imagination far beyond the bastions of Schlüsselburg?

Did not Morosoff himself, in his book, *Revelation in Tempest and Thunderstorm*, travel through space and time when, as he was reading Revelations in the Alexeivsky ravelin of the Petropavlovsky Fortress he saw thunder clouds scudding over the Isle of Patmos in the Greek Archipelago, at five o'clock in the afternoon of the 30th September in the year 395?

Do we not in sleep live in a fantastic fairy kingdom where everything is capable of transformation, where there is no stability belonging to the physical world, where one man can become another or two men at the same time, where the most improbable things look simple and natural, where events often occur in inverse order, from end to beginning, where we see the symbolical images of ideas and moods, where we talk with the dead, fly in the air, pass through walls, are drowned or burnt, die, and remain alive?

All this taken together shows us that we have no need to think that the spirits that appear or fail to appear at spiritualistic séances must be the only possible beings of four dimensions. We may have very good reason for saying that we are ourselves beings of four dimensions and are turned towards the third dimension with only one of our sides, i.e. with only a small part of our being. Only this part of us lives in three dimensions, and we are conscious only of this part as our body. The greater part of our being lives in the fourth dimension, but we are unconscious of this greater part of ourselves. Or it would be still more true to say that we live in a four-dimensional world, but are conscious of ourselves only in a three-dimensional world. This means that we live in one kind of conditions, but imagine ourselves to be in another.

The conclusions of psychology bring us to the same idea, but by a different road. Psychology comes, though very slowly, to the recognition of the possibility of awakening our consciousness, i.e. the possibility of a particular state of it, when it sees and feels itself in a real world having nothing in common with this world of things and phenomena — in a world of thoughts, mental images and ideas.

In discussing earlier the properties of the fourth dimension, I mentioned that the tessaract, that is, a^4, may be obtained by the movement of a cube in space, on the condition that all the points of the cube move.

Consequently if we suppose that from each point of the cube there is drawn a line which this movement must follow, the combination of these lines will then form the projection of a body of four dimensions. This body, that is the tessaract, as was found before, can be regarded as an infinite number of cubes growing, as it were, out of the first cube.

Let us see now whether we know of any examples of such motion, which implies the motion of all points of the given cube.

Molecular motion, that is, the motion of minute particles of matter which is increased by heating and lessened by cooling, is the most appropriate example of motion along the fourth dimension, in spite of all the erroneous ideas of physicists with regard to this motion.

In an article entitled "May we hope to see molecules?"[5] Prof. Goldgammer writes that, according to modern views, molecules are bodies the lineal section of which is something between one millionth and one tenmillionth part of a millimetre. It has been calculated that one milliardth part of a cubic millimetre, that is, one cubic microne, at a temperature of $0°$ C. and at normal pressure contains about 30 million molecules of oxygen. "Molecules move very fast; thus under normal conditions the majority of molecules of oxygen have the velocity of about 450 metres per second. Molecules do not disperse in all directions instantaneously in spite of their great velocities only because they collide every moment with one another and because of this change the direction of their motion. Owing to this the path of a molecule has the aspect of a very entangled zigzag, and a molecule actually 'marks time,' as it were, on one spot."

Leaving aside for the time the entangled zigzag and the theory of colliding molecules (Brownian movement), we must try to find what results are produced by molecular motion in the visible world.

In order to find an example of motion along the fourth dimension we have to find a motion whereby the given body would actually move and not remain in one place (or one state).

Examining all the observable kinds of motion we must admit that the *expansion* and *contraction* of bodies come nearest to the indicated conditions.

Expansion of gases, liquids and solids means that molecules retreat from one another. Contraction of solids, liquids and gases means that the molecules approach one another. The distance between them diminishes. There is space here and there are distances.

Is it not possible that this space lies in the fourth dimension?

A movement in this space means that all the points of the given geometrical body, that is, all the molecules of the given physical body, move.

The figure resulting from the movement of a cube in space when the cube expands or contracts will have the form of a cube, and we can imagine it as an infinite number of cubes.

Is it right to suppose that the assemblage of lines drawn from every point of a cube, interior as well as exterior, the lines along which the points

[5] In the review *Naoutchnoye Slovo*, February, 1903.

approach one another or retreat from each other, constitutes the projection of a four-dimensional body?

In order to answer this it is necessary to determine what these lines are and what this direction is.

These lines connect all the points of the given body with its centre. Consequently the direction of the movement indicated will be from the centre along the radii.

In investigating the paths of the movements of the points (or molecules) of a body in the case of expansion and contraction, we find in them many interesting features.

We cannot see the distance between molecules. We cannot see it in the case of solids, liquids and gases because it is extremely small, and in the case of highly rarefied matter, as for instance that in Crookes tubes, where this distance is probably increased to the proportions perceptible for us or for our apparatus, we cannot see it because the particles themselves, the molecules, are too small to be accessible to our observation. In the above-mentioned article Prof. Goldgammer states that given certain conditions molecules could be photographed if they could be made luminous. He writes that when the pressure in Crookes tubes is reduced to one-millionth part of an atmosphere one microne will contain only 30 molecules of oxygen. If they were luminous they could be photographed on a screen.

To what extent this photographing is really possible, is another question. For the present argument, a molecule as a real quantity in relation to a physical body can represent a point in its relation to a geometrical body.

All bodies must necessarily consist of molecules; consequently they must possess a certain, though a very small, dimension of inter-molecular space. Without this we cannot conceive a real body, and can conceive only imaginary geometrical bodies. A real body consists of molecules and possesses a certain inter-molecular space.

This means that the difference between a cube of three dimensions, a^3, and a cube of four dimensions, a^4, will be that a cube of four dimensions consists of molecules, whereas a cube of only three dimensions in reality does not exist and is only a projection of a four-dimensional body in three-dimensional space.

In expanding or contracting, that is, in moving along the fourth dimension, if the preceding arguments are admitted, a cube or sphere remains for us all the time a cube or sphere, changing only in size. Hinton quite rightly observed in one of his books that the passing of a cube of higher dimension transversely to our space would appear to us as a change in the properties of the matter of the cube before us. He also says that the idea of the fourth dimension ought to have arisen from observation of a series of progressively growing or diminishing spheres or cubes. This last idea brings him quite near to the right definition of motion in the fourth dimension.

One of the clearest and most comprehensible forms of motion in the fourth dimension in this sense is growth, the principle of which lies in expansion. It is not difficult to explain why it is so. Every motion within the limits of three-dimensional space is at the same time a motion in time. Molecules or points of an expanding cube do not return to their former place on contraction. They trace a certain curve, returning, not to the point of time at which they started, but to another. And if we suppose that generally they do not return, the distance between them and the original point of time will continually increase. Let us imagine the internal motion of a body in the course of which its molecules, having retreated from one another, do not approach one another again, but the distance between them is filled up with new molecules, which in their turn move asunder and make room for new ones. Such an internal motion of a body would be its growth, at least a geometrical scheme of growth. If we compare a little green apple just formed from the ovary with a large red fruit we shall realise that the molecules composing the ovary could not create the apple while moving only in three-dimensional space. They need in addition to this a continuous motion in time, a continuous deviation into the space which lies outside the three-dimensional sphere. The apple is separated from the ovary by time. From this point of view the apple represents three or four months' motion of molecules along the fourth dimension. If we imagine the whole of the way from the ovary to the apple, we shall see the direction of the fourth dimension, that is, the mysterious fourth perpendicular — the line perpendicular to all three perpendiculars of our space and parallel to none of them.

On the whole Hinton stands so near to the correct solution of the problem of the fourth dimension that he sometimes guesses the place of the "fourth dimension" in life, although he cannot determine this place exactly. Thus he says that the symmetry of the structure of living organisms can be explained only by the movement of their particles along the fourth dimension.

Everybody knows, says Hinton,[6] the means of obtaining on paper, images resembling living insects. A few blots of ink are splashed on a piece of paper and the sheet is folded in two. A very complicated symmetrical image is obtained, resembling a fantastic insect. If a whole series of these figures were seen by a man quite unacquainted with the method of their production, then, thinking purely logically, he would have to conclude that they had originated from folding the paper in two, that is to say, that their symmetrically disposed points have been in contact. In the same way, in examining and studying structural forms of organised beings which very strongly resemble the figures on paper obtained by the above-described method, we may conclude that these symmetrical forms of insects, leaves, birds and other animals are produced by means of a process similar to this folding. And we may explain the symmetrical structure of organised beings, if not by folding in two in four-dimensional space, at any rate by a disposi-

---

[6] *The Fourth Dimension*, 2nd edition, 1921, pp. 18, 19.

tion in a manner similar to the folding of the smallest particles from which they are built up.

There exists indeed in nature a very interesting phenomenon, which gives us perfectly correct diagrams of the fourth dimension. It is only necessary to know how to read these diagrams. They are seen in the fantastically varied but always symmetrical shapes of snow-flakes, and also in the designs of the flowers, stars, ferns and lacework which frost makes on window panes. Drops of water settling from the air on to a cold pane, or on to the ice al-

FIG. 1 A *diagram of the Fourth Dimension in Nature*

ready formed upon it, begin instantaneously to freeze and expand, leaving traces of their motion along the fourth dimension in the shape of intricate designs. These frost drawings on window panes, as well as the designs of snow-flakes, are figures of the fourth dimension, the mysterious a^4. The motion of a lower figure to obtain a higher one, as imagined in geometry, is here actually realised, and the resulting figure, in effect, represents the trace left by the motion of the lower figure, because the frost preserves all the stages of the expansion of freezing drops of water.

Forms of living bodies, living flowers, living ferns, are created according to the same principles, though in a more complex order. The outline of a tree gradually spreading into branches and twigs is, as it were, a diagram of the fourth dimension, a^4.

Leafless trees in winter or early spring often present very complicated and extraordinarily interesting diagrams of the fourth dimension. We pass them without noticing them because we think that a tree exists in three-dimensional space. Similar wonderful diagrams can be seen in the designs of sea-weeds, flowers, young shoots, certain seeds, etc., etc. Sometimes it is sufficient to magnify them a little in order to see the secrets of the "Great Laboratory" that are hidden from our eye.

Some very remarkable illustrations of the above statements may be found by the reader in Prof. K. Blossfeldt's book on art-forms in nature.[7]

Living organisms, the bodies of animals and human beings, are built on the principles of symmetrical motion. In order to understand these principles let us take a simple schematic example of symmetrical motion. Let us imagine a cube composed of 27 small cubes, and let us imagine this cube as expanding and contracting. During the process of expansion all the 26 cubes lying round the central cube will retreat from it and on contraction will approach it again. For the sake of convenience in reasoning and in order to increase the likeness of the cube to a body consisting of molecules, let us suppose that the cubes have no dimension, that they are nothing but points. In other words, let us take only the centres of the 27 cubes and imagine them connected by lines both with the centre and with each other.

Visualising the expansion of this cube, composed of 27 cubes, we may say that in order to avoid colliding with another cube and hindering its motion, each of these cubes must move away from the centre, that is to say, along the line which connects its centre with the centre of the central cube.

This is the first rule.

In the course of expansion and contraction molecules move along the lines which connect them with the centre.

Further, we see in our cube that the lines connecting the 26 points with the centre are not all equal. The lines drawn to the centre from the centres of the corner cubes are longer than the lines drawn to the centre from the centres of the cubes lying in the middle of the sides of the large cube.

If we suppose that the inter-molecular space is doubled by expansion, then all the lines connecting the 26 points with the centre are at the same time doubled in length. The lines are not equal; therefore molecules move with unequal speed, some of them faster, and some slower; those further removed from the centre move faster, those lying nearer the centre move slower.

From this we may deduce a second rule.

The speed of the motion of molecules in the expansion and contraction of a body is proportional to the length of the lines which connect these molecules with the centre.

Observing the expansion of the big cube, we see that the distances between *all* the 27 cubes are increased proportionally to the former distances.

If we designate by the letter *a* lines connecting the 26 points with the centre, and by the letter *b* lines connecting the 26 points with one another, then, having constructed several triangles inside the expanding and contracting cube, we shall see that lines *b* are lengthened proportionally to the lengthening of lines *a*.

---

[7] *Art Forms in Nature*, by Prof. Karl Blossfeldt, with an introduction by Karl Nierendorf (London: A. Zwemmer, 1929).

From this we deduce a third rule.

In the process of expansion the distance between molecules increases proportionally to the increase of their distance from the centre.

This means therefore that the points that were at an equal distance from the centre will remain at an equal distance from it, and two points that were at an equal distance from a third point will remain at an equal distance from it.

Moreover, if we look upon this motion not from the centre, but from any one of the points, it will appear to us that this point is the centre from which the expansion proceeds, that is to say, it will appear that all the other points retreat from or approach this point, preserving their former relation to it and to each other, while this point itself remains stationary. " The centre is everywhere! "

The laws of symmetry in the structure of living organisms are based on this last rule. But living organisms are not built by expansion alone. The element of movement in time enters into it. In the course of growth each molecule traces a curve resulting from the combination of two movements, movement in space and movement in time. Growth proceeds in the same direction, along the same lines, as expansion. Therefore the laws of growth must be analogous to the laws of expansion. The conditions of expansion, that is, the *third rule*, ensure the most rigorous symmetry in freely expanding bodies, because if points which were originally at an equal distance from the centre continue always to remain at an equal distance from it, the body will grow symmetrically.

In the figure produced by the ink spread on a sheet of paper folded in two, the symmetry of all the points was obtained because the points on one side came into contact with the points on the other side. To each point on one side there corresponded a point on the other side and, when the paper was folded, these points touched one another. From the third rule formulated above it must follow that between the opposite points of a four-dimensional body there exists some relation, some affinity, which we have not hitherto noticed. To each point there corresponds as it were one or several others linked with it in some way unintelligible to us. That is, this point is unable to move independently; its movement is connected with the movement of other corresponding points, which occupy positions analogous to its own in the expanding and contracting body. And these points are precisely the points opposite to it. It is, as it were, linked with them, linked in the fourth dimension. An expanding body appears to be folded in different ways and this establishes a certain strange connection between its opposite points.

Let us try to examine the way in which the expansion of the simplest figure is effected. We will take this figure not in space even, but on a plane. We will take a square. We will connect the four points at its angles with the centre. Then we will connect with the centre points lying in the middle of the sides, and then points lying half-way between them. The first four points, that is, those lying at the angles, we will call points A; the four points lying in the middle of the sides of the square we will call points B, and finally the points lying also on the sides of the square between A and B (there will be eight of them) we will call points C.

The points A, the points B and the points C lie at different distances from the centre, and therefore on expansion they must move with unequal speed, all the time preserving their relation to the centre. At the same time

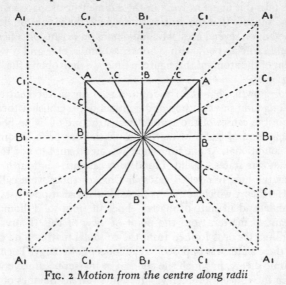

FIG. 2 *Motion from the centre along radii*

all the points A are connected among themselves, just as the points B are connected among themselves and as the points C are connected among themselves. Between the points of each group there is a strange inner connection. They must remain at *equal* distances from the centre.

Let us now suppose that the square is expanding, or in other words that all the points, A, B and C retreat from the centre along radii. As long as the expansion of the figure proceeds unhindered, the movement of the points will follow the above-mentioned rules, and the figure will remain a square and preserve a most exact symmetry. But let us suppose that suddenly some obstacle has arisen on the path of the motion of one of the points C, forcing this to stop. In such a case there are two possible alternatives. Either all the other points C will continue to move as if nothing had happened, or they also will stop. If they continue to move, the symmetry of the figure will be broken. If they stop, it will mean a strict observance of the deduction from the third rule, according to which points at an equal distance from the centre must on expansion remain at an equal distance from it. In fact if all the points C[1], obeying the mysterious affinity which exists between them and the point C which met with an obstacle, stop, while points

A and B continue to move, then the square will be transformed into a regular, perfectly symmetrical star. It is quite possible that a similar thing happens in the process of the growth of plants and living organisms. Let us take a more complicated figure, in which the centre from which the expansion starts is not a point, but a line, and in which the points retreating from the centre on expansion are disposed on both sides of that line. An analogous expansion will then produce not a star, but something resembling a dentate leaf. If we take this figure as lying in three-dimensional space instead of on a plane and suppose that the centres from which the expansion develops lie not on one but on several axes, we shall obtain on expansion a figure which may resemble a living body with symmetrical limbs, etc.; and if we suppose a movement of the atoms of this figure in time, we shall obtain the " growth " of a living body.

Laws of growth, that is, of motion originating in the centre and proceeding along radii in expansion and contraction, establish a theory which may explain the causes of the symmetrical structure of living bodies.

The definition of states of matter in physics has been becoming more and more conditional. At one time there was an attempt to add to the three generally known states — solid, liquid and gaseous — a fourth, " radiant matter," as the greatly rarefied gases in Crookes tubes were called. Then there exists a theory which considers the colloidal (gelatinous) state of matter as an independent state of matter, different from solid, liquid and gaseous. Organised matter, from the point of view of this theory, is a kind of colloidal matter or is formed from the colloidal matter. The concept of matter in these states was opposed to the concept of energy. Then appeared the electronic theory, in which the concept of matter became very little different from the concept of energy; later came various theories of the structure of the atom, which introduced many new ideas into the concept of matter.

But in this domain more than any other scientific theories differ from ordinary life conceptions. For a direct orientation in the world of phenomena it is necessary for us to distinguish matter from energy, and it is necessary to distinguish the three states of matter — solid, liquid and gaseous. At the same time it must be recognised that even these three states of matter known to us are distinguished by us clearly and indisputably only in their most " classical " forms, like a piece of iron, the water in a river, the air which we breathe. But the transitional forms overlap and are not clear. Therefore very often we do not know exactly when one state passes into the other, cannot draw a definite line of demarcation between the states of matter, cannot say when a solid has been transformed into a liquid, when a liquid has been transformed into gas. We presume that different states of matter depend on a different cohesion of molecules, on the speed and properties of molecular motion, but we distinguish these states only by their external traits, which are very inconstant and often become intermixed.

It can be said definitely that the finer the state of matter the more energetic it is considered to be, that is to say, containing as it were less substance and more motion. If matter is opposed to time, it will be possible to say that each finer state contains more time and less matter than a coarser state.

There is more " time " in a liquid than in a solid; there is more " time " in a gas than in a liquid.

If we accept the possibility of the existence of still finer states of matter, they should be more energetic than those recognised by physics; they should contain, according to the above, more time and less space, still more motion and still less substance.

The logical necessity of energetic states of matter has long been accepted in physics and is proved by very clear reasoning.

. . . What after all is substance? . . .[8] The definition of substance has never been very clear and has become still less clear since the discoveries of modern science. Is it possible, for instance, to define as a substance the mysterious agent to which physicists have recourse for the explanation of phenomena of heat and light? This agent, this medium, this mechanism — call it what you like — nevertheless exists, for it manifests itself in indisputable action. Besides, it is deprived of the qualities without which it is difficult to imagine a substance. It has no weight, and possibly it has no mass; it does not produce any direct impression on any one of our organs of sense; in a word it does not possess a single feature which would indicate what was formerly called " material." On the other hand it is not a spirit, at least nobody has ever thought of calling it that. But does it mean that it is necessary to deny its reality only because it cannot be classified as substance?

Is it necessary in the same way and for the same reason to deny the reality of the mechanism by means of which gravitation is transmitted into the depths of space with a velocity infinitely greater than the velocity of light,[9] which Laplace considered instantaneous? The great Newton considered it impossible to do without this agent. He to whom belongs the discovery of universal gravitation wrote to Bentley: " That Gravity should be innate, inherent and essential to Matter, so that one Body may act upon another at a Distance thro' a Vacuum, without the Mediation of anything else, by and through which their Action and Force may be conveyed from one to another, is to me so great an Absurdity, that I believe no Man who has in philosophical Matters a competent Faculty of thinking, can ever fall into it. Gravity must be caused by an Agent acting constantly according to certain Laws; but whether this Agent be material or immaterial, I have left to the Consideration of my Readers " (3rd letter to Bentley, 25th February, 1692).

The difficulty of allotting a place to these agents is so great that certain physicists, for example Hirn, who has unfolded this idea in his book, *Structure of Celestial Space*, consider it possible to imagine a new class of agents which occupy a position, so to speak, in the middle, between the material and the spiritual order and serve as a great source to the forces of nature. This class of

---

[8] *Essais sur la philosophie des sciences. C. de Freycinet* (Gauthier Villars & Fils, éditeurs). Paris, 1896, pp. 300–2.

[9] This was written in the nineties of last century.

agents, called dynamic by Hirn, from the conception of which he excludes all idea of mass and weight, serves, as it were, to establish relations, to provoke actions over a distance between different parts of matter.

The theory of Hirn's dynamic agents is based upon the following: we could never determine what matter and force really were, but in any case we always considered them opposite to one another, that is to say, we could define matter only as something opposite to force and force as something opposite to matter. But now the old views of matter as something solid and opposite to energy have considerably changed. A physical atom, formerly regarded as indivisible, is now recognised to be complex, composed of electrons. Electrons, however, are not material particles in the usual meaning of the word. They are better defined as moments of manifestation of energy, moments or elements of force. To put it in a different way, electrons, representing the smallest divisions of matter possible, are at the same time the smallest divisions of force. Electrons can be positive or negative. It is possible to think that the difference between matter and force consists simply in different combinations of positive and negative electrons. In one combination they produce on us the impression of matter, in another combination, the impression of force. From this point of view the difference between matter and force, which constitutes so far the basis of our view of nature, does not exist. Matter and force are one and the same thing or, rather, different manifestations of one and the same thing. In any case there is no essential difference between matter and force, and the one must pass into the other. From this point of view matter is nothing but condensed energy. And if it is so, then it is quite natural that degrees of condensation might be different. This theory explains how Hirn was unable to conceive half-material, half-energetic agents. Fine rarefied states of matter must in fact occupy a middle position between matter and force.

In his book *Unknown Forces of Nature*, C. Flammarion wrote: " Matter is not at all what it appears to our senses, to touch or vision. . . . It represents one single whole with energy and is the manifestation of the motion of invisible and imponderable elements. The Universe has a dynamic character. Guillaume de Fontenay gives the following explanation of the dynamic theory. In his opinion matter is in no way the inert substance it is usually considered to be."

Let us take a carriage wheel and place it horizontally on the axle. The wheel is not moving. Let us take a rubber ball and make it fall between the spokes. Now let us make the wheel move slightly. The ball will fairly often hit the spokes and rebound. If we increase the rotation of the wheel the ball will not pass through it at all; the wheel will become for it a kind of impenetrable disc. We may make a similar experiment placing the wheel vertically and pushing a rod through it. A bicycle wheel will serve the purpose well, as its spokes are thin. When the wheel is stationary, the rod will pass through it nine times out of ten. When in motion the wheel will repel the rod more and more often. When the speed of its motion is increased it will become impenetrable, and all efforts at piercing it will strike as against steel armour.[10]

Now having examined in the world surrounding us all that answers to the physical conditions of a higher dimensional space, we may put the question more definitely: what is the fourth dimension?

We have seen that it is impossible to prove its existence mathematically or to determine its properties and above all to define its position in relation to our world. Mathematics admits only the possibility of the existence of higher dimensions.

At the very beginning, when defining the idea of the fourth dimension, I pointed out that if it existed, it would mean that besides the three perpendiculars known to us there must exist a fourth. And this in its turn would mean that from any point of our space a line can be traced in a direction unknown and unknowable for us, and further that quite close, side by side with us, but in an unknown direction, there lies some other space which we are unable to see and into which we cannot pass.

I explained later why we are unable to see this space and I determined that it must lie not side by side with us in an unknown direction, but inside us, inside the objects of our world, inside our atmosphere, inside our space. However, this is not the solution of the whole problem, although it is a necessary stage on the way to this solution, because the fourth dimension *is not only inside us,* but we ourselves are inside it, that is, in the space of four dimensions.

I mentioned before that " spiritualists " and " occultists " of different schools often use the expression " fourth dimension " in their literature, assigning to the fourth dimension all phenomena of the " astral sphere."

The " astral sphere " of the occultists which permeates our space is an attempt to find a place for phenomena which do not fit into our space. And consequently it is to a certain extent that continuation of our world inwards which we require.

The " astral sphere " from an ordinary point of view may be defined as the *subjective world,* projected outside us and taken for the *objective world.* If anybody actually succeeded in establishing the objective existence of even a portion of what is called " astral," it would be the world of the fourth dimension.

But the very concept of the " astral sphere " or " astral matter " has changed many times in occult teachings.

On the whole, if we take the views of " occultists " of different schools on nature, we shall see that they are based upon the recognition of the possibility of studying conditions of existence other than our physical ones, and of using the knowledge of these other conditions of existence for the purpose of influencing our physical conditions. " Occult " theories generally

---

[10] Camille Flammarion, *Les forces naturelles inconnues.* Paris, 1927 (E. Flammarion, éditeur), p. 568.

start from the recognition of one basic substance, the knowledge of which provides *a key* to the knowledge of the mysteries of nature. But the concept of this substance is not definite. Sometimes it is understood as a *principle*, as a *condition of existence*, and sometimes as *matter*. In the first instance the basic substance contains in itself the roots and causes of things and events; in the second instance the basic substance is the primary matter from which everything else is obtained. The first concept is of course much more subtle and is the result of more elaborate philosophical thought. The second concept is more crude and is in most cases a sign of the decline of thought, a sign of an ignorant handling of difficult and profound ideas.

Philosopher-alchemists called this fundamental substance " Spiritus Mundi " — the spirit of the world. But alchemists — *seekers after gold* — considered it possible to put the spirit of the world into a crucible and subject it to chemical manipulations.

This should be kept in mind in order to understand the " astral hypotheses " of modern theosophists and occultists. Saint-Martin and, later, Eliphas Lévi still understood the " astral light " as a *principle*, as conditions of existence other than our physical conditions. But in the case of modern spiritualists and theosophists " astral light " has been transformed into " astral matter," which can be *seen* and even photographed. The theory of " astral matter " is based on the hypothesis of " fine states of matter." The hypothesis of fine states of matter was still possible in the last decades of the old physics, but it is difficult to find a place for it in modern physico-chemical thought. On the other hand, modern physiology deviates further and further from physico-mechanical explanations of vital processes and comes to the recognition of the enormous influence of *traces of matter*, that is, of imponderable and chemically indefinable matters, which are nevertheless clearly seen by the results of their presence, such as " hormones," " vitamines," " internal secretions " and so on.

Therefore, in spite of the fact that the hypothesis of fine states of matter does not stand in any relation whatever to new physics I shall attempt here to give a short exposition of the " astral theory."

According to this theory particles resulting from the division of physical atoms produce a kind of special fine matter — " astral matter " — unsubjected to the action of the majority of physical forces, but subjected to the action of forces not affecting physical matter. Thus this " astral matter " is subjected to the action of psychic energy, will, feelings and desires, which are real forces in the astral sphere. This means that man's will, and also his sense reactions and emotional impulses, act upon " astral matter " just as physical energy acts upon physical bodies.

Further, the transformation into the astral state of physical matter composing visible bodies and objects is recognised as possible. This is *dematerialisation*, that is, from the physical point of view, a complete disappearance of physical objects no one knows where without trace or remains. Also, the reverse process, that is, the transformation of astral matter into the physical state or into physical matter is recognised as possible. This is *materialisation,* that is, the appearance of things, objects and even living beings from no one knows where.

Moreover, it is recognised as possible that matter which enters into the composition of a physical body, after having been transformed into the astral state, may " return " to the physical state in another form. Thus one metal, having been transformed into the astral state, may " return " in the form of another metal. In this way alchemical processes are explained by the temporary transference of some body, most often some metal, into an astral state where matter is subject to the action of will (or of spirits) and may change entirely under the influence of this will and reappear in the physical world *as another metal;* thus iron can change into gold. It is recognised as possible to accomplish this transformation of matter from one state into another and the transformation of one body into another by means of mental influence, assisted by certain rituals, etc. Further it is considered possible to see in the astral sphere events which have not yet happened in the physical sphere, but which must happen and must influence both the past and the future.

All this taken together makes up the content of what is called magic.

Magic, in the usual understanding of this word, means the capacity to accomplish what cannot be accomplished by ordinary physical means. Such would be, for instance, the power to influence psychically people and objects at a distance, to see people's actions and to know their thoughts, to make them disappear from our world and appear in unexpected places; the capacity to change one's appearance and even one's physical nature, to transfer oneself in some inconceivable way to great distances, to pass through walls, etc.

" Occultists " explain all such acts by the knowledge of the properties of the " astral sphere " possessed by magicians and their ability to act mentally upon astral matter and through it upon physical matter. Certain kinds of " sorcery " can be explained by the imparting of special properties to inanimate objects. This is attained by means of influencing psychically their " astral matter," by a special kind of psychic magnetisation of them; in this way magicians could impart to objects any properties they chose, make them execute their will, bring good or evil to other people, warn them against impending disasters, give force or take force away. To such magical practices belongs, for instance, the " blessing of water," which has now become nothing but a rite in Christian and Buddhist religious services. Originally it was an operation undertaken for the purpose of saturating water psychically with certain radiations or emanations with the aim of endowing it with the desired qualities, curative or other.

In theosophical and modern occult literature there are many very picturesque descriptions of the astral sphere. But no proofs of the objective existence of the astral sphere are anywhere given.

" Spiritualistic " proofs, that is, phenomena at séances, or " mediumistic " phenomena in general, " communications," etc., ascribed to spirits, that is, to disincarnated souls, are in no sense proofs, because all these phenomena can be explained much more simply. In the chapter on dreams I point out the possible meaning of spiritualistic phenomena as the results of impersonation. Theosophical explanations based upon " clairvoyance " require first of all proof of the existence of " clairvoyance," which remains unproved in spite of the number of books in which the authors have described what they attained or what they found by means of clairvoyance.

It is not generally known that in France there exists a prize, established many years ago, which offers a considerable sum of money to anybody who would read a letter in a closed envelope. The prize remains unclaimed.

Both the spiritualistic and the theosophical theories suffer from one common defect which explains why " astral " hypotheses remain always the same and receive no proofs. " Space " and " time " are taken both in spiritualistic and in theosophical astral theories in exactly the same way as in the old physics, that is, separately from one another. " Disincarnated spirits " or " astral beings " or thought forms are taken *spatially* as bodies of the fourth dimension, but *in time* as physical bodies. In other words they remain in the same time conditions as physical bodies. And it is precisely this that is impossible. If " fine states of matter " produce bodies of different spatial existence, these bodies must have a different time existence. But this idea does not enter into theosophical or spiritualistic thought.

In this chapter there has been collected only the historical material relating to the study of the " fourth dimension," or rather that part of the historical material which brings one nearer to the solution of the problem or at least to its more exact formulation.

In this book, in the chapter " A New Model of the Universe," I show how the problems of " space-time " are connected with the problems of the structure of matter, and consequently the structure of the world, and how they lead to a right understanding of the *real* world, avoiding a whole series of unnecessary hypotheses, both pseudo-occult and pseudo-scientific.

1908–1929

Chapter III

SUPERMAN

❖

Sᴵᴰᴇ by side with the idea of hidden knowledge there runs through the whole history of human thought the idea of superman.

The idea of superman is as old as the world. Through all the centuries, through hundreds of centuries of its history, humanity has lived with the idea of superman. Sayings and legends of all ancient peoples are full of images of a superman. Heroes of myths, Titans, demi-gods, Prometheus who brought fire from heaven; prophets, messiahs and saints of all religions; heroes of fairy-tales and epic songs; knights who rescue captive princesses, awake sleeping beauties, vanquish dragons, and fight giants and ogres — all these are images of a superman.

Popular wisdom of all times and all peoples has always understood that man, as he is, cannot arrange his own life by himself; popular wisdom has never regarded man as the crowning achievement of creation. It has always understood the place of man, and always accepted and admitted the thought that there can and must be beings who, though also human, are much higher, stronger, more complex, more " miraculous," than ordinary man. It is only the opaque and sterilised thought of the last centuries of European culture which has lost touch with the idea of superman and put as its aim *man* as he is, as he always was and always will be. And in this comparatively short period of time, European thought had so thoroughly forgotten the idea of superman that, when Nietzsche threw out this idea to the West, it appeared new, original and unexpected. In reality this idea has existed from the very beginning of human thought known to us.

After all, superman has never completely vanished in modern Western thought. What, for instance, is the Napoleonic legend and what are all similar legends but attempts to create a new myth of superman? The masses in their own way still live with the idea of superman; they are never satisfied with man as he is; and the literature supplied to the masses invariably gives them a superman. What indeed is the Count of Monte Cristo, or Rocambole, or Sherlock Holmes, but a modern expression of the same idea of a strong, powerful being, against whom ordinary men cannot fight, who surpasses them in strength, bravery and cunning, and whose power always has in it something mysterious, magical, miraculous?

If we try to examine the forms in which the idea of superman has been expressed in human thought in different periods of history, we shall see that it falls into several definite categories.

The first idea of superman pictured him in the past, connected him with the legendary Golden Age. The idea has always been one and the same. People dreamt of, or remembered, times long past when their life was governed by supermen, who struggled against evil, upheld justice and acted as mediators between men and the Deity, governing them according to the will of the Deity, giving them laws, bringing them commandments. The idea of theocracy is always connected with the idea of superman. God, or gods, whatever they were called, always governed people with the help and mediation of supermen — prophets, chiefs, kings, of a mysterious superhuman origin. Gods could never deal directly with men. Man never was and never considered himself sufficiently strong to look upon the face of the Deity and receive laws directly. All religions begin with the advent of a superman. " Revelation " always comes through a superman. Man has never believed himself able to do anything of real significance.

But dreams of the past could not satisfy man; he began to dream of the future, of the time when a superman would come *again*. From this a new conception of superman resulted.

People began to expect the superman. He was to come; arrange their affairs, govern them, teach them to obey the law, or bring them a new law, a new teaching, a new knowledge, a new truth, a new revelation. The superman was to come to save men from themselves, as well as from the evil forces surrounding them. Almost all religions contain such an expectation of a superman, an expectation of a prophet, of a messiah.

In Buddhism the idea of superman completely replaces the idea of the Deity; because Buddha is not God, he is only a superman.

The idea of superman has never been absent from the consciousness of mankind. The image of a superman was shaped out of very varied elements. At times it received a strong admixture of popular fantasy which brought into it conceptions arising from the personification of nature, of fire, of thunder, of the forest, of the sea; the same fantasy sometimes united in a single image vague rumours concerning some distant people, either more savage or, on the contrary, more civilised.

Thus, travellers' tales of cannibals were united in the imagination of the ancient Greeks into the image of the Cyclops Polyphemus, who devoured the companions of Odysseus. An unknown people, an unknown race, was very easily transformed in myths into a single superhuman being.

Thus, the idea of superman in the past, or in the present in unknown countries, has always been vivid and rich in content. But the idea of a superman as a prophet or messiah, of the superman whom people were expecting, was always very obscure. People had a very dim conception of superman, they did not understand in what way superman should differ from ordinary man.

And when superman came, people stoned him or crucified him because he did not fulfil their expectations. But nevertheless the idea did not die and, even in an indistinct and confused form, it served as a measure by which the nothingness of man was measured. And the idea was gradually forgotten when man began to lose the realisation of his nothingness.

For the modern scientific view of the world the idea of superman stands apart, as a sort of philosophical curiosity unconnected with anything else. Modern Western thought does not know how to depict the idea of superman in the right tones. It always distorts this idea, it is always afraid of the final deductions from it and, in its theories of the future, it denies any connection with it.

This attitude towards the idea of superman is based upon a wrong understanding of the ideas of evolution. The chief defects of the modern understanding of evolution have been pointed out in an earlier chapter.

" Superman," if he ever enters scientific thought, is regarded as the product of the evolution of man, although as a rule this term is not used at all and is replaced by the term " a higher type of man." In this connection, evolutionary theories have become the basis of a naïve optimistic view of life and of man. It is as though people said to themselves: now that evolution exists and now that science recognises evolution, it follows that all is well and must in future become still better. In the imagination of the modern man reasoning from the point of view of the ideas of evolution, everything should have a happy ending. A story should necessarily end in a wedding. It is precisely here that the chief mistake with regard to the ideas of evolution lies. Evolution, however it be understood, is not assured for anyone or for anything. The theory of evolution means only that nothing stands still, nothing remains as it was, everything inevitably goes either up or down, but not at all necessarily up; to think that everything necessarily goes up — this is the most fantastic conception of the possibilities of evolution.

All the forms of life we know are either the result of evolution, or the result of degeneration. But we cannot discriminate between these two processes, and we very often mistake the results of degeneration for the results of evolution. Only in one respect we make no mistake: we know that nothing remains as it was. Everything " lives," everything is transformed.

Man also is transformed, but whether he is going up or down is a big question. Moreover, *evolution* in the true sense of the word has nothing in common with the anthropological change of the type, even if we consider such a change of type as established. Nor has evolution anything in common with the change of social forms, customs and laws, nor with the modification and " evolution " of forms of slavery or means of warfare. Evolution towards superman is the creation of new forms of thinking and feeling, and the abandonment of old forms.

Moreover, we must remember that the development of a new type is accomplished at the expense of the old type, which is made to disappear by the same process. The new type being created out of an old one overcomes it, so to speak, conquers it, occupies its place.

Nietzsche's Zarathustra speaks of this in the following words:

I teach you the superman. Man is something that has to be surmounted. What have you done to surmount man?

What is the ape to man? A laughing stock or a sore disgrace! And just the same shall man be to the superman — a laughing stock or a sore disgrace.[1]

Even the wisest of you is but a discord, and a hybrid of plant and phantom.

Man is a rope over an abyss. A dangerous crossing, a dangerous wayfaring, a dangerous looking back, a dangerous trembling and halting.

What is great in man is that he is a bridge and not a goal; what is lovable in man is that he is an over-going and a down-going.[2]

These words of Zarathustra have not entered into our usual thinking. And when we picture to ourselves a superman we accept and approve in him just those sides of human nature which should be discarded on the way.

Superman appears to us as a very complicated and contradictory being. In reality superman must be a clearly defined being. He cannot have within him that eternal inner conflict, that painful inner division, which men continually feel, and which they ascribe even to gods.

At the same time there cannot be two opposite types of superman. Superman is the result of a *definite* movement, of a *definite* evolution.

In ordinary thinking superman appears as a hypertrophied man with all sides of his nature greatly exaggerated. This, of course, is quite impossible, because one side of human nature can develop only at the expense of other sides, and superman can be the expression of only one, and moreover of *one very definite*, side of human nature.

These wrong conceptions of superman are due in a considerable degree to the fact that ordinary thought considers man to be a much more finished type than he really is.

The same naïve view of man lies at the base of all existing social sciences and theories. All these theories have in view only *man* and his future. They either endeavour to foresee the possible future of man, or recommend the best methods, from their point of view, of organising the life of man, of giving man all the happiness possible, of freeing man from unnecessary suffering, from injustice, and so on. But people do not see that attempts at a forcible application of such theories to life result only in increasing the amount of suffering and injustice. In trying to foresee the future all these

---

[1] *Thus Spake Zarathustra*, by F. Nietzsche (Thomas Common, 1908), Prologue, p. 11.

[2] Ibid., p. 13.

theories want to make life serve and obey man, and in doing so they do not take into account the real fact, that man himself must change. People, believing in these theories, want to build without keeping in mind that a new master must come and that a new master may not at all like what they have built or have begun to build.

Man is pre-eminently a transitional form, constant only in his contradictions and inconstancy — moving, becoming, changing under our eyes. Even without any special study it is perfectly clear that man is a quite unfinished being, differing to-day from what he was yesterday and differing to-morrow from what he is to-day.

So many opposing principles struggle in man that a harmonious coordination of them is quite impossible. This explains why a " positive " type of man is impossible. The soul of man is far too complex a combination for all the voices shouting in it to become united into one harmonious choir. All the kingdoms of nature live in man. Man is a little universe. In him proceed continual death and continual birth, the incessant swallowing of one being by another, the devouring of the weaker by the stronger, evolution and degeneration, growing and dying out. Man has within him everything from a mineral to God. And the desire of God in man, that is, the directing forces of his spirit, conscious of its unity with the infinite consciousness of the universe, cannot be in harmony with the inertia of a stone, with the inclination of particles for crystallisation, with the sleepy flow of the sap in a plant, with the plant's slow turning towards the sun, with the call of the blood in an animal, with the " three-dimensional " consciousness of man, which is based on his separating himself from the world, on his opposing to the world his own " I " and on his recognising as reality all apparent forms and divisions.

And the more man develops inwardly, the more strongly he begins to feel the different sides of his soul simultaneously; and the more strongly he feels himself the more strongly grows within him the desire to feel more and more, and at last he begins to desire so many things that he is never able to obtain at once all that he desires; his imagination carries him in different directions at the same time. One life is no longer sufficient for him, he needs ten, twenty lives at one time. He needs to be simultaneously in different places, with different people, in different situations, he wants to reconcile the irreconcilable and combine the uncombinable. His spirit does not wish to reconcile itself to the limitations of body and matter, to the limitations of time and space. His imagination travels infinitely far beyond all possibilities of realisation, just as his emotional feeling travels infinitely far beyond the formulations and attainments of his intellect.

Man outruns himself, but at the same time begins to be satisfied with imagination only, without attempts at realisation. And in his rare attempts at realisation he does not see that he obtains things diametrically opposed to what he thinks he is approaching.

The complicated system of the human soul often appears as dual, and there are serious grounds for such a view. There live in every man, as it were, two beings, one being comprising the mineral, vegetable, animal and human " time and space " world, the other being belonging to some other world. One is the being of " the past," the other the being of " the future." But which is the being of the past and which the being of the future we do not know. And the past and the future find themselves in eternal struggle and eternal conflict in the soul of man. It may be said without the slightest exaggeration that the soul of man is the battle-field of the past and the future.

Nietzsche's Zarathustra says these interesting words:

I am of to-day and heretofore, but something is in me that is of the morrow and of the day following and the hereafter (*Thus Spake Zarathustra*).

But Zarathustra speaks not of the conflict, he speaks of the fulness which includes to-day and heretofore, to-morrow and hereafter, a fulness which comes when contradictions, multiplicity and duality have been conquered.

The necessity to struggle against man for the attainment of superman is what modern thought utterly refuses to admit. This idea entirely disagrees with the exalting of man and his weaknesses which is so characteristic of our times.

At the same time this does not mean that the idea of superman plays no rôle in our time. If certain schools of modern thought reject the idea of superman or are afraid of it, others, on the contrary, are entirely based on this idea and cannot exist without it. The idea of superman separates the thought of humanity into two sharply divided and very definite categories.

1. Conception of man without the idea of superman: " scientific " conception of man, and also a considerable part of philosophical conception of man.

2. Conception of man from the point of view of the idea of superman: mystical, occult and theosophical conception of man (though here it must be noted that almost everything that is known under these names is pseudo-mystical, pseudo-occult and pseudo-esoteric conceptions).

In the first case man is taken as a completed being. Study is made of his anatomical structure, his physiological and psychological functions, his present position in the world, his historical fate, his culture and civilisation, the possibility of the better organisation of his life, his possibilities of knowledge, etc.; in all this man is taken as what he is. In this case chief attention is concentrated on the results of man's activities, his attainments, his discoveries, his inventions. And in this case these results of man's activities are regarded as proofs of his evolution, although as often happens, they demonstrate just the contrary.

The idea of evolution in this conception of man is taken as the general evolution of all men, of the whole of mankind. Mankind is regarded as evolving. And although such an evolution has nothing analogous to it in Nature and cannot be explained by any biological example, Western thought is in no way disconcerted by this and continues to speak of evolution.

In the second case man is taken as an uncompleted being, out of which something different should result. And the whole meaning of the existence of this being lies, in this case, in its transition into this new state. Man is regarded as a grain, as a larva, as something temporary and subject to transformation. And in this case all that refers to man is taken from the point of view of this transformation; in other words, the value of everything in man's life is determined by the consideration of whether it is useful for this transformation or not.

But the idea of transformation itself remains very obscure. And the conception of man from the point of view of superman cannot be regarded either as popular or as progressing. It enters as an indispensable attribute into semi-occult, semi-mystical teachings, but it plays no part in the scientific, or in the more widely-spread pseudo-scientific, philosophies of life.

The reason for this, apart from everything else, is to be seen in the complete divergence of Western culture from religious thought. If it were not for this divergence, the conception of man from the point of view of the idea of superman would not be lost, because religious thought, in its true sense, is impossible without the idea of superman.

The absence of the idea of superman from the majority of modern philosophies of life is to a considerable extent the cause of the terrible chaos of thought in which modern humanity lives. If men tried to connect the idea of superman with all the more or less accepted views, they would see that it shows everything in a new light, presenting from new angles the things which they thought they knew quite well, reminding them of the fact that man is only a temporary visitor, only a passenger, on the earth.

Naturally such a view could not be popular. Modern philosophies of life (or at least a great many of them) are built on sociology or on what is called sociology. And sociology never thinks of a time so remote that a new type will have developed out of man, but is concerned only with the present or the near and immediate future. But it is precisely this attitude which serves merely to show the scholasticism of that science. Sociology like any other scholastic science deals not with living facts, but with artificial abstractions. Sociology, dealing with the " average level " and " average man," does not see the relief of the mountains, does not understand that neither humanity nor individual man is something flat and uniform.

Humanity, as well as individual man, is a mountain chain with high snow summits and deep precipices, and, moreover, in that unsettled geological period when everything is in process of formation, when whole mountain ranges vanish, when deserts appear in the place of seas, when new volcanoes rise, when fields and forests are buried under the flow of boiling lava, when continents emerge and perish and when glacial periods come and go. An " average man," with whom alone sociology can deal, does not exist in reality any more than the " average mountain height " exists.

It is impossible to indicate the moment when a new, a more stable, type is formed. It is being formed continuously. Growth proceeds without interruptions. There is never a moment when anything is completed. A new type of man is being formed now and amongst us. The selection goes on in all races and nations of the earth, except in the most backward and degenerating races; the latter include the races usually considered the most advanced, that is, those completely absorbed in pseudo-culture.

Superman does not belong to the historical future. If superman can exist on earth, he must exist both in the past and in the present. But he does not stay in life, he appears and goes away.

Just as a grain of wheat in becoming a plant goes out of the sphere of the life of grains; just as an acorn in becoming an oak goes out of the life of acorns; just as a caterpillar in becoming a chrysalis *dies* for caterpillars and in becoming a butterfly goes completely out of the sphere of observation of caterpillars, in the same way superman goes out of the sphere of observation of other people, goes out of their historical life.

An ordinary man cannot see a superman or know of his existence, just as a caterpillar cannot know of the existence of a butterfly. This is a fact which we find extremely difficult to admit, but it is natural and psychologically inevitable. The higher type cannot in any sense be controlled by the lower type or be the subject of observation by the lower type; but the lower type may be controlled by the higher and may be under the observation of the higher. And from this point of view the whole of life and the whole of history can have a meaning and a purpose which we cannot comprehend.

This meaning, this purpose, is *superman*. All the rest exists for the sole purpose that out of the masses of humanity crawling on the earth *superman* should from time to time emerge and rise, and by this very fact go away from the masses and become inaccessible and invisible to them.

The ordinary view of life either finds no aim in life or sees the aim in the " evolution of the masses." But the evolution of the masses is as fantastic and illogical an idea as would be, for instance, the idea of an identical evolution of all the cells of a tree or all the cells of an organism. We do not realise that the idea of the evolution of the masses is equivalent to expecting *all* the cells of a tree, that is, the cells of the roots, bark, wood-fibre and leaves, to be *transformed* into cells of flowers and fruit, that is, expecting *the whole* tree to be transformed into flowers and fruit.

Evolution, which is usually regarded as evolution of the masses, can in reality never be anything but evolution of the few. And *in mankind* such an evolution can only be conscious. It is only degeneration which can proceed unconsciously in men.

Nature has in no way guaranteed a superman. She holds within herself all possibilities, including the most sinister. Man cannot be promoted to superman as a reward, either for a long term of service as a man, or for irreproachable conduct, or for his sufferings, whether accidental or created by himself unintentionally by his own stupidity or unadaptability to life, or even intentionally for the sake of the reward which he hopes to obtain.

Nothing leads to superman except the understanding of the idea of superman, and it is precisely this understanding that is becoming ever rarer and rarer.

For all its inevitability the idea of superman is not at all clear. The psychological outlines of superman elude modern man like a shadow. Men create superman according to their own likeness and image, endowing him with their qualities, tastes and defects in an exaggerated form.

To superman are ascribed features and qualities which can never belong to him, features which are entirely contradictory and incompatible, which deprive one another of any value and destroy one another. The idea of superman is generally approached from the wrong angle; it is taken either too simply, merely on one plane, or too fantastically, without any connection with reality. The result is that the idea is distorted, and men's treatment of it becomes more and more erroneous.

In order to find a right approach to this idea, we must first of all create for ourselves a harmonious picture of superman. Vagueness, indefiniteness and diffuseness are in no way necessary attributes of the picture of superman. We can know more about him than we think, if only we want to and know how to set about it. We have perfectly clear and definite lines of thought for reasoning about superman and perfectly definite notions, some connected with the idea of superman and others opposed to it. All that is required is to avoid confusing them. Then the understanding of superman, the creation of a harmonious picture of superman, will cease to be such an unattainable dream as it sometimes appears.

The inner growth of man follows quite definite paths. It is necessary to determine and to understand these paths; otherwise, when the idea of superman is already accepted in one form or another, but is not connected vitally with the life of man, it takes strange, sometimes grotesque or monstrous forms. People who think naïvely picture superman to themselves as a kind of exaggerated man, in whom both the positive and the negative sides of human nature have developed with equal freedom and have reached the utmost limits of their possible development. But this is exactly what is impossible. The most elementary acquaintance with psychology, certainly if we take psychology as real understanding of the laws of the inner being of man, shows that the development of features of one kind can only proceed at the expense of features of another kind. There are many contradictory qualities in man which can in no case develop on parallel lines.

The imagination of primitive peoples pictured superman as a giant, a man of herculean strength, extremely long-lived. We must revise the qualities of superman, that is, the qualities ascribed to superman, and determine whether these qualities can be developed only *in man*. If qualities which can exist apart from him are attributed to superman it becomes evident that these qualities are wrongly connected with him. Only those qualities must develop in superman which can develop in him alone; for instance, gigantic size cannot by any means be a quality of absolute value for super-man. Trees can be still taller; houses, towers, mountains, may be higher than the tallest giant that earth can bear. Thus height and size cannot serve as the aim of the evolution of superman. Besides, modern biology knows very well that man *cannot be* taller than a certain height, that is, his skeleton would not stand a weight greatly surpassing the weight of man's body. Nor does enormous physical strength present an absolute value. Man with his own weak hands is able to construct machines more powerful than any giant. And for " Nature," for the " Earth," the strongest man, even a giant, is just a pigmy, imperceptible on its surface. Neither is longevity, however great it may be, a sign of inner growth. Trees can exist for thousands of years. A stone can exist for tens or hundreds of thousands of years.

All these qualities are of no value in superman, because they can be mani-fested apart from him.

In superman qualities must develop which cannot exist in a tree or in a stone, qualities with which neither high mountains nor earthquakes can compete.

The development of the inner world, the evolution of consciousness, this is an absolute value, which in the world known to us can develop only in man and cannot develop apart from him.

The evolution of consciousness, the inner growth of man, is the " ascent towards superman." But inner growth proceeds not along one line, but along several lines simultaneously. These lines must be established and de-termined, because mingled with them are many deceptive, false ways, which lead man aside, turn him backward or bring him into blind alleys.

It is of course impossible to dogmatise about a form of the intellectual and emotional development of superman. But several aspects of it can be shown with perfect exactitude.

Thus the first thing that can be said is that superman cannot be thought about on the ordinary " materialistic " plane. Superman must necessarily be connected with something mysterious, something of magic and sorcery.

Consequently an interest directed towards the " mysterious " and the " inexplicable," a gravitation towards the " occult," are inevitably connected with evolution in the direction of superman. Man suddenly feels that he cannot continue to ignore much that has seemed to him, till now, unworthy of attention. Suddenly he begins to see everything as it were with new eyes, and all the " fairy-like," the " mystical," which only yesterday he smilingly rejected as a superstition, acquires unexpectedly for him some new deep meaning, either symbolical or real.

He finds new meanings in things, unexpected and strange analogies. An interest in the study of religions, old and new, appears in him. His thought penetrates the inward meaning of allegories and myths, he finds a deep and strange significance in things which formerly looked self-evident and unin-teresting.

It may be that interest in the mysterious and the miraculous creates the chief watchwords serving to unite men who begin to discover the hidden meaning of life. But the same interest in the mysterious and the miraculous also serves to test people. A man who has retained the possibilities of credulity or superstition will infallibly run on to one of the submerged rocks of which the sea of " occultism " is full; he will succumb to the seduction of some mirage — will in one way or another lose his aim.

At the same time superman cannot be simply a " great business man " or a " great conqueror " or a " great statesman " or a " great scientist." He must inevitably be either a magician or a saint. Russian heroic legends always ascribe to their heroes traits of magical wisdom, that is, of " secret knowledge."

The idea of superman is directly connected with the idea of hidden knowledge. The expectation of superman is the expectation of some new revelation, of new knowledge.

But, as has been stated before, sometimes the expectation of superman is connected with the usual theories of evolution, that is, with the idea of general evolution, and superman is regarded in this case as a possible product of the evolution of man. It is curious that this seemingly most logical theory completely destroys the idea of superman. The cause of this lies, of course, in the wrong view of evolution in general, which has already been pointed out. Moreover, for some reason superman cannot be regarded as a higher zoological type in comparison with man, as a product of the general law of evolution. There is in this view some radical mistake which is clearly felt in all attempts to form an image of the superman of the distant and unknown future. The picture appears too nebulous and diffuse; the image of superman in this case loses all colour and grows almost repulsive, as though from the very fact of becoming lawful and inevitable. Superman must have something unlawful in him, something which violates the general course of things, something unexpected, unsubjected to any general laws.

This idea is expressed by Nietzsche.

I want to teach men the sense of their existence, which is the superman, the lightning out of the dark cloud — man (*Thus Spake Zarathustra*).

Nietzsche understood that superman cannot be regarded as the product of a historical development which can be realised in the distant future, that he cannot be regarded as a new zoological species. Lightning cannot be regarded as the result of the " evolution of the cloud."

But the feeling of the " unlawfulness " of superman, his " impossibility " from the ordinary point of view, causes people to attribute to him features that are really impossible, and so superman is often pictured as a kind of Juggernaut car, crushing people in its progress.

Malice, hatred, pride, conceit, selfishness, cruelty, all are considered *superhuman*, on the sole condition that they reach the furthest possible limits and do not stop at any obstacle. Complete liberation from all moral restraint is considered superhuman or approaching superhuman. "Superman" in the vulgar and falsified sense of the word means: all is permitted.

The supposed a-morality of superman is associated with the name of Nietzsche. But Nietzsche is not guilty of this idea. On the contrary, perhaps no one has ever put into the philosophy of superman so much longing for true morality and for true love as Nietzsche. He was only destroying the old petrified morality which had long since become anti-moral. He rebelled against ready-made morality, against the invariable forms which in theory are obligatory always and for everyone, and in practice are violated always and by everyone.

Verily I have taken from you perhaps a hundred formulæ, and your virtue's favourite playthings; and now you upbraid me, as children upbraid.

They played by the sea — then came there a wave and swept their playthings into the deep; and now do they cry.

And further:

When I came unto men, then found I them resting on an old infatuation: all of them thought they had long known what was good or bad for men.

This somnolence did I disturb when I taught that no one yet knows what is good and bad — unless it be the creating one (*Thus Spake Zarathustra*).

In Nietzsche the moral feeling is the feeling of artistic creation, the feeling of service.

Often it is a very stern and merciless feeling. Zarathustra says:

Oh, my brethren, am I then cruel? But I say: what falleth, that shall one also push! (*Thus Spake Zarathustra*).

Obviously these words are doomed to misunderstanding and misinterpretation. The cruelty of Nietzsche's superman is regarded as his chief feature, as the principle underlying his treatment of men. The great majority of Nietzsche's critics do not wish to see that this cruelty of superman is turned against something inner, something *in himself*, against everything that is "human, all too human," small, vulgar, literal and inert, which makes man the corpse which Zarathustra carried on his back.

The non-understanding of Nietzsche is one of the curious examples of a non-understanding which is almost intentional. Nietzsche's idea of superman is clear and simple. It is sufficient to take the beginning of *Zarathustra*.

Thou great star! What would be thy happiness if thou hadst not those for whom thou shinest?

For ten years hast thou come up hither to my cave; thou wouldst have satiated of thy light and of thy journey, had it not been for me, my eagle and my serpent.

But we awaited thee every morning, took thy superfluity from thee and blest thee for it.

Lo! I am satiated with my wisdom, like the bee that has gathered too much honey; I need hands held out for it.

I would fain bestow and distribute . . .

Therefore I must descend into the deep, as thou dost in the evening. . . .

Bless the cup then, that is about to overflow, that the water may flow golden out of it, and carry everywhere the reflection of thy bliss.

And further:

Zarathustra went alone down the mountain and no one met with him. When, however, he entered the forest, there suddenly stood before him an old man. . . . And thus spake the old man to Zarathustra.

No stranger to me is this wanderer. Many years ago passed he by. Zarathustra was he called but he hath altered.

Then thou carriedst thine ashes into the mountains; wilt thou now carry thy fire into the valleys? Fearest thou not the incendiary's doom?

Yea, I recognized Zarathustra. Pure is his eye, and no loathing lurketh about his mouth . . .

Zarathustra answered:

I love men.

And after *this*, Nietzsche's ideas were regarded as one of the causes of German militarism and chauvinism!

All this lack of understanding of Nietzsche is curious and characteristic because it can only be compared with the lack of understanding on the part of Nietzsche himself of the ideas of Christianity and of the Gospels. Nietzsche understood Christ according to Renan. Christianity was for him the religion of the weak and the miserable. He rebelled against Christianity, opposed superman to Christ, and did not wish to see that he was fighting the very thing that had created him and his ideas.[3]

The fundamental feature of superman is power. The idea of " power " is very often connected with the idea of demonism. And then appears the demoniacal man.

Many people have been enthusiastic about demonism, but nevertheless the idea is utterly false and is in its essence not of a very high order. As a matter of fact the " beautiful demonism " we know is one of the " pseudo-ideas " by which people live. We do not know and do not want to know the real demonism, such as it must be according to a right meaning of the idea. All evil is very small and very vulgar. There can be no strong and great

---

[3] Nietzsche did not or would not understand that his superman was to a considerable extent the product of *Christian* thought. Moreover, Nietzsche was not generally very frank, even with himself, regarding the sources of his inspirations. I have never found, either in his biographies or in his letters, any indication of his acquaintance with contemporary " occult " literature. At the same time he obviously knew it well and made use of it.

It is very interesting to draw a parallel between some passages in the chapter on " The Bestowing Virtue " in Nietzsche's *Zarathustra*, and chapter IX, vol. I, in the *Dogme et Rituel de la Haute Magie* of Eliphas Lévi.

evil. Evil always consists in the transforming of something great into something small. But how can people reconcile themselves to such an idea? They must necessarily have " great evil."

Evil is one of the ideas which exist in the minds of men in a falsified form, in the form of their own " pseudo-images." Our whole life is surrounded by such pseudo-images. We have a pseudo-Christ, a pseudo-religion, a pseudo-civilisation, pseudo-sciences, etc., etc.

But generally speaking there can be two kinds of falsification: one, the more usual, where a substitute is given in place of the real thing — " instead of bread, a stone, and instead of fish, a serpent "; the other, a little more complex, when " base truth " is transformed into an " exalting lie." [4] This occurs when an idea or a phenomenon, constant and common in our life, and small and insignificant in its nature, is painted over and decorated with such zeal that at last people begin to see in it a certain disturbing beauty and some features which invite imitation.

A very beautiful " Sad demon, spirit of exile " is created precisely through such a falsification of the clear and simple idea of the " devil."

Lermontoff's " demon " or Milton's " Satan " is a pseudo-devil. The idea of the devil (the slanderer), the spirit of evil and lies, is intelligible and necessary in the dualistic philosophy of the world. But then the devil has no attractive features, whereas the " demon " or " Satan " possesses many beautiful and positive qualities: power, intelligence, contempt of everything small and vulgar. None of these are features of the devil.

The demon or Satan is an embellished, falsified devil. The real devil is, on the contrary, the falsification of everything brilliant and strong; he is counterfeit, plagiarism, vilification, vulgarisation, the " street," the " gutter."

In his book on Dostoevsky, A. L. Volynsky drew particular attention to the way in which Dostoevsky depicted the *devil* in the " Brothers Karamazoff."

The Devil whom Ivan Karamazoff sees is a parasite in check trousers, who suffers from rheumatism and has lately had himself vaccinated against smallpox.

The devil is vulgarity and triviality embodied. Everything he says is mean and vile; it is scandal, filthy insinuation, the desire to play upon the most repulsive sides of human nature. The whole sordidness of life spoke with Ivan Karamazoff in the person of the devil. We are, however, inclined to forget the real nature of the devil and are more willing to believe the poets, who embellish him and make an operatic demon out of him. The same demoniacal traits are ascribed to superman. But it is enough to look at them more closely to see that they are nothing more than pure falsification and deceit.

Speaking generally, in order to understand the idea of superman it is useful to have in mind everything opposed to the idea. From this point of

---

[4] The author quotes a well-known line from Pushkin.

view it is interesting to note that besides a devil in check trousers who has had himself vaccinated, there is another very well-known type, uniting in itself all in man that is most opposed to the superhuman. Such is the Roman procurator of Judea in the time of Jesus — Pontius Pilate.

The rôle of Pilate in the Gospel tragedy is extremely characteristic and significant, and if it was a conscious rôle, it would be one of the most difficult. But it is strange that perhaps of all the rôles of the Gospel drama the rôle of Pilate needs least of all to be a conscious one. Pilate could not " make a mistake," could not act in this way or in that way, and therefore he was taken in his natural state as a part of the surroundings and conditions, just as were the people who gathered in Jerusalem for the Passover and the crowd who shouted " crucify him." And the rôle of Pilate is identical with the rôles of the " Pilates " in life in general. It is not sufficient to say that Pilate tried Jesus, wanted to free him, and finally executed him. This does not determine the essence of his nature. The chief point lies in the fact that Pilate was almost the only one who *understood* Jesus. He understood him, of course, in his own Roman way; yet, in spite of understanding, he delivered him to be scourged and executed. Pilate was undoubtedly a very clever man, well educated and cultured. He saw very clearly that the man who stood before him was no criminal " preaching sedition to the people " or " inducing them not to pay the taxes," etc., as was declared to him by the " truly Jewish people " [5] of that time; that this man was not a pretender, not an impostor who called himself the King of Judea, but simply a " philosopher," as he could define Jesus to himself.

This " philosopher " aroused his sympathy, even his compassion. The Jews clamouring for the blood of an innocent man were repellent to him. He tried to help Jesus. But it was too much for him to fight for Jesus in earnest and incur unpleasantness, so, after a short hesitation, Pilate delivered him up to the Jews.

It was probably in his mind that he was serving Rome and in this particular case was safeguarding the peace of its rulers, maintaining order and quiet among the subject people, averting the cause of possible unrest, even sacrificing an innocent man for it. It was done in the name of politics, in the name of Rome, and the responsibility seemed to fall on Rome. Certainly Pilate could not have known that the days of Rome itself were already numbered, and that he himself was creating one of the forces that were to destroy Rome. But the thinking of Pilates never goes so far as that. Moreover, Pilate with regard to his own actions had a very convenient philosophy: everything is relative, everything is a question of point of view, nothing is of any particular value. It was a practical application of the " principle of relativity." On the whole Pilate is a very modern man. With such a philosophy it is easy to find the way amidst the difficulties of life.

Jesus even helped him; he said:

---

[5] An allusion to a patriotic organisation with strong pogrom tendencies in pre-war Russia — " truly Russian people."

For this cause came I into the world that I should bear witness unto the truth.

" What is truth? " ironically answered Pilate.

And this at once put him into his accustomed way of thinking and acting, reminded him who and where he was, showed him how he should look at things.

Pilate's essential feature is that he sees the truth but does not wish to follow it. In order to avoid following the truth which he sees, he has to create for himself a special sceptical and mocking attitude towards the very idea of truth and towards the adherents of the idea. In his own heart he is no longer able to regard them as criminals; he has outgrown this; but he must cultivate in himself a certain slightly ironical attitude towards them, which will allow him to sacrifice them when it is necessary.

Pilate went so far that he even tried to set Jesus free, but of course he would not have allowed himself to do anything that could compromise him. This would have made him ridiculous in his own eyes. When his attempts failed, as probably he could foresee, he came out to the people and washed his hands, showing by this that he disclaimed all responsibility.

The whole of Pilate is in this. The symbolical washing of hands is indissolubly connected with the image of Pilate. The whole of him is in this gesture.

For a man of real inner development there cannot be any washing of hands. This gesture of inner deceit can never belong to such a man.

" Pilate " is a type expressing that which in cultured humanity hinders the inner development of man, and forms the chief obstacle on the way to superman. Life is full of big and small Pilates. " The crucifixion of Christ " can never be accomplished without their help.

They see and understand the truth perfectly. But any " regrettable necessity," or interests of politics as understood by them, or interests of their own position, may force them to betray truth and then *to wash their hands*.

In relation to the evolution of the spirit, Pilate is a stop. Real growth consists in the harmonious development of mind, feeling and will. A one-sided development, that is, in this instance, the development of mind and will without the corresponding development of feeling, cannot go far. In order to betray truth Pilate had to make truth itself relative. And this relativity of truth adopted by Pilate helps him to find a way out of the difficult situations in which his own understanding of the truth places him. At the same time this very relativity of truth stops his inner development, the growth of his ideas. One cannot go far with relative truth. " Pilate " is bound to find himself in a closed circle.

Another remarkable type in the Gospel drama, a type also opposed to everything which in ordinary humanity leads to the superman, is Judas.

Judas is a very strange figure in the Gospel tragedy. There is no one about whom so much has been written as Judas. In modern European literature there are attempts to represent and interpret Judas from all possible points of view. Contrary to the usual " Church " interpretation of Judas as a mean and greedy " Jew " who sold Christ for thirty pieces of silver, he is sometimes represented as a figure even higher than Christ, as a man who sacrificed himself, his salvation and his " life eternal " in order that the miracle of redemption should be accomplished; or as a man who revolted against Christ, because Christ, in his opinion, spoiled the " cause," surrounded himself with worthless people, put himself in a ridiculous position, and so on.

Actually, however, Judas is not even a " rôle," and certainly not a romantic hero, not a conspirator desirous of strengthening the union of the apostles with the blood of Christ, not a man struggling for the purity of an idea. Judas is simply a small man who found himself in the wrong place, an ordinary man, full of distrust, of fears and suspicions, a man who ought not to have been among the apostles, who understood nothing of what Jesus said to his disciples, but a man who for some reason or other was accepted as one of them and was even given a responsible position and a certain authority. Judas was considered one of the favourite disciples of Jesus; he was in charge of the apostles' domestic arrangements, was their treasurer. Judas' tragedy was that he feared to be exposed; he felt himself in the wrong place and dreaded the thought that Jesus might one day reveal this to others. And at last he could bear it no longer. He did not understand some words of Jesus; perhaps he felt a threat in these words, perhaps a hint at something which only he and Jesus knew. Perturbed and frightened, Judas fled from the supper of Jesus and his disciples and decided to expose Jesus. The famous thirty pieces of silver played no part in this whatever. Judas acted under the influence of injury and fear; he wished to break and destroy that which he could not comprehend, that which revolted and humiliated him by the very fact of its being above his understanding. He needed to accuse Jesus and his disciples of crimes in order to feel himself in the right. Judas' psychology is a most human psychology, the psychology of slandering what one does not understand.

The placing of Pilate and Judas side by side with Jesus is a wonderful feature of the Gospel drama; it would be impossible to find or imagine a more striking contrast. If the Gospels were to be regarded simply as a literary work, a work of art, then the placing together of Christ, Pilate and Judas would point to the hand of a great author. In short scenes, in a few words, there are shown here contradictions which not only have not disappeared in the human race in two thousand years, but have grown and developed with great luxuriance.

Instead of approaching inner unity, man recedes farther and farther from it, but the question of attaining this unity is the most essential question of the inner development of man. Unless he attains inner unity, man can have no " I," can have no will. The concept of " will " in relation to a man who has not attained inner unity is entirely artificial.

Most of our actions are prompted by involuntary motives. The whole of life is composed of small things which we continually obey and serve. Our " I " continually changes as in a kaleidoscope. Every external event which strikes us, every suddenly aroused emotion, becomes caliph for an hour, begins to build and govern, and is in its turn as unexpectedly deposed and replaced by something else. And the inner consciousness, without attempting to disperse the illusory designs created by the shaking of the kaleidoscope and without understanding that in reality the power that decides and acts is not itself, endorses everything and says about those moments of life in which different external forces are at work, " This is I, this is I."

From this point of view " the will " can be defined only as the " resultant of desires." Consequently, so long as desires have not become permanent, man is the plaything of moods and external impressions. He never knows what he will say or do next. Not only the next day, but even the next moment, is hidden from him by the wall of accident.

What appears to be the consecutiveness of men's actions finds its explanation in the poorness of motives and desires, or in the artificial discipline grafted by " education," or, above all, in men's imitation of one another. As to the men with a so-called " strong will," these are usually men of one dominating desire, in which all other desires vanish.

If we do not understand the absence of unity in the inner world of man, we do not understand the necessity of such a unity in superman, just as we do not understand many of his other features. Thus superman appears to us a dried-up being, rational and deprived of emotions, whereas in reality the emotionality of superman, that is, his ability to feel, must far exceed ordinary human emotionality.

The psychology of superman eludes us because we do not understand the fact that the normal psychic state of superman constitutes what we call *ecstasy* in all possible meanings of this word.

Ecstasy is so far superior to all other experiences possible to man that we have neither words nor means for the description of it. Men who have experienced ecstasy have often attempted to communicate to others what they have experienced, and these descriptions, often coming from different centuries, from people who never heard of one another, are wonderfully alike and above all contain similar cognitional aspects of the Unknown. Moreover, the descriptions of real ecstasy contain a certain inner truth which cannot be mistaken and the absence of which is felt at once in cases of sham ecstasy as it occurs in descriptions of the experiences of the " saints " of the formal religions.

But speaking in general, a description in plain words of the experiences of ecstasy presents almost insurmountable difficulties. Only art, that is, poetry, music, painting, architecture, can succeed in transmitting, though in a very feeble way, the real content of ecstasy. All true art is in fact nothing but an attempt to transmit the sensation of ecstasy. And only the man who finds in it this taste of ecstasy will understand and feel art.

If we define " ecstasy " as the highest degree of emotional experience — which is probably a perfectly correct definition — it will become clear to us that the development of man towards superman cannot consist in the growth of the intellect alone. Emotional life must also evolve, in certain not easily comprehensible forms. And the chief change in man must come precisely from the evolution of emotional life.

Now if we imagine man approaching the new type, we must understand that he will live a certain peculiar life of his own, which will be very little like the lives of ordinary men and difficult for us to conceive. There will be very much suffering in his life — there will be sufferings which as yet affect us but very little and there will also be joys of which ordinary men have no idea, and even a feeble reflection of which reaches us only very rarely.

But for the man who undergoes no change through contact with the idea of superman there is in this idea a certain feature which imparts to it a very gloomy aspect. This is the remoteness of the idea, the fact that superman is very far away, cut off from us, from ordinary life. We occupy one place in life, he occupies a different place, and has no relation to us except that in some way we create him. When people begin to realise their relation to superman from this point of view, a certain vague doubt begins to creep in, and gradually develops into a more definite and very unpleasant feeling, which is shaped into a quite definitely negative view of the whole idea.

People may reason and often have reasoned in this way: let us grant that superman will come and that he will be exactly as we have pictured him, a new and enlightened being, and that he will be in a sense the result of the whole of our life. But what is it to us if it is he who will exist and not we? What are we in relation to him? Soil, on which will grow a gorgeous flower? Clay, out of which will be modelled a beautiful statue? We are promised a light which we shall never see. Why should we serve the light which will shine for others? We are beggars, we are in the dark and in the cold, and we are comforted by being shown the lights of a rich man's house. We are hungry and we are told of the magnificent feast in which we can have no part. We spend our whole life in collecting pitiful crumbs of knowledge, and then we are told that all our knowledge is illusion; that in the soul of superman a light will spring forth in which he will see in a flash all that we have so eagerly sought, aspired to and could never find.

And the misgivings which assail people when they encounter the idea of superman have a very sound basis. They cannot be passed by. They cannot be disposed of by saying that man must find happiness in being conscious of his connection with the idea of superman. These are nothing but words: " man *must* "! And what if he does not feel happiness? Man has a right to know, has a right to ask questions: why must he serve the idea of superman, why must he submit to this idea, why *must* he do anything?

In order to find the true meaning of the idea of superman it is necessary to understand that the idea is much more difficult than is generally thought. This is so because the idea requires for its right expression and understanding new words, new concepts and a knowledge which may very easily not be in the possession of man. All that is set forth here, all that portrays superman, even if it introduces something new into the understanding of the idea, is far from being sufficient. Ideas such as the idea of superman cannot be considered on the level of ordinary ideas relating to things and phenomena of the three-dimensional world. The idea of superman recedes into infinity and, like all ideas that recede into infinity, it requires a very particular approach, that is, from the direction of infinity.

In the ancient Mysteries there existed a consecutive and graduated order of initiation. In order to be raised to the next degree, to ascend the next step, the man to be initiated had to pass through a certain definite course of preparation. He was then subjected to the required tests, and only after he had passed through all the tests and had proved that his preparation had been serious and on the right lines were the next doors opened before him and he penetrated more deeply into the interior of the temple of initiation.

One of the first things that the man to be initiated learned and had to appreciate was the impossibility of following a path of his own choice and the danger which awaited him if he did not carry out all the preparatory rituals and ceremonies required before initiation, and if he failed to learn all that was required to be known, if he failed to remember all that he had to remember. He was told of the awful consequences following a violation of the order of initiation, the terrible punishments which awaited the man to be initiated who dared to enter the sanctuary without having observed all these rules. And what was required of him first was the realisation of the necessity of *advancing by steps*. He had to realise that it was impossible for him to out-distance himself, and that any attempt in this direction was certain to end tragically. A rigorous consecutiveness of inner development was a fundamental rule of the Mysteries. If we try to analyse psychologically the idea of initiation, we shall understand that *initiation* was an introduction into a circle of new ideas. Each further degree of initiation represented the disclosing of a new idea, a new point of view, a new angle of vision. And in the Mysteries new ideas were not disclosed to a man until he had proved himself sufficiently prepared to receive them.

In this order of initiation into new ideas a deep understanding of the properties of the world of ideas can be seen. The ancients understood that the reception of each new idea required special preparation; they understood that an idea caught in passing can easily be seen in a wrong light, or received in a wrong way, and that a wrongly received idea can produce very undesirable and even disastrous results.

The Mysteries and the gradual initiations were to protect people from the half-knowledge which is often much worse than no knowledge at all, particularly in questions of the Eternal, with which the Mysteries had to deal.

The same system of gradual preparation of people for the reception of new ideas is brought forward in all the rituals of magic.

The literature on magic and occultism was for a long time entirely ignored by Western scientific and philosophical thought or rejected as an absurdity and a superstition. And it is only quite recently that people are beginning to understand that all these teachings must be taken in a symbolical way, as a complex and subtle picture of psychological and cosmic relations.

A strict and unswerving observance of various small rules, which often look trivial, incomprehensible and unrelated to anything important, is demanded by all the rituals of ceremonial magic. And again the horrors are described which await the man who has broken the order of the ceremonies, or changed it of himself, or omitted something by neglect. There are many legends of magicians who invoked a spirit but lacked the power to control it. This happened either because the magician forgot the words of the invocation, or in some way broke the magic ritual, or because he invoked a spirit stronger than himself, stronger than all his invocations and magic figures.

All these instances, of the men who break the ritual of initiation in the Mysteries, or of the magicians who invoke spirits stronger than themselves, equally represent, in allegorical form, the position of a man in relation to new ideas which are too strong for him and which he cannot handle because he has not the required preparation. The same idea was expressed in the legends and tales of the sacred fire which consumed the uninitiated who incautiously approached it, and in the myths of gods and of goddesses the sight of whom was not permitted to mortals, who perished if they looked upon them. The light of certain ideas is too strong for man's eyes, especially when he sees it for the first time. Moses could not look at the burning bush; on Mount Sinai he could not look upon the face of God. All these allegories express one and the same thought, that of the terrible power and danger of new ideas which appear unexpectedly.

The Sphinx with its riddle expressed the same idea. It devoured those who approached it and could not solve the riddle. The allegory of the Sphinx means that there are questions of a certain order which man must not approach unless he knows how to answer them.

Having once come into contact with certain ideas man is unable to live as he lived before; he must either go farther or perish under a burden which is too heavy for him.

The idea of superman is closely connected with the problem of time and eternity, with the Riddle of the Sphinx. In this lie its attraction and its danger; this is why it so strongly affects the souls of men.

As was pointed out before, modern psychology does not realise the immense danger of certain themes, ideas and questions. Even in primitive philosophy, when men divided ideas into divine and human, they understood better the existence of different orders of ideas. Modern thought does not recognise this at all. Existing psychology and the theory of knowledge do not teach people to discriminate between different orders of ideas, nor point out that some ideas are very dangerous and cannot be approached without long and complicated preparation. This occurs because modern psychology generally does not take into consideration the reality of ideas, does not understand this reality. To a modern mind ideas are an abstraction from facts; in our eyes ideas have no existence of themselves. That is why we get so badly burned when we touch certain ideas. For us " facts," which do not exist, are real, and ideas, which alone exist, are unreal.

Ancient and mediæval psychology understood better the position of the human mind in relation to ideas. It understood that the mind could not deal with ideas in a right way so long as the reality of them was not clear to it. And further, the old psychology understood that the mind was incapable of receiving ideas of different kinds simultaneously or out of the right order, that is, it could not pass, without preparation, from ideas of one order to ideas of another order. It understood the danger of such irregular and disorderly dealing with ideas. The question is: in what must the preparation consist? Of what do the allegories of Mysteries and magic rituals speak?

First of all, they speak of the necessity of an adequate knowledge for every order of ideas, because there are things which cannot be approached without preliminary knowledge.

In other domains we understand this perfectly. It is impossible without adequate knowledge to handle a complicated machine; it is impossible without knowledge and practice to drive a railway engine; it is impossible without knowing all the details to touch the various parts of a high-powered electric machine.

A man is shown an electric machine; its parts are explained, and he is told: " If you touch this or that part it is death." And everybody understands this and realises that in order to know the machine it is necessary to learn a great deal and to learn for a long time. And he realises also that machines of different kinds require different knowledge and that by having learned to work a machine of one kind one does not be ɔme able to handle all kinds of machines.

An idea is a machine of enormous power.

But this is exactly what modern thought does not realise.

Every idea is a complicated and delicate machine. In order to know how to handle it, it is necessary first of all to possess a great deal of purely theoretical knowledge and, besides that, a large amount of experience and practical training. Unskilled handling of an idea may produce an explosion of the idea; a fire begins, the idea burns and consumes everything round it.

From the point of view of modern understanding, the whole danger is confined to wrong reasoning, and there it ends. In reality, however, this is far from being the end of the matter. One error in reasoning leads to a whole series of others. And certain ideas are so powerful, contain such an amount of hidden energy, that either a right or a wrong deduction from them will inevitably produce enormous results. There are ideas which reach the most hidden recesses of the soul of man and which, once they have affected them, leave an everlasting trace. Moreover, if the idea is taken wrongly, it leaves a wrong trace, leading a man astray and poisoning his life.

A wrongly received idea of superman acts precisely in this way. It detaches man from life, sows deep discord in his soul and, giving him nothing, deprives him of what he had.

It is not the fault of the idea itself, but of a wrong approach to it.

In what, then, must a right approach consist?

As the idea of superman has points of contact with the problem of time and with the idea of the infinite, it is not possible to touch the idea of superman without having cleared up the means of approach to the problem of time and to the idea of the infinite. The problem of time and the idea of the infinite contain laws of the action of the machine.

Without knowing these laws a man will not know what effect will be produced by his touching the machine, by his pulling one lever or another.

The problem of time is the greatest riddle humanity has ever had to face. Religious revelation, philosophical thought, scientific investigation and occult knowledge, all converge at one point, that is, on the problem of time, and all come to the same view of it.

Time does not exist! There exist no perpetual and eternal appearance and disappearance of phenomena, no ceaselessly flowing fountain of ever appearing and ever vanishing events. Everything exists always! There is only one eternal present, the Eternal Now, which the weak and limited human mind can neither grasp nor conceive.

But the idea of the *Eternal Now* is not at all the idea of a cold and merciless predetermination of everything, of an exact and infallible pre-existence. It would be quite wrong to say that if everything already exists, if the remote future exists now, if our actions, thoughts and feelings have existed for tens, hundreds and thousands of years and will continue to exist for ever, it means that there is no life, no movement, no growth, no evolution.

People say and think this because they do not understand the infinite and want to measure the immeasurable depths of eternity with their weak and limited finite minds. Of course they are bound to arrive at the most hopeless of all possible solutions of the problem. Everything *is*, nothing can change, everything exists beforehand and eternally. Everything is dead and immovable in frozen forms amidst which beats our consciousness, which has created for itself the illusion of the movement of everything around it, a movement which in reality does not exist.

But even such a weak and relative understanding of the idea of infinity as is possible for the limited human intellect, provided only that it develops along right lines, suffices to destroy " this gloomy phantom of hopeless immobility."

The world is a world of infinite possibilities.

Our mind follows the development of possibilities always in one direction only. But in fact every moment contains a very large number of possibilities. *And all of them are actualised,* only we do not see it and do not know it. We always see only one of the actualisations, and in this lie the poverty and limitation of the human mind. But if we try to imagine the actualisation of all the possibilities of the present moment, then of the next moment, and so on, we shall feel the world growing infinitely, incessantly multiplying by itself and becoming immeasurably rich and utterly unlike the flat and limited world we have pictured to ourselves up to this moment. Having imagined this infinite variety we shall feel a " taste " of infinity for a moment and shall understand how inadequate and impossible it is to approach the problem of time with earthly measures. We shall understand what an infinite richness of time going in all directions is necessary for the actualisation of all the possibilities that arise each moment. And we shall understand that the very idea of arising and disappearing possibilities is created by the human mind, because otherwise it would burst and perish from a single contact with the infinite actualisation. Simultaneously with this we shall feel the unreality of all our pessimistic deductions as compared with the vastness of the unfolding horizons. We shall feel that the world is so boundlessly large that a thought of the existence of any limits in it, a thought of there being anything whatever which is not contained within it, will appear to us ridiculous.

Where, then, are we to seek for a true understanding of " time " and " infinity "? Where to seek for this infinite extension in all directions from every moment? What ways lead to it? What ways lead to the future which exists now? Where to find right methods of dealing with it? Where to find right methods of dealing with the idea of superman? These are questions to which modern thought gives no answer.

But human thought has not always been so helpless in the face of these problems. There have existed and there exist other attempts to solve the riddles of life.

The idea of superman belongs to the " inner circle." Ancient religions and myths always pictured in the image of superman the higher " I " of man, man's consciousness. This higher " I," or higher consciousness, was always represented as a being almost separate from ordinary man but, in a certain sense, living within man.

It depended on man himself whether he drew nearer to this being, became it, or turned aside from it, even broke away from it altogether.

Very often the image of superman as a being belonging to the remote future or to the Golden Age or to the mythical present, symbolised this inner being, the higher " I," the superman in the past, the present and the future.

What was symbol and what was reality depended on the way of thinking of the particular man in question. People who were inclined to regard the outer as objectively existing considered the inner to be a symbol of the outer. People who understood differently and knew that the outer did not mean the objective, considered outer facts to be symbols of the possibilities of the inner world.

But in reality the idea of superman has never existed apart from the idea of higher consciousness.

The ancient world was never superficially materialistic. It always knew how to penetrate the depths of an idea and how to find in it not only one meaning but many. The world of to-day, having made the idea of superman concrete in one sense, has deprived it of its inner power and freshness. Superman as a new zoological species is above all tedious. He is possible and admissible only as " higher consciousness."

What is higher consciousness?

Here, however, it is necessary to note that any division into " higher " and " lower," as for instance the division of higher and lower mathematics, is always artificial. In reality, of course, *the lower* is nothing but a limited conception of the whole, and *the higher* is a broader and less limited conception. In relation to consciousness this question of " higher " and " lower " stands thus: the lower consciousness is a limited self-consciousness of the whole, while the higher conciousness is a fuller self-consciousness.

You have made your way from worm to man, and much is still in you of the worm. Once were ye apes, and even yet is man more of an ape than any of the apes (*Thus Spake Zarathustra*).

Of course these words of Zarathustra have nothing to do with the " theory of Darwin." Nietzsche spoke of the discord in the soul of man, of the struggle between the past and the future. He understood the tragedy of man, which lies in the fact that in his soul there live simultaneously a *worm*, an *ape* and a *man*.

In what relation, then, does such an understanding of the idea of superman stand to the problem of time and to the idea of the infinite? And where to seek for " time " and for " infinity "?

Again in the soul of man, is the answer of the ancient teachings. Everything is within man, and there is nothing outside him.

How is this to be understood?

Time is not a condition of the existence of the universe, but only a condition of the perception of the world by our psychic apparatus, which imposes on the world conditions of time, since otherwise the psychic apparatus would be unable to conceive it.

Western thought, at least the evolving part of it, the part that builds no dogmatic barriers for itself, also finds " further possibilities of studying problems of time in passing to questions of psychology " (Minkovsky).

The " passing to questions of psychology " in problems of space and time, of the necessity for which Minkovsky speaks, would mean for natural science the acceptance of Kant's proposition that time and space are nothing but forms of our sense perception and originate in our psychic apparatus.

We are, however, unable to conceive infinity without relation to space and time. Therefore, if space and time are forms of our perception and lie in our soul, it follows that the roots of infinity are to be sought also within us, within our soul. And we may perhaps define it as an infinite possibility of the expansion of our consciousness.

The depths hidden within the consciousness of man were well understood by philosopher-mystics whose thought was closely connected with parallel systems of Hermetic philosophy, alchemy, Cabala and others.

"Man contains within himself heaven and hell," they said; and their representations of man often showed him with the different faces of God and the worlds of "light and darkness" in him. They affirmed that by penetrating within the depths of himself man can find everything, attain everything. And what he will attain depends on what he seeks and how he seeks. And they did not understand this as an allegory. The soul of man actually appeared to them as a window or as several windows looking on infinity. And man in ordinary life appeared to them as living, as it were, on the surface of himself, ignorant and even unconscious of what lies in his own depths.

If he thinks of infinity he conceives it as outside him. In reality infinity is within him. And by consciously penetrating within his soul man can find infinity within himself, can come into contact with it and enter into it.

Gichtel, a mystic of the 17th century, gives a drawing of the "perfect man" in his remarkable book *Theosophia Practica*.

The perfect man is the Cabalistic Adam Kadmon, i.e. humanity or mankind, of which an individual man is a copy.

The drawing represents the figure of a man on whose head (on the forehead) is shown the Holy Ghost; in the heart, Jesus; in the "solar plexus," Jehovah. The upper part of his chest with the organs of respiration (and possibly the organs of speech) contains the "Wisdom" or the "Mirror of God," and the lower part of the body with its organs contains the "Dark World" or the "Root of Souls in the Centre of the Universe."

Thus this drawing represents in man five ways into infinity. Man can choose any of these ways; and what he will find will depend on his direction, that is, on which way he takes.

Man has become so earthly and outward, says Gichtel, that he seeks afar, beyond the starry sky, in the higher eternity, what is quite near him, within the inner centre of his soul.

When the soul begins to strive to divert its will from the exterior constellation and abandon everything visible in order to turn to God, to its Centre, this requires desperate work.

The more the soul penetrates within itself, the nearer it approaches God until it finally stops before the Holy Trinity. Then it has reached deep knowledge.[6]

---

[6] J. G. Gichtel, *Theosophia Practica* (1696), Traduite en français. Paris, 1897 (Bibliothèque Rosicrucienne), Introduction, p. 14.

Such an inward understanding of the idea of infinity is much truer and deeper than the outward understanding of it, and it gives a more correct approach to the idea of superman, a clearer understanding of it. If infinity lies in the soul of man and if he is able to come into contact with it by penetrating within himself, this means that the " future " and " superman "

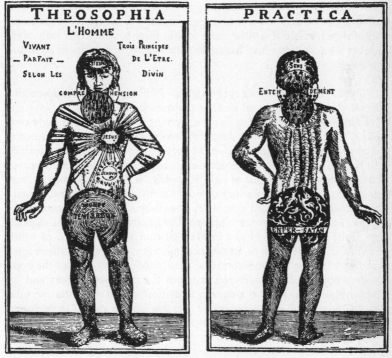

FIG. 3 *Gichtel's Perfect Man*

are in his soul, and that he can find them within himself if he seeks them in the right way.

The peculiarity and distinctive feature of the ideas of the " real " world, i.e. of *the world as it is,* are that, viewed in the light of materialism, they appear absurd. This is a necessary condition. But this condition and the necessity for it are never properly understood, and that is why the ideas of the " world of many dimensions " often produce on people such a nightmare effect.

Superman is one of the possibilities which lie within the depths of the soul of man. It rests with man himself to bring this idea nearer or to turn it aside. The nearness or remoteness of superman from man lies not in time, but in man's attitude towards the idea, and not only in a mental attitude, but in an active and practical relation to it. Man is separated from superman not by time, but by the fact that he is not prepared to receive superman. The whole of time lies within man himself. Time is the inner obstacle to a direct sensation of one thing or another, and it is nothing else. The building of the future, the serving of the future, are but symbols, symbols of man's attitude towards himself, towards his own present. It is clear that if this view is accepted and if it is recognised that all the future is contained within man himself, it will be naïve to ask: what have I to do with superman? It is evident that man has to do with superman, for superman is man himself.

Yet the view of superman as the higher " I " of man, as something within himself, does not contain all possible understanding.

Knowledge of the *world as it is* is something more subtle and more complex; it does not require any denial whatever of the outward existence of the phenomenon in question. But the outward aspect of the phenomenon is in this case known by man in its relation to the inward aspect. Moreover, the distinctive characteristic of right knowledge is the absence of any negation in it, especially the absence of negation of an opposite view. " Real," i.e. many-dimensional and complete, knowledge differs from material or logical (i.e. unreal) knowledge above all in its not excluding the opposite view. True knowledge includes in itself all contradictory views, of course after first divesting them of artificial complications and superstitious interpretations. It must be understood that the absence of negation of the opposite does not mean necessary acceptance of the false, the illusory and the superstitious. Knowledge is a correct separation of the real from the false, and this is reached not by means of negation but by means of inclusion. Truth includes all in itself, and what cannot enter it shows by this very fact its falsity and incorrectness.

In truth there are antitheses; one view does not exclude another.

Therefore in relation to the idea of superman only that understanding is true which includes both views, the outer and the inner.

We have indeed no grounds whatever for denying the possibility of a real, living superman in the past, or in the present, or in the future. At the same time we must recognise in our inner world the presence of seeds of something higher than that by which we ordinarily live, and we must recognise the possibility of the sprouting of these seeds and their manifestation in forms at present incomprehensible to us.

Superman in the past, or in the future, does not stand in contradiction to the possibility of higher consciousness in the man living now. On the contrary, the one reveals the other.

Men who are conscious of superman within them, who are conscious of the revealing of new forces within them, become by virtue of this very fact connected with the idea of superman in the past or in the future. And men who seek for a real, living superman in the present thereby reveal a higher principle in their souls.

The idea of superman is difficult to understand and therefore dangerous because it makes necessary the knowledge of how to accord two opposite views. An *outer* aspect alone of this idea, or an *inner* aspect alone, cannot satisfy man. And each of these aspects is wrong in its way. Each of them is in its way a distortion of the idea. And in a distorted form this idea becomes its own opposite and not only does not elevate man, but on the contrary thrusts him down towards pessimistic negation, or brings him to passive " non-doing," to a stop.

Disillusionment with life and the aims of life, when aroused by the idea of superman, comes from a wrong understanding of it, mostly from the feeling of the remoteness and inaccessibility of superman in outer life.

On the other hand, an exclusively inner understanding of the idea of superman also detaches a man from life and makes all activity useless and unnecessary in his eyes. If superman is within me, if it is only necessary to descend deep into myself in order to find him, what is the use of all attempts to do anything or to find him outside myself?

These are the two submerged rocks lying in the depths of the idea of superman.

Man finds superman within himself when he begins to look for him outside himself, and he can find superman outside himself when he has begun to look for him within himself.

Having understood and visualised the image of superman such as he can be, man must reconstruct the whole of his life so that it does not contradict this image . . . if he can. This will reveal the idea of superman in his soul.

An intellectual approach to the idea of superman is possible only after a very long and persistent training of the mind. Ability to think is the first necessary stage of initiation, which ensures safety in approaching this idea. What does it mean to be able to think? It means to be able to think differently from the way in which we are accustomed to think, that is to say, to conceive the world in new categories. We have simplified our conception of the world too much, we have become accustomed to picture it to ourselves as too uniform, and we must now learn anew to understand its complexity. In order to do so it is necessary to understand again, and to understand again in a new way, that we do not know at all what man is, and to realise that man is undoubtedly something quite different from what we think him to be.

In our hearts we know certain things very well; but we can never concentrate on them. We understand a certain cycle of ideas, but live in another cycle of ideas. Life turns round us, and we turn with it, and round us turn our shadows.

Nothing is outside us. But we forget this at every sound (*Thus Spake Zarathustra*).

In the Jewish legends of the Talmud there is a remarkable story about
Moses, which contains the whole idea of the evolution of man in the true
sense of the word.

THE PORTRAIT OF MOSES [7]

The whole world was shaken and enthralled by the miracle of the Exo-
dus. The name of Moses was on everyone's lips. Tidings of the great miracle
reached also the wise king of Arabistan. The king summoned to him his
best painter and bade him go to Moses, to paint his portrait and bring it
back to him. When the painter returned the king gathered together all his
sages, wise in the science of physiognomics, and asked them to define by the
portrait the character of Moses, his qualities, inclinations, habits and the
source of his miraculous power.

" King," answered the sages, " this is the portrait of a man cruel, haughty,
greedy of gain, possessed by desire for power and by all the vices which
exist in the world."

These words roused the king's indignation.

" How can it be possible," he exclaimed, " that a man whose marvellous
deeds ring through the whole world should be of such a kind? "

A dispute began between the painter and the sages. The painter affirmed
that the portrait of Moses had been painted by him quite accurately, while
the sages maintained that Moses' character had been unerringly determined by them according to the portrait.

The wise king of Arabistan decided to verify which of the disputing
parties was right, and he himself set off for the camp of Israel.

At the first glance the king became convinced that the face of Moses
had been faultlessly portrayed by the painter. On entering the tent of the
man of God he knelt down, bowed to the ground and told Moses of the
dispute between the artist and the sages.

" At first, until I saw thy face," said the king, " I thought it must be that
the artist had painted thy image badly, for my sages are men very much
experienced in the science of physiognomics. Now I am convinced that they
are quite worthless men and that their wisdom is vain and worthless."

" No," answered Moses, " it is not so; both the painter and the physiog-
nomists are men highly skilled, and both parties are right. Be it known
to thee that all the vices of which the sages spoke have indeed been assigned to me by nature and perhaps to an even higher degree than was
found by them from my portrait. But I struggled with my vices by long
and intense efforts of the will and gradually overcame and suppressed them
in myself until all opposed to them became my second nature. And in this
lies my greatest pride."

                                                                    1911–1929

 [7] *Agada*, legends, parables and sayings from the Talmud and the Midrashes, in four
parts. Compiled from original sources by I. H. Ravnitsky and H. N. Bialik. Authorised
translation into Russian with introduction by S. G. Frug. Published by S. D. Saltsman,
Berlin, Part I, p. 104.

Chapter IV

CHRISTIANITY AND THE NEW TESTAMENT

❀

THE IDEA of esotericism occupies a very important place in Christian teaching and in the New Testament if these are properly understood.

But in order to understand both the one and the other it is first of all necessary to separate strictly what relates to esotericism (or, more exactly, that in which the esoteric idea occupies the chief place) and what does not relate to esotericism, that is, does not follow from the esoteric idea.

In the New Testament the esoteric idea occupies the chief place in the four Gospels. The same can be said of the Revelation of St. John. But, with the exception of several passages, the esoteric ideas in the Apocalypse are " enciphered " still more than in the Gospels and in their ciphered parts they do not enter into the following examination.

The Acts and the Epistles are works of a quite different specific gravity from the four Gospels. In them esoteric ideas are met, but these ideas do not occupy in them a predominant place, and they could exist without these ideas.

The four Gospels are written for the few, for the very few, for the pupils of esoteric schools. However intelligent and educated in the ordinary sense a man may be, he will not understand the Gospels without *special* indications and without *special* esoteric knowledge.

At the same time it is necessary to note that the four Gospels are the sole source from which we know of Christ and of his teaching. The Acts and the " Epistles " of the Apostles add several essential features, but they also introduce a great deal that does not exist in the Gospels and that contradicts the Gospels. In any case from the Epistles it would not be possible to reconstruct either the person of Christ, or the Gospel drama, or the essence of the Gospel teaching.

The Epistles of the Apostles, and especially the Epistles of the Apostle Paul, are the building of the Church. They are the *adaptation* of the ideas of the Gospels, the materialisation of them, the application of them to life, very often an application which goes *against* the esoteric idea.

The addition of the Acts and the Epistles to the four Gospels in the New Testament has a dual meaning. First (from the point of view of the

Church), it gives the possibility to the Church, which in fact originates from the Epistles, to establish connection with the Gospels and with the " drama of Christ." And, second, (from the point of view of esotericism) it gives the possibility to a few men, who begin with Church Christianity, but are capable of understanding the esoteric idea, to come into touch with the first source and perhaps to succeed in finding the hidden truth.

Historically the chief rôle in the formation of Christianity was played not by the teaching of Christ but by the teaching of Paul. Church Christianity from the very beginning contradicted in many respects the ideas of Christ himself. Later, the divergence became still wider. It is by no means a new idea that Christ, if born on earth later, not only could not be the head of the Christian Church, but probably would not be able even to belong to it, and in the most brilliant periods of the might and power of the Church would most certainly have been declared a heretic and burned at the stake. Even in our more enlightened times, when the Christian Churches, if they have not lost their anti-Christian features, have at any rate begun to conceal them, Christ could have lived without suffering the persecutions of the " scribes and Pharisees " perhaps only somewhere in a Russian hermitage.

Thus the New Testament, and also Christian teaching, cannot be taken as one whole. It must be remembered that later cults deviate very sharply from the fundamental teaching of Christ himself, *which in the first place was never a cult.*

Further, it is certainly not possible to speak of " Christian countries," " Christian nations," " Christian culture." In reality all these concepts have only a historico-geographical meaning.

On the basis of the above propositions, in speaking of the New Testament I shall from now on have in view only the four Gospels and on two or three occasions the Apocalypse.

And in speaking of Christianity or of Christian (or Gospel) teaching, I shall have in view only the teaching which is contained in the four Gospels. All later additions, based on the Epistles of the Apostles, on decisions of the councils, on works of Fathers of the Church, on visions of mystics and on ideas of reformers, are not included within the limits of my subject.

The New Testament is a very strange book. It is written for those who already have a certain degree of understanding, for those who possess a key. It is the greatest mistake to think that the New Testament is a simple book, and that it is intelligible to the simple and humble. It is impossible to read it simply just as it is impossible to read simply a book of mathematics, full of formulæ, special expressions, open and hidden references to mathematical literature, allusions to different theories known only to the " initiated," and so on. At the same time there are in the New Testament a number of passages which can be understood emotionally, that is, which can produce a certain emotional impression, different for different people, or even for the same man at different moments of his life. But it is certainly wrong to think that these emotional impressions exhaust the whole content of the Gospels. Every phrase, every word, contains hidden ideas, and it is only when one begins to bring these hidden ideas to light, that the power of this book and its influence on people, which has lasted for two thousand years, becomes clear.

It is remarkable that by his attitude to the New Testament, by the way in which he reads it, by what he understands in it, by what he deduces from it, every man shows himself. The New Testament is a general examination for the whole of humanity. In cultured countries of the present day everyone has heard of the New Testament; for this it is not necessary to be officially a Christian. A certain knowledge of the New Testament and Christianity enters into general education. And every man by the way in which he reads the New Testament, by what he derives from it, by what he fails to derive, by the fact that he does not read it at all, shows the level of his development and his inner state.

In each of the four Gospels there are many things consciously thought out and based on great knowledge and deep understanding of the human soul. Certain passages are written with the definite calculation that one man should understand them in one way, another in another way and a third in a third way, and that these men should never be able to agree as to the interpretation and understanding of what they had read; and that at the same time all of them should be equally wrong, and the true meaning consist of something which would never even occur to them of themselves.

A mere literary analysis of the style and content of the four Gospels shows the immense power of these narratives. They were written consciously for a definite purpose by men who knew more than they wrote. The Gospels tell us in a direct and exact way of the existence of esoteric thought, and they are in themselves one of the chief literary evidences of the existence of this thought.

What meaning and what aim may such a book have if we assume that it is written consciously? Probably, not one but many aims; but first of all, indisputably, the aim of showing men that there is only *one way* to hidden knowledge, if they wish and are able to go by that way. To speak more exactly, this aim could be to show the way to those who can go by this way, and in showing the way to make a selection of those who are fit for it, to divide people into suitable and unsuitable, from this point of view.

The Christian teaching is a very stern religion, infinitely far removed from the sentimental Christianity that is created by modern preachers. Through all the teaching, in its true meaning, there runs the idea that the " Kingdom of Heaven," whatever these words may mean, *belongs to the few*, that strait is the gate and narrow is the way, and only few can pass through and thus attain " salvation," and that those who do not go in are but chaff which will be burned.

And now also the axe is laid unto the root of the trees: therefore every tree which bringeth not forth good fruit is hewn down, and cast into the fire.

. . . .

Whose fan is in his hand and he will throughly purge his floor, and gather his wheat into the garner; but he will burn up the chaff with unquenchable fire (Matt. 3. 10, 12).

The idea of the exclusiveness and difficulty of " salvation " is so definite and so often emphasized in the Gospels, that all the lies and hypocrisy of modern Christianity are indeed necessary in order to forget it and to attribute to Christ the sentimental idea of *general* salvation. These ideas are as far from true Christianity as the rôle of social reformer, which also is sometimes attributed to Christ, is from Christ.

Still farther from Christianity is of course the religion of " Hell and Sin " adopted by narrow sectarians of a particular kind who have at one time or another appeared in all branches of Christianity, but most of all in Protestantism.

In speaking of the New Testament, it is first of all necessary to establish one's views, even if only approximately, as to the existing versions of the text and the history of the Gospels.

There are no grounds whatever for supposing that the Gospels were written by the persons to whom they are ascribed, that is, by immediate disciples of Jesus. It is a much more likely supposition that all four Gospels had a very different history and were written much later than is assumed in the official church explanations. It is very probable that the Gospels appeared as the result of the joint work of many persons, who perhaps collected manuscripts, which circulated among followers of the apostles and contained records of the miraculous events which had occurred in Judea. But at the same time there is ample ground for thinking that these collections of manuscripts were edited by men who pursued a perfectly definite aim and who foresaw the enormous diffusion and significance which the New Testament was to attain.

The Gospels differ very much from one another. The first, that is, the Gospel of St. Matthew, can be considered as the principal. There is a supposition that it was originally written in Aramaic, that is, in the language in which Christ is supposed to have spoken, and that it was translated into Greek about the end of the first century, though there are also other suppositions, for instance, that Christ taught the people in Greek, as the Greek language was spoken in the Judea of that time equally with Aramaic. The Gospels of St. Mark and St. Luke were compiled from the same material as that ,which served for the Gospel according to St. Matthew. There is great probability in Renan's assertions that both these Gospels were written in Greek.

St. John's Gospel, which was written later, is of an entirely different kind. It also was written in Greek and probably by a Greek, certainly not by a Jew. One small feature points to this. In all cases in which in the other Gospels it is said " the people," in St. John's Gospel it is said " Jews."

Or for instance, the following explanation, which could in no circumstances have been made by a Jew:

Then took they the body of Jesus, and wound it in linen clothes with the spices, *as the manner of the Jews is to bury* (John 19. 40).

St. John's Gospel is a quite exceptional literary work. It is written with tremendous emotional upheaval. And it can produce an utterly inexpressible impression on a man who is himself in a highly emotional state. It is not possible to read St. John's Gospel intellectually. There is a great deal of the emotional element also in the other Gospels, but it is possible to understand them with the mind. St. John's Gospel cannot be understood by the mind at all. One feels in it an emotional excitement on the level of ecstasy. In this excited state a man rapidly speaks or writes certain words or phrases full of deep meaning for him and full of meaning for people who are in the same state as he, but entirely devoid of any sense for people who listen with ordinary hearing and think with ordinary mind. It is difficult to make such an experiment, but if anyone happens to read St. John's Gospel while in a highly emotional state, he will understand *what* is said there and will realise that this is a quite exceptional work, which cannot be measured by ordinary standards or judged on the level of books which are written intellectually and can be read and understood intellectually.

The text of all four Gospels in modern language is rather corrupt, but *less* so than might be expected. The text was undoubtedly corrupted in transcription in the early centuries and later, during our times, in translation. The original authentic text has not been preserved, but if we compare the present translations with the existing older texts, Greek, Latin and Church-Slavonic, we notice a difference of a quite definite character. The alterations and distortions are all similar to one another. Their psychological nature is always identical, that is, in every case in which an alteration is noticed it can be seen that the translator or scribe did not understand the text; something was too difficult, *too abstract*, for him. So he corrected it very slightly, adding one little word, and in this way giving to the text in question a clear and logical meaning *on the level of his own understanding*. This fact does not allow of the slightest doubt and can be verified in the later translations.

The oldest known texts, that is, the Greek and the first Latin translations, are much more abstract than the later translations. There is much in the earlier texts that is found in the form of an abstract idea, which in the later translations has become a concrete image, a concrete figure.

The most interesting transformation of this kind has occurred with the devil. In many passages in the Gospels where we are accustomed to meet him, he is entirely absent from the early texts. In the Lord's Prayer, for instance, which has entered profoundly into the habitual thought of the ordinary man, the words " deliver us from evil " in the English and German translations correspond to the Greek and Latin texts; but in Church-Slavonic and Russian it is " deliver us from *the sly one* "; in French (in some translations) it is: " mais délivre nous *du Malin* "; and in Italian: " ma liberaci *dal maligno*."

The difference between the first early Latin translation and the later translation edited by Theodore Beza (16th century) is very characteristic in this respect. In the first translation the phrase reads " sed libera nos a malo," but in the second, " sed libera nos *ab illo improbo* " (" from the wicked one ").

Speaking generally, the whole Gospel mythology has been very greatly altered. " The Devil," that is, the slanderer or tempter, was in the original text simply a name or description which could be applied to any " slanderer " or " tempter." And it is possible to suppose that these names were often used to designate the visible, deceptive, illusory, phenomenal world, " Maya." But we are too much under the influence of mediæval demonology. And it is difficult for us to understand that in the New Testament there is no *general idea* of the devil. There is the idea of evil, the idea of temptation, the idea of demons, the idea of the unclean spirit, the idea of the prince of the demons; there is Satan who tempted Jesus; but all these ideas are separate and distinct from one another, always allegorical and very far from the mediæval conception of the Devil.

In the fourth chapter of St. Matthew's Gospel, in the scene of the temptation in the wilderness, Christ says to the devil according to the Greek text, ὕπαγε ὀπίσω μου, " go after me," and according to the Church-Slavonic text, " follow me." But in the Russian, English, French and Italian texts this is translated: " Get thee hence, Satan."

In the ninth verse after this (Matt. 4. 19) Christ says to the fishermen whom he found by the lake casting their nets, almost the same words: " Go after me," or " follow me "; in Greek, δεῦτε ὀπίσω μου.

This similarity in addressing the " devil " who tempted Jesus, and the fishermen whom Jesus took as his disciples and promised to make " fishers of men," must have a definite meaning. But to the translator it of course looked an absurdity. Why should Christ wish the devil to follow him? The result was the famous phrase " *get thee hence, Satan*." Satan in this case simply represented the visible, phenomenal world, which must not " get hence " by any means, but must only serve the inner world, follow it, *go behind it*.

As a further example of distortion of the Gospel text there can be taken the well-known words about daily bread — " give us this day our daily bread."

The fact is that the qualification of bread as " насущный " " daily," " *quotidien*," " *täglich*," does not exist at all in the Greek and the Latin texts. The Greek text reads:

τὸν ἄρτον ἡμῶν τὸν ἐπιούσιον δὸς ἡμῖν σήμερον;

the Latin:

panem nostrum supersubstantialem da nobis hodie.

The Greek word ἐπιούσιος (which is translated by the Latin word *supersubstantialis*) according to the explanation of Origen did not exist in the Greek language and was specially invented for the translation of the corresponding Aramaic term. But the Aramaic text of St. Matthew's Gospel, if it ever existed, has not been preserved, and it is impossible to establish what word was translated by the word ἐπιούσιος or supersubstantialis. In any case this word was not " necessary," not " daily," since ἐπιούσιος or *supersubstantialis* means " super-existing," " super-substantial "; an idea certainly very remote from " necessary," " daily." At the same time how can we know what the Slavonic word " насущный " meant at the time when it was created? This word most probably did not exist in the old Bulgarian, just as the word ἐπιούσιος did not exist in Greek. Its meaning might have changed later, and it entered into the spoken language with an entirely different sense. In the beginning " насущный " could have meant *supersubstantial*, and later it became " necessary for life."

The possibility of translating ἐπιούσιος as " necessary " or " daily " is also explained by a play on words. There is an attempt to explain the word ἐπιούσιος by deriving it not from εἰμί " to be," but from εἶμι " to go." In this case ἐπιούσιος will mean " coming." This translation is adopted in the newly revised translations of the New Testament. But it contradicts the first Latin translation, in which we find the word *supersubstantialis* (" super-existing "), for the use of which there was evidently a certain reason.

The distortion of the sense in translation, arising from the fact that the translator failed to understand the deep *abstract* meaning of the given passage, is especially evident in a very characteristic alteration of the sense in the French translation of a passage in the Epistle to the Ephesians.

. . . that ye, being rooted and grounded in love, May be able to comprehend with all saints what is the breadth, and length, and depth, and height (Ephesians 3. 17, 18).

These strange words, of unquestionably esoteric origin, which speak of the cognition of the *dimensions of space*, were certainly not understood by the translator, and in the French translation he inserted the little word *en* which gave the meaning:

. . . et qu'étant enracinés et fondés dans la charité vous puissiez comprendre, avec tous les saints, quelle *en* est la largeur, la longueur, la profondeur, et la hauteur.

that ye, being rooted and grounded in love, may be able to comprehend with all the saints what is *its* breadth, and length, and depth, and height.

The above examples show the character of the distortions of the Gospel texts in translations. But in general they are not very important.

The idea which is sometimes met in modern occult teachings, that the existing text of the Gospels is not complete and that there is (or was) another, complete, text, has no basis in fact and will not be taken into consideration in what follows.

Further, in studying the New Testament it is necessary to separate the *legendary* element, which is often borrowed from the life stories of other Messiahs and Prophets, from the narration of the actual life of Jesus, and then to separate the legends and events described in it from the teaching.

The " drama of Christ " and its relation to the Mysteries have already been referred to. At the very beginning of this drama appears the enigmatic figure of John the Baptist. The most obscure passages in the New Testament refer to John the Baptist. There are teachings which regard him as the chief figure in the whole drama and relegate Christ to a secondary place. But too little is definitely known about these teachings to make it possible to base anything on them, and, further, the drama which was played in Judea will be spoken of as the " drama of Christ."

The events in Judea which ended with the death of Jesus occupied a very small place in the life of the peoples of that time. It is a well-known fact that *nobody* except the immediate participants knew of these events. No historical evidence that Jesus actually existed is extant besides the Gospels.

The Gospel tragedy acquired its meaning, significance and magnitude only gradually, as the teaching of Christ grew and expanded. In this a great part was played by oppressions and persecutions. But evidently there was something in the tragedy itself and in the teaching associated with it and arising from it, which distinguished both the one and the other from ordinary sectarian movements. This *something* was the connection with the Mysteries.

The legendary side introduces into the life of Christ many entirely conventional figures and, as it were, stylises him as a prophet, a teacher or a Messiah. These legends adapted to Christ are drawn from the most varied sources. There are Indian, Buddhist and Old Testament legends, and there are features taken from Greek myths.

The " massacre of the innocents " and the " flight into Egypt " are features taken from the life of Moses. The " Annunciation," that is, the appearance of the angel who announced the coming birth of Christ, is a feature from the life of Buddha. In the history of Buddha it was a white elephant which descended from the heavens and announced to Queen Maya the coming birth of Prince Gautama.

There follows the feature of the old man Simeon waiting for the infant Jesus in the temple and saying that now he might die since he had seen the newly born Saviour of the world — " Now lettest thou thy servant depart in peace." This is an episode taken entirely from the story of the life of Buddha.

When Buddha was born, Asita, an aged hermit, came down from the Himalayas to Kapilavastu. Coming to the court he made sacrifices at the feet of the child. Then Asita walked three times round the child and taking him in his hands, recognised in him the 32 signs of Buddhahood, which he saw with his opened inner sight.[1]

The strangest legend connected with Christ, which for a long time was a point of disagreement between different schools and sects in the growing Christianity and finally became the basis of the dogmatic teachings of almost all Christian creeds, is the legend of the birth of Jesus by the virgin Mary *direct of God himself*.

This legend arose later than the text of the Gospels.

Christ called himself the son of God or the son of man; he continually spoke of God as his father; he said that he and the father are one; that whoever obeys him, obeys his father also, and so forth. Yet Christ's own words do not create the legend, do not create the myth; they can be understood allegorically and mystically in the sense that Christ felt oneness with God, or felt God in himself. And above all they can be understood in the sense that every man can become the son of God if he obeys the will and laws of God.

In the Sermon on the Mount, Christ says:

Blessed are the peacemakers: for they shall be called *sons of God* (R.V. Matt. 5. 9).

And in another place:

Ye have heard that it was said, Thou shalt love thy neighbour, and hate thine enemy.

But I say unto you, Love your enemies, and pray for them that persecute you;

That ye may be sons of your Father which is in heaven: for he maketh his sun to rise on the evil and the good, and sendeth rain on the just and the unjust (R.V. Matt. 5. 43–45).

This translation agrees with the Greek, Latin, French and Russian translations. In the English Authorised Version, and also in the German, there stands "the children of God" and "the children of your father." But this is a result of the adaptation of the Gospel text by theologians for their own purposes.

These texts show that originally the expression "Son of God" had an entirely different meaning from that given to it later.

The myth of Christ being the son of God in the literal sense was created gradually during several centuries. And although the dogmatic Christian

---

[1] *Jatâkamâla*, by M. M. Higgins, Colombo, 1914, p. 205.

would certainly deny the pagan origin of this idea, it is undoubtedly taken from Greek mythology.

In no other religion are there such definite relations between gods and men as in the Greek myths. All the demi-gods, Titans and heroes of Greece were always direct *sons of gods*. In India gods themselves were incarnated in mortals, or descended on earth and assumed for a time the form of men or animals. But regarding great men as sons of gods is a purely Greek form of thinking (which later passed to Rome) of the relation between gods and their messengers on earth.

And strange though it is, this idea of the Greek myths passed into Christianity and became its chief dogma.

In dogmatic Christianity Christ is the son of God in exactly the same sense as Hercules was the son of Zeus or as Æsculapius was the son of Apollo.[2]

The erotic element, which in Greek myths very strongly permeated the idea of the birth of men or demi-gods from gods, is absent in the Christian myth, just as it is absent in the myth of the birth of Prince Gautama. This fact is connected with the very characteristic " denial of sex " in Buddhism and in Christianity, the causes of which are as yet far from being clear.

But it is beyond doubt that Christ has become the son of God according to the " pagan " idea.

Apart from the influence of Greek myths, Christ had to become a god in accordance with the general idea of the Mysteries.

The death of the god and his resurrection were the fundamental ideas of the Mysteries.

At the present time there are attempts to explain the idea of the *death of the god* in the Mysteries as a survival of the still more ancient custom of the " murder of kings " (*The Golden Bough*, by Sir J. G. Frazer. Part III). These explanations are connected with the general tendency of " evolutionary " thought to look for the origin of complex and incomprehensible manifestations in manifestations that are more simple, primitive or even pathological. From all that has been said earlier about esotericism, however, it should be clear that this tendency leads nowhere and that on the contrary more simple and primitive, or even criminal, customs are usually a degenerated form of forgotten sacraments and rites of a very high nature.

The second place in importance in " theological " Christianity, after the idea of the *sonship* and *divinity* of Christ, is occupied by the idea of *redemption* and of the *sacrifice* of Christ.

---

[2] Plato was also called a son of Apollo. Alexander the Great in the temple of Jupiter Ammon in Egypt was declared to be a son of Jupiter and he accordingly disavowed his father Philip of Macedonia and was recognised by the Egyptians as a son of God.

Justin Martyr, in his " First Apology " addressed to the emperor Hadrian, writes:

> The son of God called Jesus, even if only a man by ordinary generation, yet on account of his wisdom is worthy to be called son of God . . . and if we affirm that he was born of a virgin, accept this in common with what you accept of Perseus (*Mysticism and the Creed*, by W. F. Cobb (Macmillan, 1914), p. 144).

The idea of redemption and sacrifice, which became the basis of dogmatic Christianity, appears in the New Testament in the following words:

The next day John seeth Jesus coming unto him, and saith, Behold the Lamb of God, which taketh away the sin of the world (John 1. 29).

Thus Jesus was associated with the paschal lamb, which was a *sin-offering*.

In the Gospels the sacrifice of Christ is most spoken of in St. John. The other evangelists also make reference to sacrifice and redemption, for example, the words of Christ:

Even as the Son of man came not to be ministered unto, but to minister, and to give his life a ransom for many (Matt. 20. 28).

But all these and similar passages beginning with the words of John the Baptist and ending with the words of Christ himself, have a very wide allegorical and abstract meaning.

The idea was made concrete only in the Epistles, mainly in the Epistles of the Apostle Paul. It was necessary to explain the death of Jesus and it was necessary to explain his death at the same time indicating that he was the son of God and himself God. The idea of the Mysteries and of the " drama of Christ " could never be made common property, because for the explanation of it there were neither words nor understanding, not even in those who would have to explain it. It was necessary to find a nearer, a more comprehensible, idea, which would have given the possibility of explaining to the crowd why God had allowed worthless and criminal people to torture and kill himself. The explanation was found in the idea of concrete *redemption*. It was said that Jesus did this for men, that having sacrificed himself, he freed men from their sins; later it was added — from the original sin, from the sin of Adam.

The idea of redemptive sacrifice was understandable to the Jews, for it played a great part in the Old Testament in ritualistic offerings and ceremonies. There was a rite performed on the " Day of Atonement," when one he-goat was killed as a sin-offering for the sins of the people, and another he-goat was smeared with the blood of the goat that had been killed, and driven into the wilderness or cast down a precipice.

The idea of God sacrificing himself for the salvation of men exists also in Indian mythology. The god Shiva drank the poison which was to poison the whole of mankind; therefore many of his statues have the *throat painted blue*.

Religious ideas travelled from one country to another, and this feature, that is, concrete sacrifice for men, might have been attributed to Jesus in the same way as the features from the life of Buddha which were mentioned before.

The connecting of the idea of redemption with the idea of the transference of evil, as is done by the author of the above-mentioned book, *The Golden Bough*, has no foundation whatever.

The magical ceremony of the *transference of evil* has psychologically nothing in common with the idea of *voluntary sacrifice*. But of course this distinction can have no meaning for evolutionary thought, which does not enter into such fine distinctions.

The Old Testament idea of atonement contradicts esoteric thought. In esoteric teachings it is made perfectly clear that no one can be liberated from sin *by compulsion and without his own participation*. Men were and are now in such a position that in order to show them the way to liberation very great sacrifice is necessary. *Christ showed the way to liberation*.

And he says it direct:

I am the way (John 14. 6).

I am the door: by me if any man enter in, he shall be saved, and shall go in and out, and find pasture (John 10. 9).

And whither I go ye know, and the way ye know.
Thomas saith unto him, Lord, we know not whither thou goest; and how can we know the way?
Jesus saith unto him, I am the way, the truth, and the life: no man cometh unto the Father, but by me (John 14. 4, 5, 6).

Then said they unto him, Who art thou? And Jesus saith unto them, Even the same that I said unto you from the beginning (John 8. 25).

In order to begin to understand the Gospels and the Gospel teaching it is necessary first of all to understand what the Kingdom of Heaven or the Kingdom of God means.

These expressions are the key to the most important part of the Gospel teaching. Unless they are rightly understood, nothing can be understood. At the same time we are so accustomed to the usual, church, interpretation that the Kingdom of Heaven means either the place or the state in which the souls of the just will find themselves *after death*, that we do not even imagine the possibility of another understanding of these words.

The words of the Gospel " The Kingdom of Heaven is within you " sound for us hollow and unintelligible, and they not only do not explain the principal idea, but are more likely to obscure it. Men do not understand that within them lies *the way* to the Kingdom of Heaven and that the Kingdom of Heaven does not necessarily lie beyond the threshold of death.

The Kingdom of Heaven, the Kingdom of God, means *esotericism*, that is, the inner circle of humanity, and also the knowledge and the ideas of this circle.

The French occultist-writer, Abbé Constant, the strange and sometimes very clever Eliphas Lévi, writes in his book, *Dogme et Rituel de la Haute Magie* (1861):

After passing our life in the search for the Absolute in religion, science and justice; after revolving in the circle of Faust, we have reached the primal doctrine and the first book of Humanity. At this point we pause having discovered the secret of human omnipotence and indefinite progress, the key of all symbolisms, the first and final doctrine: have come to understand what was meant by the expression so often made use of in the Gospel — The Kingdom of God.[3]

And in another place in the same book Eliphas Lévi says:

Magic which the men of old denominated the *Sanctum Regnum*, the Holy Kingdom or Kingdom of God, *Regnum Dei* — exists only for kings and for priests. Are you priests? Are you kings?

The priesthood of Magic is not a vulgar priesthood and its royalty enters not into competition with the princes of this world. The monarchs of science are the princes of truth and their sovereignty is hidden from the multitude, like their prayers and sacrifices. The kings of science are the men who know the truth and whom the truth has made free, according to the specific promise given by the most mighty of all initiators (John 8. 32).[4]

Further he says:

To attain the *Sanctum Regnum*, in other words, the knowledge and power of the Magi, there are four indispensable conditions — an intelligence illuminated by study, an intrepidity which nothing can check, a will which cannot be broken, and a prudence which nothing can corrupt and nothing intoxicate. To KNOW, TO DARE, TO WILL, TO KEEP SILENCE, — such are the four words of the Magus . . . which can be combined after four manners and explained four times by one another.[5]

Eliphas Lévi noted a fact which has struck many who have studied the New Testament both before and after him, namely that the Kingdom of Heaven or the Kingdom of God means esotericism, the inner circle of humanity.

It does not mean a Kingdom in Heaven, but a Kingdom under the power of Heaven, under the laws of Heaven. The expression the "Kingdom of Heaven" in relation to the esoteric circle has exactly the same meaning as had the old official title of China, "The Celestial Empire." It did not mean an Empire in Heaven, but an Empire under the direct power of Heaven, under the laws of Heaven. Theologians have distorted the meaning of the Kingdom of Heaven, have connected it with the idea of Paradise, "Heaven," that is, of the place or condition in which, according to them, the souls of the just find themselves *after death*. In fact it can be seen quite clearly in the Gospels that Christ in his preaching spoke of the Kingdom of God on earth, and in the Gospels there are very definite passages showing that, as he taught, the Kingdom of Heaven can be attained during life.

---

[3] *Transcendental Magic*, translated by A. E. Waite, 1923 edition, p. 27.
[4] Ibid., p. 34.
[5] Ibid., p. 37.

Verily I say unto you, There be some standing here, which *shall not taste of death*, till they see the Son of man coming in his kingdom (Matt. 16. 28).

It is very interesting to note here that Christ speaks of his "kingdom" and at the same time calls himself the "Son of Man," that is to say, *simply a man*.

Further, in St. Mark he says:

Verily I say unto you, That there be some of them that stand here, which shall not taste of death, till they have seen the kingdom of God come with power (Mark 9. 1).

And in St. Luke:

But I tell you of a truth, there be some standing here, which shall not taste of death, till they see the kingdom of God (Luke 9. 27).

These passages were understood in the sense of the nearness of the second advent. But in this sense all their meaning was naturally lost when all Christ's personal disciples had died. But from the point of view of esoteric understanding these passages have preserved in our times the same meaning that they had in the time of Christ.

The New Testament is an introduction to the hidden knowledge or the secret wisdom. There are several definite lines of thought which can be seen quite clearly in it. All that follows refers to the two chief lines.

One line sets forth the principles of the Kingdom of Heaven or the esoteric circle and its knowledge; this line emphasises the difficulty and exclusiveness of apprehending truth. And the other line shows what men must do in order to approach truth, and what they must not do, that is, what can help them and what can hinder them; the methods and rules of study and work on oneself; occult and school rules.

To the first line belongs the saying that the approach to truth requires exceptional efforts and exceptional conditions. Only a few can approach truth. No phrase is more often repeated in the New Testament than the saying that *only those who have ears can hear*. These words are repeated nine times in the Gospels, and eight times in the Revelation of St. John, seventeen times in all.

The idea that it is necessary to know how to hear and see, and to be able to hear and see, and that not everyone can hear and see, is also brought out in the following passages:

Therefore I speak to them in parables: because they seeing see not; and hearing they hear not, neither do they understand.

And in them is fulfilled the prophecy of Esaias, which saith, By hearing ye shall hear, and shall not understand; and seeing ye shall see, and shall not per-fold, some sixtyfold, some thirtyfold.

For this people's heart is waxed gross, and their ears are dull of hearing, and their eyes they have closed; lest at any time they should see with their eyes, and hear with their ears, and should understand with their heart, and should be converted, and I should heal them.

But blessed are your eyes, for they see: and your ears, for they hear.

For verily I say unto you, That many prophets and righteous men have desired to see those things which ye see, and have not seen them; and to hear those things which ye hear, and have not heard them (Matt. 13. 13–17).

That seeing they may see, and not perceive; and hearing they may hear, and not understand; lest at any time they should be converted, and their sins should be forgiven them (Mark 4. 12).

Having eyes, see ye not? and having ears, hear ye not? and do ye not remember? (Mark 8. 18).

And he said, Unto you it is given to know the mysteries of the kingdom of God: but to others in parables; that seeing they might not see, and hearing they might not understand (Luke 8. 10).

Why do ye not understand my speech? even because ye cannot hear my word.

.   .   .   .

He that is of God heareth God's words: ye therefore hear them not, because ye are not of God (John 8. 43, 47).

I have yet many things to say unto you, but ye cannot bear them now (John 16. 12).

All these passages refer to the first line, which explains the meaning of the Kingdom of Heaven as belonging to the few, i.e. the idea of the inner circle of humanity or the idea of esotericism.

The second line refers to *the disciples*.

The mistake of the usual, church, interpretations is that what refers to "esotericism" is regarded as referring to *the future life*, and what refers to the "disciples" is regarded as referring *to all men*.

It must be further noted that the different lines of thought are intermixed in the Gospels. Often one and the same passage refers to different lines. Often different passages, or passages formulated differently, express one idea, refer to one and the same line. Sometimes passages that succeed one another and apparently follow from one another, refer in fact to entirely different ideas.

There are passages, for example " be ye as little children," which have dozens of different meanings at the same time. Our mind refuses to conceive, refuses to comprehend, these meanings. Even if we write down these different meanings when they are explained to us, or when we ourselves arrive at an understanding of them, and afterwards read the notes made at different times, they seem to us cold and empty, having no meaning, because our mind cannot simultaneously grasp more than two or three meanings of one idea.

In addition to this there are many strange words in the New Testament, the meanings of which we do not really know, such as " faith," " mercy," " redemption," " sacrifice," " prayer," " alms," " blindness," " poverty," " riches," " life," " death," " birth," and many others.

If we succeed in understanding the hidden meaning of these words and expressions, the general content at once becomes clear and intelligible and often completely opposite to what is usually supposed.

In what follows, I shall deal only with the two above-mentioned lines of thought. Thus the interpretation which I give here will in no way exhaust the contents of the Gospel teaching and will aim only at showing the possibility of explaining some of the Gospel ideas in connection with the ideas of esotericism and " hidden wisdom."

If we read the Gospels bearing in mind that the *Kingdom of Heaven* means the inner circle of humanity, everything at once acquires for us new sense and meaning.

John the Baptist says:

Repent ye: for the kingdom of heaven is at hand (Matt. 3. 2).

And he says immediately afterwards that men must not hope to receive the Kingdom of Heaven remaining as they are, that this is in no way their *right*, that in reality they deserve something quite different.

But when he saw many of the Pharisees and Sadducees come to his baptism, he said unto them, O generation of vipers, who hath warned you to flee from the wrath to come?
Bring forth therefore fruits meet for repentance:
And think not to say within yourselves, We have Abraham to our father: for I say unto you, that God is able of these stones to raise up children unto Abraham (Matt. 3. 7–9).

John the Baptist emphasised with extraordinary power the idea that the Kingdom of Heaven is attained only by a few who deserve it. For the rest, for those who do not deserve it, he leaves no hope.

And now also the axe is laid unto the root of the trees: therefore every tree which bringeth not forth good fruit is hewn down, and cast into the fire (Matt. 3. 10).

And further on, speaking of Christ, he pronounces words which are forgotten more than any others:

Whose fan is in his hand, and he will throughly purge his floor, and gather his wheat into the garner; but he will burn up the chaff with unquenchable fire (Matt. 3. 12).

Jesus, in speaking of the Kingdom of Heaven, several times points out the exceptional significance of the preaching of John the Baptist:

And from the days of John the Baptist until now the kingdom of heaven suffereth violence, and the violent take it by force (Matt. 11. 12).

The law and the prophets were until John: since that time the Kingdom of God is preached, and every man presseth into it (Luke 16. 16).

Jesus himself, when beginning to preach the Kingdom of Heaven, uses the same words as were spoken by John:

Repent: for the kingdom of heaven is at hand (Matt. 4. 17).

In the Sermon on the Mount he says:

Blessed are the poor in spirit: for theirs is the kingdom of heaven (Matt. 5. 3).

Poor in spirit is a very enigmatic expression, which has always been wrongly interpreted and has given ground for the most incredible distortions of the ideas of Christ. " Poor in spirit " of course does not mean weak in spirit, and certainly does not mean poor, that is, destitute in the material sense. In their true meaning these words contain the Buddhist idea of *non-attachment to things.* A man who by the strength of his spirit makes himself non-attached to things, as though destitute, that is, when things have for him as little meaning as if he had not had them and had not known about them, will be *poor in spirit.*

This non-attachment is a necessary condition for approaching esotericism or the Kingdom of Heaven.

Further on Jesus says:

Blessed are they which are persecuted for righteousness' sake: for theirs is the kingdom of heaven (Matt. 5. 10).

This is the second condition. The disciple of Christ might expect to be " persecuted for righteousness' sake."

People of the " outer circle " hate and persecute people of the " inner circle," particularly those who come to help them. And Jesus says:

Blessed are ye, when men shall revile you, and persecute you, and shall say all manner of evil against you falsely, *for my sake.*

Rejoice, and be exceeding glad: for great is your reward in heaven: for so persecuted they the prophets which were before you (Matt. 5. 11, 12).

He that loveth his life shall lose it: and he that hateth his life in this world shall keep it unto life eternal (John 12. 25).

If the world hate you, ye know that it hated me before it hated you.

If ye were of the world, the world would love his own: but because ye are not of the world, but I have chosen you out of the world, therefore the world hateth you.

Remember the word that I said unto you, The servant is not greater than his lord. If they have persecuted me, they will also persecute you (John 15. 18–20).

They shall put you out of the synagogues: yea, the time cometh, that who-soever killeth you will think that he doeth God service (John 16. 2).

These passages very definitely emphasise the inaccessibility of esoteric ideas for the majority, for the crowd.

All these passages contain a very definite foreseeing of the results of the preaching of Christianity. But generally this is understood as the foreseeing of the persecutions for the preaching of Christianity among the heathen, while in reality Jesus certainly meant the persecutions for the preaching of esoteric Christianity among pseudo-Christians, or for endeavours to pre-serve esoteric truths in the midst of a church Christianity that was becoming more and more distorted.

In the next chapter Jesus speaks of the meaning of esotericism and the way to it, and clearly emphasises the difference between esoteric values and earthly values.

Lay not up for yourselves treasures upon earth, where moth and rust doth corrupt, and where thieves break through and steal:

But lay up for yourselves treasures in heaven, where neither moth nor rust doth corrupt, and where thieves do not break through nor steal:

For where your treasure is, there will your heart be also.

. . . .

No man can serve two masters: for either he will hate the one, and love the other; or else he will hold to the one, and despise the other. Ye cannot serve God and mammon.

. . . .

But seek ye first the kingdom of God, and his righteousness: and all these things shall be added unto you (Matt. 6. 19, 20, 21, 24, 33).

These passages again are understood too simply, in the sense of oppos-ing the ordinary earthly desires for possessions and power to the desire for eternal salvation. Jesus was of course much more subtle than that, and in warning against amassing treasures on earth he certainly warned against outward religious forms and outward piety and outward saintliness, which later became the aim of church Christianity.

In the next chapter Jesus speaks of the necessity for guarding the ideas of esotericism and not giving them forth indiscriminately, for there are people to whom these ideas in their essence are inaccessible, who, in so far as they can grasp them, will inevitably distort them, make wrong use of them and turn them against those who are trying to give them these ideas.

Give not that which is holy unto the dogs, neither cast ye your pearls before swine, lest they trample them under their feet, and turn again and rend you (Matt. 7. 6).

But immediately after this Jesus shows that esotericism is not hidden from those who really seek it.

Ask, and it shall be given you; seek, and ye shall find; knock, and it shall be opened unto you:

For everyone that asketh receiveth; and he that seeketh findeth; and to him that knocketh it shall be opened.

Or what man is there of you, whom if his son ask bread, will he give him a stone?

Or if he ask a fish, will he give him a serpent?

If ye then, being evil, know how to give good gifts unto your children, how much more shall your Father which is in heaven give good things to them that ask him? (Matt. 7. 7–11).

There follows further a very significant warning. The idea of it is that it is better not to enter upon the path of esotericism, better not to begin the work of inner purification, than to begin and abandon it, to set out and turn back, or to begin in a right way and then to distort everything.

When the unclean spirit is gone out of a man, he walketh through dry places, seeking rest; and finding none, he saith, I will return unto my house whence I came out.

And when he cometh, he findeth it swept and garnished.

Then goeth he, and taketh to him seven other spirits more wicked than himself; and they enter in, and dwell there: and the last state of that man is worse than the first (Luke 11. 24–26).

This again may have reference to church Christianity, which may represent a house swept and garnished.

And further Jesus speaks of the difficulty of the path and of possible mistakes.

Enter ye in at the strait gate: for wide is the gate, and broad is the way, that leadeth to destruction, and many there be which go in thereat:

Because strait is the gate, and narrow is the way, which leadeth unto life, and few there be that find it.

Not every one that saith unto me, Lord, Lord, shall enter into the kingdom of heaven; but he that doeth the will of my Father which is in heaven (Matt. 7. 13, 14 and 21).

Esotericism here is called " life." This is particularly interesting in comparison with other passages, which speak of ordinary life as " death " and of people as the " dead."

In these passages one can see the relationship between the inner circle and the outer circle, that is, how large is the one, the outer, and how small the other, the inner. In another place Jesus says that the " small " can be greater than the " large."

And he said, Whereunto shall we liken the kingdom of God? or with what comparison shall we compare it?

It is like a grain of mustard seed, which, when it is sown in the earth, is less than all the seeds that be in the earth:

But when it is sown, it groweth up, and becometh greater than all herbs, and shooteth out great branches; so that the fowls of the air may lodge under the shadow of it (Mark 4. 30–32).

The next chapter speaks of the difficulty of approaching esotericism and of the fact that esotericism does not give earthly blessings and sometimes even contradicts worldly forms and obligations.

And a certain scribe came, and said unto him, Master, I will follow thee whithersoever thou goest.

And Jesus saith unto him, The foxes have holes, and the birds of the air have nests; but the Son of man hath not where to lay his head.

And another of his disciples said unto him, Lord, suffer me first to go and bury my father.

But Jesus said unto him, Follow me; and let the dead bury their dead (Matt. 8. 19–22).

At the end of the following chapter mention is made of the great need in which people stand of help from the inner circle, and of the difficulty of helping them.

But when he saw the multitudes, he was moved with compassion on them, because they fainted, and were scattered abroad, as sheep having no shepherd.

Then saith he unto his disciples, The harvest truly is plenteous, but the labourers are few:

Pray ye therefore the Lord of the harvest, that he will send forth labourers into his harvest (Matt. 9. 36–38).

In the next chapter instructions are set out to the disciples as to what their work must consist in.

And as ye go, preach, saying, The kingdom of heaven is at hand (Matt. 10. 7).

What I tell you in darkness, that speak ye in light: and what ye hear in the ear, that preach ye upon the housetops (Matt. 10. 27).

But immediately after this Jesus adds that the preaching of esotericism gives results quite different from those which, from the point of view of ordinary life, the disciples may expect. Jesus explains that by his preaching of the esoteric doctrine he has brought men anything but peace and tranquillity, and that truth divides men more than anything else, again because only few can receive truth.

Think not that I am come to send peace on earth: I came not to send peace, but a sword.

For I am come to set a man at variance against his father, and the daughter against her mother, and the daughter-in-law against her mother-in-law.

And a man's foes shall be they of his own household.

He that loveth father or mother more than me is not worthy of me (Matt. 10. 34–37).

The last verse is again the Buddhist idea that a man must not be " attached " to anyone or anything. ("Attachment" in this case certainly does not mean " sympathy " or " affection " in the sense in which these words are used in modern languages). " Attachment " in the Buddhist (and in the Gospel) sense of the word means a small, selfish and slavish feeling. This is not " love " at all, since a man may hate that to which he is attached, may try to free himself and not be able to do so. " Attachment " to things, to people, even to one's father and mother, is the chief obstacle on the way to esotericism.

Further on this idea is emphasised still more.

Then came to him his mother and his brethren, and could not come at him for the press.

And it was told him by certain which said, Thy mother and thy brethren stand without, desiring to see thee.

And he answered and said unto them, My mother and my brethren are these which hear the word of God, and do it (Luke 8. 19–21).

After this Jesus begins to speak of the Kingdom of Heaven in parables. The first is that of the sower.

And he spake many things unto them in parables, saying, Behold, a sower went forth to sow;

And when he sowed, some seeds fell by the way side, and the fowls came and devoured them up:

Some fell upon stony places, where they had not much earth: and forthwith they sprung up, because they had no deepness of earth:

And when the sun was up, they were scorched; and because they had no root, they withered away.

And some fell among thorns; and the thorns sprung up, and choked them.

But others fell into good ground, and brought forth fruit, some an hundredfold, some sixtyfold some thirtyfold.

Who hath ears to hear, let him hear (Matt. 13. 3–9).

This parable, which contains a complete and exact description of the preaching of esotericism and of all its possible results, and bears a direct relation to the preaching of Christ himself, is almost the central of all the parables.

The meaning of this parable is perfectly clear. It refers, of course, to esoteric ideas, to the ideas of the " Kingdom of Heaven," which are received and understood only by very few people and for the immense majority disappear without leaving any trace.

And this parable again ends with the words, " who hath ears to hear, let him hear."

In the subsequent conversation with the disciples Jesus points out the difference between the disciples and other people.

And the disciples came, and said unto him, Why speakest thou unto them in parables?

He answered and said unto them, Because it is given unto you to know the mysteries of the kingdom of heaven, but to them it is not given (Matt. 13. 10, 11).

This is the beginning of the explanations referring to a " school " and " school methods." As will be seen later, much of what is said in the Gospel was intended *only for the disciples* and has meaning only in a school, and only in connection with other school methods and requirements.

In this connection Jesus speaks of a psychological and perhaps even cosmic law, which seems incomprehensible without explanations, but the explanations are not set out in the Gospel, though of course they were given to the disciples.

For whoever hath, to him shall be given, and he shall have more abundance: but whosoever hath not, from him shall be taken away even that he hath (Matt. 13. 12).

Then Jesus returns to parables; i.e. to the idea of parables.

Therefore speak I to them in parables: because they seeing see not; and hearing they hear not, neither do they understand (Matt. 13. 13).

And the same in St. Luke:

Unto you it is given to know the mysteries of the kingdom of God: but to others in parables; that seeing they might not see, and hearing they might not understand (Luke 8. 10).

He hath blinded their eyes and hardened their heart; that they should not see with their eyes, nor understand with their heart, and be converted, and I should heal them (Isaiah 6. 10; John 12. 40).

For this people's heart is waxed gross, and their ears are dull of hearing, and their eyes they have closed . . .
But blessed are your eyes, for they see: and your ears, for they hear.
For verily I say unto you, That many prophets and righteous men have desired to see those things which ye see, and have not seen them; and to hear those things which ye hear, and have not heard them (Matt. 13. 15–17).

Teaching by parables was most characteristic of Christ. Renan finds that in the literature of Judaism there was nothing that could serve as a model for this form.
Renan writes:

It is particularly in the parable that the master excelled. Nothing in Judaism had given him a model for this delightful form. It is he who created it.

C'est surtout dans la parabole que le maître excellait. Rien dans le Judaisme ne lui avait donné le modèle de ce genre délicieux. C'est lui qui l'a créé.[6]

_____
[6] *Vie de Jésus*, par E. Renan (Nelson Editeurs), p. 116.

Later, with the astounding inconsequence which characterises all the "positivist" thought of the 19th century, and particularly Renan himself, he adds:

It is true that one finds in Buddhist books parables of exactly the same tone and the same composition as the Gospel parables. *But it is difficult to admit that a Buddhist influence was exerted in this.*

Il est vrai qu'on trouve dans les livres bouddhiques des paraboles exactement du même ton et de la même facture que les paraboles évangeliques. Mais il est difficile d'admettre qu'une influence bouddhique se soit exercée en ceci.[7]

In fact, the Buddhist influence in parables is beyond any doubt. And parables, more than anything else, show that Christ was acquainted with Eastern teachings and particularly with Buddhism. Renan generally tries to represent Christ as a very naïve man, who felt much, but thought little and knew little. Renan was but the expression of his own times and of the views of his epoch. The characteristic quality of European thought is that we can only think in extremes. Either Christ is God, or Christ is a naïve man. For the same reason we fail to notice the subtleties of psychological distinctions which Christ introduces into his parables and explanations of them.

The explanations of the parables which Christ gives to his disciples are not less interesting than the parables themselves.

Hear ye therefore the parable of the sower.

When any one heareth the word of the kingdom, and understandeth it not, then cometh the wicked one, and catcheth away that which was sown in his heart. This is he which received seed by the way side.

But he that received the seed into stony places, the same is he that heareth the word, and anon with joy receiveth it;

Yet hath he not root in himself, but dureth for a while: for when tribulation or persecution ariseth because of the word, by and by he is offended.

He also that received seed among the thorns is he that heareth the word; and the care of this world, and the deceitfulness of riches, choke the word, and he becometh unfruitful (Matt. 13. 18–22).

Next comes the parable of the tares:

Another parable put he forth unto them, saying, The kingdom of heaven is likened unto a man which sowed good seed in his field:

But while men slept, his enemy came and sowed tares among the wheat, and went his way.

But when the blade was sprung up, and brought forth fruit, then appeared the tares also.

So the servants of the householder came and said unto him, Sir, didst not thou sow good seed in thy field? from whence then hath it tares?

He said unto them, An enemy hath done this. The servants said unto him,

---

[7] Ibid., p. 116.

Wilt thou then that we go and gather them up? But he said, Nay; lest while ye gather up the tares, ye root up also the wheat with them.

Let both grow together until the harvest; and in the time of harvest I will say to the reapers, Gather ye together first the tares, and bind them in bundles to burn them: but gather the wheat into my barn (Matt. 13. 24–30).

The parable of the sower and that of the tares have many different meanings. First of all, it is, of course, the contrasting of pure esoteric ideas with ideas mixed with " tares " sown by the devil. In this case the grains or seeds denote ideas.

In one place Christ says:

The sower soweth the *word* (Mark 4. 14).

In other cases a seed or grain symbolises man.

The " grain " played a very important part in the ancient Mysteries. The idea of the " burial " of the grain in the earth, its " death " and " resurrection " in the form of a green sprout, symbolised the whole idea of the Mysteries. There are many naïve pseudo-scientific attempts to explain the Mysteries as an " agricultural myth," i.e. as a survival of the ancient " pagan " rites of a primitive agricultural people. In reality the idea was of course infinitely wider and deeper and was certainly conceived not by a primitive people, but by one of the long-vanished prehistoric civilisations. The grain allegorically represented " man." In the Eleusinian Mysteries every candidate for initiation carried in a particular procession a grain of wheat in a tiny earthenware bowl. The secret that was revealed to a man at the initiation was contained in the idea that man could die simply as a grain, or could rise again into some other life. This was the principal idea of the Mysteries which was expressed by many different symbols. Christ often makes use of the same idea, and there is enormous power in it. The idea contains a biological explanation of the whole series of the intricate and complex problems of life. Nature is extraordinarily generous, almost lavish, in her methods. She creates an enormous quantity of seeds in order that a few of them only may germinate and carry life further. If man is looked upon as a grain, the " cruel " law which is continually emphasised in the Gospel teaching becomes comprehensible, that the great majority of mankind are but " chaff " which shall be burned.

Christ very often returns to this idea, and in his explanations the idea loses its cruelty, because it becomes clear that in the " salvation " or " perdition " of every individual man there is nothing preordained or inevitable, that both the one and the other depend on man himself, on his own attitude towards himself, towards other men and towards the idea of the Kingdom of Heaven.

In succeeding parables Christ again emphasises the idea and meaning of esotericism in relation to life, the small external magnitude of esotericism in comparison with life, and yet the immense possibilities and the immense significance of esotericism and the particular quality of esoteric ideas: that they approach him who understands and appreciates their meaning.

These short parables about the Kingdom of Heaven, each of which includes the whole content of the Gospel teaching, are remarkable even simply as works of art.

Another parable put he forth unto them saying, The kingdom of heaven is like to a grain of mustard seed, which a man took, and sowed in his field:

Which indeed is the least of all seeds: but when it is grown, it is the greatest among herbs, and becometh a tree, so that the birds of the air come and lodge in the branches thereof.

Another parable spake he unto them: The kingdom of heaven is like unto leaven, which a woman took, and hid in three measures of meal, till the whole was leavened.

All these things spake Jesus unto the multitude in parables; and without a parable spake he not unto them.

Again, the kingdom of heaven is like unto treasure hid in a field; the which when a man hath found, he hideth, and for joy thereof goeth and selleth all that he hath, and buyeth that field.

Again, the kingdom of heaven is like unto a merchant man, seeking goodly pearls:

Who, when he had found one pearl of great price, went and sold all that he had, and bought it.

Again, the kingdom of heaven is like unto a net, that was cast into the sea, and gathered of every kind:

Which, when it was full, they drew to shore, and sat down, and gathered the good into vessels, but cast the bad away (Matt. 13. 31–34, 44–48).

In the last parable there is again the idea of separation, the idea of selection. Further on Christ says:

So shall it be at the end of the world: the angels shall come forth and sever the wicked from among the just,

And shall cast them into the furnace of fire: there shall be wailing and gnashing of teeth.

Jesus saith unto them, Have ye understood all these things? They say unto him, Yea, Lord (Matt. 13. 49–51).

But apparently the disciples did not quite understand, or understood something wrongly, confused the new interpretation with the old, because Christ said to them next:

Therefore every scribe which is instructed unto the kingdom of heaven is like unto a man that is an householder, which bringeth forth out of his treasure things new and old (Matt. 13. 52).

This refers to an intellectual study of the Gospel teaching, to attempts at rationalistic interpretations, in which elements of esoteric ideas are mixed up with barren scholastic dialectic, the *new* with the *old*.

The succeeding parables and teachings contain a development of this same idea of selection and test; only a man who creates within himself the Kingdom of Heaven with all its rules and laws can enter Christ's Kingdom of Heaven.

Therefore is the kingdom of heaven likened unto a certain king, which would take account of his servants.

And when he had begun to reckon, one was brought unto him, which owed him ten thousand talents.

But forasmuch as he had not to pay, his lord commanded him to be sold, and his wife, and children, and all that he had, and payment to be made.

The servant therefore fell down, and worshipped him, saying, Lord, have patience with me, and I will pay thee all.

Then the lord of that servant was moved with compassion, and loosed him, and forgave him the debt.

But the same servant went out, and found one of his fellow-servants, which owed him an hundred pence: and he laid hands on him, and took him by the throat, saying, Pay me that thou owest.

And his fellow-servant fell down at his feet, and besought him, saying, Have patience with me, and I will pay thee all.

And he would not; but went and cast him into prison, till he should pay the debt.

So when his fellow-servants saw what was done, they were very sorry, and came and told unto their lord all that was done.

Then his lord, after that he had called him, said unto him, O thou wicked servant, I forgave thee all that debt, because thou desiredst me:

Shouldst not thou also have had compassion on thy fellow-servant, even as I had pity on thee?

And the lord was wroth, and delivered him to the tormentors, till he should pay all that was due unto him (Matt. 18. 23–34).

Next comes the story of the rich young man, of the difficulties and trials, of the obstacles, made by life, of the attractions of life, of the power of life over people, especially over those *who have great possessions.*

The young man saith unto him, All these things have I kept from my youth up: what lack I yet?

Jesus said unto him, If thou wilt be perfect, go and sell that thou hast, and give to the poor, and thou shalt have treasure in heaven: and come and follow me.

But when the young man heard that saying, he went away sorrowful: for he had great possessions.

Then said Jesus unto his disciples, Verily I say unto you, That a rich man shall hardly enter into the kingdom of heaven.

And again I say unto you, It is easier for a camel to go through the eye of a needle, than for a rich man to enter into the kingdom of God (Matt. 19. 20–24).

"Rich" again has of course many different meanings. First of all, it contains the idea of "attachment," sometimes the idea of great knowledge, a great mind, a great talent, position, fame — all these are " riches," which close the entrance to the Kingdom of Heaven. Attachment to church religion is also " riches." Only if the " rich man " becomes " poor in spirit " does the Kingdom of Heaven open to him.

The passages that follow in St. Matthew's Gospel deal with different attitudes to esoteric ideas.

Some people grasp at them, but quickly abandon them; others resist at first but afterwards take to them seriously. These are two types of people. One type is the man who said that he would go and did not go, and the other is the man who said that he would not go and went. Then sometimes people either unsuccessful in life, or occupying a very low position in life, people even criminal from the point of view of ordinary morals, " the publicans and harlots," prove to be better from the point of view of the Kingdom of Heaven than the righteous men confident of themselves.

But what think ye? A certain man had two sons; and he came to the first, and said, Son, go work to-day in my vineyard.

He answered and said, I will not; but afterwards he repented, and went.

And he came to the second, and said likewise. And he answered and said, I go, sir: and went not.

Whether of them twain did the will of his father? They say unto him, The first. Jesus saith unto them, Verily I say unto you, That the publicans and the harlots go into the kingdom of God before you.

For John came unto you in the way of righteousness, and ye believed him not: but the publicans and the harlots believed him: and ye, when ye had seen it, repented not afterward, that ye might believe him (Matt. 21. 28–32).

Then follow the parable of the husbandmen and the explanation, in which one feels great ideas of a cosmic order, which possibly refer to the succession of cycles, this is, to the replacement of an unsuccessful experiment by a new experiment.[8] This parable may refer to the whole of humanity and to the relation between the inner circle and the outer circle of humanity.

Hear another parable: There was a certain householder, which planted a vineyard, and hedged it round about, and digged a winepress in it, and built a tower, and let it out to husbandmen, and went into a far country:

And when the time of the fruit drew near, he sent his servants to the husbandmen, that they might receive the fruits of it.

And the husbandmen took his servants, and beat one, and killed another, and stoned another.

Again, he sent other servants more than the first: and they did unto them likewise.

But last of all he sent unto them his son, saying, They will reverence my son.

But when the husbandmen saw the son, they said among themselves, This is the heir; come, let us kill him, and let us seize on his inheritance.

And they caught him, and cast him out of the vineyard, and slew him.

---

[8] Ch. I, p. 47.

When the lord therefore of the vineyard cometh, what will he do unto those husbandmen?

They say unto him, He will miserably destroy those wicked men, and will let out his vineyard unto other husbandmen, which shall render him the fruits in their seasons (Matt. 21. 33–41).

Next comes the same idea of selection and that of the different attitudes of people to the idea of the Kingdom of Heaven.

The kingdom of heaven is like unto a certain king, which made a marriage for his son,

And sent forth his servants to call them that were bidden to the wedding: and they would not come.

Again, he sent forth other servants, saying, Tell them which are bidden, Behold, I have prepared my dinner: my oxen and my fatlings are killed, and all things are ready: come unto the marriage.

But they made light of it, and went their ways, one to his farm, another to his merchandise:

And the remnant took his servants, and entreated them spitefully and slew them.

But when the king heard thereof, he was wroth: and he sent forth his armies, and destroyed those murderers, and burned up their city (Matt. 22. 2–7).

Then follows the parable of the people who are ready and not ready for esotericism.

Then saith he to his servants, The wedding is ready, but they which were bidden were not worthy.

Go ye therefore into the highways, and as many as ye shall find, bid to the marriage.

So those servants went out into the highways, and gathered together all as many as they found, both bad and good: and the wedding was furnished with guests.

And when the king came in to see the guests, he saw there a man which had not on a wedding garment:

And he saith unto him, Friend, how camest thou in hither not having a wedding garment? And he was speechless.

Then said the king to the servants, Bind him hand and foot, and take him away, and cast him into outer darkness; there shall be weeping and gnashing of teeth.

For many are called, but few are chosen (Matt. 22. 8–14).

Next there is one of the best-known parables, that of the talents.

For the kingdom of heaven is as a man travelling into a far country, who called his own servants, and delivered unto them his goods.

And unto one he gave five talents, to another two, and to another one; to every man according to his several ability; and straightway took his journey.

Then he that had received the five talents went and traded with the same, and made them other five talents.

And likewise he that had received two, he also gained other two.

But he that had received one went and digged in the earth, and hid his lord's money.

After a long time the lord of those servants cometh, and reckoneth with them.

And so he that had received five talents came and brought other five talents, saying, Lord, thou deliverest unto me five talents: behold I have gained beside them five talents more.

His lord said unto him, Well done, thou good and faithful servant: thou has been faithful over a few things, I will make thee ruler over many things: enter thou into the joy of thy lord.

He also that had received two talents came and said, Lord, thou deliveredst unto me two talents: behold, I have gained two other talents beside them.

His lord said unto him, Well done, good and faithful servant; thou hast been faithful over a few things, I will make thee ruler over many things: enter thou into the joy of thy lord.

Then he which had received the one talent came and said, Lord, I knew thee that thou art an hard man, reaping where thou hast not sown, and gathering where thou hast not strawed:

And I was afraid, and went and hid thy talent in the earth: lo, there thou hast that is thine.

His lord answered and said unto him, Thou wicked and slothful servant, thou knowest that I reap where I sowed not, and gather where I have not strawed:

Thou oughtest therefore to have put my money to the exchangers, and then at my coming I should have received mine own with usury.

Take therefore the talent from him, and give it unto him which hath ten talents.

For unto everyone that hath shall be given, and he shall have abundance: but from him that hath not shall be taken away even that which he hath.

And cast ye the unprofitable servant into outer darkness: there shall be weeping and gnashing of teeth (Matt. 25. 14–30).

This parable contains all the ideas connected with the parable of the sower, and besides this the idea of the change of cycles and of the destruction of bad material.

In St. Mark's Gospel there is an interesting parable which explains the laws under which the influence of the inner circle is exerted on outer humanity.

And he said, So is the kingdom of God, as if a man should cast seed into the ground;

And should sleep, and rise night and day, and the seed should spring and grow up, he knoweth not how.

For the earth bringeth forth fruit of herself; first the blade, then the ear, after that the full corn in the ear.

But when the fruit is brought forth, immediately he putteth in the sickle, because the harvest is come (Mark 4. 26–29).

And with many such parables spake he the word unto them, as they were able to hear it.

But without a parable spake he not unto them: and when they were alone, he expounded all things to his disciples (Mark 4. 33–34).

The continuation of this idea of the " harvest " is found in St. Luke's Gospel.

The harvest truly is great, but the labourers are few: pray ye therefore the Lord of the harvest, that he would send forth labourers into his harvest (Luke 10. 2).

In St. John's Gospel the same idea is developed in a still more interesting way.

And he that reapeth receiveth wages, and gathereth fruit unto life eternal: that both he that soweth and he that reapeth may rejoice together.

And herein is that saying true, One soweth, and another reapeth.

I sent you to reap that whereon ye bestowed no labour; other men laboured, and ye are entered into their labours (John 4. 36–38).

In the above passages, in connection with the idea of harvest several cosmic laws are touched upon. The " harvest " can only take place at a definite time, *when the corn is ripened*, and Jesus emphasises this special characteristic of the time of harvest, and also the general idea that not everything can take place at any time. Esoteric processes require time. Different moments require different action in relation to them.

Then came to him the disciples of John, saying, Why do we and the Pharisees fast oft, but thy disciples fast not?

And Jesus said unto them, Can the children of the bridechamber mourn, as long as the bridegroom is with them? but the days will come, when the bridegroom shall be taken from them, and then shall they fast (Matt. 9. 14, 15).

The same idea of the different meaning of different moments and of certain esoteric work being possible only at a definite time is found in St. John's Gospel.

I must work the works of him that sent me, while it is day: the night cometh when no man can work (John 9. 4).

Further comes the opposition between ordinary life and the way to esotericism. Life holds man. But those who enter the way to esotericism must forget all the rest.

And another also said, Lord, I will follow thee; but let me first go bid them farewell, which are at home at my house.

And Jesus said unto him, No man, having put his hand to the plough, and looking back, is fit for the kingdom of God (Luke 9. 61–62).

Further on the same idea is developed in one particular sense. In most cases life conquers. Means become aim. People give up their great possibilities for the sake of the little present.

A certain man made a great supper, and bade many:
And sent his servant at supper time to say to them that were bidden, Come; for all things are now ready.
And they all with one consent began to make excuse. The first said unto him, I have bought a piece of ground, and I must needs go and see it: I pray thee have me excused.
And another said, I have bought five yoke of oxen, and I go to prove them: I pray thee have me excused.
And another said, I have married a wife, and therefore I cannot come (Luke 14. 16–20).

In St. John's Gospel the idea of " new birth " is introduced in explanation of the principles of esotericism.

Except a man be born again, he cannot see the kingdom of God (John 3. 3).

Then follows the idea of resurrection, resuscitation. Life without the idea of esotericism is regarded as death.

For as the Father raiseth up the dead, and quickeneth them; even so the Son quickeneth whom he will (John 5. 21).

Verily, verily, I say unto you, The hour is coming, and now is, when the dead shall hear the voice of the Son of God: and they that hear shall live . . .
Marvel not at this: for the hour is coming, in the which all that are in the graves shall hear his voice (John 5. 25, 28).

Verily, verily, I say unto you, If a man keep my saying, he shall never see death (John 8. 51).

These last passages are certainly interpreted quite wrongly in existing pseudo-Christian teachings.
" Those that are in the grave " does not mean dead people who are buried in the earth, but, on the contrary, those who are living in the ordinary sense, but dead from the point of view of esotericism.
This idea is met with several times in the Gospels where men are compared to sepulchres or graves. The same idea is expressed in the wonderful Easter hymn of the Orthodox Church, which was mentioned earlier.[9]

Christ is risen from the dead.
He has conquered death with death,
And given life to those who were in tombs.

" Those in tombs " are precisely those who are regarded as living. This idea is expressed quite clearly in Revelations:

Thou hast a name that thou livest, and art dead (Rev. 3. 1).

---

[9] Ch. I, p. 26.

The comparison of people with sepulchres or graves is met with several times in St. Matthew and St. Luke:

Woe unto you, scribes and Pharisees, hypocrites! for ye are like unto whited sepulchres, which indeed appear beautiful outward, but are within full of dead men's bones, and of all uncleanness (Matt. 23. 27).

Woe unto you, scribes and Pharisees, hypocrites! for ye are as graves which appear not, and the men that walk over them are not aware of them (Luke 11. 44).

The same idea is developed further in Revelations. Esotericism gives life. In the esoteric circle there is no death.

He that hath an ear, let him hear what the Spirit saith unto the churches; To him that overcometh will I give to eat of the tree of life, which is in the midst of the paradise of God . . .
He that hath an ear, let him hear what the Spirit saith unto the churches, He that overcometh shall not be hurt of the second death (Rev. 2. 7 and 11).

To this refer also the words in St. John's Gospel which connect the teachings of the Gospels with the teaching of the Mysteries.

Verily, verily, I say unto you, Except a corn of wheat fall into the ground and die, it abideth alone: but if it die, it bringeth forth much fruit (John 12. 24).

In Revelations there are some remarkable words in the third chapter which acquire particular significance in connection with the meaning which Jesus himself always attached to the words " rich " and " poor," " blind " and " he who sees."

Because thou sayest, I am rich, and increased with goods, and have need of nothing; and knowest not that thou art wretched, and miserable, and poor, and blind, and naked:
I counsel thee to buy of me gold tried in the fire, that thou mayest be rich; and white raiment, that thou mayest be clothed, and that the shame of thy nakedness do not appear; and anoint thine eyes with eyesalve, that thou mayest see (Rev. 3. 17, 18).

Of the " blind " and " those who can see " Christ speaks in St. John's Gospel.

For judgment I am come into this world, that they which see not might see; and that they which see might be made blind.
And some of the Pharisees which were with them heard these words, and said unto him, Are we blind also?
Jesus said unto them, if ye were blind, ye should have no sin: but now ye say, We see; therefore your sin remaineth (John 9. 39, 41).

The expressions " blind " and " blindness " generally have several meanings in the New Testament. And it is necessary to understand that blindness can be outward and physical, or inner blindness, just as there can be inner leprosy, inner death — which are much worse than outward.

This brings us to the question of "miracles." All "miracles" — the healing of the blind, the cleansing of the lepers, the casting out of devils, the raising of the dead — can be explained in two ways if the Gospel terminology is understood rightly, either as outward physical miracles or as inner miracles, the healing of inner blindness, inner cleansing and inner resurrection.

The man born blind, whom Jesus heals, uses remarkable words when the Pharisees and Sadducees tried to convince him that from their point of view Jesus had no right to heal him.

Then again called they the man that was blind, and said unto him, Give God the praise: we know that this man is a sinner.

He answered and said, Whether he be a sinner or no, I know not: one thing I know, that, whereas I was blind, now I see (John 9. 24, 25).

The idea of inner miracle and inner conviction of miracle are very closely connected with Christ's definite words as to the meaning of the Kingdom of Heaven in the following passage.

And when he was demanded of the Pharisees, when the kingdom of God should come, he answered them and said, The kingdom of God cometh not with observation:

Neither shall they say, Lo here! or, lo there! for behold, the kingdom of God is within you (Luke 17. 20, 21).

All that has been said until now and all the passages that have been quoted belong to one line of thought, which goes through all the Gospel teaching, namely the line which develops the idea of the meaning of esotericism or the Kingdom of Heaven.

The other line which also goes through all the Gospels deals with the methods of occult or *school* work. First of all, it shows the meaning of occult work in relation to life.

Follow me, and I will make you fishers of men (Matt. 4. 19).

These words show that the man who enters upon the way of esotericism must have in view that he has to work for esotericism, and work in a very definite sense, that is, find people suitable for esoteric work and prepare them for it. People are not born in the "inner circle." The inner circle feeds on the outer circle. But only very few of the people of the outer circle are suitable for esotericism. Therefore the work of preparing people for the inner circle, the work of "fishers of men," is a very important part of esoteric work.

These words, "Follow me, and I will make you fishers of men," like many others, certainly cannot refer to all men.

And they straightway left their nets, and followed him (Matt. 4. 20).

Further on Jesus says, again addressing himself only to the disciples and explaining the meaning of esotericism and the rôle and place of people belonging to esotericism:

Ye are the salt of the earth: but if the salt have lost his savour, wherewith shall it be salted? it is thenceforth good for nothing, but to be cast out, and to be trodden under fo, of men.

Ye are the light of the world. A city that is set on a hill cannot be hid.

Neither do men light a candle, and put it under a bushel, but on a candlestick; and it giveth light unto all that are in the house.

Let your light so shine before men, that they may see your good works, and glorify your Father which is in heaven (Matt. 5. 13-16).

After this he explains the requirements which are set before people approaching esotericism.

For I say unto you, That except your righteousness shall exceed the righteousness of the scribes and Pharisees, ye shall in no case enter into the kingdom of heaven (Matt. 5. 20).

In the ordinary interpretation of the Gospels this second line, referring only to the disciples, is taken as wrongly as the first, referring to the Kingdom of Heaven or esotericism. Everything contained in the first line of thought is taken, in the ordinary interpretation, as referring to *the future life*. Everything contained in the second line of thought is taken as *moral teaching*, referring to all people in general. In reality these are rules for the disciples.

To the disciples also, refers all that is said about *watchfulness*, that is, about the constant attention and observation which are required of them.

This idea is first met with in the parable of the ten virgins.

Then shall the kingdom of heaven be likened unto ten virgins, which took their lamps, and went forth to meet the bridegroom.

And five of them were wise, and five were foolish.

They that were foolish took their lamps, and took no oil with them:

But the wise took oil in their vessels with their lamps.

While the bridegroom tarried, they all slumbered and slept.

And at midnight there was a cry made, Behold, the bridegroom cometh; go ye out to meet him.

Then all those virgins arose, and trimmed their lamps.

And the foolish said unto the wise, Give us of your oil; for our lamps are gone out.

But the wise answered, saying, Not so; lest there be not enough for us and you: but go ye rather to them that sell, and buy for yourselves.

And while they went to buy, the bridegroom came; and they that were ready went in with him to the marriage: and the door was shut.

Afterward came also the other virgins, saying, Lord, Lord, open to us.

But he answered and said, Verily I say unto you, I know you not.

Watch therefore, for ye know neither the day nor the hour wherein the Son of man cometh (Matt. 25. 1–13).

The idea that the disciples cannot know when active work will be required of them and that they must be ready at any moment is emphasised in the following words.

Watch therefore: for ye know not what hour your Lord doth come.

But know this, that if the goodman of the house had known in what watch the thief would come, he would have watched, and would not have suffered his house to be broken up.

Therefore be ye also ready: for in such an hour as ye think not the Son of man cometh (Matt. 24. 42–44).

Further on the work of the master himself is mentioned and the fact that he can receive very little help even from his disciples.

Then saith he unto them, My soul is exceeding sorrowful, even unto death: tarry ye here, and watch with me.

. . . .

And he cometh unto his disciples, and findeth them asleep, and saith unto Peter, What, could ye not watch with me one hour?

Watch and pray, that ye enter not into temptation: the spirit indeed is willing, but the flesh is weak.

. . . .

Then cometh he to his disciples, and saith unto them, Sleep on now, and take your rest: behold, the hour is at hand, and the Son of man is betrayed into the hands of sinners (Matt. 26. 38, 40, 41, 45).

Great importance is evidently attached to the idea of " watching." It is repeated many times in all the Gospels.

In St. Mark:

Take ye heed, watch and pray: for ye know not when the time is.

For the Son of man is as a man taking a far journey, who left his house, and gave authority to his servants, and to every man his work, and commanded the porter to watch.

Watch ye therefore: for ye know not when the master of the house cometh, at even, or at midnight, or at the cockcrowing, or in the morning:

Lest coming suddenly he find you sleeping.

And what I say unto you I say unto all, Watch (Mark 13. 33–37).

In St. Luke there are again emphasised the necessity for being ready at any moment and the impossibility of knowing beforehand.

Let your loins be girded about, and your lights burning.

. . . .

Blessed are those servants whom the lord when he cometh shall find watching: verily I say unto you, that he shall gird himself, and make them to sit down to meat, and will come forth and serve them.

And if he shall come in the second watch, or come in the third watch, and find them so, blessed are those servants.

And this know, that if the goodman of the house had known what hour the thief would come, he would have watched, and not have suffered his house to be broken through.

Be ye therefore ready also: for the Son of man cometh at an hour when ye think not (Luke 12. 35, 37–40).

And further on:

Watch ye therefore, and pray always, that ye may be accounted worthy to escape all these things that shall come to pass, and to stand before the Son of man (Luke 21. 36).

All the preceding passages refer to " watchfulness." But this word has many different meanings. It is quite insufficient to understand it in the simple or everyday sense — to be ready. The word " watchfulness " contains a whole doctrine of esoteric psychology which is explained only in occult schools.

Christ's precepts on watchfulness are very similar to precepts of Buddha on the same subject. But in Buddha's teaching the purpose and the meaning of watchfulness are still clearer. All the inner work of a " monk " Buddha resolves into watchfulness, and he points to the necessity of incessant exercising in watchfulness for the attainment of clear consciousness, for the overcoming of suffering and for the achieving of liberation.[10]

Following upon this, the second important requirement of " occult rules " is that of the knowledge and capacity to keep secrets, that is, the knowledge and capacity to be silent.

Christ attaches special importance to this, and the requirement of silence is repeated in the Gospels in a literal form also seventeen times (like the words, only those who have ears can hear).

And immediately his leprosy was cleansed.
And Jesus saith unto him, See thou tell no man (Matt. 8. 3, 4).

And their eyes were opened; and Jesus straitly charged them, saying, See that no man know it (Matt. 9. 30).

And as they came down from the mountain, Jesus charged them, saying, Tell the vision to no man (Matt. 17. 9; Mark 9. 9).

And there was in their synagogue a man with an unclean spirit; and he cried out,
Saying, Let us alone; what have we to do with thee, thou Jesus of Nazareth? art thou come to destroy us? I know thee who thou art, the Holy One of God.

---

[10] Die Reden Gotamo Buddhos aus der mittleren Sammlung Majjhimanikayo des Pali-Kanons, übersetzt von Karl Eugen Neumann (R. Piper & Co., München, 1922), vol. I, pp. 122–123 and 634–635.

And Jesus rebuked him, saying, Hold thy peace, and come out of him (Mark 1. 23–25; Luke 4. 33–35).

And he healed many that were sick of divers diseases, and cast out many devils; and suffered not the devils to speak, because they knew him (Mark 1. 34; Luke 4. 41).

And as soon as he had spoken, immediately the leprosy departed from him, and he was cleansed.
And he straitly charged him, and forthwith sent him away;
And saith unto him, See thou say nothing to any man: but go thy way (Mark 1. 42–44; Luke 5. 13, 14).

And unclean spirits, when they saw him, fell down before him, and cried, saying, Thou art the Son of God.
And he straitly charged them that they should not make him known (Mark 3. 11, 12).

And straightway the damsel arose, and walked . . .
And he charged them straitly that no man should know it (Mark 5. 42, 43).

And straightway his ears were opened, and the string of his tongue was loosed, and he spake plain.
And he charged them that they should tell no man (Mark 7. 35, 36).

After that he put his hands again upon his eyes, and made him look up: and he was restored, and saw every man clearly.
And he sent him away to his house, saying, Neither go into the town, nor tell it to any in the town (Mark 8. 25, 26).

And he saith unto them, But whom say ye that I am? And Peter answereth and saith unto him, Thou art the Christ.
And he charged them that they should tell no man of him (Mark 8. 29, 30; Luke 9. 20, 21; Matt. 16. 20).

The idea of keeping secrets is connected in esotericism with the idea of conserving energy. Silence, secrecy, create a closed circle, that is, an " accumulator." This idea runs through all occult systems. The ability to keep silence or to say only what is necessary and when it is necessary, is the first degree of control of oneself. In school work the ability to keep silence is a definite degree of attainment. The ability to keep silent includes the art of concealing oneself, not showing oneself. The " initiated " is always hidden from the " uninitiated " even though the uninitiated may deceive himself by thinking that he sees, or can see, the motives and actions of the " initiated." The " initiated," according to esoteric rules, has not the right to and must not disclose the positive side of his activity or of himself to anyone except those whose level is near his own, who have already passed the test and have shown that their attitude and their understanding are right.

Take heed that ye do not your alms before men, to be seen of them: otherwise ye have no reward of your Father which is in heaven.

Therefore when thou doest thine alms, do not sound a trumpet before thee, as the hypocrites do in the synagogues and in the streets, that they may have glory of men. Verily I say unto you, They have their reward.

But when thou doest alms, let not thy left hand know what thy right hand doeth:

That thine alms may be in secret: and thy Father which seeth in secret himself shall reward thee openly.

And when thou prayest, thou shalt not be as the hypocrites are: for they love to pray standing in the synagogues and in the corners of the streets, that they may be seen of men. Verily I say unto you, They have their reward.

But thou, when thou prayest, enter into thy closet and when thou hast shut thy door, pray to thy Father which is in secret; and thy Father which seeth in secret shall reward thee openly.

But when ye pray, use not vain repetitions, as the heathen do: for they think that they shall be heard for their much speaking (Matt. 6. 1–7).

One of the chief occult rules, one of the first principles of esoteric work, which the disciples must learn, is embodied in Christ's words:

Let not thy left hand know what thy right hand doeth.

The study of the theoretical and practical meaning of this principle constitutes one of the most important parts of school work in all esoteric schools without exception. This element of secrecy was very strong in the Christian communities of the first centuries. And the requirement of secrecy was not based on the fear of persecution, as is now generally thought, but on the still existing traditions of esoteric schools, with which Christian communities were undoubtedly connected in the beginning.[11]

After this come conversations with the disciples, in which what Christ says refers only to the disciples and cannot refer to other people.

Then answered Peter and said unto him, Behold we have forsaken all, and followed thee; what shall we have therefore?

And Jesus said unto them, Verily I say unto you, That ye which have followed me, in the regeneration when the Son of man shall sit in the throne of his glory, ye also shall sit upon twelve thrones, judging the twelve tribes of Israel.

---

[11] " Nothing can be stronger than the language of the Fathers of the Church down to the fifth century on the care with which the creed was to be kept a secret. It was to be preserved in the memory only. The name Symbolum is used for it, of which the most probable explanation is that it meant a password whereby Christians recognised each other. St. Augustine says: ' You must not write down anything about the creed because God said, " I will put my law in their hearts and in their minds I will write it." Therefore the Creed is learned by hearing and is not written on tablets or on any material substance but in the heart.'

" It is therefore not surprising that there is no specimen of a creed until the end of the second century, and really the most ancient public written creed is about the end of the third century." (Extracted from *The History of the Creeds*, by J. R. Lumby, D.D. (Deighton Bell & Co.), 1887, pp. 2 and 3.)

And every one that hath forsaken houses, or brethren, or sisters, or father, or mother, or wife, or children, or lands, for my name's sake, shall receive an hundredfold, and shall inherit everlasting life.

But many that are first shall be last; and the last shall be first (Matt. 19. 27–30).

It is also to the disciples that the beginning of the next chapter, that is, the parable of the labourers in the vineyard, refers. The parable loses all its meaning if applied to all people.

For the kingdom of heaven is like unto a man that is an householder, which went out early in the morning to hire labourers into his vineyard.

And when he had agreed with the labourers for a penny a day, he sent them into his vineyard.

And he went out about the third hour, and saw others standing idle in the market place,

And said unto them, Go ye also into the vineyard, and whatsoever is right I will give you. And they went their way.

Again he went out about the sixth and ninth hour, and did likewise.

And about the eleventh hour he went out, and found others standing idle, and saith unto them, Why stand ye here all the day idle?

They say unto him, Because no man hath hired us. He saith unto them, Go ye also into the vineyard; and whatsoever is right, that shall ye receive.

So when even was come, the lord of the vineyard saith unto his steward, Call the labourers, and give them their hire, beginning from the last unto the first.

And when they came that were hired about the eleventh hour, they received every man a penny.

But when the first came, they supposed that they should have received more; and they likewise received every man a penny.

And when they had received it, they murmured against the goodman of the house.

Saying, These last have wrought but one hour, and thou hast made them equal unto us, which have borne the burden and heat of the day.

But he answered one of them, and said, Friend, I do thee no wrong: didst not thou agree with me for a penny?

Take that thine is, and go thy way: I will give unto this last, even as unto thee.

Is it not lawful for me to do what I will with mine own? Is thine eye evil, because I am good?

So the last shall be first, and the first last: for many be called, but few chosen (Matt. 20. 1–16).

Further, there is an interesting passage in St. Luke's Gospel explaining that the disciples should not expect special reward for what they are doing. It is *their duty* to do it.

But which of you, having a servant plowing or feeding cattle, will say unto him by and by, when he is come from the field, Go and sit down to meat?

And will not rather say unto him, Make ready wherewith I may sup, and

gird thyself, and serve me, till I have eaten and drunken; and afterward thou
shalt eat and drink?

Doth he thank that servant because he did the things that were commanded
him? I trow not.

So likewise ye, when ye have done all those things which are commanded
you, say, We are unprofitable servants: we have done that which was our duty
to do (Luke 17. 7–10).

All these passages refer only to the " disciples." Having explained whom
he is addressing, Jesus in the following passages establishes his own position
in relation to the " Law," that is, to those principles of esotericism which
were already known before from the teachings of the prophets:

Think not that I am come to destroy the law, or the prophets: I am not come
to destroy, but to fulfil (Matt. 5. 17).

These words have another meaning. Christ very definitely emphasised
that he was not a social reformer and that it was not his aim to change old
laws or to point out weak features in them. On the contrary he often stressed
and intensified them, that is, found the Old Testament requirements insufficient, as relating to the outward side alone.

In some cases rules for disciples were created in this way. Such, for
instance, are the passages:

Ye have heard that it was said by them of old time, Thou shalt not commit
adultery:

But I say unto you, That whosoever looketh on a woman to lust after her
hath committed adultery with her already in his heart (Matt. 5. 27, 28).

This means of course that the disciples could never justify themselves
by being formally innocent in something when they were inwardly guilty.

In other cases Jesus, in commenting on old laws, simply repeated or again
stressed life-precepts, such for instance as the precepts as to divorce, which
really had no relation to his teaching, except as indications of the necessity
for inner truth and the insufficiency of outward truth.

It hath been said, Whosoever shall put away his wife, let him give her a
writing of divorcement:

But I say unto you, That whosoever shall put away his wife, saving for the
cause of fornication, causeth her to commit adultery: and whosoever shall marry
her that is divorced committeth adultery (Matt. 5. 31, 32).

The aim in this case was to make out of these precepts, together with
the rules for the disciples, a " context " which would allow Jesus to say what
he intended and what could not be said without a certain introduction.
Thus the passages quoted above, both those which constitute rules for the
disciples and those which constitute precepts as to divorce, are necessary
in the Gospels only in order to introduce the following two verses, and at
the same time partly to distract attention from these verses.

And if thy right eye offend thee, pluck it out, and cast it from thee: for it is profitable for thee that one of thy members should perish, and not that thy whole body should be cast into hell.

And if thy right hand offend thee, cut it off, and cast it from thee: for it is profitable for thee that one of thy members should perish, and not that thy whole body should be cast into hell (Matt. 5. 29, 30).

These two verses, together with one verse from the 19th chapter of St. Matthew, have probably created more misunderstanding than all the Gospels taken together. And they actually contain dozens of possibilities of wrong interpretation. For the right *psychological* understanding of them they must first of all be entirely separated from the *body* and from *sex*. They refer to different "I"s, to different personalities, of man. At the same time they have another, occult or esoteric, meaning, of which I will speak later, in the chapter "Sex and Evolution." The disciples could have understood the meaning of these words. But in the Gospels they certainly remained totally incomprehensible. The presence in the Gospels of the precepts as to divorce was also never understood. These precepts entered into the text of the New Testament and aroused very numerous comments as the genuine words of Christ. The Apostle Paul and succeeding preachers of the new religion based whole codes of law on these passages, entirely refusing to see that these passages were only screens and could not have an independent meaning in Christ's teaching.

At the same time Christ says that to fulfil the law is not sufficient for the disciples. They are subject to a far more rigid discipline, based on far subtler principles.

That except your righteousness shall exceed the righteousness of the scribes and Pharisees, ye shall in no case enter into the kingdom of heaven.

Ye have heard that it was said by them of old time, Thou shalt not kill; and whosoever shall kill shall be in danger of the judgment:

But I say unto you, That whosoever is angry with his brother without a cause shall be in danger of the judgment: and whosoever shall say to his brother, Raca, shall be in danger of the council: but whosoever shall say, Thou fool, shall be in danger of hell fire.

Therefore if thou bring thy gift to the altar, and there rememberest that thy brother hath aught against thee;

Leave there thy gift before the altar, and go thy way; first be reconciled to thy brother, and then come and offer thy gift (Matt. 5. 20–24).

After this follow the most perplexing and difficult passages in the Gospels, because these passages can be understood rightly only in connection with the esoteric idea. But ordinarily they are understood as general moral rules, constituting what is considered to be Christian morality and Christian virtue. At the same time all men's conduct contradicts these rules. Men cannot fulfil these rules and even cannot understand them. The result is an enormous amount of deceit and self-deceit. Christian teachings are based on the Gospels, but the whole order and structure of the life of Christian peoples goes against the Gospels.

And it is characteristic in this case that all this hypocrisy and all this lying are quite useless. Christ never taught *all men* not to resist evil, to turn the left cheek when they are smitten on the right, and to give their cloaks to those who want to take away their coats. These passages in no way constitute general moral rules, and they are not a code of Christian virtues. They are *rules for the disciples*, and not general rules of conduct. The true meaning of these rules can be explained only in an occult school. And the key to this meaning is in the words:

Be ye therefore perfect, even as your Father which is in heaven is perfect (Matt. 5. 48).

Further on follow the explanations:

Ye have heard that it hath been said, An eye for an eye, and a tooth for a tooth:

But I say unto you, That ye resist not evil: but whosoever shall smite thee on thy right cheek, turn to him the other also.

And if any man will sue thee at the law, and take away thy coat, let him have thy cloak also.

Give to him that asketh thee, and from him that would borrow of thee turn not thou away.

Ye have heard that it hath been said, Thou shalt love thy neighbour, and hate thine enemy.

But I say unto you, Love your enemies, bless them that curse you, do good to them that hate you, and pray for them which despitefully use you, and persecute you;

That ye may be the children of your Father which is in heaven; for he maketh his sun to rise on the evil and on the good, and sendeth rain on the just and on the unjust.

For if ye love them which love you, what reward have ye? do not even the publicans the same?

Be ye therefore perfect, even as your Father which is in heaven is perfect (Matt. 5. 38–40, 42–46, 48).

Each of these passages forms the content of a special, complex and practical teaching. These practical teachings, taken together, constitute an occult or esoteric system of self-training and self-education based on principles unknown outside occult schools.

Nothing can be more useless and more naïve than an endeavour to understand their content without adequate instruction.

After this comes the prayer given by Christ, which sums up the whole content of the Gospel teaching and can be regarded as a synopsis of it, the Lord's Prayer. The distortions in the text of this prayer have already been mentioned. The origin of the prayer is unknown, but in Plato's *Second Alcibiades* Socrates quotes a prayer, which very much resembles the Lord's

Prayer and is most probably the original form of the Lord's Prayer. This prayer is thought to be of Pythagorean origin.

Zeus the King, give us all that is good whether we ask for it or not, but command all that is evil to leave us even when we ask it of thee.[12]

The likeness is so obvious that it requires no comment.

This prayer quoted by Socrates explains an incomprehensible point in the Lord's Prayer, namely, the word " but " after the words " lead us not into temptation, *but* deliver us from evil." This *but* points to a continuation of the phrase which had existed before but which is missing from the Gospel prayer. This omitted continuation, " even when we ask them (evil things) of thee," explains " but " in the preceding sentence.

Afterwards follow the inner rules, again for the disciples, the rules which *cannot* refer to all people.

Therefore I say unto you, Take no thought for your life, what ye shall eat, or what ye shall drink, nor yet for your body, what ye shall put on. Is not the life more than meat, and the body than raiment?

Behold the fowls of the air: for they sow not, neither do they reap, nor gather into barns; yet your heavenly Father feedeth them. Are ye not much better than they?

Which of you by taking thought can add one cubit unto his stature?

And why take ye thought for raiment? Consider the lilies of the field, how they grow; they toil not, neither do they spin:

And yet I say unto you, That even Solomon in all his glory was not arrayed like one of these.

Wherefore, if God so clothe the grass of the field, which to-day is, and to-morrow is cast into the oven, shall he not much more clothe you, O ye of little faith?

Therefore take no thought, saying, What shall we eat? or, What shall we drink? or, Wherewithal shall we be clothed?

(For after all these things do the Gentiles seek:) for your heavenly Father knoweth that ye have need of all these things.

But seek ye first the kingdom of God, and his righteousness; and all these things shall be added unto you.

Take therefore no thought for the morrow: for the morrow shall take thought for the things of itself. Sufficient unto the day is the evil thereof (Matt. 6. 25–34).

Further on come the rules governing the relations of the " disciples " to one another, again having no relation to *all men*.

Judge not, that ye be not judged.

For with what judgment ye judge, ye shall be judged: and with what measure ye mete, it shall be measured to you again.

And why beholdest thou the mote that is in thy brother's eye, but considerest not the beam that is in thine own eye?

---

[12] Ζεῦ βασιλεῦ, τὰ μὲν ἐσθλά, φησί, καὶ εὐχομένοις καὶ ἀνεύκτοις ἄμμι, δίδου, τὰ δὲ δεινὰ καὶ εὐχομένοις ἀπαλέξειν κελεύει (Plato, *Alcibiades II*, 143Α).

Or how wilt thou say to thy brother, Let me pull out the mote out of thine eye; and, behold, a beam is in thine own eye?

Thou hypocrite, first cast out the beam out of thine own eye; and then shalt thou see clearly to cast out the mote out of thy brother's eye (Matt. 7. 1–5).

The general tendency of the usual interpretations, again, is to regard these passages as rules of Christian morality and at the same time to take them as an unattainable ideal.

But Christ was much more practical; he did not teach impracticable things. The rules that he gave were meant to be carried out, but not by all, only by those to whom the carrying out of them could bring benefit and *who were able to carry them out.*

There is an interesting similarity between certain very well-known passages in the Gospels and certain passages in Buddhist books.

For instance, in *The Buddhist Catechism* there are the following words:

The fault of others is easily perceived but that of oneself is difficult to perceive; a man winnows his neighbour's faults like chaff, but his own fault he hides, as a cheat hides the bad die from the gambler.[13]

In the 9th chapter of St. Matthew the general direction of occult work and its basic principles are spoken of. The first of them is that people must themselves become aware of what they need. Until people have felt a need for esotericism, it cannot be useful for them and cannot exist for them.

They that be whole need not a physician, but they that are sick (Matt. 9. 12).

Then follow very significant words:

But go ye and learn what that meaneth, I will have mercy, and not sacrifice: for I am not come to call the righteous, but sinners to repentance (Matt. 9. 13).

And in another place Jesus says:

But if ye had known what this meaneth, I will have mercy, and not sacrifice, ye would not have condemned the guiltless (Matt. 12. 7).

The ordinary interpretations are very far from the true meaning of these passages. The cause of this lies in the fact that we do not understand what " mercy " means, that is, we do not understand what the word means which is translated into European languages as mercy, miséricorde, Barmherzigkeit. This word has some quite different meaning which eludes us. But the etymology of the Russian word милость, if we derive it from the word милый (as слабость from слабый and хилость from хилый), gives some idea of the possible correct meaning of this word and of passages in which it occurs. The word милый cannot be fully translated into English. Very often it means *darling*. If we could coin the word " *darlingness* " it would

---

13 *The Buddhist Catechism* (1915), p. 49, by Henry S. Olcott.

be very near to милость, i.e. to the word translated as *mercy*. Further, the following passages refer to occult rules:

At the same time came the disciples unto Jesus, saying, Who is the greatest in the kingdom of heaven?
And Jesus called a little child unto him, and set him in the midst of them.
And said Verily I say unto you, Except ye be converted, and become as little children, ye shall not enter into the kingdom of heaven (Matt. 18. 1–3).

The following passages have very great occult meaning. But they refer to *principles*, and not to rules.

Then were there brought unto him little children, that he should put his hands on them, and pray: and the disciples rebuked them.
But Jesus said, Suffer little children, and forbid them not, to come unto me: for of such is the kingdom of heaven (Matt. 19. 13, 14).

Passages referring to children are repeated in the other Gospels.

And he sat down, and called the twelve, and saith unto them, if any man desire to be first, the same shall be last of all, and servant of all.
And he took a child, and set him in the midst of them: and when he had taken him in his arms, he said unto them,
Whosoever shall receive one of such children in my name, receiveth me: and whosoever shall receive me, receiveth not me, but him that sent me (Mark 9. 35–37).
And they brought unto him also infants, that he would touch them: but when his disciples saw it, they rebuked them.
But Jesus called them unto him, and said, Suffer little children to come unto me, and forbid them not: for of such is the kingdom of God. Verily I say unto you, Whosoever shall not receive the kingdom of God as a little child shall in no wise enter therein (Luke 18. 15–17).

All these passages are full of the deepest meaning, but again they are meant only for the disciples. On the path of school work a man grown-up and rich in experience must very soon become as a child. He must accept the authority of other men who know more than he does. He must trust them and obey them, and hope for their help. He must understand that alone, without their guidance, he can do nothing. He must feel a child in relation to them. He must tell them the whole truth and never conceal anything from them. He must understand that he must not judge them. And he must use all his powers and all his endeavours for becoming able to help them. Unless a man passes through this stage, unless he temporarily becomes as a child, unless he sacrifices the results of his life-experience, he will never enter the inner circle, that is, the " Kingdom of Heaven." For Christ the " child " was a symbol of the *disciple*.
The relation of disciple to teacher is the relation of a *son* to a *father* and of a child to a grown-up man. In this connection the fact that Christ always called himself *son* and called God *father* acquires new significance.

The disciples of Jesus often argued among themselves. One of the constant subjects of their conversations was: which of them was the greatest; and Jesus always condemned these disputes from the point of view of occult principles and rules.

Ye know that the princes of the Gentiles exercise dominion over them, and they that are great exercise authority upon them.
But it shall not be so among you: but whosoever will be great among you, let him be your minister (Matt. 20. 25, 26).

Sometimes these disputes as to who was the greatest took on a truly tragic character. Once Jesus spoke to his disciples of his forthcoming death and resurrection.

And they departed thence, and passed through Galilee; and he would not that any man should know it.
For he taught his disciples, and said unto them, The Son of man is delivered into the hands of men, and they shall kill him; and after that he is killed, he shall rise the third day.
But they understood not that saying, and were afraid to ask him.
And he came to Capernaum: and being in the house he asked them, What was it that ye disputed among yourselves by the way?
But they held their peace: for by the way they had disputed among themselves, who should be the greatest (Mark 9. 30–34).

In these last words is felt the most tragic feature of the Gospel drama, whether it was enacted or real — the failure of the disciples to understand Jesus, their naïve behaviour in relation to him and their much " too human " attitude towards each other. " Who is greatest? "

In the Gospel of St. Luke there is an interesting explanation of the word " neighbour " which is full of occult meaning. This word is usually taken in a wrong meaning, as *any man*, or as he with whom one has to do. This sentimental interpretation of the word " neighbour " is very far from the Gospel meaning.

And behold, a certain lawyer stood up, and tempted him, saying, Master, what shall I do to inherit eternal life?
He said unto him, What is written in the law? How readest thou?
And he answering said, Thou shalt love the Lord thy God with all thy heart, and with all thy soul, and with all thy strength, and with all thy mind; and thy neighbour as thyself.
And he said unto him, Thou hast answered right: this do, and thou shalt live.
But he, willing to justify himself, said unto Jesus, And who is my neighbour?
And Jesus answering said, A certain man went down from Jerusalem to Jericho, and fell among thieves, which stripped him of his raiment, and wounded him, and departed, leaving him half dead.

And by chance there came down a certain priest that way: and when he saw him, he passed by on the other side.

And likewise a Levite, when he was at the place, came and looked on him, and passed by on the other side.

But a certain Samaritan, as he journeyed, came where he was: and when he saw him, he had compassion on him,

And went to him, and bound up his wounds, pouring in oil and wine, and set him on his own beast, and brought him to an inn, and took care of him.

And on the morrow when he departed, he took out two pence, and gave them to the host, and said unto him, Take care of him; and whatsoever thou spendest more, when I come again, I will repay thee.

Which now of these three, thinkest thou, was neighbour unto him that fell among the thieves?

And he said, He that showed mercy on him. Then said Jesus unto him, Go, and do thou likewise (Luke 10. 25–37).

The parable of the " good Samaritan " shows that " neighbour " is not "any man " as it is ordinarily interpreted in sentimental Christianity. The thieves who robbed and wounded him, the priest who having seen him passed by on the other side, the Levite who came and looked on him and also passed by, are most certainly not " neighbours" to the man who was helped by the Samaritan. *The Samaritan became his neighbour by helping him.* If he also had passed by, he, just like the others, would not have been his neighbour. From the esoteric point of view a man's neighbours are those who help him or may help him in his striving either to know esoteric truths or to approach esoteric work.

Side by side with the line of occult rules in the New Testament can be seen the line of unmerciful condemnation of pseudo-religion.

Ye hypocrites, well did Esaias prophesy of you, saying, This people draweth nigh unto me with their mouth, and honoureth me with their lips; but their heart is far from me (Matt. 15. 7, 8).

Then there follow a number of biting and sarcastic remarks which unfortunately are as alive in our times as they were in the time of Christ:

Let them alone: they be blind leaders of the blind. And if the blind lead the blind, both shall fall into the ditch (Matt. 15. 14).

After a very caustic conversation with the Pharisees and Sadducees Jesus says:

Take heed and beware of the leaven of the Pharisees and of the Sadducees (Matt. 16. 6).

But this warning was forgotten almost before Christ died. In St. Luke the same warning is given, only still more clearly:

Beware ye of the leaven of the Pharisees, which is hypocrisy (Luke 12. 1).

This is followed by a whole chapter on pseudo-religion which shows all its features, manifestations, effects and results.

Then spake Jesus to the multitude, and to his disciples, saying, The scribes and the Pharisees sit in Moses' seat: All therefore whatsoever they bid you observe, that observe and do; but do ye not after their works: for they say, and do not.

For they bind heavy burdens and grievous to be borne, and lay them on men's shoulders; but they themselves will not move them with one of their fingers.

But all their works they do for to be seen of men: they make broad their phylacteries, and enlarge the borders of their garments,

And love the uppermost rooms at feasts, and the chief seats in the synagogues,

And greetings in the markets, and to be called of men, Rabbi, Rabbi.

But be ye not called Rabbi: for one is your Master, even Christ; and all ye are brethren.

And call no man your father upon the earth: for one is your Father, which is in heaven.

Neither be ye called masters: for one is your Master, even Christ.

But he that is greatest among you shall be your servant.

And whosoever shall exalt himself shall be abased; and he that shall humble himself shall be exalted.

But woe unto you, scribes and Pharisees, hypocrites! for ye shut up the kingdom of heaven against men: for ye neither go in yourselves, neither suffer ye them that are entering to go in.

Woe unto you, scribes and Pharisees, hypocrites! for ye devour widows' houses and for a pretence make long prayer: therefore ye shall receive the greater damnation.

Woe unto you, scribes and Pharisees, hypocrites! for ye compass sea and land to make one proselyte, and when he is made, ye make him twofold more the child of hell than yourselves.

. . . .

Woe unto you, scribes and Pharisees, hypocrites! for ye pay tithe of mint and anise and cummin, and have omitted the weightier matters of the law, judgment, mercy, and faith: these ought ye to have done, and not to leave the other undone.

Ye blind guides, which strain at a gnat, and swallow a camel.

Woe unto you, scribes and Pharisees, hypocrites! for ye make clean the outside of the cup and of the platter, but within they are full of extortion and excess.

Thou blind Pharisee, cleanse first that which is within the cup and platter, that the outside of them may be clean also.

Woe unto you, scribes and Pharisees, hypocrites! for ye are like whited sepulchres, which indeed appear beautiful outward, but are within full of dead men's bones, and of all uncleanness.

Even so ye also outwardly appear righteous unto men, but within ye are full of hypocrisy and iniquity.

Woe unto you, scribes and Pharisees, hypocrites! because ye build the tombs of the prophets, and garnish the sepulchres of the righteous,

And say, If we had been in the days of our fathers, we would not have been partakers with them in the blood of the prophets.

Wherefore ye be witnesses unto yourselves, that ye are the children of them which killed the prophets.

Fill ye up then the measure of your fathers.

Ye serpents, ye generation of vipers, how can ye escape the damnation of hell?

Wherefore, behold, I send unto you prophets, and wise men, and scribes: and some of them ye shall kill and crucify; and some of them ye shall scourge in your synagogues, and persecute them from city to city (Matt. 23. 1–15, 23–24).

In another place are found other remarkable words connected with the above:

Woe unto you, lawyers! for ye have taken away the key of knowledge: ye entered not in yourselves, and them that were entering in ye hindered (Luke 11. 52).

What is most striking in the story of Jesus is that his teaching, after all that he said, should have become, like all other teachings in the world, the source of pseudo-religions.

The "scribes" and "Pharisees" have appropriated his teaching and in his name continue to do exactly what they did before.

The crucifixion of Christ is a symbol. It occurs without cessation always and everywhere. This would have to be considered the most tragic part of the story of Christ, if it were not possible to suppose that it also entered into the general plan, and that the capacity of men to distort and adapt everything to their own level was calculated and weighed.

This distortion of the teaching is spoken of in the Gospels. According to the Gospel terminology this is "offence."

But whoso shall offend one of these little ones which believe in me, it were better for him that a millstone were hanged about his neck, and that he were drowned in the depth of the sea.

Woe unto the world because of offences! for it must needs be that offences come; but woe to that man by whom the offence cometh [14] (Matt. 18. 6, 7).

The "offence," that is, "seduction" or "corruption," is certainly first of all the distortion of esoteric truths, the distortion of the teachings given to people, against which above all Christ revolted and against which he especially struggled.

Many questions and many misunderstandings usually arise from the parable of the *unjust steward*, in the 16th chapter of St. Luke.

---

[14] The word "offence" is a translation of the Greek word σκάνδαλον; in Church-Slavonic and in Russian this word is translated as "seduction," which is nearer to the meaning of the Greek word. Other possible translations are: "corruption," "leading astray," "ensnaring." So in order to understand the English text it is necessary to replace the word "offence" by the word "seduction" or "corruption," and "offend" by "seduce" or "corrupt." The meaning then becomes clear.

And he said also unto his disciples, There was a certain rich man, which had a steward; and the same was accused unto him that he had wasted his goods.

And he called him, and said unto him, How is it that I hear this of thee? give an account of thy stewardship; for thou mayest be no longer steward.

Then the steward said within himself, What shall I do? for my lord taketh away from me the stewardship: I cannot dig; to beg I am ashamed.

I am resolved what to do, that, when I am put out of the stewardship, they may receive me into their houses.

So he called every one of his lord's debtors unto him, and said unto the first, How much owest thou unto my lord?

And he said, An hundred measures of oil. And he said unto him, Take thy bill, and sit down quickly, and write fifty.

Then said he to another, And how much owest thou? And he said, An hundred measures of wheat. And he said unto him, Take thy bill, and write fourscore.

And the lord commended the unjust steward, because he had done wisely: for the children of this world are in their generation wiser than the children of light.

And I say unto you, Make to yourselves friends of the mammon of unrighteousness; that, when ye fail, they may receive you into everlasting habitations.

He that is faithful in that which is least is faithful also in much: and he that is unjust in the least is unjust also in much.

If therefore ye have not been faithful in the unrighteous mammon, who will commit to your trust the true riches?

And if ye have not been faithful in that which is another man's, who shall give you that which is your own? (Luke 16. 1–12).

How is this parable to be understood? This question raises a whole series of other questions in regard to the interpretation of Gospel passages in general. Without going into details, it can be said that the understanding of difficult passages may be based sometimes on passages adjoining them, or on passages near to them in meaning, though far removed from them in the text; sometimes on the understanding of the "line of thought" to which they belong; and sometimes on passages which express the obverse side of the idea and often seem to have no logical connection with the first.

In the present instance with regard to the parable of the unjust steward it can be said at once that it relates to occult principles, that is, to rules of esoteric work. But this is not sufficient for the understanding of it. There is something strange in this demand for falsehood, demand for deceit.

This demand only begins to be comprehensible when we consider the nature of the falsehoods that are demanded. The steward *cuts down* the debts of his lord's debtors, "forgives" them a part of their debts, and for this his lord afterwards praises him.

Is not this *forgiveness of sins?* In the passage immediately following the Lord's Prayer, Jesus says:

For if ye forgive men their trespasses, your heavenly Father will also forgive you:

But if ye forgive not men their trespasses, neither will your Father forgive your trespasses (Matt. 6. 14, 15).

Usually these passages are understood as advice to people to forgive those who sin *against them*. But actually this is not said at all. What is said is simply " forgive people their sins." And if we take the passage literally as it is written, the parable of the unjust steward begins to be more comprehensible. It is recommended in this parable to forgive people their sins, *not against us*, but all their sins generally, whatever they may be.

The question may arise as to how we can forgive the sins of other people, sins which have no relation to ourselves. The parable of the unjust steward gives the answer to this.

We can do it by means of a certain illegal practice, by means of a falsification of " bills," that is, by means of a certain intentional alteration of that which we see. In other words, we can, as it were, forgive other people their sins by representing them to ourselves as better than they really are.

This is a form of falsehood which not only is not condemned but is actually approved in the Gospel teaching. By means of such a falsehood a man insures himself against certain dangers, " acquires friends," and *on the strength of this falsehood* proves deserving of confidence.

A very interesting development of the same idea, though without reference to the parable of the unjust steward, can be found in St. Paul's Epistles. In reality many of his paradoxical statements are an expression of this idea. Paul understood that " forgiveness of sins " will not bring any benefit to the " lord's debtors," though it brings benefit to him who *sincerely* forgives them. In exactly the same way " love of enemies " will not bring benefit to enemies, but on the contrary will be the most cruel revenge.

Therefore if thine enemy hunger, feed him; if he thirst, give him drink: for in so doing thou shalt heap coals of fire on his head (Rom. 12. 20).

The difficulty is that it must be *sincere* love. If a man " loves his enemies " in order to heap coals of fire on their heads, he will certainly heap coals on his own head.

The idea of the parable of the unjust steward, that is, the idea of the benefit of seeing things as better than they are, enters also into Paul's well-known affirmations as to " power " and " rulers."

Let every soul be subject unto the higher powers. For there is no power but of God: the powers that be are ordained of God.

Whosoever therefore resisteth the power, resisteth the ordinance of God: and they that resist shall receive to themselves damnation.

For rulers are not a terror to good works, but to the evil. Wilt thou then not be afraid of the power? do that which is good, and thou shalt have praise of the same:

For he is the minister of God to thee for good. But if thou do that which is evil, be afraid; for he beareth not the sword in vain: for he is the minister of God, a revenger to execute wrath upon him that doeth evil.

Wherefore ye must needs be subject, not only for wrath, but also for conscience sake.

But for this cause pay ye tribute also: for they are God's ministers, attending continually upon this very thing.

Render therefore to all their dues: tribute to whom tribute is due; custom to whom custom; fear to whom fear; honour to whom honour (Rom. 13. 1–7).

Jesus also said once: " Render therefore unto Cæsar the things which are Cæsar's." But he never said that Cæsar is of God. Here the difference between Christ and Paul, between that which is esoteric and that which, though very high, is human, becomes particularly clear. In the idea of the parable of the unjust steward there is no *self-suggestion*. Paul introduces self-suggestion; his followers were expected to believe in " falsified bills."

The meaning of the parable of the unjust steward becomes still clearer if we find the passages which include the obverse side of the same idea.

These are the passages speaking of the blasphemy against the Holy Ghost. These passages include the obverse side of the idea expressed in the parable of the unjust steward, because they speak not of what people may *acquire*, but of what people may *lose* and in what way.

Wherefore I say unto you, All manner of sin and blasphemy shall be forgiven unto men: but the blasphemy against the Holy Ghost shall not be forgiven unto men.

And whosoever speaketh a word against the Son of man, it shall be forgiven him: but whosoever speaketh against the Holy Ghost, it shall not be forgiven him, neither in this world, neither in the world to come (Matt. 12. 31, 32).

Verily I say unto you, All sins shall be forgiven unto the sons of men, and blasphemies wherewith soever they shall blaspheme:

But he that shall blaspheme against the Holy Ghost hath never forgiveness, but is in danger of eternal damnation (Mark 3. 28, 29).

And whosoever shall speak a word against the Son of man, it shall be forgiven him; but unto him that blasphemeth against the Holy Ghost it shall not be forgiven (Luke 12. 10).

A good man out of the good treasure of the heart bringeth forth good things: and an evil man out of the evil treasure bringeth forth evil things.

But I say unto you, That every idle word that men shall speak, they shall give account thereof in the day of judgment (Matt. 12. 35, 36).

What is the connection between these passages and the parable of the unjust steward? What is meant by the blasphemy against the Holy Ghost? Why is this blasphemy not to be forgiven, and what is the Holy Ghost?

The Holy Ghost is that which is *good* in everything. In every object, in every man, in every event, there is something good, not in a philosophical and not in a mystical sense, but in the simplest, psychological and everyday sense. If a man does not see this good, if he condemns everything irrevocably, if he seeks and sees only the bad, if he is incapable of seeing the good in things and people — then this is the blasphemy against the Holy Ghost. There are different types of men. Some are capable of seeing the good even where there is very little of it. They are sometimes even inclined to exaggerate it to themselves. Others, on the contrary, are inclined to see everything worse than it is in reality, are incapable of seeing anything good. First of all, always and in everything, they find something bad, always begin with suspicion, with accusation, with calumny. This is the blasphemy against the Holy Ghost. This blasphemy *is not forgiven*; that means that it leaves a very deep trace on the inner nature of the man himself.

Usually in life people take slander too lightly, excuse it too easily in themselves and in others. Slander constitutes half their lives, fills half their interests. People slander without themselves noticing what they are doing and automatically they expect nothing but slander from others. They answer the slander of others with slander and strive only to forestall them. A particularly noticeable tendency to slander is called either a critical mind or wit. Men do not understand that even the usual everyday slander is the beginning of the blasphemy against the Holy Ghost. It is not for nothing that the *Devil* means *slanderer*. The passage in the Gospel, that they shall give account even of every idle word in the day of judgement, sounds so strange and incomprehensible to men because they do not understand that even a small slander is the beginning of the blasphemy against the Holy Ghost. They do not understand that even every idle word remains and that by slandering everything around them they may unintentionally touch something belonging to a different order of things and find themselves chained to the wheel of eternity in the rôle of a small and impotent slanderer.

Thus the idea of the slander which will not be forgiven to man relates even to ordinary life. Slander leaves a deeper trace on them than men think.

But slander has a special meaning in esoteric work, and Christ pointed to this meaning.

And whosoever speaketh a word against the Son of man, it shall be forgiven him: but whosoever speaketh against the Holy Ghost, it shall not be forgiven him, neither in this world, neither in the world to come.

These remarkable words mean that calumny and slander directed *against Christ personally* can be forgiven. But as the head of a school, as master of a school, he could not forgive slander directed against the school, against the idea of school work, against the idea of esotericism.

This form of *blasphemy against the Holy Ghost* remains with man for ever.

The parable of the unjust steward refers to the creation of the other, of the contrary, tendency, that is to say, the tendency to see the Holy Ghost or the " good " even where there is very little of it, and in this way to increase the good in oneself and liberate oneself from sins, that is from " evil."

Man finds what he looks for. Who looks for the evil finds the evil; who looks for the good, finds the good.

A good man out of the good treasure of the heart bringeth forth good things: and an evil man out of the evil treasure bringeth forth evil things.

At the same time nothing is more dangerous than to understand this idea of Christ's in a literal or sentimental sense, and to begin to see the " good " where it does not exist at all.

The idea that in every object, in every man and in every event there is something good is right only in relation to normal and natural manifestations. This idea cannot be equally right in relation to abnormal and unnatural manifestations. There can be no Holy Ghost in the blasphemy against the Holy Ghost; and there are things, people and events that are by their very nature the blasphemy against the Holy Ghost. Justification of them is the blasphemy against the Holy Ghost.

A great amount of evil in life occurs just because people, afraid of committing a sin or afraid of appearing not sufficiently charitable or not sufficiently broad-minded, justify what does not deserve justification. Christ was not sentimental, he was never afraid to tell an unpleasant truth, and he was not afraid to act. The expulsion of the money-changers from the temple is a most remarkable allegory, showing Christ's attitude towards " life," which tries to turn even the temple to its own ends.

And Jesus went into the temple of God, and cast out all them that sold and bought in the temple, and overthrew the tables of the moneychangers, and the seats of them that sold doves,
And said unto them, It is written, My house shall be called the house of prayer; but ye have made it a den of thieves (Matt. 21. 12, 13).

There remain to be mentioned two ideas, which are often associated with the Gospel teaching and which throw an equally wrong light both on principles and on Christ himself.

The first idea is that the Gospel teaching does not refer to earthly life, that Christ did not build anything upon earth, that the whole idea of Christianity is to prepare man for eternal life, for the life beyond the threshold of death.

And the second idea is that Christian teaching is too ideal for men and is therefore impracticable, that Christ was a poet and philosopher in his dreams, but that sober reality cannot dwell on these dreams and cannot seriously take them into consideration.

But both these ideas are wrong. Christ taught not for death, but for life, but his teaching never included and never could include *the whole of life*. In his words, especially in his parables, there continually appear many people who stand entirely outside his ideas: all kings, rich men, thieves, priests, Levites, servants of the rich, merchants, scribes and Pharisees, and so on. And this huge, absurd life, to which his teaching had no relation, was in his eyes the Mammon which one could not serve at the same time as God.

And Christ was never an unpractical " poet " or " philosopher." His teaching is not for all, but it is strictly practical in all its details. *It is practical first of all because it is not for all.* Many people are unable to take anything from his teaching but entirely false ideas, and to them Christ had nothing to say.

1911–1929

Chapter V

THE SYMBOLISM OF THE TAROT

I

IN occult or symbolic literature, that is to say, in the literature based on the recognition of the existence of hidden knowledge, there is one phenomenon of great interest.

This is the Tarot.

The Tarot is a pack of cards which is still used in southern Europe for card-playing and fortune-telling. It differs very little from ordinary playing cards, which are a reduced Tarot pack. It has the same Kings, Queens, Aces, tens, and so on.

The Tarot cards have been known since the end of the fourteenth century, when they already existed among the Spanish gipsies. They were the first cards that appeared in Europe.

There are several variations of the Tarot, consisting of different numbers of cards. It is considered that the most exact reproduction of the oldest Tarot is the so-called "Tarot of Marseilles."

This pack consists of 78 cards. Of these, 52 are ordinary playing cards with the addition of one "picture" card in each suit, namely the "Knight," which is placed between the Queen and the Knave. This makes 56 cards divided into four suits, two black and two red, named as follows: Wands (clubs), Cups (hearts), Swords (spades), and Pentacles or discs (diamonds).

There are in addition 22 numbered cards with special names which are outside the four suits.

1. The Juggler.
2. The High Priestess.
3. The Empress.
4. The Emperor.
5. The Hierophant.
6. Temptation.
7. The Chariot.
8. Justice.
9. The Hermit.
10. The Wheel of Fortune.
11. Strength.

12. The Hanged Man.
13. Death.
14. Temperance (Time).
15. The Devil.
16. The Tower.
17. The Star.
18. The Moon.
19. The Sun.
20. The Day of Judgement.
21. The World.
0. The Fool.

The pack of Tarot cards, according to the legend, represents an Egyptian hieroglyphic book, consisting of 78 tablets, which have come down to us in a miraculous manner.

It is known that in the library of Alexandria, besides papyri and parchments, there were many such books, consisting often of a great number of clay or wooden tablets.

With regard to the further history of the Tarot cards, it has been said that in the beginning they were medallions stamped with designs and numbers, later metallic plates, then leather cards, and finally paper cards.

Outwardly the Tarot is a pack of cards, but in its inner meaning it is something altogether different. It is a " book " of philosophical and psychological content, which can be read in many different ways.

I will give an example of a philosophical interpretation of the whole idea or general content of the *Book of the Tarot*, its metaphysical title, as it were, which will plainly show the reader that this " book " could not have been devised by the illiterate gipsies of the 14th century.

The Tarot is divided into three parts.

1st part — 21 numbered cards, from 1 to 21.

2nd part — one card numbered 0.

3rd part — 56 cards, i.e. four suits of 14 cards each.

The second part is a link between the first and the third, because all the 56 cards of the third part together are considered equal to the card numbered zero.[1]

Let us imagine the 21 cards of the first part laid out in the form of a triangle, with seven cards to each side; in the centre of the triangle a point represented by the zero card (the second part), and the triangle enclosed in a square consisting of 56 cards (the third part), 14 to each side of the square. Now we have a representation of the metaphysical relation between *God, Man and the Universe*, or between (1) the noumenal world (or objective world), (2) the psychic world of man, and (3) the phenomenal world (or subjective world), i.e. the physical world.

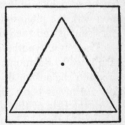

FIG. 4

The triangle is God (the Trinity) or the noumenal world.

The square (four elements) is the visible, physical or phenomenal world.

The point is the soul of man, and both worlds are reflected in man's soul.

The square is equal to the point. This means that all the visible world

---

[1] The French philosopher and mystic of the 18th century, Saint Martin (Le Philosophe Inconnu), called his principal book *Tableau Naturel des Rapports qui existent entre Dieu, l'Homme et l'Univers*. The book consists of 22 chapters representing commentaries on the 22 principal Tarot cards.

is contained in the consciousness of man, that is to say, is created in the soul of man and is his representation. And the soul of man is a point having no dimension in the centre of the triangle of the objective world.

It is clear that such an idea could not have appeared among ignorant people, and it is clear that the Tarot is more than a pack of playing and fortune-telling cards.

It is possible to express the idea of the Tarot also in the form of a triangle in which is enclosed a square (the material universe) in which is enclosed a point (man).

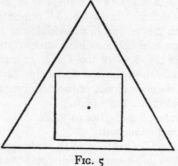

FIG. 5

It is very interesting to try to determine the aim, purpose and application of the book of the Tarot.

First of all it is necessary to observe that the Tarot is a " philosophical machine," which in its meaning and possible application has much in common with the philosophical machines that the philosophers of the Middle Ages sought and tried to invent.

There is a hypothesis according to which the invention of the Tarot is attributed to Raymond Lully, a philosopher and alchemist of the 13th century and the author of many mystical and occult books, who actually put forward in his book *Ars Magna* a scheme of a " philosophical machine." With the help of this machine it was possible to put questions and receive answers to them. The machine consisted of concentric circles with words designating the ideas of different worlds arranged on them in a certain order. When certain words were put in a definite position one in relation to the other for the formation of a question, other words gave the answer.

The Tarot has a great deal in common with this " machine." In its purpose it is a kind of philosophical abacus.

(*a*) It gives a possibility of *setting out* in different graphic forms (like the above-mentioned triangle, point and square) ideas which are difficult if not impossible to put into words.

(*b*) It is an instrument of the mind, an instrument which can serve for training the capacity for combination and so on.

(*c*) It is an appliance for exercising the mind, for accustoming it to new and wider concepts, to thinking in a world of higher dimensions, and to the understanding of symbols.

The system of the Tarot, in its deeper, wider and more varied sense, stands in the same relation to metaphysics and mysticism as a system of notation, decimal or other, stands in relation to mathematics. The Tarot may be only an attempt to create such a system, but even the attempt is interesting.

In order to become acquainted with the Tarot it is necessary to be familiar with the idea of the Cabala, Alchemy, Magic and Astrology.

According to the very probable opinion of several commentators on the Tarot, it is a synopsis of the Hermetic sciences with their various subdivisions, or an attempt at such a synopsis.

All these sciences constitute a single system of the psychological study of man in his relations to the world of noumena (to God, to the world of spirit) and to the world of phenomena (the visible physical world).

The letters of the Hebrew alphabet and the various allegories in the Cabala; the names of metals, acids and salts in alchemy; the names of planets and constellations in astrology; the names of good and evil spirits in magic — all these were but a conventional hidden language for psychological ideas.

Open study of psychology, especially in its wider sense, was impossible. Torture and the stake awaited investigators.

If we look still further into past ages we shall see still more fear of all attempts to study man. How was it possible amidst all the darkness, ignorance and superstition of those times to speak and act openly? The open study of psychology is under suspicion even in our time, which is considered enlightened.

The true essence of Hermetic sciences was therefore hidden beneath the symbols of Alchemy, Astrology and the Cabala. Of these, Alchemy took as its outer aim the preparation of gold, or the discovery of the elixir of life; Astrology and the Cabala, divination; and Magic, the subjugation of spirits. But when the true alchemist spoke of the search for gold, he spoke of the search for gold in the soul of man. And when he spoke of the elixir of life, he spoke of the search for eternal life and the ways to immortality. In these cases he called " *gold* " what in the Gospels is called the Kingdom of Heaven, and what in Buddhism is called Nirvana. When the true astrologer spoke of constellations and planets, he spoke of the constellations and planets in the soul of man, i.e. of the properties of the human soul and its relations to God and the world. When the true Cabalist spoke of the *Name of God* he searched for this Name in the soul of man and in Nature, and not in dead books, not in the Biblical text, as did the scholastic Cabalists. When the true Magician spoke of the subjugation of " spirits," elementals and the like to the will of man, he understood by this the subjugation to one single will of the different " I "s of man, his different desires and tendencies. The

Cabala, Alchemy, Astrology and Magic are parallel symbolical systems of psychology and metaphysics.

Oswald Wirth speaks in a very interesting way about Alchemy in one of his books: [2]

Alchemy in reality studies metaphysical metallurgy, i.e. the operations which Nature works in living beings; the deepest *science of life* was here hidden under strange symbols. . . .

But such immense ideas would burst brains that were too narrow. Not all alchemists were geniuses. Greed attracted to Alchemy men who were looking for gold, who were alien to any esotericism; they understood everything *literally*, and their follies often knew no bounds.

From this fantastic kitchen of vulgar charlatans came modern chemistry. But true philosophers, worthy of the name, lovers or friends of wisdom, carefully *separated the fine from the coarse, with caution and foresight*, as was required by the *Emerald Tablet* of Hermes Trismegistus; i.e. they rejected the meaning belonging to the dead letter and left for themselves only the inner spirit of the doctrine.

In our time we confound the wise with the foolish and reject entirely all that does not bear the official seal.

The study of the Name of God in its manifestations constitutes the basis of the Cabala. " Jehovah " is spelt in Hebrew with four letters, Yod, He, Vau and He. These four letters have been given a symbolical meaning. The first letter expresses the active principle, initiative; the second, the passive principle, inertia; the third, equilibrium, " form "; and the fourth, result or latent energy. The Cabalists affirm that every phenomenon and every object consists of these four principles, i.e. that every object and every phenomenon consists of the Divine Name. The study of this name (in Greek the Tetragrammaton or the word of four letters) and the finding of it in everything constitute the chief aim of Cabalistic philosophy.

What is the real meaning of this?

According to the Cabalists, the four principles permeate and compose each and every thing. Therefore, by finding these four principles in things and phenomena of quite different categories, between which he had previously seen nothing in common, a man begins to see the analogy between these things. And gradually he becomes convinced that everything in the world is constructed according to the same laws, according to the same plan. From a certain point of view the enriching of the intellect and its growth consist in the widening of its capacity for finding analogies. The study of the law of the four letters, or of the Name of Jehovah, can therefore constitute a means for widening consciousness. The idea is quite clear. If the Name of God is really in everything (if God is present in everything), then everything should be analogous to everything else, the smallest part should be analo-

---

[2] *L'imposition des mains et la médecine philosophale* (Paris, Chamuel éditeur, 1897), pp. 146–7.

gous to the whole, the speck of dust analogous to the Universe and all analogous to God. " As above, so below."

Speculative philosophy arrives at the conclusion that the world undoubtedly exists, but that our conception of the world is false. This means that the causes of our sensations which lie outside ourselves really exist, but that our conception of these causes is false. Or, to put it in another way, it means that the *world in itself*, i.e. the world by itself, without our perception of it, exists, but we do not know it and can never reach it, because all that is accessible to our study, i.e. the whole world of phenomena or manifestations, is *only our percept of the world*. We are surrounded by the wall of our own percepts and are unable to look over this wall into the real world.

The Cabala aims at studying the world as it is, the world in itself. The other "mystical" sciences have precisely the same object.

In Alchemy the four principles of which the world consists are called the four elements. These are fire, water, air and earth, which exactly correspond in their meaning to the four letters of the name of Jehovah.

In Magic the four elements correspond to the four classes of spirits; — spirits of fire, water, air and earth (elves, water-sprites, sylphs and gnomes).

In Astrology, the four elements correspond, very remotely, to the four cardinal points, the east, the south, the west and the north, which, in their turn, sometimes serve to designate various divisions of the human being.

In the Apocalypse they are the four beasts, one with the head of a bull, the second with the head of a lion, the third with the head of an eagle and the fourth with the head of a man.

And all these together are the Sphinx, the image of the four principles merged into one.

The Tarot is, as it were, a combination of the Cabala, Alchemy, Magic and Astrology.

The four principles of the four letters of the Name of God, or the four alchemical elements, or the four classes of spirits, or the four divisions of man (the four Apocalyptic beasts) correspond to the four suits of the Tarot: wands, cups, swords and pentacles.

Each suit, each side of the square which as a whole is equal to the point, represents one of the elements, or governs one of the four classes of spirits. Wands are fire or elves, cups are water or water-sprites, swords are air or sylphs and pentacles are earth or gnomes.

Moreover, in each suit the King stands for the first principle or fire, the Queen for the second principle or water, the Knight for the third principle or air, and the Page (Knave) for the fourth principle or earth.

The ace again signifies fire, the two — water, the three — air, the four — earth. Then the fourth principle, combining in itself the first three, becomes the beginning of a new square. The four becomes the first principle, the five

— the second, the six — the third, and the seven — the fourth. Further, the seven again is the first principle, the eight — the second, the nine — the third, and the ten — the fourth, thus completing the last square.

Further, the black suits (wands and swords) express active qualities, energy, will, initiative, and the red suits (cups and pentacles) express passive qualities and inertia. Then, the first two suits, wands and cups, signify good, that is, favourable conditions or friendly relations, and the last two, swords and pentacles, signify evil, that is, unfavourable conditions or hostile relations.

In this way each of the 56 cards signifies something active or passive, good or evil, arising either from man's will or coming to him from without. Further, the meanings of the cards are complicated in different ways by a combination of the symbolical meanings of the suits and the numbers. Altogether the 56 cards present, as it were, a complete picture of all the possibilities of the life of man. This is the principle on which is based the use of the Tarot for divination.

But the philosophical significance of the Tarot is incomplete without the 22 cards or the " Major Arcana." These cards have, first a numerical meaning, and then a very complicated symbolical one. Taken in their numerical aspect, the cards form equilateral triangles, squares and similar figures, which have different meanings, according to the cards composing them.

The literature devoted to the Tarot consists for the greater part in an interpretation of the symbolical pictures of the 22 cards. Many authors of mystical books have modelled their works on the plan of the Tarot. But their readers often do not even suspect this, as the Tarot is not always mentioned.

I have already referred to the book by the " Unknown Philosopher," Saint Martin, A *Natural Table of the Relations between God, Man and the Universe.*

It is precisely in the Tarot, says one of the modern followers of St. Martin, that the Unknown Philosopher has found the mysterious links connecting God, Man and the Universe.

Dogme et Rituel de la Haute Magie, by Eliphas Lévi (1853),[3] is also written on the plan of the Tarot. To each of the 22 cards Eliphas Lévi dedicated two chapters, one chapter in the first part and one chapter in the second part. Eliphas Lévi refers to the Tarot in his other books, *Histoire de la Magie, La Clef des Grands Mystères, La Grande Arcane,* and others.

The commentators of the Tarot always refer to the *History of Magic,* by Christian (in French, 1854). This book gives an astrological interpretation of the 56 cards.

---

[3] *Transcendental Magic, its Doctrine and Ritual,* by Eliphas Lévi. Translated, annotated and introduced by Arthur Edward Waite (William Rider & Son, London, 1923).

Further, there are books by Guaita with strange allegorical titles: *Au Seuil du Mystère, Le Temple de Satan,* and *La Clef de la Magie Noire.* The first of these books is an introduction, the second is dedicated to the first seven cards from 1 to 7 (of the 22), the third, to the second seven cards, while the fourth, which should have completed this detailed commentary on the Tarot, did not appear.

Interesting material for the study of the Tarot is given by the works of Oswald Wirth, who restored the Tarot cards and published besides several books dedicated to Hermetic and Masonic symbolism.

In English there are books by A. Waite, who gives short commentaries on the Tarot pack as printed in England and furnishes a small bibliographical index of works on the Tarot. Further certain material for the study of the Tarot is given by Bourgeat, Decrespe, Pickard and by the English translator of the Cabala, MacGregor Mathers.

The French occultist, " Dr. Papus," has two books specially devoted to the Tarot (*Tarot des Bohémiens* and *Tarot Divinatoire*). And in his other books also there are numerous references to and indications of the Tarot, although they are obscured by a great deal of cheap fantasy and pseudomysticism.

This list does not of course include all the literature relating to the Tarot. It must also be noted that the bibliography of the Tarot can never be complete, since the most valuable information and the keys to the understanding of the Tarot are to be found in works on Alchemy, Astrology and Mysticism in general, the authors of which may not even have thought of the Tarot or have not mentioned it. Thus, for instance, for the understanding of the picture of man, as presented by the Tarot, much is given by Gichtel's *Theosophia Practica* (17th century) and especially by the drawings in this book. Poisson's book, *Théories et Symboles des Alchimistes,* is useful for the understanding of the four symbols of the Tarot.

There are references to the Tarot in H. P. Blavatsky's books, both in the *Secret Doctrine* and in *Isis Unveiled,* and there are reasons for believing that Blavatsky attached great importance to the Tarot. In the theosophical publication which appeared during Blavatsky's life (*Theosophical Siftings*) there were two unsigned articles on the Tarot, in one of which much stress was laid on the phallic element contained in the Tarot.

But speaking generally of the literature on the Tarot, acquaintance with it is most disappointing, as is acquaintance with occult and especially theosophical literature, because all this literature promises too much in comparison with what it gives.

Each of the books mentioned contains something interesting about the Tarot. But side by side with valuable and interesting material they contain a great deal of rubbish, which is characteristic of all " occult " literature in general. Namely, there is first a purely scholastic search for the meaning in the letter, second, too hasty conclusions, covering with words what the author himself has not understood, skipping difficult problems, unfinished speculations, and third, unnecessary complexity and unsymmetrical constructions. The books of "Dr. Papus," who was in his time the most popular commentator on the Tarot, are particularly rich in all this.

Yet Papus himself says that all complexity points to the imperfection of a system. He says, "Nature is very synthetic in her manifestations, and simplicity lies at the base of her outwardly most intricate phenomena." This is certainly quite correct, but precisely this simplicity is lacking in all explanations of the system of the Tarot.

For this reason even a sufficiently thorough study of all these works does not carry a reader far towards the understanding of the system and symbolism of the Tarot, and gives no indication whatever as to the practical application of the Tarot as a key to metaphysics or psychology. All the authors who have written about the Tarot have exalted this system and called it the Universal Key, but have not shown how this key is to be used.

I will give here a few extracts from the works of authors who have attempted to explain and interpret the Tarot and its idea.

Eliphas Lévi says in his above-mentioned book, *Dogme et Rituel:* [4]

The universal key of magical works is that of all ancient religious dogmas — the key of the Kabalah and the Bible, the Little Key of Solomon.

Now, this Clavicle, regarded as lost for centuries, has been recovered by us, and we have been able to open the sepulchres of the ancient world, to make the dead speak, to behold the monuments of the past in all their splendour, to understand the enigmas of every sphinx and to penetrate all sanctuaries.

Among the ancients the use of this key was permitted to none but the high priests, and even so its secret was confined only to the flower of initiates. . . .

Now this was the key in question: a hieroglyphic and numeral alphabet, expressing by characters and numbers a series of universal and absolute ideas. . . .

The symbolical tetrad, represented in the Mysteries of Memphis and Thebes by the four forms of the sphinx — man, eagle, lion and bull — corresponded with the four elements of the old world (water, air, fire and earth). . . .

Now these four signs, with all their analogies, explain the one word hidden in all sanctuaries. . . . Moreover, the sacred word was not pronounced: it was spelt, and expressed in four words, which are the four sacred words — Jod He Vau He.

The Tarot is a truly philosophical machine, which keeps the mind from wandering, while leaving it initiative and liberty; it is mathematics applied to the Absolute, the alliance of the positive and the ideal, a lottery of thoughts as exact as numbers, perhaps the simplest and grandest conception of human genius.

An imprisoned person, with no other book than the Tarot, if he knew how to use it, could in a few years acquire universal knowledge and would be able to speak on all subjects with unequalled learning and inexhaustible eloquence.

---

[4] *Transcendental Magic, its Doctrine and Ritual*, pp. 462, 479, 480.

P. Christian in his *History of Magic* [5] describes (referring to Iamblichus) the ritual of initiation into the Egyptian Mysteries in which a rôle was played by pictures similar to the 22 Arcana of the Tarot.

The initiate sees a long gallery, supported by caryatides in the form of twenty-four sphinxes, twelve on each side. On each part of the wall between two sphinxes there are fresco paintings, representing mystical figures and symbols. These twenty-two pictures face one another in pairs. . . .

As he passes the twenty-two pictures of the gallery, the initiate receives instruction from the priest. . . .

Each *arcanum*, made visible and tangible by each of these pictures, is a formula of the law of human activity in its relation to spiritual and material forces, the combination of which produces the phenomena of life.

In this connection I must point out that in the Egyptian symbolism which is accessible for study there are actually *no traces of the 22 Tarot cards*. This being so, we have to accept the proposition of Christian on faith and to assume that, as he says, it refers to the " secret crypts in the temple of Osiris," of which no trace whatever has remained and with which those Egyptian monuments that have been preserved have little in common.

The same can be said about India. There is no trace of the 22 *Tarot cards*, i.e. the Major Arcana, in Indian paintings or sculpture.

Oswald Wirth, in his book *Le Symbolisme Hermétique*, [6] speaks of the language of the symbols in a very interesting way:

A symbol can always be studied from an infinite number of points of view; and each thinker has the right to discover in the symbol a new meaning corresponding to the logic of his own conceptions.

As a matter of fact symbols are precisely intended to awaken ideas sleeping in our consciousness. They arouse a thought by means of suggestion and thus cause the truth which lies hidden in the depths of our spirit to reveal itself.

In order that symbols could speak, it is essential that we should have in ourselves the germs of the ideas, the revelation of which constitutes the mission of the symbols. But no revelation whatever is possible if the mind is empty, sterile and inert.

For this reason symbols do not appeal to everyone, cannot speak to everyone. They especially elude minds which claim to be positive and which base their reasoning only on inert scientific and dogmatic formulæ. The practical utility of these formulæ cannot be contested, but from the philosophical point of view they represent only frozen thought, artificially limited, made immovable to such an extent, that it seems dead in comparison with the living thought, indefinite, complex and mobile, which is reflected in symbols.

It is perfectly clear that symbols are not created for expounding what are called scientific truths.

---

[5] *Histoire de la Magie du Monde Surnaturel et de la Fatalité à travers les temps et les peuples*, par P. Christian, pp. 112–113 (Paris, Furne, Jouvet & Cie, éditeurs).

[6] *Le Symbolisme Hermétique*, par O. Wirth, pp. 38–40 and 83 (Publications initiatiques).

By their very nature the symbols must remain elastic, vague and ambiguous, like the sayings of an oracle. Their rôle is to unveil mysteries, leaving the mind all its freedom.

Unlike despotic orthodoxies, a symbol favours independence. Only a symbol can deliver a man from the slavery of words and formulæ and allow him to attain to the possibility of thinking freely. It is impossible to avoid the use of symbols if one desires to penetrate into the secrets (mysteries), that is to say, into those truths which can so easily be transformed into monstrous delusions as soon as people attempt to express them in direct language without the help of symbolical allegories. The silence which was imposed on initiates finds its justification in this. Occult secrets require for their understanding an effort of the mind, they can illuminate the mind inwardly, but they cannot serve as a theme for rhetorical arguments. Occult knowledge cannot be transmitted either orally or in writing. It can only be acquired by deep meditation. It is necessary to penetrate deep into oneself in order to discover it. And those who seek it outside themselves are on the wrong path. It is in this sense that the words of Socrates " Know thyself " must be understood.

In the realm of symbolism one must not attempt to be too exact. Symbols correspond to ideas which by their very nature are difficult to embrace, and which are quite impossible to reduce to scholastic definitions.

Scholastics bring to the ultimate analysis only words, that is to say, something entirely artificial. By its very nature a word is an instrument of paradox. Any theme can be defended by means of argumentation. This is so because every discipline deals not with realities reaching our consciousness by themselves, but only with their oral representations, with the fantasies of our spirit which often allows itself to be deceived with this false coin of our thought.

Hermetic philosophy is distinguished by its being able to move away from words and to immerse itself in the contemplation of things taken by themselves, in their own essence.

And there is nothing surprising in the fact that under these conditions philosophy divided into two streams. One had its origin in the logic of Aristotle and maintained the possibility of arriving at truth by way of reasonings based on premises regarded as incontestable.

This was the official philosophy that was taught at (ordinary) schools, whence the term " scholastic."

The other philosophy followed another direction, always more or less occult, in the sense that it was always cloaked in mystery and passed on its teachings only under the cover of enigmas, allegories and symbols. Through Plato and Pythagoras this philosophy claimed to have come down from the Egyptian Hierophants and from the very founder of their science, Hermes Trismegistus, whence it was called " Hermetic."

The disciple of Hermes was silent, he never disputed nor did he try to convince any one about anything. Enclosed within himself, he was absorbed in deep meditation and finally by this means penetrated into the secrets of Nature. He earned the confidence of Isis and entered into relations with the true initiates. Gnosis opened to him the principles of the holy ancient sciences, from which Astrology, Magic and the Cabala were gradually formed.

These sciences officially called " dead " all refer to the same subject, to the discovery of hidden laws which govern the universe. And they differ from the official science of physics by their more mysterious and transcendental character. These sciences constitute the Hermetic philosophy.

This philosophy is further distinguished by the fact that it was never content to be purely speculative (theoretical). As a matter of fact, it always followed a practical aim, seeking for actual results; its problem was always concerned with which is called the Realisation of the Great Work.

In the book already mentioned (*L'imposition des mains*, pp. 140–1), Oswald Wirth writes on the same subject:

A special reason explains why theories which were so famous in the Middle Ages and down to the 18th century have lost credit in our eyes. We have lost the key to the language in which these theories were expressed. We have quite a different way of speaking. In past times people did not pretend to assume that they used strictly exact terms about everything. They considered that approximations were quite sufficient, because the pure truth was fatally inexpressible. The ideal truth will not allow itself to be confined to any formula. It follows from this that in a certain sense every word is a lie. The inner side of thought, its fundamental spirit, eludes us. This is the Deity, which continually reveals itself and which nevertheless allows itself to be seen only in its reflections. For this reason Moses could not see the face of Jehovah.

It follows from this that when it is necessary to express transcendental ideas one is forced to have recourse to figurative language. It is impossible to do without allegories and symbols. This is not at all a matter of choice, very often there is no other way of making oneself understood.

Pure thought cannot be transmitted, it is necessary to clothe it with something. But this clothing is always transparent for him who knows how to see.

Therefore Hermetism addresses itself to those thinkers who are compelled by an inner voice to go into the depths of all things and remains incomprehensible to those who stop at the external meaning of words.

S. Guaita says in his book, *Au Seuil du Mystère*:

To enclose all truth in spoken language, to express the highest occult mysteries in an abstract style, this would not only be useless, dangerous and sacrilegious, but also impossible. There are truths of a subtle, synthetic and divine order, to express which in all their inviolate completeness, human language is incapable. Only music can sometimes make the soul feel them, only ecstasy can show them in absolute vision, and only esoteric symbolism can reveal them to the spirit in a concrete way.[7]

In examining the 22 cards of the Tarot in different combinations and in trying to establish possible and permanent relations existing between them, we find it possible to lay out the cards in pairs, the first with the last, the second with the last but one, and so on. And we see that when laid out in this way the cards acquire a very interesting meaning.

The possibility of such a disposition of the Tarot cards is shown by the

---

[7] *Au Seuil du Mystère*, par Stanislas de Guaita (nouvelle édition, Georges Carré, éditeur, Paris, 1890), pp. 176–177.

order of the Tarot pictures in the gallery of the mythical " temple of initiation " of which Christian speaks.

The cards are laid out thus:

1 — 0	6 — 17
2 — 21	7 — 16
3 — 20	8 — 15
4 — 19	9 — 14
5 — 18	10 — 13
	11 — 12

Disposed in this way, one card explains the other and, what is most important, shows that they can be explained only together and can never be explained separately (as in the case of cards 1 and 0).

In studying these pairs of cards, the mind becomes accustomed to seeing unity in duality.

1. The Juggler.	0. The Fool.
2. The Priestess.	21. The World.
3. The Empress.	20. The Day of Judgement.
4. The Emperor.	19. The Sun.
5. The Hierophant.	18. The Moon.
6. Temptation.	17. The Star.
7. The Chariot.	16. The Tower.
8. Justice.	15. The Devil.
9. The Hermit.	14. Temperance (Time).
10. The Wheel of Fortune.	13. Death.
11. Strength.	12. The Hanged Man.

The 1st card, " The Juggler," depicts the Superman, or mankind as a whole, connecting earth and heaven. Its opposite is " The Fool," card 0. This is an individual man, a weak man. The two cards together represent the two poles, the beginning and the end.

The 2nd card, " The High Priestess," is Isis, or Hidden Knowledge. Its opposite is card 21, " The World " in the circle of Time, in the midst of the four principles, that is, the object of knowledge.

The 3rd card, " The Empress," is Nature. Its opposite is card 20, " The Day of Judgement " or " The Resurrection of the Dead." This is Nature, its eternally regenerating and revivifying activity.

The 4th card, " The Emperor," is the Law of Four, the life-bearing principle, and its opposite is card 19, " The Sun," as the real expression of this law and the visible source of life.

The 5th card, " The Hierophant," is Religion, and its opposite is card 18, " The Moon," which can be understood as the opposing principle, hostile to religion, or as " Astrology," that is as the basis of religion. In some old Tarot cards, instead of the wolf and the dog, on the 18th card there is a picture of two men making astronomical observations.

The 6th card, "Temptation" or Love, is the emotional side of life, and card 17, "The Star" (The Astral World), is the emotional side of Nature.

The 7th card, "The Chariot," is Magic in the sense of incomplete knowledge, in the sense of "the house built upon the sand," and its opposite, card 16, "The Tower," is the fall which inevitably follows an artificial rise.

The 8th card, "Justice," is Truth, and card 15, "The Devil," is Lie.

The 9th card, "The Hermit," is wisdom, or knowledge and the search for knowledge, and card 14, "Time," is the subject of knowledge, or what is conquered by knowledge, or what serves as the measure of knowledge. As long as a man does not understand time, or as long as a man's knowledge does not change his relation to time, his knowledge is worth nothing. Moreover, the first meaning of card 14, "Temperance," points to self-command or the control of emotions as the necessary condition of "wisdom."

The 10th card is "The Wheel of Fortune," and its opposite is card 15, "Death." Life and death are one. Death only indicates the turning of the wheel of life.

The 11th card is "Strength," and its opposite is card 12, "The Hanged Man," Sacrifice, that is, what gives strength. The greater a man's sacrifice, the greater will his strength be. Strength is proportionate to sacrifice. He who can sacrifice all, *can do all.*

Having approximately established these correspondences, it is interesting to try to re-design the Tarot cards in pen-pictures, imagining the cards with the meaning which they should have; in other words simply imagining what they may mean.

The following "pictures of the Tarot" are in many cases the result of a purely subjective understanding, for instance the 18th card. The same card, as has been mentioned before, has in some old Tarots the meaning of "Astrology." And in that case its relation to the fifth card is quite different.[8]

Further, in continuing to examine possible meanings of the Tarot pack, it is necessary to say that in many of the books which have already been mentioned 21 cards out of the 22 Major Arcana are taken as a trinity or as a triangle, each side of which consists of seven cards. The three parts of Guaita's work are each devoted to one of the three sides of the triangle, and in this case as in many others the sevens are taken in order from 1 to 22 (that is to 0).

But the fact is that constructed in this way the triangles, though quite accurate numerically, have no meaning symbolically. This means that they are quite heterogeneous as regards the pictures. In none of the sides of the

---

[8] In addition to this I find it necessary to point out that in 1911, when I wrote *The Symbolism of the Tarot*, I had the modern English pack of the Tarot, which had been re-designed and in many cases altered according to theosophical interpretation. Only in some cases in which the alterations appeared to me utterly unfounded and detracting from the idea, as for instance in card 0 (The Fool), I used the Tarot of Oswald Wirth as it appears in Papus' book, *Le Tarot des Bohémiens*. Later on I re-wrote some other of my pen-pictures in accordance with the old cards and the Tarot of Oswald Wirth. — P.O.

triangle do the pictures represent anything whole and connected, but appear an entirely fortuitous arrangement.

The conclusion can be drawn that the pictures must be taken according to their meaning and not according to their order in the pack. In other words, cards which are next to one another in the pack may have no connection in their meaning.

And then, in examining the meaning of the Tarot cards as revealed in the " pen-pictures," it can be seen that the 22 cards fall into three sets of seven, each homogeneous in itself as regards the meaning of the pictures, plus one card which is a result of all the three sevens; and this card can be either 0 or 21.

In these three sets of seven, which cannot be found by the numbers and must be looked for in the meaning of the symbols, there is again the secret doctrine (or an attempt at a secret doctrine), the expression of which is the Tarot. In accordance with this, the " Major Arcana " contain in themselves the same division as the whole Tarot, i.e. the " Major Arcana " are also divided into God, Man and the Universe.

One set of seven refers to Man.

Another set refers to Nature. And the third set refers to the world of ideas (i.e. to God or the Spirit).

The first seven: *Man*. The " Juggler " or " Magician " (Adam Kadmon), humanity or Superman; the " Fool " (individual man); " Temptation " (love), mankind; the " Devil " (the fall); the " Chariot " (the illusory quest); the " Hermit " (the real quest); the " Hanged Man " (attainment). Cards 1, 0, 6, 15, 7, 9, 12.

The second seven: the *Universe*. The Sun, the Moon, the Star, the Lightning (The Tower), the Resurrection of the Dead, Life, and Death. Cards 19, 18, 17, 16, 20, 10, 13.

The third seven: *God*. The High Priestess (knowledge); the Empress (creative power); the Emperor (the four elements); the Hierophant (religion); Time (eternity); Strength (love, union and infinity); Truth. Cards 2, 3, 4, 5, 14, 11, 8.

The first seven represents the seven steps on the path of man if taken in time, or the seven faces of man which co-exist in him, the seven faces which are expressed in the changes of the personality of man — the latter if they are taken in the mystical sense of the secret doctrine of the Tarot.

The second and third sevens — the Universe and the world of ideas or God — each represents separately, and also in combination with the first, a wide field for study. Each of the seven symbolical pictures which refer to the Universe connects man in a certain way with the world of ideas. And each of the seven ideas connects man in a certain way with the Universe.

None of the three sevens includes the 21st card, " The World," which in this case contains in itself all the 21 cards, that is, the whole triangle.

Now if we construct a triangle each side of which is formed by one of the seven, place the 21st card in its centre and arrange the four suits in a square round the triangle, then the interrelation between the square, the triangle and the point becomes still clearer.

When we placed card o in the centre we had to use a certain figurative interpretation, saying that the world is contained in the mind of man. But now we obtain the world at the centre too: the 21st card equal to the triangle and the square taken together. The world is in the circle of time, among the four principles (or four elements) represented by the four beings of the Apocalypse. The square also represents the world (or the four elements of which the world consists).

In conclusion it is interesting to quote several curious speculations from the book *Le Tarot des Bohémiens* referring to the origin of other games known to us: chess, dominoes and others, and also a legend about the origin of the Tarot.

The Tarot is composed of numbers and figures, which mutually react upon and explain each other, writes the author of *Le Tarot des Bohémiens*.[9]

But if we separate the figures and arrange them upon paper in the form of a wheel, making the numbers move in the shape of dice, we produce the Game of Goose, with which Ulysses, according to Homer, practised cheating beneath the walls of Troy.

If we fix the numbers upon alternate black and white squares, and allow the lesser figures of our game to move upon them — the King, Queen, Knight, Foolish Man or Knave, Tower or Ace — we have the Game of Chess. In fact, the primitive chessboards bore numbers, and philosophers used them to solve problems of logic.

If leaving the figures on one side, we confine ourselves to the use of numbers, the Game of Dice appears, and if we weary of throwing the dice, we can mark the characters upon horizontal plates and create the Game of Dominoes.

Chess degenerates in the same way into the Game of Draughts.

Lastly, our pack of cards, instead of first appearing under Charles VI, according to the common report, is of far older date. Spanish regulations were in existence long before this reign, forbidding the nobles to play at cards, and the Tarot itself is of very ancient origin.

The sceptres of the Tarot have become clubs, the cups hearts, the swords spades, and the pentacles or money diamonds. We have also lost the twenty-two symbolical figures and the four knights.

Of the origin of the Tarot Papus in the same book tells a story, probably invented by himself:

A time followed when Egypt, no longer able to struggle against her invaders, prepared to die honourably. Then the Egyptian savants (at least so my mysterious informant asserts) held a great assembly to arrange how the knowl-

---

[9] *The Tarot of the Bohemians*, by Papus, translated by A. P. Morton. Second revised edition with preface by A. E. Waite. Chapter XXI, p. 338. (William Rider & Son, London, 1919.)

edge, which until that date had been confined to men judged worthy to receive it, should be saved from destruction.

At first they thought of confiding these secrets to virtuous men secretly recruited by the Initiates themselves, who would transmit them from generation to generation.

But one priest, observing that virtue is a most fragile thing, and most difficult to find, at all events in a continuous line, proposed to confide the scientific traditions to vice.

The latter, he said, would never fail completely, and through it we are sure of a long and durable preservation of our principles.

This opinion was evidently adopted, and the game chosen as a vice was preferred. The small plates were then engraved with the mysterious figures which formerly taught the most important scientific secrets, and since then the players have transmitted this Tarot from generation to generation, far better than the most virtuous men upon earth would have done.

These fantasies of the French " occultist " might be interesting if he did not pretend to esoteric knowledge. But of course they contain nothing historical, and I quote them here because they express well the general feeling aroused by the Tarot and the idea of its incomprehensible origin.

II

Card 1, The Juggler

I saw a strange-looking man.

His figure clad in a multi-coloured jester's dress stood between earth and sky. His feet were hidden in grass and flowers; and his head, in a large hat with strangely turned-up brim, resembling the sign of eternity, disappeared in the clouds.

In one hand he held the magic wand, the sign of fire, with one end pointing to the sky; and with the other hand he was touching the pentacle, the sign of earth, which lay in front of him on a travelling juggler's stall, side by side with the cup and the sword, the signs of water and air.

Like lightning there flashed in me the realisation that I saw the four magical symbols in action.

The face of the *Juggler* was radiant and confident. His hands flitted about swiftly as though playing with the four signs of the elements, and I felt that he held some mysterious threads which connected the earth with the distant luminaries.

His every movement was full of significance, and every new combination of the four symbols created long series of unexpected phenomena. My eyes were dazzled. I could not follow everything that was presented.

For whom is all this performance? I asked myself. Where are the spectators?

And I heard the Voice saying:

"Are spectators necessary? Look at him more closely."

I again lifted my eyes to the man in a jester's dress, and I saw that he was changing all the time. Innumerable crowds seemed to pass and pass in him before me, disappearing before I could tell myself what I saw. And I understood that he himself was both the *Juggler* and the *spectators*.

At the same time I saw myself in him, reflected as in a mirror, and it seemed to me that I was looking at myself through his eyes. But another feeling told me that there was nothing in front of me but the blue sky and that within myself a window opened, through which I saw unearthly things and heard unearthly words.

Card 0, The Fool

And I saw another Man.

Weary and lame he dragged himself along a dusty road, across a lifeless plain beneath the scorching rays of the sun.

Gazing stupidly sideways with fixed eyes, with a half-smile, half-grimace frozen upon his face, he crawled along neither seeing nor knowing whither, plunged in his own chimerical dreams, which moved eternally in the same circle.

The fool's cap and bells was on his head back to front. His clothes were torn down the back. A wild lynx with burning eyes leaped at him from behind a stone and drove its teeth into his leg.

He stumbled, nearly falling, but dragged himself ever further, carrying over his shoulder a sack full of unnecessary, useless things, which only his madness forced him to carry.

In front the road was cleft by a ravine. A deep precipice awaited the crazy wanderer . . . and a huge crocodile with gaping jaws crept out of the abyss.

And I heard the Voice saying to me:

"Behold. This is the same Man."

Everything became confused in my head.

"What has he in his sack?" I asked, not knowing why I did so.

After a long silence the Voice answered:

"The four magic symbols, the wand, the cup, the sword and the pentacle. The fool always carries them with him, but he does not understand what they mean."

"Do you not see that is you, yourself?"

And with a thrill of horror, I felt that this also was I.

Card 2, THE HIGH PRIESTESS

When I had lifted the first veil and entered the outer court of the Temple of Initiations, I saw in the half-darkness the figure of a Woman, sitting on a high throne between two columns of the temple, one white and one black.

Mystery breathed from her and around her.

Sacred symbols gleamed on her green robes. On her head was a golden tiara surmounted with a two-horned moon. On her knees she held two crossed keys and an open book.

Between the two columns behind the Woman hung a second veil all embroidered with green leaves and pomegranate fruits.

And the Voice said to me:

" In order to enter the temple it is necessary to lift the second veil and pass between the two columns. And in order to pass between them it is necessary to obtain possession of the keys, to read the book and understand the symbols. The knowledge of good and evil awaits you.

" Are you ready? "

And with deep suffering I felt that I was afraid to enter the Temple.

" Are you ready? " repeated the Voice.

I was silent. My heart nearly stopped with fear. I could not utter a word. I felt that a precipice was opening before me and that I should not dare to take a single step.

Then the Woman sitting between the two columns turned her face to me and looked at me without saying a word.

And I understood that she was speaking to me, but my fear only grew greater.

I knew that I should not enter the Temple.

Card 21, THE WORLD

An unexpected vision rose before me.

A circle resembling a wreath woven from rainbows and lightning revolved between sky and earth.

It revolved with frenzied speed, blinding me with its brilliance, and in this radiance and fire music sounded and soft singing was heard and also the peals of thunder and the roar of a hurricane and the noise of mountain avalanches and the rumble of earthquakes.

The circle whirled with a terrible noise, touching earth and sky, and in its centre I saw the dancing figure of a young and beautiful woman, wrapped in a light transparent scarf, with a magic wand in her hand.

And at the sides of the circle there became visible to me the four beasts of the Apocalypse — one like a lion, the second like a calf, the third with the face of a man and the fourth like a flying eagle.

The vision disappeared as suddenly as it had appeared.
A strange stillness descended on the earth.
" What does this mean? " I asked in astonishment.
" It is the image of the World," said the Voice. " It must be understood before one can pass through the gates of the Temple. This is the World in the circle of time, amid the four principles — this is what you always see, but never understand.

" Understand that all that you see, things and phenomena, are but the hieroglyphs of higher ideas."

Card 3, THE EMPRESS

I felt the breath of spring; and with the fragrance of violets, lilies of the valley and the wild cherry the soft singing of elves was borne towards me.

Brooks murmured, green tree-tops rustled, innumerable choirs of birds were singing, bees were droning and everywhere was the joyful living breath of Nature.

The sun shone softly and mildly, a small white cloud hung over the woods.

In the midst of a green glade where bloomed the first yellow primroses, on a throne encircled with ivy and blossoming lilac, I saw the Empress.

A green wreath adorned her golden hair. Twelve stars shone above her head. Two snow-white wings were visible behind her back, and in one hand she held a sceptre.

With a tender smile the Empress looked about her, and beneath her glance flowers opened and buds unfolded their sticky green leaves.

The whole of her dress was covered with flowers, as though every flower that opened was reflected or imprinted on it and became a part of her garment.

The sign of Venus, the Goddess of Love, was carved upon her marble throne.

" Oh, Queen of Life," I said, " why is everything so radiant and joyful and happy around you? Do you not know that there is the grey, weary autumn, the cold, white winter? Do you not know that there is death, black graves, cold damp sepulchres, cemeteries?

" How can you smile joyfully looking at the unfolding flowers, when all dies and all will die, when all is condemned to death — even that which is not yet born? "

The Empress looked at me smiling, and beneath her smile I suddenly felt that in my soul the flower of some bright understanding was opening, as though something was being revealed to me, and the terror of death began to depart from me.

Card 20, THE RESURRECTION OF THE DEAD

I saw an icy plain. A chain of snow mountains shut off the horizon. A cloud arose and grew until it covered a quarter of the sky. And in the midst of the cloud there appeared two fiery wings. And I saw the messenger of the Empress.

He raised his trumpet and blew a loud and imperious blast.

And in response the plain trembled, and with loud reverberating echoes the mountain answered.

And one after the other the graves in the plain began to open and out of them people came forth — young children and old folk and men and women. And they stretched out their arms to the messenger of the Empress, and tried to catch the sound of the trumpet.

And in the sound of the trumpet I felt the smile of the Empress. And in the opening graves I saw the unfolding flowers, and in the extended hands I smelt the fragrance of flowers.

And I understood the mystery of birth in death.

Card 4, THE EMPEROR

After I had studied the first three numbers it was given to me to understand the great Law of Four — the Alpha and Omega of all.

I saw the Emperor on a high throne of stone which was decorated with four rams' heads.

A golden helmet gleamed on his brow. His white beard fell over his purple mantle. In one hand he held a sphere, the symbol of his possessions, and in the other a sceptre in the form of the Egyptian cross — the sign of his power over birth.

" I am the Great Law," said the Emperor.

" I am the Name of God.

" The four letters of His Name are in me and I am in everything.

" I am in the four principles, I am in the four elements. I am in the four seasons. I am in the four quarters of the earth.

" I am in the four signs of the Tarot.

" I am action, I am resistance, I am completion, I am result.

" For him who knows the way to see me, there are no mysteries on the earth.

" As the earth contains fire, water and air, as the fourth letter of the name contains the first three and itself becomes the first, so my sceptre contains the complete triangle and bears in itself the seed of a new triangle."

And while the Emperor spoke, his helmet and the golden armour visible beneath his mantle shone ever more and more fiercely, until I could no longer bear their radiance and dropped my eyes.

And when I tried to raise them again, before me was an all-pervading radiance, and light and fire.

And I fell prostrate worshipping the Fiery Word.

Card 19, THE SUN

After this, when I first saw the Sun, I understood that it is itself the expression of the Fiery Word and the sign of the Emperor.

The great luminary shone and gave warmth. Below, tall golden sunflowers nodded their heads.

And I saw two children in a garden behind a high enclosure. The Sun poured its hot rays on them, and it seemed to me that a golden rain was falling upon them, as though the Sun poured molten gold over the earth.

For an instant I closed my eyes, and when I opened them again I saw that every ray of the Sun was the sceptre of the Emperor, which bore within it life. And I saw how beneath the sharp points of these rays the mystical flowers of the Waters were unfolding everywhere, and how the rays penetrated into these flowers, and how the whole of Nature was continually born from the mysterious union of the two principles.

Card 5, THE HIEROPHANT

I saw the great Master in the Temple.

He was seated on a golden throne, set upon a purple dais; he wore the robes of a high priest and a golden tiara.

Under his feet I saw two crossed keys, and two Initiates were bowed before him. And he spoke to them.

I heard the sound of his voice, but could not understand one word that he said. Either he spoke in a language unknown to me, or there was something that prevented me from understanding the meaning of his words.

And the Voice said to me: "He speaks only for those who have ears to hear.

"But woe unto them who believe that they hear before they have really heard, or hear that which he does not say, or put their own words in place of his words. They will never receive the keys of understanding. And it is of them that it was said that they neither go in themselves, neither suffer them that are entering to go in."

Card 18, The Moon

A desolate plain stretched out before me. The full moon looked down as if wrapped in meditation. Under her wavering light the shadows lived their own peculiar lives. There were black hills on the horizon.

Between two grey towers wound a path, losing itself in the distance. On either side of the path, facing one another, a wolf and a dog were sitting and howling, with their muzzles raised to the moon. From a stream a great black crayfish clambered on to the sand. A cold heavy dew was falling.

A feeling of dread overcame me. I felt the presence of a mysterious world, a world of hostile spirits, of corpses rising from the grave, of tormented ghosts.

In the pale light of the moon I seemed to feel the presence of phantoms: shadows seemed to be crossing the path, someone was waiting for me behind the towers — and it was dangerous to look back.

Card 6, Temptation

I saw a flowering garden in a green valley surrounded by soft blue hills.

In the garden I saw a Man and a Woman. Elves, water-nymphs, sylphs and gnomes came to them freely; three kingdoms of nature, stones, plants and animals, served them.

To them was revealed the mystery of universal equilibrium, and they themselves were the symbol and expression of that equilibrium.

Two triangles were united in them into a six-pointed star, two bow-shaped magnets merged into one ellipse.

High above them I saw floating the Genie, who, unseen, guided them, and whose presence they always felt.

And I noticed how from a tree, on which the golden fruit was ripening, a snake crept down and whispered in the ear of the woman; and the woman listened, smiled at first incredulously, then with curiosity. Then I saw her speak to the man, and he also smiled, pointing with his hand to the garden all around him. Suddenly a cloud appeared and hid the picture from me.

"This is the picture of temptation," said the Voice. "But what constitutes the temptation? Can you understand its nature?"

"Life is so good," I said, "and the world so beautiful, the three kingdoms of Nature and the four elements so obedient, that they wished to believe themselves the lords and masters of the world, and they could not withstand this temptation."

" Yes," said the Voice; " the wisdom which crawls on the ground said to them that they knew themselves what was good and what was evil. And they believed this, because it was pleasant to think so. And then they ceased to hear the guiding voice. Equilibrium was destroyed. The enchanted world was closed to them. Everything appeared to them in a false light. And they became mortal. This Fall is the first sin of man, and is perpetually repeated, because man never ceases to believe in himself, and lives by this belief. Only when man has atoned this sin *by great suffering* can he pass out of the power of death and return to life."

Card 17, The Star

In the midst of the heavens shone a great star, and around it were seven smaller stars. Their rays were intertwined, filling space with an endless radiance and light. And each of the eight stars contained in itself all the eight stars.

And beneath the shining stars, beside a blue stream I saw a naked girl, young and beautiful. Kneeling on one knee she poured water from two vessels, one of gold and one of silver; a small bird on a bush raised its wings and prepared for flight.

For an instant I understood that I was seeing the soul of Nature.
" This is the imagination of Nature," said the Voice softly. " Nature dreams, imagines, creates worlds. Learn to unite your imagination with her imagination; and nothing will ever be impossible for you.
" But remember that it is impossible to see both rightly and wrongly at the same time. Once for all you must make a choice and then there can be no return."

Card 7, The Chariot

I saw a chariot drawn by two sphinxes, a white and a black. Four pillars supported a sky-blue canopy, spangled with five-pointed stars.
Beneath the canopy, driving the sphinxes, stood the Conqueror in armour of steel, and in his hand was a sceptre, surmounted with a sphere, a triangle and a square.
A golden pentagram shone on his crown. On the front of the chariot, above the sphinxes, was fastened a two-winged sphere and the mystic lingam and yoni, the symbol of union.
" Everything in this picture has a meaning. Look and try to understand," said the Voice to me.
" This is the conqueror who has not yet conquered himself. Here are both will and knowledge. But in all this there is more of the desire to attain than real attainment.

" The man in the chariot began to consider himself conqueror before he actually conquered. He decided that conquest must come to a conqueror. In this there are many real possibilities, but also many deceiving lights, and great dangers await the man in the chariot.

" He drives the chariot by the strength of his will and of the magic sword, but the tension of his will may weaken and the sphinxes may pull in different directions and tear him and his chariot in two.

" This is the conqueror against whom the conquered may still rise. Do you see behind him the towers of the conquered city? Perhaps the flame of revolt burns there already.

" And he does not know that within himself lies the conquered city, that within himself the sphinxes are watching his every movement, and that within himself great dangers await him.

" And realise that this is the same man whom you saw connecting heaven and earth, and the same man whom you saw dragging himself along a dusty road towards the precipice where the crocodile awaited him."

Card 16, The Tower

I saw rising from earth to heaven a high tower, whose top reached beyond the clouds.

Black night was all around and thunder rumbled.

And suddenly the sky opened, a thunderclap shook the whole earth, and the lightning struck the top of the tower.

Tongues of flame shot out of heaven; the whole tower filled with fire and smoke — and I saw the builders of the tower falling from its top.

" Look, " said the Voice; " Nature hates deceit, and man cannot subjugate himself to her laws. Nature is patient for a long time and then suddenly with one blow she annihilates all that goes against her.

" If only men could see that almost all that they know consists of the ruins of destroyed towers, perhaps they would cease to build them."

Card 8, Truth

When I became possessed of the keys, had read the book and understood the symbols, I was permitted to lift the veil of the Temple and enter the inner sanctuary. And there I saw a woman with a gold crown and a purple mantle. In one hand she held an uplifted sword, and in the other a pair of scales. Seeing her I trembled with fear, because her look was infinitely deep and terrible, and drew me like an abyss.

" You are seeing Truth," said the Voice. " Everything is weighed in these scales. That sword is eternally lifted in defence of justice and nothing can escape it.

"But why do you turn your eyes from the scales and the sword? Are you afraid?

"Yes, they deprive you of your last illusions. How will you live on earth without these illusions?

"You wished to see Truth and now you see her.

"But remember what awaits a mortal when he has seen the goddess. He will never again be able to shut his eyes to what does not please him, as he has done hitherto. He will see truth perpetually, always and in everything. Can you bear this? You have seen truth. Now you have to go further even if you do not wish to."

Card 15, THE DEVIL

Terrifying black night enveloped the earth, and in the distance burned a lurid red flame.

A strange fantastic figure became visible to me as I drew nearer.

High above the earth I saw the hideous red face of the devil, with large hairy ears, a pointed beard and the curved horns of a goat. Between the horns of the devil's forehead an inverted pentagram shone with phosphorescent light. Two grey wings, membranous, like the wings of a bat, were extended. The devil held up one naked fat arm with elbow bent and fingers outspread, and on the palm I recognized the sign of black magic. In the other hand he held a burning torch, pointing downwards, from which rose clouds of black suffocating smoke. The devil sat on a great black cube, gripped between the claws of his beast-like shaggy legs.

A man and a woman were chained to an iron ring in the front of the cube.

And I saw that they were the same man and woman whom I had seen in the garden, but now they had horns and tails with fiery tips.

"This is the picture of the fall, the picture of weakness," said the Voice, "the picture of lies and evil.

"These are the same people, but they began to believe in themselves and in their own powers. They said that they knew themselves what was good and what was evil. They mistook their weakness for strength and then Deceit subjugated them."

And I heard the voice of the devil.

"I am Evil," he said, "in so far as evil can exist in this best of all worlds. In order to perceive me one must see crookedly, wrongly and narrowly. Three paths lead to me: conceit, suspicion and accusation. My chief virtues are calumny and slander. I complete the triangle, the two other sides of which are death and time.

"In order to escape from this triangle it is only necessary to see that it does not exist.

"But how to do that is not for me to tell.

"For I am Evil, which men invented in order to have a justification for themselves and in order to regard me as the cause of all the wrongdoing of which they are guilty themselves.

"I am called the King of Lies, and truly I am the King of Lies, for I am the greatest product of human lies."

Card 9, THE HERMIT

After long wanderings in a sandy, waterless desert, where nothing lived but snakes, I met a Hermit.

He was wrapped in a long cloak, with a hood drawn over his head; in one hand he held a long staff and in the other a lighted lantern, although it was broad daylight and the sun was shining.

"I searched for man," said the Hermit; "but I have long since abandoned the search.

"Now I am searching for buried treasure. Do you also wish to search for it? First you must get a lantern. Without a lantern you will always be finding treasures, but your gold will turn to dust.

"And understand the first mystery — we do not know what treasure it is we search for, whether it is that which was buried by our ancestors, or that which will be buried by our descendants."

Card 14, TEMPERANCE (TIME)

I saw an Angel standing between earth and heaven, clothed in a white robe, with wings of flame and a golden halo round his head. He stood with one foot on the land and the other on the sea, and behind him the sun was rising.

On the angel's breast was the sign of the Sacred book of the Tarot — the square, and within it the triangle. On his brow was the sign of eternity and life — the circle.

In his hands the angel held two cups — one of gold and one of silver, and between the cups there flowed an incessant stream, which sparkled with all the colours of the rainbow. But I could not say from which cup it flowed and into which it was flowing.

And with terror I understood that I had come to the last mysteries, from which there is no return.

I looked at the angel, at his signs, at his cups, at the rainbow stream between the cups, and my human heart fluttered with fear, and my human mind was wrought with the anguish of incomprehension.

" The name of the angel is Time," said the Voice.

" On his forehead is the circle. This is the sign of Eternity and the sign of Life.

" In the angel's hands are two cups, golden and silver. One cup is the past, the other the future. The rainbow stream between them is the present. You see that it is flowing in both directions.

" This is Time in its most incomprehensible aspect for man.

"Men think that everything is incessantly flowing in one direction. They do not see that everything eternally meets, that one thing comes from the past and another from the future, and that time is a multitude of circles turning in different directions.

" Understand this mystery and learn to distinguish the opposite currents in the rainbow stream of the present."

Card 10, The Wheel of Fortune

I walked on absorbed in deep meditation, endeavouring to understand my vision of the Angel.

And suddenly raising my head, I saw in the midst of the sky an immense revolving circle covered with cabalistic letters and signs.

The circle revolved with fearful speed, and together with it, now rising, now falling, revolved the symbolic figures of the serpent and the dog; and on the top of the circle, motionless, sat the sphinx.

At the four quarters of the sky I saw on the clouds the four winged beasts of the Apocalypse — one like a lion, another like a calf, the third with the face of a man and the fourth like a flying eagle — and each of them was reading an open book.

And I heard the voice of the animals of Zarathustra:

" *Everything goes, everything returns; eternally rolls the wheel of being. Everything dies, everything blossoms forth again; eternally runs the year of being.*

" *Everything breaks, everything is united anew; eternally builds itself the same house of being. Everything parts, everything meets again; the ring of being remains eternally true to itself.*

" *Being begins in every Now, around every 'Here' rolls the sphere of 'There.' The middle is everywhere. Crooked is the path of eternity.*" [10]

Card 13, Death

Wearied by the flashing of the wheel of life, I sank on the ground and closed my eyes. But it seemed to me that the wheel was still revolving

---

[10] *Also sprach Zarathustra*, III.

before me and that the four beasts on the clouds still sat and read their books.

And suddenly, opening my eyes, I saw a gigantic horseman on a white charger, clad in black armour with a black helmet and a black plume.

The face of a skeleton looked out from under the helmet. One bony hand held a great black gently waving banner, and the other held black reins, ornamented with a skull and cross-bones.

And wherever the white steed passed, night and death followed, flowers withered, leaves fell, the earth was covered with a white shroud, grave-yards appeared, towers, palaces and cities fell into ruins.

Kings in the full splendour of their glory and power, beautiful women, loving and beloved, high priests invested with power from God, innocent children — all, at the approach of the white steed, fell on their knees before it in terror and stretched out their hands in despair and anguish — and then fell to rise no more.

In the distance behind the towers the sun was setting.

The chill of death took hold of me. It seemed to me that already I felt the white hoofs of the steed on my breast, and I saw the whole world falling down into an abyss.

But suddenly I felt something familiar in the measured step of the horse, something I had heard and seen before. Another instant — and I heard in its step the movement of the wheel of life.

Light broke in upon me, and looking at the disappearing horseman and the setting sun, I understood that the path of life consists of the hoof-marks of the steed of Death.

The sun, setting on one side, rises on the other.

Every moment of its motion is a setting at one point and a rising at another.

I understood that just as the sun rises in its setting and sets in its rising, so life dies when it is born, and is born when it dies.

"Yes," said the Voice; "you think that the sun has only one aim, to set and to rise. Does the sun know anything of the earth, of people of the sunset and sunrise? It goes its own way, over its own orbit, round an Unknown Centre. Life, Death, sunrise, sunset, are you not aware that all these are but the thoughts, dreams, and fears of the Fool?"

Card 11, STRENGTH

In the midst of a green plain, bordered by gently-rolling blue hills, I saw a woman with a lion.

Garlanded with roses, the sign of Eternity over her head, the woman calmly and confidently closed the lion's mouth, and the lion gently licked her hand.

"This is the picture of strength," said the Voice; "understand all its meanings.

"First of all it shows the strength of love. There is nothing stronger than love. Only love can conquer evil. Hatred always breeds hatred. Evil always bears evil.

"You see those garlands of roses? They speak of the magic chain. Union of desires, union of efforts, create such strength that all wild unconscious strength bows before it.

"And further it is the strength of Eternity.

"Here you pass into the realm of mysteries. For a consciousness that is aware of the sign of Eternity above it, there are no obstacles, nor can there be any resistance from the infinite."

Card 12, The Hanged Man

And I saw a man with his hands tied behind his back, hanging by one leg from a high gallows with his head downwards, and in fearful torments.

Round his head was a golden halo.

And I heard a Voice which spoke to me:

"Behold, this is the man who has seen the Truth.

"New suffering, such as no earthly misfortune can ever cause, that is what awaits man on earth when he finds the path to Eternity and the understanding of the Infinite.

"He is still a man, but he already knows many things inaccessible even to gods. And this conflict between the big and the little in his soul makes his torture and his Golgotha.

"In his own soul a high gallows is raised on which he hangs in suffering, feeling as though he was turned head downwards.

"He himself chose this way.

"It is for this that he went a long journey from trial to trial, from initiation to initiation, through failures and through falls.

"And now he has found Truth and has known himself.

"He now knows that it is he who stands between earth and heaven controlling the elements with the magical symbols, and it is also he who walks in the Fool's cap along a dusty road beneath the blazing sun towards the abyss where the crocodile awaits him. It is he with his companion in the Garden of Eden under the protection of the beneficent genie; it is also he who is bound with her to the black cube of lies; it is he who stands as the conqueror for a moment in the deceptive chariot, drawn by the sphinxes ready to rush in opposite directions; and it is he again in the desert who looks for Truth with a lantern in the bright light of day.

"And now he has found Truth."

1911–1929

Chapter VI

WHAT IS YOGA?

❊

THE MYSTERY OF THE EAST

For the West the East has always been the land of mystery and enigmas. About India in particular many legends and fantastic tales have existed and still exist, chiefly about the mysterious knowledge of Indian sages, philosophers, fakirs and saints.

Indeed many facts have long since shown that apart from the knowledge contained in the ancient books of India, in its holy scriptures, legends, songs, poems and myths, there exists certain other knowledge which cannot be drawn from books and which is not revealed openly, but traces of which are quite clearly seen.

It is impossible to deny that the philosophy and the religions of India contain inexhaustible sources of thought. And European philosophy has made and is making wide use of these sources, but strangely enough it can never take from them what is most important and most essential in them.

This fact has been realised by many Europeans who have studied the religious and philosophical teachings of the East. They have felt that they receive from the books not all that the Indians know, and this feeling has strengthened the idea that besides the knowledge contained in books there exists another, a secret, knowledge, concealed from the "uninitiated," or that besides the known books there are others, kept hidden, containing the "secret teaching."

A great deal of energy and time has been spent on the search for this secret doctrine of the East. And there is good ground for believing that in fact there exist not only one, but many doctrines unknown to the West, which grow from one general root.

But apart from *doctrines*, known and unknown, there exist also a number of systems of self-discipline which are known under the name of *Yoga*.

The word Yoga can be translated by the word *unity* or *union* or *subjugation*; in the first meaning it corresponds to the word " harnessing," from the Sanskrit word *yug*, to which correspond the English word *yoke* and the Russian иго (eego).

One of the meanings of the word "Yoga" is "right action."

To follow Yoga means to subjugate to the control of one or another system of Yoga thought, feeling, internal and external movements, etc., that is, the functions, most of which ordinarily work without control.

"Yogis," is the name given to those who live and act according to "Yoga." These are men who pass or have passed through a certain school and live according to rules that are known only to themselves and are incomprehensible to the uninitiated, and according to knowledge which infinitely increases their powers as compared with the powers of ordinary men.

There are many tales and beliefs about "Yogis"; sometimes they are said to be mystics leading a life of contemplation, indifferent to food and clothing; at other times, to be men possessing miraculous powers, able to see and hear at a distance, men whom wild beasts and the forces of nature obey. These powers and capacities are acquired by methods and exercises which constitute the secret of Yoga and which enable Yogis to understand people and to act rightly and expediently in all circumstances and on all occasions in life.

Yogis have nothing in common with "fakirs," that is, with men who endeavour to subjugate the physical body to the will by the way of suffering, and who are very often ignorant fanatics torturing themselves in order to attain heavenly beatitude, or conjurors who for money perform "miracles," which are based upon skill, patience and the accustoming of the body to assume incredible postures or to exercise its functions in an abnormal way.

These conjurors and fakirs often call themselves Yogis, but a true Yogi can always be recognised, for he can never have the fanaticism and frenzied sectarianism of fakirs; he will display nothing for payment, and above all he will possess knowledge surpassing the knowledge of ordinary men.

"The science of Yogis," that is, the methods used by Yogis for the development in themselves of extraordinary powers and capacities, comes from remote antiquity. Thousands of years ago the sages of ancient India knew that the powers of man in all the spheres and provinces of his activity can be greatly increased by means of right training and by accustoming man to control his body, mind, attention, will, emotions and desires.

In connection with this the study of man in ancient India was on a level quite inconceivable to us. This can only be explained by the fact that the philosophical schools existing at that time were directly connected with esoteric schools.

Man was considered not as a completed entity, but as containing in himself a multitude of latent powers. The idea was that in ordinary life and in ordinary man these powers are dormant but can be awakened and developed by means of a certain mode of life, by certain exercises, by certain work upon oneself. This is what is called Yoga. An acquaintance with the ideas of Yoga enables man first to know himself better, to understand his latent capacities and inclinations, to find out and determine the direction in which they ought to be developed; and second, to awaken his latent capacities and learn how to use them in all paths of life.

"The science of Yogis," or, to put it more correctly, the cycle of the sciences of Yogis, consists in descriptions of these methods, adapted to men of different types and different activities in life, and also in the exposition of the theories connected with these methods.

Each of the "sciences" composing Yoga falls into two parts: the theoretical part and the practical part.

The theoretical part aims at setting forth the fundamental principles and general outline of the given subject as a complete and connected whole, without descending into unnecessary details.

The practical part teaches the methods and ways of the best training for the desired activity, the methods and means of development of latent powers and capacities.

It is necessary to mention here that even the theoretical part can never really be learned from books. Books can at best serve as synopses only for the purpose of repetition and for remembering, while the study of the ideas of Yoga requires direct oral tuition and explanation.

As regards the practical part, very little of it can be expounded in writing. Consequently even if there are books containing attempts at an exposition of the practical methods of Yoga, they cannot possibly serve as a manual for practical and independent work.

In general, in speaking about Yoga it is necessary to point out that the relationship between its practical and theoretical parts is analogous to the relationship between practical and theoretical sides in art. There exists a theory of painting, but the study of the theory of painting does not enable one to paint pictures. There exists a theory of music, but the study of the theory of music will not enable one to play any musical instrument.

In the practice of art as in the practice of Yoga there is something which does not exist and cannot exist in the theory. Practice is not built up according to theory. Theory is derived from practice.

The sciences of Yoga in India were for a long time kept secret, and these methods, which increase the power of man in an almost miraculous way, were the privilege of special schools or the secret of ascetics and hermits who had completely renounced the world. In Indian temples (or in connection with them) there were schools where the pupils, *Chelas*, who had traversed a long path of tests and preparatory education, were initiated into the science of the Yogis by special teachers, *Gurus*. Europeans were unable to obtain any information about Yoga, and what was usually related by travellers concerning this question bore a purely fantastic character.

The first correct information about Yoga began to appear only in the second half of the 19th century, though many methods of Yogis were known in mystical societies much earlier.

But though Europeans had borrowed a great deal from the Yogis, they were nevertheless unable to understand and realise all the significance of the "sciences of Yogis" taken as a whole.

In reality *Yoga is the key to all the ancient wisdom of the East.*

The ancient books of India cannot be comprehensible to Western scientists. That is because all these books were written by *Yogis*, that is, by men possessing not merely a developed intellect, but powers and capacities infinitely surpassing the powers and capacities of an ordinary man.

The powers which Yoga gives are not limited to the strengthening of the capacity of understanding. Yoga increases the creative capacity of man in all the spheres and domains of life, gives him the possibility of *direct* penetration into the mysteries of nature, discloses to him the secrets of eternity and the enigmas of existence.

At the same time Yoga increases the powers of man, first, for the struggle with life, that is, with all the physical conditions in which man is born and which are all hostile to him; second, for the struggle with Nature, who always wishes to use man for her own ends; and third, for the struggle with the illusions of his own consciousness, which being dependent on his limited psychic apparatus, creates an enormous number of mirages and delusions. Yoga helps man to struggle against the deception of words, shows him clearly that a thought expressed in words cannot be true, that there can be no truth in words, that at best they can only hint at truth, reveal it for a moment and then hide it. Yoga teaches the way to find the hidden truth concealed in things, in the actions of men, in the writings of great sages of all times and peoples.

Yoga falls into five divisions:

1. Raja-Yoga or the Yoga of the development of consciousness.
2. Jnana-Yoga (Gnyana or Gnana-Yoga), the Yoga of knowledge.
3. Karma-Yoga or the Yoga of right actions.
4. Hatha-Yoga, the Yoga of power over the body.
5. Bhakti-Yoga, the Yoga of right religious action.

The five Yogas are five paths leading to the same goal: to perfection, to the transition to higher levels of knowledge and life.

The divisions of the five Yogas depends on the division of types of man, his capacities, preparation, and so on. One man can begin with contemplation, with the study of his own " I." Another needs the objective study of nature. A third must first of all understand the rules of conduct in ordinary life. For a fourth before anything else it is necessary to acquire control over the physical body. For a fifth it is necessary to " learn to pray," to understand his religious feelings and to learn how to govern them.

Yoga teaches the way to do rightly everything that man does. Only by studying Yoga can man see how wrongly he has acted on all occasions in his life; how much of his strength he has spent quite uselessly, attaining only the poorest results with an enormous expenditure of energy.

Yoga teaches man the principles of the right economy of forces. It teaches him to be able to do whatever he does, consciously, *when this is necessary*. This immeasurably increases man's powers and improves the results of his work.

The study of Yoga first of all shows man how greatly he has been mistaken about himself.

Man becomes convinced that he is far weaker and much more insignificant than he has considered himself to be, and at the same time that he can become stronger and more powerful than the strongest and most powerful man he can imagine.

He sees not only what he is, but what he may become. His conception of life, of man's place, rôle and purpose in life, undergoes a complete change. He loses the feeling of separateness, and the feeling of the senseless and chaotic nature of life. He begins to understand his aim and to see that his pursuit of this aim brings him into contact with other people going in the same direction.

Yoga does not seek, as its primary object, to guide man. Yoga only increases his powers in any of the directions of his activity. But at the same time, in using the powers given by Yoga man can follow one direction only. Should he change this direction, Yoga itself will turn against him, will stop him, will deprive him of all powers, and may possibly even destroy him altogether. Yoga carries enormous power, but this power can be used only in a certain direction. This is a law which becomes clear to any one who studies Yoga.

In everything it touches Yoga teaches man to discriminate between the real and the false, and this capacity for proper discrimination helps man to find hidden truths where hitherto he had seen or supposed nothing hidden.

When a man studying Yoga takes up certain books which he thought he knew quite well, to his profound astonishment he suddenly finds in them an infinite amount that is new. Some hidden depth seems to be revealed to him in these books, and with surprise and awe he feels this depth and understands that until now he has seen nothing but the surface.

Such an effect is produced by many books belonging to the holy scriptures of India. There is no necessity for these books to be kept hidden. They may be accessible to all and yet hidden from all except those who know how to read them. And such hidden books exist in all countries and among all peoples. One of the most occult books, the New Testament, is the most widely known. But of all books this is the one people least know how to read, the one they most distort in their understanding of it.

Yoga teaches how to search for truth and how to find truth in everything. It teaches that there is nothing that could not serve as a starting point for the finding of truth.

Yoga is not accessible all at once in its entirety. It has many degrees of varying difficulty. This is the first thing to be realised by anyone who wishes to study Yoga.

The limits of Yoga cannot be seen all at once or from a distance at the beginning of the way. For the man who studies Yoga new horizons open before him as he continues on his way. Each new step shows him something new ahead, something that he has not seen and could not have seen before. But a man cannot see very far ahead. And at the beginning of the study of Yoga he cannot know all that this study will give. Yoga is an entirely new way, and on entering upon it it is impossible to know where it will lead.

To put it in another way, Yoga cannot be defined as one can define what medicine is, what chemistry is, what mathematics is. In order to define what Yoga is, study and *knowledge* of Yoga are necessary.

Yoga is a closed door. Anyone may knock if he wishes to enter. But until he has entered he cannot know what he will find behind this door.

A man who enters the path of Yoga with the aim of reaching its summits must give himself up entirely to Yoga, give to Yoga all his time and all his energy, all his thoughts, feelings and motives. He must endeavour to harmonise himself, to achieve an inner unity, *to create in himself a permanent " I,"* to protect himself from continual strivings, moods and desires, which sway him now in one direction, now in another. He must compel all his powers to serve one aim. Yoga demands all this, but it also helps to attain it by showing the means and methods by which it can be reached. For every kind of activity there are special conditions which are favourable to it and which Yoga helps to define.

The study of Yoga is impossible in the scattered condition of thoughts, desires and feelings amidst which an ordinary man lives. Yoga demands the whole of man, the whole of his time, all his energy, all his thoughts, all his feelings, the whole of his life. Only Karma-Yoga allows man to remain in the conditions of his ordinary life. All the other Yogas demand immediate and complete withdrawal from life, *even if only for a certain time.* The study of Yogas, with the exception of Karma-Yoga, is impossible in life circumstances. Equally impossible is the study of Yoga without a teacher, without his constant and incessant watch over the pupil.

A man who hopes to know Yoga by reading a few books will be greatly disappointed. In a book, in written exposition, it is impossible to transmit to a man any practical knowledge — everything depends on the work of the teacher upon him and on his own work upon himself.

The common aim of all the forms of Yoga is the changing of man, the broadening of his consciousness. At the basis of all the Yogas there lies one principle, which is that man as he is born and lives is an uncompleted and imperfect being, but one who can be altered and brought to the development possible to him by means of suitable instruction and training.

From the point of view of the principles of Yoga man is simply material upon which it is possible and necessary to work.

This refers first of all to man's inner world, to his consciousness, his psychic apparatus, his mental capacities, his knowledge, which according to the teachings of Yogis can be completely changed, freed from all the usual limitations and strengthened to a degree surpassing all imagination. As a result, man acquires new possibilities of knowing the truth and new powers for surmounting obstacles on his way, no matter whence these obstacles arise. Further, it refers to the physical body of man, which is studied and gradually subjected to the control of mind and consciousness, even in those of its functions of which man is not usually aware in himself at all.

The opening up of higher consciousness is the aim of all the Yogas.

Following the way of Yoga a man must reach the state of samadhi, that is, of ecstasy or enlightenment, in which alone truth can be understood.

THE FIVE YOGAS

HATHA-YOGA

Hatha-Yoga is the Yoga of power over the body and over the physical nature of man.

According to the teaching of Yogis, a practical study of Hatha-Yoga gives man ideal health, lengthens his life and gives him many new powers and capacities which an ordinary man does not possess and which seem almost miraculous.

Yogis affirm that a healthy and normally functioning body is more easily subjected to the control of consciousness and mind than a body which is sick, disordered and unbalanced and from which one never knows what is to be expected. Moreover, it is easier to disregard a healthy body, whereas a sick body subjects man to itself, makes him think too much of it, demands too much attention for itself.

Therefore the first aim of Hatha-Yoga is a healthy body.

At the same time, Hatha-Yoga prepares the physical body of man to bear all the hardships connected with the functioning in him of the higher psychic forces: higher consciousness, will, intense emotions, etc. These forces do not function in ordinary man. Their awakening and development produce terrific strain and pressure on the physical body. And if the physical body is not trained and prepared by special exercises, if it is in its usual sickly condition, it is unable to withstand this pressure and cannot keep up with the unusually intensive work of the organs of perception and consciousness, which is inevitably connected with the development of the higher forces and possibilities of man. In order to enable the heart, brain and nervous system (and also *other organs* the rôle of which in the psychic life of man is little, if at all, known to Western science) to bear the pressure of new functions the whole body must be well balanced, harmonised, purified, put in order and prepared for the new and tremendously hard work which awaits it.

There are many rules evolved by Yogis with regard to the regulation and control of the activities of different organs of the body. Yogis assume that the body cannot be left to itself. Instincts do not guide its activity with sufficient vigour; the intervention of the intellect is imperative.

One of the fundamental ideas of Yogis regarding the body is that in its natural state the body can by no means be taken as the ideal apparatus it is often thought to be. Many functions are only necessary to preserve the existence of the body in various unfavourable conditions; and there are functions which are the result of other, wrong, functions.

Further, Yogis think that many of these unfavourable conditions have already disappeared, whereas the functions created by them continue to exist. And Yogis affirm that by abolishing these needless functions it is possible greatly to increase the energy which can be used for useful work.

Again there are many functions which are in a rudimentary state but which may be developed to an inconceivable degree.

The body given by nature is from the Yogis' point of view only material. And a man on his way to his highest aims can make use of this material and, after reshaping and remodelling it in a suitable way, can create for himself a weapon which will enable him to attain his aims. Yogis affirm that the possibilities latent in the body are enormous.

And Yogis possess numerous methods and means for decreasing the useless functions of the body and for awakening and bringing to light the new powers and capacities which lie dormant in it.

Yogis say that only an insignificant proportion of the energy of the body is used profitably, (that is, in preserving the life of the body and in serving the higher aims of man). The greater part of the energy produced by the body is, in their opinion, spent quite uselessly.

But they consider it possible to make all the organs of the body work for a single aim, that is, to take all the energy created by the organs and make it serve the higher aims, which at present it often only hinders.

Hatha-Yoga deals with the physical nature of man in the strictest sense of the word, that is, with vegetable and animal functions. And with regard to this physical nature Yogis have long known certain laws which have only in quite recent times been perceived by Western science. First, the extraordinary independence of the separate organs of the body and the absence of one common centre governing the life of the organism; and second, the capacity of one organ to do, to a certain extent and in certain cases, the work of another.

In observing the independence of various organs and parts of the body Yogis came to the conclusion that the life of the body consists of thousands of separate lives. Each such " life " presupposes a " soul " or a " consciousness." Yogis recognise these independent " lives " possessing separate " souls " not only in all the various organs, but also in all the tissues and in all the substances of the body. This is the " occult " side of Hatha-Yoga.

These " lives " and these " consciousnesses " are the " spirits " of the body. According to the theory of Hatha-Yoga, man is able to subordinate them to himself, to make them serve his aims.

Hatha-Yogis learn to control the breathing, the circulation of the blood and nervous energy. They are said to be able, by holding the breath, almost to stop all the functions of the body, sink it into a lethargy in which a man can remain for any length of time without food or air, and without harm to himself. On the other hand they are said to be able to intensify the breathing and by making it rhythmic with the beating of the heart to take in an enormous supply of vital force, and to use this force, for instance, for the treatment of diseases, both their own and other people's. By an effort of will Yogis are supposed to be able to suspend the circulation of the blood in any part of the body or, on the contrary, to direct to it an increased supply of fresh arterial blood and nervous energy. It is precisely on this that their method of treatment is based.

By learning to govern their own bodies Yogis at the same time learn to govern the whole of the material universe.

The human body represents a universe in miniature. It contains everything from mineral to God. And this is for them not a mere figure of speech, but the most real truth. Through his body man is in contact with the whole of the universe, and with everything in it. The water contained in the human body connects man with all the water of the earth and the atmosphere; the oxygen contained in the human body connects man with the oxygen in the whole universe; the carbon with the carbon; the vital principle with everything living in the world.

It is quite clear why this must be so. The water entering into the composition of man's body is not separated from the water outside the body, it is only as if it flowed through man; it is the same with the air, and with all the chemical substances of the body, etc.; they all merely travel through the body.

By learning to control the various principles (" spirits " according to occult terminology) composing his body a man becomes able to control the same principles in the world, that is, " the spirits of nature."

At the same time a right understanding of the principles of Hatha-Yoga teaches a man to understand the laws of the universe and his own place in the world.

Even an elementary acquaintance with the principles and methods of Hatha-Yoga shows the impossibility of studying Yoga without a teacher and without his constant supervision. The results attained by the methods of Hatha-Yoga are equally the work of the pupil himself and the work of the teacher on the pupil.

In other Yogas this may not be so clear. But in Hatha-Yoga there cannot be the slightest doubt about it, especially when the man who studies it has understood the principles of " Asanas."

" Asanas " is the name given in Hatha-Yoga to certain special postures of the body which a Yogi must learn to assume. Many of these postures appear quite impossible at the first glance. They look as if a man either must have no bones at all or else must break all his tendons. There already exists a sufficient number of photographic and even cinematographic pictures of the " Asanas," and the difficulty of these postures is evident to anyone who has had the opportunity of seeing such pictures. Even the description of the " Asanas " which can be found in certain books of Hatha-Yoga shows their difficulty and their practical impossibility for any ordinary man. Nevertheless the Hatha-Yogis study these " Asanas," that is, they train the body to assume all these incredible postures.

Everyone can try one of the easiest " Asanas." This is the " posture of Buddha," so-called because the sitting Buddha is usually represented in this " Asana." The simplest form of this " Asana " is when a Yogi sits cross-legged, not " Turkish fashion," but with one foot placed on the opposite knee, and the other knee on the other foot; the legs being tightly pressed to the ground and to each other. Even this " Asana," the simplest of all, is impossible without long and persistent training. But as a matter of fact the posture just described is not a complete " Asana." If one looks closely at statues of the Buddha, it will be seen that both feet lie on the knees, heels upward. In such a position the legs are interwoven in a manner which looks quite impossible without bones being broken. But people who have been in India have seen and *photographed* this " Asana " in its complete form.

Apart from the outward " Asanas " there also exist inward " Asanas," which consist in changing various inner functions, as for instance a slowing down or quickening of the action of the heart and the entire circulation of the blood. They further enable man to control a whole series of inner functions which ordinarily are not only outside the control of man, but in many cases completely unknown to European science or only beginning to be suspected.

The meaning and ultimate aim of the outward " Asanas " is precisely the attainment of control over the inner functions.

Self-instruction in the " Asanas " presents insurmountable difficulties. There exist descriptions of over seventy " Asanas." But even the most complete and detailed description does not give the order in which they should be studied. And this order cannot be indicated in books because it depends on the physical type of a man.

That is to say that for every physical type a different order is necessary. For every man there exists one or several " Asanas " which he can learn and practise more easily than the others. But the man himself does not know his own physical type, and does not know which " Asanas " are the easier for him and with which he should begin. Moreover, he does not know the *preparatory exercises*, which are different for every " Asana " and for every physical type.

All this can be determined for him only by a teacher possessing complete knowledge of Hatha-Yoga.

After a certain period of observation and after certain trial exercises which he sets his pupil the teacher determines his physical type and tells him with which of the " Asanas " he should begin. One pupil must begin with the seventeenth " Asana," another with the thirty-fifth, a third with the fifty-seventh, a fourth with the first, and so on.

Having established which of the " Asanas " the pupil must try to master, the teacher gives him special and successive exercises which he demonstrates to him. These exercises gradually bring him to the desired " Asana," that is, enable him to assume and keep for a certain time the requisite posture of the body.

When the first " Asana " is attained, the teacher determines the next " Asana " which the pupil must try to attain, and again gives him exercises which in the course of time bring him to this " Asana."

The study of a wrong " Asana " contains almost insurmountable difficulties. And, moreover, as is quite definitely pointed out in books expounding the principles of Hatha-Yoga, " a wrong Asana kills a man."

All this taken together shows quite clearly that the study of Hatha-Yoga as well as the study of other Yogas is impossible without a teacher.

The chief method of Hatha-Yoga, the method which makes possible the subordination to the will of the physical body and even of the " unconscious " physical functions, is continuous work on the *overcoming of pain.*

The overcoming of pain, the overcoming of the fear of physical suffering, the overcoming of continual and incessant desire for quiet, ease and comfort, create the force which transfers a Hatha-Yogi to another level of being.

In the literature, chiefly theosophical,[1] relating to the history of the principles and methods of Yoga there exists a difference of opinion which has a certain significance. There are authors who maintain that the study of Yoga must necessarily begin with Hatha-Yoga and that without Hatha-Yoga it cannot give any results. And there are other authors who maintain that Hatha-Yoga may be studied after the other Yogas, especially after Raja-Yoga, when the pupil is already in possession of all the powers given by new consciousness.

The most correct solution of the question would be to assume that in this case, as well as in many other cases, the difference depends upon the type; that is, there are types of men who must necessarily begin with Hatha-Yoga, and there are types for whom paths through the other Yogas are possible.

In the scientific records of investigators on " Indian Asceticism " which exist in Western literature, Hatha-Yogis are unfortunately often confused with " fakirs." The causes of such a confusion can be easily understood. The investigators who observe external phenomena and do not understand the principles of Yoga cannot distinguish original phenomena from imitation.[2] Fakirs imitate Hatha-Yogis. But what is done by Hatha-Yogis for the attainment of a definite aim, which is clearly understood by them, becomes itself the aim for Fakirs. Fakirs begin therefore with the most difficult, with extremes, and mostly with practices which *injure* the physical body. They hold their arms, or one arm, stretched upwards until the arms wither; they

---

[1] For instance, *Old Diary Leaves*, by H. S. Olcott, Vols. II and III.
[2] E.g. *Fakire und Fakirtum*, by Richard Schmidt.

look at the fire or at the sun until they become blind; they deliver themselves to be eaten by insects and the like. For a certain period of time some of them in this way develop in themselves strange and supernormal capacities, but their way has nothing in common with the way of Hatha-Yogis.

RAJA-YOGA

Raja-Yoga is the Yoga of the education of consciousness. The man who studies Raja-Yoga practically, acquires consciousness of his " I." At the same time he acquires extraordinary inner powers, control over himself and the capacity to influence other people.

Raja-Yoga in relation to the psychic world of man, to his self-consciousness, has the same meaning as Hatha-Yoga has in relation to the physical world. Hatha-Yoga is the Yoga of the overcoming of the body, the acquiring of control over the body and its functions; Raja-Yoga is the Yoga of the overcoming of the illusory and erroneous self-consciousness of man and of the acquiring of control over consciousness.

Raja-Yoga teaches man that which constitutes the basis of the philosophy of the whole world — *knowledge of himself*.

Just as Hatha-Yoga regards the physical body as imperfect but capable of being changed for the better, so Raja-Yoga regards the psychic apparatus of man as being far from ideal, but capable of being set right and improved.

The task of Raja-Yoga is the " placing of consciousness," which is completely analogous to the " placing of the voice " in singing. Ordinary Western thought does not in the least realise the necessity of " placing the consciousness," finds in general that ordinary consciousness is quite sufficient, and that man can have nothing else.

Raja-Yoga establishes that consciousness, like a powerful voice, requires proper " placing," which would multiply its power and quality tenfold, increase its efficiency, make it " sound better," reproduce better, reconstruct the interrelation of ideas, embrace more at one time.

The first assertion of Raja-Yoga is that man does not know himself at all, has a completely false, distorted idea of himself.

This lack of understanding of himself is man's chief difficulty on his way, the chief cause of his weakness. If we imagine a man who does not know his body, does not know the parts of his body, their number and relative position, does not know that he has two arms, two legs, one head and so on, it will give an exact illustration of our position in relation to our psychic world.

From the point of view of Raja-Yoga man's psychic apparatus is a system of darkened and crooked lenses through which his consciousness looks upon the world and upon itself, receiving a picture which in no way corresponds to the reality. The chief defect of the psychic apparatus is that it makes man accept as separate that which it shows as separate. A man who believes in his psychic apparatus is a man who believes in the field of view of the binoculars through which he looks, in the full conviction that what enters the field of view of his binoculars at that moment exists separately from that which does not enter it.

The new self-knowledge is attained in Raja-Yoga through a study of the principles of man's psychic world and through a long series of exercises of the consciousness.

A study of the principles of psychic life shows man the four states of consciousness possible for him, which in the usual Indian psychology are called:

deep sleep,
sleep with dreams,
waking state,
Turiya or the state of enlightenment.

(In esoteric teachings these states of consciousness are defined somewhat differently, but they remain four and their mutual relations remain near to the above.)

After this follows the study of psychic functions, thinking, feeling, sensing and so on, both separately and in their relation to each other; the study of dreams, the study of semi-conscious and unconscious psychic processes, the study of illusions and self-deceptions, the study of various forms of self-hypnosis and self-suggestion, *with the object of freeing oneself from them.*

One of the first practical tasks set before a man who begins to study Raja-Yoga is the attainment of the ability to stop thoughts, the capacity *not to think,* that is, entirely to stop the mind at will, to give a complete rest to the psychic apparatus.

This ability to stop thought is regarded as a necessary condition for awakening certain powers and possibilities latent within man, and as a necessary condition for subordinating the unconscious psychic processes to the will. Only when a man has created in himself this capacity for stopping the flow of his thoughts can he approach the possibility of hearing the thoughts of other people, and all the voices which incessantly speak in nature, the voices of various " small lives," which are component parts of himself, and the voices of " big lives," of which he is a component part. Only when he has acquired the capacity to create a passive state of his mind can a man hope to hear the *voice of the silence,* which alone can reveal to him the truths and secrets hidden from him.

Moreover (and this is the first thing that is attained), in learning to stop thinking at will man acquires the power of reducing the useless expenditure of psychic energy consumed in unnecessary thinking. Unnecessary thinking is one of the chief evils of our inner life. How often it happens that some thought gets into our mind, and the mind, having no power to throw it out, turns the thought over and over endlessly, just as a stream turns a stone over and over in its bed.

This happens especially when a man is agitated or annoyed or hurt, is afraid of something, is suspicious of something, and so on. And people do not realise what an enormous amount of energy is spent on this unnecessary turning over in the mind of the same thoughts, of the same words. People do not realise that a man, without noticing it, may repeat many thousand times in the course of an hour or two some silly sentence or fragment of verse, which has stuck in his mind without any reason.

When the " disciple " has learned *not to think*, he is taught *to think* — to think of what he wants to think of, and not of anything that comes into his head. This is a method of concentration. Complete concentration of mind on one subject and the capacity for not thinking of anything else at the same time, the capacity for not being drawn aside by accidental associations, give a man enormous powers. He can then force himself not only to think, but also not to feel, not to hear, not to see anything happening around him; he can avoid having the sensation of any kind of physical discomfort, either of heat or of cold or of suffering; he is able by a single effort to make himself insensible to any pain, even the most terrible. This explains one of the theories that Hatha-Yoga becomes easy after Raja-Yoga.

The next step, the third, is meditation. The man who has studied concentration is taught to use it, that is, to meditate, to enter deeply into a given question, to examine its different sides one after another, to find in it correlations and analogies with everything he knows, everything he has thought or heard before. Right meditation discloses to man an infinite amount that is new to him in things which he previously thought were known to him. It shows him depths about which it has never occurred to him to think and, above all, it brings him nearer the " new consciousness," flashes of which, like lightning, begin to illuminate his meditations, revealing to him for a moment infinitely remote horizons.

The next step — the fourth — is contemplation. Man is taught, having placed before himself one or another question, to enter into it as deeply as possible *without thinking;* or even without putting any question before himself, to enter deeply into an idea, a mental picture, landscape, phenomenon of nature, sound, number.

A man who has learned to contemplate awakens the higher faculties of his soul, lays himself open to influences which come from the higher spheres of the life of the world and, as it were, communes with the deepest mysteries of the universe.

At the same time Raja-Yoga makes man's " I " the object of concentration, meditation and contemplation. Having taught man to economise his mental powers and direct them at will, Raja-Yoga requires him to direct them upon self-knowledge, knowledge of his real " I."

The altering of man's self-consciousness and of his " self-feeling " is the principal aim of Raja-Yoga. Its object is to make man really feel and become conscious of the heights and depths in himself, by which he comes into contact with eternity and infinity, that is, to make man feel that he is not a mortal, temporary and finite speck of dust in the infinite universe, but an immortal, eternal and infinite quantity equal to the whole universe, a drop in the ocean of the spirit, but a drop which may contain the whole ocean. The broadening of the " I " according to the methods of Raja-Yoga is precisely this bringing together of the self-consciousness of man with the self-consciousness of the world, the transferring of the focus of self-consciousness from a small separate unit into infinity. Raja-Yoga broadens man's " I " and reconstructs his view of himself and his feeling of himself.

As a result man attains a state of extraordinary freedom and power. He not only controls himself but is able to control others. He can read the thoughts of other people whether they are near him or at a distance; he can suggest to them his own thoughts and desires and subordinate them to himself. He can acquire clairvoyance, he can know the past and the future.

All this may appear fantastic and impossible to a European reader, but much of the " miraculous " is in reality not at all as impossible as it seems at the first glance. In the methods of Raja-Yoga everything is based on the understanding of laws which are incomprehensible to us, and on the strictly consecutive and gradual character of work on oneself.

The idea of " separation of self," of " non-attachment," occupies a very important place in the practice of Raja-Yoga. After this follows the idea of the absence of permanency and unity in man and in his " I " — and further the idea of the non-existence of the *separateness* of man, the absence of any division between man, humanity and nature.

The study of Raja-Yoga is impossible without the constant and direct guidance of a teacher. Before the pupil begins to study himself he is studied by the teacher, who determines the way he must follow, that is, the sequence of exercises he must do, since the exercises can never be the same for different men.

The aim of Raja-Yoga is to bring man nearer to higher consciousness, proving to him the possibility of a new state of consciousness, similar to awakening after sleep. As long as a man does not know the taste and sensation of this awakening, as long as his mind is still asleep, Raja-Yoga aims at making the idea of awakening understandable to him by telling him of the people who have awakened, teaching him to recognise the fruits of their thought and activity, which are entirely different from the results of the activity of ordinary people.

KARMA-YOGA

Karma-Yoga teaches right living. Karma-Yoga is the Yoga of activity.

Karma-Yoga teaches the right relation towards people and the right action in the ordinary circumstances of life. Karma-Yoga teaches how to become a Yogi in life without going into the desert or entering a school of

Yogis. Karma-Yoga is a necessary supplement to all other Yogas; only with the help of Karma-Yoga can a man always remember his aim and never lose sight of it. Without Karma-Yoga all other Yogas either give no results or degenerate into something opposite to themselves. Raja-Yoga and Hatha-Yoga degenerate into a search for external miracles, for the mysterious, for the terrible, that is, into pseudo-occultism. Bhakti-Yoga degenerates into pseudo-mysticism, into superstition, into a personal adoration or into a striving for personal salvation. Jnana-Yoga degenerates into scholasticism or at best into metaphysics.

Karma-Yoga is always connected with the aim of inner development, of inner improvement. It helps man not to fall asleep inwardly amidst the entangling influences of life, especially in the midst of the *hypnotising influence of activity*. It makes him remember that nothing external has any significance, that everything must be done without caring about results. Without Karma-Yoga man becomes absorbed in the nearest, the visible, aims and forgets the chief aim.

Karma-Yoga teaches man to change his fate, to direct it at will. According to the fundamental idea of Karma-Yoga this is attained only by altering the inner attitude of man towards things and towards his own actions.

The same action can be performed differently, one and the same event can be lived through differently. And if a man alters his attitude towards what happens to him, this will in the course of time inevitably change the character of the events which he encounters on his way.

Karma-Yoga teaches man to understand that when it seems to him that he himself is acting, in reality it is not he who acts, but only a power passing through him. Karma-Yoga asserts that a man is not at all what he thinks himself to be, and teaches man to understand that only in very rare cases does he act of himself and independently, and that in most cases he acts only as a part of one or another great whole. This is the " occult " side of Karma-Yoga, the teaching concerning the forces and laws which govern man.

A man who understands the ideas of Karma-Yoga feels all the time that he is but a tiny screw or a tiny wheel in the big machine, and that the success or non-success of what he thinks he is doing depends very little on his own actions.

Acting and feeling in this way, a man can never meet with failure in anything, because the greatest failure, the greatest unsuccess, may further success in his inner work, in his struggle with himself, if he only finds the right attitude towards this unsuccess.

A life governed by the principles of Karma-Yoga differs greatly from an ordinary life. In ordinary life, no matter what the conditions may be, the chief aim of man consists in avoiding all unpleasantnesses, difficulties and discomforts, so far as this is possible.

In a life governed by the principles of Karma-Yoga, a man does not seek to avoid unpleasantnesses or discomforts. On the contrary, he welcomes them, for they afford him a chance of overcoming them. From the point of view of Karma-Yoga, if life offered no difficulties it would be necessary to create them artificially. And therefore the difficulties which are met with in life are regarded not as something unpleasant which one must try to avoid, but as very useful conditions for the aims of inner work and inner development.

When a man realises this and feels it constantly, life itself becomes his teacher.

The chief principle of Karma-Yoga is *non-attachment*. A man who follows the methods of Karma-Yoga must practise *non-attachment* always and in everything, whether to good or to evil, to pleasure or to pain. Non-attachment does not mean indifference. It is a certain kind of separation of self from what happens or from what a man is doing. It is not coldness, nor is it the desire to shut oneself off from life. It is the recognition and the constant realisation that everything is done according to certain laws and that everything in the world has its own fate.

From an ordinary point of view the following of the principles of Karma-Yoga appears as fatalism. But it is not fatalism in the sense of the accepting of the exact and unalterable preordination of everything without the possibility of any change whatever. On the contrary, Karma-Yoga teaches how to change the karma — how to influence the karma. But from the point of view of Karma-Yoga this influencing is an entirely inner process. Karma-Yoga teaches that a man may change the people and events around him by changing his attitude towards them.

The idea of this is very clear. Every man from his birth is surrounded by a certain karma, by certain people and certain events. And in accordance with his nature, education, tastes and habits he adopts a certain definite attitude towards things, people and events. So long as his attitude remains unchanged, people, things and events also remain unchanged, that is, corresponding to his karma. If he is not satisfied with his karma, if he wants something new and unknown he must change his attitude towards what he has and then the new events will come.

Karma-Yoga is the only way possible for people who are tied to life, who are unable to free themselves from the external forms of life, for people who either through their birth or through their own powers and capacities are placed at the head of human communities or groups, for people who are connected with the progress of the life of humanity, for historical personages, for people whose personal life seems to be the expression of the life of an epoch or a nation. These people cannot change themselves visibly; they can change themselves only internally, while externally remaining the same as before, saying the same things, doing the same things, but *without attachment*, as actors on the stage. Having become such actors in relation to their life, they become *Yogis* in the midst of the most varied and intense activity. There can be peace in their soul whatever their troubles may be.

Their thought can work without hindrance, independently of anything that may surround it.

Karma-Yoga gives freedom to the prisoner in a gaol and to the king on a throne, if only they can feel that they are actors playing their rôles.

BHAKTI-YOGA

Bhakti-Yoga is the Yoga of the religious way. Bhakti-Yoga teaches how to believe, how to pray and how to attain certain salvation. Bhakti-Yoga can be applied to any religion. Differences in religions do not exist for Bhakti-Yoga. There is only the idea of the religious way.

The Yogi Ramakrishna, who in the eighties of the last century lived in the monastery of Dakshineswar, near Calcutta, and became known through the works of his disciples (Vivekananda, Abedananda and others), was a Bhakti-Yogi. He recognised as equal all religions with all their dogmas, sacraments and rituals. He himself belonged simultaneously to all religions. Twelve years of his life were spent in following over and over again the way of asceticism according to the rules of each of the great religions in turn. And always he came to the same result, to the state of samadhi or ecstasy, which he became convinced constitutes the aim of all religions. Ramakrishna used therefore to say to his disciples that from personal experience he had arrived at the conclusion that all great religions are one, and was convinced that all of them lead alike to God, that is, to the Highest Knowledge.

In bringing man nearer to samadhi, Bhakti-Yoga, if practised separately from other Yogas, carries him away completely from the world. Man acquires enormous powers, but at the same time loses the capacity for using them (as well as the capacity for using his ordinary powers) for earthly purposes.

Ramakrishna told his disciples that after he had been several times in the state of samadhi he began to feel that he was no longer able to take care of himself. He told his disciples how once he cried, thinking that now he must die of starvation. This frightened him at first, until he became convinced that somebody was always taking care of him.

In the book *The Gospel of Ramakrishna* a remarkable conversation is quoted between the sick Ramakrishna, who was already nearing death, and an Indian sage, a Pundit, who came to visit him.

Pundit Sashadhar came one day to pay his respects to Bhagavan Ramakrishna. Seeing his illness, he asked:

Bhagavan, why dost thou not concentrate thy mind upon the diseased part and thus cure thyself?

The Bhagavan replied:

How can I fix my mind, which I have given to God, upon this cage of flesh and blood?

Sashadhar said:

Why dost thou not pray to thy divine mother for cure of thy illness?

The Bhagavan answered:

When I think of my mother the physical body vanishes and I am entirely out of it, so it is impossible for me to pray for anything concerning the body.[3]

Thus all that man attains on this way has no value from the earthly point of view and cannot be used for the acquisition of earthly comforts.

The impossibility of proving by argument to another man the existence of what he does not himself feel emotionally, caused Ramakrishna to teach that Bhakti-Yoga is the best of all the ways of Yoga because it does not require proof. Bhakti-Yoga addresses itself directly to the feelings and brings together, not people who think alike, but people who feel alike.

Ramakrishna also considered Bhakti-Yoga the simplest and the easiest of all the ways because this way demands the destruction of attachment to anything earthly, self-renunciation, the giving up of one's will and the unconditional surrender of oneself to God.

But since for many people precisely this may seem to be the most difficult, that alone shows that Bhakti-Yoga is a way for people of a certain definite type and of a definite mentality, and that Bhakti-Yoga cannot be considered a way accessible to all.

Bhakti-Yoga has much in common with Raja-Yoga. Like Raja-Yoga, Bhakti-Yoga includes methods of concentration, meditation and contemplation, but the object of concentration, meditation and contemplation is not " I," but " God," that is, the *All*, in which the little spark of human consciousness completely vanishes.

The practical significance of Bhakti-Yoga lies in the emotional training. Bhakti-Yoga is a method of " breaking in " and " harnessing " emotions for those whose emotions are particularly strong but whose religious emotions, which ought to control other emotions, are scattered, not concentrated, carry them at once very far but produce strong reactions. At the same time it is a method for developing religious emotions for those in whom they are weak. Bhakti-Yoga is in a sense a supplement to any religion or an introduction to religion for a man of a non-religious type.

The ideas of Bhakti-Yoga are nearer and more intelligible for the West than the ideas of other Yogas, owing to the existence in Western literature of works on " religious practice " akin to Bhakti-Yoga in their spirit and meaning, although quite different in quality.

Works of such a kind in Protestant countries, for instance, the books of the German mystics of the 16th, 17th and 18th centuries, are often interesting, but Protestantism cut itself off too thoroughly from tradition, and the authors of these works were obliged to seek, either openly or stealthily, for a support of their methods in " occultism " or in " theosophy " of one

---

[3] *The Gospel of Ramakrishna*, published by The Vedanta Society, New York, 1907, p. 419.

kind or another. Thus the Protestant works are not purely religious.

In Catholicism everything that had any life in it was probably killed in the times of the Inquisition, and Catholic works on religious practice, such as the well-known book of Ignatius Loyola, are nothing but manuals for creating hallucinations of a definite and stereotyped character — Jesus on the Cross, The Virgin Mary with the Infant, Saints, Martyrs, "Hell," "Heaven," and so on. In other words they teach the transference of dreams into the waking state and the formation of these dreams into certain definite images — a process quite possible and called in pseudo-occultism "clairvoyance." The very same methods for creating pseudo-clairvoyance exist and play a very important part in modern occultism.

A very amusing parody of these methods is to be found in Eliphas Lévi's book *Dogme et Rituel de la Haute Magie*, where he describes an evocation of the devil (*Rituel*, p. 243). Unfortunately very few readers of Eliphas Lévi understand that this is a parody.

Pseudo-clairvoyance, "dreams in the waking state," desired and expected hallucinations, are called in Orthodox mystic literature "beauty." [4] It is very characteristic of Orthodox mysticism that it warns people and cautions them precisely against what Catholic mysticism and pseudo-occultism advise and suggest.

The most interesting works on religious practice are to be found in the literature of the Eastern Orthodox church. First, there is a collection of writings in six volumes bearing the title *Dobrotolubiye* ($\phi\iota\lambda o\kappa a\lambda i a$) (the greater part of which was translated from the Greek), which contains descriptions of mystical experiences, statutes and regulations of monastic life, rules of prayer and contemplation, and descriptions of methods very near methods of Hatha-Yoga (adopted in Bhakti-Yoga), as for instance methods of breathing, of different postures and positions of the body, and so on.

Besides the *Dobrotolubiye* itself there must be noted a small book belonging to the middle of the 19th century which was sold in Russia before the war in the third edition of 1884. This book is called *The Sincere Narrations of a Pilgrim to his Spiritual Father*. It is by an unknown author and is in a sense an introduction to the *Dobrotolubiye*, though at the same time it is a quite independent treatise on religious practice very near to Bhakti-Yoga. An acquaintance with this small book gives an exact idea of the character and the spirit of Bhakti-Yoga.

"The Narrations of a Pilgrim" is extremely interesting even from a literary point of view alone. It is one of the little known gems of Russian literature. Both the pilgrim himself and the people he met and spoke of are all

---

[4] The word "прелесть" is the translation of the Greek $\pi\lambda\acute{a}\nu\eta$, temptation, seduction. But the Russian word прелесть besides its first meaning, "allurement," has a great many associations connected with its second meaning, "charm" or "beauty." And in the English translation I have left the word "beauty," because it renders best the meaning put into this word in the *Dobrotolubiye* and "The Narrations of a Pilgrim." Also it shows clearly the character of the experiences preferred in Catholic mysticism and in pseudo-occultism, that is their external and formal "beauty" as opposed to their inner meaning and content.

living Russian types, many of whom have existed up to our own times and whom we who are living now have seen and met.

It is difficult to tell whether the pilgrim actually existed and whether his narrations were written down from his words by the Archimandrite Paissy, the author of the foreword to the book, or whether these narrations are Paissy's own or those of some other educated monk. Much in these narrations leads one to suspect the pen and the thought not only of an educated but of a highly educated and highly talented man. On the other hand those who know in what an extraordinarily artistic way some Russians such as this " pilgrim " can tell stories about themselves and everything else, will not think it impossible for the pilgrim to have been a real living person who was actually speaking about himself.

" The Narrations of a Pilgrim " contains a schematic explanation of the principles of a special exercise of *Bhakti-Yoga*, which is called constant or mental prayer, and a description of the results this prayer gives.

The " pilgrim " repeated his prayer, " *Lord Jesus Christ, Son of God, have mercy upon me,*" at first three thousand times consecutively in a day, then six thousand times, then twelve thousand and finally without counting. When the prayer had become quite automatic in him, did not require any effort and was repeated involuntarily, he began to " bring it into the heart," that is, to make it emotional, to connect a definite feeling with it. After a certain time the prayer began to evoke this feeling and to strengthen it, enriching it to an extraordinary degree of acuteness and intensity.

" The Narrations of a Pilgrim " cannot serve as a manual for the practical study of " mental prayer," because the description of the method of study contains a certain probably intentional incorrectness, namely, far too great an ease and rapidity in the pilgrim's study of " mental prayer." Nevertheless, this book gives a very clear idea of the principles of work upon self according to the methods of Bhakti-Yoga and is, in many respects, a unique production of its kind.

The methods of the *Dobrotolubiye* have not vanished from real life, as is shown by a very interesting, though unfortunately too short, description of Mount Athos by B. Zaitseff which was published in Russian in Paris in 1928.

B. Zaitseff describes the everyday life and the character of the religious practice in the Russian monastery of St. Panteleimon at Mount Athos. It can be seen from his description that " mental prayer " (the cell duty) plays a very important part in monastic life.

The basis of this life is the cutting off of the personal will and an absolute submission to hierarchic authority. No monk may go out of the gates of the monastery without having received the " blessing " (permission) from the abbot. The abbot assigns to every monk his " obedience," that is, the particular work he has to do. Thus there are monks who are fishermen, wood-cutters, kitchen-gardeners, agricultural labourers, vineyard workers, sawyers, and more intellectual workers—monk-librarians, "grammarians," ikon-painters, photographers, and so on. At present the monastery of St. Panteleimon contains about five hundred brothers.

. . . .

The arrangement of the day in the monastery is fixed once for all and everything moves in obedience only to the hands of the clock. But as everything is unusual at Mount Athos, so time also is astonishing. To the day of my departure I could not get used to it. It is the ancient East. At sunset the hand of the tower clock is moved to midnight. The whole system changes according to the time of the year, and one must move with the seasons and adapt oneself to the sunset. In May the difference between Mount Athos and European time amounts to about five hours.

Thus Matins in St. Panteleimon's monastery began, while I was there, at six o'clock in the morning (one in the morning by our time). Matins continue until four or four-thirty in the morning. (In this case and afterwards I give the European time.) After Matins there follows immediately the mass (liturgy), which continues until six in the morning; thus almost the whole night is spent in church services; this is a characteristic feature of Mount Athos. Then everybody rests till seven. From seven to nine is " obedience " [5] for nearly everyone. Even the oldest monks come out to work if they are even relatively in good health (they go to the forest, to vineyards, to kitchen-gardens; they load oxen with timber and mules with hay and firewood). The first meal is at nine o'clock, then " obedience " again till one. At one o'clock tea and rest till three; then " obedience " till six o'clock. From five-thirty to six-thirty vespers are said in the churches. Very few monks attend these day services, for most of them are at work. But vespers are read for them at their work. At six in the evening there is the second meal, if it is not a fast day. If it is Monday, Wednesday or Friday, instead of a meal they have only bread and tea. After the second meal the church-bells ring for complines, which continue from seven to eight o'clock. Then follows " cell-duty," that is, prayer with bowings in the cell. After each short prayer [6] the monk moves one bead of his rosary and makes a bow from the waist. At the eleventh bead, a large one, he bows to the ground. Thus a cassocked monk (the lowest monastic degree) makes daily six hundred bows from the waist; a "mantled" monk makes about a thousand; and a monk invested with a schema makes about fifteen hundred (not counting corresponding bows to the ground). In the case of a cassocked monk it takes about an hour and a half, in the case of a monk of the highest rank from three to three and a half hours. Consequently a cassocked monk is free about ten o'clock and the others about eleven. Till one o'clock, when Matins begin, is the monks' sleeping-time (two to three hours). To this is sometimes added an hour in the morning, and perhaps, an hour in the afternoon, after tea. But as every monk has his own small things to do which take time, it may be supposed that the monks sleep not more than four hours, or even less.

To us laymen who have seen this life, the essence of which is that the monks pray through the night, work through the day and have very little sleep and very poor food, it is a mystery how they can stand it. And yet they live, and live

---

[5] The daily work given to each monk by the abbot.
[6] Such as the Jesus prayer, Ave Maria, prayer for the dead, prayer for the living, etc.

to a very old age (at present the majority of them are old men). Moreover, the commonest type of Mount Athos monk seems to me a healthy, calm and balanced type.[7]

Monastic life, whatever severity and difficulties it may involve, is certainly not Bhakti-Yoga. Bhakti-Yoga can be applied to every religion (of course to a real religion, not to an invented one); this means that Bhakti-Yoga includes all religions and recognises no difference between them. Moreover, Bhakti-Yoga, as well as all the other Yogas, does not require a final abandonment of life, but only temporary withdrawal from life for the attainment of a definite aim. When the aim is attained, the Yoga becomes unnecessary. Also, the Yoga requires more initiative and more understanding. Yoga is a more active way. Monastic life is a more passive way.

Nevertheless the study of monastic life and of monastic asceticism is of great interest from the psychological point of view, because here many ideas of Yoga can be seen in practical application, though possibly in a setting different from true Yoga.

As well as in Orthodox monasteries, the ideas of Bhakti-Yoga occupy a very important place in Mahomedan monasteries of Sufis and Dervishes, and also in Buddhist monasteries, especially in Ceylon, where Buddhism has been preserved in its purest form.

Ramakrishna, whom I have mentioned, was both a Yogi and a monk at the same time, but more a monk than a Yogi. His followers, so far as can be judged by information to be found in literature, have gone partly in a religious, partly in a philosophical direction, although they call it Yoga. In reality the school of Ramakrishna has not left behind any ways to a practical Yoga, having deviated into theoretical descriptions of these ways.

JNANA-YOGA

Jnana (Gnyana or Gnana) Yoga, as it is pronounced in different parts of India, is the Yoga of knowledge. The root *jna, gnya, gna* (Russian *zna*) corresponds to the roots of the words: modern English *know*, German *kennen*, Anglo-Saxon *cnawan*, Latin (*g*)*noscere*, Greek γιγνώσχειν. Jnana-Yoga leads men towards perfection by changing his knowledge both in relation to himself and in relation to the world surrounding him. This is the Yoga of men of the intellectual way. It liberates the human mind from the fetters of an illusory conception of the world, leads it to true knowledge, showing the fundamental laws of the universe.

Jnana-Yoga uses all the methods of Raja-Yoga. It starts from the affirmation that the weak human mind, brought up in contemplation of illusions, will never solve the enigmas of life, that this demands a better instrument specially adapted for the task. Together therefore with the study of the principles lying at the basis of things Jnana-Yoga requires the special work

---

[7] B. Zaitseff, *Athos*, Y.M.C.A. Press (in Russian), Paris, 1928, pp. 32–34.

of the education of the mind. The mind is trained for contemplation, for concentration, for thinking in new and unaccustomed directions and on new planes, connected not with the outward aspect of things but with their fundamental principles; and above all the mind is trained to think quickly and exactly, always keeping in view the essential, and wasting no time on external and unimportant details.

Jnana-Yoga starts from the fact that the chief cause of human misfortunes and disasters is *Avidya* — Ignorance. And the object of Jnana-Yoga is to overcome Avidya and bring man nearer to what is called Brahma-vidya, divine knowledge.

The aim of Jnana-Yoga is the liberation of the human mind from those limited conditions of knowledge in which it is placed by the forms of sense perception and by logical thinking based on opposites. From the point of view of Jnana-Yoga a man must first of all learn right thinking. Right thinking and the broadening of ideas and conceptions must lead to the broadening of perception, while the broadening of perception must finally lead to a change in sensations, that is, to the abolition of all false and illusory sensations.

Indian teachers (Gurus) do not in the least aim at making their disciples accumulate as much miscellaneous knowledge as possible. On the contrary, they want their disciples to see in everything they study, however small it may be, the principles that lie at the basis of everything. Usually the disciple is given for meditation either some verse from ancient scriptures or some symbol, and he meditates for a year, two years, possibly for ten years, from time to time bringing to his teacher the results of his meditations. This seems strange to a Western mind, which always aims at going ever forward, but possibly it is the right method for penetrating to the root of ideas instead of acquiring a superficial acquaintance with their external side by making enormous mental collections of words and facts.

In studying Jnana-Yoga man sees clearly that Yoga cannot be only a method. A right method must necessarily lead to certain truths, and in expounding a method it is impossible not to touch on these truths. Nevertheless, it must be remembered that in its nature Yoga cannot be a doctrine and that there can therefore be no synopsis or general outline of the ideas of Jnana-Yoga. In using Yoga as a method man must himself find, feel and realise the truths which form the content of the philosophy of the Yogis. The same truths received in the form of a doctrine from another person or from books will not have the same effect upon the mind and soul as truths which man has found for himself, truths he has long sought for and long struggled with before accepting them.

Jnana-Yoga teaches that the truth for a man can only be that which he has felt as truth. Moreover, it teaches man to verify one truth by another, to ascend slowly towards the summit of knowledge, never losing sight of the point of departure and constantly returning to it, in order to preserve a right orientation.

Jnana-Yoga teaches that the truths realised by the logical mind, educated on observation of the three-dimensional world, are not truths at all from the point of view of higher consciousness.

Jnana-Yoga teaches man to distrust himself, to distrust his sensations, mental images, concepts, ideas, thoughts and words; above all to distrust words, to verify everything and always to look round at every step, to demand that everything that has been found should accord with the testimony of experience and with fundamental principles.

The ideas of Jnana-Yoga have been transmitted up to now in a symbolical form only. The images of Indian gods and the figures of Indian mythology contain many ideas of Jnana-Yoga. But the understanding of them requires oral explanations and commentaries.

The study of Jnana-Yoga from books is impossible because there exists a whole series of principles which have never been expounded in writing. Indications of these, and even some definitions of them, can be found in books, but these indications are intelligible only to those who have already received direct tuition. The difficulty of understanding these principles is especially great because it is not enough to understand them intellectually; it is necessary to learn to apply and use them for the division and classification not only of abstract ideas, but also the concrete things and occurrences which man meets in life.

The idea of *Dharma* in one of its meanings in Indian philosophy is an introduction to the study of one of these principles, which may be called the principle of relativity.

The principle of relativity in the science of Yogis has nothing in common with the principle of relativity in modern physics and is studied not in its application to one class of phenomena only, but in relation to all the phenomena of the universe on all planes and levels, and thus, by penetrating everything, it connects everything into one single whole.

All that has gone before is a short summary of what can be learned about Yoga from the existing and generally accessible literature in European languages.

But in order to understand rightly the meaning and significance of the different Yogas it is necessary to realise clearly that all five Yogas, that is, each one separately, are an abbreviation and adaptation for different types of people of *one and the same general system*. This system is taught orally in particular schools, which differ from the Yogis' schools as much as the Yogis' schools differ from monasteries.

This system has no name and has never been made public; allusions to it are only rarely met with in Eastern writings. Much of what has been ascribed to Yoga belongs in reality to this system. At the same time the system cannot be regarded simply as a combination of the five Yogas. All the Yogas have originated from this system; each of the Yogas is in a sense a one-sided understanding of it. One is wider, another is narrower, but all of them expound one and the same system. The combination of all five Yogas does not reconstruct it because it contains many ideas, principles and methods which do not enter into any of the Yogas.

Fragments of this system, so far as the author has succeeded in becoming acquainted with them, will be set forth in the book *Man and the World in which he lives — Fragments of an Unknown Teaching*, which is being prepared for publication.

1912–1934

Chapter VII

ON THE STUDY OF DREAMS AND ON HYPNOTISM

❄

Possibly the most interesting first impressions of my life came from the world of dreams. And from my earliest years the world of dreams attracted me, made me search for explanations of its incomprehensible phenomena and try to determine the interrelation of the real and the unreal in dreams. Certain quite extraordinary experiences were, for me, connected with dreams. When still a child I woke on several occasions with the distinct feeling of having experienced something so interesting and enthralling that all that I had known before, all I had come into contact with or seen in life, appeared to me afterwards to be unworthy of attention and devoid of any interest. Moreover, I was always struck by recurring dreams, dreams which occurred in the same form, in the same surroundings, led to the same results, to the same end, and always left behind the same feelings.

About 1900, when I had already read almost all I could find on dreams in psychological literature,[1] I decided to try to observe my dreams systematically.

---

[1] In speaking of the literature on dreams I do not have in mind so-called psycho-analysis, that is, the theories of Freud and his followers, Jung, Adler and others. The reason for this is first, that when I began to be interested in dreams psychoanalysis was not yet in existence, or was very little known, and secondly, that, as I subsequently became convinced, there is and there was in psychoanalysis nothing of value, nothing that would make me alter the least of my conclusions though they are invariably all opposed to the psychoanalytical.

In order not to return again to this question I want to remark here that other aspects of psychoanalysis besides the unsuccessful attempt to study dreams are just as weak and often harmful, because they promise very much and there are people who believe in these promises and owing to this they completely lose the ability of distinguishing between the real and the false.

The only service psychoanalysis has rendered psychology as a whole is a precise formulation of the principle of the necessity of more and more observations in regions which so far have not entered into the subject of psychology. But it is exactly this principle which psychoanalysis itself has failed to follow because, having brought forward in the first stages of its existence a series of very doubtful hypotheses and generalisations, in the next stage it dogmatised them and in this way stopped any possibility of its own development. The specific " psychoanalytical " terminology which has grown out of these dogmatised hypotheses and become a kind of jargon helps us to recognise the adherents of psychoanalysis and their followers no matter how they call themselves and no matter

My observations pursued a double purpose:

1. I wanted to collect as much material as possible for judging the structure and origin of dreams and I began, as is usually recommended, to write down my dreams immediately on awakening.

2. I wanted to verify a rather fantastic idea of my own which had made its appearance almost in my childhood: *was it not possible to preserve consciousness in dreams,* that is, to know while dreaming that one is asleep and *to think consciously* as we think when awake.

The first, that is, writing down dreams and so on, very soon brought me to the understanding of the impossibility of a practical realisation of the usually recommended methods of observing dreams. *Dreams do not stand observation; observations change them.* And I very soon noticed that I was observing, not those dreams which I used to have before, but new dreams *which were created by the very fact of observation.* There was something in me which at once began *to invent dreams* directly it felt that they were

---

how much they try to deny the connection between different schools and divisions of psychoanalysis and their origin in a common source.

The characteristic feature of this jargon is that it consists of words relating to non-existing phenomena which are accepted by the followers of psychoanalysis as existing. On the imaginary existence of these phenomena and on their imaginary relations to one another psychoanalysis has constructed a fairly complicated system something like the "natural philosophy" of the beginning of the 19th century, or like certain mediæval systems which also consisted in the description and classification of non-existing phenomena, as, for instance, various very exact and detailed *demonologies.*

The funny side of psychoanalysis, as a study of its history shows, is that all the principal features of the latest psychoanalysis were deduced by Dr. Freud on the basis of observations on *one case* in the middle eighties of last century. These observations of *one female patient* form the entire basis of psychoanalysis and of all its theories and, what is particularly interesting, these observations were made while using a method which was later condemned by Freud himself. The method consisted in hypnotising the patient and putting questions to her about herself which she could not answer in a normal state. As it has been established with an undoubted accuracy, both before and after this experiment, this method can lead to nothing because by persisting in questions of this kind either the hypnotiser without knowing it suggests answers to the hypnotised subject or the hypnotised subject invents fantastic theories and tells imaginary tales. In such a manner the famous "father complex" was found which brought along with it the "mother complex" and later on the whole box of tricks, the "Œdipus myth," etcetera.

The principal facts referring to this tragi-comic aspect of psychoanalysis can be found in a book by Stefan Zweig, one of the chief apologists of Freud. Fortunately the author brings out these facts obviously entirely without realising their significance.

The later tendency of psychoanalysis is to call itself *psychology* and to speak in the name of psychology in general.

The amusing side to this is that, under the mask of psychology psychoanalysis has penetrated into the domains of university science in several countries and forms a part of the compulsory curricula in some medical schools and faculties, so that students are obliged to undergo examinations in all this muddle.

The undoubted success of psychoanalysis in modern thought is explained by the poverty of the ideas, the timidity of the methods and the complete absence of inclination towards any practical application of its theories on the part of psychology which remains scientific, and then, most of all, by the very painfully felt need of a *general system.*

The popularity of psychoanalysis in certain literary and art circles and among certain classes of the public is explained by the justification and defence of homo-sexuality by psychoanalysis.

attracting attention. This made the usual methods of observation obviously useless.

The second, that is, *attempts to preserve consciousness in sleep,* created, most unexpectedly for me, a new way of observing dreams which I had not before suspected. Namely, they created a particular half-dream state. And I was very quickly convinced that without the help of half-dream states it was quite impossible to observe dreams without changing them.

"Half-dream states" began to appear probably as a result of my efforts to observe dreams at moments of falling asleep or in half-sleep after awaking. I cannot say exactly when these states began to come in full form. Probably they developed gradually. I think they began to appear for a short time before the moment of falling asleep, but if I allowed my attention to dwell on them I could not sleep afterwards. I came therefore gradually, by experience, to the conclusion that it was much easier to observe "half-dream states" in the morning, when already awake but still in bed.

Wishing to create these states, after waking I again closed my eyes and began to doze, at the same time keeping my mind on some definite image, or some thought. And sometimes in such cases there began those strange states which I call "half-dream states." Without definite efforts such states would not come. Like all other people I either slept or did not sleep, but in these "half-dream states" I both slept and did not sleep at the same time.

If I take the time when these "half-dream states" were just beginning, i.e. when they came at the moment of going to sleep, then usually the first sign of their approach was the "hypnagogic hallucinations" many times described in psychological literature. I will not dwell on this. But when "half-dream states" began to occur chiefly in the morning, they usually started without being preceded by any visual impressions.

In order to describe these "half-dream states" and all that was connected with them, it is necessary to say a great deal. But I shall try to be as brief as possible because at the present moment I am concerned not with them but with their results.

The first sensation they produced was one of astonishment. I expected to find one thing and found another. The next was a feeling of extraordinary joy which the "half-dream states," and the possibility of seeing and understanding things in quite a new way, gave me. And the third was a certain fear of them, because I very soon noticed that if I let them take their own course they would begin to grow and expand and encroach both upon sleep and upon the waking state.

Thus "half-dream states" attracted me on the one hand and frightened me on the other. I felt in them enormous possibilities and also a great danger. But what I became absolutely convinced of was that *without these "half-dream states" no study of dreams is possible* and that all attempts at such study are inevitably doomed to failure, to wrong deductions, to fantastic hypotheses, and the like.

From the point of view, therefore, of my original idea of the study of dreams I could be very content with the results obtained. I possessed a key to the world of dreams, and all that was vague and incomprehensible in them gradually cleared up and became comprehensible and visible.

The fact is that in "half-dream states" I was having all the dreams I usually had. But I was fully conscious, I could see and understand how these dreams were created, what they were built from, what was their cause, and in general what was cause and what was effect. Further, I saw that in "half-dream states" I had a certain control over dreams. I could create them and could see what I wanted to see, although this was not always successful and must not be understood too literally. Usually I only gave the first impetus, and after that the dreams developed as it were of their own accord, sometimes greatly astonishing me by the unexpected and strange turns which they took.

I had in "half-dream states" all the dreams I was able to have in the ordinary way. Gradually my whole repertoire of dreams passed before me. And I was able to observe these dreams quite consciously, could see how they were created, how they passed one into another, and could understand all their mechanism.

The dreams, observed in this way, became gradually classified and divided into definite categories.

To one of these categories I assigned all the constantly recurring dreams which I had had from time to time during the whole of my life from early childhood.

Some of these dreams used previously to frighten me by their persistence, their frequent repetition and a certain strange character, and made me look for a hidden or allegorical meaning, prophecy or warning in them. It had seemed to me that these dreams must have a certain significance, that they must refer to something in my life.

Speaking generally, naïve thinking about dreams always begins with the idea that all, and especially persistently recurring, dreams must have a certain meaning, must foretell the future, show the hidden traits of one's character, express physical qualities, inclinations, hidden pathological states, and so on. In reality, however, as I very soon became convinced, my recurring dreams were in no way connected with any traits or qualities of my nature, or with any events in my life. And I found for them clear and simple explanations which left no doubt as to their real nature.

I will describe several of these dreams with their explanations.

The first and most characteristic dream, which I had very often, was one in which I saw a quagmire or bog of a peculiar character which I was never able to describe to myself afterwards. Often this quagmire or bog, or merely deep mud, such as is seen on Russian roads and even in Moscow streets, appeared before me on the ground or even on the floor of my room, without any association with the plot of the dream. I did my utmost to avoid this mud, not to step into it, even not to touch it. But I invariably got into it, and it began to suck me in and generally sucked my legs in up to the knees. I made every conceivable effort to get out of this mud or mire, and sometimes I succeeded, but then I usually awoke.

It was very tempting to interpret this dream allegorically, as a threat or a warning. But when I began to have this dream in " half-dream states " it was explained very simply. The whole content of this dream was created by the sensation of my legs being entangled in the blanket or sheets, so that I could neither move nor turn them. If I succeeded in turning over, I escaped from this mud, but then I invariably woke up, because I made a violent movement. As regards the mud itself and its " peculiar " character, this was connected, as I again became convinced in " half-dream states," with the more imaginary than real " fear of bogs " I had in childhood. This fear, which children and sometimes even grown-up people often have in Russia, is created by tales of quagmires and bogs and " windows." [2] And in my case, observing this dream in " half-dream state " I could reconstruct where the sensation of the peculiar mud came from. This sensation and the visual images were quite definitely associated with tales of quagmires and " windows " which were said to have a " peculiar " character, that they could be recognised, that they always differed from an ordinary swamp, that they " sucked in " what fell into them, that they were filled with a *peculiar* soft mire, and so on, and so on.

In " half-dream states " the sequence of associations in the whole dream was quite clear. First appeared the sensation of bound legs, then the signal: bog, mire, window, *peculiar* soft mud. Then fear, desire to tear oneself away and usually the awakening. There was nothing, absolutely nothing, mystical or psychologically significant in these dreams.

Second, there was a dream which also frightened me. *I dreamed that I was blind.* Something was happening around me, I heard voices, sounds, noises, movement, felt some danger threatening me; and I had to move somewhere with hands stretched out in front of me in order to avoid knocking against something, making all the time terrible efforts to see what was around me.

In " half-dream states " I understood that the effort I was making was not an effort to see, but an effort to open my eyes. And it was this effort, together with the *sensation of closed eyelids* which I could not lift, that created the sensation of " blindness." Sometimes as the result of this effort I woke up. This happened when I actually succeeded in opening my eyes.

Even these first observations of recurring dreams showed me that dreams depend much more on the direct sensations of a given moment than on any general causes. Gradually I became convinced that almost all recurring dreams were connected with the sensation not even of a state, but simply with the sensation of the posture of the body at the given moment.

When I happened to press my hand with my knee and the hand became numb, I dreamt that a dog was biting my hand. When I wanted to take

_____

[2] " Window " is the name given to a small spot, sometimes only a few yards across, of " bottomless " quagmire in an ordinary swamp.

something in my hands or lift it, it fell out of my hands because my hands were as limp as rags and refused to obey me. I remember once in a dream I had to break something with a hammer, and the hammer was as if made of indiarubber; it rebounded from the object I was striking, and I could not give any force to my blows. This, of course, was simply the sensation of relaxed muscles.

There was another recurring dream which always frightened me. In this dream I was a paralytic or a cripple; I fell down and could not get up, because my legs did not obey me. This dream also seemed to be a presentiment of what was going to happen to me, until in " half-dream states " I became convinced that it was merely the sensation of motionless legs with relaxed muscles, which of course could not obey moving impulses.

Altogether I saw that our movements, especially our impulses to movements, and the sense of impotence in making a particular movement, play the most important rôle in the creation of dreams.

To the category of constantly recurring dreams belonged also dreams of flying. I used to fly fairly often and was very fond of these dreams. In " half-dream states " I saw that flying depended on a slight giddiness which occurs in sleep from time to time without any pathological cause, but probably simply in connection with the horizontal position of the body. There was no erotic element in the dreams of flying.

Amusing dreams which occur very often, those in which one sees oneself undressed or half-dressed walking in the street or among people, also required no complicated theories for their explanation. This was simply the sensation of one's half-dressed body. As I noticed in " half-dream states," these dreams occurred chiefly when I was feeling cold during sleep. The cold made me realise that I was undressed, and this sensation penetrated into my dreams.

Some of the recurring dreams could be explained only in connection with others. Such were the dreams of stairs, often described in psychological literature. These are strange dreams, and many people have them. You go up huge, gloomy, endless staircases, find certain passages leading out, remember the way, then lose it again, come upon unfamiliar landings, turnings, doors, etc. This is one of the most typical recurring dreams. And as a rule you meet no one, you are usually alone amidst these large empty staircases.

As I understood in " half-dream states," these dreams are a combination of two motives or recollections. The first motive is created by motor memory, the memory of direction. These dreams of stairs are in no way different from dreams of long corridors, with endless court-yards through which you pass, with streets, alleys, gardens, parks, fields, woods; in a word these are dreams of *roads* or *ways*. We all know many roads and ways; in houses, up stairs and along corridors; in towns, in the country, in the mountains; and we can see all these roads in dreams, although very often we see not the roads themselves but, if it can be so expressed, the general feeling of them. Each way has its own particular sensation. These sensations are created by thousands of small details reflected and impressed in various corners of our memory. Later these sensations are reproduced in dreams, though for the creation of the desired sensations dreams very often use the accidental material of images. Because of this the "road" you see in dreams may not resemble outwardly the road you actually know and remember when awake, but it will produce the same impressions as the road you know and are familiar with, and will give you the same sensations.

"Stairs" are similar "roads," only, as has already been said, they contain another motive as well. This motive consists in a certain mystical significance which stairs have in the life of every man. Everybody in his life often experiences on the stairs a sense of something new and unknown awaiting him that very moment on the next floor, behind a closed door. Everyone can recollect many such moments in his life. A man ascends the stairs not knowing what awaits him. For children it is often their arrival at school, or generally the first impression of school, and such impressions remain throughout life. Further, stairs are often the scene of hesitations, decisions, change of decisions, and so on. All this taken together and united with memories of motion creates dreams about staircases.

To continue the general description of dreams, I must note that visual images in sleep often do not correspond to visual images in waking states. A man you know very well in life can look quite different in a dream. In spite of that, however, you do not doubt for a minute that it is really he, and his unfamiliar aspect does not surprise you in the least. It often happens that the quite fantastic, and even unnatural and impossible, aspect of a man expresses certain traits and qualities you know in him. In a word, the outward form of things, people and events in dreams is much more plastic than it is in a waking state and it is much more susceptible to the influence of the accidental thoughts, feelings and moods that pass through us.

As regards recurring dreams, their simple nature and the absence of any allegorical meaning in them became quite unquestionable for me after they had all occurred several times in my " half-dream states." I saw how they began, I could explain clearly where they came from and how they were created.

There was only one dream which I was unable to explain. That was the dream in which I saw myself *running on all fours,* and sometimes very fast. It seemed to be in certain cases the swiftest, safest and most reliable means of locomotion. In a moment of danger, or in general in any difficult situation, I always preferred in the dream this means of locomotion to any other.

For some reason I do not remember this dream in " half-dream states." And I understood the origin of this " running on all fours " only later when I was observing a small child who was only just beginning to walk. He could walk, but to him it was still a great adventure and his position on two legs was still very uncertain, unstable and unreliable. He apparently distrusted himself in this position. If therefore anything unexpected happened, if a door opened, or a noise was heard from the street, or even if the cat jumped off the sofa, he dropped immediately on all fours. In observing him I understood that somewhere, deep in the innermost recesses of our memory, are preserved recollections of these first motor impressions and of all the sensations, fears and motor impulses connected with them. Evidently there was a time when new and unexpected impressions created the impulse to drop on all fours, that is, to assume a steadier and firmer position. In a waking state this impulse is not sufficiently strong, but it acts in dreams and creates strange pictures, which had also appeared to me to be allegorical or to have some hidden meaning.

Observations of the same child also explained to me a great deal about staircases. When he began to feel quite sure of himself on the floor, the stairs were still for him a great adventure. And nothing attracted him more than the stairs. Besides, he was forbidden to go near them. And of course in the next period of his life he practically lived on the stairs. In all the houses in which he lived the stairs attracted him first of all. And when I was observing him I had no doubts that the impressions of stairs would remain in him all his life and would be connected with all emotions of a strange, attractive and dangerous character.

Returning to the methods of my observations, I must note a curious fact demonstrating that dreams change by the fact of their being observed, namely that several times I *dreamed* that I was observing my dreams. My original aim was to create consciousness in dreams, i.e. to attain the capacity of realising in sleep that I was sleeping. In " half-dream states " this was there from the very beginning. As I have already said, I both slept and did not sleep at the same time. But soon there began to appear " false observations," i.e. merely new dreams. I remember once seeing myself in a large empty room without windows. Besides myself there was in the room only a small black kitten. " I am dreaming," I say to myself. " How can I know whether I am really asleep or not? Suppose I try this way. Let this black kitten be transformed into a large white dog. In a waking state it is impossible and if it comes off it will mean that I am asleep." I say this to myself and immediately the black kitten becomes transformed into a large white dog. At the same time the opposite wall disappears, disclosing a mountain landscape with a river like a ribbon receding into the distance.

" This is curious," I say to myself; " I did not order this landscape. Where did it come from? " Some faint recollection begins to stir in me, a recollection of having seen this landscape somewhere and of its being somehow connected with the white dog. But I feel that if I let myself go into it I shall forget the most important thing that I have to remember, namely, *that I am asleep and am conscious of myself*, i.e. that I am in the state for which I have long wished and which I have been trying to attain. I make an effort not to think about the landscape, but at that moment some power seems to drag me *backwards*. I fly swiftly through the back wall of the room and go on flying in a straight line, all the time backwards and with a terrible noise in my ears, suddenly come to a stop and awake.

The description of this *backward* flying and the accompanying noise can be found in occult literature, where some special meaning is ascribed to them. But in reality there is no meaning in them except probably that of an inconvenient position of the head or slightly deranged circulation of the blood.

It was in this way, *flying backwards*, that people used to return from the witches' Sabbath.

And speaking generally, false observations, i.e. dreams within dreams, must have played a great part in the history of " magic," miraculous transformations, etc.

False observations like the one described occurred several times, remained in my memory very vividly and helped me very much in elucidating the general mechanism of sleep and dreams.

I wish now to say a few words on this general mechanism of sleep.

First, it is necessary to understand clearly that sleep may be of different degrees, of different depths. We can be more asleep or less asleep, nearer to the possibility of awaking or further from the possibility of awaking. We usually remember only those dreams which we have when near to the possibility of awakening. Dreams which we have in deep sleep, i.e. far from the possibility of awaking, we do not remember at all. People who say they do not remember dreams sleep very soundly. People who remember all their dreams or at any rate many of them are really only half asleep. The whole time they are near the possibility of awaking. And, as a certain part of the inner instinctive work of our organism is best performed in deep sleep and cannot be well carried out when a man is only half asleep, it is obvious that the absence of deep sleep weakens the organism, prevents it renewing its spent forces and eliminating the used-up substances, and so on. The organism does not rest sufficiently. As a result it cannot produce sufficiently good work, is sooner worn out, more easily falls ill. In a word, deep sleep, that is, sleep without dreams, is in all respects more useful than sleep with dreams. And the experimenters who encourage people to remember their dreams render them a truly bad service. The less a man remembers his dreams the more soundly he sleeps and the better it is for him.

Further, it is necessary to note that we make a very great mistake when we speak about the creation of mental pictures in sleep.

Thus, we speak only of the head, brain thinking, and we ascribe to it the chief part of the work of creating dreams as well as all our thinking. This is utterly wrong. Our legs also think, think quite independently of and quite differently from the head. Arms also think: they have their own memory, their own mental images, their own associations. The back thinks, the stomach thinks, each part of the body thinks independently. Not one of these thinking processes reaches our consciousness in a waking state, when the head-thinking, operating chiefly by words and visual images, dominates everything else. But when the head consciousness calms down and becomes clouded in the state of sleep, especially in the deeper forms of sleep, immediately other consciousnesses begin to speak, namely those of feet, hands, fingers, stomach, those of other organs, of various groups of muscles. These separate consciousnesses in us possess their own conceptions of many things and phenomena, for which we sometimes have also head-conceptions and sometimes have not. This is precisely what most prevents us understanding our dreams. In sleep the mental images which belong to the legs, arms, nose, tips of the fingers, to the various groups of motor muscles, become mixed with our ordinary verbal-visual images. We have no words and no forms for the expression of conceptions of one kind in conceptions of another kind. The visual-verbal part of our psychic apparatus cannot remember all these utterly incomprehensible and foreign images. In our dreams, however, these images play the same rôle as the visual-verbal images, if not a greater one.

The following two reservations that I make here should be remembered in every attempt at the description and classification of dreams. The first is that there are different states of sleep. We can only catch the dreams which pass near the surface; as soon as they go deeper, we lose them. And the second is that no matter how we try to remember and exactly describe our dreams, we remember and describe only *head-dreams*, i.e. dreams consisting of visual-verbal images; all the rest, i.e. the enormous majority of dreams, will escape us.

To this must be added another circumstance of very great importance. In sleep the head-consciousness itself changes. This means that man cannot in sleep think about himself *unless the thought is itself a dream*. A man can never pronounce his own name in sleep.

If I pronounced my name in sleep, I immediately woke up. And I understood that we do not realise that the knowledge of one's name for oneself is already a different degree of consciousness as compared with sleep. In sleep we are not aware of our own existence, we do not separate ourselves from the general picture which moves around us, but we, so to speak, move with it. Our " I " feeling is much more obscured in sleep than in a waking state. This is really the chief psychological feature which determines the state of sleep and expresses the whole difference between sleep and the waking state.

As I pointed out above, observation of dreams very soon brought me to the necessity for classification. I became convinced that our dreams differ very greatly in their nature. The general name of " dreams " confuses us. In reality dreams differ from one another as much as things and events which we see in a waking state. It would be quite insufficient to speak simply about " things," including in this planets, children's toys, prime ministers and paintings of the palæolithic period. This is exactly what we do in relation to " dreams." This certainly makes the understanding of dreams practically impossible and creates many false theories, because it is equally impossible to explain different categories of dreams on the basis of one common principle, as it would be prime ministers and palæolithic paintings.

Most of our dreams are entirely accidental, entirely chaotic, unconnected with anything and *meaningless*. These dreams depend on accidental associations. There is no consecutiveness in them, no direction, no idea.

I will describe one such dream, which was noted in *a half-dream state*. I am falling asleep. Golden dots, sparks and tiny stars appear and disappear before my eyes. These sparks and stars gradually merge into a golden net with diagonal meshes which moves slowly and regularly in rhythm with the beating of my heart, which I feel quite distinctly. The next moment the golden net is transformed into rows of brass helmets belonging to Roman soldiers marching along the street below. I hear their measured tread and watch them from the window of a high house in Galata, in Constantinople, in a narrow lane, one end of which leads to the old wharf and the Golden Horn with its ships and steamers and the minarets of Stamboul behind them. The Roman soldiers march on and on in close ranks along the lane. I hear their heavy measured tread, and see the sun shining on their helmets. Then suddenly I detach myself from the window-sill on which I am lying, and in the same reclining position fly slowly over the lane, over the houses, and then over the Golden Horn in the direction of Stamboul. I smell the sea, feel the wind, the warm sun. This flying gives me a wonderfully pleasant sensation, and I cannot help opening my eyes.

This is a typical dream of the first category, i.e. of dreams which depend on accidental associations. Looking for a meaning in these dreams is exactly the same as telling fortunes by coffee grounds. The whole of this dream passed before me when in a " half-dream state." From the first moment to the last I observed how pictures appeared and how they were transformed into one another. The golden sparks and dots were transformed into a net with regular meshes. Then the golden net was transformed into the helmets of the Roman soldiers. The pulsation which I heard was transformed into the measured tread of the marching detachment. The sensation of this pulsation means the relaxation of many small muscles, which in its turn produces a sensation of slight giddiness. This sensation of slight giddiness was immediately manifested in my seeing the soldiers, while lying on the window-sill of a *high* house and looking down; and when this giddiness increased a little, I rose from the window and flew over the gulf. This at once brought with it by association the sensation of the sea, the wind and the sun, and if I had not awakened, probably at the next moment of the dream I should have seen myself in the open sea, on a ship, and so on.

These dreams are sometimes remarkable for a particular absurdity, for quite impossible combinations and associations.

I remember one dream, in which for some reason a very great part was played by a large number of geese. Then somebody asks: " Would you like to see a *gosling*? you have certainly never seen a gosling." And at this moment I agree that I have never seen goslings. Next moment they bring me on an orange silk cushion a very strange-looking sleeping grey kitten, twice as long and thin as an ordinary kitten. And with great interest I examine the *gosling* and say that I never thought they were so strange.

If we place those dreams of which I have now spoken, that is, chaotic or incoherent, in the first category, we must place in the second category dramatic or invented dreams. Usually these two categories are intermixed, that is, an element of invention and fantasy enters into chaotic dreams, while invented dreams contain many accidental associations, images and scenes, which very often completely change their original direction. Dreams of the second category are the easiest to remember, for they are most like ordinary day-dreaming.

In these dreams a man sees himself in all kinds of dramatic situations. He travels in various distant lands, fights in wars, saves himself from some danger, chases somebody, sees himself surrounded by a crowd of people, meets all his friends and acquaintances dead and alive, sees himself at different periods of his life; though grown-up he sees himself at school, and so on.

It happens that some dreams of this kind are very interesting in their technique. They contain a quantity of such subtle material of observation, memory and imagination as man does not possess while awake. This is the first thing that struck me in dreams of this kind when I began to understand something about them.

If I saw in my dream one of my friends whom perhaps I had not seen for several years, he spoke to me in his own language, in his own voice, with his own intonations and inflections, with his own characteristic gestures; and he said precisely what only he could say.

Every man has his own manner of expressing himself, his own manner of thinking, his own manner of reacting to outward phenomena. No man can speak or act for another. And what first attracted my attention in these dreams was their wonderful artistic exactitude. The style of each man was kept throughout to the smallest detail. It happened that certain features were exaggerated or expressed symbolically. But there was never anything incorrect, anything inconsistent with the type.

In dreams of such a kind it happened that I saw more than once ten or twenty people simultaneously whom I had known at different periods of my life, and in not one of them was there ever the slightest mistake or the slightest inexactitude.

This was something more than memory; it was artistic creation, because it was quite clear to me that many details which had obviously gone from my memory were reconstructed, so to speak, on the spot, and they corresponded completely to what ought actually to have been there.

Other dreams of this kind surprised me by their thoroughly thought out and elaborated plan. They had a clear and well-conceived plot which was unknown to me beforehand. All the dramatis personæ appeared at the right moment and said and did everything they had to do and say in conformity with the plot. The action could take place and develop in the most varied conditions, could be transferred from the town to the country, to lands unknown to me, to the sea; the strangest types could enter into these dramas. I remember, for instance, one dream, full of movement, dramatic situations and the most varied emotions. If I am not mistaken it was during the Japanese war. In the dream it was a war in Russia itself. A part of Russia was occupied by the armies of some strange people, called by a strange name, which I have forgotten. I had to pass at all costs through the enemy lines on some extremely important personal affairs. In connection with this a whole series of tragic, amusing, melodramatic incidents occurred. All this would have made a complete scenario for cinema production; and everything was in its right place, nothing was out of tune with the general course of the play. There were many interesting types and scenes. The monk with whom I spoke in a monastery still lives in my memory; he was entirely outside life and outside all that took place around him, and at the same time he was full of little cares and little anxieties connected at that moment with me. The strange colonel of the enemy army with a pointed grey beard and incessantly blinking eyes was fully a living man and at the same time a very clear and definite type of man-machine, whose life is divided into several compartments with impenetrable partitions. Even the type of his imaginary nationality, the sound of the language he spoke with other officers, all this was in perfect keeping. The dream was full of small realistic details. I galloped through the enemy lines on a big white horse, and during one of the halts I brushed some white hairs off my coat with my sleeve.

I remember that this dream interested me very much because it showed me quite clearly that there was in me an artist, sometimes very naïve, sometimes very subtle, who worked at these dreams and created them out of the material which I possessed but could never use in full measure while awake. And I saw that this artist was extraordinarily versatile in his knowledge, capacities and talents. He was a playwright, a producer, a scene-painter, and a remarkable *actor-impersonator*. This last capacity in him was possibly the most astonishing of all. It especially struck me because I have very little of this capacity when awake. I never could imitate people, never could reproduce their voices, intonations, gestures, movements; never could repeat the most characteristic words or phrases even of the people most familiar to me; in the same way I never could reconstruct accents and peculiarities of speech. But I could do all this in dreams. The striking capacity for impersonation which manifested itself in dreams would undoubtedly have been a great talent had I been able to make use of it when awake. And I understood that this was not peculiar to me alone. This capacity for impersonation, for dramatisation, for arranging the picture, for stylisation, for symbolisation, lies within every man and is manifested in his dreams.

Dreams in which people see their dead friends or relations strike their imagination so strongly because of this remarkable capacity for impersonation inherent in themselves. This capacity can sometimes function in a waking state when man is absorbed in himself or separates himself from the immediate influences of life, and from usual associations.

After my observations of impersonation in dreams I entirely ceased to be surprised at tales of spiritualistic phenomena, of voices of people long dead, of " communications " and advice coming from them, etc. It can even be admitted that by following this advice people have found lost things, bundles of letters, old wills, family jewels or buried treasures. Certainly the majority of such tales are pure invention, but sometimes, although possibly very seldom, such things happen, and in that case they are undoubtedly based on impersonation. Impersonation is an art, although unconscious, and art always contains a strong " magic " element; and the magic element implies new discoveries, new revelations. A true and exact impersonation of a man long since dead can be magic like this. The impersonated image not only can say in this case what the man who reproduces it knows consciously or subconsciously, that is, without accounting for it to himself, but it can say definitely even things such as the man does not know, things which follow from the very nature of its being, from the nature of its life, that is, something that actually happened and that only it could know.

My own observation of impersonation did not go beyond observing the reproduction of what I had once known, heard or seen, with very small additions.

I remember two cases which explained to me a great deal in relation both to the origin of dreams and to " spiritualistic communications " from the world beyond. It happened after the time when I was occupied with the problem of dreams, on the way to India. I was alone. My friend S., with whom I had travelled in the East previously and with whom I had planned to go to India, had died a year before, and involuntarily, especially at the beginning of the journey, I thought about him and felt his absence.

And it happened twice — once on a boat in the North Sea and a second time in India, — that I distinctly heard his voice, as though he was entering my mental conversation with myself. On both occasions he spoke in the manner in which he alone could speak and said what he alone could say. Everything, his style, his intonation, his manner of speech, his way with me, all was in these few sentences.

Both times it happened on quite unimportant occasions, both times he joked with me in his usual manner. Of course I never thought for a moment that there could be anything " spiritualistic " in it; obviously he was in me, in my memory of him, and something within me reproduced him, " impersonated " him in these moments.

This kind of impersonation sometimes occurs in mental conversations with absent friends. And in these mental conversations, exactly as people who are dead can do, they can tell us things which we do not know.

In the case of people who are alive such incidents are explained by telepathy; in the case of the dead, by their existence after death and the possibility of their entering into telepathic communications with those alive. This is the way things are usually explained in spiritualistic works. It is very interesting to read these spiritualistic books from the point of view of the study of dreams. I could distinguish different categories of dreams in the spiritualistic phenomena described: unconscious and chaotic dreams, invented dreams, dramatic dreams and one more, a very important category, which I would call imitative. This imitative category is curious in many respects, because although in many cases the material of these dreams is quite clear in our waking state, we should not be able to use it so skilfully as we do when asleep. Here again "the artist" is at work. Sometimes he is a producer, sometimes a translator, sometimes *an obvious plagiarist* changing in his own way and ascribing to himself what he has read or heard.

The phenomena of *impersonation* have also been described in scientific literature on the study of spiritualism. F. Podmore in his book *Modern Spiritualism* (London, 1902, Vol. II, pp. 302–303), cites an interesting case from *The Proceedings of the Society for Psychical Research* (Vol. XI, pp. 309–316).

Mr. C. H. Tout, principal of Buckland College, Vancouver, describes his experiences at spiritualistic séances. During these séances some persons were afflicted with spasmodic twitchings in their hands and arms and with other involuntary movements. Tout himself in these cases felt a strong impulse to imitate these movements.

At later séances he on several occasions yielded to similar impulses to assume a foreign personality. In this way he acted the part of a deceased woman, the mother of a friend then present. He put his arm round his friend and caressed him, as his mother might have done, and the personation was recognised by the spectators as a genuine case of " spirit control."

On another occasion Mr. Tout, having under the influence of music given various impersonations, was finally oppressed by a feeling of coldness and loneliness, as of a recently disembodied spirit. His wretchedness and misery were terrible, and he was only kept from falling to the floor by some of the other sitters. At this point one of the sitters made the remark, which I remember to have overheard, " It is father controlling him," and I then seemed to realise who I was and whom I was seeking. I began to be distressed in my lungs, and should have fallen if they had not held me by the hands and let me back gently upon the floor. As my head sank back on the carpet I experienced dreadful distress in my lungs and could not breathe. I made signs to them to put something under my head. They immediately put the sofa cushions under me, but this was not sufficient — I was not raised high enough yet to breathe easily — and they then added a pillow. I have the most distinct recollection of a sigh of relief I now gave as I sank back like a sick, weak person upon the cool pillow. I was in a measure still conscious of my actions, though not of my surroundings, and I have a clear memory of seeing myself in the character of my dying father lying in the bed and in the room in which he died. It was a most curious sensation. I saw his shrunken hands and face, and lived again through his dying moments;

only now I was both myself — in some indistinct sort of way — and my father, with his feelings and appearance.

I remember a curious case of this category of pseudo-authorship. It must have been about thirty years ago.

I awoke with a clear memory of a long and, as it seemed to me, very interesting story, which I thought I had written in my dreams. I remembered it in every detail and decided to write it down at the first free moment, first as a specimen of "creative" dreams, second, thinking that I might use the theme some day, although the story had nothing in common with my usual writings and entirely differed from them in type and character. But about two hours later, when I began to write down the story, I noticed in it something very familiar and suddenly, to my great amazement, I saw that it was a story by Paul Bourget, which I had read not long before. The story was altered in a curious way. The action which in Bourget's book unfolded from one end, started in my dream from the other end. The action took place in Russia, all the characters had Russian names, and a new person was added introducing a definitely Russian atmosphere. I rather regret now that I did not write down the story at the time as I constructed it in my dream. It undoubtedly contained much of interest. First of all there was the extraordinary quickness of the work. In normal conditions, when awake, such a turning inside out of somebody else's story of similar length, transplanting the action into another country and adding a new person who appears in almost every scene, would require, according to my estimate, at least a week's work. In sleep, however, it was done without any expenditure of time, simply in the course of the progress of the action.

This extraordinary speed of mental work in sleep has many times attracted the attention of investigators, and their observations have given rise to many wrong deductions.

There is a well-known dream, much quoted but never fully understood, which is described by Maury in his book *Sleep and Dreams*, which in his opinion establishes that one moment is sufficient for a very long dream.

I was slightly indisposed and was lying in my room; my mother was near my bed. I am dreaming of the Terror. I am present at scenes of massacre; I appear before the Revolutionary Tribunal; I see Robespierre, Marat, Fouquier-Tinville, all the most villainous figures of this terrible epoch; I argue with them; at last, after many events which I remember only vaguely, I am judged, condemned to death, taken in a cart, amidst an enormous crowd, to the square of the Revolution; I ascend the scaffold; the executioner binds me to the fatal board, he pushes it, the knife falls; I feel my head being severed from the body; I awake seized by the most violent terror, and I feel on my neck the rod of my bed which had become suddenly detached and had fallen on my neck as would the knife of the guillotine. This happened in one instant, as my mother confirmed to me, and yet it was this external sensation that was taken by me for the starting point of the dream with a whole series of successive incidents. At the moment that I was struck the memory of the terrible machine, the effect of which was so well reproduced by the rod of the bed's canopy, had awakened in me all the images of that epoch of which the guillotine was the symbol.[3]

Maury explained his dream by the extraordinary speed of the work of imagination in sleep, and it followed from his explanations that in some tenth or hundredth parts of a second, which passed between the moment when the bar struck his neck and his awakening, he constructed the whole dream, which was full of movement and dramatic effect, and seemed to last a long time.

But Maury's explanation is not sufficient and is wrong in its essence. It overlooks one most important circumstance. In reality the dream took a little longer than Maury thought, possibly several seconds, a fairly long period of time for a mental process; whereas for his mother his awakening might have appeared instantaneous or *very quick*.

What happened in reality was as follows. The fall of the rod brought Maury into a " half-dream state." In this " half-dream state " the chief feeling was fear. He was afraid to wake up, afraid to explain to himself what had happened to him. The whole of his dream is created by this question: what has happened to me? This suspense, the uncertainty, the gradual disappearance of hope, are very well rendered in his dream as he tells it.

But there is one more very characteristic feature in Maury's dream which he did not notice. This is that events in his dream followed not in the order which he describes, but *from the end towards the beginning*.

This often happens in invented dreams, and it is one of the curious qualities of dreams, which may even have been noted somewhere in special literature on the subject. Unfortunately the importance and meaning of this quality have not been pointed out and the idea has not entered the usage of ordinary thought, though this capacity of dreams to develop backwards explains a great deal.

The backward development of dreams means that when we awake, we awake at the moment of the *beginning* of the dream and remember it as starting from this moment, that is, in the normal succession of events. Maury's first impression was: Oh God, what has happened to me? Answer: I am guillotined. Imagination at once draws the picture of the execution, the scaffold, the guillotine, the executioner. At the same time the question arises: how can it all have happened? How can I have got on to the scaffold? In answer there again come pictures of the Paris streets, of the crowds of the time of the Revolution, of the tumbril in which the condemned were driven to the scaffold. Then again a question, with the same anguish wringing the heart and with the same feeling that something terrible and irreparable has happened. And in answer to these questions there appear pictures of the Tribunal, the figures of Robespierre, Marat, scenes of massacre, general pictures of the Terror, explaining all that happened. At this moment

---

[3] *Le sommeil et les rêves, études psychologiques sur ces phénomènes*, by L. F. Alfred Maury, Paris, Didier et Cie, éditeurs, 1861, pp. 133–134.

Maury awoke, that means, he opened his eyes. In reality he awoke long ago, possibly several seconds before. But having opened his eyes and remembering the last moment of the dream, the scenes of the Terror and massacre, he began at once to reconstruct the dream in his mind, starting from that moment. The dream began to unfold before him in the normal order, from the beginning of events to the end, from the scene at the tribunal to the fall of the knife of the guillotine, or, in reality, to the fall of the rod.

Later when writing down or telling his dream he never doubted for a second that he actually had the dream in this order, that is to say, he never imagined the possibility of dreaming a dream in one order of events and remembering it in another. Another problem arose therefore before him: how such a long and complex dream could flash past in one moment, for he was certain that he awoke at once (he did not remember the "half-dream state"). This he explained by the extraordinary swiftness of the development of dreams, whereas in reality the explanation requires the understanding first of "half-dream states" and second of the fact that dreams can develop in *reverse order*, from end to beginning, and be remembered in the *right order*, from beginning to end.

The development of dreams from end to beginning happens fairly often, but of course we always remember these dreams in the normal order because they end with the moment from which they would begin in the normal development of events, but are remembered or imagined from this moment.

The emotional states in which we may be during sleep often produce very curious dreams. They colour with one shade or another the usual half-chaotic, half-invented dreams, make them wonderfully alive and real, and cause us to seek in them a deep meaning and significance.

I will cite here one dream which undoubtedly could be interpreted spiritualistically, though of course there is no spiritualism in it (I had this dream when I was seventeen or eighteen).

I dreamed of Lermontoff. I do not remember the visual image, but he told me in a strange hollow and strangled voice that he did not die when he was thought to have been killed. "I was saved," he said, slowly and in a low voice. "My friends arranged it. The Circassian who jumped into the grave and knocked off the earth with his dagger, pretending that it was necessary to help the coffin to pass. . . . It was connected with that. At night they dug me out. I went abroad and lived there for a long time, only I did not write anything more. No one knew about it except my sisters. Later I really died."

I awoke from this dream in an unusually depressed state. I was lying on my left side, my heart was beating fast, and I was feeling inexpressible anguish. This anguish was really the chief motive which, in connection with accidental images and associations, created the whole dream. So far as I can remember, my first impression of "Lermontoff" was the hollow strangled voice, full of some peculiar sadness. Why I replied to myself that it was Lermontoff it is difficult to say. It is possible that there was in this an emotional association. Very likely the description of the death and burial of Lermontoff might have produced a similar impression on me at one time. Lermontoff's saying that he did not die, that he was buried alive, accentuated this emotional tone still more. A curious feature of this dream was the attempt to connect the dream with facts. In the description of Lermontoff's burial in some biographies, it is stated, on the strength of the accounts of eye-witnesses, that the coffin could not pass into the recess at the side of the grave and that a mountaineer jumped down and knocked off the earth with his dagger. In my dream something was connected with this incident. Then " Lermontoff's sisters," who alone knew that he was alive. I thought even in my dream that he said " sisters " meaning " cousins," as though for some reason or other he did not wish to speak clearly. All this followed from the chief motive of the dream, a feeling of depression and mystery.

There is no doubt that this dream would have been interpreted by spiritualists in a spiritualistic sense. Speaking generally, the study of dreams is the study of " spiritualism," because " spiritualism " draws all its contents from dreams. And as I pointed out before, spiritualistic literature gave me very interesting material for the explanation of dreams.

But apart from this, spiritualistic literature undoubtedly creates whole series of " spiritualistic " dreams, just as the cinematograph or detective novels undoubtedly play a very important part in the creation of dreams.

Modern attempts at the investigation of dreams as a rule hardly take into consideration the character of a man's reading and still less his favourite amusements like theatres, cinemas, races, etc., whereas it is precisely from these that the chief material of dreams comes, especially in the case of people whose everyday life contains but few impressions. It is reading and spectacular sights that create allegorical, symbolical and similar dreams. The rôle played by advertisements and posters in creating dreams is also quite disregarded.

The building up of visual images is sometimes very strange in dreams. I have already mentioned the fact that dreams are principally built according to associations of impressions and not according to associations of facts. And, for instance, in visual images entirely different people, with whom we come into contact at entirely different periods of our lives, very often become merged and united into one person.

A young girl, a political prisoner who spent a long time in the Boutirsky prison in Moscow (in 1906–1908), told me during my visits, from behind two rows of bars, that in her dreams the impressions of the prison were completely mixed up with the impressions of the " Institute " [4] which she had left only six years before. In her dreams the prison warders became confused with former " class-ladies " and " inspectresses " (house-mistresses). Summonses before the prosecutor and cross-examination were les-

---

[4] A privileged government school for girls, of the type established in Russia in the 18th century and having the character of French convents.

sons, the coming trial was the final examination, and everything was similarly confused.

In this case the connecting link was undoubtedly the similarity of emotional experiences, the boredom, the continual constraint and the general absurdity of all the surroundings.

Another dream has remained in my memory, this time merely an amusing one, in which was manifested the principle of the personification of ideas opposite to the one described.

Long ago when I was quite young I had a friend in Moscow who accepted a situation in the south of Russia and went there. I remember seeing him off at the Kursk railway station.

About ten years later I saw him in my dream. We were sitting at a table in the station restaurant drinking beer exactly as we had done when I saw him off. But *we were three:* I, my friend as I remembered him, and my friend as he probably must have become in some part of my mental picture of him, a stout middle-aged man much older than he could have been in reality, dressed in an overcoat with a fur collar and having slow and assured movements. As usually happens in dreams this combination did not surprise me in the least, and I took it as though it was the most ordinary thing in the world.

I have now mentioned several categories of dreams, but these by no means cover all possible and existing categories. One of the reasons for the wrong interpretation of dreams is the inadequate understanding of the categories and a wrong division of dreams.

I have already pointed out that dreams differ among themselves not less than phenomena of the real world. All the examples given up to now relate to " simple " dreams, that is, to dreams which take place on the same level as our ordinary life, as our thinking and feeling in a waking state. But there are other categories of dreams. These dreams have their origin in the innermost recesses of life and rise high above the common level of our understanding and perception of things. These dreams can disclose a great deal that is unknown to us on the ordinary level of life, for instance, in showing us the future or the thoughts and feelings of other people or events unknown to us or remote from us. And they can also disclose to us the mysteries of being, show the laws governing life, bring us into contact with higher forces. These are very rare dreams, and one of the errors of the usual treatment of dreams is that these dreams are regarded as much more frequent than they are in actual fact. Their principles and ideas became to a certain extent comprehensible to me only after the experiments which I describe in the next chapter.

It must be understood that all that can be found about dreams in psychological literature refers to " simple " dreams. The confusion of ideas about these dreams depends, apart from wrong classification of the dreams themselves, to a considerable degree on wrong definition of the material of which dreams are made. Dreams are regarded as being created from *fresh* material, from the same material as that which goes to create the thoughts, feelings and emotions of our waking life. This is the reason why dreams in which a man performs actions or experiences emotions, which he could not have performed or experienced when awake, give rise to such multitudes of questions. The interpreters of dreams take it all quite seriously and create their own picture of a man's soul on the basis of these features. All this is of course quite wrong.

With the exception of dreams like those described in the beginning, such as dream of the " quagmire " or " blindness," which are created by sensations received during sleep, the chief material which goes to make up dreams is the refuse or used-up material of our psychic life.

It is the gravest mistake to think that ordinary dreams reveal us as we are somewhere in the unknown depths of our nature. To ourselves dreams cannot do this; they picture either what has been and has gone by, or, still more often, what has not been and could not have been. Dreams are always a caricature, always a comic exaggeration, but an exaggeration which in most cases relates to some non-existent moment in the past or non-existent situation in the present.

The question is, what are the principles which create this caricature? Why do dreams so contradict reality? And here we meet with a principle which though not fully understood has nevertheless been noted in " psycho-analytical" literature. This is the principle of "compensation." But the word itself is unsuccessful, and probably this unsuccessful word creates its own successful associations, which is the reason why the principle has never been wholly understood, but has on the contrary given rise to utterly wrong theories.

This idea of "compensation" has been connected with the idea of dissatisfaction. The action of the principle is understood in the sense that a man who is dissatisfied with something in life in regard either to himself or to others, compensates himself in dreams. A weak, unhappy, cowardly man sees himself brave, strong, attaining everything he desires. Some friend suffering from an incurable disease is seen by us in dreams as cured, full of strength and hope. Similarly, people who have had a long illness or have died in painful conditions appear to us in dreams, cured, content and happy. In this instance the interpretation is very near the truth, but nevertheless it is only half the truth.

In reality the principle is much wider, and the material of dreams is created not on the principle of compensation taken in a simple, psychological or life sense, but on the basis of what I would call the principle of *complementary tones* entirely without relation to our emotional feeling of those tones. This principle is very simple. If you look for some time at a red spot and then turn your eyes to a white wall, you will see a green spot. If you look for some time at a green spot and then take your eyes off you will see a red spot. Exactly the same thing happens in dreams. There exist for us no morals in dreams, *because* for good or bad our life is controlled by different moral rules. Every moment of our life is surrounded by different kinds of " thou shalt not," and therefore " thou shalt not " does not exist in dreams. There exists for us nothing extraordinary in dreams, because in life we are astonished at every new or unusual combination of circumstances. There exists for us no law of the consecutiveness of phenomena in dreams, because this law governs everything in life, and so on.

The principle of complementary tones plays the chief rôle in our dreams, as much in those we remember as in those we do not remember; and without keeping this principle in view it is impossible to explain a whole series of dreams in which we do and apparently feel what we never do and never feel in life.

Very many things happen in dreams only because they never happen and never can happen in life. Dreams are very often the *negative* in relation to the *positive* of life. But again it should be remembered that this refers only to details. The composition of dreams is not the simple opposite of life, but an " opposite " turned inside out several times and in several senses. Therefore attempts to reconstruct from dreams the hidden causes of dreams are quite useless, and it is merely senseless to suppose that the hidden causes of dreams are the hidden motives of life in a waking state.

It remains for me to make a few remarks about the conclusions which resulted from my attempts to study dreams.

The more I observed dreams the wider became the field of my observations. At first I thought that we have dreams only in a definite state of sleep, near awakening. Later I became convinced that we have dreams all the time, from the moment we fall asleep to the moment we awake, but *remember* only the dreams near awakening. And still later I realised that we have dreams continuously, *both in sleep and in a waking state*. We never cease to have dreams, though we are not aware of this.

As the result of the above I came to the conclusion that dreams can be observed while awake. It is not at all necessary to be asleep in order to observe dreams. Dreams never stop. We do not notice them in a waking state, amidst the continuous flow of visual, auditory and other sensations, for the same reason for which we do not see stars in the light of the sun. But just as we can see the stars from the bottom of a deep well, so we can see the dreams which go on in us if, even for a short time, we isolate ourselves whether accidentally or intentionally, from the inflow of external impressions. It is not easy to explain how this is to be done. Concentration upon one idea cannot produce this isolation. An arrest of the current of usual thoughts and mental images is necessary. It is necessary to achieve for a short period " consciousness without thought." When this consciousness comes dream images begin slowly to emerge through the usual sensations, and with astonishment you suddenly see yourself surrounded by a strange world of shadows, moods, conversations, sounds, pictures. And you understand then that this world is always in you, that it never disappears.

You come to a very clear although somewhat unexpected conclusion: sleep and the waking state are not two states that *succeed one another*, or follow one upon another. The names themselves are incorrect. The two states are not *sleep* and *waking state*. They may be called *sleep* and *sleep plus waking state*. This means that when we awake sleep does not disappear, but to the state of sleep *there is added* the waking state, which muffles the voices of dreams and makes dream images invisible.

The observation of " dreams " in a waking state presents far fewer difficulties than observation in sleep and, moreover, observation in this case does not change their character, does not create new dreams.

After some experience, even the arresting of thoughts, the creation of consciousness without thought, becomes unnecessary. Dreams are always there. It is sufficient only to divide the attention, and you see how into the usual thoughts of the day, into the usual conversations, there enter thoughts, words, figures, faces, scenes, either from the past, from childhood, from school years, from travels, or from what has been read or heard at some time, or from that which has never happened but of which one was one day thinking or talking.

To the dreams observable only in a waking state belongs (in my case) the strange sensation which is known to many people and has many times been described, though it has never been fully explained — *the sensation that this has happened before.*

Suddenly in some *new* combination of circumstances, among new people, in a new place, a man stops and looks with astonishment about him — this has happened before! But when? He cannot say. Later he tells himself that it *could not be so*, he has never been here or in these surroundings, has never seen these people.

Sometimes it happens that these sensations are very persistent and long, sometimes very quick and elusive. The most interesting of them occur with children.

A distinct realisation that it has happened before is sometimes absent in these sensations. But it happens sometimes without any visible or explainable cause that some definite thing, a book, a toy, a dress, a certain face, a house, a landscape, a sound, a tune, a poem, a smell, strikes the imagination as something familiar, well known, touching upon the most hidden feelings, evokes whole series of vague and fleeting associations and remains in the memory for the whole lifetime.

With me these sensations (with a clear and distinct idea that this has happened before, that I have seen it before) began when I was about six years old. After eleven they became much rarer. One of them, extraordinary for its vividness and persistence, occurred when I was nineteen.

The same sensations, but without a clearly pronounced feeling of repetition, began still earlier, from very early childhood, and were particularly vivid during the years when the sensations of repetition appeared, that is, from six to eleven; and they also came later from time to time in various conditions.

Usually when these sensations are treated of in psychological literature, only the first kind is meant, namely, the sensations with a clearly pronounced idea of repetition.

According to psychological theories, sensations of this kind are produced by two causes. Firstly, they depend on breaks in consciousness, when consciousness suddenly disappears for one quite imperceptible moment and then flashes out again. In this case the situation in which one finds oneself, that is, all that surrounds one, seems to one to have happened before, possibly long ago in the unknown past. The " breaks " themselves are explained by the possibility of the same psychic function being carried out by different parts of the thinking apparatus. As a result of this, one function having accidentally stopped in one part is immediately taken up and continued in another, producing the impression that the same situation has occurred some time previously. Secondly, the same sensation may be produced by an associative resemblance between totally different experiences, when a stone or a tree or any object may remind one of somebody one knew very well, or of some place, or of a certain incident in one's life. This happens when for instance one feature or line of a stone reminds you of some feature in a man or in another object; this can also give the sensation that *this has happened before.*

Neither of these theories explains the reason why in most cases the sensation that *this has happened before* occurs chiefly in children and almost always disappears later. On the contrary, according to these theories, the sensations described should grow more frequent with age.

Both the above theories are deficient in that they do not explain *all* the existing facts of the sensation of repetition. Exact observations show *three categories* of such sensations. The first two categories are explained (although not fully) by the above psychological theories. The peculiarity of these two categories is that they usually occur in a partly clouded consciousness, almost in a half-dream state, although this may not be realised by the man himself.

The third category of sensations that this has happened before stands quite apart, and its peculiarity is that the *sensations of repetition* are connected in these cases with an especially clear waking state of consciousness and a heightened self-feeling.

I shall speak of these sensations and their meaning in another place.[5]

In speaking of the study of dreams it is impossible to pass over another phenomenon, which is directly connected with it and which remains unexplained up to the present time, in spite of some possibility of experimenting with it.

I refer to *hypnotism.* The nature of hypnotism, i.e. its causes, and also the forces and laws that make it possible, remains unknown. All that can be

---

[5] Chapter XI, p. 419.

done is to establish conditions in which phenomena of hypnotism may occur, and the possible limits, results and consequences of these phenomena.

In this connection it must be noted that the general reading public has attached to the word hypnotism such a number of wrong conceptions that before speaking of what is possible under the term hypnotism it must be made clear what is impossible.

Hypnotism in the popular and fantastic meaning of the word and hypnotism in the scientific or real meaning of the word are two entirely different ideas.

In the real meaning the content of all the facts united under the general name of hypnotism is very limited.

By being subjected to special kinds of treatment a man can be brought to a particular state, called the hypnotic state. Although there exists a school which asserts that any man can be hypnotised at any time, facts tell against this. In order to be hypnotised, to fall into a hypnotic state, a man must be perfectly passive, i.e. know that he is being hypnotised and not resist it. If he does not know, the ordinary course of thoughts and actions suffices to protect him from the possibility of hypnotic action. Children, drunken men, madmen, do not submit to hypnosis, or submit very badly.

There exist many forms and degrees of the hypnotic state. They can be created by various methods. Passes and strokings of a certain kind, which provoke relaxation of the muscles, a fixed gaze into the eyes, flashing mirrors, sudden impressions, a loud shout, monotonous music: all these are means of hypnotising. Besides this narcotics are used, although the use of narcotics in hypnosis has been very little studied, and description of their use is hard to find even in special literature on the subject. But narcotics are used far more often than is thought, and for two purposes: first for the weakening of the resistance to hypnotic action, and second for the strengthening of the capacity to hypnotise. There are narcotics which act differently on different people, and there are narcotics which have a more or less uniform action. Almost all professional hypnotists use morphia or cocaine in order to be able to hypnotise. Different narcotics are used also for the person hypnotised; a weak dose of chloroform very much increases the capacity of a man to submit to hypnosis.

What actually occurs in a man when he is hypnotised and by what force another man hypnotises him, are questions which science cannot answer. All that we know up to now gives us the possibility of establishing only the external form of the hypnotic state and its results. The hypnotic state begins with simple weakening of the will. Control of ordinary consciousness and ordinary logic weakens. *But it never disappears altogether.* With skilful action, the hypnotic state is intensified. The man thus passes into a state of a particular kind; the external side of this state is characterised by its resemblance to sleep (in deep states unconsciousness and even insensibility appear), and the internal side by an increase of suggestibility. The hypnotic state is therefore defined as the *state of maximum suggestibility*.

In itself hypnosis does not comprise any suggestion, and is possible without any suggestion, particularly if purely mechanical means are used, such as mirrors, etc. But suggestion may play a certain part in the creation of the hypnotic state, particularly in repeated hypnotising. This fact, and also in general the confusion of ideas as to the possible limits of hypnotic action, makes it very difficult for nonspecialists (as well as for many specialists) to distinguish exactly between hypnosis and suggestion. In actual fact they are two entirely different phenomena. Hypnosis is possible without suggestion, and suggestion is possible without hypnosis.

But if suggestion, whatever it be, takes place while the subject is in a hypnotic state, it will give notably greater results. There is no resistance, or almost none. A man can be made under hypnosis to do things which seem to him a complete absurdity, though only things which have no serious importance. It is equally possible to suggest to a man something for the future (post-hypnotic suggestion), i.e. it is possible to order some action, thought or feeling for a certain moment, on the following day or later. Then the man can be awakened. He will remember nothing. But at the appointed time, like a wound-up clockwork mechanism, he will do or at least will attempt to do what has been " suggested" to him. But again only up to a certain limit. It is impossible to make a man, when hypnotised or through post-hypnotic suggestion, do anything which would contradict his nature, tastes, habits, education, convictions or even merely his ordinary actions; it is impossible to make him do anything which would provoke inner struggle in him. If such a struggle begins, the man *does not do* what has been suggested to him. The success of suggestion under hypnosis or of post-hypnotic suggestion consists precisely in suggesting to a man a series of *indifferent* actions which provoke in him no struggle. Suppositions that a man under hypnosis can be made to *know* something which he did not know in a normal state and which the hypnotiser does not know, or that a man under hypnosis can show a capacity for " clairvoyance," that is, for knowing the future or seeing events occurring at a distance, are not confirmed by any facts. At the same time there are known many cases of unconscious suggestion on the part of the hypnotiser and a certain capacity for reading his thoughts on the part of the person hypnotised.

All that takes place in the mind of the hypnotiser, that is, the semiconscious associations, imagination and anticipation of what according to him must happen, can be transferred to the person hypnotised by him. How the transference takes place it is impossible to establish, but the fact of this transference is very easy to prove if that which is known by the one is compared with that which is known by the other.

To this category are related phenomena of so-called " mediumism."

There is a very curious book by a French author, de Rochas, who describes experiments with persons whom he hypnotised and made " remember" their previous " incarnations" on earth. In reading this book I was many times amazed that the author could avoid seeing that he himself was the creator of all these " incarnations," *anticipating* what the hypnotised subject would say and *in this way suggesting to him what to say*.

This book gives very interesting material for the understanding of the process of the formation of dreams. It might have given even more important material for the study of the methods and forms of unconscious suggestion and unconscious thought-transference. But, unfortunately, the author, in his pursuit of fantastic " remembrances " of incarnations, did not see what was really valuable in his experiments and did not note many small details and particulars which would have given the possibility of reconstructing the processes of suggestion and transference of thoughts.

Hypnotism is applied in medicine as a means of action on the emotional nature of a man; for the struggle through suggestion with gloomy and depressed moods, with morbid fears and unhealthy tendencies and habits. And in those cases in which the pathological manifestations are not dependent on deep-seated physical causes, the use of hypnotism gives favourable results. However, with regard to these results, the opinions of specialists differ, and many assert that the use of hypnotism gives only short-lived useful results with a very strong reaction in the direction of the increase of undesirable tendencies, or, in the presence of seemingly favourable results, gives concomitant negative results, weakens the will and capacity of resistance to undesirable influences and makes a man even less stable than he was.

In general, hypnotism, in those cases in which the *psychical* nature of the patient is the object of action, stands on the level of a serious operation, and unfortunately is often applied without sufficient grounds and without sufficient understanding of the consequences of its use.

There exists another sphere in which hypnotism could be applied in medicine without any harm, namely the sphere of direct action (i.e. not through the mediation of the patient's psychical nature) on nerve centres, tissues, inner organs and inner processes. But unfortunately this sphere has been very little studied up to the present time.

Thus the limits of possible influence on a man with the aim of bringing him to a hypnotic state, as well as the limits of possible action on a man who is in a hypnotic state, are very well known and contain nothing enigmatic. The strengthening of the influence is possible only in the direction of strengthening the influence on the physical nature of man apart from his psychic apparatus. But it is precisely in this direction that attention has been turned least of all. On the contrary, current conceptions of hypnotism admit far greater possibilities of action on man's psychical nature than exist in actual fact.

There exist, for instance, very many stories about *mass hypnosis*, but all these stories, in spite of their wide circulation, are the purest invention, and most often are merely repetitions of similar stories which existed earlier.

In 1913 and 1914 I tried to find in India and Ceylon examples of mass hypnosis, with which, according to the descriptions of travellers, the performances of Indian jugglers or " fakirs " and some religious ceremonies are accompanied. But I did not succeed in seeing one single instance. Most of the performances, such, for example, as the raising of a plant from a seed ("mango trick") were mere tricks. And the often described "rope trick," in which a rope is thrown "up to the sky" and a boy climbs up it, etc., has obviously never existed, because not only did I not succeed in seeing it myself, but I never found a *single man* (European) who had seen it *himself*; they all knew of it only by what they had been told. A few educated Hindoos told me they had seen the "rope trick," but I cannot accept their statements as credible because, besides a very fertile imagination, I noticed in them a strange reluctance to disappoint people who look in India for miracles.

I heard later that during the Prince of Wales' travels in India (in 1921 and 1922) the "rope trick" was sought for specially for him, but could not be found. In the same way India was searched for the "rope trick" for the Wembley exhibition of 1924, but it could not be found.

A man who knew India very well told me once that the only thing resembling the "rope trick" he had ever seen was some juggling by a Hindoo conjurer with a thin wooden hoop at the end of a long bamboo rod. The juggler made the hoop run up and down the rod. Possibly it is this that started the legend.

In the 2nd and 3rd issues of the *Revue Métapsychique* (Mars-Avril, Mai-Juin) for the year 1928 there is an article (by M. C. de Vesme) "La légende de l'hallucination collective à propos du tour de la corde pendue au ciel." The author gives a very interesting survey of the history of the "rope trick," citing descriptions of the "rope trick" by eye-witnesses, stories told by people who had only heard about it, and the history of attempts to find and establish the real existence of this trick. Unfortunately, however, while denying the miraculous he himself makes several naïve assertions. For instance, he recognises the possibility of a " mechanical device concealed inside the rope," which enables the rope to stand upright so that a boy can climb it. In another place he speaks of a photograph of the "rope trick," in which one can distinguish a bamboo *inside the rope*.

Actually, if such a thing as a mechanical appliance inside the rope were possible it would be even more miraculous than the "rope trick" as it is usually described. I doubt whether even European technique could contrive such a device to be placed *inside* a thin and, presumably, fairly long rope, which would make the rope stand upright and allow a boy to climb it. But how a half-naked Hindoo juggler could have such a rope is totally incomprehensible. The "bamboo" inside the rope is still more interesting. The question arises here how the rope could be coiled if it had a bamboo inside it. Altogether the author of this very interesting survey of the study of Indian miracles has got, on this point, into a very strange position.

But stories of the miracles of fakirs make a necessary part of the descriptions of impressions of India and Ceylon. Not very long ago I happened to see a French book the author of which relates his adventures and experiences in Ceylon in recent years. To do him justice he caricatures everything he describes and makes no pretensions to seriousness. But he describes another " rope trick " in Kandy, this time with certain variations. Thus, the author, who was hidden on a verandah, was not hypnotised by the " fakir " and therefore did not see what his friends saw. Besides this, one of them photographed the whole of the performance with a cinematograph camera.

" *But when we developed the film* the same night," writes the author, " there was nothing on it."

What is most amusing is that the author does not realise in what *the most miraculous* part of his last statement consists. But this persistence in the description of the " rope trick " and " mass hypnotism," that is, precisely what does not exist, is very characteristic.

In speaking of hypnotism it is necessary to mention *self-hypnosis*.

The possibilities of self-hypnosis also are exaggerated. In reality self-hypnosis without the help of artificial means is possible only in a very feeble degree. By creating in himself a certain passive state a man can weaken the resistance which comes, for example, from logic or common sense, and surrender himself wholly to some desire. This is the possible form of self-hypnosis. But self-hypnosis never attains the forms of sleep or catalepsy. If a man seeks to overcome some great resistance in himself, he uses narcotics. Alcohol is one of the chief means of self-hypnosis. The rôle of alcohol, as a means of self-hypnosis, is still entirely unstudied.

Suggestion must be studied separately from hypnotism.

Hypnotism and suggestion are constantly confused; the place therefore which they occupy in life is quite undetermined.

In reality, *suggestion* is the fundamental fact. Hypnotism might not exist in our life, nothing would be altered by this, but *suggestion* is one of the chief factors both in individual and in social life. If there were no suggestion, men's lives would have an entirely different form, thousands of the phenomena of the life surrounding us would be quite impossible.

Suggestion can be conscious and unconscious, intentional and unintentional. The sphere of conscious and intentional suggestion is extremely small in comparison with the sphere of unconscious and unintentional suggestion.

Man's *suggestibility*, i.e. his capacity to submit to surrounding suggestions, can be different. A man can be entirely dependent on suggestions, have nothing in himself but the results of suggestions and submit to all sufficiently strong suggestions, however contradictory they may be; or he can show some resistance to suggestions, at least yield to suggestions only of certain definite kinds and repel others. But resistance to suggestion even of such a kind is a very rare phenomenon. Ordinarily a man is wholly dependent on suggestions; and his whole inner make-up (and also his outer make-up) is entirely created and conditioned by prevailing suggestions.

From earliest childhood, from the moment of first conscious reception of external impressions, a man falls under the action of suggestions, intentional and unintentional. In this case certain feelings, rules, principles and habits are suggested to him intentionally; and the ways of acting, thinking and feeling against these rules, principles and habits are suggested unintentionally.

This latter suggestion acts owing to the tendency to imitation which everyone possesses. People say one thing and do another. A child listens to one thing and imitates another.

The capacity for imitation in children and also in grown-up people greatly increases their suggestibility.

The dual character of suggestions gradually develops duality in man himself. From very early years he learns to remember that he must show the feelings and thoughts demanded of him at the given moment and never show what he really thinks and feels. This habit becomes his second nature. As time passes, he begins, also through imitation, to trust alike the two opposite sides in himself which have developed under the influence of opposite suggestions. But their contradictions do not trouble him, first because he can never see them together, and second because the capacity not to be troubled by these contradictions is *suggested* to him *because nobody ever is troubled.*

Home-education, the family, elder brothers and sisters, parents, relatives, servants, friends, school, games, reading, the theatre, newspapers, conversations, further education, work, women (or men), *fashion*, art, music, the cinema, sport, the jargon accepted in his circle, the accepted wit, obligatory amusements, obligatory tastes and obligatory taboos — all these and many other things are the source of new and ever new suggestions. All these suggestions are invariably dual, i.e. they create simultaneously what must be shown and what must be hidden.

It is impossible even to imagine a man free from suggestions, who really thinks, feels and acts as he himself can think, feel and act. In his beliefs, in his views, in his convictions, in his ideas, in his feelings, in his tastes, in what he likes, in what he dislikes, in every movement and in every thought, a man is bound by a thousand suggestions, to which he submits, even without noticing them, *suggesting to himself* that it is he himself who thinks in this way and feels in this way.

This submission to external influences so far permeates the whole life of a man, and his suggestibility is so great, that his ordinary, normal state can be called *semi-hypnotic.* And we know very well that at certain moments and in certain situations a man's suggestibility can increase still more and he can reach complete loss of any independent decision or choice whatever. This is particularly clearly seen in the psychology of a crowd, in mass movements of various kinds, in religious, revolutionary, patriotic or panic moods, when the seeming independence of the individual man completely disappears.

All this taken together constitutes one side of the " life of suggestion " in a man. The other side lies in himself and consists, first, in the submission of his so-called " conscious," i.e. intellectual-emotional, functions to influences and suggestions coming from the so-called " unconscious " (i.e. unperceived by the mind) voices of the body, the countless obscure consciousnesses of the inner organs and inner lives; and second, in the submission of all these inner lives to the completely unconscious and unintentional suggestions of the reason and the emotions.

The first, i.e. the submission of the intellectual-emotional functions to the instinctive, has been more elaborated in psychological literature; though the greater part of what is written on these subjects must be taken very cautiously. The second, i.e. the submission of the inner functions to the *unconscious* influences of the nerve-brain apparatus, has been very little studied. Meanwhile, this last side offers enormous interest from the point of view of the understanding of suggestion and suggestibility in general.

A man consists of a countless number of lives. Each part of the body which has a definite function, each organ, each tissue, each cell, has its separate life and its own separate consciousness. These consciousnesses differ very greatly in their content and in their functions from the intellectual-emotional consciousness which is known to us and which belongs to the whole organism. But this last consciousness is by no means the only one. It is not even the strongest or the clearest. Solely by virtue of its position, so to say, on the border of the inner and outer worlds it receives predominant significance and the possibility of suggesting very many ideas to the obscure inner consciousnesses. The inner consciousnesses are constantly listening to the voice of reason and of the emotions. This voice attracts them, subjugates them to its power. Why? It may seem strange, seeing that the inner consciousnesses are often more subtle and keen than the brain-consciousness. It is true that they are more subtle and keen, but they live in the dark, within the organism. The brain-consciousness appears to them as knowing more than they, as it is turned to the outer world. And the whole crowd of obscure inner consciousnesses incessantly follows the life of the outer consciousness and strives to imitate it. The head-consciousness is entirely ignorant of this and gives them thousands of different suggestions, which are very often contradictory, absurd and harmful to the organism.

The inner consciousnesses are a provincial crowd listening to the opinions of inhabitants of the capital, following their tastes, imitating their manners. What the " mind " and " feeling " say, what they do, what they wish, what they fear, becomes instantly known in the most distant, in the darkest, corners of the organism, and of course it is interpreted and understood in each of them in a different way. A perfectly casual, paradoxical idea of the brain-consciousness, which " comes into the head " casually and is forgotten casually, is taken as a revelation by some " connective tissue," which of course remodels it in its own way and begins to " live " in conformity with this idea. The stomach can be entirely hypnotised by certain absurd tastes and aversions of a purely " æsthetic " character; heart, liver, kidneys, nerves, muscles, may all in this or some other way submit to suggestions which are unconsciously given to them by thoughts and emotions. A considerable number of the phenomena of our inner life, particularly of undesirable phenomena, is in reality dependent on these suggestions. The existence and character of these obscure consciousnesses also explain a great deal in the world of dreams.

The mind and feeling forget or know nothing about this crowd which listens to their voices, and they often talk too loud when it would be better for them to be silent or not to express their opinions, since sometimes their opinions, unimportant and transient for themselves, may produce a very strong impression on the inner consciousnesses. If we do not wish to be in the power of unconscious self-suggestions, we must be careful of the words we use when we speak to ourselves and of the intonations with which we pronounce these words, although consciously we do not attach importance to these words and intonations. We must remember about all these obscure people, listening at the doors of our consciousness, drawing their own conclusions from what they hear, submitting with incredible ease to temptations and fears of every kind and starting to rush about in panic at some simple thought, that we may miss the train or lose a key. We must learn to consider the importance of these inner panics, or, for example, of the terrible depression that suddenly seizes us at the sight of a grey sky and rain beginning. This means that the inner consciousnesses have caught a casual phrase: " What nasty weather," which was said with great feeling, and they have understood it in their own way, that now the weather will always be nasty, that there is no way out and that it is not worth while living or working any longer.

But all this refers to unconscious self-suggestion. The limits of voluntary self-suggestion in our ordinary state are so insignificant that it is impossible to speak of any practical application of this force. Yet against all facts the idea of *self-suggestion* inspires confidence. And at the same time the study of involuntary suggestions and of involuntary suggestibility can never be popular because, more than anything else can do, it destroys millions of illusions and shows a man what he really is. And a man in no case wishes to know this, and he does not wish it because against it there acts the strongest suggestion existing in life, the suggestion which persuades a man to be and to appear other than he is.

1905-1929

Chapter VIII

EXPERIMENTAL MYSTICISM

❈

In 1910 and 1911, as a result of a fairly complete acquaintance with existing literature on " theosophy " and "occultism " and also with the not very numerous scientific investigations of phenomena of *witchcraft, sorcery, magic,* etc., I came to certain definite conclusions, which I was able to formulate in the following propositions:

1. All manifestations of any unusual and supernormal forces of man, both internal and external, should be divided into two main categories — *magic* and *mysticism.* Definition of these concepts presents great difficulties, because, first, in general as well as in special literature both terms are very often used in an entirely wrong sense; second, there remains much that is unexplained in respect both of magic and of mysticism taken separately; and third, the relation of magic and mysticism to one another remains similarly unexplained.

2. Having ascertained the difficulty of exact definition I decided to accept an approximate definition.

I called *magic* all cases of intensified doing or of concrete knowing through other than ordinary means, and I divided magic into *objective,* i.e. with real results, and *subjective,* i.e. with imaginary results. And I called *mysticism* all cases of intensified feeling and abstract knowing.

I called objective magic intensified doing and concrete knowing. " Intensified doing " means in this case the *real* possibility of influencing things, events and people without the aid of ordinary means, at a distance, through walls, or in time, that is, either in the past or in the future, and further, the possibility of influencing the " astral " world, if such a world exists, that is, the souls of the dead, " elementals," forces unknown to us, whether good or evil. Concrete knowing includes clairvoyance in space and time, " telepathy," thought-reading, psychometry, seeing " spirits," " thought-forms," " auras " and the like, again if all these exist.

I called subjective magic all cases of *imaginary* doing and *imaginary* knowing; in this are included artificially evoked hallucinations, dreams taken as reality, the reading of *one's own* thoughts taken as communications, the semi-intentional creation of astral visions, "Akashic records" and similar miracles.

Mysticism in its nature is subjective. I did not therefore put objective mysticism into a special group. I nevertheless found it possible sometimes to call *subjective mysticism* the false mystical states or pseudo-mystical states which are not connected with *intensified* feeling, but come near hysteria and pseudo-magic; in other words religious visions or religious dreams in concrete forms, that is, all that in Orthodox literature is called "beauty." [1]

3. The existence of *objective magic* cannot be considered established. Scientific thought has long denied it and recognised only subjective magic, that is, a kind of self-hypnosis, or hypnosis. In recent times certain admissions are met with in scientific literature or in literature that is intended to be scientific, for instance in the direction of "spiritualism." But these latest admissions are as unreliable as previous denials. "Theosophical" and "occult" thought recognises the possibility of objective magic, but in some cases evidently confuses it with mysticism, and in other cases opposes it to mysticism as a phenomenon *useless* and *immoral*, or at any rate *dangerous*, both for the man who practises "magic" and for other people, and even for the whole of humanity. But all this is affirmed though satisfactory proofs of the real existence and possibility of objective magic are absent.

4. Of all the unusual states of man there can be regarded as fully established only mystical states of consciousness and certain phenomena of subjective magic, these latter being almost all confined to the artificial creation of the visions desired.

5. All the established facts relating to the manifestations of any unusual forces of man, both in the domain of magic, even though subjective, and in the domain of mysticism, are connected with greatly intensified emotional states of a particular kind and never occur without them.

6. The greater part of the religious practice of all religions, and also various magic rituals, ceremonies and the like, have as their aim the creation of these emotional states, to which, according to the original intention, either "magical" or "mystical" powers are ascribed.

7. In many cases of deliberate creation of mystical states or production of magical phenomena the use of narcotics can be traced. In all religions of ancient origin, even in their modern form, there still survives the use of incense, perfumes, unguents, which may primarily have been connected with the use of drugs affecting the emotional and intellectual functions of man. As can be traced, drugs of that kind were very largely used in the ancient Mysteries. Many authors have pointed out the rôle of the sacred drink which was given to candidates for initiation, for instance in the Eleusinian Mysteries, and which may have had a very real and not in the least a symbolical meaning. The legendary sacred drink, the "Soma," which plays a very important part in Indian mythology and in the description of

---

[1] See footnote, Chapter VI, p. 235.

different kinds of mystical ceremonies, may have actually existed as a drink which brought people into a definite, desired state. In all descriptions of witchcraft and sorcery in all countries and among all peoples, the use of narcotics is invariably mentioned. The witches' ointments which served for flying to the Sabbath, different kinds of enchanted and magical drinks, were prepared either from plants possessing stimulant, intoxicant and narcotic properties, or from organic extracts of the same character, or from those vegetable or animal substances to which these properties were ascribed. It is known that in these cases as well as in all kinds of sorcery, belladonna, datura, extracts of poppy (opium), and, especially, of hemp (hashish) were used. All this can be traced and verified, and leaves no doubts as to its meaning. The African wizards, with regard to whom it is possible to find very interesting descriptions in the accounts of modern explorers, use hashish very largely. Siberian Shamans in order to produce in themselves a particular excited state, in which they can foretell the future (real or imaginary), or influence those about them, make use of poisonous mushrooms (*crimson fly-agaric*).

Interesting observations on the meaning of mystical states of consciousness and on the part which may be played by narcotics in the creation of mystical states can be found in Prof. James' book *Varieties of Religious Experience* (New York, 1902).

Various exercises of Yogis: breathing exercises, unusual postures, movements, " sacred dances," etc., have the same object, that is, the creation of mystical states of consciousness. But these methods are still very little known.

In examining the above propositions from the point of view of different methods I came to the conclusion that a new experimental verification of the possible results of the application of these methods was necessary, and I decided to start a series of experiments.

The following is a description of the effects I obtained by applying to myself certain methods, the details of which I had partly found in the literature on these subjects, and partly derived from all that has been set forth above.

I do not describe the actual methods I used. First, because it is not the methods but the results that matter, and second, because the description of methods would divert attention from the facts I intend to examine.

I hope some time later to return specially to these " methods."

My task, as I formulated it to myself at the beginning of my experiments, was to elucidate the questions of the relation of subjective magic to objective magic and then of the relation of objective and subjective magic, taken together, to mysticism.

All this took the shape of three questions:

1. Can the real existence of objective magic be recognised?
2. Does objective magic exist without subjective?

3. Does objective magic exist without mysticism?

Mysticism as such interested me less. However, I said to myself that if we could find a means of deliberately changing our state of consciousness, while at the same time preserving the faculty of self-observation, that would give us completely new material for self-study. We always see ourselves from one and the same angle. If what I supposed should prove to be right, it would mean that we could see ourselves from entirely new and unexpected angles.

The very first experiments showed me the difficulty of the task I had set myself and partly explained to me the failure of many experiments which had been tried by others before me.

A change in the state of consciousness as a result of my experiments began to take place very soon, much more quickly and easily than I thought. But the chief difficulty was that the new state of consciousness which was obtained gave at once so much that was new and unexpected, and these new and unexpected experiences came upon me and flashed by so quickly, that I could not find words, could not find forms of speech, could not find concepts, which would enable me to remember what had occurred even for myself, still less to convey it to anyone else.

The first new psychic sensation which appeared was a sensation of strange duality in myself. Such sensations occur, for instance, in moments of great danger or, in general, under the stress of strong emotions, when a man does or says something almost automatically and at the same time observes himself. This sensation of duality was the first new psychic sensation which appeared in my experiments, and it usually remained throughout even the strangest and most fantastic experiences. There was always a certain point which observed. Unfortunately it could not always remember what it had observed.

The changes in psychic states, this "duality of personality" that occurred, and many other things which were connected with it, usually began about twenty minutes after the beginning of the experiment. When this change came I found myself in a world entirely new and entirely unknown to me, which had nothing in common with the world in which we live, still less with the world which we assume to be the continuation of our world in the direction of the unknown.

That was one of the first strange sensations which struck me. Whether we confess it to ourselves or not, we have a certain conception of the unknowable and of the unknown, or, to be more exact, a certain expectation of it. We expect to see a world which is strange but which consists on the whole of the same kind of phenomena we are accustomed to, or which exists according to the same laws, or has at least something in common with the world we know. We cannot imagine anything *new*, just as we should not be able to imagine an entirely new animal which does not resemble in any way any of the animals we know.

And in this case I saw from the very beginning that all that we half-consciously construct with regard to the unknown is completely and utterly wrong. The unknown is unlike anything that we can suppose about it. The complete unexpectedness of everything that is met with in these experiences, from great to small, makes the description of them difficult. First of all, everything is unified, everything is linked together, everything is explained by something else and in its turn explains another thing. There is nothing separate, that is, nothing that can be named or described *separately*. In order to describe the first impressions, the first sensations, it is necessary to describe *all* at once. The new world with which one comes into contact has no sides, so that it is impossible to describe first one side and then the other. All of it is visible at once at every point; but how in fact to describe anything in these conditions — that question I could not answer.

I understood why all descriptions of mystical experiences are so poor, so monotonous and obviously invented. A man becomes lost amidst the infinite number of totally new impressions, for the expression of which he has neither words nor forms. When he wishes to express or convey them to somebody else he involuntarily uses words which in his ordinary language correspond to the greatest, the most powerful, the most unusual and the most extraordinary, though these words do not in the least correspond to what he sees, learns or experiences. The fact is that he has no other words. But in most cases the man is not even aware of this substitution because his experiences are preserved in his memory as they actually were only for a few moments. Very soon they fade, grow flat, are replaced by the words which were hurriedly and accidentally attached to them to keep them in memory. Very soon nothing remains but these words. This explains why a man who has had mystical experiences uses, for expressing and transmitting them, those forms of images, words and speech which are best known to him, which he is accustomed to use most often and which are the most typical and characteristic for him. In this way it may easily happen that different people describe and convey an entirely identical experience quite differently. A religious man will make use of the usual clichés of his religion. He will speak of the Crucified Jesus, of the Virgin Mary, of the Holy Trinity, and so on. A philosopher will try to render his experiences in the language of the metaphysics to which he is accustomed. For instance he will speak of " categories " or of " monads," or of " transcendental qualities," or something of the sort. A theosophist will speak of the " astral " world, of " thought forms " and of " Teachers." A spiritualist will speak of the spirits of the dead and of communication with them. A poet will speak of his experiences in the language of fairy-tales or ancient myths, or by describing them as sensations of love, rapture, ecstasy.

My personal impression was that in the world with which I came into contact there was nothing resembling any of the descriptions which I had read or heard of before.

One of the first impressions which astonished me was that in this world there was absolutely nothing in any way resembling the theosophical or spiritualistic "astral world." I say "astonished," not because I actually believed in this astral world, but because probably I had unconsciously thought about the unknown in forms of the astral world. As a matter of fact, at that time I was to a certain extent under the influence of theosophical literature, in so far, at any rate, as refers to nomenclature. To put it more correctly, I evidently thought, without formulating it quite clearly, that something must lie behind those perfectly concrete descriptions of the invisible world which are to be found in theosophical books. So that at first it was difficult for me to admit that the whole astral world that was described in such detail by different authors did not exist at all. Later, I found that many other things also did not exist.

I will try to describe in short what I met with in this strange world in which I saw myself.

What I first noticed, simultaneously with the "division of myself into two," was that the relation between the objective and the subjective was broken, entirely altered, and took certain forms incomprehensible to us. But "objective" and "subjective" are only words. I do not wish to hide behind these words, but I wish to describe as exactly as possible what I really felt. For this purpose I must explain what it is that I call "objective" and "subjective." My hand, the pen with which I write, the table, these are objective phenomena. My thoughts, my mental images, the pictures of my imagination, these are subjective phenomena. The world is divided for us along these lines when we are in our ordinary state of consciousness, and all our ordinary orientation works along the lines of this division. In the new state all this was completely upset. First of all we are accustomed to the constancy of the relation between the subjective and the objective — what is objective is always objective, what is subjective is always subjective. Here I saw that the objective and the subjective could change places. The one could become the other. It is very difficult to express this. The habitual mistrust of the subjective disappeared; every thought, every feeling, every image, was immediately objectified in real substantial forms which differed in no way from the forms of objective phenomena; and at the same time objective phenomena somehow disappeared, lost all reality, appeared entirely subjective, fictitious, invented, having no real existence.

This was the first experience. Further, in trying to describe this strange world in which I saw myself, I must say that it resembled more than anything a world of *very complicated mathematical relations*.

Imagine a world in which all relations of quantities, from the simplest to the most complicated, have a form.

Certainly it is easy to say "imagine such a world."

I understand perfectly well that to "imagine" it is impossible. Yet at the same time what I am saying is the closest approximation to the truth which can be made.

"A world of mathematical relations" — this means a world in which everything is connected, in which nothing exists separately and in which at the same time the relations between things have a real existence apart from the things themselves; or, possibly, "things" do not even exist and only "relations" exist.

I am not deceiving myself, and I realise that my descriptions are very poor and will probably not convey what I myself remember. But I remember seeing mathematical laws in operation, and the world as the result of the operation of these laws. Thus the process of the world's creation, when I thought of it, appeared to me under the aspect of the differentiation of some very simple basic principles or basic quantities. This differentiation always proceeded before my eyes in certain forms, sometimes for instance taking the form of a very complicated design developing out of a very simple basic *motif*, which was continually repeated and entered into every combination throughout the design. Thus the whole of the design consisted of nothing but combinations and repetitions of the basic *motif* and could at any point, so to speak, be resolved into its component elements. Sometimes it was music, which began similarly with some very simple sounds and gradually passed into complicated harmonious combinations expressed in visible forms, resembling the design which I have just described, or completely merging into it. The music and the design made a single whole; the one as it were expressed the other.

Throughout the strangest experiences I always felt that nothing of them would remain when I returned to my ordinary state. I understood that in order to remember what I had seen and felt it had all to be translated into words. But for many things there were no words, while other things passed before me so quickly that I had no time to connect them with any words. Even at the time, in the middle of these experiences, I felt that what I was remembering was only an insignificant part of what had passed through my consciousness. I continually said to myself: " I must at least remember that *this is*, that *this was*, and that this is the only reality, while everything else in comparison with it is not real at all."

I tried my experiments under the most varied conditions and in the most varied surroundings. Gradually I became convinced that it was best to be alone. Verification of the experiments, that is, observation by another person, or the recording of the experiences at the very moment they took place, was quite impossible. In any case I never obtained any results in this way.

When I tried having someone near me during these experiments, I found that no kind of conversation could be carried on. I began to say something, but between the first and second words of my sentence such an enormous number of ideas occurred to me and passed before me, that the two words were so widely separated as to make it impossible to find any connection between them. And the third word I usually forgot before it was pronounced, and in trying to recall it I found a million new ideas, but completely forgot where I had begun. I remember for instance the beginning of a sentence:

"I said yesterday" . . .

No sooner had I pronounced the word "I" than a number of ideas began to turn in my head about the meaning of the word, in a philosophical, in a psychological and in every other sense. This was all so important, so new and profound, that when I pronounced the word "said," I could not understand in the least what I meant by it. Tearing myself away with difficulty from the first cycle of thoughts about "I," I passed to the idea "said," and immediately found in it an infinite content. The idea of speech, the possibility of expressing thoughts in words, the past tense of the verb, each of these ideas produced an explosion of thoughts, conjectures, comparisons and associations. Thus, when I pronounced the word "yesterday" I was already quite unable to understand why I had said it. But it in its turn immediately dragged me into the depths of the problems of time, of past, present and future, and before me such possibilities of approach to these problems began to open up that my breath was taken away.

It was precisely these attempts at conversation, made in these strange states of consciousness, which gave me the sensation of change in time which is described by almost everyone who has made experiments like mine. This is a feeling of the extraordinary lengthening of time, in which seconds seem to be years or decades.

Nevertheless, the usual feeling of time did not disappear; only together with it or within it there appeared as it were another feeling of time, and two moments of ordinary time, like two words of my sentence, could be separated by long periods of another time.

I remember how much I was struck by this sensation the first time I had it. My companion was saying something. Between each sound of his voice, between each movement of his lips, long periods of time passed. When he had finished a short sentence, the meaning of which did not reach me at all, I felt I had lived through so much during that time that we should never be able to understand one another again, that I had gone too far from him. It seemed to me that we were still able to speak and to a certain extent understand one another at the beginning of this sentence, but by the end it had become quite impossible, because there were no means of conveying to him all that I had lived through in between.

Attempts at writing also gave no results, except on two or three occasions, when short formulations of my thoughts, written down during the experiment, enabled me afterwards to understand and decipher something out of a series of confused and indefinite recollections. But generally everything ended with the first word. It was very rarely that I went further. Sometimes I succeeded in writing down a sentence, but usually as I was finishing it I did not remember and did not understand what it meant or why I had written it, nor could I remember this afterwards.

I will try to describe consecutively how my experiments proceeded.

I omit the physiological phenomena which preceded the change in my psychic state. I will mention only that the pulsation now quickened, reaching a very high rate, now slowed down.

In this connection I several times observed a very interesting phenomenon.

In the ordinary state *intentional* slowing down or acceleration of the breathing equally produces accelerated beating of the heart. But in this case, entirely without intention on my part, there was established between the breathing and the beating of the heart a connection which ordinarily does not exist; namely, by accelerating the breathing I accelerated the beating of the heart, by slowing down the breathing I slowed down the beating of the heart. I felt that behind this new capacity lay very great possibilities. I tried therefore not to interfere with the work of the organism but to let things follow their natural course.

Left to itself, the pulsation was intensified and was gradually felt in various parts of the body as though gaining more and more ground, and at the same time it became gradually balanced until at last it began to be felt throughout the body simultaneously and after that continued as *one beat*.

This synchronised pulsation went on quickening, and suddenly a shock was felt through the whole body as though a spring clicked, and at the same instant something opened in me. Everything suddenly changed, there began something strange, new, entirely unlike anything that occurs in life. This I called the first threshold.

There was in this new state a great deal that was incomprehensible and unexpected, chiefly in the sense of still greater confusion of objective and subjective; and there were also other new phenomena of which I will now speak. But this state was not yet complete. It should more properly be called the transitional state. In many cases my experiments did not take me further than this state. Sometimes, however, it happened that this state deepened and widened as though I was gradually plunged in light. After that there came a moment of yet another transition, again a kind of shock throughout the body. And only after this began the most interesting state which I attained in my experiments.

The " transitional state " contained almost all the elements of this state, but at the same time it lacked something most important and essential. The " transitional state " did not differ much in its essence from dreams, especially from dreams in the " half-dream state," though it had its own very characteristic forms. And the " transitional state " might perhaps have taken me in by a certain sensation of the miraculous that was connected with it, if I had not been able to adopt a sufficiently critical attitude towards it, based chiefly on my earlier experiments in the study of dreams.

In the " transitional state," which, as I learned very soon, was entirely subjective, I usually began almost at once to hear " voices." These " voices " were a characteristic feature of the " transitional state."

The voices spoke to me and often said very strange things which seemed to have a quality of trick in them. Sometimes in the first moments I was excited by what I heard in this way, particularly as it answered certain vague and unformulated expectations that I had. Sometimes I heard music which evoked in me very varied and powerful emotions.

But strangely enough I felt from the first day a distrust of these states. They contained too many promises, too many things I wanted to have. The voices spoke about every possible kind of thing. They warned me. They proved and explained to me everything in the world, but somehow they did it too simply. I began to ask myself whether I might not myself have invented all that they said, whether it might not be my own imagination, that unconscious imagination which creates our dreams, in which we can see people, talk to them, hear their voices, receive advice from them, etc. After thinking in this way I had to say to myself that the voices told me nothing that I could not have thought myself.

At the same time what came in this way was often very similar to the "communications" received at mediumistic séances, or by means of automatic writing. The voices often gave themselves different names, said various flattering things to me and undertook to answer all kinds of questions. Sometimes I had long conversations with these voices.

Once I asked a question referring to alchemy. I cannot now remember the exact question, but I think it was something either about the different denominations of the four elements: fire, water, air and earth; or about the relation of the four elements to one another. I put the question in connection with what I was reading at the time.

In answer to this question a voice which called itself by a well-known name told me that the answer to my question would be found in a certain book. When I said that I had not got this book the voice told me that I should find it in the Public Library (this happened in St. Petersburg) and advised me to read the book very carefully.

I enquired at the Public Library, but the book (published in English) was not there. There was only a German translation of it in twenty parts, the first three being missing.

But soon I obtained the book elsewhere in English and actually found there certain hints very closely connected with my question, though they did not give a complete answer to it.

This instance, and a number of others like it, showed me that in these transitional states I went through the same experiences as do mediums, clairvoyants and the like. One voice told me something very interesting about the Temple of Solomon in Jerusalem, something that I thought I did not know before, or, if I had ever read it anywhere, had entirely forgotten. Among other things, in describing the temple, the voice said that there were *swarms of flies* there. Logically this was quite comprehensible and even inevitable. In a temple where sacrifices were made, where animals were killed and where there was certainly a great deal of blood and every kind of filth, there must undoubtedly have been many flies. At the same time this sounded new and, so far as I remember, I had never read of flies in connection with ancient temples. But not long before that I had been in the East myself and knew what quantities of flies can be there even under ordinary conditions.

These descriptions of Solomon's Temple, and particularly the " flies," gave me a complete explanation of many strange things which I had come across in my reading and which I could call neither deliberate falsification nor real clairvoyance. Thus the " clairvoyance" of Leadbeater and Dr. Steiner, all the " Akashic records," the descriptions of what happened tens of thousands of years ago in mythical Atlantis or in other prehistoric countries, were undoubtedly of the same nature as the flies in Solomon's Temple. The only difference was that I did not believe in my experiences, while the " Akashic records" were believed and are believed by both their authors and readers.

It very soon became evident to me that neither in these nor in the other experiences was there anything real. It was all reflected, it all came from the memory, from the imagination. The voices immediately became silent as soon as I passed to something familiar and concrete which could be verified.

This explained to me why it is that authors who describe Atlantis are unable with the aid of their " clairvoyance" to solve any practical problems relating to the present which are always so easy to find, but which for some reason they always avoid touching on. Why do they know everything that happened thirty thousand years ago and not know what is happening at the time of their experiments but in another place?

During all these experiments I felt that if I were to believe these voices I should come to a standstill and go no further. This frightened me. I felt that it was all self-deception; that however inviting all that was said and promised by the voices might be, it would all lead nowhere, but would leave me exactly where I was. I understood that it was precisely this that was " beauty," i.e. that it all came from the imagination.

I decided to struggle with these transitional states, adopting towards them a very critical attitude and rejecting as unworthy of credence *all that I might have imagined myself*. This immediately began to give results. As soon as I began rejecting everything I *heard*, realising it to be the same " stuff as dreams are made of," and firmly discarded it for some time, refusing to listen to anything or pay attention to anything, my state and my experiences changed.

I passed the second threshold, which I have already mentioned, beyond which *a new world* began. The " voices" disappeared; in their place there sounded sometimes one voice, which could always be recognised whatever forms it might take. At the same time this new state differed from the transitional state by its extraordinary lucidity of consciousness. I then found myself in the world of mathematical relations, in which there was nothing at all resembling what occurs in life.

In this state also, after passing the second threshold and finding myself in the " world of mathematical relations," I obtained answers to all my questions, but the answers often took a very strange form. In order to understand them it must be realised that the world of mathematical relations in which I was did not remain immovable; this means — there was nothing in it that remained as it was the moment before. Everything moved, changed, was transformed and became something else. Sometimes I suddenly saw all mathematical relations disappear one after another into infinity. Infinity swallowed everything, filled everything; all distinctions were effaced. And I felt that one moment more and I myself should disappear into infinity. I was overcome with terror at the imminence of this abyss. Sometimes this terror made me jump to my feet, move about, in order to drive away the nightmare which had seized me. Then I felt that someone was laughing at me; sometimes I seemed to hear the laugh. Suddenly I caught myself realising that it was I laughing at myself — that I had again fallen into the snare of " beauty," that is, of a wrong approach. Infinity attracted me and at the same time frightened and repelled me. And I came to understand it quite differently. Infinity was not infinite continuation in one direction, but infinite variation at one point. I understood that the terror of infinity results from a wrong approach to it, from a wrong attitude to it. I understood that with a right approach to it infinity is precisely what explains everything, and that nothing can be explained without it.

At the same time I felt that in infinity there was a real menace and a real danger.

To describe consecutively the course of my experiences, the course of the ideas that came to me and the course of fleeting thoughts, is quite impossible, mainly because no one experiment was ever like another. Each time I learned something new about the same thing in such a way as fundamentally to alter all I had learned about it before.

A characteristic feature of the world in which I found myself was, as I have already said, its mathematical structure and the complete absence of anything that could be expressed in the language of ordinary concepts. To use the theosophical terminology I was in the *mental world* " *Arupa*," but the peculiarity of my observations was that only this world " Arupa " really existed. All the rest was the creation of imagination. The real world was a " world without forms." It is an interesting fact that in my first experiment I found myself probably at once or almost at once in this world, escaping the " world of illusions." But in subsequent experiments " voices " seemed to try to detain me in the imaginary world, and I was able to get out of it only when I struggled firmly and resolutely with the illusions as they arose. All this strongly reminded me of something I had read before. It seemed to me that, in existing literature, in the descriptions of magical experiments or in the descriptions of initiations and preceding tests, there was something very similar to what I had experienced and felt — but of course this does not refer to modern " séances " or even to attempts at ceremonial magic, which is complete immersion in the world of illusions.

An interesting phenomenon in my experiments was the consciousness of danger which threatened me from infinity and the constant warnings received from *somebody*, as though there was *somebody* who watched me all the time and often tried to persuade me to stop my experiments, not to attempt to go along this path, which was wrong and unlawful from the point of view of certain principles which I at that time felt and understood only dimly.

What I have called " mathematical relations " were continually changing round me and within me, sometimes taking the form of sounds, of music, sometimes the form of a design, sometimes the form of light filling the whole of space, of a kind of visible vibration of light rays, crossing, interweaving with one another, pervading everything. In this connection there was an unmistakable feeling that through these sounds, through the design, through the light, I was learning something I had not known before. But to convey what I learned, to tell about it or put it into writing was very difficult. The difficulty of explaining was increased by the fact that words express badly, and really cannot express, the essence of the intense emotional state in which I was during these experiences.

This emotional state was perhaps the most vivid characteristic of the experiences which I am describing. Without it there would have been nothing. Everything came through it, that is, everything was understood through it. In order to understand my experiences it must be realised that I was not at all indifferent to the sounds and the light mentioned above. I took in everything through feeling, and experienced emotions which never exist in life. The new knowledge that came to me came when I was in an exceedingly intense emotional state. My attitude towards this new knowledge was in no way indifferent; I either loved it or was horrified by it, strove towards it or was amazed by it; and it was these very emotions, with a thousand others, which gave me the possibility of understanding the nature of the new world that I came to know.

The number " *three* " played a very important part in the world in which I found myself. In a way quite incomprehensible to our mathematics it entered into all the relations of magnitudes, created them and originated from them. All taken together, that is, the entire universe, sometimes appeared in the form of a " triad," composing one whole, and looking like some great trefoil. Each part of the " triad," by some inner process, was again transformed into a " triad," and this process continued until all was filled with " triads," which were transformed into music, or light, or designs. Once again I must say that all these descriptions express very badly what occurred, as they do not give the emotional element of joy, wonder, rapture, horror, continually changing one into the other.

As I have already said, the experiments were most successful when I was by myself and lying down. Sometimes, however, I tried being among people or walking in the streets. These experiments were usually unsuccessful. Something began, but ended almost at once, passing into a heavy physical state. But sometimes I found myself in another world. On such occasions the whole of the ordinary world changed in a very subtle and strange way. Everything became different, but it is absolutely impossible to describe what happened to it. The first thing that can be said is that there was nothing which remained indifferent for me. All taken together and each thing separately affected me in one way or another. In other words, I took everything emotionally, reacted to everything emotionally. Further, in this new world which surrounded me, there was nothing separate, nothing that had no connection with other things or with me personally. All things were connected with one another, and not accidentally, but by incomprehensible chains of causes and effects. All things were dependent on one another, all things lived in one another. Further, in this world there was nothing dead, nothing inanimate, nothing that did not think, nothing that did not feel, nothing unconscious. Everything was living, everything was conscious of itself. Everything spoke to me and I could speak to everything. Particularly interesting were the houses and other buildings which I passed, especially the old houses. They were living beings, full of thoughts, feelings, moods and memories. The people who lived in them were their *thoughts, feelings, moods*. I mean that the people in relation to the " houses " played approximately the same rôle which the different " I "s of our personality play in relation to us. They come and go, sometimes live in us for a long time, sometimes appear only for short moments.

I remember once being struck by an ordinary cab-horse in the Nevsky, by its head, its face. It expressed the whole being of the horse. Looking at the horse's face I understood all that could be understood about a horse. All the traits of horse-nature, all of which a horse is capable, all of which it is incapable, all that it can do, all that it cannot do; all this was expressed in the lines and features of the horse's face. A dog once gave me a similar sensation. At the same time the horse and the dog were not simply horse and dog; they were " atoms," conscious, moving " atoms " of great beings — " the great horse " and " the great dog." I understood then that we also are atoms of a great being, " the great man." Each thing is an atom of a " great thing." A glass is an atom of a " great glass." A fork is an atom of a " great fork."

This idea and several other thoughts that remained in my memory from my experiences entered into my book *Tertium Organum*, which was actually written during these experiments. Thus the formulations of the laws of the noumenal world and several other ideas referring to higher dimensions were taken from what I learned during these experiments.

Sometimes I felt during these experiments that I understood many things particularly clearly, and I felt if I could in some way preserve what I understood at this moment, then I should know how to make myself pass into this state at any moment I might want it; I should know how to fix this state and how to make use of it.

The question as to how to fix this state arose continually and I put it to myself many times when I was in the state in which I could receive answers to my questions; but I could never get a direct answer to it, that is, the answer which I wanted. Usually the answer began far away and, gradually widening, included everything, so that finally the answer to the question included the answers to all possible questions. Naturally, for that reason I could not retain it in my memory.

Once, I remember, in a particularly vividly-expressed new state, that is, when I understood very clearly all I wished to understand, I decided to find some formula, some key, which I should be able, so to speak, to throw across to myself for the next day. I decided to sum up shortly all I understood at that moment and write down, if possible in one sentence, what it was necessary to do in order to bring myself into the same state immediately, by one turn of thought without any preliminary preparation, since this appeared possible to me all the time. I found this formula and wrote it down with a pencil on a piece of paper.

On the following day I read the sentence, " Think in other categories." These were the words, but what was their meaning? Where was everything I had associated with these words when I wrote them? It had all disappeared, had vanished like a dream. Certainly the sentence " think in other categories " had a meaning; only I could not recollect it, could not reach it.

Later on exactly the same thing happened with this sentence as had happened with many other words and fragments of ideas that had remained in the memory after my experiences. In the beginning, these sentences seemed to be entirely empty. I even laughed at them, finding in them complete proof of the impossibility of transferring anything from there to here. But gradually something began to revive in my memory, and in the course of two or three weeks I remembered more and more of what was connected with these words. And though all of it still remained very vague, as if seen from afar, I began to *see meaning*, that is, special meaning, in words which in the beginning seemed merely abstract designations of something without any practical significance.

The same process was repeated almost every time. On the day after the experiment I remembered very little. Sometimes towards evening some vague memories began to return. Next day I could remember more; during the following two or three weeks I was able to recollect separate details of the experiences, though I was always perfectly aware that in general only an infinitesimal part was remembered. When I tried to make experiments more often than every two or three weeks, I spoiled the results, that is, everything was confused, I could remember nothing.

But I will continue the description of successful experiments. Many times, perhaps always, I had the feeling that when I passed the second threshold I came into contact with *myself*, with the self which was always within me, which always saw me and always told me something that I could not understand and could not even hear in ordinary states of consciousness.

Why can I not understand?

I answered: merely because in the ordinary state thousands of voices sound at once creating what we call our " consciousness," our thoughts, our feelings, our moods, our imagination. These voices drown the sound of that inner voice. My experiments added nothing to the ordinary " consciousness "; they *reduced* it, yet by reducing it they intensified it to an incomprehensible degree. What did they actually do? They compelled these other voices of the ordinary consciousness to keep silence, put them to sleep, or made them inaudible. Then I began to hear the other voice, which came as it were from above, from a certain point *above my head*. I understood then that the whole problem and the whole object consisted in being able to hear this voice *constantly*, in being in constant communication with it. The being to whom this voice belonged knew everything, understood everything and above all was free from thousands of small and distracting " personal " thoughts and moods. He could take everything calmly, could take everything objectively, as it was in reality. And at the same time *this was I*. How this could be so and why in the ordinary state I was so far from myself, if this was I — that I could not explain. Sometimes during the experiments I called my ordinary self " I " and the other one — " he." Sometimes, on the contrary, I called the ordinary self " he " and the other one — " I." But I shall return later to the problem of " I " in general and the realisation of " I " in the new state of consciousness, because all this was much more complicated than the mere superseding of one " I " by the other.

At present I want to try to describe, so far as it has been preserved in my memory, how this " he " or this " I " looked at things as distinct from an ordinary " I."

I remember once sitting on a sofa smoking and looking at an ash-tray. It was an ordinary copper ash-tray. Suddenly I felt that I was beginning to understand what the ash-tray was, and at the same time, with a certain wonder and almost with fear, I felt that I had never understood it before and that we do not understand the simplest things around us.

The ash-tray roused a whirlwind of thoughts and images. It contained such an infinite number of facts, of events; it was linked with such an immense number of things. First of all, with everything connected with smoking and tobacco. This at once roused thousands of images, pictures, memories. Then the ash-tray itself. How had it come into being? All the materials of which it could have been made? Copper, in this case — what was copper? How had people discovered it for the first time? How had they learned to make use of it? How and where was the copper obtained from which this ash-tray was made? Through what kind of treatment had it passed, how had it been transported from place to place, how many people had worked on it or in connection with it? How had the copper been transformed into an ash-tray? These and other questions about the history of the ash-tray up to the day when it had appeared on my table.

I remember writing a few words on a piece of paper in order to retain something of these thoughts on the following day. And next day I read:

" *A man can go mad from one ash-tray.*"

The meaning of all that I felt was that in one ash-tray it was possible to know *all*. By invisible threads the ash-tray was connected with everything in the world, not only with the present, but with all the past and with all the future. To know an ash-tray meant to know all.

My description does not in the least express the sensation as it actually was, because the first and principal impression was that the ash-tray was alive, that it thought, understood and told me all about itself. All I learned I learned from the ash-tray itself. The second impression was the extraordinary emotional character of all connected with what I had learned about the ash-tray.

"Everything is alive," I said to myself in the midst of these observations; " there is nothing dead, it is only we who are dead. If we become alive for a moment, we shall feel that everything is alive, that all things live, think, feel and can speak to us."

The case of the ash-tray reminds me of another instance in which the answer to my question came in the form of a visual image, very characteristic in its structure.

Once when I was in the state into which my experiments brought me, I asked myself: " What is the world? "

Immediately I saw a semblance of some big flower, like a rose or a lotus, the petals of which were continually unfolding from the middle, growing, increasing in size, reaching the outside of the flower and then in some way again returning to the middle and starting again at the beginning. Words in no way express it. In this flower there was an incredible quantity of light, movement, colour, music, emotion, agitation, knowledge, intelligence, mathematics, and continuous unceasing growth. And while I was looking at this flower *someone* seemed to explain to me that this was the " World " or " Brahma " in its clearest aspect and in the nearest possible approximation to what it is in reality — " If the approximation were made still nearer, it would be Brahma himself, as he is," said the voice.

These last words seemed to contain a kind of warning, as though Brahma in his real aspect was dangerous and could swallow up and annihilate me. This again was " infinity."

This incident and the symbol of Brahma or " the world," which remained in my memory, greatly interested me because it explained to me the origin of other symbols and allegorical images. I thought later that I understood the principle of the formation of the different attributes of gods and the meaning of many myths.

Moreover, this incident brings me to another very important feature of my experiments, namely, to the method by which ideas were communicated to me in these strange states after the second threshold.

As I have already said, ideas were transmitted not in words but in sounds, forms, "designs" or symbols. Usually everything began with the appearance of these forms. As was mentioned before, "voices" were the characteristic feature of the transitional state. When they ceased they were replaced by these forms, i.e. sounds, "designs," etc.; and after these followed visual images possessing very special properties and demanding detailed explanation. Brahma seen as a flower might serve as an example of these visual images, though ordinarily they were much simpler, something in the nature of conventional signs or hieroglyphs.

These signs constituted the form of speech or thought, or of what corresponded to speech or thought, in the state of consciousness which I attained. Signs or hieroglyphs moved and changed before me with dizzy rapidity, expressing in this way transitions, changes, combinations and correlations of ideas. Only this manner of "speech" was sufficiently quick for the quickness of thought which was here arrived at. No other forms were quick enough. And these *moving signs of things* indicated the beginning of new thinking, a new state of consciousness. Thinking in words became quite impossible. As I have already said, between two words of the same sentence long periods of time passed. Thinking in words could never keep pace with thought as it worked in this state.

It is curious that in mystical literature a number of references to these "signatures of things" can be found. I give them the name which was given to them by Jacob Boehme (*Tertium Organum*, Ch. XXII, p. 281). I do not doubt that Boehme spoke of exactly the same signs that I saw. For myself I call them "Symbols." By their outer form it would be more correct to call them moving hieroglyphs. I tried to draw some of them and, though I sometimes succeeded in it, on the following day it was very difficult to connect the figures obtained with any ideas. Once, however, I obtained something very interesting.

I drew a figure like this:

FIG. 6

The number of lateral projections is immaterial, but the important point is that they are disposed at unequal distances from one another along the horizontal line.

I obtained this figure in the following way.

In connection with certain facts in the lives of people whom I knew, which happened to come into my mind, I asked myself the rather complicated question as to how the fate of one man might influence the fate of another man. I cannot now reconstruct my question exactly, but I remember that it was connected with the idea of the laws of cause and effect, of free choice or accident. While still continuing to think in an ordinary way,

I imagined the life of a man I knew and the accident in his life through which he had come across other people whose lives he had most decisively influenced, and who in their turn had changed many things in his own life. Thinking in this way, I suddenly noticed, or caught myself seeing, all these intercrossing lives in the form of simple signs, namely in the form of short lines with small projections on one side. The number of these projections diminished or increased; they either approached one another or separated. And in their appearance, in their approach or separation, and also in the combination of different lines with different projections, were expressed the ideas and laws governing men's lives.

I will return later to the meaning of this symbol. At present I wish only to explain the actual method of obtaining new ideas in the state of consciousness described.

A separate part of my experiences constituted what I could call my relation to myself, or more correctly to my body. It all became alive, became thinking and conscious. I could speak to any part of my body as if it was a separate being, and could learn from it what attracted it, what it liked, what it disliked, what it was afraid of, what it lived by, what were its interests and needs. These conversations with the consciousnesses of the physical body revealed a whole new world.

I have tried to describe some of the results of these impressions in *Tertium Organum*, in speaking of consciousness *not parallel to our own*.

These consciousnesses, which I now call the consciousnesses of the physical body, had very little in common with our consciousness which objectivises the external world and distinguishes " I " from " not I ": These consciousnesses, i.e. the consciousnesses of the physical body, were completely immersed in themselves. They knew only themselves, only " I "; " not I " did not exist for them. They could think only of themselves — they could speak only of themselves. But, as against that, they knew everything about themselves that could be known. I then understood that their nature and the form of their existence consisted in their continually speaking of themselves — what they were, what they needed, what they wished, what was pleasant for them, what was unpleasant, what dangers threatened them, what could ward off or remove these dangers.

In the ordinary state we do not hear these voices separately; only the noise produced by them or their general tone is felt by us as our physical state or mood.

I have no doubt that if we could consciously enter into communication with these " beings " we should be able to learn from them all the details of the state of every function of our organism. The first idea that comes to one's mind in this connection is the consideration that this would be particularly useful, in the case of diseases and functional disorders, for right diagnosis, for the prevention of possible illnesses and for the treatment of those already existing. If a method could be found for entering into communication with these consciousnesses and for receiving from them information as to the state and demands of the organism, medicine would stand on firm ground.

In continuing my experiments I tried all the time to find a means of passing from abstract to concrete facts. I wanted to find out whether there was not a possibility of strengthening the ordinary powers of perception or of discovering new powers, especially with regard to events in time, to the past or future. I definitely put myself the question, whether the power can exist of seeing without the aid of eyes, or at a great distance, or through a wall, or of seeing things in closed receptacles, reading letters in sealed envelopes, reading a book on a shelf between other books, and so on. It had never been clear to me whether such things were possible. On the contrary, I knew that all attempts at verification of the phenomena of clairvoyance, which are sometimes described, invariably ended in failure.

During my experiments I many times attempted to " see," for instance, when I was myself in the house, what was happening in the street, which I could not see in the natural way, or to " see " some man or other whom I knew well, what he was doing at that moment; or to reconstruct fully scenes from the past of which I knew only some parts.

Then I sealed some old photographs from an album into envelopes of the same size, mixed them up and tried to " see " whose portrait I held in my hand. I tried the same thing with playing-cards.

When I became convinced that I was not succeeding, I tried to reconstruct as a clear visual image what was undoubtedly in my memory, though in the ordinary state I could not visualise it at will. For instance I tried to " see " the Nevsky, beginning from Znamensky Square, with all the houses and shop-signs in their order. But this also was never successful when done intentionally. Unintentionally and in various circumstances I more than once saw myself walking along the Nevsky, and then I " saw " both the houses and the signs exactly as they would be in reality.

Finally I had to recognise as unsuccessful all attempts to pass to concrete facts. Either it is quite impossible, or else I attempted it in the wrong way.

But there were two cases which showed that there is a possibility of a very great strengthening of our capacities of perception in relation to the ordinary events of life.

Once I obtained not exactly clairvoyance, but undoubtedly a very great strengthening of the capacity of vision. It was in Moscow in the street, half an hour after an experiment which had seemed to me to be entirely unsuccessful. For a few seconds my vision suddenly became extraordinarily acute. I could quite clearly see the faces of people at a distance at which normally one would have difficulty in distinguishing one figure from another.

Another instance occurred during the second winter of my experiments in St. Petersburg. Circumstances were such that the whole of that winter I was unable to go to Moscow, although at the time I very much wanted to go there in connection with several different matters. Finally I remember that about the middle of February I definitely decided that I would go to Moscow for Easter. Soon after this I again began my experiments. Once, quite accidentally, when I was in the state in which moving signs or hieroglyphs were beginning to appear, I had a thought about Moscow, or about someone whom I had to see there at Easter. Suddenly without any warning I received the comment that I should not go to Moscow at Easter. Why? In answer to this I saw how, starting from the day of the experiment I have described, events began to develop in a definite order and sequence. Nothing new happened. But the causes, which I could see quite well and which were all there on the day of my experiment, were evolving, and having come to the results which unavoidably followed from them, they formed just before Easter a whole series of difficulties which in the end prevented me going to Moscow. The fact in itself, as I looked at it, had a merely curious character, but the interesting side of it was that I saw what looked like a possibility of calculating the future — the whole future was contained in the present. I saw that all that had happened before Easter resulted directly from what had already existed two months earlier.

Then in my experiment I probably passed on to other thoughts, and on the following day I remembered only the bare result, that "somebody" had told me I should not go to Moscow at Easter. This was ridiculous, because I saw nothing that could prevent it. Then I forgot all about my experiment. It came to my memory again only a week before Easter, when suddenly a whole succession of small circumstances brought it about that I did not go to Moscow. The circumstances were precisely those which I had "seen" during my experiment, and they quite definitely resulted from what had existed two months before that. Nothing new had happened.

When everything fell out exactly as I had seen, or foreseen, in that strange state, I remembered my experiment, remembered all the details, remembered that I saw and knew then what had to happen.

In this incident I undoubtedly came into contact with the possibility of a different vision in the world of things and events. But, speaking generally, all the questions which I asked myself referring to real life or to concrete knowledge led to nothing.

I think that this is connected with a principle which became clear to me during my experiments.

In ordinary life we think by thesis and antithesis; always and everywhere there is "yes" or "no," "no" or "yes." In thinking differently, in thinking in a new way, in thinking by means of signs of things, I came to understand the fundamental errors of our mental process.

In reality, everywhere and in every case there were not two but three elements. There were not only "yes" and "no," but "yes," "no" and something else besides. And it was precisely the nature of this "third" element, inaccessible to the understanding, which made all ordinary reasonings unsuitable and demanded a change in the basic method. I saw that the solution of all problems always came from a *third*, unknown, element, that is to say, it came from a third and unknown side, and that without this *third* element it was impossible to arrive at a right solution.

Further, when I asked a question I very often began to see that the question itself was wrongly put. Instead of giving an immediate answer to my question, the "consciousness" to which I was speaking began to move my question round and turn it about, showing me that it was wrong. Gradually I began to see what was wrong. As soon as I understood clearly what was wrong in my question, *I saw the answer*. But the answer always included a *third element* which I could not see before, because my question was always built upon *two* elements only, thesis and antithesis. I formulated this for myself in the following way: that the whole difficulty lay in the putting of the question. If we could put questions rightly, we should know the answers. A question rightly put contains the answer in itself. But the answer will be quite unlike what we expect, it will always be on another plane, on a plane not included in the ordinary question.

In several cases in which I attempted to think with certain ready-made words or with ready-made ideas I experienced a strange sensation like a physical shock. Before me complete emptiness opened out, because in the real world with which I had come into contact there was nothing corresponding to these words or ideas. The sensation was very curious — the sensation of unexpected emptiness where I had counted upon finding something, which, if not solid and definite, would be at least existent.

I have already said that I found nothing corresponding to the theosophical "astral bodies," or "astral world," nothing corresponding to "reincarnation," nothing corresponding to the "future life" in the ordinary sense of the word, that is, to one or another form of existence of the souls of the dead. All this had no meaning, and not only did it not express any truth, but *it did not directly contradict truth*. When I tried to introduce into my thoughts the questions connected with these ideas, there were no replies to them; words remained only words *and could not be expressed by any hieroglyphs*.

The same thing happened with many other ideas, for example with the idea of "evolution" as it is understood in "scientific" thinking. It did not fit in anywhere and did not mean anything at all. There was no place for it in the world of realities.

I realised that I felt which ideas were alive and which were dead; dead ideas were not expressed in hieroglyphs, they remained words. I found an enormous number of such dead ideas in the general usage of thought. Besides the ideas already mentioned, all so-called "social theories" belonged to the dead ideas. They simply did not exist. There were words behind which lay no reality; similarly the idea of "justice," as it is ordinarily understood in the sense of "compensation" or "retribution," was utterly dead. One thing could never compensate for another, one act of violence never destroy the results of another act of violence. At the same time the idea of justice in the sense of "desire for the general good" was also dead. And, speaking generally, there was some great misunderstanding in this idea. The idea assumed that a thing could exist by itself and be " unjust," that is, contradict a certain law; but in the real world *everything was one,* and there were no two things that could contradict each other. And therefore there was nothing that could be called justice or injustice. The only difference that existed was between dead and living things. But this distinction was exactly what we did not understand, and though we strove to express the same idea in our language we hardly succeeded in doing so.

All these are only examples. In fact almost all the usual ideas and concepts by which people live proved to be *non-existent.*

With great amazement I became convinced that only a very small number of ideas corresponds to real facts, that is, actually exists. We live in an entirely unreal, fictitious world, we argue about non-existent ideas, we pursue non-existent aims, invent everything, even ourselves.

But as opposed to dead ideas which did not exist *anywhere,* there were on the other hand living ideas incessantly recurring always and everywhere and constantly present in everything I thought, learned and understood at that time.

First there was the idea of the *triad,* or the trinity, which entered into everything. Then a very important place was occupied and much was explained by the idea of the four elements: *fire, water, air* and *earth.* This was a real idea, and during the experiments, in the new state of consciousness, I understood how it entered into everything and was connected with everything through the triad. But in the ordinary state the significance and connection of these two ideas eluded me.

Further, there was the idea of *cause and effect.* As I have already mentioned, this idea was expressed in hieroglyphs in a very definite way. But it was in no way connected with the idea of " reincarnation," and referred entirely to ordinary earthly life.

A very great place — perhaps the chief place — in all that I had learned was occupied by the idea of " I." That is to say, the feeling or sensation of " I " in some strange way changed within me. It is very difficult to express this in words. Ordinarily we do not sufficiently understand that at different moments of our life we feel our " I " differently. In this case, as in many others, I was helped by my earlier experiments and observations of dreams. I knew that in sleep " I " is felt differently, not as it is felt in a waking state; just as differently, but in quite another way, " I " was felt in these experiences. The nearest possible approximation would be if I were to say that everything which is ordinarily felt as " I " became " not I," and everything which is felt as " not I " became " I." But this is far from being an exact statement of what I felt and learned. I think that an exact statement is impossible. It is necessary only to note that the new sensation of " I " during the first experiments, so far as I can remember it, and a very terrifying sensation. I felt that I was disappearing, vanishing, turning into nothing. This was the same terror of infinity of which I have already spoken, but it was reversed: in one case it was All that swallowed me up, in the other it was Nothing. But this made no difference, because All was equivalent to Nothing.

But it is remarkable that later, in subsequent experiments, the same sensation of the disappearance of " I " began to produce in me a feeling of extraordinary calmness and confidence, which nothing can equal in our ordinary sensations. I seemed to understand at that time that all the usual troubles, cares and anxieties are connected with the usual sensation of " I," result from it, and, at the same time, constitute and sustain it. Therefore, when " I " disappeared, all troubles, cares and anxieties disappeared. When I felt that I did not exist, everything else became very simple and easy. At these moments I even regarded it as strange that we could take upon ourselves so terrible a responsibility as to bring " I " into everything and start from " I " in everything. In the idea of " I," in the sensation of " I," such as we ordinarily have, there was something almost abnormal, a kind of fantastic conceit which bordered on blasphemy, as if each one of us called himself God. I felt then that only God could call himself " I," that only God was " I." But we also call ourselves " I " and do not see and do not notice the irony of it.

As I have already said, the strange experiences connected with my experiments began with the change in the sensation of " I," and it is difficult to imagine that they would be possible in the case of retention of the ordinary sensation of " I." This change constituted their very essence, and everything else that I felt and learned depended upon it.

With regard to what I learned during my experiments, particularly with regard to the increase of the possibility of cognition, I came to know much that was strange and that did not enter into any theories that I had known before.

The consciousness which communicated with me by means of moving hieroglyphs attached the greatest importance to this question and strove to impress on my mind, perhaps more than anything else, all that related to this question, that is, to the methods of cognition.

I mean that the hieroglyphs explained to me that besides the ordinary cognition based on the evidence of the sense organs, on calculation and on logical thinking, there exist *three other different cognitions*, which differ from one another and from the ordinary cognition, not in degree, not in form, not in quality, but in their very nature, as phenomena of utterly different orders which cannot be measured by the same measure. In our language we call these three phenomena together, where we recognise their existence, intensified cognition, that is, we admit their difference from the ordinary cognition, but do not understand their difference from one another. This, according to the hieroglyphs, is the chief factor in preventing us from understanding rightly our relation to the world.

Before attempting to define the " three kinds of cognition " I must remark that the communication about the forms of cognition always began from some question of mine which had no definite relation to the problems of cognition, but evidently contradicted in some way laws of cognition that were unknown to us. For example, this nearly always happened when from the domain of abstract questions I tried to pass to concrete phenomena, asking questions referring to living people or real things, or to myself in the past, present or future.

In those cases I received the answer that what I wished to know could be known in three ways or that, speaking generally, there were three ways of cognition, apart of course from the ordinary way of cognition with the help of the sense-organs, calculation and logical reasoning, which did not enter into the question, and the limits of which were assumed to be known.

Further, there usually followed a description of the characteristics and properties of each way.

It was as though someone anxious to give me right ideas of things found it particularly important that I should understand *this* rightly.

I will try to set forth as exactly as possible all that refers to this question. But I doubt whether I shall succeed in fully expressing even what I understand myself.

The first cognition is learning in an unusual way, as though through inner vision, anything relating to things and events with which I am directly connected and in which I am directly and personally interested. For instance, if I learn something which must happen in the near future to me or to someone closely connected with me, and if I learn it not in the ordinary way but through inner vision, this would be cognition of that kind. If I learn that a steamer on which I have to sail will be wrecked, or if I learn that on a definite day serious danger will threaten one of my friends, and if I learn that by taking such and such a step I can avert the danger — this will be cognition of the first kind or *the first cognition*. Personal interest constitutes a necessary condition of this cognition. Personal interest connects a man in a certain way with things and events and enables him to occupy in relation to them a definite " position of cognition." Personal interest, that is, the presence of the person interested, is an almost necessary condition of " fortune-telling," " clairvoyance," " prediction of the future "; without personal interest these are almost impossible.

The second cognition is also cognition of ordinary things and events in our life, for knowing which we have no ordinary means — just as in the first case — but with which nothing connects us personally. If I learn that a steamer will be wrecked, in the fate of which I am not personally interested at all, on which neither I nor any of my friends is sailing; if I learn that which is happening in my neighbour's house, but which has no relation to myself; if I learn for certain who actually were the persons who are considered historical enigmas, like the Man in the Iron Mask or Dmitry the Pretender or the Comte de Saint-Germain, or if I learn somebody's future or past, again having no relation to myself, this will be the second kind of cognition. The second kind of cognition is the most difficult, and is almost impossible, because if a man accidentally, or with the aid of special means or methods, learned more than other people can know he would certainly do so in the first way.

The second kind of cognition contains something unlawful. It is " magic," in the full sense of the word. The first and third ways of cognition in comparison with it appear simple and natural, though the first way, based on emotional apprehension, presentiment or desire of some kind, looks like a psychological trick; and the third way appears as a continuation of ordinary cognition, but along new lines and on new principles.

The third cognition is cognition based on knowledge of the mechanism of everything existing. By knowing all the mechanism and by knowing all the relations of the separate parts, it is easy to arrive at the smallest detail and determine with absolute precision everything connected with this detail. The third cognition is cognition based on calculation. Everything can be calculated. If the mechanism of everything is known it is possible to calculate what kind of weather there will be in a month's time, or in a year's time; it would be possible to calculate the day and hour of every occurrence. It would be possible to calculate the meaning and significance of every small event that is observed. The difficulty of the third order of cognition consists first in the necessity of knowing the whole mechanism for the cognition of the smallest thing, and second, in the necessity for putting into motion the whole colossal machine of knowledge in order to know something quite small and insignificant.

This is roughly what I " learned " or " understood " in reference to the three kinds of cognition. I see quite clearly that in this description the idea is inadequately conveyed; many things, probably the most important, escaped my memory long ago. This is true not only in relation to the question of cognition, but, generally, in relation to all that I have written here about my experiments. All these descriptions must be taken very cautiously, on the understanding that in the description, ninety-nine per cent. of what was felt and understood during the experiments has been lost.

A very strange place in my experiments was occupied by attempts to know something concerning the dead. Questions of this kind usually remained without an answer, and I was vaguely aware that there was some essential fault in the questions themselves. But once I received a very clear answer to my question. Moreover, this answer was associated with another case of unusual sensation of death, which I experienced about ten years before the experiments described and which was caused by a state of intense emotion.

In speaking of both cases I shall have to touch on entirely personal matters.

The experience was connected with the death of a certain person closely related to me. I was very young at the time and was very much depressed by his death. I could not think of anything else and was trying to understand, to solve the riddle of disappearance and of men's interconnection with one another. And suddenly within me there rose a wave of new thoughts and new sensations, leaving after it a feeling of astonishing calm. I saw for a moment why we cannot understand death, why death frightens us, why we cannot find answers to any questions which we put to ourselves in connection with the problem of death. This person who had died, and of whom I was thinking, could not have died because he had never existed. This was the solution. Ordinarily, I had seen not him himself, but something that was like his shadow. The shadow had disappeared. The man who had really existed could not have disappeared. He was bigger than I had seen him, " longer," as I formulated it to myself, and in this " length " of his there was contained, in a certain way, the answer to all the questions.

This sudden and vivid current of thought disappeared as quickly as it had appeared. For a few seconds only there remained of it something like a mental picture. I saw before me two figures. One, quite small, was like the vague silhouette of a man. This figure represented the man as I had known him. The other figure was like a road in the mountains which you see winding among the hills, crossing rivers and disappearing into the distance. This was what he had been in reality and this was what I could neither understand nor express. The memory of this experience gave me for a long time a feeling of calm and confidence. Later, the ideas of higher dimensions gave me the possibility of finding a formulation for this strange " dream in a waking state," as I called my experience.

Something closely resembling this happened again in connection with my experiments.

I was thinking about another person also closely related to me who had died two years before. In the circumstances of this person's death, as also in the events of the last years of his life, there was much that was not clear to me, and there were things for which I might have blamed myself psychologically, chiefly for my having drifted away from him, not having been sufficiently near him when he might have needed me. There was much to be said against these thoughts, but I could not get rid of them entirely, and they again brought me to the problem of death and to the problem of the possibility of a life beyond the grave.

I remember saying to myself once during the experiment that if I believed in " spiritualistic " theories and in the possibility of communication with the dead I should like to see this person and ask him one question, just one question.

And suddenly, without any preparation, my wish was satisfied, and I *saw* him. It was not a visual sensation, and what I saw was not his external appearance, but *the whole of his life*, which flashed quickly before me. This life — this was he. The man whom I had known and who had died had never existed. That which existed was something quite different, because his life was not simply a series of events, as we ordinarily picture the life of a man to ourselves, but a thinking and feeling *being* who did not change by the fact of his death. The man whom I had known was the *face*, as it were, of this being — the face which changed with the years, but behind which stood always the same unchanging reality. To express myself figuratively I may say that I saw the man and spoke to him. In actual fact there were no visual impressions which could be described, nor anything like ordinary conversation. Nevertheless, I know that it was *he*, and that it was he who communicated to me much more about himself than I could have asked. I saw quite clearly that the events of the last years of his life were as inseparably linked with him as the features of his face which I had known during his life. These events of the last years were the features of the face of his life of the last years. Nobody could have changed anything in them, just as nobody could have changed the colour of his hair or eyes, or the shape of his nose; and just in the same way it could not have been anybody's fault that this man had these facial features and not others.

The features of his face, like the features of his life of the last years — these were his qualities, these were he. To regard him without the events of the last years of his life would have been just as strange as to imagine him with a different face — it would not have been he. At the same time I understood that nobody could be responsible that he was as he was and not different. I realised that we depend upon one another much less than we think. We are no more responsible for the events in one another's lives than we are for the features of one another's faces. Each has his own face, with its own peculiar lines and features, and each has his own fate, in which another man may occupy a certain place, but in which he can change nothing.

But having realised this I saw also that we are far more closely bound to our past and to the people we come into contact with than we ordinarily think, and I understood quite clearly that death does not change anything in this. We remain bound with all with whom we have been bound. But for communication with them it is necessary to be in a special state.

I could explain in the following way the ideas which I understood in this connection: if one takes the branch of a tree with the twigs, the cross-section of the branch will correspond to a man as we ordinarily see him; the branch itself will be the life of the man, and the twigs will be the lives of the people with whom he comes into contact.

The hieroglyph described earlier, a line with lateral projections, signifies precisely this branch with twigs.

I have endeavoured in my book *Tertium Organum* to set forth the idea of the " long body " of man from birth to death. The term used in Indian philosophy, " Linga Sharira," designates precisely this " *long body of life*."

The conception of man or the life of man as a branch, with offshoots representing the lives of people with whom he is connected, linked together many things in my understanding and explained a great deal to me. Each man is for himself such a branch, other people with whom he is connected are his offshoots. But each of these people is for himself a main branch and the first man for him is his offshoot. Each of the offshoots, if attention is concentrated upon it, becomes itself a branch with offshoots. In this way the life of each man is connected with a number of other lives, one life enters, in a sense, into another, and all taken together forms a single whole, the nature of which we do not understand.

This idea of the unity of everything, in whatever sense and on whatever scale it be taken, occupied a very important place in the conception of the world and of life that was formed in me in these strange states of consciousness. This conception of the world included something entirely opposed to our ordinary view of the world or conception of the world. Ordinarily each thing and each event has for us some value of its own, some significance of its own, some meaning of its own. This separate meaning that each thing, each event, has, is much more comprehensible and familiar to us than its possible general meaning and general significance, even in cases in which we can suppose or think of this general significance. But in this new conception of the world everything was different. Each thing appeared, first of all, not as a separate whole, but as a part of another whole, in most cases incomprehensible and unknown to us. The meaning and significance of the thing were determined by the nature of this great whole and by the place which it occupied in this whole. This completely changed the entire picture of the world. We are accustomed to take everything separately. Here there was nothing separate, and it was extraordinarily strange to feel oneself in a world in which all things were connected one with another and all things followed one from another. Nothing existed separately. I felt that the separate existence of anything — including myself — was a fiction, something non-existent, impossible. The sensation of absence of separateness and the sensation of connectedness and oneness united with the emotional part of my conceptions. At the beginning the combined sensation was felt as something terrifying, oppressive and hopeless; but later, without changing its nature, it began to be felt as the most joyous and radiant sensation that could exist.

Further, there was a picture or mental image which entered into everything and appeared as a necessary part of every logical or illogical construction. This image showed two aspects, both of everything taken together, that is, the whole world, and of every separate part of it, that is, each separate side of the world and of life. One aspect was connected with the First Principle. I saw, as it were, the origin of the whole world or the origin of any given phenomenon or any given idea. The other aspect was connected with separate things: I saw the world, or those events which interested me at the particular moment, in their final manifestation, that is, as we see them around us, but connected into a whole, incomprehensible to us. But between the first aspect and the second aspect there always occurred an interruption like a gap or blank space. Graphically I might represent this approximately in the following way: Imagine that from above three lines appear from one point; each of these three lines is again transformed into three lines; each of these three lines again into three lines. Gradually the lines break more and more and gradually become more and more varied in properties, acquiring colour, form and other qualities, but not reaching real facts, and transforming themselves into a kind of invisible current proceeding from above. From below, imagine the infinite variety of phenomena collected and classified into groups; these groups again unite, and as a result great numbers of very varied phenomena are actually bound into wholes and can be expressed by one sign or one hieroglyph. A series of these hieroglyphs represents life or the visible world at a certain distance from the surface. From above goes the process of differentiation, and from below goes the process of integration. But differentiation and integration do not meet. Between what is above and what is below is formed a blank space in which nothing is visible. The upper differentiating lines, multiplying and acquiring different colours, merge quickly together and disappear into a blank space which separates what is above from what is below. From below all the infinitely varied phenomena are very soon transformed into principles, extraordinarily rich in meaning and in hieroglyphic designation, but nevertheless smaller than the last of the visible upper lines.

It was approximately in this graphic representation that these two aspects of the world and things appeared to me. Or I might say that both above and below the world was represented on different scales, and these scales never met for me, never passed into one another, remained entirely incommensurable. The whole difficulty was precisely in this, and this difficulty was felt all the time. I realised that if I could throw a bridge from what was below to what was above or, still better, in the opposite direction, from what was above to what was below, I should understand everything that was below, because starting from above, the fundamental principles, it would have been easy and simple to understand anything below. But I never succeeded in connecting principles with facts because, though, as I have already said, all the facts very quickly became merged into complicated hieroglyphs, these hieroglyphs still differed very much from the *upper* principles.

Nothing that I am writing, nothing that can be said, about my experiences, will be comprehensible if the continuous emotional tone of these experiences is not taken into consideration. There were no calm, dispassionate, unexciting moments at all; everything was full of emotion, feeling, almost passion.

The strangest thing in all these experiences was the coming back, the return to the ordinary state, to the state which we call life. This was something very similar to dying or to what I thought dying must be.

Usually this coming back occurred when I woke up in the morning after an interesting experiment the night before. The experiments almost always ended in sleep. During this sleep I evidently passed into the usual state and awoke in the ordinary world, in the world in which we awake every morning. But this world contained something extraordinarily oppressive, it was incredibly empty, colourless and lifeless. It was as though everything in it was wooden, as if it was an enormous wooden machine with creaking wooden wheels, wooden thoughts, wooden moods, wooden sensations; everything was terribly slow, scarcely moved, or moved with a melancholy wooden creaking. Everything was dead, soulless, feelingless.

They were terrible, these moments of awakening in an unreal world after a real one, in a dead world after a living, in a limited world, cut into small pieces, after an infinite and entire world.

I did not obtain particularly new facts through my experiments, but I got many thoughts. When I saw that my first aim, i.e. objective magic, remained unattainable, I began to think that the artificial creation of mystical states might become the beginning of a new method in psychology. This aim would have been attained if I had found it possible to change my state of consciousness while at the same time retaining full power of observation. This proved to be impossible to the full extent. The state of consciousness changed, but I could not control the change, could never say *for certain* in what the experiment would result, and even could not always observe; ideas followed upon one another and vanished too quickly. I had to recognise that though my experiments had established many possibilities, they did not give material for exact conclusions. The fundamental questions as to the relation of subjective magic to objective magic and to mysticism remained without decisive answers.

But after my experiments I began to understand many things differently. I began to understand that many philosophical and metaphysical speculations, entirely different in theme, form and terminology, might in actual fact have been attempts to express precisely that which I came to know, and which I have tried to describe. I understood that behind many of the systems of the study of the world and man there might lie experiences and sensations very similar to my own, perhaps identical with them. I understood that for centuries and thousands of years human thought has been circling and circling round something that it has never succeeded in expressing.

In any case my experiments established for me with indisputable clearness the possibility of coming into contact with the *real* world that lies behind the wavering mirage of the visible world. I saw that knowledge of the real world was possible but, as became clearer and clearer to me during my experiments, it required a different approach and a different preparation.

Putting together all that I had read and heard of, I could not but see that many before me had come to the same result, and many, most probably, had gone much further than I. But all of them had always been inevitably confronted with the same difficulty, namely the impossibility of conveying in the language of the dead the impressions of the living world. All of them except those who knew another approach. . . . I came to the conclusion that without the help of those who know another approach it is impossible to do anything.

1912–1929

Chapter IX

IN SEARCH OF THE MIRACULOUS

I

NOTRE DAME DE PARIS

MANY strange thoughts have always been evoked in me by the view from the top of the towers of Notre Dame. How many centuries have passed beneath these towers, how many changes and how few changes!

A small mediæval town surrounded by fields, vineyards and woods. A growing Paris which several times outgrows its walls. The Paris of the last centuries, "which changes its face every fifty years," as Victor Hugo remarked. And the people . . . for ever going somewhere past these towers, for ever hurrying somewhere, and always remaining where they were, seeing nothing, noticing nothing, always the same people. And the towers, always the same, with the same gargoyles looking on at this town, which is for ever changing, for ever disappearing and yet always remaining the same.

Here two lines in the life of humanity are clearly seen. One is the line of the life of these people below; and the other, the line of the life of those who built Notre Dame. And looking down from these towers you feel that the *real* history of humanity, the history worth speaking of, is the history of the people who built Notre Dame and not that of those below. And you understand that these are two quite different histories.

One history passes by in full view and, strictly speaking, is the *history of crime*, for if there were no crimes there would be no history. All the most important turning-points and stages of this history are marked by crimes: murders, acts of violence, robberies, wars, rebellions, massacres, tortures, executions. Fathers murdering children, children murdering fathers, brothers murdering one another, husbands murdering wives, wives murdering husbands, kings massacring subjects, subjects assassinating kings.

This is one history, the history which everybody knows, the history which is taught in schools.

The other history is the history which is known to very few. For the majority it is not seen at all behind the history of crime. But what is created by this hidden history exists long afterwards, sometimes for many centuries, as does Notre Dame. The visible history, the history proceeding on the surface, the history of crime, attributes to itself what the hidden history has created. But actually the visible history is always deceived by what the hidden history has created.

So much has been written about the Cathedral of Notre Dame, and so little is actually known about it. One who has never tried to find out anything about it for himself, or to make something out of the material available, would never believe how little in fact is known about the building of the cathedral. It took many years to build; the dates when it was begun and when it was finished are known; the bishops who, in one way or another, contributed to this construction are also known, and so are the popes and kings of that time. But nothing has remained concerning the *builders* themselves with the exception of names, and even that seldom.[1] And no facts have remained concerning the schools which stood behind all that was created by that strange period which began about the year one thousand and lasted for about four centuries.

It is known that there existed *Schools of Builders*. Of course they had to exist, for every master worked and ordinarily lived with his pupils. In this way painters worked, in this way sculptors worked. In this way, naturally, architects worked. But behind these individual schools stood other institutions of very complex origin. And these were not merely architectural schools or schools of masons. The building of cathedrals was part of a colossal and cleverly devised plan which permitted the existence of entirely free philosophical and psychological schools in the rude, absurd, cruel, superstitious, bigoted and scholastic Middle Ages. These schools have left us an immense heritage, almost all of which we have already wasted without understanding its meaning and value.

These schools, which built the " Gothic " cathedrals, concealed themselves so well that traces of them can now be found only by those *who already know that such schools must have existed*. Certainly the Catholic Church of the 11th and 12th centuries, which already used the torture and the stake for heretics and stifled all free thought, did not build Notre Dame. There is not the slightest doubt that for a time the Church was made an instrument for the preservation and propagation of the ideas of *true Christianity*, that is, of true religion or true knowledge, which were absolutely foreign to it.

And there is nothing improbable in the fact that the whole scheme of the building of cathedrals and of the organisation of schools under cover of this building activity was created because of the growing " heretic-mania "

---

[1] " In the voluminous records of the church of Notre Dame, which go back beyond the 12th century, there is not a single word about the actual work of the construction of the cathedral. According to the chronicles of the period before the Gothic the libraries of monasteries were full of descriptions of the construction of their buildings and of the biographies and praises of their builders. But with the coming of the Gothic period suddenly all became silent. Until the 12th century there is no mention of any of the architects." (From a book by Viollet-le-Duc.)

in the Catholic Church and because the Church was rapidly losing those qualities which had made it a refuge for knowledge.

By the end of the first thousand years of the Christian era the monasteries had gathered all the science, all the knowledge, of that time. But the legalisation of the hunting and prosecution of heretics, and the approach of the Inquisition, made it impossible for knowledge to reside in monasteries.

There was then found or, to speak more accurately, *created*, for this knowledge a new and convenient refuge. Knowledge left the monasteries and passed into Schools of Builders, Schools of Masons. The style later called "Gothic" and at the time known as the "new" or "modern," of which the characteristic feature was the pointed arch, was accepted as the distinctive sign of the schools. The schools within presented a complex organisation and were divided into different degrees; this means that in every "school of masons" where all the sciences necessary for architects were taught there were inner schools in which the true meaning of religious allegories and symbols was explained and in which was studied "esoteric philosophy" or the *science of the relations between God, man and the universe*, that is, the very "magic," for a mere thought of which people were put on the rack and burnt at the stake. The schools lasted up to the Renaissance, when the existence of "secular science" became possible. The new science, carried away by the novelty of free thought and free investigation, very soon forgot its origin and beginning, and forgot also the rôle of the "Gothic" cathedrals in the preservation and successive transmission of knowledge.

But Notre Dame has remained, and to this day guards and shows us the ideas of the schools and the ideas of the true "freemasons."

It is known that Notre Dame, at least in its exterior, is at present nearer to what it was originally than it has been during the past three centuries. After an incalculable number of ignorant pious alterations, after the storm of revolution which destroyed what had survived these alterations, Notre Dame was restored in the second part of the 19th century by a man who had deep understanding of its idea. But what has remained of the really old and what is new it is difficult to say, not for lack of historical data, but because the "new" is often in fact the "old."

Such, for instance, is the tall, slender, pierced spire over the eastern part of the cathedral, from which the twelve Apostles, preceded by the apocalyptic beasts, are descending to the four corners of the world. The old spire was demolished in 1787. What we now see is a structure of the 19th century and is the work of Viollet-le-Duc, the restorer of the cathedral during the Second Empire.

But not even Viollet-le-Duc could create the *view* from the big towers over the city including this spire and the Apostles; he could not create the whole scenic effect which was undoubtedly a part of the builders' design. The spire with the Apostles is an inseparable part of this view. You stand on the top of one of the big towers and look towards the east. The city, the houses, the river, the bridges, the tiny, microscopic people. . . . And not one of these people sees the spire, or sees the Teachers descending upon the earth preceded by the apocalyptic beasts. This is quite natural, because *from there*, from the earth, it is difficult to distinguish them. If you go there, to the embankment of the Seine, to the bridge, the Apostles will appear from there almost as small as the people appear from here, and they will merge into the details of the roof of the cathedral. They can be seen only if one knows of their existence, like so many other things in the world. But who cares to know?

And the gargoyles? They are regarded either simply as an ornament, or as individual creations of different artists at different times. In actual fact, however, they are one of the most important features of the design of the whole building.

This design was very complex. To be more exact, it is not even one design, but several designs completing one another. The builders wished to put all their knowledge, all their ideas, into Notre Dame. You find there mathematics, astronomy; some very strange ideas of biology or " evolution " in the stone bushes, on which human heads grow, on the balustrade of the large platform under the flying buttresses.

The gargoyles and other figures of Notre Dame transmit to us the psychological ideas of its builders, chiefly the idea of the *complexity of the soul*. These figures are the soul of Notre Dame, *its different " I "s*: pensive, melancholy, watching, derisive, malignant, absorbed in themselves, devouring something, looking intensely into a distance invisible to us, as does the strange woman in the headdress of a nun, which can be seen above the capitals of the columns of a small turret high up on the south side of the cathedral.

The gargoyles and all the other figures of Notre Dame possess one very strange property: beside them people cannot be drawn, painted or photographed; beside them people appear dead, expressionless stone images.

It is difficult to explain these " I "s of Notre Dame; they must be felt, and they *can* be felt. But it is necessary to choose the time when Paris becomes quiet. This happens before daybreak, when it is not yet quite light but when it is already possible to distinguish some of these strange beings sleeping above.

I remember such a night; it was before the war. I was making a short stay in Paris on the way to India and was wandering about the town for the last time. It was already growing light, and the air was becoming cold. The moon moved swiftly among the clouds. I walked round the whole cathedral. The huge massive towers stood as though on the alert. But I already understood their secret. And I knew that I was taking with me a firm conviction, which nothing could shake, that *this* exists, that is, that there is another history apart from the *history of crime*, and that there is another thought, which created Notre Dame and its figures. I was going to search for other traces of this thought, and I was sure that I should find them.

Eight years passed before I saw Notre Dame again. These were the years of almost unprecedented commotion and destruction. And it seemed to me that something had changed in Notre Dame, as though it was beginning to have a presentiment of its approaching end. During these years, which have written such brilliant pages into the history of crime, bombs dropped over Notre Dame, shells burst, and it was only by accident that Notre Dame did not share the fate of that wonderful fairy-tale of the twelfth century, Rheims Cathedral, which perished a victim of progress and civilisation.

And when I went up the tower and again saw the descending Apostles I was struck by the vainness and almost complete uselessness of attempts to teach people something they have no desire whatever to know.

And again, as many times before, I could find only one argument against this, namely, that perhaps the aim both of the teaching of the Apostles and of the construction of Notre Dame was not to teach *all* the people, but only to transmit *certain* ideas to a *few* men through the " space of time." Modern science conquers space within the limits of the surface of the small earth. Esoteric science *has conquered time,* and it knows methods of transferring its ideas intact and of establishing communications between schools through hundreds and thousands of years.

1922

II

Egypt and the Pyramids

The first strange sensation of Egypt that I experienced was on the way from Cairo to the pyramids.

On the bridge across the Nile I was filled with a strange and almost frightening sense of expectation. Something was changing around me. In the air, in the colours, in the lines, there was a magic which I did not yet understand.

Arab and European Cairo quickly disappeared, and in its place, in everything that surrounded me, I felt Egypt, which enveloped me.

I felt Egypt in the air blowing softly from the Nile, in the large boats with their triangular sails, in the groups of palms, in the wonderful rose tints of the rocks of Mokattam, in the silhouettes of the camels moving on the road in the distance, in the figures of women in their long black cloaks with bundles of reeds on their heads.

And this Egypt was felt as extraordinarily real, as though I was suddenly transferred into another world, which to my own astonishment I seemed to know very well. At the same time I was aware that this other world was the distant past. But here it ceased to be past, appeared in everything, surrounded me, became the present. This was a very strong sensation and strangely definite.

The sensation surprised me all the more because Egypt had never attracted me particularly; books and Egyptian antiquities in museums made it appear not very interesting and even tedious. But here I suddenly felt something extraordinarily alluring in it and, above all, something close and familiar.

Later, when I analysed my impressions, I was able to find certain explanations for them, but at first they only astonished me, and I arrived at the pyramids strangely agitated by all that I had encountered on the way.

The pyramids appeared in the distance as soon as we crossed the bridge; then they were hidden behind gardens and again appeared before us and grew larger and larger.

When approaching them one sees that the pyramids do not stand on the level of the plain which stretches between them and Cairo, but on a high rocky plateau rising sharply from it.

The plateau is reached by a winding and ascending road which goes through a cutting in the rock. Having walked to the end of this road you find yourself on a level with the pyramids, before the so-called Pyramid of Kheops, on the same side as the entrance into it. To the right in the distance is the second pyramid, and behind it, the third.

Here, having ascended to the pyramids, you are in a different world, not in the world you were in ten minutes ago. There — fields, foliage, palms, were still about you. Here it is a different country, a different landscape, a kingdom of sand and stone. *This is the desert*. The transition is sharp and unexpected.

The sensation which I had experienced on the way came over me with renewed force. The incomprehensible past became the present and felt quite close to me, as if I could stretch out my arm into it, and our present disappeared and became strange, alien and distant.

I walked towards the first pyramid. On a close view you see that it is built of huge blocks of stone, each more than half the height of a man. At about the level of a three-storied house there is a triangular opening — the entrance into the pyramid.

From the very beginning, as soon as I had gone up to the plateau where the pyramids stand, had seen them close and had inhaled the air which surrounds them, I felt that they were alive. And I had no need to analyse my thoughts on this subject. I felt it as real and unquestionable truth. And I understood at the same time why all these little people who were to be seen near the pyramids took them merely as dead stones. It was because all the people were themselves dead. Anyone who is at all alive cannot but feel that the pyramids are alive.

I now understood this and many other things.

The pyramids are just like ourselves, with the same thoughts and feelings, only they are very, very old and know much. And so they stand there and think and turn over their memories. How many thousands of years have passed over them! They alone know.

And they are far older than historical science supposes.

All is quiet around them. Neither tourists, nor guides, nor the British military camp, visible not far off, disturb their calm and that impression of extraordinarily concentrated stillness which surrounds them. People disappear near the pyramids. The pyramids are bigger and occupy more room than we imagine. The Great Pyramid is nearly three quarters of a mile round its base and the second only a little less. People are unnoticeable beside them. And if you go as far as the third pyramid you are swallowed up in the real desert.

The first time I went there I passed a whole day by the pyramids and early the following morning went there again. And during the two or three weeks I spent that time at Cairo I went there almost every day.

I realised that I was attracted and held by sensations which I had never experienced before anywhere. Usually I sat on the sand somewhere between the second and the third pyramids and tried to stop the flow of my thoughts, and at times it seemed to me that I heard the thoughts of the pyramids.

I did not examine anything as people do; I only wandered from place to place and drank in the general impression of the desert and of this strange corner of the earth where the pyramids stand.

Everything here was familiar to me. Sun, wind, sand, stones, together made one whole from which I found it hard to go away. It became quite clear to me that I should not be able to leave Egypt as easily as I had left every other place. There was something here that I had to find, something that I had to understand.

The entrance into the Great Pyramid is on the north side and rather high from the ground. The opening is in the form of a triangle. From it there leads a narrow passage which at once begins to descend at a steep angle. The floor is very slippery; there are no steps, but on the polished stone there are horizontal notches, worn smooth, into which it is possible to put one's feet sideways. Moreover, the floor is covered with fine sand and it is very difficult to keep oneself from sliding the whole way down. The Bedouin guide clambers down in front. In one hand he holds a lighted candle; the other he stretches out to you. You go down this sloping well in a bent attitude. You at once become very hot from the effort and the unaccustomed attitude. The descent seems rather long — at last it ends. You now find yourself in the place where a massive granite block once shut off the entrance, that is to say, approximately on the level of the base of the pyramid. From here it is possible to continue the descent to the " lower chamber," which is at a considerable depth below the level of the rock — and it is also possible to climb up to the so-called " Chambers " of the King and Queen, which are approximately at the centre of the pyramid. In order to do this it is necessary first of all to get round the granite block of which I have spoken.

Some time, long ago — according to one account at the time of the last Pharaohs, and according to others in the times of the Arabs — the conquerors who tried to penetrate to the interior of the pyramid, where there were supposed to be untold treasures, were stopped by this granite block. They

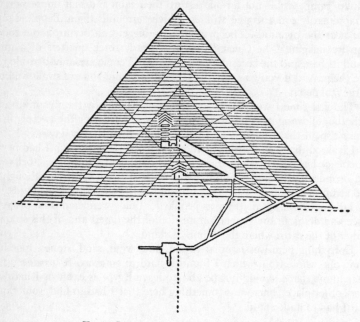

FIG. 7 *Cross-section of the Great Pyramid*

could neither move nor pierce the block, and so they made a passage round it in the softer stone from which the pyramid was built.

The guide holds up his candle. You are now standing in a fairly large cavern and in front of you there is an obstacle which you must overcome in order to go further. This obstacle is something in the nature of a frozen or petrified waterfall by which you have to ascend. Two Arabs scramble up and reach their hands down to you. You climb up and pressing yourself against the " waterfall " make your way sideways along a narrow ledge round the middle part of the frozen, stone cascade. Your feet slip, and there is nothing to hold by. At last you are there. Now it is necessary to ascend a little further, and before you there appears the narrow black entrance of another corridor. It leads upwards. Holding on to the walls, breathing the stifling air with difficulty and drenched with sweat, you slowly make your way forward. The candles of the guides before and behind you feebly light the uneven stone walls. Your back begins to ache from the bent position.

To all this is added a feeling of weight hanging over you, like that felt beneath the earth in the deep galleries of mines and pits.

At last you come out again into a place where you can stand upright. After a short rest you look round and in the feeble light of the candles you make out that you are standing before the entrance to a narrow, straight corridor, along which you can go without bending. This corridor leads straight to the " Chamber of the Queen."

To your right, if you stand facing the entrance to the corridor, you see the irregular black opening of a well, also made by treasure-seekers and communicating with the lower subterranean chamber.

At the level of your head, over the entrance to the corridor leading to the " Chamber of the Queen," another corridor begins, leading to the " Chamber of the King." But this second corridor is not parallel with the first, but forms an angle with it; that is, it goes upwards like a steep staircase which begins a little above the ground.

In the construction of this upper corridor-staircase there is much that is difficult to understand and that at once strikes the eye. In examining it I very soon understood that this corridor is the key to the whole pyramid.

From the place where I stood, it could be seen that the upper corridor was very high, and along its sides, like the banisters of a staircase, were broad stone parapets, descending to the ground, that is, to the level where I stood. The floor of the corridor did not reach down to the ground, being cut short, as I have already mentioned, at about a man's height from the floor. In order to get into the upper corridor from where I stood, one had to go up first by one of the side-parapets and then drop down to the " staircase " itself. I call this corridor a " staircase " only because it ascends steeply. It has no steps, only worn-down notches for the feet.

Feeling that the floor behind you falls away, you begin to climb, holding on to one of the " parapets."

What strikes you first is that everything in this corridor is of very exact and fine workmanship. The lines are straight, the angles are correct. At the same time there is no doubt that this corridor was not made for walking along. Then for what was it made?

The answer to this is given by the " parapets." When you turn your attention to them, you see on them mathematically correct notched divisions at strictly equal distances from one another. These divisions are so precise that they immediately attract your attention. There is some idea, some intention, in them. And suddenly it becomes clear to you that up and down this " corridor " some kind of stone or metal plate, or " carriage," must have moved, which possibly, in its turn, served as a support for some measuring apparatus and could be fixed in any position. The divisions on the parapet show clearly that they were used for some kind of measurement, for finding certain angles.

No doubt remained in my mind that this corridor with its parapets was the most important place in the whole pyramid. It cannot be explained without the supposition of a " carriage " moving up and down the incline. And this, in its turn, alters the whole conception of the pyramid and opens up entirely new possibilities.

At a definite time of the year the rays of certain stars can penetrate into the pyramid through the opening by which we entered it (until these stars become displaced in the progress of the great astronomical cycle). If we suppose that somewhere on the path of the rays mirrors are fixed, the rays penetrating through the opening of the pyramid will be thrown into the corridor on the apparatus fixed on the movable carriage. There is no doubt that some kind of observations were carried out here, some kind of cycles were recorded, some data were established.

The granite block, round which goes what I called the *stone waterfall*, bars the way to these rays. But the meaning, the purpose and the *epoch* of this block are completely unknown.

It is very difficult to define in our language the object and purpose of the pyramid. The pyramid was an observatory, but not only an " observatory " in the modern meaning of the word, for it was also a " scientific instrument "; and not only an instrument or a collection of instruments, but also a " scientific treatise," or rather a whole library on physics, mathematics and astronomy; or, to be still more exact, it was a " physico-mathematical faculty " and at the same time a " depository of measures," which is quite clearly shown by the measurements of the pyramid, the numerical interrelation of its height, base, sides, angles, and so on.

I had a very concrete feeling of the idea of the pyramid later, when I visited the famous observatory of Jay Singh at Jaipur, in Rajputana. The " observatory " is a huge square surrounded by walls, with strange *buildings*: stone triangles, the height of a large house; huge circles with divisions; empty cisterns resembling ponds with bridges across them and with polished brass bottoms for reflecting the stars; mysterious stone mazes which serve to find a definite constellation. All these are gigantic physical and astronomical apparatus, gnomons, quadrants, sextants and others, that is, instruments that are now made of brass and kept in cases. If one imagines all these apparatus, and many others unknown to us, *combined into one* and supposes that their very measurements and the interrelation of their parts express the fundamental relations between the measurements of the different parts of, say, the solar system, the result will be the idea of the pyramid.

But I will continue the description of the pyramid as I saw it.

At the top the inclined corridor with parapets becomes horizontal and then leads into the " Chamber of the King." Candles are not sufficient to light the high smooth stone walls. It is rather stifling. By one wall there is something resembling a sarcophagus with high chipped sides.

I sent the guides away into the corridor and for some minutes remained alone.

I had a very strange feeling in this stone cell enclosed in the mass of the pyramid. The pulsation of life which filled the pyramid and emanated from it was felt here more strongly than anywhere. But besides this it appeared to me that this " Chamber " was telling me something about itself. I felt myself surrounded by different voices. But their words seemed to sound from behind a wall. I could hear but could not understand them. It seemed to me that it was necessary to make only quite a small effort and I should then hear everything. But I did not succeed in making this effort and probably it was not a question of effort at all, something much more important separated me from these voices.

" The Chamber of the Queen " differs little from the " Chamber of the King," but for some reason does not give the same sensations. The lower subterranean chamber, which is more difficult to reach and is very stifling, is a little larger than the " King's Chamber " and is also full of thoughts and inaudible voices which are trying to impress something on you.

From the top of the pyramid my attention was attracted by the Dahshur Pyramid with irregular sides which is seen in the distance through field-glasses, the strange Step Pyramid situated nearer, and not far from it a large white pyramid.

A few days after, I rode out from Gizeh to these distant pyramids. I did not want to see anything in particular, but wished to form a general impression of this part of the desert.

Having passed the Pyramid of Kheops and the Sphinx I found myself on a broad road leading to Aboussir. As a matter of fact there was no road, but a broad track covered with traces of horses, donkeys and camels. On the left, towards the Nile, lay ploughed fields. To the right there stretched a rocky cliff, beyond which the desert began.

From the very beginning of the road from Gizeh I began to experience this strange sensation of past as present which for some reason was produced in me by the Egyptian landscape. But this time I felt a desire to understand this sensation better, and I looked with particular intentness at everything round me, trying to decipher the secret of this magic of Egypt. And I came to think that the secret might lie in the astonishing changelessness of the Egyptian landscape and its colours. In other countries nature changes its face several times a year. Even where for centuries the main features have been preserved, as in forests and steppes, the outer cover of nature, the grass, the leaves, is all new, just born. But here this sand and these stones are the same as those which had seen the people who built the pyramids, the Pharaohs and the Caliphs.

And it seemed to me that in these stones which had seen so much, something of what they had seen was preserved, and that because of this a certain link was established through them with the life which existed in these places before and seemed still to be invisibly present here.

My grey Arab pony galloped quickly along by the uneven stone wall which lay on the right of the road, now nearer and now further off. And I was more and more immersed in a strange feeling of liberation from everything by which we ordinarily live.

The whole present receded, appeared transparent like mist, and through it the past became more and more visible all around me, not taking any definite form but penetrating me by a thousand different sensations and emotions.

Nowhere had I ever felt before so clearly and definitely the unreality of the present. I felt here that all that we consider as actually existing is nothing but a mirage which passes over the face of the earth, perhaps the shadow or the reflection of some other life, or perhaps only dreams created in our imagination as a result of some obscure impacts and vague sounds which reach our consciousness from the Unknown which surrounds us.

I felt that everything vanished — St. Petersburg, London, Cairo, hotels, railways, steamers, people; everything became a mirage. But the desert round me existed, and I existed, though in a very strange way, without any connection with the present, but conscious of a very strong connection with the unknown past.

And in everything I felt there was a not easily comprehensible but very subtle joy. I would describe it as the joy of liberation from oneself and the joy of feeling the incredible richness of life, which never dies but exists in an infinite variety of forms invisible and intangible for us.

Having passed Sakkara with the Step Pyramid and the white pyramid I went further to the Dahshur Pyramids. Here there was no road at all. The sand changed to small flints which formed what looked like enormous waves. When I came to level places and my pony began to gallop it seemed to me several times that I was dropping money, for the flints flew up from the hoofs and tinkled like silver.

Even the first of the Dahshur Pyramids produces an extraordinary and peculiar impression, as though it were sunk in its own thoughts but would presently notice you and would speak to you definitely and clearly. I rode slowly round it. There was not a soul near it, and nothing was visible but the sand and the pyramid with irregular sides in the distance.

I rode up to it. It is the strangest pyramid of all. I was only sorry that I could not be transported to this pyramid straight from Cairo, without seeing and feeling anything else. I was already too much saturated with impressions and could not fully appreciate what I felt here. But I felt that the stones here were animate and entrusted with a definite task. The south Dahshur Pyramid with the irregular lines of its sides struck me by its very definiteness, which was almost frightening.

At the same time I did not wish to formulate, even to myself, all that I felt. It was too much like imagination.

But my thoughts went on without obeying me and at times it appeared to me that I was really beginning to imagine things. But the sensation was quite different from that produced by imagination. There was something inexpressibly real in it. I turned my pony round and slowly rode back. Some

distance off something seemed suddenly to push me. I quickly turned in the
saddle. The pyramid was looking at me as though expecting something.

"Till next time!" I said.

I could not fully analyse all the feelings that I had at that moment.
But I felt that precisely here, if only I could remain here alone sufficiently
long, my thoughts and sensations would reach such a degree of tension that
I should really see and hear what is ordinarily invisible and inaudible. How
far this was really connected with this strange pyramid or how far it was the
result of the whole day and the whole week of unusual sensations, I could
not say. But I felt that here my sensations of Egypt reached their highest
intensity.

At the present time views on the pyramids can be divided into two categories. To the first category belongs the theory of tombs, and to the second,
astronomical and mathematical theories.

Historical science, that is, Egyptology, keeps almost exclusively to the
theory of tombs, with very small and feeble admissions in the direction of
the possibility of the *utilisation* of pyramids for astronomical observations.
Thus Professor Petrie in his book A *History of Egypt* speaks of three deep
trenches which were cut in the rock and were about 160 feet long, 20 feet
deep, and not over five or six feet wide. "The purpose of such trenches is
quite unknown; but there may have been some system of observing azimuths
of stars by a surface of water at the bottom, and a cord stretched from end
to end at the top; by noting the moment of the transit of the reflections of
the star past the cord, an accurate observation of azimuth might be made"
(p. 41).

But speaking generally, historical science is not interested in the astronomical and mathematical meaning of the pyramids.

If Egyptologists ever touch upon this side of the question, it is acting
only as amateurs and in this case no great importance is attached to their
opinions. R. A. Proctor's book, which I mention later, is an example of this.

The description of the construction of the pyramids (chiefly of the
Great Pyramid) to be found in Herodotus is accepted as final and decisive.

Herodotus relates what he was told about the construction of the Great
Pyramid two or three thousand years before his time. He says that on the
granite blocks covering the pyramid hieroglyphic inscriptions were cut
referring to various facts connected with its construction. Among other
things there was recorded the amount of garlic, onions and radishes that
was eaten by the slaves who built the pyramid, and from the amount of
garlic, etc., it was possible to draw conclusions as to the number of slaves
and the duration of the work.

Herodotus says that before the Great Pyramid was built, a causeway had
to be made through the desert on an embankment for the transport of the
material. He himself saw this causeway, which, according to his words, was
a construction not less great than the pyramid itself.

The approximate date of the construction given by Herodotus is, owing to the profusion of small details pointed out by him, regarded in Egyptology as indisputable.

In reality all that Herodotus says is not in the least convincing. It must be remembered that Herodotus himself could not read hieroglyphs. This knowledge was carefully guarded and was the privilege of the priests. Herodotus could record only what was translated to him, and that certainly would have been only what confirmed and established the official version of the construction of the pyramids. This official version accepted in Egyptology may actually be far removed from truth. And the truth may be that what is regarded as the construction of the Great Pyramid was in reality its restoration. The pyramids may be much older than we think.

The Sphinx, which may have been constructed at the same time as the pyramids, or still earlier, is quite rightly considered prehistoric. What does this mean? It means that some thousands of years before our era, possibly many thousands of years, the people or peoples who are known to us under the name of " ancient Egyptians " occupied the valley of the Nile and found, half buried in the sands, the pyramids and the Sphinx, the meaning and significance of which were quite incomprehensible to them. The Sphinx looked towards the East, so it was called the image of Harmakuti or the " Sun on the Horizon." Very much later the king to whom is ascribed the name of Kheops (Egyptologists have, of course, quite a different name for him) restored one of the pyramids and made of it a mausoleum or sepulchre for himself. Moreover, the inscriptions cut into the facing of this pyramid described the doings of the king in a laudatory and exaggerated tone, and the *restoration* was of course called *construction*. These inscriptions misled Herodotus, who took them for exact historical data.

The restoration of the pyramids was not their construction. The brother of Kheops, Khephren (the spelling and pronunciation of these names are very uncertain and unreliable), restored another pyramid. Gradually this became a custom, and so it happened that some of the Pharaohs built for themselves new pyramids, usually of smaller dimensions, and some restored the old, which were of larger dimensions. It is also possible that the first to be restored were the Dahshur Pyramids and the Step Pyramid at Sakkara. Gradually all the pyramids were converted into sepulchres, for a sepulchre was the most important thing in the life of the Egyptians of that period. But it was only an accidental episode in the history of the pyramids, which in no way explains their origin.

At the present time many interesting facts have been established concerning the Great Pyramid. But these discoveries belong either to astronomers or to mathematicians. And if it happens that any Egyptologists speak of them, there are only very few who do so, and their opinions are usually suppressed by others.

In a way the reason for this is understandable, for too much charlatanism has accumulated round the study of the astronomical and mathematical significance of the pyramids. Theories, for instance, exist and books are published proving that the measurements of the various parts of corridors and walls inside the Great Pyramid represent the whole history of mankind from Adam to " the end of general history." According to the author of one such book prophecies contained in the pyramid refer chiefly to England and even give the length of the duration of post-war cabinets.

The existence of such " theories " of course makes it clear why science is afraid of new discoveries concerning the pyramids. But this in no way diminishes the value of existing attempts to establish the astronomical and mathematical meaning of the pyramids, in most cases so far only *the Great Pyramid*.

R. A. Proctor in his book *The Great Pyramid* (London, 1883) regards the pyramid as a kind of telescope or transit apparatus. He draws special attention to the slots on the parapets of the grand gallery and finds that they were made for moving up and down the incline instruments used for carrying out observations. Further he points to the possible existence of a water-mirror at the junction of the ascending and descending passages and asserts that the pyramid was a *clock* for Egyptian priests and chiefly an astronomical clock.

L'Abbé Moreux has collected in his book *Les Enigmes de la Science* almost all the existing material relating to the Great Pyramid as a " depository of measures " or as a mathematical compendium. The sum of the sides of the base of the pyramid divided by its height doubled gives the relation of circumference to diameter, the number π, which plays such an important rôle in the history of mathematics. The height of the pyramid is *one thousand millionth* part of the distance of the earth from the sun (which, by the way, was established in science with sufficient accuracy only in the second half of the 19th century), etc., etc.

All this and many other things show the astounding narrowness of modern scientific views and the absence of even ordinary curiosity in the Egyptologists who come to a standstill at the theory of tombs and the story of Herodotus, and do not wish to know anything more. In reality the pyramids contain a great enigma. The pyramids, more than anything else in the world, tell us that we are quite wrong in considering that our ancestor was a " hairy, tailed quadruped, probably arboreal in its habits, and an inhabitant of the Old World." In actual fact our genealogy is much more interesting. Our ancestors were very rich and eminent people, and they left us an enormous inheritance, which we have completely forgotten, especially since the time when we began to consider ourselves the descendants of a monkey.

                                                            1914–1925

III

THE SPHINX

Yellowish-grey sand. Deep blue sky. In the distance the triangle of the Pyramid of Khephren, and just before me this strange, great face with its gaze directed into the distance.

I used often to go to Gizeh from Cairo, sit down on the sand before the Sphinx, look at it and try to understand it, understand the idea of the artists who created it. And on each and every occasion I experienced the same fear and terror of annihilation. I was swallowed up in its glance, a glance that spoke of mysteries beyond our power of comprehension.

The Sphinx lies on the Gizeh plateau, where the great pyramids stand, and where there are many other monuments, already discovered and still to be discovered, and a number of tombs of different epochs. The Sphinx lies in a hollow, above the level of which only its head, neck and part of its back project.

By whom, when, and why the Sphinx was erected — of this nothing is known. Present-day archæology takes the Sphinx to be prehistoric.

This means that even for the most ancient of the ancient Egyptians, those of the first dynasties six to seven thousand years before the birth of Christ, the Sphinx was the same riddle as it is for us to-day.

From the stone tablet, inscribed with drawings and hieroglyphs, found between the paws of the Sphinx, it was once surmised that the figure represented the image of the Egyptian god Harmakuti, "The Sun on the Horizon." But it has long been agreed that this is an altogether unsatisfactory interpretation and that the inscription probably refers to the occasion of some partial restoration made comparatively recently.

As a matter of fact the Sphinx is older than historical Egypt, older than her gods, older than the pyramids, which, in their turn, are much older than is thought.

The Sphinx is indisputably one of the most remarkable, if not the most remarkable, of the world's works of art. I know nothing that it would be possible to put side by side with it. It belongs indeed to quite another art than the art we know. Beings such as ourselves could not create a Sphinx. Nor can our culture create anything like it. The Sphinx appears unmistakably to be a relic of another, a very ancient culture, which was possessed of knowledge far greater than ours.

There is a tradition or theory that the Sphinx is a great, complex hieroglyph, or a book in stone, which contains the whole totality of ancient knowledge, and reveals itself to the man who can read this strange cipher which is embodied in the forms, correlations and measurements of the different parts of the Sphinx. This is the famous riddle of the Sphinx, which from the most ancient times so many wise men have attempted to solve.

Previously, when reading about the Sphinx, it had seemed to me that it would be necessary to approach it with the full equipment of a knowledge different from ours, with some new form of perception, some special kind of mathematics, and that without these aids it would be impossible to discover anything in it.

But when I saw the Sphinx for myself, I felt something in it that I had never read and never heard of, something that at once placed it for me among the most enigmatic and at the same time fundamental problems of life and the world.

The face of the Sphinx strikes one with wonder at the first glance. To begin with, it is quite a *modern* face. With the exception of the head-ornament there is nothing of "ancient history" about it. For some reason I had feared that there would be. I had thought that the Sphinx would have a very "alien" face. But this is not the case. Its face is simple and understandable. It is only the way that it looks that is strange. The face is a good deal disfigured. But if you move away a little and look for a long time at the Sphinx, it is as if a kind of veil falls from its face, the triangles of the head-ornament behind the ears become invisible, and before you there emerges clearly a complete and undamaged face with eyes which look over and beyond you into the unknown distance.

I remember sitting on the sand in front of the Sphinx — on the spot from which the second pyramid in the distance makes an exact triangle behind the Sphinx — and trying to understand, to read its glance. At first I saw only that the Sphinx looked beyond me into the distance. But soon I began to have a kind of vague, then a growing, uneasiness. Another moment, and I felt that the Sphinx was not seeing me, and not only was it not seeing, it could not see me; and not because I was too small in comparison with it or too insignificant in comparison with the profundity of wisdom it contained and guarded. Not at all. That would have been natural and comprehensible. The sense of annihilation and the terror of vanishing came from feeling myself in some way too transient for the Sphinx to be able to notice me. I felt that not only did these fleeting moments or hours which I could pass before it not exist for it, but that if I could stay under its gaze from birth to death, the whole of my life would flash by so swiftly for it that it could not notice me. Its glance was fixed on something else. It was the glance of a being who thinks in centuries and millenniums. I did not eixst and could not exist for it. And I could not answer my own question — do I exist for myself? Do I, indeed, exist in any sort of sense, in any sort of relation? And in this thought, in this feeling, under this strange glance, there was an icy coldness. We are so accustomed to feel that we are, that we exist. Yet all at once, here, I felt that I did not exist, that there was no I, that I could not be so much as perceived.

And the Sphinx before me looked into the distance, beyond me, and its face seemed to reflect something that it saw, something which I could neither see nor understand.

Eternity! This word flashed into my consciousness and went through me with a sort of cold shudder. All ideas about time, about things, about life, were becoming confused. I felt that in these moments, in which I stood before the Sphinx, it lived through all the events and happenings of thousands of years — and that on the other hand centuries passed for it like moments. How this could be I did not understand. But I felt that my consciousness grasped the shadow of the exalted fantasy or clairvoyance of the artists who had created the Sphinx. I touched the mystery but could neither define nor formulate it.

And only later, when all these impressions began to unite with those which I had formerly known and felt, the fringe of the curtain seemed to move, and I felt that I was beginning, slowly, slowly, to understand.

The problem of Eternity, of which the face of the Sphinx speaks, takes us into the realm of the Impossible. Even the problem of Time is simple in comparison with the problem of Eternity.

Hints towards the solution of the problem of Eternity can be found in the various symbols and allegories of ancient religions and in some of the modern as well as the ancient philosophies.

The circle is the image of Eternity. A line going into space and returning to its starting-point. In symbolism it is the snake biting its own tail. But where is the beginning in a closed circle? Our thought, caught in a circle, also cannot escape from it.

A heroic effort of imagination, a complete break with everything logically comprehensible, natural and possible, is necessary in order to divine the secret of this circle, and to find the point where the end unites with the beginning, where the head of the snake bites its own tail.

The idea of eternal recurrence, which for us is connected with the name of Pythagoras and in modern times with that of Nietzsche, is precisely such a sweep of the sword over the knot of the Gordian car.

Only in the idea of return, of endless repetition, can we understand and imagine Eternity. But it must be remembered that in this case we shall have no knot before us, but only its severed parts. And having understood the nature of the knot in this divided aspect, we shall afterwards have to unite these fragments again in thought and create from them a whole.

1908–1914

IV

The Buddha with the Sapphire Eyes

Green Ceylon. A lace-work of coco-nut palms along the sandy shores of the ocean. Fishermen's hamlets amidst the green. Lagoons, lakes, paddy-fields. Panoramas of valley and mountain landscapes. The sharp-pointed Adam's Peak. Ruins of ancient cities. Gigantic statues of Buddha under green branches of trees from which monkeys stare down at you. White Buddhist temples amongst flowers and foliage. Monks in yellow robes. Cingalese with tortoise-shell combs in their hair, wearing close-fitting white skirts, reaching to the ground. Laughing black-eyed girls in light carts drawn by quick-trotting bullocks. Huge trees, thickly covered with scarlet blossoms. The broad leaves of banana trees. Again palms. Rose-red earth — and sun, sun, sun.

I stayed at a hotel outside Colombo, on the sea-shore, and from there I made a number of excursions — going south to Galle, to the Buddhist monasteries, north to the toy town of Kandy, where stands the holy Temple of the Tooth, its white stones covered with green moss — and further, to the ruins of Anaradhapura, a city which long before the birth of Christ had a population of two millions, and was destroyed during the invasion of the Tamils at the beginning of our era. It has long been overrun and swallowed up by the green jungle through which now for nearly fifteen miles stretch streets and squares overgrown with grass and bushes, foundations and the half-demolished walls of houses, temples, monasteries, palaces, reservoirs and tanks, fragments of broken statues, gigantic dagobas, bell-shaped brick buildings and so on.

On returning to my hotel after one of these excursions, I stayed indoors for a few days, trying to write down my impressions, above all my conversations with the Buddhist monks who had been explaining the teaching of Buddha. These conversations had left me with a strange feeling of dissatisfaction. I could not give up the thought that in Buddhism many things existed on which we were not able to come to any understanding and which I should define by the words " miraculous " or " magical " — that is to say, precisely what Buddhists denied in Buddhism.

Buddhism appeared to me in two aspects simultaneously. On the one hand I saw it as a religion full of light, full of softness and warmth, of all religions the furthest removed from what may be called " paganism," a religion which even in its extreme church-forms never blessed the sword, never employed compulsion in any form whatever; a religion which one might embrace while remaining in one's former religion. All this on the one hand. On the other hand a strange philosophy which tries to deny that which constitutes the essence and principal content of every religion — the idea of the miraculous.

The bright side of Buddhism I felt immediately on entering any Buddhist temple, especially in the southern part of Ceylon. Buddhist temples are little green nooks resembling the hermitages in Russian monasteries. A white stone enclosure and within it a few small, white buildings and a little belfry. Everything is always very clean and there is much verdure, many shadows, sun-flecks and flowers. A traditional dagoba, a broad bell-shaped building with a surmounting spire, standing over buried treasure or relics. Beneath the trees a semi-circle of carved stone altars, and on them flowers brought by pilgrims, and in the evening the lights of oil-lamps; and the inevitable sacred Bo-tree, which in appearance resembles the elm. And pervading all a sense of quietude and serenity that carries you away from the clamour and contradictions of life.

But as soon as you seek to come nearer to Buddhism, you immediately encounter a whole series of formal obstacles and evasions. " Concerning this we must not speak; about this Buddha has forbidden us even to think; this we have not at all, never have had and never can have." Buddhism teaches only how one can liberate oneself from suffering. And liberation from suffering is possible only by overcoming in oneself the desire for life, the desire for pleasure, all desires in general. In this is the beginning and the end of Buddhism, there is no mysticism, no hidden knowledge, no ideas about the miraculous, no future except the possibility of liberation from suffering — and annihilation.

But as I heard all this, I was inwardly convinced that it was not so, and that in Buddhism there were many things to which perhaps I could not give a name, but which were definitely connected with the very name of Buddha, i.e. " The Enlightened One "; and that precisely the idea of " illumination " or " enlightenment," and assuredly not the arid and materialistic theories of liberation from suffering, constituted the principal essence of Buddhism.

This contradiction, which I felt so strongly, would not allow me to write; it prevented me from formulating my impressions even to myself; it made me dispute mentally with the Buddhists with whom I had talked; it made me contradict them, argue with them, wish to compel them to recognise and talk of something of which they did not wish to speak.

Consequently my work went badly. For several days I tried to write in the morning, but seeing that nothing came of it, I used to go for a stroll along the sea-shore, or take a train to the town.

Once, on a Sunday morning, when our usually half-empty and sleepy hotel was filled with people from the town, I went out early. This time I did not go by the sea but along the road which led from the shore inland, through green meadows, past clumps of trees and now and again one or two huts.

The path along which I went led out on to the main road running south from Colombo. I remembered that somewhere about here must be a Buddhist temple to which I had not yet been, and I asked an old Cingalese, who was selling green coco-nuts in a little stall by the side of the road, where the temple was. Some other people came along and by their united efforts they somehow managed to understand what I wanted, and told me that the temple was on this road towards Colombo and that a small path on the right would lead to it.

After going some distance I found at last among the trees the path of which they had told me and which led to the temple. Soon I caught sight of the enclosure and gates. I was met by the gate-keeper, a very talkative Cingalese with a thick beard and the inevitable comb in his hair. First he took me into the new shrine, where some modern and quite uninteresting statues of Buddha and his disciples stood in a row. Then we looked at the vihare, where the monks live and where there is a school for children and a hall for preaching; then the dagoba, on the spire of which is set a large moonstone which is shown to tourists and, so far as I could understand, was considered the most remarkable object in the whole temple; then a huge spreading and apparently very ancient Bo-tree, which by its age showed the antiquity of the temple. Under this tree there was deep shade, into which obviously the sun never penetrated, for the stone altars which stood in it were covered with fine green moss.

There were some extraordinarily picturesque spots among the buildings and trees; and I remembered that I had seen photographs of them before.

Finally we went to look at the old shrine. It was undoubtedly a very ancient building, long, one-storied, columned, with a verandah. As is always the case with these shrines, the walls inside were covered with bright painting representing various episodes from the life of Prince Gautama and from other incarnations of Buddha. In the second room, the guide told me, was a very ancient statue of Buddha *with sapphire eyes*. Statues of Buddha are either standing, sitting or reclining. This was a reclining Buddha. When we entered the second room of the shrine it was quite dark, as the light from the door through which we came could not reach it. I struck a match and saw behind a latticed glass frame running the whole length of the wall a huge statue lying on its side with one hand under its head, and the strange gaze of eyes which were not looking at me and yet appeared to see me.

The gate-keeper opened another door and in the faint light that penetrated to where I was standing the face of the Buddha appeared before me. It was a face about a yard in length, painted yellow, with strongly marked dark lines round the nostrils, mouth and eyebrows — and with great blue eyes.

" Those eyes are real sapphires," my guide told me. " Nobody knows when this statue was made; but it is certainly more than a thousand years old."

" Will not the frame open? " I asked the guide.

" It does not open," he replied. " It has not been opened for over sixty years."

He went on talking, but I was not listening. The gaze of those great blue eyes attracted me.

A second or two passed and I understood that I was in the presence of a miracle.

The guide quietly went out behind me and sat on the steps of the verandah, and I was left alone with the Buddha.

The face of the Buddha was quite alive; he was not looking straight at me, and yet he saw me. At first I felt nothing but wonder. I had not expected and could not have expected anything like it. But very soon wonder and all other feelings and thoughts disappeared in new and strange sensations. The Buddha *saw* me, saw in me that which I could not see myself, all that was hidden in the most secret recesses of my soul. And under his gaze, which, as it were, passed me by, I began to see all this myself. Everything that was small, superfluous, uneasy and troubled came to the surface and displayed itself under this glance. The face of the Buddha was quite calm, but not expressionless, and full of deep thought and feeling. He was lying here deep in thought, and I had come, opened the doors and stood before him, and now he was involuntarily judging me. But there was no blame or reproach in his glance. His look was extraordinarily serious, calm and full of understanding. But when I attempted to ask myself what the face of the Buddha expressed, I realised that there could be no answer. His face was neither cold nor indifferent. On the other hand it would be quite wrong to say that it expressed warmth, sympathy or compassion. All this would be too small to ascribe to him. At the same time it would also be wrong to say that the face of the Buddha expressed unearthly grandeur or divine wisdom. No, it was a human face, yet at the same time a face which men do not happen to have. I felt that all the words I could command would be wrong if applied to the expression of this face. I can only say that here was *understanding*.

Simultaneously I began to feel the strange effect which the Buddha's face produced on me. All the gloom that rose from the depths of my soul seemed to clear up. It was as if the Buddha's face communicated its calm to me. Everything that up to now had troubled me and appeared so serious and important, now became so small, insignificant and unworthy of notice, that I only wondered how it could ever have affected me. And I felt that no matter how agitated, troubled, irritated and torn with contradictory thoughts and feelings a man might be when he came here, he would go away calm, quiet, enlightened, *understanding*.

I remembered my work, remembered the conversations with the Buddhists, remembered how I had failed to make clear to myself certain things relating to Buddhism. And I nearly laughed: so utterly useless had it all been. All Buddhism was in this face, in this gaze. And suddenly I seemed to understand certain things Buddha had forbidden men to speak of, things above human reason and above human words. Was it not right? Here I saw this face and felt it, and yet I was not able to say what it expressed. If nevertheless I tried to put it into words that would be even worse, because it would be a lie. In this perhaps lay the explanation of Buddha's prohibition. And Buddha had said also that he had imparted the whole of the teaching, and that no secret doctrine existed. Might this not mean that the secret was hidden not in secret words, but in words known to all, but not understood by men? Was it not possible that this Buddha was the solution of the mystery, the key to it? The whole statue was here before me, there was nothing secret or hidden in it; but even so, could I say that I saw it? And would others see it and understand it even to the extent that I did? Why was it unknown? It must be that people fail to notice it, just as they fail to see the truth hidden in Buddha's words about liberation from suffering.

I looked at those deep blue eyes and felt that though my thoughts were near the truth they were not yet the truth, because the truth is richer and more varied than anything that can possibly be expressed in thoughts or words. At the same time I felt that this face really contained the whole of Buddhism. No books are necessary, no philosophical discourse — in Buddha's glance is everything. One need only come here and be moved by this glance.

I went out of the shrine with the intention of returning on the following day and trying to photograph the Buddha. But for this purpose it would be necessary to open the frame. The gate-keeper to whom I spoke about the frame told me again that it could not be opened. However, I left with the hope of managing it somehow on the following day.

On the way back to the hotel I wondered how it could have happened that this Buddha was so little known. I was quite sure that it was not mentioned in any of the books on Ceylon which I had. And so it proved. In Cave's large *Book of Ceylon* there was actually a picture of this temple — the inner court with the little stone stairway leading to the belfry and the old shrine in which the Buddha is, and even with the same gate-keeper who took me round. But not one word about the statue. And this seemed all the more strange, because, apart from the mystical significance of this Buddha and its value as a work of art, it was certainly one of the largest Buddhas I had seen in Ceylon, and, moreover, had sapphire eyes. How it had been overlooked or forgotten I could not imagine. The cause is of course to be found in the intensely " barbarian " character of the Western crowd which penetrates into the East, and in its deep contempt for all that does not serve the immediate purposes of profit or entertainment. At some time or other the Buddha was probably seen and described by somebody, but afterwards it was forgotten. The Cingalese certainly know of the Buddha with the Sapphire Eyes, but for them it just *exists*, in the same way that the sea or the mountains exist.

Next day I went again to the temple.

I went fearing that on this occasion I should neither see nor feel what I had experienced the day before, that the Buddha with the Sapphire Eyes would suddenly prove to be just an ordinary stone statue with a painted face. But my fears were not confirmed. The Buddha's gaze was exactly the same, penetrating my soul, illuminating everything in it and, as it were, putting everything in order.

A day or two later I was in the temple again, and the gate-keeper now met me as an old acquaintance. And again the face of the Buddha communicated something to me that I could neither understand nor express. I intended to try and find out something about the history of the Buddha with the Sapphire Eyes. But it happened that almost immediately I had to leave for India. Then the war began, and the face of the Buddha remained far from me across the gulf of men's madness.

One thing is certain. This Buddha is quite an exceptional work of art. I do not know of any work in Christian art which stands on the same level as the Buddha with the Sapphire Eyes, that is to say, I know of no work which expresses in itself so completely the idea of Christianity as the face of this Buddha expresses the idea of Buddhism. To understand this face is to understand Buddhism.

And there is no need to read large volumes on Buddhism, or to talk with professors who study Eastern religions or with learned *bhikshus*. One must come here, stand before the Buddha and let the gaze of those blue eyes penetrate one's soul, and one will understand what Buddhism is.

Often when I think of the Buddha I remember another face, the face of the Sphinx and the gaze of those eyes which do not see you. These are two quite different faces. Yet they have something in common, both of them speak of another life, of another consciousness, which is higher than man's consciousness. Therefore we have no words to describe them. When, by whom, or for what purpose these faces were created we do not know, but they speak to us of a real existence, of another life, and of the existence of men who know something of that life and can transmit it to us by the magic of art.

1914

V

THE SOUL OF THE EMPRESS MUMTAZ-I-MAHAL

It was my last summer in India. The rains were already beginning when I left Bombay for Agra and Delhi. For several weeks before that I had been collecting and reading everything I could find about Agra, about the palace of the Great Moguls and about the Taj Mahal, the famous mausoleum of the Empress who died at the beginning of the 17th century.

But everything that I had read, either then or before, left me with a kind of indefinite feeling as though all who had attempted to describe Agra and the Taj Mahal had missed what was most important.

Neither the romantic history of the Taj Mahal, nor the architectural beauty, the luxuriance and opulence of the decoration and ornaments, could explain for me the impression of fairy-tale unreality, of something beautiful, but infinitely remote from life, the impression which was felt behind all the descriptions, but which nobody has been able to put into words or explain.

And it seemed to me that here there was a mystery. The Taj Mahal had a secret which was felt by everybody but to which nobody could give a name.

Photographs told me nothing at all. A large and massive building, and four tapering minarets, one at each corner. In all this I saw no particular beauty, but rather something incomplete. And the four minarets, standing separate, like four candles at the corners of a table, looked strange and almost unpleasant.

In what then lies the strength of the impression made by the Taj Mahal? Whence comes the irresistible effect which it produces on all who see it? Neither the marble lace-work of the trellises, nor the delicate carving which covers its walls, neither the mosaic flowers, nor the fate of the beautiful Empress, none of these by itself could produce such an impression. It must lie in something else. But in what? I tried not to think of it, in order not to create a preconceived idea. But something fascinated me and agitated me. I could not be sure, but it seemed to me that the enigma of the Taj Mahal was connected with the mystery of death, that is, with the mystery regarding which, according to the expression of one of the Upanishads, " even the gods have doubted formerly."

The creation of the Taj Mahal dates back to the time of the conquest of India by the Mahomedans. The grandson of Akbar, Shah Jehan, was one of the conquerors who changed the very face of India. Soldier and statesman, Shah Jehan was at the same time a fine judge of art and philosophy; and his court at Agra attracted all the most eminent scholars and artists of Persia, which was at that time the centre of culture for the whole of Western Asia.

Shah Jehan passed most of his life, however, on campaign and in fighting. And on all his campaigns he was invariably accompanied by his favorite wife, the beautiful Arjumand Banu, or, as she was also called, Mumtaz-i-Mahal — " The Treasure of the Palace." Arjumand Banu was Shah Jehan's constant adviser in all matters of subtle and intricate Oriental diplomacy, and she also shared his interest in the philosophy to which the invincible Emperor devoted all his leisure.

During one of these campaigns the Empress, who as usual was accompanying Shah Jehan, died, and before her death she asked him to build for her a tomb — " the most beautiful in the world."

And Shah Jehan decided to build for the interment of the dead Empress an immense mausoleum of white marble on the bank of the river Jumna in his capital Agra, and later to throw a silver bridge across the Jumna and on the other bank to build a mausoleum of black marble for himself.

Only half these plans was destined to be realised, for twenty years later, when the building of the Empress' mausoleum was being completed, a rebellion was raised against Shah Jehan by his son Aurungzeb, who later destroyed Benares. Aurungzeb accused his father of having spent on the building of the mausoleum the whole revenue of the state for the last twenty years. And having taken Shah Jehan captive Aurungzeb shut him up in a subterranean mosque in one of the inner courts of the fortress-palace of Agra.

Shah Jehan lived seven years in this subterranean mosque and when he felt the approach of death, he asked to be moved to the fortress wall into the so-called "Jasmine Pavilion," a tower of lace-like marble, which had contained the favourite room of the Empress Arjumand Banu. And on the balcony of the "Jasmine Pavilion" overlooking the Jumna, whence the Taj Mahal can be seen in the distance, Shah Jehan breathed his last.

Such, briefly, is the history of the Taj Mahal. Since those days the mausoleum of the Empress has survived many vicissitudes of fortune. During the constant wars that took place in India in the 17th and 18th centuries, Agra changed hands many times and was frequently pillaged. Conquerors carried off from the Taj Mahal the great silver doors and the precious lamps and candlesticks; and they stripped the walls of the ornaments of precious stones. The building itself, however, and the greater part of the interior decoration has been preserved.

In the thirties of the last century the British Governor-General proposed to sell the Taj Mahal for demolition. The Taj Mahal has now been restored and is carefully guarded.

I arrived at Agra in the evening and decided to go at once to see the Taj Mahal by moonlight. It was not full moon, but there was sufficient light.

Leaving the hotel, I drove for a long time through the European part of Agra, along broad streets all running between gardens. At last we left the town and, driving through a long avenue, on the left of which the river could be seen, we came out upon a broad square paved with flagstones and surrounded by red stone walls. In the walls, right and left, there were gates with high towers. The gate on the right, my guide explained, led into the old town, which had been the private property of the Empress Arjumand Banu, and remains in almost the same state as it was during her lifetime. The gate in the left-hand tower led to the Taj Mahal.

It was already growing dark, but in the light of the broad crescent of the moon every line of the buildings stood out distinctly against the pale sky. I walked in the direction of the high, dark-red gate-tower with its arrow-shaped arch and horizontal row of small white characteristically Indian cupolas surmounted by sharp-pointed spires. A few broad steps led from the square to the entrance under the arch. It was quite dark there. My footsteps along the mosaic paving echoed resoundingly in the side niches from which stairways led up to a landing on the top of the tower, and to the museum which is inside the tower.

Through the arch the garden is seen, a large expanse of verdure and in the distance some white outlines resembling a white cloud that had descended and taken symmetrical forms. These were the walls, cupolas and minarets of the Taj Mahal.

I passed through the arch and out on to the broad stone platform, and stopped to look about me. Straight in front of me and right across the garden led a long broad avenue of dark cypresses, divided down the middle by a strip of water with a row of jutting arms of fountains. At the further end the avenue of cypresses was closed by the white cloud of the Taj Mahal. At the sides of the Taj, a little below it, the cupolas of two large mosques could be seen under the trees.

I walked slowly along the main avenue in the direction of the white building, by the strip of water with its fountains. The first thing that struck me, and that I had not foreseen, was the immense size of the Taj. It is in fact a very large structure, but it appears even larger than it is, owing chiefly to the ingenious design of the builders, who surrounded it with a garden and so arranged the gates and avenues that the building from this side is not seen all at once, but is disclosed little by little as you approach it. I realised that everything about it had been exactly planned and calculated, and that everything was designed to supplement and reinforce the chief impression. It became clear to me why it was that in photographs the Taj Mahal had appeared unfinished and almost plain. It cannot be separated from the garden and from the mosques on either side, which appear as its continuation. I saw now why the minarets at the corners of the marble platform on which the main building stands had given me the impression of a defect. For in photographs I had seen the picture of the Taj as ending on both sides with these minarets. Actually, it does not end there, but imperceptibly passes into the garden and the adjacent buildings. And again, the minarets are not actually seen in all their height as they are in photographs. From the avenue along which I walked only their tops were visible behind the trees.

The white building of the mausoleum itself was still far away, and as I walked towards it, it rose before me higher and higher. Though in the uncertain and changing light of the crescent moon I could distinguish none of the details, a strange sense of expectation forced me to continue looking intently, as if something was about to be revealed to me.

In the shadow of the cypresses it was nearly dark; the garden was filled with the scent of flowers, above all with that of jasmine, and peacocks were miauing. And this sound harmonised strangely with the surroundings, and somehow still further intensified the feeling of expectation which was coming over me.

Already I could see, brightly outlined in front of me, the central portion of the Taj Mahal rising from the high marble platform. A little light glimmered through the doors.

I reached the middle of the path leading from the arched entrance to the mausoleum. Here, in the centre of the avenue, is a square tank with lotuses in it and with marble seats on one side.

In the faint light of the half moon the Taj Mahal appeared luminous. Wonderfully soft, but at the same time quite distinct, white cupolas and white minarets came into view against the pale sky, and seemed to radiate a light of their own.

I sat on one of the marble seats and looked at the Taj Mahal, trying to seize and impress on my memory all the details of the building itself as I saw it and of everything else around me.

I could not have said what went on in my mind during this time, nor could I have been sure whether I thought about anything at all, but gradually, growing stronger and stronger, a strange feeling stole over me, which no words can describe.

Reality, that everyday actual reality in which we live, seemed somehow to be lifted, to fade and float away; but it did not disappear, it only underwent some strange sort of transformation, losing all actuality; every object in it, taken by itself, lost its ordinary meaning and became something quite different. In place of the familiar, habitual reality another reality opened out, a reality which usually we neither know, nor see, nor feel, but which is the one true and genuine reality.

I feel and know that words cannot convey what I wish to say. Only those will understand me who have themselves experienced something of this kind, who know the " taste " of such feelings.

Before me glimmered the small light in the doors of the Taj Mahal. The white cupolas and white minarets seemed to stir in the changing light of the white half moon. From the garden came the scent of jasmine and the miauing of the peacocks.

I had the sensation of being in two worlds at once. In the first place, the ordinary world of things and people had entirely changed, and it was ridiculous even to think of it; so imaginary, artificial and unreal did it appear now. Everything that belonged to this world had become remote, foreign and unintelligible to me — and I myself most of all, this very I that had arrived two hours before with all sorts of luggage and had hurried off to see the Taj Mahal by moonlight. All this — and the whole of the life of which it formed a part — seemed a puppet-show, which moreover was most clumsily put together and crudely painted, thus not resembling any reality whatsoever. Quite as grotesquely senseless and tragically ineffective appeared all my previous thoughts about the Taj Mahal and its riddle.

The riddle was here before me, but now it was no longer a riddle. It had been made a riddle only by that absurd, non-existent reality from which I had looked at it. And now I experienced the wonderful joy of liberation, as if I had come out into the light from some deep underground passages.

Yes, this was the mystery of death! But a revealed and visible mystery. And there was nothing dreadful or terrifyng about it. On the contrary, it was infinite radiance and joy.

Writing this now, I find it strange to recall that there was scarcely any transitional state. From my usual sensation of myself and everything else I passed into this new state immediately, while I was in this garden, in the avenue of cypresses, with the white outline of the Taj Mahal in front of me.

I remember that an unusually rapid stream of thoughts passed through my mind, as if they were detached from me and choosing or finding their own way.

At one time my thought seemed to be concentrated upon the artists who had built the Taj Mahal. I knew that they had been Sufis, whose mystical philosophy, inseparable from poetry, has become the esotericism of Mahomedanism and in brilliant and earthly forms of passion and joy expressed the ideas of eternity, unreality and renunciation. And here the image of the Empress Arjumand Banu and her memorial, " the most beautiful in the world," became by their invisible sides connected with the idea of death, yet death not as annihilation, but as a new life.

I got up and walked forward with my eyes on the light glimmering in the doors, above which rose the immense shape of the Taj Mahal.

And suddenly, quite independently of me, something began to be formulated in my mind.

The light, I knew, burned above the tomb where the body of the Empress lay. Above it and around it are the marble arches, cupolas and minarets of the Taj Mahal, which carry it upwards, merging it into one whole with the sky and the moonlight.

I felt that precisely here was the beginning of the solution of the riddle.

The light — glimmering above the tomb where lies the dust of her body — this light that is so small and insignificant in comparison with the marble shape of the Taj Mahal, this is life, the life which we know in ourselves and others, in contrast with that other life which we do not know, which is hidden from us by the mystery of death.

The light which can so easily be extinguished, that is the little, transitory, earthly life. The Taj Mahal — that is the future or *eternal* life.

I began to understand the idea of the artists who had built the mausoleum of the Empress, who had surrounded it with this garden, with these gates, towers, pavilions, fountains, mosques — who had made it so immense, so white, so unbelievably beautiful, merging into the sky with its cupolas and minarets.

Before me and all around me was the soul of the Empress Mumtaz-i-Mahal.

The soul, so infinitely great, radiant and beautiful in comparison with the little body that had lived on earth and was now enclosed in the tomb.

In that moment I understood that the soul is not enclosed in the body, but that the body lives and moves in the soul. And then I remembered and understood a mystical expression which had arrested my attention in old books:

The soul and the future life are one and the same.

It even seemed strange to me that I had not been able to understand this before. Of course they were the same. Life, as a process, and that which lives, can be differentiated in our understanding only so long as there is the idea of disappearance, of death. Here, as in eternity, everything was united, dimensions merged, and our little earthly world disappeared in the infinite world.

I cannot reconstruct all the thoughts and feelings of those moments, and I feel that I am expressing a negligible part of them.

I now approached the marble platform on which stands the Taj Mahal with its four minarets at the corners. Broad marble stairs at the sides of the cypress avenue lead up to the platform from the garden.

I went up and came to the doors where the light was burning. I was met by Mahomedan gate-keepers, with slow, quiet movements, dressed in white robes and white turbans.

One of them lit a lantern, and I followed him into the interior of the mausoleum.

In the middle, surrounded by a carved marble trellis, were two white tombs; in the centre the tomb of the Empress, and beside it that of Shah Jehan. The tombs were covered with red flowers, and above them a light burned in a pierced brass lantern.

In the semi-darkness the indistinct outlines of the white walls vanished into the high dome, where the moonlight, penetrating from without, seemed to form a mist of changing colour.

I stood there a long time without moving, and the calm, grave Mahomedans in their white turbans left me undisturbed, and themselves stood in silence near the trellis which surrounded the tombs.

This trellis is itself a miracle of art. The word " trellis " conveys nothing, because it is really not a trellis, but a lace of white marble of wonderful workmanship. It is difficult to believe that the flowers and decorative ornamentation of this white filigree lace are neither moulded nor cast, but carved directly in thin marble panels.

Observing that I was examining the trellis, one of the gate-keepers quietly approached me and began to explain the plan of the interior of the Taj Mahal.

The tombstones before me were not real tombs. The real tombs in which the bodies lay were underneath in the crypt.

The middle part of the mausoleum, where we now stood, was under the great central dome; and it was separated from the outer walls by a wide corridor running between the four corner recesses, each beneath one of the four smaller cupolas.

" It is never light here," said the man, lifting up his hand. " Light only comes through the trellises of the side galleries."

" Listen, master."

He stepped back a few paces and, raising his head, cried slowly in a loud voice:

" Allah! "

His voice filled the whole of the enormous space of the dome above our heads, and as it began slowly, slowly, to die away, suddenly a clear and powerful echo resounded in the side cupolas from all four sides simultaneously:

" Allah! "

The arches of the galleries immediately responded, but not all at once; one after another voices rose from every side as though calling to one another.

" Allah! Allah! "

And then, like the chorus of a thousand voices or like an organ, the great dome itself resounded, drowning everything in its solemn, deep bass: " Allah! "

Then again, but more quietly, the side-galleries and cupolas answered, and the great dome, less loudly, resounded once more, and the faint, almost whispering tones of the inner arches re-echoed its voice.

The echo fell into silence. But even in the silence it seemed as if a far, far-away note went on sounding.

I stood and listened to it, and with an intensified sense of joy I felt that this marvellous echo also was a calculated part of the plan of the artists who had given to the Taj Mahal a voice, bidding it repeat for ever the name of God.

Slowly I followed the guide, who, raising his lantern, showed me the ornaments covering the walls: violet, rose, blue, yellow and bright red flowers mingled with the green, some life-size and others larger than life-size, stone flowers that looked alive and that were beyond the reach of time; and after that, the whole of the walls covered with white marble flowers, carved doors and carved windows — all of white marble.

The longer I looked and listened, the more clearly, and with a greater and greater sense of gladness, I felt the idea of the artists who had striven to express the infinite richness, variety and beauty of the *soul* or of *eternal life* as compared with the small and insignificant earthly life.

We ascended to the roof of the Taj Mahal, where the cupolas stand at the corners, and from there I looked down on the broad, dark Jumna. Right and left stood large mosques of red stone with white cupolas. Then I crossed to the side of the roof which overlooks the garden. Below, all was still, only the trees rustled in the breeze, and from time to time there came from afar the low and melodious miauing of the peacocks.

All this was so like a dream, so like the " India " one may see in dreams, that I should not have been in the least surprised had I suddenly found myself flying over the garden to the gate-tower, which was now growing black, at the end of the cypress avenue.

Then we descended and walked round the white building of the Taj Mahal on the marble platform, at the corners of which stand the four minarets, and by the light of the moon we examined the decorations and ornaments of the outer walls.

Afterwards we went below into the white marble crypt, where, as above, a lamp was burning and where red flowers lay on the white tombs of the Emperor and Empress.

The following morning I drove to the fortress, where the palace of Shah Jehan and the Empress Arjumand Banu is still preserved.

The fortress of Agra is a whole town in itself. Enormous towers built of brick stand above the gates. The walls are many feet thick, and enclose a lybyrinth of courtyards, barracks, warehouses and buildings of all kinds. A considerable part of the fortress indeed is devoted to modern uses and is of no particular interest. At last I came upon the Pearl Mosque, which I had known from Verestchagin's picture. Here begins the kingdom of white marble and blue sky. There are only two colours, white and blue. The Pearl Mosque is very much larger than I had imagined. Great heavy gates encased in copper, and behind them, under a glittering sky, a dazzling white marble yard with a fountain, and further on a hall for sermons, with wonderful carved arches with gold ornaments and with marble latticed windows into the inner parts of the palace, through which the wives of the Emperor and the ladies of the court could see into the mosque.

Then the palace itself. This is not one building, but a whole series of marble buildings and courts contained within the brick buildings and courts of the fortress itself.

The throne of Akbar, a black marble slab in the fortress wall on a level with the higher battlements, and in front of it the " Court of Justice." Then Shah Jehan's " Hall of Audience," with more carved arches similar to those in the Pearl Mosque, and finally the residential quarters of the palace and the Jasmine Pavilion.

These palace apartments are situated on the fortress wall which looks out over the Jumna. They consist of a series of rooms, not very large according to modern standards, but the walls of which are covered with rare and beautiful carving. Everything is so wonderfully preserved that it might have been only yesterday that here, with their women, lived those emperor-conquerors, philosophers, poets, sages, fanatics, madmen, who destroyed one India and created another. Most of the residential part of the palace is under the floor of the marble courts and passages which extend from the Hall of Audience to the fortress wall. The rooms are joined by corridors and passages and by small courts enclosed in marble trellises.

Beyond the fortress wall there is a deep inner court where tourneys of warriors were held, and where wild beasts fought with one another or with men. Above is the small court surrounded by lattices, from which the ladies of the palace viewed the combats of elephants against tigers and gazed at the contests of the warriors. Here, too, with their wares, came merchants from far countries, Arabians, Greeks, Venetians and Frenchmen. A " chessboard " court paved with rows of black and white slabs in chess-board pattern, where dancers and dancing-girls in special costumes acted as chessmen. Further on, the apartments of the Emperor's wives; in the walls carved cupboards for jewelry still exist, as well as small round apertures, leading to secret cupboards, into which only very small hands could penetrate. A bathroom lined with rock crystal which causes its walls to sparkle with changing colours when a light is lit. Small, almost toy rooms, like bonbonnières. Tiny balconies. Rooms under the floor of the inner court, into which the light passes only through thin marble panels, and where it is never hot — and then at last, the miracle of miracles, the Jasmine Pavilion, which used to contain the favourite apartment of the Empress Mumtaz-i-Mahal.

It is a circular tower, surrounded by a balcony hanging over the fortress wall above the Jumna. Eight doors lead within from the balcony. There is literally not one inch of the walls of the Jasmine Pavilion or of the balustrades and pillars of the balcony, that is not covered with the most delicate, beautiful carving. Ornament within ornament, and again in every ornament still another ornament, almost like jewellers' work. The whole of the Jasmine Pavilion is like this, and so is the small hall with a fountain and rows of carved columns.

In all this there is nothing grandiose or mystical, but the whole produces an impression of unusual intimacy. I felt the life of the people who had lived there. In some strange way I seemed to be in touch with it, as if the people were still living; and I caught glimpses of the most intimate and secret aspects of their lives. In this palace time is not felt at all. The past connected with these marble rooms is felt as the present, so real and living does it stand out, and so strange is it even to think while here that it is no more.

As we were leaving the palace the guide told me of the subterranean maze beneath the whole fortress where, it is said, innumerable treasures lie concealed. And I remembered that I had read about it before. But the entrances to these underground passages had been closed and covered over many years ago, after a party of curious travellers had lost their way and perished in them. It is said that there are many snakes there, among them some gigantic cobras larger than any to be found elsewhere, which were perhaps alive in the days of Shah Jehan. And they say that sometimes on moonlight nights they crawl out to the river.

From the palace I drove again to the Taj Mahal, and on the way I bought photographs taken from old miniatures, portraits of Shah Jehan and the Empress Arjumand Banu. Once seen, their faces remain in the memory. The Empress' head is slightly inclined, and she holds a rose in her delicate hand. The portrait is very much stylised, but in the shape of the mouth and in the large eyes one feels a deep inner life, strength and thought; and in the whole face the irresistible charm of mystery and fairy-tale. Shah Jehan is in profile. He has a very strange look, ecstatic yet at the same time balanced. In this portrait he sees something which no one but himself could see or perhaps would dare to see. Also he appears to be looking at himself, observing his every thought and feeling. It is the look of a clairvoyant, a dreamer, as well as that of a man of extraordinary strength and courage.

The impression of the Taj Mahal not only is not weakened by the light of day, rather it is strengthened. The white marble amidst the green stands out so astonishingly against the deep blue sky; and in a single glance you seize more particulars and details than at night. Inside the building you are still more struck by the luxuriance of the decoration, the fairy-tale flowers, red, yellow and blue, and the garlands of green; the garlands of marble leaves and marble flowers and lace-work trellises. . . . And all this is the soul of the Empress Mumtaz-i-Mahal.

I spent the whole of the next day until evening in the garden that surrounds the Taj Mahal. Above all things I liked to sit on the wide balcony on the top of the gate-tower. Beneath me lay the garden intersected by the cypress avenue and the line of fountains reaching as far as the marble platform on which the Taj Mahal stands. Under the cypresses slowly moved groups of Mahomedan visitors in robes and turbans of soft colours that can only be imagined: turquoise, lemon-yellow, pale green, yellow-rose. For a long time I watched through my glasses a pale orange turban side by side with an emerald shawl. Every now and again they vanished behind the trees, again they appeared on the marble stairs leading to the mausoleum. Then they disappeared in the entrances to the Taj Mahal, and again could be seen amongst the cupolas on the roof. And all the time along the avenue of cypresses moved the procession of coloured robes and turbans, blue, yellow, green, rose turbans, shawls and caftans — not a single European was in sight.

The Taj Mahal is the place of pilgrimage and the place for promenades from the town. Lovers meet here; you see children with their large dark eyes, calm and quiet, like all Indian children; ancient and decrepit men, women with babies, beggars, fakirs, musicians. . . .

All faces, all types of Mahomedan India pass before you.

And I had a strange feeling all the time that this, too, was part of the plan of the builders of the Taj Mahal, part of their mystical idea of the contact of the *soul* with the whole world and with all the life that from all sides unceasingly flows into the soul.

1914

VI

The Mevlevi Dervishes

I saw them for the first time in 1908. Constantinople then was still alive. Later it died. *They* were the soul of Constantinople, though nobody knew of this.

I remember entering the court of the " Tekke " at the top of *Yuksek Kalderym,* that noisy and, in those days, still so typically Eastern street, with its steps, which climbs high up the hill from the bridge across the Golden Horn and joins the main street of Pera.

Whirling dervishes! I expected maniacal rage, frenzy — an unpleasant and painful spectacle. I had even hesitated whether I should go or not. But the court of the Tekke with its old green plane-trees and the ancient tombs of an old graveyard overgrown with high grass struck me with its wonderful air of peace and quiet.

The ceremony had already begun. As I approached the doors of the Tekke I heard strange soft music — flutes and muffled drums. It was an unexpected and unusually pleasant impression.

There followed conversations at the entrance — some business about boots and slippers — then to the right, to the left — then a dark passage. . . . But I knew already that I had come to a place where I should see something.

A round hall strewn with carpets and surrounded by a breast-high wooden partition. Behind the partition, in a circular corridor, spectators. The ceremony of salutation was in progress.

Men in black robes with wide sleeves, with tall yellow camel-hair hats narrowing a little towards the top (kulas), one after another, to the accompaniment of music, approached the sheikh, who sat on cushions with his back to the princes' box. They made low bows to him, first standing at his right, then, having taken a few steps, repeated the same low bows standing at his left. And then, one after another, like black monks, slowly and calmly they sat down along the circular partition of the round room. The music still played.

Now the music stopped. Silence. The men in tall kulas were sitting with lowered eyes.

The sheikh began a long speech. He spoke of the history of Mevlevi, of all the sultans who had ruled in Turkey, enumerated their names, spoke of interest and sympathy towards the Order of Dervishes. The Arabic words sounded strange. My friend, who had lived for a long time in the East, translated to me in a low voice.

But I was looking rather than listening. What struck me in these dervishes was that *they were all different*.

When you see many people together wearing the same dress, you do not as a rule distinguish their faces. All of them seem to have one and the same face.

But what particularly struck the eye here and what at once arrested my attention was the fact that they were all *different*. Not one face was like another. And each face at once impressed itself on the memory. I had never experienced anything like it. In the first ten or fifteen minutes while I was watching the ceremony of salutations, the faces of all the dervishes in the circle became near and familiar to me, like the faces of school-friends. I already knew them all, and with an incredibly pleasant feeling waited for what would follow.

Again, as though from a distance, came the sound of music. One after another, without haste — some throwing off their robes and remaining in short jackets reaching to the waist and a sort of long white skirt, and others keeping their robes — the dervishes rose and with calm and assured movements, lifting the right arm, bent, the head turned to the right and the left arm outstretched, slowly stepped into the circle and with extraordinary seriousness began to turn, at the same time moving round the circle. And in the centre, his arms bent in the same way, looking at his right hand, a dervish with a short grey beard and a calm pleasant face slowly turned on one spot, shuffling his feet with a peculiar motion. All the others, some very young men, others middle-aged, and some quite old men, turned round him. And all of them turned round and moved along the circle at a different speed; the older ones turned slowly, others, the younger ones, with a speed that took one's breath away. Some appeared as they turned to have their eyes closed, others merely looked down, but no one of them ever touched another.

In their midst, not turning like the others, slowly walked a dervish with a grey beard, in a black robe and with a green turban wound round his camel-hair kula, with the palms of his hands pressed against his breast and his eyes lowered. He walked strangely, moving now to the right, now to the left, now advancing, now receding a little, but all the time proceeding round the circle, only sometimes passing as though from one orbit to another and back again. But he never touched anyone, just as no one touched him.

How could this be? I could not understand it. But I did not even think about it because at that moment all my attention was taken in watching the *faces*.

The sheikh sitting on cushions in his place opposite me, the dervish turning in the middle, the other dervish in the green turban moving slowly among the turning dervishes, the very, very old man slowly turning among the young ones — all of them reminded me of something.

I could not explain it to myself.

And the dervishes continued to turn round and move along the circle. Thirteen of them were whirling at the same time. Now and then one or another stopped and, slowly and calmly, with face illumined and concentrated, sat down by the wall. Others rose and took their places in the circle.

And involuntarily I began to think that this is what is described as a mad whirling which drives them into a frenzy! If there is anything in the world which is the complete opposite of frenzy, it is precisely this whirling. There was a system in it which I could not understand, but which made itself clearly felt, and, what was most important, there was some intellectual concentration and mental effort, as though they were not only turning, but at the same time solving difficult problems in their minds.

I walked out of the Tekke into the street, full of strange and disturbing impressions. I felt that I had found something, something extraordinarily valuable and important, but I felt at the same time that I had no means of understanding it, that I had no possibility of drawing nearer, that I even had no language.

All that I had known and read about Dervishes before did not explain to me the enigma which I felt. I knew that the order of Mevlevi was founded in the 13th century by the Persian poet and philosopher, Jalal-ud-

Din Rumi, that the whirling dervishes represent schematically the solar system and the planets revolving round the sun, that the dervishes have carried through all those centuries, quite intact, their statutes, their regulations, even their dress. And I knew that an acquaintance with existing literature on dervishes is terribly disappointing because one feels that what is most important is lacking in it. Now that I had seen them myself I formulated to myself what I considered the *most important* problems about them. First, how do they manage not to knock against one another and even not to touch one another? And second, in what lies the secret of this intense mental effort connected with the whirling, the effort which I *saw*, but was unable to define? Later I learned that the answer to one question replies also to the other.

Constantinople passed like a dream. I went to other Tekkes, in Eyoub, in Scutari, saw other dervishes. And all the time the sense of enigma became stronger in me.

Whirling dervishes, " Mevlevi," and others, *howling* dervishes, " Rifa'is " in Scutari, were something quite apart by themselves, different from anything I had ever known or met in life. And in thinking about them I recalled the words of a well-known man in Moscow who had laughed at me when I said once that the East holds much that is still unknown.

" Do you really believe that there still remains something unepxlored in the East? " he said. " So many books have been written about the East, so many serious scientists have given up their whole lives to the study of every small piece of land there, of every tribe, of every custom. It is simply naïve to think that anything miraculous and unknown has remained in the East. I could more easily believe in miracles on Kuznetsky Most."

All that he said was very clever, and I almost agreed with him. But here I was in the East myself. And the first thing I saw was a miracle. And this miracle was there for all to see, it was almost in the street. The main street of Pera was precisely the " Kuznetsky Most " of Constantinople. And nobody could explain this miracle to me *because nobody knew anything about it.*

Twelve years passed before I saw the dervishes again.

Many countries had passed before my eyes, many events had occurred around me during that time. No one was left of those who were with me when I was first in Constantinople. *And there was even no Russia.* For during these last three years the ground had fallen away behind me. It was a quite inconceivable period, when there was no *way back*, when I experienced in relation to places and people the same sensation which we ordinarily feel in relation to time.

To no place that I had left was it possible to return. From nobody from whom I had parted did I have any more news.

But when from the ship I saw in the mist the minarets of Stamboul and the Galata Tower on the other side, the first thought that came to me was that I should soon see the dervishes.

And soon I saw them. Constantinople had become still noisier, if that was possible, but looked empty in spite of the new crowds. During those years the poor town had lost half its Eastern colour and was rapidly acquiring Western drabness and hideousness. But in the Tekke of the dervishes at Pera all was as before: the same old tomb-stones, the same plane-trees, the same soft music and the same or similar calm faces. I could not be certain after twelve years, but it seemed to me that I recognised several faces.

And now I knew more about them. I knew a part of their secret. I knew *how they did it*. I knew in what the mental work connected with the whirling consisted. Not the details of course, because only a man who takes part in the ceremonies or exercises can know the details. But I knew *the principle*.

All this did not make the miracle less. It only came nearer and became more significant. And at the same time I understood why they do not reveal their secret. It is easy to tell what they do and how they do it. But in order to understand it fully one must first know *why they do it*. And this cannot be told.

Again I went away and again, soon after, the ground fell away behind me and to return to Constantinople had become impossible.

And soon the dervishes themselves disappeared. The enlightened rulers of the new Turkey forbade all activity to " astrologers, fortune-tellers and dervishes." And in the Tekke at Pera there is now a police-station.

1909–1925

Chapter X

A NEW MODEL OF THE UNIVERSE

I

AT every attempt to study the world and nature man inevitably finds himself confronted with a series of definite questions to which he is unable to give direct answers. But upon his recognition or non-recognition of these questions, upon his way of formulating them, and upon his attitude towards them, depends the whole further process of his thinking about the world and, consequently, about himself.

The most important of these questions are the following:

1. *What form has the world?*
2. *Is the world a chaos or a system?*
3. *Did the world come into being accidentally, or was it created according to plan?*

And strange though it may appear at the first glance, one or another solution of the first question, that of the form of the world, actually determines the possible solution both of the second and of the third questions.

If the questions as to whether the world is a chaos or a system, and whether the world came into being accidentally or was created according to plan, are solved without being preceded by a definition of the form of the world, and do not result from such a definition, those solutions lack weight, demand " faith " and fail to satisfy the mind. It is only when the answers to these questions are derived from the definition of the form of the world that they can be sufficiently exact and complete.

It is not difficult to prove that the predominating general philosophies of life of our time are based on such solutions of these three fundamental questions as might have been considered scientific during the 19th century. The discoveries of the 20th century and even those of the end of the 19th century have not as yet affected ordinary thought or have affected it very little.

And it is not difficult to prove that all further questions concerning the world, the development and elaboration of which constitute the object of scientific, philosophical and religious thought, arise from these three fundamental questions.

But in spite of its predominant importance, the question of the form of the world has comparatively seldom arisen independently, being usually included in other problems, cosmogonical, cosmological, astronomical, geometrical, physical and other. The average man would be greatly surprised if he were told that the world may have a form. For him the *world* has no form.

Yet in order to understand the world one must be able to build some model of the universe, however imperfect. Such a model of the world, such a model of the universe, cannot be built without a definite conception of the form of the universe. To make a model of a house one must know the form of the house, to make a model of an apple, one must know the form of the apple.

Therefore, before passing to principles upon which a new model of the universe can be built, we must examine, though only summarily, the history of the question as to the form of the world, the present state of this question in science, and the "models" which have been built up to the present day.

The ancient and mediæval cosmogonical and cosmological conceptions of exoteric systems (which alone became known to science) were never very clear or very interesting. Moreover, the universe they pictured was a very small universe, much smaller than the modern astronomical world. I shall not therefore speak of them.

Our study of different views of the question concerning the form of the world will begin from the moment when astronomical and physico-mechanical systems freed themselves from the idea that the earth is the centre of the world. The period in question embraces several centuries. But actually we shall occupy ourselves only with the last century, almost precisely from the end of the first quarter of the 19th century.

By that time the sciences which studied the world of nature had long been divided and stood then in the same relation to one another in which they stand now, or stood at any rate quite recently.

Physics studied phenomena in matter around us.

Astronomy studied the "movements of celestial bodies."

Chemistry endeavoured to penetrate the mystery of the structure and composition of matter.

These three physical sciences based their conceptions of the form of the world entirely upon the geometry of Euclid. Geometrical space was taken as physical space. No difference was distinguished between them, and space was taken apart from matter, just as a box and its capacity may be examined independently of its contents.

Space was understood as an "infinite sphere." The infinite sphere was geometrically determined only from the centre, that is, from any point, by three radii at right angles to one another. And an infinite sphere was regarded as entirely similar in all its physical properties to a finite sphere.

The question of the non-correspondence of geometrical, that is, of Euclidean, three-dimensional space (whether infinite or finite) on the one hand with physical space on the other hand arose only very occasionally and did not interfere with the development of physics in the directions which were possible to it.

It was only about the end of the 18th and the beginning of the 19th century that the idea of this non-correspondence and the doubt as to the correctness of identifying physical space with geometrical space became so insistent that it was no longer possible to pass them over in silence.

This doubt was aroused, first: by attempts at a revaluation of geometrical values, that is, attempts either to *prove* the axioms of Euclid, or to prove their incorrectness; and second: by the very development of physics, or more exactly of mechanics, that is, the part of physics dealing with motion, for this development led to the conviction that physical space could not be housed in geometrical space and continually reached beyond it. Geometrical space could be taken as physical space only by closing the eyes to the fact that in geometrical space everything is immovable, that it contains no *time* necessary for motion, and that the calculation of any figure resulting from motion, such as a screw, for instance, requires four coordinates.

Later on, the study of phenomena of light, electricity and magnetism, and also the study of the structure of the atom, necessitated a similar broadening of the concept of space.

The result of purely geometrical speculations concerning the correctness or incorrectness of the axioms of Euclid was twofold. On the one hand a conviction arose that geometry was a purely speculative science, dealing solely with principles and entirely completed, which could neither be added to nor altered; also a science which could not be applied to all the facts that are met with, which is true only under certain definite conditions, but within those conditions is perfectly reliable and irreplaceable by anything else. On the other hand there arose a certain disappointment in the geometry of Euclid and a desire to remodel it, to rebuild it on a new basis, to broaden it, to make it a physical science which could be applied to all the facts that are met with, without the necessity for arranging these facts in an artificial order. The first view on geometry was right; the second was wrong, but this second attitude can be said to have triumphed in science and thus considerably delayed its development. But I shall revert to this later.

Kant's ideas of categories of space and time taken as categories of perception and thought have never entered into scientific, i.e. physical thought, in spite of certain later attempts to introduce them into physics. Scientific (physical) thought proceeded apart from philosophical and psychological thought. And scientific thought always took time and space as having an objective existence outside us. And in virtue of this it was always considered possible to express their relations mathematically.

But the development of mechanics and other branches of physics led to the necessity for recognising a fourth coordinate of space in addition to the three fundamental coordinates: length, breadth and height. And the idea of the fourth coordinate or the fourth dimension of space gradually became more and more inevitable, though for a long time it remained a kind of " taboo."

Material for the construction of new hypotheses of space remained in the works of the mathematicians: Gauss, Lobatchevsky, Saccheri, Bolyai and especially Riemann, who in the fifties of the 19th century was already considering the question of the possibility of a totally new understanding of space. There were no serious attempts at a psychological study of the problem of space and time. The idea of the fourth dimension remained for a long time shelved, and by specialists was regarded as purely mathematical and by non-specialists as mystical or occult.

But if we start from the moment of the appearance of this idea at the beginning of the 19th century and make a brief survey of the development of scientific thought from that moment up to the present day, it may help us to understand the course which the further development of the idea may take. At the same time we may see what this idea tells us or can tell us in regard to the fundamental problem of the form of the world.

The first and essential question which arises at this point is that of the relation of the physical sciences to mathematics. From the ordinary point of view it is taken as an admitted fact that mathematics studies the relation of quantities in the same world of things and phenomena as that studied by the physical sciences. From this follow two more propositions: first, that every mathematical proposition must have a physical equivalent, though it may still be undiscovered at the given moment; and second, that every physical phenomenon can be expressed mathematically.

As a matter of fact neither of these propositions has any foundation whatever, and the acceptance of them as axioms arrests the progress of thought along the very lines where progress is most necessary. But this will be dealt with later.

In the discussions which follow of all the physical sciences we shall examine only physics proper. And in physics we shall have to pay most attention at first to mechanics: for since about the middle of the 18th century mechanics has assumed a predominant position in physics; so much so that until quite recently it was considered both possible and probable that a means would be found of interpreting all physical phenomena as mechanical phenomena, that is, as phenomena of motion. Some scientists even went much further in this direction and, not content with admitting the possibility of finding a means of interpreting physical phenomena as phenomena of motion, asserted that this means had already been found and that it explained not only physical phenomena, but also phenomena of life and thought.

At present one often meets with a division of physics into *old* and *new*, and in its chief lines this division may be accepted. But it should not be understood too literally.

I will now try to make a brief survey of the fundamental ideas of old physics which led to the necessity for building " new physics," which has unexpectedly destroyed old physics; and then I will come to the ideas of new physics which lead to the possibility of building a " new model of the universe," which destroys new physics just as new physics destroyed old physics.

Old physics lasted until the discovery of the electron. But even the electron was conceived by old physics as existing in the same artificial world, governed by Aristotelian and Newtonian laws, in which it studied visible phenomena; in other words, the electron was accepted as existing in the same world in which our bodies and other objects commensurable with them exist. Physicists did not understand that the electron belongs to another world.

Old physics was based on certain immovable foundations. The space and time of old physics possessed very definite properties. First of all, they could be examined and calculated *separately*, i.e. the being of a thing in space in no way affected or touched its being in time. Further, there was one space for all that exists, and all that occurred in this space. Time also was one for all that exists and was measured always and for everything by one scale. In other words, it was considered possible to measure with one measure all movements possible in the universe.

The corner-stone of the whole understanding of the laws of the universe was the principle of Aristotle concerning the unity of laws in the universe.

This principle in its modern meaning can be formulated in the following way: in the whole of the universe and under all possible conditions the laws of nature must be identical; in other words, a law which has been established at one place in the universe must hold good at any other place in the universe. On the basis of this, science, in studying phenomena on the earth and in the solar system, assumed the existence of the same phenomena on other planets and in other solar systems.

This principle, attributed to Aristotle, in reality was certainly never understood by him in the sense which it had acquired in our times. The universe of Aristotle differed greatly from the universe as we conceive it. The thinking of the people of Aristotle's time differed greatly from the thinking of the people of our time. Many fundamental principles and many starting-points of thought, which we can accept as firmly established, had to be proved and established by Aristotle.

Aristotle endeavoured to establish the unity of laws in the sense of a protest against superstitions, against naïve magic, against naïve miracles, and so on. In order to understand the " principle of Aristotle " it is necessary to realise that he had still to prove that, if in general dogs cannot speak in human language, then one particular dog, say, in the island of Crete, *also* cannot speak; or that if in general trees cannot move of themselves, then one particular tree *also* cannot move, and so on.

All this has of course been forgotten long ago, and from the principle of Aristotle there follows now the idea of the permanency of all physical concepts, such as motion, velocity, force, energy, etc. This means that what has once been regarded as motion always remains motion; what has once been regarded as velocity always remains velocity, becoming " infinite velocity."

In its primary meaning the "principle of Aristotle" is comprehensible and necessary and is nothing else than the law of the general consecutiveness of phenomena which belongs to logic. But in its modern meaning the "principle of Aristotle" is entirely wrong.

Even for new physics the concept of infinite velocity, which is exclusively based on the "principle of Aristotle," has become impossible, and the "principle of Aristotle" must be completely abandoned before the planning of a new model of the universe becomes possible. I shall return to this question later.

In speaking of physics it is first of all necessary to analyse the very definition of the subject. According to the definition of text-books of this science, physics studies "matter in space and phenomena in this matter."

And here we are at once faced with the fact that physics operates with undefined and unknown quantities which, for the sake of convenience (or owing to the difficulty of definition), are taken as known quantities and even as quantities requiring no definition.

There are formally distinguished in physics first: quantities requiring definition; and second: "primary" quantities, the idea of which is considered to be inherent in all people. Prof. Chwolson in his *Text-book* [1] enumerates as primary quantities:

Extensions — linear-extension, area-extension and volume-extension, that is, the length of a straight line, the area of a portion of surface and the volume of a portion of space limited by surfaces; extension being the measure of size and distance.

Time.

Velocity of uniform rectilinear motion.

These are naturally only examples, and Prof. Chwolson does not insist on the completeness of the list. In reality, the list is very long; it includes space, infinity, matter, motion, mass and so on. In a word, practically all the concepts with which physics operates refer to undefined and undefinable quantities.

Of course in a great many cases it is impossible to avoid operating with unknown quantities, but it has become the traditional "scientific" method not to recognise anything as unknown, and to regard the "quantities" which elude definition as "primary," the idea of which is inherent in everyone. The natural result has been that the whole of the vast edifice erected with tremendous labour has become artificial and unreal.

In the definition of physics given above we meet with two undefined concepts: *space* and *matter*.

---

[1] As an example of a text-book on physics from which quotations can be made the author has taken Prof. O. D. Chwolson's *Text-book on Physics* (in Russian), (5th edition, in five volumes, Berlin, 1923). This book is neither better nor worse than any other text-book on physics and it can very well be taken as an example of text-book opinions and views. It is even better than many other books bceause of Prof. Chwolson's impartiality towards new theories.

I have already referred to space in the preceding pages. As regards matter, Prof. Chwolson writes (*Text-book of Physics*, Vol. I, Introduction):

In objectifying the cause of a sensation, that is, transferring this cause into a definite place in space, we conceive this space as containing something which we call *matter* or substance (page 2).

Further Prof. Chwolson says:

The use of the term " matter " was reserved exclusively for matter which is able to affect our organ of touch more or less directly (page 7).

Further, matter is divided into organised matter (of which living bodies and plants are composed) and non-organised matter.

This method of division instead of definition is applied in physics whenever definition is difficult or impossible, that is, in relation to all fundamental concepts. Later we shall often meet with this fact.

The difference between organised matter and non-organised matter is determined only by external characteristics. The origin of organised matter is admitted to be unknown. The transition of non-organised matter into organised matter may be observed (feeding, breathing), and it is admitted that such a transition takes place only in the presence and through the action of already existing organised matter. The mystery of the first transition remains hidden (Chwolson).

On the other hand we see that organised matter easily passes into non-organised matter, losing certain undefinable properties which we call *life*.

Many attempts have been made to regard organised matter as a particular case of non-organised matter, and to explain all the phenomena that take place in organised matter (i.e. phenomena of life), as a combination of physical phenomena. But these attempts, as well as attempts at the artificial creation of organised matter from non-organised matter, led to nothing and could neither create nor prove anything. In spite of this they left a very strong impress on general philosophies of life of a scientific kind, from the standpoint of which the " artificial creation of life " is recognised as not only possible but already partly attained. Followers of these philosophies regard the very name of *organic chemistry*, i.e. chemistry studying organised matter, as having merely a historical meaning, and define it as the " chemistry of carbon compounds," although at the same time they cannot help admitting the special position of the chemistry of carbon compounds and its difference from general inorganic chemistry.

Non-organised matter is in its turn divided into simple matter and composite matter (this becomes the province of chemistry). Composite matter consists of a so-called chemical compound of several simple matters. Every matter can be divided into very small parts, called " particles." A *particle* is the smallest quantity of the given matter which is still capable of exhibiting at least the chief properties of this matter. The further divisions of matter, molecule, atom, electron, are so small that, taken separately, they do not possess any material properties, though this last fact is never sufficiently taken into account.

According to the most recent scientific ideas, non-organised matter consists of 92 elements or simple matters, though not all of them have as yet been discovered. There exists a hypothesis that the atoms of various elements are nothing but a combination of a certain number of atoms of hydrogen, which, in this case, is taken as fundamental or primary matter. Several theories exist concerning the possibility or the impossibility of the transition of one element into another. And in some cases such a transition has been established, which again contradicts the " principle of Aristotle."

Organised matter, or " carbon compounds," actually consists of four elements — hydrogen, oxygen, carbon and nitrogen, with a negligible admixture of other elements.

Matter possesses many properties, such as mass, volume, density, etc., which are in most cases only definable one relatively to another.

The temperature of a body is recognised as depending on the motion of molecules. Molecules are considered to be in perpetual motion; as physics defines it, they are constantly colliding and scattering in all directions and returning again. The greater the motion, the greater the shocks when they collide, the higher the temperature (Brownian movement).

If this were possible in reality, it would mean approximately that, for instance, several hundreds of motor-cars, swiftly moving in different directions in a large square of a big city, crash into one another every minute and disperse in various directions, remaining intact.

It is very curious that a *quick-motion* cinematographic film produces such an illusion. Moving objects lose their individuality and appear to collide and fly off in different directions or pass through one another.[2]

How it can be that material bodies possessing mass, weight and very complicated structure and moving at great velocity, collide and scatter without being broken up and destroyed, is not explained by physics.

One of the most important conquests of physics was the establishment of the principle of the conservation of matter. This principle consists in the recognition of the fact that matter is never and in no physical or chemical conditions created anew, nor does it disappear. Its total amount remains constant. With the principle of conservation of matter are connected the principles established later, the principle of conservation of energy and the principle of conservation of mass.

Mechanics is the name given to the science of the motion of physical bodies and of the causes upon which the character of this motion may depend in various particular cases (Chwolson).

---

[2] The author once saw a quick-motion cinematograph picture of the Place de la Concorde, with motor-cars rushing from all directions and in all directions. And the impression was exactly as if the cars violently collided with one another every moment and flew apart, remaining all the time in the square and never leaving it.

But, just as in the case of all other physical concepts, *motion* is not defined by physics. Physics only establishes the properties of motion — duration, velocity and direction in space, without which properties a phenomenon cannot be called motion.

The division and sometimes the definition of these properties take the place of the definition of motion itself, and the established characteristics of the properties of motion are referred to motion itself. Thus motion is divided into rectilinear and curvilinear, continuous and non-continuous, accelerating and retarding, uniform and variable.

The establishment of the principle of the relativity of motion led to a whole series of conclusions. The question arose: if the motion of a material point can be determined only by its position in relation to other bodies or points, then how is the motion to be determined if the other bodies or points also move? And this question became especially complicated when it was established, not merely philosophically in the sense of πάντα ῥεῖ, but fully scientifically, with calculations and diagrams, that nothing is motionless in the universe, that everything without exception moves in one way or another, and that one motion can be established only relatively to another. But at the same time there were established cases of apparent immobility in motion. Thus it was established that separate component parts of a uniformly moving system of bodies maintain the same position in relation to one another as though the system were stationary. Thus, things inside a swiftly moving railway carriage behave in exactly the same way as when the carriage is standing still. And in the case of two or more moving systems of bodies, for instance in the case of two trains running on different tracks in the same direction or in different directions, it was established that their relative velocity is equal to the difference between, or the sum of, their respective velocities, according to the direction of the movement. Thus two trains approaching one another will approach with a velocity equal to the sum of their respective velocities. For one train overtaking another, the second train will run in a direction opposite to its own with a velocity equal to the difference between the respective velocities of the two trains. What is usually called the velocity of a train is the velocity which is ascribed to the train observed during its passage between two objects which are stationary for it, for instance between two stations, and so on.

The study of motion in general and of vibratory and undulatory movements in particular exercised a tremendous influence on the development of physics. Wave movements began to be regarded as a universal principle, and many attempts were made to reduce all physical phenomena to vibratory movements.

One of the fundamental methods of physics was the measurement of quantities.

The measurement of quantities was based upon certain principles, the most important of which was the principle of homogeneity, namely, quantities conforming to the same definition and differing from one another merely quantitatively were called homogeneous quantities and it was considered possible to compare them and measure one in relation to another. As to quantities which differed in definition, it was considered impossible to measure them one in relation to another.

Unfortunately, as has already been shown, there were very few *definitions* of quantities in physics and therefore definitions were generally replaced by their denominations.

But as mistakes in the denomination could always occur, and qualitatively different quantities could be named similarly, while qualitatively identical quantities could be named differently, physical measurements were unreliable. And the more so because here again the principle of Aristotle was felt — that is, a quantity once recognised as a quantity of a certain order always remained a quantity of that order. Different forms of energy passed into one another, matter passed from one state into another, but space (or a part of space) always remained space, time always remained time, motion always remained motion, velocity always remained velocity, and so on.

On these grounds it was agreed to regard as *incommensurable* only those quantities which were qualitatively different. Quantities which differed merely quantitatively were regarded as *commensurable*.

Continuing the subject of the measurement of quantities, it is necessary to point out that the units of measure used in physics are quite arbitrary and have no connection with the quantities that are measured. All the units of measure have only one thing in common — they are always borrowed from *elsewhere*. There is not a single case in which a characteristic of the given quantity itself is taken as the measure.

The artificiality of measures in physics has certainly never been a secret, and from the realisation of this artificiality follow attempts to establish, for instance, the measure of length *as a part of the meridian*. Naturally these attempts alter nothing, and parts of the human body, an " ell " or a " foot," taken as units of measure, or a " metre," i.e. a part of the meridian, are equally arbitrary. In reality things bear their own measure in themselves. And to find the measure of things is to understand the world. Physicists have dimly guessed this, though they have never succeeded in even approaching these measures.

Prof. Planck in 1900 (this really belongs to new physics) constructed a system of " absolute units," taking as its basis " universal constants," namely: first, the velocity of light in a vacuum; second, the constant unit of gravitation; third, a constant quantity which plays an important part in thermodynamics (energy divided by temperature); and fourth, a constant quantity which is called " action " (energy multiplied by time) and is the smallest possible quantity of action or its atom.

Using these quantities Planck obtains a system of units which he considers to be absolute and entirely independent of any arbitrary choice of man, and which he regards as *natural*.

Planck affirms that these quantities will retain their natural meaning so long as the laws of universal gravitation and of the propagation of light in a vacuum, and the two fundamental principles of thermo-dynamics, remain unchanged; they will always be the same by whatever intelligent beings and by whatever methods they are determined.

But the law of universal gravitation and the law of the propagation of light in a vacuum are the two weakest points in physics, because in reality they are not what they are taken for. And therefore Planck's whole system of measures is very unreliable. What is interesting in it is not the result but only the principle, i.e. the recognition of the necessity for finding natural measures of things. The actual determination of absolute units of measure lies beyond the new model of the universe.

The law of universal gravitation was stated by Newton in his book: *Philosophiæ naturalis principia mathematica*, which was published in London in 1687. This law from the very beginning received two formulations: one scientific, the other popular.

The scientific formulation is as follows:

There are observed phenomena between two bodies in space which *can be described* by presuming that two bodies attract one another with a force directly proportional to the product of their masses and inversely proportional to the square of the distance separating them.

And the popular formulation is:

Two bodies *attract* one another with a force directly proportional to the product of their masses and inversely proportional to the square of the distance separating them.

In this second formulation the fact is entirely forgotten that the force of attraction is merely a fictitious quantity accepted only for a convenient description of phenomena. *And the force of attraction* is regarded as really existing both between the sun and the earth and between the earth and a falling stone.[3]

Prof. Chwolson writes in his *Text-book of Physics:* [4]

The tremendous development of celestial mechanics, entirely based on the law of universal gravitation taken as a fact, made scientists forget the purely descriptive character of this law and see in it the final formulation of an actually existent physical phenomenon.

What is important in Newton's law is that it gives a very simple mathematical formulation which can be applied throughout the universe, and on the basis of which it is possible to calculate all movements, in particular

---

[3] The most recent electro-magnetic theory of gravitational fields dogmatises the *second* view.

[4] Vol. I, p. 182.

the movements of celestial bodies, with astonishing accuracy. Newton certainly never established it as a fact that bodies are actually attracted by one another, nor did he establish *why* they are attracted or *through the mediation of what.*

How can the sun influence the motion of the earth through the void of space? How in general is it possible to conceive action through empty space? The law of gravitation does not give an answer to this question, and Newton himself was perfectly aware of this fact. Both he and his contemporaries, Huygens and Leibnitz, definitely gave warning against attempts to see in Newton's law the solution of the problem of action through empty space, and regarded this law merely as a *formula for calculation.* Nevertheless the tremendous achievements of physics and astronomy attained through the application of Newton's law caused scientists to forget this warning, and the opinion was gradually established that Newton had discovered the force of attraction.

Prof. Chwolson writes in his *Text-book of Physics* (Vol. I, pp. 181, 182, 183):

The term " actio in distans," that is, " action at a distance," designates one of the most harmful doctrines that ever prevailed in physics and retarded its progress; this doctrine admitted the possibility of immediate action by one object on another object at a certain distance from it, at a distance so great as to make immediate contact between the two impossible.

In the first half of the 19th century the idea of action at a distance reigned supreme in science. Faraday was the first to point out the impossibility of the admission that a body should *without mediation* excite forces and produce motion at a point where that body is not situated. Leaving aside the question of universal gravitation, he turned his special attention to magnetic and electric phenomena and pointed out the supremely important part played in these phenomena by the *intervening medium* which fills the space between the bodies that appear to act upon one another without mediation. . . .

At the present time the conviction that action at a distance should not be admitted in any domain of physical phenomena has obtained universal recognition.

But the old physics was able to abandon action at a distance only after it had accepted the hypothesis of the *universal medium* or æther. The acceptance of that hypothesis was equally necessary for the theories of light and electric phenomena as they were understood by old physics.

In the 18th century phenomena of light were explained by the hypothesis of emission put forward by Newton in 1704. This hypothesis assumed that luminous bodies emit in all directions minute particles of a special light-substance which travel through space with tremendous velocity and, entering the eye, produce in it the impression of light. In this hypothesis Newton developed the ideas of the ancients. In Plato the expression, " light filled my eyes," is often found.

Later, mainly in the 19th century, when the attention of investigators was drawn to those results of the phenomena of light which could not be explained on the hypothesis of emission, another hypothesis obtained wide recognition, namely, the hypothesis of undulatory vibrations in æther. This hypothesis was first advanced by the Dutch physicist Huygens in 1690, but for a long time it was not accepted by science. Later on, investigations of the phenomena of diffraction definitely turned the scale in favour of the hypothesis of light waves as against the hypothesis of emission; and the subsequent work of physicists, mainly on the polarisation of light, for a time gained general recognition for this hypothesis.

In this hypothesis the phenomena of light are explained as analogous to the phenomena of sound. Just as sound results from the vibration of particles of the sonant body and is propagated through the vibration of particles of the air or some other elastic medium, so, on this hypothesis, light results from the vibration of molecules of the luminous body and is propagated by means of vibrations in an exceedingly elastic æther which fills both interstellar space and the space between molecules.

During the 19th century the theory of vibrations gradually became the basis of the whole of physics. Electricity, magnetism, heat, light, even *life* and *thought* (purely dialectically, it is true), were explained by the theory of vibrations. And it cannot be denied that in the case of the phenomena of light and electro-magnetics the theory of vibrations gave remarkably convenient and simple formulæ for calculation. A whole series of remarkable discoveries and inventions was made on the basis of the theory of vibrations.

But the theory of vibrations required æther. Æther as a hypothesis was created for the explanation of very heterogeneous phenomena, and it was therefore endowed with strange and contradictory properties. It is omnipresent, it fills the whole universe, pervades all its points, all atoms and all interatomic space. It is continuous, it possesses perfect elasticity. Yet æther is so rarefied, thin and permeable that all earthly and heavenly bodies pass through it without meeting with perceptible resistance to their movement. Its rarity is so great that if æther were to be condensed into a liquid, the whole of its mass within the limits of the system of the Milky Way could be contained in one cubic centimetre.

At the same time Sir Oliver Lodge considers the density of æther to be approximately a *billion times* greater than the density of water. From the latter point of view the world proves to be composed of a solid substance — " æther " — which is millions of times denser than a diamond; and matter, even the densest matter we know, is merely *empty space*, a bubble in the mass of æther.

Many attempts have been made to prove the existence of æther or to discover facts confirming its existence.

Thus it was recognised that the existence of æther would be established if it were once proved that a ray of light moving faster than another ray of light changes its character in a certain way.

It is a known fact that the pitch of a sound rises or falls as the hearer approaches or retreats from it (Doppler's principle). Theoretically this principle was considered applicable to light. This would have meant that a swiftly approaching or retreating object should change its colour (as the sound of an engine-whistle changes its pitch as it approaches or retreats). But owing to the structure of the eye and the speed of its perception it was impossible to expect that the eye would notice the change of colour even if such a change actually took place.

In order to establish the fact of the change of colour it was necessary to have recourse to the spectroscope, that is, to decompose a ray of light and observe every colour of the spectrum separately.

These experiments gave no positive results whatever and to prove the existence of the æther by them was not possible.

In order to settle once and for all the question of the existence or the non-existence of the æther the American scientists Michelson and Morley, in the middle eighties of the last century, began a whole series of experiments assisted by special apparatus invented by themselves.[5]

The apparatus was mounted on a stone slab fixed upon a wooden float revolving in a tank filled with mercury, and made one full revolution in six minutes. A ray of light from a special lamp fell on mirrors attached to the revolving float and partly passed through them and partly was reflected, one half going in the direction of the movement of the earth and the other at right angles to it. This means that in accordance with the plan of the experiment one half of the ray moved with the normal speed of light and the other with the speed of light *plus* the speed of the rotation of the earth. At the union of the divided ray, there should have appeared, according to the plan of the experiment, certain light phenomena resulting from a difference in speed and showing the relative movement between the earth and the æther, that is, indirectly proving the existence of the æther.

Observations were made over a long period at all times of the day and night, and nothing was discovered.

From the standpoint of the original problem it was necessary to recognise that the experiment failed. But it disclosed another phenomenon, possibly much more significant than that which it attempted to establish. This was the fact that the speed of a ray of light cannot be increased. The ray of light moving with the earth differed in no way from the ray of light moving at right angles to the direction of the movement of the earth in its orbit.

It was necessary to recognise as *a law* that the velocity of a ray of light is a constant and limiting quantity, which cannot be increased. And this, in its turn, explained why Doppler's principle was inapplicable to phenomena of light. At the same time it established the fact that the general law of the composition of velocities, which was the basis of mechanics, could not be applied to the velocity of light.

In his book on relativity, Prof. Einstein explains that if we imagine a

---

[5] For the detailed description of the experiment of Michelson and Morley, see the *American Journal of Science* (Third Series), 1887, Vol. 34, pp. 333 *et seq.*

train moving at the rate of 30 kilometres a second, i.e. with the velocity of the movement of the earth, and a ray of light overtaking or meeting it, then the composition of velocities will in this case be impossible. The velocity of light will not be increased by the addition to it of the velocity of the train and will not be decreased by the subtraction from it of the velocity of the train.

At the same time it was established that no existing instruments or means of observation can *intercept a moving ray*. In other words, it is never possible to catch the end of a ray which has not yet reached its destination. In theory we may speak of rays which have not yet reached a certain point, but in practice we are unable to observe such rays. Consequently, for us, with our means of observation, the propagation of light is virtually instantaneous.

At the same time the physicists who analysed the results of the Michelson-Morley experiment explained its failure by the presence of new and unknown phenomena resulting from great velocities.

The first attempts to solve this question were made by Lorentz and Fitzgerald. *The experiment could not succeed,* was Lorentz's formulation of his propositions, for every body moving in æther *itself* undergoes deformation, namely, for an observer at rest it contracts in the direction of the motion. Basing his reasonings on the fundamental laws of mechanics and physics, he showed by means of a series of mathematical constructions that the Michelson-Morley installation necessarily suffered a contraction and that the amount of the contraction was exactly such as to counterbalance the displacement of the light waves consequent upon their direction in space, and thus to annul the results of the difference in velocity of the two rays.

Lorentz's conclusions as to the presumed contraction of a moving body gave rise in their turn to many explanations, and one of these explanations was put forward from the point of view of Prof. Einstein's special principle of relativity.

But this relates to the new physics.

The old physics was indissolubly connected with the theory of vibrations.

The new theory, which came to replace the mechanical theory of vibrations, was the theory of the atomic structure of light and electricity, taken as independently existing matters composed of *quanta*.

The new teaching, says Prof. Chwolson,[6] appears to be a return to the Newtonian emission theory although considerably altered. This new teaching is far from being completed. And its most important part, the *quantum* itself, still remains undefined. What a quantum is cannot be defined by new physics.

The theory of the atomic structure of light and electricity entirely altered the view on electrical and light phenomena. Science has ceased to see the fundamental cause of electrical phenomena in special states of æther and

---
[6] Vol. I, p. 9.

has returned to the old doctrine which admitted electricity to be a kind of substance which has real existence.

The same thing has happened with light. According to modern theories, light is a stream of minute particles rushing through space at the rate of 300,000 kilometres a second. They are not the corpuscles of Newton, but a special kind of *matter-energy*, formed by electro-magnetic vortices.

The materiality of the light stream was established by the experiments of Prof. Lebedeff of Moscow. Prof. Lebedeff proved that light has weight, that is to say, that light when falling on bodies produces a mechanical pressure on them. It is characteristic that at the beginning of his experiments to determine the weight of light Prof. Lebedeff based them on the theory of the vibrations of the æther. This shows how the old physics confuted itself.

Prof. Lebedeff's discovery was very important for astronomy; for instance it explained certain phenomena which had been observed at the passing of the tail of a comet near the sun. But it was chiefly important for physics, as it supplied a further confirmation of the unity of the structure of radiant energy.

The impossibility of proving the existence of the æther, the establishment of the limiting and constant velocity of light, new theories of light and electricity and, above all, the study of the structure of the atom, indicated the most interesting lines of the development of the new physics.

Another part of new physics has developed from that particular formation of physics which was called mathematical physics. According to the definition which was given to it, mathematical physics usually started from some fact confirmed by experiment and expressing a certain orderly connection between phenomena. It enveloped this connection in a mathematical form and further, as it were, transformed itself almost into pure mathematics and began to elaborate, exclusively by means of mathematical analysis, those consequences which followed from the basic proposition (Chwolson).

Thus it is presumed that the success or unsuccess of the conclusions of mathematical physics might depend upon three factors: first, on the correctness of the definition of the fundamental fact, second, on the correctness of its mathematical expression, and third, on the correctness of the subsequent mathematical analysis.

There was a time when the importance of mathematical physics was greatly exaggerated, writes Prof. Chwolson (Vol. I, p. 13).

It was expected that it was precisely mathematical physics which should have served the principal course of the development of physics as a science. This, however, is quite erroneous. In the deductions of mathematical physics there are a great number of essential defects. In the first place, in almost every case it is only in the first rough approximation that they correspond with the results of direct observation. This is caused by the fact that the premises of mathematical physics can be considered sufficiently exact only within the narrowest limits: moreover these premises generally disregard a whole series of collateral circumstances the influence of which outside these narrow limits cannot be neglected. Therefore, the deductions of mathematical physics correspond to ideal cases, which cannot be practically realised and are often far removed from actuality.

And further:

It should be added that the methods of mathematical physics make it possible to solve special problems in hardly any but the simplest cases, especially so far as the *form* of the body is concerned. But practical physics cannot limit itself to these cases and is continually faced with problems which mathematical physics is incapable of solving. Moreover the results of the deductions of mathematical physics are often so complicated that their practical application proves to be impossible.

In addition to this should be mentioned yet another very characteristic property of mathematical physics, namely, that as a rule its deductions cannot be formulated otherwise than mathematically, and lose all their meaning and importance if an attempt be made to interpret them in the language of facts.

The new physics which developed from mathematical physics possesses many of the properties of the latter.

Prof. Einstein's theory of relativity is a separate chapter in new physics, which has developed from mathematical physics. It is wrong to identify the theory of relativity with new physics as is done by some followers of Prof. Einstein. New physics can exist without the theory of relativity. But for us, from the standpoint of the construction of a model of the universe, the theory of relativity is of great interest because it deals before anything else with the fundamental question of the form of the world.

There exists an enormous literature devoted to the exposition, explanation, popularisation, criticism and elaboration of the principles of Einstein, but, owing to the close relationship between the theory of relativity and mathematical physics, deductions from this theory are difficult to formulate logically. And the fact must be accepted that neither Prof. Einstein himself nor any of his numerous followers and interpreters have succeeded in explaining the meaning and essence of his theories in a clear and comprehensible way.

One of the first reasons for this fact is pointed out by Mr. Bertrand Russell in his popular book, *The A B C of Relativity*. He writes that the name "the theory of relativity" misleads people, and that a tendency to prove that *everything is relative* is generally ascribed to Prof. Einstein, while in reality he endeavours to discover and establish *that which is not relative*. And it would be still more correct to say that Prof. Einstein endeavours to establish the relation between what is relative and what is not relative.

Further Prof. Chwolson, in his *Text-book of Physics*, writes of the theory of relativity (Vol. V, p. 350):

The foremost place in Einstein's theory of relativity is occupied by a perfectly new and, at first glance, incomprehensibly strange conception of time. Much effort and prolonged work on oneself are needed to become used to it. But it is infinitely more difficult to accept the numerous consequences which follow from the principle of relativity and affect all branches of physics without exception. Many of these consequences obviously contradict what is usually, though often without adequate motive, called " common sense." Some of these may be called the paradoxes of the new doctrine.

Einstein's ideas about time may be formulated as follows:

Each of two systems moving relatively to each other has in fact its own time, perceived and measured by an observer moving with the particular system.

The concept of simultaneity in the general sense does not exist. Two events which occur at different places may appear simultaneous to an observer at one point, whereas for an observer at another point they may occur at different times. It is possible that for the first observer the same phenomenon may occur earlier, and for the second, later (Chwolson).

Further, of the ideas of Prof. Einstein, Prof. Chwolson singles out the following:

The æther does not exist.

The concept of space, taken separately, has no meaning whatever. Only co-existence of space and time makes reality.

Energy possesses inert mass. Energy is an analogue of matter, and the transformation of what we call the mass of ponderable matter into the mass of energy, and vice versa, is possible.

It is necessary to distinguish the geometrical form of a body from its kinetic form.

The last points to a definite connection between Einstein's theory and the supposition of Fitzgerald and Lorentz as to the lengthwise contraction of moving bodies. Einstein accepts this supposition, although he says that he bases it on other principles than those of Fitzgerald and Lorentz, namely, on the special principle of relativity. At the same time the theory of the lengthwise contraction of bodies, deduced not from facts but from Lorentz's transformations, becomes the necessary foundation of the theory of relativity.

In making use exclusively of Lorentz's transformations, Einstein affirms that a rigid rod moving in the direction of its length is shorter than the same rod when it is in a state of rest, and the more quickly such a rod moves, the shorter it becomes. A rod moving with the velocity of light would lose its third dimension. It would become a cross-section of itself.

Lorentz himself affirmed that an electron actually disappeared when moving with the velocity of light.

These affirmations cannot be proved, since the contractions, even if they really occur, are too negligible with all possible velocities. A body moving with the velocity of the earth, i.e. 30 kilometres a second, must, according to the calculations of Lorentz and Einstein, undergo contraction by $\frac{1}{200,000}$ of its length; that is, a body 200 metres long would contract by 1 millimetre.

Further it is interesting to note that the supposition as to the *contraction of a moving body* radically contradicts the principle established by new physics, of the *increment of energy and mass in the moving body*. This latter principle is perfectly correct, although it has remained unelaborated.

As will be seen later, this principle, in its full meaning, which had not yet been revealed in new physics, is one of the foundations of the new model of the universe.

Passing to Einstein's own exposition of his fundamental theory, we see that it consists of two " principles of relativity," the " special principle " and the " general principle."

The "special principle of relativity" is supposed to establish the possibility of examining together and on the basis of a general law facts of the general relativity of motion which appear from the ordinary point of view to be contradictory, or to speak more accurately, the fact that all velocities are relative and that at the same time the velocity of light is non-relative, limiting and "maximal." Einstein finds a way out of the difficulty created by all this, first: by understanding time itself, according to the formula of Minkovsky, as an imaginary quantity resulting from the relation of the given velocity to the velocity of light; second: by making a whole series of altogether arbitrary assumptions on the border line of physics and geometry; and third: by replacing direct investigations of physical phenomena and observations of their correlations by purely mathematical operations with Lorentz's transformations, the results of which show, in his opinion, the laws governing physical phenomena.

The "general principle of relativity" is introduced where it becomes necessary to make the idea of the infinity of space-time agree with the laws of the density of matter and the laws of gravitation in the space accessible to observation.

To put it briefly, the " special " and the " general " principles of relativity are necessary for agreement between contradictory theories on the border line of old and new physics.

The fundamental tendency of Einstein is to regard mathematics, geometry and physics as one whole.

The principle is certainly quite correct; the three *ought to* constitute one. But " *ought to constitute* " does not mean that they *do constitute*.

The confusion of these two concepts is the chief defect of the theories of relativity.

In his book *The Theory of Relativity* Prof. Einstein writes:

Space is a three-dimensional continuum. . . . Similarly the world of physical phenomena which was briefly called " world " by Minkovsky is naturally four-dimensional in the space-time sense. For it is composed of individual events, each of which is described by four numbers, namely, three space-coordinates and a time-coordinate. . . .

That we have not been accustomed to regard the world in this sense as a four-dimensional continuum is due to the fact that in physics, before the advent of the theory of relativity, time played a different and more independent rôle, as compared with the space-coordinates. It is for this reason that we have been in the habit of treating time as an independent continuum. As a matter of fact, according to classical mechanics, time is absolute, i.e., it is independent of the position and the condition of motion of the system of coordinates. . . .

The four-dimensional mode of consideration of the "world" is natural on the theory of relativity, since according to this theory time is robbed of its independence.

. . . .

But the discovery of Minkovsky which was of importance for the formal development of the theory of relativity, does not lie here. It is to be found rather in the fact of his recognition that the four-dimensional space-time continuum of the theory of relativity, in its most essential formal properties, shows a pronounced relationship to the three-dimensional continuum of Euclidean geometrical space. In order to give due prominence to this relationship, however, we must replace the usual time coordinate t by an imaginary magnitude $\sqrt{-1}$. ct proportional to it. Under these conditions the natural laws satisfying the demands of the (special) theory of relativity assume mathematical forms, in which the time-coordinate plays exactly the same rôle as the three space-coordinates. Formally these four coordinates correspond exactly to the space-coordinates in Euclidean geometry.[7]

The formula $\sqrt{-1}$. ct means that the time of every event is taken not simply by itself, but as an imaginary quantity in relation to the velocity of light, i.e. that a purely physical concept is introduced into the presumed "meta-geometrical" expression.

The time-duration t is multiplied by the velocity of light c and by the square root of minus one, $\sqrt{-1}$, which without changing the magnitude makes it an imaginary quantity.

This is quite clear. But what is necessary to note in relation to the passage quoted above is that Einstein regards Minkovsky's "world" as a development of the theory of relativity, whereas in reality the special principle of relativity *is built on the theory of Minkovsky*. If we suppose that the theory of Minkovsky is derived from the principle of relativity, then again, just as in the case of the theory of Fitzgerald and Lorentz relating to the lengthwise contraction of moving bodies, *it remains incomprehensible on what basis the principle of relativity is actually built.*

In any case, the building of the principle of relativity requires specially prepared material.

---

[7] A. Einstein, *Relativity, the Special and the General Theory.* Translated by R. W. Lawson. 4th edition. Methuen & Co., London, pp. 55, 56, 57.

In the very beginning of his book Prof. Einstein writes that in order to make certain deductions from the observation of physical phenomena agree with one another it is necessary to revise certain *geometrical* concepts. " Geometry " means " land measuring," he writes.[8] " Both mathematics and geometry owe their origin to the need to know something of the properties of real things." On the basis of this, Prof. Einstein considers it possible to " supplement geometry," that is, for instance, to replace the concept of *straight lines* by the concept of *rigid rods*. Rigid rods are subject to changes under the influence of temperature, pressure, etc.; they can expand and contract. All this must of course greatly alter " geometry."

Geometry which has been supplemented in this way is obviously a natural science, says Einstein, and is to be treated as a branch of physics.[9]

I attach special importance to the view on geometry expounded here, because without it it would have been impossible to construct the theory of relativity.[10]

. . . .

Euclidean geometry must be abandoned.[10]

The next important point in Einstein's theory is his justification of the mathematical method that he applies.

Experience has led to the conviction, he says, that, on the one hand, the principle of relativity (in the restricted sense) [11] holds true, and that on the other hand the velocity of the transmission of light in vacuo has to be considered to be a constant (*Relativity*, p. 42).

According to Prof. Einstein, the combination of these two propositions supplies the law of transformations for the four coordinates determining the place and the time of an event.

He writes:

Every general law of nature must be so constituted that it is transformed into a law of exactly the same form when, instead of the space-time variables of the original coordinate system, we introduce new space-time variables of another co-ordinate system. In this connection the mathematical relation between the magnitudes of the first order and the magnitudes of the second order is given by the Lorentz transformation. Or, in brief: General Laws of nature are co-variant with respect to Lorentz transformations (p. 42).

Einstein's assertion that the laws of nature are co-variant with Lorentz's transformations is the clearest illustration of his position. Starting from this point he considers it possible to ascribe to phenomena the changes which he finds in the transformations. This is precisely the method of

---

[8] *On the Physical Nature of Space.*
[9] Ibid.
[10] Ibid.
[11] I.e. the principle of the relativity of velocities in classical mechanics.

mathematical physics which was condemned long ago, and which is mentioned by Prof. Chwolson in the passage quoted above.

In *The Theory of Relativity*, there is a chapter under the title " Experience and the Special Theory of Relativity."

To what extent is the special theory of relativity supported by experience? This question is not easily answered, writes Prof. Einstein (p. 49).

.   .   .   .

The special theory of relativity has crystallised out from the Maxwell-Lorentz theory of electro-magnetic phenomena. Thus all facts of experience which support the electro-magnetic theory also support the theory of relativity (p. 49).

Prof. Einstein feels very acutely the necessity of facts for establishing his theories on firm ground. But he succeeds in finding these facts only in respect of invisible quantities — electrons and ions.

He writes:

Classical mechanics required to be modified before it could come into line with the demands of the special theory of relativity. For the main part, however, this modification affects only the laws for rapid motions, in which the velocities of matter are not very small as compared with the velocity of light. We have experience of such rapid motions only in the case of electrons and ions; for other motions the variations from the laws of classical mechanics are too small to make themselves evident in practice (p. 44).

Passing to the general theory of relativity, Prof. Einstein writes:

The classical principle of relativity, relating to three-dimensional space with the coordinate of time *t* (a real quantity) is violated by the fact of the constant velocity of light.

But the fact of the constant velocity of light is violated by the curvature of a ray of light in gravitational fields. This requires a new theory of relativity and a space, determined by Gaussian coordinates, applicable to non-Euclidean continua.

Gaussian coordinates differ from the Cartesian by the fact that they can be applied to any kind of space, independently of the properties of that space. They adapt themselves automatically to any space, whereas the Cartesian coordinates require a space of special definite properties, i.e. geometrical space.

In continuing the comparison of the special and the general theories of relativity Prof. Einstein writes:

The special theory of relativity has reference to domains in which no gravitational field exists. In this connection a rigid body in the state of motion serves as a body of reference, i.e. a rigid body the state of motion of which is so chosen that the proposition of the uniform rectilinear motion of " isolated " material points holds relatively to it (p. 98).

In order to make clear the principles of the general theory of relativity, Einstein takes the space-time domain as a disc uniformly rotating round its centre on its own plane. An observer situated on this disc regards the disc as being " at rest." He regards the force acting upon him, and generally upon all bodies which are at rest in relation to the disc, as the action of the gravitational field.

The observer performs experiments on his circular disc with clocks and measuring-rods. In doing so, it is his intention to arrive at exact definitions for the signification of time and space data with reference to the circular disc.

To start with, he places one of two identically constructed clocks at the centre of the circular disc, and the other on the edge of the disc, so that they are at rest relative to it (p. 80).

. . . .

Thus on our circular disc, or, to make the case more general, in every gravitational field, a clock will go more quickly or less quickly, according to the position in which the clock is situated (at rest). For this reason it is not possible to obtain a reasonable definition of time with the aid of clocks which are arranged at rest with respect to the body of reference. A similar difficulty presents itself when we attempt to apply our earlier definition of simultaneity in such a case (p. 81).

. . . .

The definition of the space coordinates also presents insurmountable difficulties. If the observer (moving with the disc) applies his standard measuring-rod (a rod which is short as compared with the radius of the disc) tangentially to the edge of the disc, then, . . . the length of this rod will be less since moving bodies suffer a shortening in the direction of the motion. On the other hand, the measuring-rod will not experience a shortening in length, if it is applied to the disc in the direction of the radius (p. 81).

. . . .

For this reason non-rigid (elastic) reference-bodies are used, which are as a whole not only moving in any way whatsoever, but which also suffer alterations in form *ad lib.* during their motion. Clocks, for which the law of motion is of any kind, however irregular, serve for the definition of time. We have to imagine each of these clocks fixed at a point on the non-rigid (elastic) reference-body. These clocks satisfy only the one condition, that the " readings " which are observed simultaneously on adjacent clocks (in space) differ from each other by an infinitely small amount. This non-rigid (elastic) reference-body which might appropriately be termed a " reference-mollusc," is in the main equivalent to a Gaussian four-dimensional coordinate system chosen arbitrarily. That which gives the " mollusc " a certain comprehensibleness as compared with the Gauss coordinate system is the (really unjustified) formal retention of the separate existence of the space-coordinates as opposed to the time-coordinate. Every point of the mollusc is treated as a space-point, and every material point which is at rest relatively to it as at rest, so long as the mollusc is considered as reference-body. The general principle of relativity requires that all these molluscs can be used as reference-bodies with equal right and equal success in the formulation of the general laws of nature; the laws themselves must be quite independent of the choice of molluscs (p. 99).

In respect of the fundamental question as to the form of the world Einstein writes:

If we ponder over the question as to how the universe, considered as a whole, is to be regarded, the first answer that suggests itself is surely this: As regards space (and time) the universe is infinite. There are stars everywhere, so that the density of matter, although very variable in detail, is nevertheless on the average everywhere the same. In other words: However far we might travel through space, we should find everywhere an attenuated swarm of fixed stars of approximately the same kind and density (p. 105).

This view is not in harmony with the theory of Newton. The latter theory rather requires that the universe should have a kind of centre in which the density of the stars is a maximum, and that as we proceed outwards from this centre the group-density of the stars should diminish, until finally, at great distances, it is succeeded by an infinite region of emptiness. The stellar universe ought to be a finite island in the infinite ocean of space (pp. 105, 106).

The reason why an unbounded universe is impossible is that, according to the theory of Newton, the intensity of the gravitational field at the surface of a sphere filled with matter, even if this matter is of a very small density, would increase with increasing radius of the sphere, and would ultimately become infinite, which is impossible (p. 106).

The development of non-Euclidean geometry led to the recognition of the fact, that we can cast doubt on the infiniteness of our space without coming into conflict with the laws of thought or with experience (p. 108).

Admitting the possibility of similar conclusions Einstein describes the world of two-dimensional beings on a spherical surface.

In contrast to ours, the universe of these beings is two-dimensional; but, like ours, it extends to infinity (p. 108).

This surface of the world of two-dimensional beings would constitute " space " for them. This space would possess very strange properties. If the spherical-surface beings were to draw circles in their " space," that is, on the surface of their sphere, these circles would increase up to a certain limit, and would then *begin to decrease*.

The universe of these beings is finite and yet has no limits (p. 109).

Einstein comes to the conclusion that the spherical-surface beings would be able to determine that they are living on a sphere and might even find the radius of this sphere if they were able to examine a sufficiently great part of the surface.

But if this part is very small indeed, they will no longer be able to demonstrate that they are on a spherical " world " and not on a Euclidean plane, for a small part of a spherical surface differs only slightly from a piece of a plane of the same size (p. 110).

Thus if the spherical-surface beings are living on a planet of which the solar system occupies only a negligibly small part of the spherical universe, they have no means of determining whether they are living in a finite or an infinite universe, because the " piece of universe " to which they have access is in both cases practically plane, or Euclidean (p. 110).

. . . .

To this two-dimensional sphere-universe there is a three-dimensional analogy, namely, the three-dimensional spherical space which was discovered by Riemann. Its points are likewise all equivalent. It possesses a finite volume which is determined by its " radius " (p. 111).

It is easily seen that the three-dimensional spherical space is quite analogous to the two-dimensional spherical surface. It is finite (that is of finite volume) and has no bounds (p. 112).

It may be mentioned that there is yet another kind of curved space, " elliptical space." It can be regarded as a curved space in which the two " counterparts " are identical. . . . An elliptical universe can thus be considered to some extent as a curved universe possessing central symmetry (p. 112).

It follows from what has been said, that closed spaces without limits are conceivable. From amongst these, the spherical space (and the elliptical) excels in its simplicity, since all points in it are equivalent. As a result of this discussion, a most interesting question arises for astronomers and physicists, and that is whether the universe in which we live is infinite, or whether it is finite in the manner of the spherical universe. Our experience is far from being sufficient to enable us to answer this question. But the general theory of relativity permits of our answering it with a moderate degree of certainty, and in this connection the difficulty mentioned earlier (from the point of view of the Newtonian theory) finds its solution (p. 112).

The structure of space according to the general theory of relativity differs from that generally recognised.

According to the general theory of relativity, the geometrical properties of space are not independent, but they are determined by matter. Thus we can draw conclusions about the geometrical structure of the universe only if we base our considerations on the state of the matter as being something that is known. We know from experience that . . . the velocities of the stars are small as compared with the velocity of transmission of light. We can thus as a rough approximation arrive at a conclusion as to the nature of the universe as a whole, if we treat the matter as being at rest (p. 113).

. . . .

We might imagine that as regards geometry, our universe behaves analogously to a surface which is irregularly curved in its individual parts, but which nowhere departs appreciably from a plane: something like the rippled surface of a lake. Such a universe might fittingly be called a quasi-Euclidean universe. As regards its space it would be infinite. But calculation shows that in a quasi-Euclidean universe the average density of matter would necessarily be nil. Thus such a universe could not be inhabited by matter everywhere: it would present to us an unsatisfactory picture (p. 114).

If we are to have in the universe an average density of matter which differs from zero, however small may be that difference, then the universe cannot be quasi-Euclidean. On the contrary the results of calculation indicate that if matter be distributed uniformly, the universe would necessarily be spherical (or elliptical). Since in reality the detailed distribution of matter is not uniform, the real universe will deviate in individual parts from the spherical, i.e. the universe will be quasi-spherical. But it will be necessarily finite. In fact, the theory supplies us with a simple connection between the space-expanse of the universe and the average density of matter in it (p. 114).

The last proposition is treated in a somewhat different manner by Prof. A. S. Eddington in his book: *Space, Time and Gravitation.*

After mass and energy there is one physical quantity which plays a very fundamental part in modern physics, known as *Action.*[12] *Action* here is a very technical term, and is not to be confused with Newton's "Action and Reaction." In the relativity theory in particular this seems in many respects to be the most fundamental thing of all. The reason is not difficult to see. If we wish to speak of the continuous matter present *at* any particular point of space and time, we must use the term *density. Density multiplied by volume in space gives us mass,* or what appears to be the same thing, *energy.* But from our space-time point of view, a far more important thing is density multiplied by a four-dimensional volume of space and time; this is *action.* The multiplication by three dimensions gives mass or energy; and the fourth multiplication gives mass or energy multiplied by time. Action is thus mass multiplied by time, or energy multiplied by time, and is more fundamental than either.

Action is the curvature of the world. It is scarcely possible to visualize this statement, because our notion of curvature is derived from surfaces of two dimensions in a three-dimensional space, and this gives too limited an idea of the possibilities of a four-dimensional surface in space of five or more dimensions. In two dimensions there is just one total curvature and if that vanishes the surface is flat or at least can be unrolled into a plane.

. . . .

Wherever there is matter there is action and therefore curvature; and it is interesting to notice that in ordinary matter the curvature of the space-time world is by no means insignificant. For example, in water of ordinary density the curvature is the same as that of space in the form of a sphere of radius 570,-000,000 kilometres. The result is even more surprising if expressed in time units; the radius is about half an hour.

It is difficult to picture quite what this means; but at least we can predict that a globe of water of 570,000,000 km. radius would have extraordinary properties. Presumably there must be an upper limit to the possible size of a globe of water. So far as I can make out a homogeneous mass of water of about this size (and no larger) could exist. It would have no centre, and no boundary, every point of it being in the same position with respect to the whole mass as every other point of it — like points on the *surface* of a sphere with respect to the surface. Any ray of light after travelling for an hour or two would come back to the starting point. Nothing could enter or leave the mass, because there is no boundary to enter or leave by; in fact it is co-extensive with space. There could

---

[12] Action is determined as energy multiplied by time (Chwolson).

be no other world anywhere else, because there isn't an " anywhere else " (pp. 147, 148).

An exposition of the theories of new physics which stand apart from " relativity " would take too much space. The study of the structure of light and electricity, the study of the atom (the theories of Bohr), and especially the study of the electron (the quantum theory), lead physics along entirely right lines, and if physics really succeeded in freeing itself from the above-mentioned impediments, which arrest its progress, and also from unnecessarily paradoxical theories of relativism, it would some day discover that it knows much more about the true nature of things than might be supposed.

OLD PHYSICS

Geometrical conception of space, that is, consideration of space apart from time. Conception of space as emptiness in which there may or may not be " bodies."

One time for all that exists. Time measurable on one scale.

Aristotle's principle of the constancy and unity of laws in the whole universe, and, as deduction from this principle, confidence in immutability of recognised phenomena.

Elementary understanding of measure, measurability and incommensurability. Measures taken for everything from outside.

Recognition of a whole series of concepts, difficult to define, such as time, velocity, etc., as primary concepts requiring no definition.

Law of gravitation or attraction and extension of this law to phenomena of falling (weight).

" Universe of flying balls," both in celestial space and inside atom.

Theories of vibrations, undulatory movements, etc.

Tendency to interpret all phenomena of radiant energy by undulatory vibrations.

Necessity of hypothesis of " æther " in some form or another. Æther as substance of greatest density, and " æther " as substance of greatest rarity.

NEW PHYSICS

Attempts to escape from three-dimensional space by means of mathematics and metageometry. Four coordinates.

Study of the structure of matter and of radiant energy. Study of the atom. Discovery of electrons.

Recognition of velocity of light as limiting velocity. Velocity of light as universal constant.

Definition of fourth coordinate in connection with velocity of light. Time as imaginary quantity. Minkovsky. Recognition of necessity for taking time together with space. Space-time four-dimensional continuum.

New ideas in mechanics. Recognition of possible incorrectness of principle of conservation of energy. Recognition of possible transformation of matter into energy and vice versa.

Attempts to build systems of absolute units of measure.

Establishment of fact of weight of light and of materiality of electricity. Principle of increase of energy and mass of body in motion.

Special and general principles of relativity; and the idea of necessity for *finite* space in connection with laws of gravitation and distribution of matter in the universe.

Curvature of space-time continuum. Unlimited, but finite universe, measurements of which are determined by density of matter which constitutes it. Spherical or elliptical space.

" Elastic " space.

New theories of structure of atom. Study of electron. Quantum theory. Study of structure of radiant energy.

II

Now having examined the principal features of both the " old " and the " new " physics, we may ask ourselves whether, on the basis of the material we possess, it is possible to predict the direction which the future development of physical knowledge will take, and whether it is possible to build from these predictions a model of the universe, the separate parts of which will not contradict and mutually destroy one another. The answer will be that it would not be difficult to build such a model, or at any rate it would be quite possible, if we had at our disposal all the necessary measurements of the universe accessible to us. A new question arises: " Have we all the necessary measurements? " And the answer must undoubtedly be: " No, we have not." Our measurements of the universe are inadequate and incomplete. In a " geometrical " three-dimensional universe this is quite clear; the world cannot be fitted into the space of three coordinates. Too many things are left out, things which cannot be measured. It is equally clear also in the " metageometrical " universe of four coordinates. The world with all its variety of phenomena does not fit into four-dimensional space, no matter how we take the fourth coordinate, whether as a quantity analogous to the first three or as an imaginary quantity determinable relatively to the ultimate physical velocity that has been found, i.e. the velocity of light.

The proof of the artificiality of the four-dimensional world in new physics lies first of all in the extreme complexity of its construction, which requires a *curved space*. It is quite clear that this *curvature* of space indicates the presence in it of yet another dimension or dimensions.

The universe of four coordinates is as unsatisfactory as the universe of three coordinates. And to be more exact we can say that we do not possess all the measurements necessary for the construction of a model of the universe, because neither the three coordinates of old physics nor the four coordinates of new physics are sufficient for the description of all the variety of phenomena in the universe; or, in other words, because we have not enough dimensions.

Let us imagine that somebody builds a model of a house, having only the floor, one wall and the roof. This will be a model corresponding to a *three-dimensional* model of the universe. It will give a general impression of the house, but only on condition that both the model itself and the observer remain motionless. The slightest movement will destroy the whole illusion.

The *four-dimensional* model of the universe of new physics is the same model, only arranged so that it rotates, turning its front always to the observer. This can prolong the illusion for some time, but only on the condition of there being not more than *one observer*. Two people observing such a model from different sides will very soon see in what the trick consists.

Before attempting to make clear without any analogies what it actually means to say that the universe does not fit into three-dimensional or four-dimensional space, and before attempting to discover what number of coordinates really determines the universe, I must eliminate one of the most essential misunderstandings which exists with regard to dimensions.

That is to say, I must repeat that there is no approach from mathematics to the study of the dimensions of space or space-time. And mathematicians who assert that the whole problem of the fourth dimension in philosophy, in psychology, in mysticism, etc., has arisen because " someone once overheard a conversation between two mathematicians on subjects they alone could understand," are greatly mistaken, whether voluntarily or involuntarily is best known to themselves.

Mathematics detaches itself easily and simply from three-dimensional physics and Euclidean geometry, because really it does not belong there at all.

It is quite wrong to think that all mathematical relations must have physical or geometrical meanings. On the contrary, only a very small and the most elementary part of mathematics has a permanent connection with geometry and with physics, and only very few geometrical and physical quantities can have permanent mathematical expression.

For us it is necessary to understand exactly that dimensions cannot be expressed mathematically and that consequently mathematics cannot serve as an instrument for the investigation of problems of space and time. Only measurements along previously agreed-upon coordinates can be expressed mathematically. It can, for instance, be said that the length of an object is

5 metres, the breadth 10 metres and the height 15 metres. But the difference between the *length*, the *breadth* and the *height* themselves cannot be expressed; mathematically they are equivalent. Mathematics *does not feel* dimensions as geometry and physics feel them. Mathematics cannot feel the difference between a point, a line, a surface and a solid. The point, the line, the surface and the solid can be expressed mathematically only by means of *powers*, that is to say, simply for the sake of designation: a, a line; a^2, a surface; a^3, a solid. But the fact is that the same designations would serve also for segments of a line of different lengths: — a, 10 metres; a^2, 100 metres; a^3, 1000 metres.

The artificiality of designating dimensions by powers becomes perfectly clear if we reason in the following way:

We assume that a is a line, a^2 is a square, a^3 is a cube, a^4 is a body of four dimensions; a^5 and a^6, as will be seen later, can be explained. But what will a^{25} mean, or a^{125}, or a^{1000}? Once we allow that dimensions correspond to powers, this will mean that powers *actually* express the dimensions. Consequently the number of dimensions must be the same as the number of powers. This would be an obvious absurdity, as the limitation of the universe in relation to number of dimensions is quite obvious, and no one would seriously assert the possibility of an infinite or even of a large number of dimensions.

Having established this point, we may note once more, though it should be quite clear already, that three coordinates are not sufficient for the description of the universe, for such a universe would contain no motion, or, putting it differently, every observable motion would immediately destroy the universe.

The fourth coordinate takes time into consideration. Space is no longer taken separately. Four-dimensional space-time allows of motion.

But motion by itself is a very complex phenomenon. At the very first approach to motion we meet with an interesting fact. Motion has in itself three clearly expressed dimensions: duration, velocity and " direction." But this direction does not lie in Euclidean space, as was assumed by old physics; it is a direction from before to after, which for us never changes and never disappears.

Time is the measure of motion. If we represent time by a line, then the only line which will satisfy all the demands of time will be a *spiral*. A spiral is a " three-dimensional line," so to speak, that is, a line which requires three coordinates for its construction and designation.

The three-dimensionality of time is completely analogous to the three-dimensionality of space. We do not measure space by *cubes*, we measure it linearly in different directions, and we do exactly the same with time, although in time we can measure only two coordinates out of three, namely the duration and the velocity; the direction of time for us is not a quantity but an absolute condition. Another difference is that in regard to space we realise that we are dealing with a three-dimensional continuum, whereas in regard to time we do not realise it. But, as has been said already, if we attempt to unite the three coordinates of time into one whole, we shall obtain a spiral.

This explains at once why the " fourth coordinate " is insufficient to describe time. Although it is admitted to be a curved line, its curvature remains undefined. Only three coordinates, or the " three-dimensional line," that is, the spiral, give an adequate description of time.

The three-dimensionality of time explains many phenomena which have hitherto remained incomprehensible, and makes unnecessary most of the elaborate hypotheses and suppositions which have been indispensable in the attempts to squeeze the universe into the boundaries of a three- or even four-dimensional continuum.

This also explains the failure of relativism to give a comprehensible form to its explanations. Excessive complexity in any construction is always the result of something having been omitted or wrongly taken at the outset. The cause of the complexity in this case lies in the above-mentioned impossibility of squeezing the universe into the boundaries of a three-dimensional or four-dimensional continuum. If we try to regard three-dimensional space as two-dimensional and to explain all physical phenomena as occurring on a surface, several further " principles of relativity " will be required.

The three dimensions of time can be regarded as the continuation of the dimensions of space, i.e. as the " fourth," the " fifth " and the " sixth " dimensions of space. A " six-dimensional " space is undoubtedly a " Euclidean continuum," but of properties and forms totally incomprehensible to us. The six-dimensional form of a body is inconceivable for us, and if we were able to apprehend it with our senses we should undoubtedly see and feel it as three-dimensional. Three-dimensionality is a function of our senses. Time is the boundary of our senses. Six-dimensional space is reality, the world as it is. This reality we perceive only through the slit of our senses, touch and vision, and define as three-dimensional space, ascribing to it Euclidean properties. Every six-dimensional body becomes for us a three-dimensional body *existing in time*, and the properties of the fifth and the sixth dimensions remain for us imperceptible.

Six dimensions constitute a " period," beyond which there can be nothing except the repetition of the same period on a different scale. The period of dimensions is limited at one end by the point, and at the other end by infinity of space multiplied by infinity of time, which in ancient symbolism was represented by two intersecting triangles, or a six-pointed star.

Just as in space one dimension, a line, or two dimensions, a surface, cannot exist by themselves and when taken separately are nothing but imaginary figures, while the *solid* exists in reality, so in time only the three-dimensional *solid of time* exists in reality.

In spite of the fact that the counting of dimensions in geometry begins with the line, actually, in the real physical sense, only the material point and the solid are objects which exist. Lines and surfaces are merely features and properties of a solid. They can also be regarded in another way: a line as the path of the motion of a point in space, and a surface as the path of the motion of a line along the direction perpendicular to it (or its rotation). The same may be applied to the solid of time. In it only the point (the moment) and the solid are real. The *moment* can change, that is, it can contract and disappear or expand and become a solid. The *solid* also can contract and become a point, or can expand and become an infinity.

The number of dimensions can neither be infinite nor very great; *it cannot be more than six.* The reason for this lies in the property of the sixth dimension which includes in itself *All Possibilities* of the given scale.

In order to understand this it is necessary to examine the content of the three dimensions of time taken in their " space " sense, that is, as the fourth, the fifth and the sixth dimensions of space.

If we take a three-dimensional body as a point, the line of the existence or motion of this point will be a line of the fourth dimension.

Let us take the line of time as we usually conceive it.

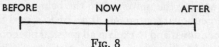

BEFORE   NOW   AFTER

FIG. 8

The line determined by the three points " before," " now," " after," is a line of the fourth dimension.

Let us imagine several lines perpendicular to this line, before-now-after. These lines, each of which designates *now* for a given moment, will express the perpetual existence of past and possibly of future moments.

NOW	NOW	NOW	NOW	NOW
1612	1712	1812	1912	2012
1612	1712	1812	1912	2012
1612	1712	1812	1912	2012
1612	1712	1812	1912	2012
NOW	NOW	NOW	NOW	NOW

BEFORE ---- 1612 ---- 1712 ---- 1812 ---- 1912 ---- 2012 ---- AFTER

FIG. 9

Each of these perpendicular lines is the *perpetual now* for some moment, and every moment has such a line of *perpetual now*.

This is the fifth dimension.

The fifth dimension forms a surface in relation to the line of time.

Everything we know, everything we recognize as existing, lies on the line of the fourth dimension; the line of the fourth dimension is the " historical time " of our section of existence. This is the only " time " we know, the only time we feel, the only time we recognise. But though we are not aware of it, sensations of the existence of other " times," both parallel and perpendicular, continually enter into our consciousness. These parallel " times " are completely analogous to our time and consist of before-now-after, whereas the perpendicular " times " consist only of now, and are, as it were, cross-threads, the *woof* in a fabric, in their relation to the parallel lines of time which in this case represent the *warp*.

But each moment of " now " on the line of time, that is, on one of the parallel lines, contains not one, but a certain number of possibilities, at times a great, at others a small number. The number of possibilities contained in every moment must necessarily be limited, for if the number of possibilities were not limited, there would be no impossibilities. Thus each moment of time, within certain limited conditions of being or physical existence, contains a definite number of possibilities and an infinite number of impossibilities. But impossibilities can also be of different kinds. If, walking through a familiar rye-field, I suddenly saw a big birch tree which was not there yesterday, it would be an impossible phenomenon (precisely the " material miracle " which is not admitted by the principle of Aristotle). But if, walking through a rye-field, I saw in the middle of it a coconut palm, this would be an impossible phenomenon of a different kind, also a " material miracle," but of a much higher or more difficult order. This difference between impossibilities should be kept in mind.

On the table before me there are many different things. I may deal with these things in different ways. But I cannot, for instance, take from the table something that is not there. I cannot take from the table an orange that is not there, just as I cannot take from it the Pyramid of Kheops or St. Isaac's Cathedral. It looks as though there was actually no difference in this respect between an orange and a pyramid, and yet there is a difference. An orange *could be* on the table, but a pyramid *could not be*. However elementary all this is, it shows that there are different degrees of impossibility.

But at present we are concerned only with possibilities. As I have already mentioned, each moment contains a definite number of possibilities. I may actualise one of the existing possibilities, that is, I may do something. I may do nothing. But whatever I do, that is, whichever of the possibilities contained in the given moment is actualised, the actualisation of this possibility will determine *the following moment of time*, the following *now*. This second moment of time will again contain a certain number of possibilities, and the actualisation of one of these possibilities will determine *the following moment of time*, the following *now*, and so on.

Thus the line of the direction of time can be defined as the line of the actualisation of one possibility out of the number of possibilities which were contained in the preceding point.

The line of this actualisation will be the line of the fourth dimension, the line of time. We visualise it as a straight line, but it would be more correct to think of it as a zigzag line.

The perpetual existence of this actualisation, the line perpendicular to the line of time, will be the line of the fifth dimension, or the line of eternity.

For the modern mind eternity is an indefinite concept. In ordinary conversational language eternity is taken as a limitless extension of time. But religious and philosophical thought put into the concept of eternity ideas which distinguish it from mere infinite extension homogeneous with finite extension. This is most clearly seen in Indian philosophy with its idea of the *Eternal Now* as the state of Brahma.

In fact, the concept of eternity in relation to time is the same as the concept of a surface in relation to a line. A surface is a quantity incommensurable with a line. Infinity for a line need not necessarily be a line without end; it may be a surface, that is an infinite number of finite lines.

Eternity can be an infinite number of finite " times."

It is difficult for us to think of " time " in the plural. Our thought is too much accustomed to the idea of one time, and though in theory the idea of the plurality of " times " is already accepted by new physics, in practice we still think of time as one and the same always and everywhere.

What will the sixth dimension be?

The sixth dimension will be the line of the actualisation of other possibilities which were contained in the preceding moment but were not actualised in " time." In every moment and at every point of the three-dimensional world there are a certain number of possibilities; in " time," that is, in the fourth dimension, one possibility is actualised every moment, and these actualised possibilities are laid out, one beside another, in the fifth dimension. The line of time, repeated infinitely in eternity, leaves at every point unactualised possibilities. But these possibilities, which have not been actualised in one time, are actualised in the sixth dimension, which is an aggregate of " all times." The lines of the fifth dimension, which run perpendicular to the line of " time," form as it were a surface. The lines of the sixth dimension, which start from every point of " time " in all possible directions, form the solid or three-dimensional continuum of time, of which we know only one dimension. We are one-dimensional beings in relation to time. Because of this we do not see parallel time or parallel times; for the same reason we do not see the angles and turns of time, but see time as a straight line.

Until now we have taken all the lines of the fourth, the fifth and the sixth dimensions as straight lines, as coordinates. But we must remember that these straight lines cannot be regarded as really existing. They are merely an imaginary system of coordinates for determining the spiral.

Generally speaking, it is impossible to establish and prove the real existence of straight lines beyond a certain definite scale and outside certain definite conditions. And even these " conditional straight lines " cease to be straight if we imagine them on a revolving body which possesses, besides, a whole series of other movements. This is quite clear as regards space lines: straight lines are nothing but imaginary coordinates which serve to measure the length, the breadth and the depth of spirals. But time lines are geometrically in no way different from space lines. The only difference lies in the fact that in space we know three dimensions and are able to establish the *spiral* character of all cosmic movements, that is, movements which we take on a sufficiently large scale. But we dare not do this as regards " time." We try to lay out the whole space of time on one line of the great time which is general for everybody and everything. But this is an illusion; general time does not exist, and each separately existing body, each separately existing " system " (or what is accepted as such), has its own time. This is recognised by new physics. But what it means and what a separate existence means is not explained by new physics.

Separate time is always a completed circle. We can think of time as a straight line only on the great straight line of the great time. If the great time does not exist, every separate time can only be a circle, that is, a closed curve. But a circle or any closed curve requires two coordinates for its definition. The circle (circumference) is a two-dimensional figure. If the second dimension of time is eternity, this means that eternity enters into every circle of time and into every moment of the circle of time. Eternity is the curvature of time. Eternity is also movement, an *eternal movement*. And if we imagine time as a circle or as any other closed curve, *eternity* will signify eternal movement along this curve, eternal repetition, eternal recurrence.

The fifth dimension is movement in the circle, repetition, recurrence. The sixth dimension is the way out of the circle. If we imagine that one end of the curve rises from the surface, we visualise the third dimension of time — the sixth dimension of space. The line of time becomes a spiral. But the spiral, of which I have spoken before, is only a very feeble approximation to the spiral of time, only its possible geometrical representation. The actual spiral of time is not analogous to any of the lines we know, for it branches off at every point. And as there can be many possibilities in every moment, so there can be many branches at every point. Our mind refuses not only to visualise, but even to think of the resulting figure in curved lines, and we should lose the direction of our thought in this impasse if *straight lines* did not come to our aid.

In this connection we can understand the meaning and purpose of the straight lines of the system of coordinates. Straight lines are not a naïveté of Euclid, as non-Euclidean geometry and the " new physics " connected with it are trying to make out. Straight lines are a concession to the weakness of our thinking apparatus, a concession thanks to which we are able to think of reality in approximate forms.

A figure of three-dimensional time will appear to us in the form of a complicated structure consisting of radii diverging from every moment of time, each of them bearing within it its own time and throwing out new radii at every point. Taken together these radii will form the three-dimensional continuum of time.

We live and think and exist on one of the lines of time. But the second and third dimensions of time, that is, the surface on which this line lies and the solid in which this surface is included, enter every moment into our life and into our consciousness, and influence our "time." When we begin to feel the three dimensions of time we call them direction, duration and velocity. But if we wish to understand the true interrelation of things even approximately, we must bear in mind the fact that direction, duration and velocity are not real dimensions, but merely the reflections of the real dimensions in our consciousness.

In thinking of the *time solid* formed by the lines of all the possibilities included in each moment, we must remember that beyond these there can be nothing.

This is the point at which we can understand the *limitedness of the infinite universe*.

As has been said before, the three dimensions of space plus the zero dimension and plus the three dimensions of time form the *period of dimensions*. It is necessary to understand the properties of this period. It includes both space and time. The period of dimensions may be taken as *space-time*, that is, the space of six dimensions or the space of the actualisation of all possibilities. Outside this space we can think only of repetitions of the period of dimensions either on the scale of zero or on the scale of infinity. But these are different spaces, which have nothing in common with the space of six dimensions and may or may not exist, without changing anything in the space of six dimensions.

The counting of dimensions in geometry begins with the line, the first dimension, and in a certain sense this is right. But both space and time have yet another, the *zero dimension* — the point or the moment. And it must be understood that any space solid, up to the *infinite sphere* of old physics, is a *point* or a *moment* when taken in time.

The zero dimension, the first, the second, the third, the fourth, the fifth and the sixth dimensions form the period of dimensions. But a " figure " of the zero dimension, a point, is *a solid of another scale*. A figure of the first dimension, a line, is infinity in relation to a point. For itself a line is a solid, but a solid of another scale than a point. For a surface, that is, for a figure of two dimensions, a line is a *point*. A surface is three-dimensional for itself, whereas for a solid it becomes a point, and so on. A line and a surface are for us only geometrical concepts, and it is incomprehensible at the first glance how they can be three-dimensional bodies for themselves. But it becomes more comprehensible if we begin with the solid which represents a really existent physical body. We know that a body is three-dimensional for itself as well as for other three-dimensional bodies of a scale near its own. It is also infinity for a surface, which is *zero* in relation to it, because no number of surfaces will make a solid. And the solid is also a point, a zero, a figure of the zero dimension, for the fourth dimension, first, because, however big it may be, a solid is a point, that is, a moment for time, and, second, because no number of solids will make time. The whole of three-dimensional space is but a moment in time. It should be understood that " lines " and " surfaces " are only names which we give to dimensions which for us lie between the point and the solid. They have no real existence for us. Our universe consists only of points and solids. A point is zero dimension, a solid is three dimensions. On another scale a solid must be taken as a time point, and on yet another scale again as a solid, but as a solid of three dimensions of *time*.

In such a simplified universe there would be no time and no motion. Time and motion are created precisely by these *incompletely perceived solids*, that is, by space and time lines and space and time surfaces. And the period of dimensions of the real universe actually consists of *seven powers of solids* (a power is of course only a name in this case). (1) A point, — the hidden solid. (2) A line, — the solid of the second power. (3) A surface, — the solid of the third power. (4) A body or a solid, — the solid of the fourth power. (5) Time, or the existence of a body or a solid in time, — the solid of the fifth power. (6) Eternity, or the existence of time, — the solid of the sixth power. (7) That for which we have no name, the " six-pointed star," or the existence of eternity, — the solid of the seventh power.

Further it should be observed that dimensions are movable, i.e. any three consecutive dimensions form either " time " or " space," and the " period " can move upwards and downwards when one degree is added above and one is taken away from below or when one degree is added below and one is taken away from above. Thus, if one dimension from " below " is added to the six dimensions we possess, then one dimension from " above " must disappear. The difficulty of understanding this eternally changing universe, which contracts and expands according to the *size of the observer* and the speed of his perception, is counterbalanced by the constancy of laws and relative positions in these changing conditions.

The " seventh dimension " is impossible, for it would be a line leading nowhere, running in a non-existent direction.

The line of impossibilities is the line of the seventh, the eighth and the other non-existent dimensions, a line which leads nowhere and comes from nowhere. No matter what strange universe we may imagine, we can never admit the real existence of a solar system in which the moon is made of green cheese. In the same way, whatever strange scientific manipulations we may think of, we cannot imagine that Prof. Einstein would really erect a pole on the Potsdamer Platz in order to measure the distance between the earth and the clouds, as he threatens to do in his book.

One could find many such examples. The whole of our life actually consists of phenomena of the " seventh dimension," that is, of phenomena of fictitious possibility, fictitious importance and fictitious value. We live in the seventh dimension and cannot escape from it. And our model of the universe can never be complete if we do not realise the place occupied in it by the " seventh dimension." But it is very difficult to realise this. We never even come near to understanding how many *non-existent* things play a rôle in our life, govern our fate and our actions. But again, as has been said before, even the non-existent and the impossible can be of different degrees — and therefore it is perfectly justifiable to speak not of the seventh dimension, but generally of *imaginary dimensions*, the number of which is also imaginary.

In order to establish with complete exactitude the necessity for regarding the world as a world of six coordinates, it is necessary to examine the fundamental concepts of physics, which have remained without definition, and see whether it is not possible to find definitions for them with the help of some of the principles we have established above.

We will deal with matter, space, motion, velocity, infinity, mass, light, etc.

We will begin with motion.

In the usual views of both the old and the new physics motion remains always the same. Distinction is made only between its properties: duration, velocity, direction in space, discontinuity, continuity, periodicity, acceleration, retardation and so on, and the characteristics of these properties are attributed to motion itself, so that motion is divided into rectilinear, curvilinear, continuous, non-continuous, accelerated, retarded, etc. The principle of the relativity of motion led to the principle of the composition of velocities, and the working out of the principle of relativity led to the denial of the possibility of the composition of velocities when " terrestrial " velocities are compared with the velocity of light. This led to many other conclusions, suppositions and hypotheses. But these do not interest us for the moment. One fact, however, must be established, namely, that the very concept " motion " is not defined. Equally " velocity " is not defined. In regard to " light," opinions of physicists diverge.

For the present it is only important for us to realise that motion is always taken as a phenomenon of one kind. There are no attempts to establish different kinds of phenomena in motion itself. And this is especially strange, because for direct observation there definitely exist four kinds of motion as four perfectly distinct phenomena.

In certain cases direct observation deceives us, for instance when it shows much non-existent motion. But phenomena themselves are one thing, and the division of them is another. In this particular case direct observation brings us to real and unquestionable facts. One cannot reason about motion without having understood the division of motion into four kinds.

These four kinds of motion are as follows:

1. *Slow motion, invisible as motion, for instance the movement of the hour-hand of a clock.*

2. *Visible motion.*

3. *Quick motion, when a point becomes a line, for instance the movement of a smouldering match waved quickly in the dark.*

4. *Motion so quick that it does not leave any visual impression, but produces definite physical effects, for instance the motion of a flying bullet.*

In order to understand the difference between the four kinds of motion let us imagine a simple experiment. Let us imagine that we are looking at a white wall at a certain distance from us on which a black point is moving, now faster, now slower, then stopping altogether.

It is possible to determine exactly when we begin to see the point move and when we cease to see it move.

We see the movement of the point *as movement* if the point covers in $\frac{1}{10}$th of a second one or two minutes of the arc of a circle, taking as the radius our distance from the wall. If the point moves more slowly it will appear to us motionless.

Let us suppose first that the point moves with the velocity of the hour-hand of a clock. Comparing its position with other, motionless, points, first, we establish the fact of the movement of the point and, second, we determine the velocity of its movement; but we do not see the movement itself.

This will be the first kind of motion, *invisible motion.*

Further, if the point moves more quickly, covering two minutes of arc or more in $\frac{1}{10}$th of a second, we see its motion as motion.

This is the second kind of motion, *visible motion.* It can be very varied in its character and cover a large scale of velocities, but when velocity is increased 4,000 to 5,000 times, and in certain cases less, it passes into the *third kind of motion.*

This means that if the point moves very fast, covering in $\frac{1}{10}$th of a second the whole field of our vision, i.e. 160° or 9,600 minutes of arc, we shall see it not as a moving point but *as a line.*

This is the third kind of motion, with a visible trace, or motion in which the moving point is transformed into a line, motion with the apparent addition of one dimension.

And, finally, if the point starts off at once with the velocity of, say, a rifle bullet, we shall not see it at all, but if the " point " possesses weight and mass, its motion may have many physical effects which we can observe and study. For instance we can hear the motion, we can see other motions aroused by the invisible motion, and so on.

This is the fourth kind of motion, motion with an invisible but perceptible trace.

These four kinds of motion are absolutely real facts upon which depend the whole form, aspect and correlation of phenomena in our universe. This is so because the distinction of the four kinds of motion is not only subjective, i.e. they differ not only in our perception, but they *differ physically* in their results and in their action on other phenomena; and above all they are different in relation to one another, and this relation is permanent.

The ideas that have been set forth here may appear very naïve to a learned physicist. — What is the eye? he would say. The eye has a strange capacity for "remembering" for about $\frac{1}{10}$th of a second what it has seen; if the point moves sufficiently fast for the *memory* of each $\frac{1}{10}$th of a second to merge with another *memory*, the result will be a line. There is no transformation of a point into a line here. It is all entirely subjective, that is, it all takes place only in us, only in our perception. In reality a moving point remains a moving point.

This is how the matter appears from the scientific point of view.

The objection is based on the supposition that we *know* that the observed phenomenon is produced by the motion of a point. But suppose we do not know? How can we ascertain it if we cannot come sufficiently near the line we observe, or arrest the motion, stop the supposed moving point?

Our eye sees a line; with a certain velocity of motion, a photographic camera will also "see" a line or a streak. The moving point is actually transformed into a line. We are quite wrong in not trusting our eye in this case. This is just a case in which our eye does not deceive us. The eye establishes an exact principle of division of velocities. The eye certainly establishes these divisions for itself, on its own level, on its own scale. And this scale may change. What will not change, for instance in connection with the distance, what will remain the same on any scale, is, first, the number of different kinds of motion — there will always be four — and next, the *interrelation* of the four velocities with their derivatives, i.e. with their results, or the interrelation of the four kinds of motion. This interrelation between the four kinds of motion creates the whole visible world. And the essence of this interrelation consists in the fact that one motion is not necessarily motion relatively to another motion, but only if the velocities which are compared do not differ greatly from one another.

Thus in the above example the visible motion of the point on the wall is *motion* in comparison both with invisible motion and with motion fast enough to form a line. But it will not be motion in relation to a flying bullet, for which it will be immobility, just as the line formed by a swiftly moving point will be a line and not motion for a slowly (invisibly) moving point. This can be formulated in the following way:

Dividing motion into four kinds, according to the above principles, we observe that motion is motion (with increased or decreased velocity) only for kinds of motion that are near one another, that is, within the limits of a definite correlation of velocities, or, to put it more precisely, within the limits of a certain definite increase or decrease of velocity, which can probably be determined exactly. More remote kinds of motion, i.e. motions with very different velocities, for instance, 4,000 or 5,000 times slower or faster than another, are for one another not motions of different velocity, but phenomena of a greater or lesser number of dimensions.

But what is velocity? What is this mysterious property of motion which exists only in middle degrees and disappears in small and large degrees, thus subtracting or adding one dimension? And what is motion itself?

Motion is an apparent phenomenon dependent upon the extension of a body in the three dimensions of time. This means that every three-dimensional body possesses also three time-dimensions which we do not see as such and which we call the properties of motion or of existence. Our mind cannot embrace time-dimensions in their entirety, there exist no concepts which would express their essence in all their variety, for all existent " time concepts " express only one side, or only one dimension, each. Therefore the extension of three-dimensional bodies in the indefinable (for us) three dimensions of time appears to us as motion with all its properties.

We stand in exactly the same position in relation to dimensions of time as animals stand in relation to the third dimension of space.

I wrote in *Tertium Organum* about the perception of the third dimension by animals. All apparent movements are real for them. A house turns about when a horse runs past it, a tree jumps into the road. Even if an animal is motionless and only examines an equally motionless object, this object begins to manifest strange movements. The animal's own body, even in the state of rest, may manifest for it many strange movements, which our bodies do not manifest for us.

Our relation to motion and especially to velocity is very similar to this. Velocity can be a property of space. The sensation of a velocity may be the sensation of the penetration into our consciousness of one of the dimensions of a higher space unknown to us.

Velocity can be regarded as an *angle*. And this at once explains all the properties of velocity and especially the fact that both great and small velocities cease to be velocities. An angle has naturally a limit both in one direction and in the other.

Let us again imagine a world of flat beings. Let us imagine these flat beings in the shape of squares with their organs of perception situated on one side of the square. Let us call this percipient side *a*.

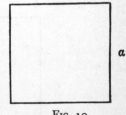

Fig. 10

Let us imagine that the " square " is turned with its percipient side towards two figures, let us say two " triangles " ABC and DEF, in the position shown in Fig. 11.

Of the triangle ABC it knows only the line AC, and this line is motionless for it. Of the triangle DEF it knows the lines DE and DF, which appear to it as one line, and these lines, which go out of the field of its vision, must undoubtedly differ from the line AC, possess some property which the line AC does not possess. The "square" will call this property *motion*.

If the "square" happens to meet the triangle GHI, the lines GH and GI will also be "motion" for it, but a slower motion.

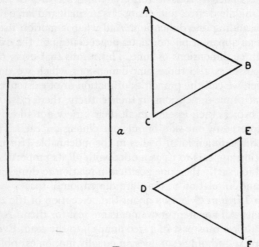

FIG. 11

And if the "square" meets the triangle JKL, the lines JK and JL will be a swifter motion.

And finally, if the "square" meets lines almost perpendicular to its percipient side, like the lines MN and MO, it will say that this is the limiting, maximal velocity and that there can be no higher velocity.

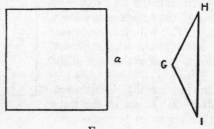

FIG. 12

The idea of velocity as an angle makes not only clear but necessary the idea of a limiting velocity beyond which there can exist no other velocity, and also the idea of the impossibility of an infinite velocity, because an angle cannot be infinite and must have a limit which can always be established and measured.

So far, in all the above examples velocity has been taken as uniform and unchangeable. But, on the basis of the same principle, it is easy to establish the meaning of acceleration, variable velocity, and so on.

Let us imagine that the receding line PQ (Fig. 15) is not a straight line but a line with an angle.

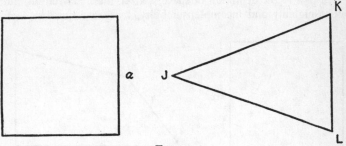

FIG. 13

The flat being in examining such a line from the point P will see this line as motion starting with one speed and then accelerating.

The line ST (Fig. 16) will appear to it as a motion alternately accelerated and retarded. And further, lines with angles, curves of different kinds, lines lying at various or changing angles to the percipient side, will represent different kinds of velocity: constant, variable, uniformly accelerated, uniformly retarded, periodically accelerated and retarded and so on.

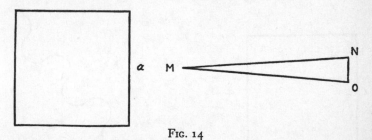

FIG. 14

The essence of all that has been said is that a line receding at an angle will appear as motion only if it lies at angles of certain definite degrees. A line lying at a very small angle to a motionless line which is parallel to the percipient side would appear motionless; at a greater angle it would appear as motion, and a line lying at an angle approaching the limit would appear something altogether different from motion. Thus " velocity " is only the property of certain definite angles, and as the angle does not depend on scale, it is quite possible that " velocity " is the only constant phenomenon in the universe.

This principle is in no way changed by the alteration of the angles on a spherical surface, or for instance on the saddle-shaped surface used by Lobatchevsky, in comparison with the angles on a flat surface, because for every kind of surface the angles will remain unchangeable.

Now, starting from the above definitions of time, motion and velocity, we shall pass to the definition of space, matter, mass, gravitation, infinity, commensurability and incommensurability, "negative quantity," etc.

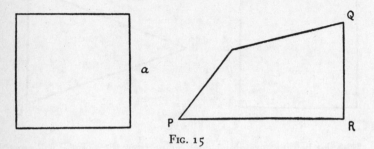

FIG. 15

As regards space, the first fact we come upon is that space is much too readily accepted as *homogeneous*. The very question of the possible heterogeneity of space never arises. And if such a question ever arose, it was only in the domain of purely mathematical speculation and never passed into conceptions of the real world from the point of view of heterogeneous space.

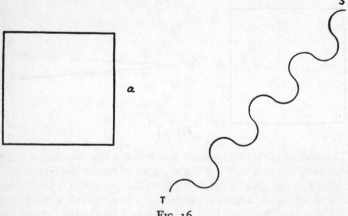

FIG. 16

Even the most complex mathematical and metageometrical views assert themselves each to the exclusion of all the others. " Spherical " space, " elliptical " space, space determined by the density of matter and by the laws of gravitation, " finite and yet limitless " space — in each case this is *the whole* of space, and in each case the whole of space is uniform and homogeneous.[13]

Of all the latest definitions of space the most interesting is the "mollusc" of Einstein. The "mollusc" anticipates many future discoveries. The "mollusc" is able to move by itself, to expand and to contract. The "mollusc" can be unequal to itself and heterogeneous with itself.

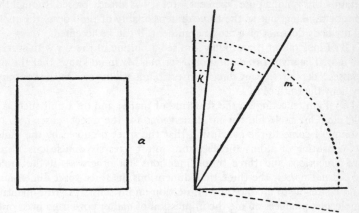

FIG. 17

Angle k — small velocity, the beginning of motion
Angle l — greater velocity, visible motion
Angle m — limiting velocity, the end of motion
Dotted line below — an impossible acceleration

But still the "mollusc" is only an analogy, only a very timid example of the way in which space can and should be regarded. And behind this example, in order to make it possible, the whole arsenal of mathematics, metageometry and new physics with the "special" and "general" principles of relativity is necessary.

[13] The present chapter in its essential features was completed in 1912. The first part was written later, but in making a survey of the present state of physics I did not try to bring it fully up to date and to mention *all* the theories that had appeared by that time, because not one of them changed anything in my principal conclusions. The most complete exposition of views on space will be found by the reader in Prof. Eddington's book, *Space, Time and Gravitation*, particularly in the chapter, "Kinds of Space." At the beginning of this chapter Prof. Eddington quotes W. K. Clifford (1845–1879) who wrote in his book, *Common Sense of the Exact Sciences:*

"The danger of asserting dogmatically that an axiom based on the experience of a limited region holds universally will now be to some extent apparent to the reader. It may lead us to entirely overlook, or when suggested at once reject, a possible explanation of phenomena. The hypothesis that space is not flat, and again that its geometrical character may change with the time, may or may not be destined to play a great part in the physics of the future; yet we cannot refuse to consider them as possible explanations of physical phenomena, because they may be opposed to the popular dogmatic belief in the universality of certain geometrical axioms — a belief which has risen from centuries of indiscriminating worship of the genius of Euclid."

This may have a connection with the idea of the heterogeneity of space.

In reality all this could be done much more simply, if only the possible heterogeneity of space were understood.

Let us take space just as we took motion, from the point of view of direct observation.

(A) The space, occupied by the house in which I live, by the room in which I am now and by my body, is perceived by me as three-dimensional. Certainly this is not a pure " percept," for it has already passed through the prism of thinking, but as the three-dimensionality of the house, the room and my body does not give rise to argument, it can be accepted.

(B) I look out of the window and see a portion of the sky with several stars in it. *The sky is two-dimensional for me*. My mind knows that the sky possesses " depth." But my direct senses do not tell me so. On the contrary, they deny the truth of it.

(C) I am reflecting on the structure of matter and on a unit such as a molecule. One molecule has no dimensions for the direct senses but, by reasoning, I come to the conclusion that the space occupied by the molecule, consisting of atoms and electrons, must have six dimensions: three space-dimensions and three time-dimensions, for otherwise, if the molecule did not possess the three time-dimensions, its three space-dimensions would be unable to produce any impression on my senses. A great quantity of molecules produces on me the impression of *matter* possessing mass only because of the six-dimensionality of the space occupied by every molecule.

Thus " space " is not homogeneous for me. The room is three-dimensional, the sky two-dimensional. The molecule has no dimension for direct perception; atoms and electrons have still less dimension, but owing to their six-dimensionality a multitude of molecules produces on me the impression of matter. If the molecules had no time-dimensions *matter* would be emptiness for me.

What has been said above must leave several points requiring explanation. First, if the molecule has *no dimension* how can atoms and electrons have *still less*? And second, how do time-dimensions affect our senses and why would not space-dimensions by themselves produce any effect on us?

In order to answer these questions it is necessary to enlarge upon the above considerations.

A star which appears to me as a twinkling point actually consists of two enormous suns each surrounded by a whole series of planets and separated by colossal distances. This twinkling point in reality occupies an enormous expanse of three-dimensional space.

Here again the objection may be raised, just as in the case of the four kinds of motion, that I take purely subjective sensations and attribute to them real meaning. And again, as in the case of the four kinds of motion, I may reply to this that what interests me is not sensations, but the interrelations of their *causes*. The causes are not subjective, but depend upon perfectly definite and perfectly objective conditions, namely, comparative magnitude and distance.

The house and the room are three-dimensional for me, by virtue of their commensurability with my body. The " sky " is two-dimensional, because it is remote. The " star " is a point because it is small as compared with the " sky." The " molecule " may be six-dimensional, but as a point, i.e. taken as a zero-dimensional body, it cannot produce any effect on my senses. These are all facts, there is nothing subjective in them.

But this is by no means all.

The dimensions of my space depend upon the size of my body. If the size of my body could change, the dimensions of the space around me would change also. " Dimension " corresponds to " size." If the dimensions of my world can change with a change in my size, then the size of my world also can change.

But in what respect?

A right answer to this question will at once put us on the right road.

The smaller the " reference-body " or " reference-system," the smaller the world. Space is proportionate to the size of the reference-body, and all measurements of space are proportionate to the measurements of the reference-body. And yet it is the same space. Let us take an electron on the sun in its relation to visible space and to the earth. For the electron the whole of visible space will be (of course only approximately) a sphere one kilometre in diameter; the distance from the sun to the earth will be a few centimetres, and the earth itself will be almost a " material point." A ray of light from the sun reaches the earth (for the electron) instantaneously. This explains why we can never intercept a ray of light half-way.

If instead of an electron we take the earth, then for the earth distances will necessarily be much longer than they are for us. They will be longer by exactly as many times as the earth is bigger than the human body. This is necessarily so if only because otherwise the earth could not feel itself the three-dimensional body we know it to be, but would be for itself some incomprehensible six-dimensional continuum. But such a self-feeling would contradict the rightly understood principle of the unity of laws. The reason is that if the earth could be for itself a six-dimensional continuum, then we also should have to be for ourselves six-dimensional continua. And since we are for ourselves three-dimensional bodies, the earth also must be for itself a three-dimensional body; although at the same time it is not possible to assert with certainty that the earth's conception of itself must necessarily coincide with our conception of it.

If we now try to imagine what the space occupied by terrestrial objects must be for the electron on the one hand and for the earth on the other, we shall come to a very strange and at first glance paradoxical conclusion. Things which surround us, tables, chairs, objects of daily use, other people, etc., cannot exist for the earth, for they are too small for it. It is impossible to conceive a chair in the planetary world. It is impossible to conceive an individual man in relation to the earth. An individual man cannot exist in relation to the earth. The whole of humanity cannot exist by itself in relation to the earth. It exists only together with all the vegetable and animal world and with all that has been made by the hand of man.

There can be no serious objection to this, because a particle of matter that is as small in relation to the human body as the human body, or even all humanity, is in relation to the earth certainly cannot exist for us. And it is quite obvious that a chair cannot exist in the planetary world because it is too small. What is strange and what is paradoxical is the inference that a chair cannot exist *for the electron or in the world of electrons also, and also because it is too small.*

This seems an absurdity. "Logically" it ought to be that a chair cannot exist for the electron, because a chair is too big compared with the electron. But it would be so only in a "logical," that is, in a three-dimensional, universe with a permanent space. The six-dimensional universe is illogical and the space in it can contract and expand on an incredibly large scale, preserving only one permanent property, namely *angles*. Therefore, the space existing for the electron which is proportionate to its size will be so small that a *chair* will occupy practically no room in this space.

Thus we have come to a space which expands and contracts in accordance with the size of the "reference-body" — an expandable and contractible space. Einstein's "mollusc" is the nearest approximation to this idea in new physics. But like most of the ideas of new physics, the "mollusc" is not so much a formulation of something new as an attempt to show that the old will not do. The "old" in this case is immovable and unchanging space. The same can be said of the general idea of the space-time continuum. New physics recognises that space cannot be examined apart from time, time cannot be examined apart from space, but what actually constitutes the essence of the relation of space to time and why phenomena of space and phenomena of time appear to be different for direct perception, new physics does not state.

The new model of the universe establishes exactly the unity of space and time, and the difference between them; it establishes also the principle that space can pass into time and time into space.

In old physics space is always space, and time is always time. In the new physics the two categories make one, *space-time*. In the new model of the universe the phenomena of one category can pass into the phenomena of the other category, and vice versa.

When I write of space, space-concepts and space-dimensions, I mean space for us. For the electron, and most probably even for bodies much larger than the electron, our space is time.

The six-pointed star which represented the world in ancient symbolism is in reality the representation of space-time or the "period of dimensions," i.e. of the three space-dimensions and the three time-dimensions in their perfect union, where every point of space includes the whole of time and every moment of time includes the whole of space; when *everything* is *everywhere* and *always*.

But this state of six-dimensional space is incomprehensible and inaccessible to us, for our sense-organs and our mind enable us to establish a connection only with the material world, that is, with a world of certain definite limitations in relation to higher space. We can never see a six-pointed star.

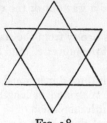

FIG. 18

What does material world mean? What does materiality mean? What does matter mean?

Earlier in this chapter a definition by Prof. Chwolson was quoted:

In objectifying the cause of a sensation, that is, transferring this cause into a definite place in space, we conceive this place as containing something which we call *matter* or substance (Vol. I, p. 2).

And further:

The use of the term "matter" was reserved exclusively for matter which is able to affect our organ of touch more or less directly (Vol. I, p. 6).

Modern physics and chemistry have achieved much in the study of the structure and composition of matter, and they do not limit themselves by a definition of matter like that made by Prof. Chwolson and apparently regard as *matter* everything that admits of objective study, everything that can be measured and weighed, even indirectly. In studying the structure and composition of matter these sciences deal with divisions of matter which are so small that they can produce no effect on our organs of touch, but are nevertheless recognised as material.

In fact both the old view, which limited the concept of matter too closely, and the new view, which extends it too far, are incorrect.

In order to avoid contradictions, indefiniteness and confusion of terms, it is necessary to establish the existence of several *degrees of materiality*.

1. Solid, liquid and gaseous states of matter (up to a certain degree of rarefaction), that is, states in which matter can be divided into "particles."

2. Very rarefied gases, consisting of separate molecules, and molecules resolved into component atoms.

3. Radiant energy (light, electricity, etc.), that is, the *electronic state of matter*, or electrons with their derivatives not bound into atoms. Certain physicists regard this state as *decomposition of matter*. But there are no data which justify this view.

It is not known how electrons become combined into atoms, just as it is not known how molecules become combined into cells and into protoplasm in living or organised matter.

It is necessary to keep in view these divisions because without applying them it is impossible to find a way out of the chaos in which physical sciences find themselves.

What do these divisions signify from the standpoint of the above principles of " the new model of the universe," and how can the degrees of materiality be defined?

Matter of the first kind is three-dimensional, i.e. any part of this matter and any " particle " can be measured in length, breadth and height and exists in time, i.e. in the fourth dimension.

Matter of the second and third kinds, i.e. its components, molecules, atoms and electrons, have no space-dimensions in comparison with particles of matter of the first kind, and reach our consciousness only in large masses and only through their time-dimensions, the fourth, the fifth and the sixth; in other words, they reach it only by virtue of their motion and the repetition of their motion.

Thus only the first degree of matter can be taken as existing in geometrical forms and in three-dimensional space. Atomic and electronic matter can with every right be regarded as matter belonging not to our, but to another, space, for it requires for its description six dimensions. And its units, molecules, atoms and electrons, if taken by themselves, can with every right be called *immaterial*.

" Materiality " is divided for us into three categories or three degrees.

The first kind of materiality is the state of matter of which our bodies consist. This matter and any part of it must possess (for us) three space-dimensions and one time-dimension; their fifth and sixth dimensions we cannot perceive.

In the materiality of the first kind there is (for us) more space than time.

The second and the third kinds of materiality are the states of molecules, atoms and electrons, which (for the direct senses) have the zero dimension in space and reach our consciousness by virtue of their three dimensions of time.

In the materiality of the second and third kinds there is (for us) more time than space.

The change of the state of matter from solid to liquid and from liquid to gaseous concerns molecules only, i.e. the distance between them and their cohesion. But inside the molecules, in all three states of matter, the solid, the liquid and the gaseous, everything remains the same, i.e. the proportion of matter and emptiness does not alter. "Electrons" remain equally far one from another inside the atoms and revolve in their orbits in the same way in all states of cohesion of molecules. Changes in the density of matter, i.e. transition from the solid state into the liquid or the gaseous state, do not reach them and do not affect them in any way.

The world inside the molecules is completely analogous to the great space in which celestial bodies move. Electrons, atoms, molecules, planets, solar systems, agglomerations of stars — all these are phenomena of the same order. Electrons move in their orbits in the atom just as planets move in the solar system. Electrons are the same celestial bodies as planets, even their velocity is the same as the velocities of the planets. In the world of electrons and atoms it is possible to observe all the phenomena which are observed in the astronomical world. There are comets in this world which travel from one system to another, there are shooting stars, there are streams of meteorites. "As above so below." Science seems to have proved the old formula of the Hermetists. Unfortunately, however, *it only seems so*, for in actual fact the model of the universe which science builds is too unstable and can fall to pieces at a single touch.

Indeed, what links together all these revolving particles or aggregations of matter? Why do not the planets of the solar system fly apart in different directions? Why do they continue to revolve in their orbits round the central luminary? Why do electrons remain linked with one another, thus constituting an atom? Why do they not fly apart, why does matter not resolve into nothing?

Science has always been confronted with these questions in one form or another, and even in our day it is unable to answer them without introducing two new unknown quantities: "attraction" or "gravitation" and "æther."

"Attraction" — replies science to the above question — keeps the planets near the sun and binds electrons into one whole; attraction, that mysterious force, the influence of a larger mass upon a smaller mass. This again produces a question: how can one mass influence another, even a smaller one, when it is at a great distance from it? If we imagine the sun as a large apple, the earth will be a poppy seed at a distance of twelve paces from this apple. How can the apple influence the poppy seed twelve paces from it? They must be linked in some way, for otherwise the influence of one body upon another remains totally incomprehensible and is in fact impossible.

Scientists have tried to find an answer to this problem by imagining a certain *medium* through which influence is transmitted and in which electrons and (possibly) also celestial bodies revolve.

All these hypotheses, and also the hypothesis of gravitation, are entirely unnecessary, from the point of view of the new model of the universe.

Atomic matter makes our consciousness aware of its existence through its motion. If the motion inside atoms were to stop, matter would turn into emptiness, into nothing. The effect of materiality, the impression of mass, is produced by the *motion* of the minutest particles, which *demands time*. If we take away time, if we imagine atoms without time, that is, if we imagine all the electrons constituting the atom as immovable, *there will be no matter*. *Motionless* small quantities are outside our scale of perception. We perceive not them, but their orbits, or the orbits of their orbits.

Celestial space is emptiness for us, that is, precisely what matter would be without time.

But in the case of celestial space we have learned sooner than we learned in the case of matter that what we see does not correspond to reality, though our science is still far from the right understanding of this reality.

Luminous points have turned into worlds moving in space. The universe of flying globes has come into being. But this picture is not the end of the possible understanding of celestial space.

If we represent schematically the interrelation of celestial bodies, we shall represent them as discs or points at a great distance from one another. But we know that they are not immovable, we know that they revolve round one another, and we know that they are not points. The moon revolves round the earth, the earth revolves round the sun, the sun in its turn revolves round some other luminary unknown to us, or, at any rate, moves in a definite direction along a definite line. Consequently the moon in revolving round the earth at the same time revolves round the sun and at the same time moves somewhere together with the sun. And the earth in revolving round the sun at the same time revolves round an unknown centre.

If we wish to represent graphically the paths of this motion, we shall represent the path of the sun as a line, the path of the earth as a spiral winding round this line, and the path of the moon as a spiral winding round the spiral of the earth. If we wish to represent the path of the whole solar system, we shall have to represent the paths of all the planets and asteroids as spirals winding round the central line of the sun, and the paths of the planets' satellites as spirals round the spirals of the planets. Such a drawing would be very difficult to make, in fact with asteroids it would be impossible; and it would be still more difficult to construct an exact model from this drawing, especially if all the interrelations, distances, exact thickness of the spirals, etc., were to be strictly observed. But if we were to succeed in building such a model, it would be an exact model of a small particle of *matter* enlarged many times. The same model, reduced a required number of times, would appear to us as impenetrable matter, exactly identical with all the matter which surrounds us.

Matter or substances of which our bodies and all the objects surrounding us consist is built in exactly the same way as the solar system; only we are incapable of perceiving electrons and atoms as immovable points but perceive them in the form of the complex, and entangled traces of their movement which produce the effect of mass. If we were able to perceive the solar system on a much smaller scale, it would produce on us the effect of matter. There would be no emptiness in the solar system for us, just as there is no emptiness in the matter surrounding us.

The emptiness or fulness of space depends entirely upon the dimensions in which we perceive the matter or particles of matter contained in that space. And the dimensions in which we perceive this matter depend upon the size of the particles of this matter in comparison with our body, upon the greater or lesser distance separating us from them, and upon our perception of their motion (which depends upon the velocity of their own motion and the rate of our perception), which creates the subjective aspect of the world.

All these conditions, taken together, determine the dimensions in which we perceive various agglomerations of matter.

A whole world, consisting of several suns, with their surrounding planets and satellites, rushing with terrific velocity through space, but separated from us by great distances, is perceived by us as an immovable point.

The almost immeasurably small electrons when moving are transformed into lines, and these lines intertwining among themselves create for us the impression of mass, i.e. of hard, impenetrable matter, of which the three-dimensional bodies surrounding us consist.

Matter is created by the fine web made by the traces of the motion of the smallest " material points."

The study of the principles of this motion is necessary for the understanding of the world, because it is only when we make these principles clear to ourselves that we shall have an exact conception of how the web created by the motion of the electrons is woven and thickened, and how the whole world of infinite variety of phenomena is constructed from this web.

The main principle of the structure of matter from the point of view of the new model of the universe is the idea of *gradations* in this structure. Matter of one kind cannot be described as consisting of units of matter of another kind. It is the greatest mistake to say that tangible matter consists of atoms and electrons. *Atoms* consist of positive and negative electrons. *Molecules* consist of atoms. *Particles of matter* consist of molecules. *Material bodies* consist of matter. It cannot be said that material bodies consist of molecules or of atoms. Atoms and molecules cannot be regarded as material particles; they belong to a different space-time. It was pointed out earlier that they contain more time than space. An electron is much more a time unit than a space unit.

To regard, for instance, the body of man as consisting of electrons or even of molecules is as wrong as it would be wrong to regard the population of a large town or a company of soldiers or any gathering of people as consisting of *cells*. It is evident that the population of a large and even of a small town, or a company of soldiers, consists not of microscopic cells, but of individual men. Precisely in the same way the body of man consists of individual cells, or simply physically, of matter. Of course I have not in view a metaphor which would regard a gathering of people as an organism and individual people as cells of this organism.

A whole series of unnecessary hypotheses falls away as soon as we realise the general connectedness and cohesion which follow from the above definitions of matter and mass.

The first which falls away is the hypothesis of gravitation. Gravitation is necessary only in the " world of flying balls "; in the world of *interconnected spirals* it becomes unnecessary. Similarly there disappears the necessity of recognising a " medium " through which gravitation, or " action at a distance," is transmitted. Everything is connected. The world constitutes One Whole.

Another interesting problem is disclosed at the same time. The hypothesis of gravitation was connected with observations of phenomena of weight and falling. According to the Newtonian legend indeed (the apple which Newton saw fall from the tree), these observations gave grounds for the building up of the whole hypothesis. It occurred to nobody that the phenomena which were explained by " gravitation " or " attraction " on the one hand, and the phenomena of " weight " on the other hand, are *totally different phenomena* having nothing whatever in common.

The sun, the moon, the stars, which we see, are cross-sections of spirals which we do not see. These cross-sections do not fall out of the spirals because of the same principle by reason of which the *cross-section of an apple* cannot fall out of the apple.

But the apple falls to the ground *as though aiming at the centre of the earth* in virtue of an entirely different principle, namely the " *principle of symmetry*." In Chapter II of this book there is a description of that particular movement which I called movement from the centre and towards the centre along radii, and which, with its laws enumerated there, is the foundation and cause of the phenomena of symmetry.

The laws of symmetry, when they are established and elaborated, will occupy a very important place in the new model of the universe. And it is quite possible that what is called the law of gravitation, in the sense of the formula for calculation, will prove to be a partial expression of the law of symmetry.

The definition of mass as the result of the motion of invisible points dispenses with any necessity for the hypothesis of æther. A ray of light has material structure, and so has electric current; but light and electricity are matter not formed into atoms, but remaining in the electronic state.

Returning to the concepts of physics and geometry, I must repeat that the wrong development of scientific thought which has led in new physics to the unnecessary complication of problems which were simple in their essence was to a great extent due to operating with *undefined* concepts.

One of these undefined concepts is " infinity."

Infinity has a definite meaning only in mathematics. In geometry infinity needs to be defined, and still more does it need to be defined in physics. These definitions do not exist, nor have there even been attempts at such definitions that are worthy of attention. " Infinity " is taken merely as something very big, bigger than anything else we can conceive, and at the same time as something completely homogeneous with the finite, yet incalculable. In other words, it is never said anywhere in a definite and exact form that the infinite is *not homogeneous* with the finite. I mean that it has not been established exactly *what* distinguishes the infinite from the finite either physically or geometrically.

In reality, both in the domain of geometry and in the domain of physics, infinity has a distinctive meaning, which differs very greatly from the strictly mathematical meaning. And the establishment of different meanings of infinity solves a number of otherwise insoluble problems and leads our thought out of a series of mazes and blind alleys created either artificially or through misunderstanding.

First of all, an exact definition of infinity dispenses with the necessity for mixing up physics with geometry, which is the favourite idea of Einstein and the foundation of non-Euclidean geometry. I have pointed out earlier that the mixing up of physics and geometry, that is to say, the introduction of physics into geometry, or a physical revaluation of geometrical values (all these rigid rods and non-rigid rods and so on), which follows from an identical mathematical valuation of geometrical and physical values, is unnecessary either for arguments concerning relativity, or for anything else.

Physicists are quite right in feeling that geometry is not sufficient for them; in Euclidean space there is not enough room for them with their luggage. But the remarkable feature of the geometry of Euclid (and this is exactly why Euclidean geometry *should be preserved intact*) consists in the fact that it contains within itself an indication of the way out. There is no need to break up and destroy the geometry of Euclid. It can very well adapt itself to any kind of physical discovery. *And the key to this is infinity*.

The difference between infinity in mathematics and infinity in geometry is quite clear at the first glance. Mathematics does not establish two infinities for one finite quantity. Geometry begins with this.

Let us take any finite line. What is infinity for this line? We have two answers: a line continued into infinity, or the square, of which the given line is a side. What is infinity for a square? An infinite plane, or the cube of which the given square constitutes a side. What is infinity for a cube? Infinite three-dimensional space, or a figure of four dimensions.

Thus the usual concept of an infinite line remains, but to it there is added another, the concept of infinity as a plane resulting from the motion of the line in a direction perpendicular to itself.

The infinite three-dimensional sphere remains; but a four-dimensional body constitutes infinity for a three-dimensional body.

Moreover, the problem becomes even simpler if we bear in mind that an "infinite" line, an "infinite" plane and an "infinite" solid are pure abstractions; whereas a (finite) line in relation to a point, a square in relation to a line and a cube in relation to a square, are real concrete facts.

So, remaining within the domain of facts, the principle of infinity in geometry can be formulated as follows: for every figure of a given number of dimensions infinity is a figure of the given number of dimensions plus one.

At the same time the figure of the lower number of dimensions is *incommensurable* with the figure of the higher number of dimensions. Incommensurability (in figures of different numbers of dimensions) creates infinity.

All this is very elementary. But if we firmly bear in mind the inferences to be drawn from these elementary propositions, they will enable us to free ourselves from the influence of the wrongly interpreted Aristotelian principle of the constancy of phenomena. The principle of Aristotle is true only within the limits of the finite, within the limits of commensurability. As soon as the infinite begins, we know nothing and have no right to assert anything in relation to the unity of phenomena and laws.

Continuing these arguments, we meet with another still more interesting fact, that is, that *physical* infinity differs from *geometrical* infinity as greatly as geometrical infinity differs from *mathematical* infinity. Or, to be more precise, physical infinity begins *much sooner* than geometrical infinity. And if mathematical infinity has only one meaning and geometrical infinity two meanings, physical infinity can have many meanings, that is, the mathematical meaning (incomputability), the geometrical meaning (the presence of an additional dimension or immeasurable extension) and purely physical meanings, that is, difference in function.

Infinity is created by incommensurability. But incommensurability can be arrived at in different ways. And in the physical world incommensurability can be brought about because of the *quantitative* difference alone. As a rule, only quantities which are different qualitatively are regarded as incommensurable, and the qualitative difference is regarded as independent of the quantitative difference. But this is precisely where the chief mistake lies. Quantitative difference brings about qualitative difference.

In the mathematical world incommensurability is created by the *incomputability* of one of the quantities compared; in the geometrical world it is created either by the infinite extension of one of the quantities which are being compared, or by the presence in it of a new dimension. In the physical world it is brought about simply by a difference in size which sometimes even permits of calculation.

All this means that infinity in geometry differs from infinity in mathematics in being *relative*. Mathematical infinity is equally infinity for any finite number. But geometrical infinity has no absolute meaning. A square is infinity for a line, but it is merely *bigger* than another smaller square or smaller than another bigger square.

In the physical world a large body is often incommensurable with a small one, and the small body bigger than the large one. A mountain is incommensurable with a mouse, and the mouse is *bigger* than the mountain by the perfection of its functions and by reason of its belonging to another level of being.

Further, it must be mentioned that *the function of every individual thing is possible only if the thing itself has a definite size*. The reason why this has not been noticed and established long ago is to be found in a wrong understanding of the principle of Aristotle.

Physicists have often come upon manifestations of this law, namely, that the function of every individual thing is possible only if the thing itself has a definite size, but it has never arrested their attention and never led them to put together observations obtained in different domains. In the formulation of many physical laws we find qualifications that the particular law is true only of medium quantities, and that in the case of larger quantities or smaller quantities the law changes. This law is still more clearly seen in the phenomena studied by biology and sociology.

The conclusion from what has been said can be formulated in the following way:

All that exists is what it is only within the limits of a certain and very restricted scale. On a different scale it becomes something else. In other words, every thing and every event has a certain meaning only within the limits of a certain scale, when compared with things and events of proportions not very far removed from its own, that is, existing within the same scale.

A chair cannot be a chair in the planetary world. Similarly, a chair cannot be a chair in the world of electrons. A chair has its meaning and its three dimensions only among objects created by the hand of man, serving the needs and requirements of man, and commensurable with man. On the planetary scale a chair cannot have individual existence because it cannot have any function. It is simply a small particle of matter inseparable from the matter surrounding it. As has been explained before, in the world of electrons *also* a chair becomes too small for its function and therefore loses all its meaning and all its significance. A *chair* actually does not exist in comparison even with things which differ from it much less than planets or electrons. A chair in the midst of the ocean, or a chair in the midst of the Alpine ranges, would be a point having no dimension.

All this shows that incommensurability exists not only among things of different categories and denominations, and not only among things of a different number of dimensions, but also among things which merely differ considerably in size. A big object is incommensurable with a small object. A big object is often infinite in comparison with a small one.

Every separate thing and every separate phenomenon, in becoming bigger or smaller, ceases to be what it was and becomes something else — something belonging to another category.

This principle is still utterly foreign to physics, both to the old and to the new. On the contrary, every separate thing and every separate phenomenon remains for physics what it was originally recognised as being — matter remains matter, motion remains motion, velocity remains velocity. And yet it is precisely this possibility of the transition of space phenomena into time phenomena and of time phenomena into space phenomena which conditions the eternal fluctuation of life. And this transition takes place when the given phenomenon becomes infinity in relation to another phenomenon.

From the point of view of old physics, velocity, which was considered a generally understood phenomenon requiring no definition, always remained velocity; it could grow, increase, become an *infinite velocity*. It occurred to no one to doubt it. And having only accidentally stumbled upon the fact that the velocity of light is a limiting velocity, physicists were forced to admit that all was not well, and that the idea of velocity needed revision.

But physicists certainly could not surrender at once and admit that velocity can cease to be velocity and can become something else.

What did they actually stumble upon?

They stumbled upon an instance of infinity. The velocity of light is infinity as compared with all the velocities which can be observed or created experimentally. And, as such, it cannot be increased. In actual fact it ceases to be velocity and becomes an *extension*.

A ray of light possesses an additional dimension as compared with any object moving with " terrestrial velocities."

A line is infinity in relation to a point. And the motion of the point does not alter this relation; a line will always remain a line.

The idea of limiting velocity presented itself when physicists hit upon a case of obvious infinity. But even apart from this, all the inconsistencies and contradictions in the old physics which were discovered and calculated by Prof. Einstein and supplied him with material for the building of his theories, all these without exception result from the difference between the infinite and the finite. He himself often alludes to this.

Einstein's description of the example of " the behaviour of clocks and measuring rods on a rotating marble disc " suffers from one defect. Prof. Einstein forgot to say that the diameter of the " marble disc " to which are fastened the clocks which begin to go at different speeds with the movement of the disc, according to their distance from the centre of the disc, should be approximately equal to the distance from the earth to Sirius; or else, the " clocks " must be the size of an atom (about five million of which can be put in the diameter of a full-stop). With such a difference in size strange phenomena can actually occur, such as the unequal speed of the clocks or the change in the length of the measuring rods. But there could not be a " disc " with a diameter equal to the distance from the earth to Sirius, or clocks the size of an atom. Such clocks will cease to exist before they change their speed, though this cannot be intelligible to modern physics, which, as I pointed out before, cannot get free of the Aristotelian principle of the constancy of phenomena and cannot therefore notice that constancy is always destroyed by incommensurability. It can be assumed generally that within the limits of terrestrial possibilities the behaviour of both the clocks and the measuring-rods will be quite respectable, and for all practical purposes we can safely rely upon them. There is only one thing we must not do — we must not set them any " problems with infinity."

After all, all the misunderstandings are caused by problems with infinity, chiefly because infinity is introduced on a level with finite quantities. The result will of course be different from what is expected; an unexpected result demands adaptation. The " special principle of relativity " and the " general principle of relativity " are very complicated and cumbersome adaptations for the explanation of the strange and unexpected results of " problems with infinity."

Prof. Einstein himself writes that proofs of his theories can be found either in astronomical phenomena or in the phenomena of electricity and light. In other words, he affirms by this that all problems that require particular principles of relativity arise from problems with infinity or with incommensurability.

The special principle of relativity is based on the difficulty of establishing the simultaneity of two events separated by space, and above all on the impossibility of the composition of velocities in comparing terrestrial velocities with the velocity of light. This is precisely a case of the established heterogeneity of the finite and the infinite.

Of this heterogeneity I have spoken earlier; as regards the impossibility of establishing the simultaneity of two events Prof. Einstein does not specify at what distance between two events the establishment of their simultaneity becomes impossible. And if we insist upon an explanation we shall certainly receive the answer that the distance must be " very great." This " very great " distance again shows that Prof. Einstein presumes a problem with infinity.

Time is really different for different moving systems of bodies. But it is incommensurable (or it cannot be synchronised) only if the moving systems are separated by a large space which is actually infinity for them, or when they differ greatly in size or velocity, that is, when one of them is infinity in comparison with the other, or contains infinity.

And to this may be added that not only time, but also space, is different for them, changing according to their size and velocity.

The general proposition is quite correct —

" Every separately existing system has its own time."

But what does " separately existing " mean? And how can there be separate systems in a *world of connected spirals*? All that exists in the world constitutes one whole; there can be nothing separate.

The principle of the absence of separateness, of the impossibility of separateness, constitutes a very important part of certain philosophical teachings, for instance of Buddhism, where one of the first conditions for a right understanding of the world is considered to be the destruction of the " sense of separateness " in oneself.

From the point of view of the new model of the universe separateness exists, but only relatively.

Let us imagine a system of cog-wheels, rotating with different velocities, which depend upon their size and upon the place occupied by each of them in the system. The system, for instance the mechanism of an ordinary watch, constitutes one whole, and from this point of view there can be nothing separate in it. From another point of view each separate cog-wheel moves at its own velocity, i.e. it has a separate existence and *its own time*.

In analysing the problem of *infinity* and infinite quantities we touch upon several other problems, the elucidation of which is equally necessary for a right understanding of the new model of the universe. Some of these problems have already been examined. There remain the problems of *zero quantities* and *negative quantities*.

Let us try to begin the examination of these quantities in the same way as we began the examination of infinity and infinite quantities, that is, let us try to compare their meanings in mathematics, in geometry and in physics.

Zero in mathematics has always one meaning. There is no reason to speak of *zero quantities* in mathematics.

Zero in mathematics and the point in geometry have approximately the same meaning, with the difference that the point in geometry indicates the *place* at which something begins or at which something ends, or at which something happens, for instance where two lines intersect one another; whereas in mathematics zero indicates the limit of certain possible operations. But in their essence there is no difference between zero and the point, because neither has independent existence.

The case is quite different in physics. The *material point* is a point only on a given scale. If the scale is changed the point can prove to be a very complex and many-dimensional system of immense measurements.

Let us imagine a small map on which even the biggest towns are points. Let us suppose that we have found the means to bring out the content of these points or to fill them with content. Then, what looked like a point will manifest a great many new properties and characteristics, and the extensions and measurements included in it. In the town will appear streets, parks, houses, people. How are the measurements of these streets, squares and people to be understood?

When the town was for us a point, they were *smaller than a point*. Is it not possible to call them *negative dimensions*?

The uninitiated, in most cases, do not know that the concept " *negative quantity* " has no definition in mathematics. It has a certain meaning only in elementary arithmetic, and also in algebraical formulæ, where it designates the *operation* to be performed, rather than the difference in the properties of the quantities. In physics "negative quantity" does not mean anything at all. Nevertheless we have already come upon negative quantities. It was when speaking of dimensions inside the atom, that I had to point out that although the atom (or the molecule) has no dimension for the direct senses, i.e. is equal to zero, these dimensions or extensions *inside the atom* are still smaller, i.e. *smaller than zero.*

So we need no metaphors or analogies in order to speak about negative dimensions. These are the dimensions within what appears to be a material point. And this explains exactly why it is wrong to regard small particles of matter such as atoms or electrons as material. They are not material, because they are *negative* physically, i.e. smaller than *physical* zero.

Putting together all that has been set forth hitherto, we see that besides the *period of six dimensions*, we have *imaginary dimensions*, the seventh, the eighth and so on, which proceed in non-existent directions and differ in the degree of impossibility; and *negative dimensions* within the smallest particles representing for us material points.

In new physics the conflict between the old and the new ideas of time and space is especially marked in conceptions as to the ray of light, but at the same time a right understanding of the ray of light will solve all points at issue in the question of time and space.

I will complete the new model of the universe by an analysis of a ray of light, but before beginning this analysis I must examine certain further properties of time taken as a three-dimensional continuum.

Until now I have taken time as the measure of motion. But motion in itself is the sensation of an *incomplete* perception of the space in question. For a dog, for a horse, for a cat, our third dimension is motion. For us motion begins in the fourth dimension and is a partial sensation of the fourth dimension. But as for animals the imaginary movements of objects which in reality constitute their third dimension merge into those movements which are movements for us, that is into the fourth dimension, so for us movements of the fourth dimension merge into movements of the fifth and sixth dimensions. Starting from this we must endeavour to establish something which will allow us to judge the properties of the fifth and sixth dimensions. Their relation to the fourth dimension must be analogous to the relation of the fourth dimension to the third, of the third to the second, and so on. This means that first of all the new, the higher, dimension must be incommensurable with the lower dimension and form infinity for it, seeming to repeat its characteristics an infinite number of times.

Thus, if we take " time " (that is extension from before to after) as the fourth dimension, what will be the fifth dimension in this case, that is, what forms infinity for time, what is incommensurable with time?

It is precisely phenomena of light that enable us to come into immediate contact with movements of the fifth and sixth dimensions.

The line of the fourth dimension is always and everywhere a closed curve, although on the scale of our three-dimensional perception we do not see either that this line is curved or that it is closed. This closed curve of the fourth dimension, or the circle of time, is the life or existence of every separate object, of every separate system, which is examined in time. But the circle of time does not break up or disappear. It continues to exist, and joining other, previously formed circles, it passes into eternity. Eternity is the infinite repetition of the completed circle of life, an infinite repetition of *existence*. Eternity is incommensurable with time. Eternity is infinity for time.

Quanta of light are precisely such circles of *eternity*.

The third dimension of time (the sixth dimension of space) is the stretching out of these eternal circles into a spiral or a cylinder with a screw-thread in which each circle is locked in itself (and motion along it is eternal) and simultaneously passes into another circle which is also eternal, and so on.

This hollow cylinder with two kinds of thread would be a model of a ray of light — a model of three-dimensional time.

The next question is, where is the electron? What happens to the electron of the luminous molecule which sends out quanta of light? This is one of the most difficult questions for new physics.

From the point of view of the new model of the universe the answer is clear and simple.

The electron is transformed into quanta, it becomes a ray of light. The point is transformed into a line, into a spiral, into a hollow cylinder.

As three-dimensional bodies electrons do not exist for us. The fourth dimension of electrons, that is *their existence* (the completed circle), also has no measurement for us. It is too small, has too short duration, is shorter than our thought. We cannot know about them, i.e. we cannot perceive them in a direct way.

Only the fifth and sixth dimensions of electrons have certain measurements in our space-time. The fifth dimension constitutes the thickness of the ray, and the sixth dimension its length.

Therefore in radiant energy we deal not with electrons themselves, but with their time dimensions, with the traces of their movement and existence, of which the primary web of any matter is woven.

Now if we accept the approximate description of the ray of light as a hollow cylinder consisting of quanta lying close to one another lengthwise along the ray, the picture becomes clearer.

First of all, the conflict between the theory of undulatory movements and the emission theory is settled, and it is settled in the sense that both theories prove to be equally true and equally necessary, though they refer to different phenomena or to different sides of the same kind of phenomenon.

Vibrations or undulatory movements, which were taken for the cause of light, are undulatory movements transmitted *along already existing rays of light*. What is called the " velocity of light " is probably the velocity of these vibrations passing along the ray. This explains why the calculations made on the basis of the theory of vibrations proved to be correct and made new discoveries possible. In itself a ray has no velocity; it is a line, a space concept, not a time concept.

No æther is necessary, for vibrations travel *by light itself*. At the same time light has " atomic structure," for a cross-section of a beam of light would show a network through the mesh of which the molecules of the gas it meets can easily slip.

In spite of the fact that scientists speak of the very accurate methods which they possess for counting electrons and measuring their velocities, it is permissible to have doubts whether they really mean electrons and not their extensions along the sixth dimension, the extensions which have already acquired space meaning for us.

The material structure of a ray of light explains also its possible deviations under the influence of forces acting upon it. But it is certain that these forces are not " attraction " in the Newtonian sense, although they may very possibly be magnetic attraction.

There still remains one question I have intentionally left untouched until now. This is the question of the duration of the existence of small particles, molecules, atoms and electrons. This question has never received serious consideration in physics; small units are regarded as *constant*, like matter and energy, that is, as existing for an indefinitely long time. If there were ever any doubts about this, they have not left a noticeable trace, and physicists speak of molecules, atoms and electrons, first (as has already been pointed out), as *particles of matter*, and, second, as particles which exist parallel with ourselves, occupying a certain time within our time. This is never said directly, but on this point doubt never arises. And yet in reality the existence of small units of matter is so short that it is quite impossible to speak of them in the same language as that in which we speak of physical bodies when they are the subject of our examination.

It was made clear before that the space of small units is proportionate to their size, and in exactly the same way their time is proportionate to their size. This means that their time, i.e. the time of their existence, is almost non-existent in comparison with our time.

Physics speaks of observing electrons and calculating their weight, velocity, etc. But an electron is for us only a *phenomenon*, and a phenomenon which is quicker than anything visible to our eyes; an atom as a whole is perhaps only a longer phenomenon, but longer on the same scale, just as there are various instantaneous speeds in a photographic camera. But both the atom and the electron are only time phenomena for us and, moreover, " instantaneous " phenomena; they are not bodies, not objects. Some scientists assert that they have succeeded in seeing molecules. But do they know how long by their clock a molecule can exist? During its very short existence, a molecule of gas (which alone may be accessible to observation, if this be possible at all) travels through immense distances and will in no case appear either to our eye or to the photographic camera as a moving point. And seen as a line it would inevitably intersect with other lines, so that it would be more than difficult to trace a single molecule, even for the period of a small fraction of a second; and even if this became possible in some way it would require such magnification as is actually impossible up to the present time.

All this must be kept in view in speaking, for instance, of phenomena of light. A great many misunderstandings fall away at once if we realise and carefully bear in mind the fact that an " electron " exists for an immeasurably small part of a second, which means that it can never under any condition be seen or measured by us, as we are.

It is impossible with existing *scientific* material to find firm ground for any theory as to the short existence of small units of matter. The material for such a theory is to be found in the idea of " different time in different cosmoses," which forms part of a special doctrine on the world, which will be the subject of another book.

1911–1929

Chapter XI

ETERNAL RECURRENCE AND THE LAWS OF MANU

❀

T HE FUNDAMENTAL problems of being, that is, the enigmas of birth and death, of coming into existence and of disappearance, never leave man. Whatever he may think about, he is actually thinking of these enigmas or problems. And even when he decides with himself to leave these questions alone, in reality he seizes upon every possibility, even the most remote, and tries once more to understand something in the enigmas which he had recognised to be insoluble.

Speaking generally, by their attitude towards the problems of life and death people can be divided into two categories. Most people approach these problems just as they approach all other problems and somehow solve them for themselves either positively or negatively. In order to arrive at these solutions they use ordinary methods of thought, the same methods and the same categories of thought as they use for thinking of the ordinary things that happen in life. They say either that after death there will be nothing, that beyond the threshold of death there is not and cannot be any existence; or else, that there will be an existence of some sort, either like the earthly existence or different from it, and consisting either entirely of suffering or entirely of joy.

But others know more than that. They realise that the problems of life and death cannot be approached in an ordinary way, that it is impossible to think of these problems in the same forms in which people think of something that happened yesterday or will happen to-morrow. But they do not go further than this. They feel that it is impossible, or at any rate useless, to think of these things *simply*, but what it means to think *not simply* they do not know.

In order to arrive at a right form of thinking in relation to these problems it is necessary to remember that they are connected with the idea of Time. We understand these problems to the extent to which we understand Time.

From the ordinary standpoint man's life is taken as a line from birth to death.

```
1854                                                    1904
 |—————————————————————————————————————————|
```

A man was born, lived fifty years and died. But where he was before 1854 and where he may be after 1904 is unknown. This is the general formulation of all questions of life and death.

Science deals only with man's body and according to it the body did not exist before it was born and is disintegrated after death. Philosophy does not take these questions seriously, and considers them to be unanswerable and consequently naïve.

Religious teachings and various pseudo-occult, spiritualistic and theosophical systems claim to know the solutions of these problems.

In reality, of course, no one knows anything.

The mystery of existence before birth and existence after death, if there is such existence, *is the mystery of time*. And " time " guards its secrets better than many people think. In order to approach these mysteries it is necessary first to understand time itself.

All ordinary attempts to answer questions about " what was before " and " what will be after " are based on the ordinary conception of time:

```
| BEFORE      |    NOW    |   AFTER    |
|             |           |            |
```

And the same formula is applied to the problems of existence before birth and after death, whenever such existence is admitted, i.e. the formula is taken thus:

```
| BEFORE       |   NOW    |   AFTER     |
| BEFORE BIRTH |   LIFE   | AFTER DEATH |
```

It is precisely here that the fundamental mistake lies. Time in the sense of before, now, after, is the product of our life, of our being, of our perception and, above all, of our thinking. Outside this life, outside the usual perception, the interrelation of the three phases of time can change; in any case we have no guarantee that it will remain the same. And yet, in ordinary thought, including religious, theosophical and " occult " thought, this question is never even raised. " Time " is regarded as something which is not subject to discussion, as something which belongs to us once and for all and cannot be taken away from us, and which is always the same. Whatever may happen to us, " time " will always belong to us, and not only " time," but even " eternity."

We use this word without understanding its true meaning. We take " eternity " to be an infinite extension of time, while really " eternity " means another dimension of time.

In the 19th century certain Eastern and pseudo-Eastern theories began to penetrate Western thought, among others the idea of " reincarnation," that is, of the periodical reappearance on earth of the same souls. This idea was not entirely unknown before, but belonged to hidden mystical thought. The popularisation of this idea is chiefly due to modern theosophy with all its ramifications.

The origin of the idea of reincarnation as it is expounded in modern theosophy is open to argument. It was adopted by theosophists practically without alteration from the cult of Krishna, which is a religion of Vedic origin, considerably retouched by reformers. But even the cult of Krishna does not contain the " democratic principle " of universal and equal reincarnation which is so characteristic of modern theosophy. In the real cult of Krishna only heroes, leaders and teachers of humanity reincarnate. Reincarnation for the masses, for the crowd, for " householders," assumes much vaguer forms.

Side by side with the idea of reincarnation there exists in India the idea of the " transmigration of souls," i.e. the reincarnation of the souls of human beings into animals. The idea of the transmigration of souls connects reincarnation with reward and punishment. Theosophists regard the transmigration of souls as a distortion of the idea of reincarnation by popular beliefs. But this can in no way be regarded as certain. And both the idea of reincarnation and belief in the transmigration of souls may be regarded as having originated from one common source, namely, the teaching of the repetition of everything and of eternal recurrence.

The idea of the eternal recurrence of things and phenomena, the idea of eternal repetition, is connected in European thought with the name of Pythagoras and with the vague notions of the periodicity of the universe which are found in Indian philosophy and cosmogony. This idea of periodicity cannot be clear to European thought because it becomes complete and connected only with the aid of oral commentaries which up to the present time have never and nowhere been made public.

The " life of Brahma," the " days and nights of Brahma," the " breath of Brahma," kalpas and manvantaras; all these ideas are very obscure for European thought, but by their inner content they are invariably associated with Pythagorean ideas of eternal recurrence.

The name of Gautama the Buddha, who was almost if not exactly a contemporary of Pythagoras and who also taught eternal recurrence, is very seldom mentioned in connection with this idea, in spite of the fact that in Buddha's teaching of the " wheel of lives " the idea is clearer than anywhere else, although it is obscured almost beyond recognition by ignorant interpretations and translations.

Nietzsche contributed a great deal to the popularisation of the idea of eternal recurrence, but he has added nothing new to it. On the contrary, he introduced several wrong concepts into it, as for instance his calculation, which mathematically is altogether wrong, of the mathematical necessity for the repetition of identical worlds in the universe.[1]

But though he made mistakes in the attempts to prove his theories, Nietzsche felt emotionally the idea of eternal recurrence very strongly. He felt the idea as a poet. And several passages in his *Zarathustra*, and in other books where he touches upon the idea, are perhaps the best he ever wrote.

But repetition cannot be proved on our plane, that is, in the three-dimensional world with time as the fourth dimension, no matter whether time is taken as a real or as an imaginary quantity. Repetition requires five dimensions, i.e. an entirely new " space-time-eternity."

The Pythagorean ideas of the repetition of everything were referred to among others by Eudemus, a pupil of Aristotle. Eudemus' "Physics" has been lost, and what he wrote about the Pythagoreans is known to us only through the later commentaries of Simplicius. It is very interesting to observe that, according to Eudemus, the Pythagoreans distinguished two kinds of repetition.

Simplicius wrote:

The Pythagoreans said that the same things are repeated again and again.

In this connection it is interesting to note the words of Eudemus, Aristotle's disciple (in the 3rd book of Physics). He says: Some people accept and some people deny that time repeats itself. Repetition is understood in different senses. One kind of repetition may be in the natural order of things ($\epsilon\delta os$), like repetition of summers and winters and other seasons, when a new one comes after another has disappeared; to this order of things belong the movements of the heavenly bodies and the phenomena produced by them, such as solstices and equinoxes, which are produced by the movement of the sun.

But if we are to believe the Pythagoreans there is another kind of repetition. That means that I shall talk to you and sit exactly like this and I shall have in my hand the same stick, and everything will be the same as it is now and time, as it can be supposed, will be the same. Because if movements (of heavenly

---

[1] Nietzsche attempts to prove the necessity for repetition in Euclidean space, and in ordinary, i.e. one-dimensional, time. His understanding of the idea of repetition was that somewhere in the infinite space of the universe an earth exactly like the one we live on must be repeated. And then the same causes will create the same effects; and as a result there will be a room somewhere, exactly like that in which I am sitting, and in that room a man exactly like me with an exactly similar pen will write what I am writing now. Such a construction is possible only with a naïve understanding of time.

Nietzsche proves the necessity for repetition roughly in the following way. According to him, if we take a certain number of units and examine their possible combinations, the combinations that occurred once are bound to recur in the course of time. If the number of units is large, repetitions will be more frequent, and if the number of units is infinite, everything is bound to repeat.

This is in fact wrong simply because Nietzsche fails to see that the number of possible combinations will grow in a much higher ratio than the number of units. And consequently the number of possible repetitions, instead of increasing, will diminish. Thus, with a certain, not even infinite, but merely large number of units, the number of combinations will be infinite and the probability of repetition will equal zero. Given an infinite number of units even the possibility of repetition is out of the question.

bodies) and many other things are the same, what occurred before and what will occur afterwards are also the same. This applies also to repetition, which is always the same. Everything is the same and therefore time is the same.[2]

The preceding passage from Simplicius is particularly interesting in that it gives a key for the translation of other Pythagorean fragments, that is, notes on Pythagoras and his teaching, which have been preserved in certain authors. The basis of the view on Pythagoras which is accepted in textbooks of the history of philosophy is the idea that in the philosophy of Pythagoras and in his conception of the world the chief place was occupied by *number*. In reality it is simply a bad translation. The word " number " is in fact constantly met with in Pythagorean fragments. But only the word; and in most cases this word merely completes verbs which do not express the repeated or iterative action which the author aims at describing. At the same time this word is always translated as having independent significance, which entirely distorts its meaning. The preceding passage from Simplicius loses all meaning in the usual translation.

These two kinds of repetition, which Eudemus called repetition in the natural order of things and repetition in number of existences, are, of course, repetition in time and repetition in eternity. It follows from this that the Pythagoreans distinguished these two ideas, which are confused by modern Buddhists and were confused by Nietzsche.

Jesus undoubtedly knew of repetition and spoke of it with his disciples. In the Gospels there are many allusions to this, but the most unquestionable passage, which has a quite definite meaning in the Greek, Slavonic and German texts, has lost its meaning in translations into other languages, which took the most important word from the Latin translation.

And Jesus said unto them, Verily I say unto you, That ye which have followed me, in the regeneration . . . (Matt. 19. 28).

In Greek: ὁ δὲ Ἰησοῦς εἶπεν αὐτοῖς Ἀμὴν λέγω ὑμῖν ὅτι ὑμεῖς οἱ ἀκολουθήσαντές μοι, ἐν τῇ παλιγγενεσίᾳ. . .

In German the words ἐν τῇ παλιγγενεσίᾳ are translated " in der Wiedergeburt."

The Greek παλιγγενεσία, the Slavonic and Russian word пакибытие, the

---

Οὕτω δὲ οἱ Πυθαγόρειοι τὰ αὐτά πως καὶ τῷ ἀριθμῷ τῷ πάλιν καὶ πάλιν ἔλεγον γίνεσθαι. οὐδὲν δὲ ἴσως χεῖρον καὶ τῆς Εὐδήμου ῥήσεως ἐκ τοῦ τρίτου τῶν Φυσικῶν τὰ ἐνταῦθα λεγόμενα παραφράζουσης ἀκούειν· " ὁ δὲ αὐτὸς χρόνος πότερον γίνεται ὥσπερ ἔνιοί φασίν ἢ οὔ, ἀπορήσειεν ἄν τις· πλεοναχῶς δὴ λεγομένου τοῦ ταὐτοῦ τῷ μὲν εἴδει φαίνεται γίνεσθαι τὸ αὐτὸ οἷον θέρος καὶ χειμὼν καὶ αἱ λοιπαὶ ὧραί τε καὶ περίοδοι, ὁμοίως δὲ καὶ αἱ κινήσεις αἱ αὐταὶ γίνονται τῷ εἴδει, τροπὰς γὰρ καὶ ἰσημερίας καὶ τὰς λοιπὰς πορείας ὁ ἥλιος ἀποτελεῖ· εἰ δέ τις πιστεύσειε τοῖς Πυθαγορείοις, ὥστε πάλιν τὰ αὐτὰ ἀριθμῷ, κἀγὼ μυθολογήσω τὸ ῥαββίον ἔχων ὑμῖν καθημένοις οὕτω, καὶ τὰ ἄλλα πάντα ὁμοίως ἕξει, καὶ τὸν χρόνον εὔλογός ἐστι τὸν αὐτὸν εἶναι· μιᾶς γὰρ καὶ τῆς αὐτῆς κινήσεως, ὁμοίως δὲ καὶ πολλῶν τῶν αὐτῶν τὸ πρότερον καὶ ὕστερον ἓν καὶ ταυτόν, καὶ ὁ τούτων δὴ ἀριθμός· πάντα ἄρα τὰ αὐτά, ὥστε καὶ ὁ χρόνος." *Simplicii in Physicorum, IV, 12. Commentaria in Aristotelem Græca* [ed. H. Diels, 1882], Vol. 9, p. 732.

German Wiedergeburt, can be translated only as *repeated existence* (again-existence) or repeated birth (again-birth).

In Latin this word was translated regeneratio, which in the first meaning corresponded to *repeated birth*. But later, owing to the use of the word regeneratio (and its derivatives) in the sense of *renovation*, it lost its original meaning.

The Apostle Paul undoubtedly knew of the idea of repetition, but had a negative attitude towards it. This idea was too esoteric for him.

For Christ is not entered into the holy places made with hands

. . . .

Nor yet that he should offer himself often, as the high priest entereth into the holy place every year with blood of others;

For then must he often have suffered since the foundation of the world: but now once in the end of the world hath he appeared to put away sin by the sacrifice of himself (Heb. 9. 24–26).

It must be noted that the Epistle to the Hebrews is ascribed also to certain other authors as well as to the Apostle Paul, and really there is no definite information on this question.

Origen (3rd century) in his book *On First Principles* also refers to the idea of repetition, but speaks about it negatively.

And now I do not understand by what proofs they can maintain their position, who assert that worlds sometimes come into existence which are not dissimilar to each other, but in all respects equal. For if there is said to be a world similar in all respects (to the present), then it will come to pass that Adam and Eve will do the same things which they did before: there will be a second time the same deluge, and the same Moses will again lead a nation numbering nearly six hundred thousand out of Egypt; Judas will also a second time betray the Lord; Paul will a second time keep the garments of those who stoned Stephen; and everything which has been done in this life will be said to be repeated.[3]

At the same time Origen was very near to the correct understanding of *eternity*. And it is possible that he denied the idea of repetition not quite sincerely. It is very probable that because of the conditions of his time this idea could not be introduced without being denied.

But it is an interesting fact that this idea was known in the first centuries of Christianity; but later it entirely disappeared from " Christian thought."

If we try to trace the idea of eternal recurrence in European literature it is necessary to mention the remarkable " fable " by R. L. Stevenson, *The Song of the Morrow* (1895); and C. H. Hinton's story " An Unfinished Communication " in the second book of his *Scientific Romances* (1898), and also one or two pages in his story " Stella " in the same book.

---

[3] Origen, περὶ Ἀρχῶν, Book II, Chapter III. The writings of Origen, translated by the Rev. Frederick Crombie (T. & T. Clark, Edinburgh, 1878), Vol. I, p. 84.

There are also two interesting poems on the same subject. One is by Alexis Tolstoy: [4]

Through the slush and the ruts of the roadway —
By the side of the dam of the stream;
Where the wet fishing nets are drying,
The carriage jogs on, and I muse.

I muse and I look at the roadway,
At the damp and the dull grey weather,
At the shelving bank of the lake,
And the far-off smoke of the villages.

By the dam, with a cheerless face,
Is walking a tattered old Jew.
From the lake, with a splashing of foam,
The waters rush through the weir.

A little boy plays on a pipe,
He has made it out of a reed.
The startled wild-ducks have flown,
And call as they sweep from the lake.

Near the old tumbling-down mill
Some labourers sit on the grass.
An old worn horse in a cart
Is lazily dragging some sacks.

And I know it all, oh! so well,
Though I never have been here before,
The roof there, far away yonder,
And the boy, and the wood, and the weir,

And the mournful voice of the mill,
And the crumbling barn in the field —
I have been here and seen it before,
And forgotten it all long ago.

This very same horse plodded on,
It was dragging the very same sacks;
And under the mouldering mill
The labourers sat on the grass.

And the Jew, with his beard, walked by,
And the weir made just such a noise.
All this has happened before,
Only, I cannot tell when.

The other is by D. G. Rossetti.

Sudden Light

I have been here before,
But when or how I cannot tell:
I know the grass beyond the door,

---

[4] Translated by the Hon. Maurice Baring, *The Oxford Book of Russian Verse.*

> The sweet keen smell,
> The sighing sound, the lights around the shore.
>
> You have been mine before —
> How long ago I may not know:
> But just when at that swallow's soar
> Your neck turn'd so,
> Some veil did fall — I knew it all of yore.
>
> Then, now — perchance again! . . .
> O round mine eyes your tresses shake!
> Shall we not lie as we have lain
> Thus for Love's sake,
> And sleep, and wake, yet never break the chain?

There is a variant to the last stanza:

> Has this been thus before
> And shall not thus time's eddying flight
> Still with our lives our love restore
> In death's despite
> And day and night yield one delight once more?

Both poems were written in the fifties of last century.

Tolstoy's poem is usually regarded as simply recording strange passing moods. But A. Tolstoy, who was much interested in mystical literature and was in contact with several occult circles which existed in Europe at his time, may have known of the idea of eternal recurrence quite definitely.

The feeling of the repetition of events was very strong in Lermontoff. He is full of presentiments, expectations, "memories." He constantly alludes to these sensations, especially in his prose. "The Fatalist" is practically written on the theme of repetition and of remembering that which seems to have happened in some unknown past. Many passages in "The Princess" and in "Bela," especially the philosophical digressions, produce the impression that Lermontoff himself is trying to remember something that he has forgotten.

We think in general that we know Lermontoff. But who has asked himself what the following passage in "Bela" means?

. . . I was exhilarated to feel myself so high above the world. It was a childish feeling, of course, but when we get away from artificial conditions and approach nearer to Nature we cannot help becoming children. All that we have acquired falls away from our being and we become once more what we were and what we shall one day assuredly be again.[5]

Personally I do not remember a single attempt to analyse these words in all the literature on Lermontoff. But the idea of the possibility of some kind of "return" undoubtedly disturbed Lermontoff, now carried him away, now appeared an unrealisable dream:

---

[5] "A Hero of our Time," by M. Y. Lermontoff (Philip Allan). London, 1928. *Bela*, pp. 49 and 50.

> Would it not be better to finish the path of life in self-forgetting
> And to fall into an unending sleep
> Looking for a near awakening.
>
> ("Valerik.")

In our time the idea of recurrence and even of the possibility of half-conscious remembering becomes more and more pressing and necessary. In the *Life of Napoleon* (1928), D. S. Merejkovsky constantly alludes to Napoleon in the phrase "he knew" ("remembered"). And later, in dealing with Napoleon's last years in Europe, "he forgot" ("he ceased to remember").

This list does not claim to be complete. I wished only to show that the idea of repetition and recollection of the *past* which is not in our time is far from being foreign to Western thought.

But the psychological apprehension of the idea of eternal recurrence does not necessarily lead to a logical understanding and explanation of it. In order to understand the idea of eternal recurrence and its different aspects it is necessary to go back to the ideas of the "New Model of the Universe."

The idea of time as the fourth dimension does not contradict the ordinary views of life, so long as we take time as a straight line. This idea only brings with it a sensation of greater preordination, of greater inevitability. But the idea of time as a *curve* of the fourth dimension entirely changes our conception of life. If we clearly understand the meaning of this curvature and especially when we begin to see how the curve of the fourth dimension is transformed into the curves of the fifth and the sixth dimensions, our views of things and of ourselves cannot remain any longer what they were.

As has been said in the preceding chapter, according to the initial scheme of dimensions, in which dimensions are still taken as straight lines, the fifth dimension is a line perpendicular to the line of the fourth dimension and intersecting it, that is, a line which passes through every moment of time, the line of the infinite existence of a moment.

But how is this line formed, where does it come from and what follows out of it? This can be understood to a certain extent if life is taken as a series of undulatory vibrations.

As we should know from the study of undulatory vibrations in the world of physical phenomena, every wave comprises in itself a complete circle, that is, the matter of the wave moves in a completed curve in the same place and for as long as the force acts which creates the wave.

We should know also that every wave consists of smaller waves and is in its turn a component part of a bigger wave.

If we take, simply for the sake of argument, *days* as the smaller waves which form the bigger waves of *years*, then the waves of years will form one great wave of *life*. And so long as this wave of life rolls on, the waves

ESET416 ETERNAL RECURRENCE AND THE LAWS OF MANU

of days and the waves of years must rotate at their appointed places, repeating and repeating themselves. Thus the line of the fourth dimension,

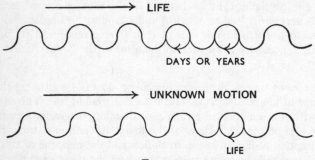

FIG. 19

the line of life or *time*, consists of wheels of ever-repeating *days*, of small circles of the fifth dimension, just as a ray of light consists of quanta of light, each rotating in its place so long as the primary shock which sends forth the particular ray persists. But in itself a *ray* may be a curve, a component part of some other bigger wave. The same applies to the line of life. If we take it as one great wave consisting of the waves of days and

FIG. 20

years, we shall have to admit that the line of life moves in a curve and makes a complete revolution, coming back to the point of its departure. And if a day or a year is a wave in the undulatory movement of our life, then our whole life is a wave in some other undulatory movement of which we know nothing.

As I have already pointed out, in our ordinary conception life appears as a straight line drawn between the moments of birth and death.

But if we imagine that life is a wave, we shall get this figure:

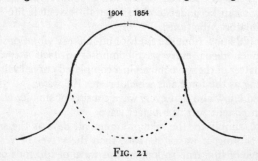

FIG. 21

The point of death coincides with the point of birth.

For one who has followed the development of the ideas which touch on " dimensions of time," in the preceding chapter and in this one, this point does not present any difficulty but on the contrary results naturally from all that has been said earlier. But usually after this point there comes a question which is more difficult to answer, namely, how an identical relation between the births of different people is preserved when we know that the relation between their deaths is quite different, i.e. that it does not correspond with the relation of their births. To put it more shortly, what will happen to a man who has died before his grandmother? He must be born immediately, and his mother is as yet unborn. Two answers are possible. First, it is possible to say that at the moment when the soul touches infinity different relations of time become adjusted, because a moment of eternity can have different time value. And, second, it is possible to say that our usual conceptions of " dimensions of time " are wrong. For instance, for us time can have different duration — five years, ten years, a hundred years — but it always has the same speed. But where are proofs of this? Why not suppose that time in certain limits (for instance, in relation to human life) always has the same duration but *different speed*? One is not more arbitrary than the other, but with the admission of this possibility the question disappears.

In my book *Tertium Organum* I gave a drawing of the figure of the fourth dimension taken from a book by Van Manen. This figure consists of two circles, one inside the other. It is the figure of life. The small circle stands for man; the large circle for the life of man. The small circle rolls inside the large circle, which first widens, then gradually becomes more narrow and brings the small circle to the same point from which it started. In rolling along the large circle the small circle continually rotates on its own axis. This rotation is *eternity* in relation to *time*, which is movement along the large circle.

Here again we meet what appears to be a paradox — the fifth dimension inside the fourth dimension; movement along the fifth dimension creating movement along the fourth dimension. How are we to find here the beginning and the end? Which is the driving force? And which is driven? Is it the small circle that rotates, driven by the shock which sends it round the large circle, or is it the large circle itself which is driven by the rotation of the small circles? The one drives the other. But in relation to *life* taken as the large circle, *eternity* is to be found, first, in the small circles of repeating moments, days and years, and, second, in the repetition of the large

ONE LIFE   ANOTHER LIFE   A THIRD LIFE

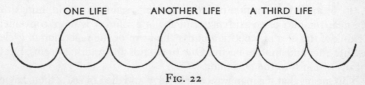

FIG. 22

circle itself, in the repetition of life, that is, in the repetition of the waves.

Just as in the case of the fourth dimension, we are again faced with the fact that a higher dimension is both above and below the lower dimension.

As above so below.

The fourth dimension *for us* lies in the world of celestial bodies and in the world of molecules.

The fifth dimension lies in the moments of life eternally remaining where they are, and in the repetition of life itself, taken as a whole.

Life in itself is *time* for man. For man there is not and cannot be any other time outside the time of his life. *Man is his life.* His life is his time.

The way of measuring time, *for all*, by means of such phenomena as the apparent or real movement of the sun or the moon, is comprehensible as being convenient for practical purposes. But it is generally forgotten that this is only a formal time accepted by common agreement. Absolute time for man is his life. There can be no other time outside this time.

If I die to-day, to-morrow will not exist *for me*. But, as has been said before, all theories of the future life, of existence after death, of reincarnation, etc., contain one obvious mistake. They are all based on the usual understanding of time, that is, on the idea that *to-morrow* will exist after death. In reality it is just in this that life differs from death. Man dies because his time ends. There can be no to-morrow after death. But all usual conceptions of the " future life " require the existence of " to-morrow." What future life can there be, if it suddenly appears that there is no future, no " to-morrow," no time, no " after "? Spiritualists, theosophists, theologians and others who know everything about the future life, may find themselves in a very strange situation if the fact is realised that no " after " exists.

What then is possible? And what may the meaning of life as a circle be?

I have pointed out in the preceding chapter that the very curvature of the line of time implies the presence in it of yet another dimension, namely, the *fifth dimension*, or eternity. And if in the usual understanding the *fourth dimension* is extension of time, what can the fifth dimension, or eternity, be?

Eternity for our mind is conceivable only under two forms: either under the form of *co-existence* or under the form of *repetition*. The form of co-existence requires space conceptions — *somewhere there* exist things identical with those here; identical people, an identical world. The form of repetition requires time conceptions — *some time* everything will be repeated or is repeated, either immediately after the completion of the particular cycle, that is, of the particular life, or after every moment. The latter, i.e. the immediate repetition of every moment again and again, brings this idea near the idea of co-existence. But for our mind it is more convenient to think of the idea of repetition under the form of the repetition of cycles. One life ends and another begins. One time ends and another begins. Death is really a return to the beginning.

This means that if a man was born in 1877 and died in 1912, then, having died, he finds himself again in 1877 and must live the same life all over again. In dying, in completing the circle of life, he enters the same life from the other end. He is born again in the same town, in the same street, of the same parents, in the same year and on the same day. He will have the same brothers and sisters, the same uncles and aunts, the same toys, the same kittens, the same friends, the same women. He will make the same mistakes, laugh and cry in the same way, rejoice and suffer in the same way. And when the time comes he will die in exactly the same way as he did before, and again at the moment of his death it will be as though all the clocks were put back to 7.35 a.m. on the 2nd September 1877, and from this moment started again with their usual movement.

The new life begins in exactly the same conditions as the preceding one, and it cannot begin in any other conditions. The only thing that can and even must be admitted, is the fact of the strengthening with every life of the tendencies of the preceding life, of those tendencies which grew and increased during life, both bad and good tendencies, those which were a manifestation of strength and those which were a manifestation of weakness.

There exists, indeed, much more psychological material for the idea of eternal recurrence than is supposed. But the existence of this material is not fully realised by scientific thought.

Everybody knows the sensation, or descriptions of the sensation, that is experienced sometimes by people, especially in childhood, the sensation that *this has happened before*. The two poems quoted earlier could have been inspired by the same sensation.

I spoke of this sensation in the chapter on dreams, and I pointed out there that the usual explanations account for two categories out of three of these sensations but leave the third category unexplained. This third category is characterised by the fact that the sensation that *this has happened before*, though very vivid and frequent in childhood, disappears in adult life. In some cases this special kind of foreknowledge of people, things, places and events can be verified and established. The very rare " trustworthy " cases of clairvoyance belong to such foreknowledge.

But in itself the fact of these accidental recollections, even if they are really recollections, is too small to allow anything to be built on it.

A man may be perfectly justified in asking: " if such a tremendous phenomenon as the repetition of lives really exists, why do we know nothing of it, why do we not remember *more*? And why did not people realise it long ago, why is it only now presented to us as a new discovery? "

All these questions are quite well-founded; but at the same time it is not difficult to answer them.

Earlier in this book the transformation of a butterfly was given as an example of evolution. What is especially characteristic for us in the transformation of a butterfly from the point of view in question is the fact that in passing to a new level of transformation the " butterfly " *completely* vanishes from the preceding level, *dies* on the preceding level, ceases to exist *there*, that is, loses all connection with its former existence. If a butterfly sees and learns more, it is unable to tell the caterpillars anything about it. It is already dead as a caterpillar, it has vanished from the world of caterpillars.

Something analogous must happen to people to whom the mysteries of time and eternity are revealed. They know and can speak of what they know, but people will neither hear nor understand them.

Why did not people long ago come to the idea of eternal recurrence?

But they did in fact come to it long ago. I have pointed to the teaching of Pythagoras, to Buddhism, to theories of reincarnation and transmigration of souls, which, in their modern forms are actually only a distortion of the idea of eternal recurrence. Many other ideas of the future life, various allusions in " occult " teachings, for instance, the very strange idea of the possibility of *changing the past*, various popular beliefs, such as the cult of ancestors — all these are connected with the idea of recurrence.

It is quite clear that the idea of recurrence cannot be popular in its pure form, primarily because it seems absurd from the standpoint of ordinary logic, since there is nothing similar to it in the world of " three-dimensional " sensations or in the usually accepted " time." The usual view of time leaves no place for recurrence. On the contrary, according to the ordinary wisdom of the world " nothing ever returns." So even in those teachings in which originally the idea of recurrence undoubtedly existed in its pure form, as for example in Buddhism, it has become distorted and adapted to the usual understanding of time. According to recent interpretations of learned Buddhists, a man is born into a new life at the very moment of his death. But this is a *continuation in time*. Buddhists have rejected the " absurd " idea of a return into the past, and their " wheel of lives " rolls along with the calendar. In this way certainly they have taken away all force from the idea, but they have made it acceptable to the masses and capable of logical explanation and interpretation.

In speaking of the idea of eternal recurrence, it is necessary to understand that it cannot be proved in the ordinary way, that is, by the usual methods of observation and verification. We know but one line of time, the one on which we now live. We are one-dimensional beings in relation to time; we have no knowledge of parallel lines. Suppositions as to the existence of parallel lines cannot be proved so long as we remain on one line. In my book *Tertium Organum* I described what the universe of one-dimensional beings must be. These beings know nothing besides their own line. If they supposed the existence of something new, something they did not know before, for them it would have to be on their own line, either in front of them or behind them. Our position in relation to time is exactly the same. Everything that exists must occupy a certain place in time either in front of us or behind us. There can be nothing parallel to us. This means that we cannot prove the existence of anything parallel so long as we remain on our line. But if we attempt to break away from ordinary views and bear in mind that the supposition of the possible existence of other lines of " time " parallel to ours is more " scientific " than the usual naïve one-dimensional conception of time, then the conception of life as a recurring phenomenon will prove to be easier than we imagine.

Ordinary views are based upon the assumption that the life of a man, that is, the whole of his inner world, his desires, tastes, sympathies, antipathies, tendencies, habits, inclinations, capacities, talents, vices, arise out of nothing and vanish into nothing. Christian teachings speak of the possibility of a future life, that is, of life beyond the grave, but they do not speak of life before birth. According to their view, " souls " are born with bodies. In actual fact, however, it is very difficult to think of life (that is, of the soul) or of the inner being of man, as being that arises out of nothing. And it is much easier to think that this being existed earlier, before birth. But people do not know how to begin thinking in this direction. The theosophical theories of reincarnation which try to stretch the life of an individual man along the line of the life of the earth will not bear criticism from the point of view of a rightly understood idea of time.

There exist dozens, perhaps even hundreds, of various ingenious theories which claim to explain all the angles and curves of man's inner world by a combination of hereditary influences and the suppressed voices of hidden inner instincts. All these theories are acceptable, each in its own way, but none of them explains *everything* in man. One theory explains one thing better, another explains another thing better. But much, very much, remains unexplained. It could not be otherwise, for theories of heredity, even of a dim far-away heredity, theories of hidden instincts, of unconscious memory, can explain certain sides of man, but other sides they cannot explain. And until we find it possible to recognize that we have lived before, very much will remain in us that we shall never be able to understand.

It is very difficult to accept the idea of the absolute and inevitable repetition of *everything*. It seems to us that if we were to remember at least something, we should be able to avoid some of the most unpleasant things. Moreover the idea of absolute repetition does not agree with the idea of growing tendencies, which is also necessary.

In this connection it must be recognised that as regards the character of the repetition of their lives people fall into several types or categories.

There are people of absolute repetition, in whose case everything, both big and little, is transmitted from one life to another.

There are people whose lives have each time the same beginning, but go on with slight variations, upwards or downwards, coming to approximately the same end.

There are people in whose case lives go with a definitely ascending tendency, becoming richer and stronger *outwardly*.

There are people whose lives, on the contrary, display a clearly marked descending line, which gradually destroys all that is alive in them and reduces them to nothing.

And there are people whose life contains an *inner* ascending line, which gradually leads them out of the circle of eternal repetition and causes them to pass to another plane of being.

Let us first examine the type of lives in which absolute repetition is inevitable.

These are, first of all, people of " *byt*," [6] of deeply-rooted, petrified, routine life. Their lives succeed one another with the monotony of the hand of the clock moving on the dial. There can be in their lives nothing unexpected, nothing accidental, no adventures. They are born and die in the same house where their fathers and grandfathers were born and died and where their children and grandchildren will be born and will die. National calamities, wars, earthquakes, plagues, sometimes wipe thousands and hundreds of thousands of them from the face of the earth at one stroke. But apart from such events their whole life is strictly ordered and organised on a plan. Let us imagine a merchant in an old Eastern town living in the fixed conditions of the established routine life which has gone on unchanged for whole centuries. He sells carpets in the same shop where his father and grandfather, and probably his great-grandfather, sold carpets. His whole life from birth to death can be seen as on a map. In a certain year he takes a wife, in a certain year he puts his eldest son in the shop, in a certain year he wins a lawsuit against his neighbour, always using the same obvious method, and always in the same year, day and hour he dies, always of the same cause — of having eaten too much pilaff.

There can be no new events in the lives of such people. But it is just this absoluteness of repetition that creates in them some vague consciousness of the inevitability of everything that happens, a belief in fate, fatalism and, at times, a strange sort of wisdom and calmness, in some cases passing into a kind of ironical contempt for people who are restless, seeking for something, striving after something.

To another type of people of the same category of exact repetition belong historical personages: people whose lives are linked with the great cycles of life, that is to say, with the life of peoples, states, countries — great conquerors, reformers, leaders of the masses, revolutionaries, kings who build up empires, kings who destroy great empires, their own or their enemies', all these belong to this category. There can be no change in the lives of these people either. Every word they pronounce affects the destiny of nations. And they must know their parts perfectly. They can add nothing of their own, they can omit nothing, nor change the meaning of what they have to say.

This type is especially clear if we take weak historical personages, those men whom history puts forward as though intentionally for responsible

---

[6] An untranslatable Russian word, signifying in its first meaning — *life* (in relation to external forms); in its second meaning, as used in literature — life in firmly established forms: peasants' *byt*, merchants' *byt*, country landowners' *byt*; " *byt* circumstance."

The word *byt* is very largely used in connection with the theatre — *byt* play, *byt* actor (different from a character actor), *byt* voice, *byt* intonations or inflexions.

parts when empires or whole cultures are to be destroyed, such people, for instance, as Louis XVI or Nicholas II.

They do nothing, and they do not want to do anything, they only wish to be left in peace, and yet each movement, each gesture, each word of theirs, even words that seem to be uttered by mistake, such as the famous " senseless dreams," [7] have significance and either begin or end a historical period; and all of them, without exception, lead to the ultimate catastrophe. Not a single word can be left out, and even mistakes must be repeated.

" Strong personages " — Napoleons, Cæsars, Genghis Khans — are in no way different from weak personages. They are pieces on the same board, and equally they cannot do anything themselves, cannot say one word of themselves, cannot either add anything to or subtract anything from what they *must* say or do.

In the case also of people who constitute the crowd on the world's stage repetition is inevitable. The crowd must know its rôle very well at any particular moment. No expression of popular feeling during patriotic manifestations or armed revolutions and insurrections, during coronations or revolutions, would be possible if the crowd could be ignorant of its rôle or forget its rôle. And this knowledge is possible only through constant repetition of the same thing.

But if we pass to the separate lives of the people who form the crowd, we shall see that with different people " growing tendencies " produce very different results. " Growing tendencies " may be of two kinds, those which raise the vitality (though only outwardly) and those which lower the vitality.

Let us take the type which lowers the vitality, the type with the growing tendency to degeneration. Failures, drunkards, criminals, prostitutes, suicides, belong to this category. With each new life they " fall " more and more easily, offer less and less resistance. Their vital force gradually weakens, they become living automatons, shadows of themselves, with a single tendency, a single desire, which constitutes their chief passion, their chief vice or their chief weakness. If their life is linked up with the lives of other people, this link gradually weakens and at last disappears altogether. These people pass slowly out of life. This is exactly what happens to suicides. They are surrounded by an atmosphere of strange fatality, and at times they do not even live up to the moment of their suicide, but begin to die sooner and finally cease to be born.

This is real death, for *death* exists just as *birth* exists.

Souls are born and die just like bodies. *The birth* of all souls is the same. How it occurs is perhaps the greatest mystery in life. But the death of souls may be different. The soul may die on one plane of being and pass to a higher plane of being. And it may die altogether, become gradually reduced to nothing, vanish, cease to be.

To the category of dying souls belong people who are known by their

---

[7] The words of the Emperor Nicholas II which were used by mistake when receiving representatives of the " zemstvos " and towns in 1895.

424 ETERNAL RECURRENCE AND THE LAWS OF MANU

tragic fate and especially by their tragic end. It is to these people that the remarkable rule of the Eleusinian Mysteries referred, a rule that has never been rightly understood and interpreted.

Participation in the Mysteries was barred, first, to criminals, second, to foreigners (that is, barbarians) and finally to *people in whose lives great calamities occurred.*

This rule has usually been interpreted in the sense that great calamities in people's lives meant the hostility of the gods or the anger of the gods caused by something that those people had done or omitted to do. But in esoteric understanding it was certainly clear that people whose lives consist of a series of catastrophes could not be admitted to participation in the Mysteries or to initiation, because the fact of these continuous catastrophes showed that they were going down hill and could not be stopped.

In seeming contrast to the descending or unsuccessful type, but in reality in exactly the same position, are people who are successful from the ordinary point of view, but successful through adaptation to the darkest or most senseless sides of life: people who quickly amass enormous fortunes, millionaires and super-millionaires; successful statesmen of opportunist or definitely criminal activities; " scientists " who create bogus theories, which become fashionable and arrest the development of true knowledge; " philanthropists " who support all forms of prohibitive legislation; inventors of high explosives and poisonous gases; sport-addicts of every kind and description; prize-fighters, world champions, record-breakers, cinema-clowns and " stars "; novelists, poets, musicians, painters, actors, commercially successful, but having no other value; founders of crazy sects and cults, and the like. In each new life these people continue to do what they did before, spend less and less time on preparatory training, grasp sooner and sooner the technique of their business and the technique of success, attain greater and greater celebrity or fame. Some of them become " infant prodigies " and show their special capacities from the earliest years.

The danger for the successful type of people is their success. Success hypnotises them, makes them believe that they themselves are the cause of their success. Success makes them follow the line of least resistance, that is, sacrifice everything to success. Therefore nothing changes in their lives, save that success is attained ever more easily and ever more mechanically. Without formulating it they feel that their strength lies precisely in this mechanicalness, and they suppress in themselves all other desires, interests and inclinations.

Men of real science, of real art, of real thought or action, differ from these chiefly in very seldom attaining success. As a rule, they begin to be recognised only long after the end of their earthly life. And this is an exceedingly favourable factor from the point of view of the repetition of their lives. The inner decomposition which almost inevitably comes with success never sets in with them. And they start each new life striving towards their unattainable aim, every time with new strength, and they sometimes begin and " remember " astoundingly early, like some famous musicians or thinkers.

Evolution, that is, inner growth, inner development, cannot be either accidental or mechanical. The ways of evolution are the ways of Jnana-Yoga, Raja-Yoga, Karma-Yoga, Hatha-Yoga and Bhakti-Yoga, or the way of the special doctrine accessible only to few, which was mentioned earlier, in the chapter on Yoga. The five Yogas and the way of the special doctrine are the ways of work on oneself for people of different inner type. But all the ways are equally difficult, all the ways equally demand *the whole of man*.

People of the descending type are excluded from the outset. No evolution is possible for them, for they are incapable of any long and sustained effort, whereas evolution is the result of long and persistent work in a definite direction. In exactly the same position are people of the successful type. People of the failing type are hindered by their failure, people of the successful type are hindered by their success.

For people of " byt " and for historical personages evolution is possible only through very difficult, hidden, Karma-Yoga. They can make no outward changes. And if by some miracle they begin to realise their position and solve the chief enigma of life, they must play a rôle, must pretend that they do not notice or understand anything. Besides Karma-Yoga, Bhakti-Yoga is possible for them in some cases. Karma-Yoga shows them that it is possible to change inwardly without changing outwardly and that only the inward change is of importance. This is an extremely difficult way, an almost impossible way, and it requires a great amount of help from somebody who can help.

Evolution for all categories of people is connected with recollections. Recollection of an *unknown past* has been spoken of earlier. And recollection may be very different in quality and may have very different properties. The evolving individual remembers, although vaguely, his previous lives. But as evolution means escaping from the wheel of the fifth dimension and passing into the spiral of the sixth dimension, recollection has importance only when it bears an active character in a certain definite direction, when it creates discontent with what exists and a longing for new ways.

By this I mean that recollection by itself does not create evolution; on the contrary, it may be the cause of a still worse bondage in life, that is, in the fifth dimension. In these cases, " recollection " takes either " routine life " forms, or pathological forms, hiding itself behind one or another kind of emotional or practical attitude to life.

Sometimes a man definitely begins to think that he knows what is bound to happen. If he is of the successful type, he ascribes it to his sagacity, astuteness, clearness of mind and so on. In reality it is all recollection, though unconscious recollection. A man feels that he has already walked along this road, he almost knows what will be beyond the next turning, and naturally in all these cases recollection produces pride, self-assurance and conceit instead of dissatisfaction.

People of absolute repetition, that is, people of " routine life," and also "historical personages," can have sometimes almost conscious recollection, but it does not awaken them and only binds them more and more to trifles, to things, to customs, to words, to rituals, to gestures, and makes it still more difficult for them to stand apart from themselves and to look at themselves from outside.

A business man explains this recollection by his experience, his capacity to think quickly, to guess correctly, by his " flair," by his " business instinct," by his " intuition." In the case of " great " soldiers, statesmen, revolutionary leaders, navigators who discover new lands, inventors, scientists who create new theories, writers, musicians, artists, it is explained by " talent " or " genius " or " inspiration." In some people recollection evokes mad bravery, or a continual desire to play with their lives. They feel that *this* cannot happen to them, they cannot be killed like other ordinary people. Such are many historical personages, " men of destiny."

With people of the descending type also recollection can be very vivid, but it only intensifies their feeling of the ground crumbling beneath their feet; it intensifies their despair and discontent, which manifest themselves in the form of hatred, spite or impotent anguish, in crimes or excesses.

Thus recollection does not by itself lead to evolution, but evolution, at a certain stage, arouses recollection. In this case, however, recollection is not clouded by a superior or inferior personal interpretation, but becomes more and more conscious.

This is almost all that can be said about eternal recurrence, making use of material within general reach. There remains to be established the relation of the idea of eternal recurrence to the idea of " reincarnation," as it is treated in some teachings.

I have mentioned before that the idea of reincarnation can be regarded as a distortion of the idea of eternal recurrence. And in many cases this is true, although at the same time there are grounds for thinking that the idea of reincarnation has an independent meaning. This meaning can be found only in certain allusions contained in Indian scriptures and in a very few authors in later mystical literature.

But before passing to the origin of the idea of reincarnation or of its independent meaning, I want to set forth in a short form some of the best-known interpretations of this idea.

In modern theosophy, which, as has been said before, of all Indian teachings stands nearest to the cult of Krishna, man is regarded as a complex being consisting of " seven bodies." The higher or the finer of these bodies, the seventh, the sixth and the fifth, are but *principles* contained in the fourth body. The fourth body of man is immortal and can reincarnate. This means that after the death of the physical body and after the successive " deaths " of the second (the astral) and the third (the mental) bodies, which sometimes live very long after the death of the physical body, the fourth, *the causal body*, reincarnates in a new human being, born after a considerable lapse of time in entirely different, new, conditions. According to theosophical authors, several hundred years, and very often a thousand or even two thousand years, elapse between one reincarnation and another.

It must also be noted that the state of the higher bodies, that is, the astral, the mental and the causal, is very different at different stages of man's evolution. In a man who is but little developed, the causal body is hardly more than a principle. It carries with it no recollections. A new reincarnation is, as it were, an independent life. It is only in comparatively high stages of development that the causal body may carry some dim recollections of a former life.

The idea of reincarnation is connected with the idea of "karma." Karma is understood as a chain of causes and effects handed down from one life to another. But into the abstract idea of karma is introduced the idea of retribution. Thus a man's actions towards other people in one life may provoke similar actions on the part of those or of other people towards him in another life; or the same results may be the outcome of accidental causes. Thus, the existence of cripples or of people suffering from painful and revolting diseases is explained by the cruelties committed by these people in their past lives. This is supposed to mean that their own suffering redeems suffering caused by them. In reality in the idea of karma suffering in itself has no redeeming power. A man must only understand something from suffering, must change inwardly and must then begin to act in a different way from before. Then the new karma will, so to speak, wipe out the old one, and a man's sufferings will cease.

Other teachings which accept the idea of reincarnation differ from theosophy only formally, in certain details. Thus European " spiritualistic " teachings recognise the possibility of a quicker reincarnation, not after hundreds or thousands of years, but after a few years or months. Modern Buddhism, as was mentioned before, recognises *immediate* reincarnation after death. In this last case the reincarnating principle (in view of the fact that the existence of the " soul " is denied in Buddhism) is " the *last thought* of the dying man."

In all these conceptions of reincarnation there does not appear to be the slightest doubt regarding the correctness of the usual conception of *time*. And it is this above all which deprives them of all force and all significance. Time is taken as though it actually existed and were such as it is conceived to be in ordinary thinking. And it is taken as such without any limitation or without any argument. The clock, the calendar, history, geological periods, astronomical cycles, evoke no doubt in ordinary thought. But unfortunately, this " old-fashioned time " is in need of very serious amendment.

I pointed out in *Tertium Organum* that in relation to the idea of time Eastern writings have gone much further than Western philosophy. European theosophists are very fond of quoting words from the Vedanta about the " Eternal Now," etc. But between the " Eternal Now " and the calendar there are many intermediate stages, and it is just of these intermediate stages that they know nothing.

A man dies, the cycle of his life is closed, and even if the consciousness or the soul is preserved time disappears. This means that there is no time for the soul; the soul finds itself in eternity. The next day after death, the next year, the next century, do not exist for the soul. In eternity there can be no direction " before " → " after "; there cannot be " before " on one side in one direction and " after " on another side, but there must be both " before " and " after " on all sides. If the soul, that is, the completed life, is attracted anywhere, it can be attracted either into " before " or into " after " along any " great line " at the point of intersection of which it is found. It follows that if reincarnation is possible, it is possible in any direction of eternity. Let us imagine that for the completed cycle of the life of a man, the " great line " is the line of the existence of the earth. Then the path of the soul can lie along this line in both directions, not necessarily in one direction only. The errors in our reckoning of time lie in the fact that when we think of time we straighten out several curves simultaneously: the life of man, the lives of the big organisms of human societies, the life of the whole of humanity, the life of the earth, the life of the sun, and take them as parallel lines and, moreover, as commensurable lines capable of being expressed in the same units of measure. In reality this is impossible, for these curves are both incommensurable and not parallel. We ascribe to them this parallel quality only owing to the linear quality of our thinking and the linear quality of our conception of time.

Difficult though it is for us to get rid of linear thinking and linear conceptions, we nevertheless know enough to be able to understand that *one* time, measured by hours, days, geological periods and light years, does not exist. And therefore it is possible to speak of time for a completed circle only when this circle catches again on to some large circle; but where it will catch on, to the right, or to the left, " before " or " after," is in no way predetermined. We overlook the fact that the predetermination presumed by us is exclusively based on the imaginary analogy of the division of a small circle with the divisions of large circles. And this analogy is built on the supposition that a large circle must be divided into " before " and " after " at the point at which a small circle, a " life " or a " soul," happens to be on it, like the division of the small circle into " before " and " after " during the life of man, with the condition that the direction from " before " to " after " must be the same in both cases.

It is perfectly clear that all these suppositions and analogies have no basis and that the direction of the possible motion of the small circle in eternity is not in any way predetermined.

It is possible to admit that this " small circle," that is, the " soul " or " life," is subject to some kind of magnetic influences which may attract it to one or another point of one or another large circle, but these influences must come from very varied directions.

One may not agree with all the deductions from the above arguments, but with a certain understanding of the matter it is no longer possible to dispute the impossibility of a non-relative time, that is, a general time taken for everything that exists. In every given case time is only the period of the existence of the subject in question. And even this alone makes it impossible to regard time after death in the same way as time before death.

What does the change we call " death " actually mean? As was shown earlier, this change means that the time of the given individual ends. Death means that there is no more time. When the Angel of the Apocalypse says that " there should be time no longer," he speaks of the death of humanity.

All this makes quite clear the impossibility of an elementary treatment of the question without an analysis of the problems of time. Reincarnation, if it exists at all, is a much more complicated phenomenon, to understand which one must have a certain knowledge of the laws of time and eternity.

The laws of time and eternity are illogical laws. They cannot be studied with the four rules of arithmetic. In order to understand them one must be able to think irrationally and without " facts." There is nothing more deceptive than facts, when we cannot have all the facts referring to the matter under discussion and are forced to deal with accessible facts which instead of helping us only distort our vision. And how can we know that we have a sufficient quantity of facts for judgment in one direction or another if we have no general plan of things and know no general system? Our scientific systems based on facts are as deficient as the facts themselves. In order to come to the laws of time and eternity we must start with the understanding of the state in which there is no time and no eternity opposed to one another.

The " Eternal Now " is the state of Brahma, the state in which " everything is everywhere and always," that is, in which every point of space touches every point of time, and which in symbolism is expressed by two intersecting triangles, a six-pointed star.

In this combination time is three-dimensional, just as space is three-dimensional.

But there is a great difference between the three-dimensional time of Brahma and ordinary human one-dimensional time — the line of time which comes from an unknown past and disappears into an unknown future. And this difference is not merely subjective. Man is *in fact* a one-dimensional being in relation to time. This means that in leaving the line of time, i.e. in dying, man does not immediately find himself in the state of Brahma, or the " Eternal Now." There must be many intermediate states, and it is these intermediate states that we must now examine.

If we take as the point of departure the proposition that the aim of the evolution of the human soul must be the attainment of the state of Brahma, of the "*Eternal Now*," then the direction of our thought becomes clear.

From this point of view man, that is, his soul (taking this word without any sophistry, simply in the sense of man's inner being, of his inner existence, of which his body is the temporary receptacle) is a spark of Brahma, a seed of Brahma, which by evolving and developing can attain to the state of Brahma in the same way as the seed of an oak by sprouting and growing becomes an oak and in its turn produces similar seeds.

But the analogy with an oak, a butterfly or any other living being, while demonstrating correctly certain aspects of the evolution of man, obscures other sides of this evolution. The analogy of an oak, etc., does not contain the "Eternal Now." If we want to introduce the "Eternal Now," we must use another analogy.

Let us compare Brahma to a river. He is the source of the river, he is the river itself and he is also the sea into which the river flows. A drop of water in the river, having emerged from Brahma, wishes to return to Brahma. Brahma is All. He is the river, the sea and the source. But to return to Brahma means to return to the source, because otherwise, if the drop is satisfied with a philosophical contemplation of its own possibilities, it may say to itself that it is already in Brahma because Brahma is All, and once the drop is in the river, it is in Brahma, and once it flows with the river towards the sea which is also Brahma, it approaches still nearer to the merging with Brahma. But actually, in this way, it may be further and further removed from the source; and Brahma is the source.

In order to unite with Brahma the drop must return to the source. How can the drop return to the source? Only by moving against the current of the river, against the current of time. "The river" flows in the direction of time. A return to the source must be a movement against time, a movement not into the future, but into the past.

"Life" as we know it, all the external and all the internal life of everything living, flows in one direction, from the past to the future. And all the examples of "evolution" we are able to find also proceed from the past towards the future. Of course it only appears to us to be so, and it appears so because we build our *straight* line of time from a multitude of curves such as the lives of men, the lives of peoples, races, etc. For this purpose we artificially straighten out these curves. But they remain straight only so long as we keep them in our mind, that is, so long as we deliberately see them as straight lines. As soon as we let our attention relax, as soon as we leave some of these lines and pass to others, or to the imaginary whole, they immediately become curves again and thus destroy the entire picture of the whole. At the same time, so long as we see only one line of time, only one current, and cannot see the parallel and the perpendicular currents, we cannot see the reverse currents which must undoubtedly exist, because, after all, time taken as a surface is not a flat surface, but must necessarily be a kind of spherical surface, on which the beginning of a line is also its end, and the end is its beginning.

Let us take again the idea of return to Brahma. Brahma has created the world, or the world has emerged and is emerging from Brahma. Three ways must lead to Brahma: movement forward into the future, movement backward into the past and movement on one spot in the present.

What is movement into the future?

It is the process of life, the process of reproducing oneself in others, the process of the growth and development of human groups and of the whole of humanity. Whether there is evolution in this process is a question open to dispute. What is clear is the picture of the formation, existence and dying, of the big jelly-like organisms which fight each other and devour each other, that is, of human societies, peoples, and races.

What is movement on one spot, in the present?

It is movement along the circle of eternal recurrence, the repetition of life, and the inner growth of the soul which becomes possible owing to that repetition.

What is movement backward into the past?

It is the path of reincarnation, which, if it is possible and exists, probably exists only in the form of reincarnation into the past.

This is precisely the hidden " esoteric " side of the idea of reincarnation, which is so completely forgotten that even allusions to it are difficult to find. But such allusions exist. I will only point to some strange expressions, in the Old Testament.

King David says in dying:

I go the way of all the earth (1 Kings 2. 2).

Joshua says:

And, behold, this day I am going the way of all the earth (Joshua 23. 14).

What is the meaning of these words, what does " the way of the earth " mean?

The way of the earth is its past. " I go the way of the earth " can mean only one thing: I go into time, *I go into the past.*

There are also other expressions:

Aaron shall be gathered unto his people . . . (God says this to Moses and Aaron in mount Hor) (Numbers 20. 24).

And die in the mount whither thou goest up, and be gathered unto thy people; as Aaron thy brother died in mount Hor, and was gathered unto his people (God says to Moses) (Deuteronomy 32. 50).

Then Abraham gave up the ghost, and died in a good old age, an old man, and full of years; and was gathered to his people (Genesis 25. 8).

And Isaac gave up the ghost, and died, and was gathered unto his people . . . (Genesis 35. 29).

I am to be gathered unto my people . . . (Jacob) (Genesis 49. 29).

And yielded up the ghost, and was gathered unto his people (Jacob) (Genesis 49. 33).

Behold therefore, I will gather thee unto thy fathers, and thou shalt be gathered into thy grave in peace; *and thine eyes shall not see all the evil which I will bring upon this place* (2 Kings 22. 20). (God says this to Josiah through the prophetess.)

The words " to be gathered unto his people " have exactly the same meaning as the words "to go the way of all the earth." And the last passage — " I will gather thee unto thy fathers " — even points out the benefit resulting from it, that is, escape from the evil of the present. In the usual interpretation these words are regarded either as indicating a life after death in which a man joins his ancestors, who have passed there before him, or, in a more materialistic sense, as burial in family tombs.

But the first, that is, the interpretation explaining these words by existence after death, does not bear criticism, for it is well known that Judaism contained no idea of existence after death. Had there been such an idea, it would necessarily have been expounded and interpreted in the Bible. Neither does the second explanation, that is, burial in family tombs, answer all the indications mentioned, for the same words also refer to Aaron and to Moses, who died and were buried in the desert.

And, what is particularly important, the expressions, " to go the way of all the earth," " to be gathered unto one's fathers," or " to be gathered unto one's people," never refer to ordinary men or women; these expressions are used only in relation to very few: patriarchs, prophets and leaders of the people. This points to the hidden meaning and hidden aim of " reincarnation in the past."

In the great stream of life which flows from its source there must necessarily be contrary and transverse currents, just as in a tree there is a flow of sap from roots to leaves and a flow of sap from leaves to roots. In the great stream of life the evolutionary movement must be a movement contrary to the general process of growth, a movement against the current, a movement towards the beginning of Time, which is the beginning of All.

Bound to his wheel of repeating lives, man would be unable to avail himself of the possibility of a reverse movement against time, if there were no possibility of reincarnation in another age, in another epoch, near or distant, but at any rate in one nearer to the beginning, that is, one which is in the past.

This is a very strange theory at the first glance. The idea of a *backward* movement in time is unknown and incomprehensible to us.

Actually, however, this idea alone explains the possibility of " evolution " in the true and large meaning of the word.

Evolution, i.e. improvement, must come from the past. It is not enough to evolve in the future, even if this were possible. We cannot leave behind us the sins of our past. We must not forget that nothing disappears. Everything is eternal. Everything that has been is still in existence. The whole history of humanity is "the history of crime," and the material for this history continually grows. We cannot go far forward with such a past as ours. The past still exists, and it gives and will give its results, creating new and ever new crimes. Evil begets evil. In order to destroy the evil-consequence it is necessary to destroy the evil-cause. If the cause of the evil lies in the past, it is useless to look for it in the present. And man must go back, seek for and destroy the causes of evil, however far back they may lie. It is only in this idea that a hint of the possibility of a general evolution can be found. It is only in this idea that the possibility of changing the karma of humanity lies, because changing the karma means changing the past.

The theosophical theory is that every man receives as much evil as he produces. This is "karma" according to theosophical conception. But in this way evil cannot diminish and must necessarily grow. And humanity has no right to dream of a beautiful and bright future while it drags behind it such a trail of evil and crime, which is automatically renewed. The idea of what humanity should do with the load of evil and crime it has accumulated, occupied the minds of many thinkers. Dostoevsky could never get free of the horror of the past sufferings of people long since dead and vanished. And, fundamentally, he was undoubtedly right. Evil, once created, remains and breeds new evil.

Of the better known great teachers of humanity and founders of religions only Christ and the Buddha never advocated any form of struggle with evil by means of violence, that is, by means of new evil. But what has been the outcome of the preaching of love and mercy we know very well.

If evil can be uprooted and its consequences destroyed this can only be if it is arrested at the moment of its inception, *and arrested not by means of another evil*.

All the absurdity of the struggle for a better organisation of life on earth is due to the fact that people attempt to fight the results, leaving the causes of evil and creating new causes of new evil. As yet the precept: "do not oppose evil by evil," cannot produce any results because on their level of development people can only be either indifferent to evil or struggle with evil (or with what they call evil) by means of violence, that is by means of another evil. This struggle is always a struggle against results. People can never reach the causes of evil. It is easy to understand why this is so. The causes of evil are not in the present. They are in the past.

There would be no possibility of thinking of the *evolution of humanity*, if the possibility did not exist for individually evolving men to go into the past and struggle against the causes of the present evil which lie there. This explains *where those people disappear who have remembered their past lives*.

From the ordinary point of view this sounds like an absurdity. But the idea of reincarnation contains this absurdity, or this possibility.

In order to admit the possibility of reincarnation into the past, it becomes necessary to presume plurality of existence, or again co-existence, that is to say, it becomes necessary to suppose that the life of man, while repeating according to the law of eternal recurrence at one " place in time," if it can be put thus, *simultaneously* occurs at another " place in time." And it can be said with almost complete certainty that a man, even approaching the super-human state, will not be conscious of that *simultaneity* of lives and will *remember* one life or the life at one " place in time " as past and feel the other as present.

In the conditions of three-dimensional space and one-dimensional time plurality of existence is impossible. But under the conditions of six-dimensional space-time it is quite natural, because in it " every point of time touches every point of space " and " everything is everywhere and always." In the space-time represented by two intersecting triangles there is nothing strange or impossible in the idea of plurality of existence. And even an approach to these conditions creates for a man the possibility to " go the way of all the earth," to " be gathered to his fathers," which enables him to influence his ancestors or their contemporaries, gradually to change and to make more favourable the conditions of his birth and gradually to surround himself with people who also " remember."

Let us try to imagine such a situation in a more concrete form. Let us suppose that we know that the whole life of a certain man has shaped in a certain way owing to certain things having been done or not done by his grandfather, who died before his birth. Let us now imagine that the man has the possibility of influencing his grandfather in a certain way at a right moment through some of his contemporaries, perhaps simply of opening his eyes to something that he did not know. This may entirely change the conditions of that man's subsequent (in time) life, afford him new possibilities, and so on.

Let us suppose again that a certain man who has actual power in his hands, a statesman or politician or reigning sovereign of some past epoch, manifested an interest in the direction of real knowledge. This would have given the possibility of influencing him if there had been a man near him who could do it. Let us suppose that such a man happens to be beside him. This might give unexpected results of a very useful character, opening up new possibilities for a large number of people.

The privilege of the position of reincarnating into the past for the man who remembers what he has learned in his past life is explained by the fact that he *knows the results*, knows what has sprung from the actions of the people of the time into which he reincarnates.

This does not of course mean that *everything* or *many things* can be altered by one man being reincarnated into the past. The possibilities of altering external events are very small, but they must exist. If in every moment there were only one possibility (see Ch. X) we should live in a world of absolute predetermination, and nothing could be altered. But " moments" differ from one another very greatly in this respect. There are moments with only one possibility; there are moments with several possibilities; and there are moments with many and very varied possibilities. We can understand this by studying our own life. Let us suppose that in our own life we were able to go back ten, fifteen or twenty years. There is great probability in the supposition that we should then like to alter many things, to do many things differently, not to do many things at all. Whether we could do so or not, is a different question.[8] But in the case of reincarnation into the past this question is much simpler because only that man can reincarnate who has already attained great consciousness and power.

By this means, that is, by means of the reincarnation into the past of people who have reached a certain degree of inner development, a reverse current is created in the midst of the stream of life. This reverse current is the *evolutionary movement*, the movement which gradually makes life better and nobler, and itself returns enriched to the source from which it originated.

In comparison with this idea, the idea of reincarnation into the future seems not only fruitless, but almost a mockery of the poor reincarnating souls.

Imagine a man who lived in ancient Rome, a very clever and, for his time, an educated man, who reincarnates in our times into the circumstances of the average life of the educated classes in Europe. He would be totally out of place in these circumstances. He would have kept thousands of inclinations and desires for which there is no room in modern life. He would be full of strange superstitions, beliefs and tendencies, bordering on the criminal. What is for him perfectly natural, normal and even necessary would be for the people surrounding him immoral, against nature and vicious. What is for him perfectly lawful and right would be in their eyes criminal and revolting, and so on. The position of the poor Roman in our times would be very hard and difficult both for himself and for those round him.

In the same way a man of our times transferred into an unknown and remote future would find himself surrounded by entirely unfamiliar conditions and among people living with interests incomprehensible to him. He would feel alien in this new life, and it would require many turns of the wheel of eternal recurrence and the creation of extensive unnecessary karma before he adapted himself to the new surroundings and to the new forms of thinking.

But a man of our times reincarnated in ancient Rome would extract for himself an immense amount of profit out of his observations and comparison of the lives of two epochs so different from one another. And, certainly, wherever he appeared he would bring with him a civilising current, not because our times are more civilised, but because he himself, owing to his inadaptability to the Roman forms of life, would feel very strongly the bar-

---

[8] This subject is touched on by the author in a novel, *The Wheel of Fortune*.

barousness of the epoch; he would feel himself standing outside everything, and could not share the enthusiasm of his new contemporaries in any direction whatever.

Reincarnation into the past is connected with eternal recurrence also in the following way. Reincarnation is possible only into *places* which become free, into "vacancies." These vacancies can occur in two ways.

The first way is when a soul, after many lives of conscious struggle, obtains freedom, leaves the circle of lives in the particular " place in time " and goes in the direction of its source, that is, into the past.

The second way is when a soul dies, that is, when, after many lives spent in sliding down an incline, in moving along a diminishing spiral, with a quicker and quicker end, a soul ceases to be born.

Both the first and the second cases leave *vacant places* for reincarnation.

In the first case, that is, in the case of incarnation in the place of a man who has completed his task and has gone into the past, the soul receives a definite and usually a very complicated and difficult part, which it has to play through life, the part of the man who has gone away. The man has gone having freed himself internally, but externally having a large and varied karma. His place must be filled. The man who has gone cannot disappear from life. A new actor must impersonate the old one.

In the other case, where the soul is born in the place of a soul who has died, it also receives a very difficult part, though the difficulty here is of a quite different kind and may have been created by the personal qualities of the man who has gone or by the external conditions of his life. The difference in comparison with the first case is that the incarnating soul in this case must not play any part. It can create its own karma from the very beginning. But the conditions of birth in this case can be very unfavourable. Many souls die just because of the hard conditions of their birth, without being able to stand the circumstances in which they have to live. Such are people with a heavy and pathological heredity, the children of vicious, criminal or abnormal parents. And such also are people who are born during epochs of long wars, revolutions, barbarian invasions, during the epochs of the fall of civilisations and the destruction of nations, when people are born only to perish among tens and hundreds of thousands of others, always in the same way, without any hope of salvation and without any possibility of altering their fate.

Birth under such conditions is a very difficult examination for the reincarnating soul. But stronger and more resistant souls overcome these conditions and live in them, gradually creating round them a kind of island to which other souls in peril may swim.

Besides these, so to speak, natural parts, there are moreover in history specially created parts for the reincarnation of people who have already attained a certain degree of consciousness. Some of these parts are known, for they belong to historical personages behind whom the influence of esoteric schools can be supposed. Other parts of this kind belong to personages who are also sometimes known in history, but who appear outwardly to stand very far from any esotericism. And there are still other parts which belong to entirely unknown people who have done great work, but have left no visible traces.

As to personages who belong to schools but appear outwardly to have no relation to esotericism, very little can be said. If such people exist, their inner life must be quite independent of their outer life. And reincarnation in the place of such people can be admitted only for those souls who have had a special training for such a double life. For a man who has developed in ordinary conditions such reincarnation would be impossible.

But even for people specially trained for difficult parts there cannot be a reincarnation the predominant tendency of which contradicts esoteric work.

There is not a single esoteric tradition which shows the possibility of an *inner contradiction* between the outer part in life and the inner work. This means that a man who belongs to schools secretly cannot act against them openly. Still less is it possible that a man belonging to an esoteric school should wear a mask of pseudo-occultism or by his conduct degrade the idea of schools. Such assertions are sometimes met with, having originated from people who once had, but afterwards lost, a connection with esoteric schools, or who make esoteric ideas a means for serving their personal aims.

It never can happen otherwise. It is the greatest error to think it possible that " good " may hide under the mask of " evil," that " truth " may hide under the mask of " deceit." This is just as impossible as *conscious evil* is impossible. Evil, by its very nature, must necessarily be unconscious and blind. Therefore a life which serves unconscious and blind powers, or a life which serves deceit or is based on deceit, cannot be *a conscious part*.

The rôle of a man in life, when he belongs to an esoteric school, always expresses his inner being, and for this very reason his life sometimes remains a historical enigma.

Such rôles belong, for instance, to certain persons in the Gospel drama. I have referred before to the drama of Christ. But the drama of Christ was not the drama of Christ alone. It was a drama with a great number of *dramatis personae* who played definite rôles which were firmly fixed in their minds. The drama of Christ, the whole story told in the Gospels, is of intense interest from the point of view of the mechanism of eternal recurrence and reincarnation in the past.

The first question that arises from the point of view of eternal recurrence is this:

Is it possible that all the *dramatis personae* of the Gospel drama are destined eternally to play their parts, eternally to say the same words, eternally to do the same thing?

In order to answer this question it is necessary to understand clearly that in the Gospel drama there are two kinds of part and two kinds of actor. The same words must be said, the same deeds must be done, the same scenes must be enacted before the spectators and before history. But in the one case the actors are always the same, in the other they may be different. The actor who once played Judas will always play Judas, but the actor who once played Christ may next time play some other conscious part, for instance, that of John the Baptist. The Apostles may exchange rôles. But there may have been some among them who did not know their rôles thoroughly enough or who attempted to alter them, to introduce something of their own, to " improve " something. These will have to play the same rôles over and over again until they have learned them to perfection and remember them word for word. We do not know their mistakes, for mistakes were corrected in the Gospels, which were written by men who understood the meaning and purpose of the drama of Christ. But the actual story might easily have differed in its details from the story described in the Gospels. The Apostles may not only exchange rôles or act better the next time, but they may pass over to more important, more central, rôles in the drama, and each of them may hope some day to play Christ.

These are conscious rôles. Unconscious rôles cannot change. The priests who tried Jesus and incited the people against him; all the people who formed the crowd that demanded his death; the soldiers who parted his garments, and so on, will play their rôles without the slightest change. The unconscious rôles of the Gospel drama are firmly fixed in their invariable repetition. What else can a man cry who has cried " *crucify him* "? It is absolutely impossible for him to cry anything else or even to think of anything else. And he will go on crying it through all the cycles of eternity. What can Pilate do or say *differently*? He can do nothing. He can only " wash his hands " again. All these people have crucified themselves, have nailed themselves to the cross of Jesus, for all eternity. And no power can tear them from this cross.

There is deep meaning in the myth of the " Wandering " or " Eternal Jew." He *eternally* says and will say his " *Go on quicker!* " [9]

There can be no mistake in the unconscious rôles because each man played his unconscious rôle for the first time according to his type, education, environment, epoch, in obeying the crowd instinct, in imitating other people and so on. The next time his rôle was repeated mechanically, and the more he played it, the more thoroughly he knew his rôle, the less possibility was there of mistake or misunderstanding. " Eternal repetition " took control of his rôle, and no mistake was any longer possible. The producer of the drama of Christ could rely on the unconscious rôles as surely as he could rely on the scenery of Judea, on customs, on feast-days, and the like.

But conscious rôles require preparation.

---

[9] The legend of the " Wandering Jew " (or " Eternal Jew ") refers to the man at whose doors Jesus wished to rest while carrying the cross, and who cried to him: " Go on quicker! " and was cursed by Jesus and made to wander eternally, having no possibility either of dying or of resting. The legend has been known in literature since the beginning of the 17th century. There is another version of it which existed in the 13th century.

In the further development of Christianity, esoteric Christianity became a school for training actors for this drama. The drama itself, so to speak, was an examination performance. All this together gave a very interesting picture. The drama as the beginning, as the source, created religion, and the religion as the result, as the " river," by its reverse current fed the " source." The mental image of all this suggested the cosmic process.

The transformation of Christianity into the Church, the pact between Church and State, the distortion and perversion of the original idea of the *religion of love* until it descended to the preaching of Christianity sword in hand, the slaughter of heretics, the Inquisition; all these were a result of the Gospel drama. Such was the inevitable outcome of the work of the selection and separation of people capable of taking up esoteric work from among the masses of ordinary humanity. People incapable of esoteric work also heard the teaching of the Gospels and naturally had to appropriate the tenets and principles of the Gospels and adapt them to their own understanding, to their own life, to the struggle against one another, to their crimes, and so on.

But nothing is wasted in the economics of esotericism, and the distorted forms of Christianity also have their significance, because many people are able to receive ideas of a higher order only in a distorted form, while some of these people having received these ideas in a distorted form can sometimes feel that they are distorted and can begin to search for truth and sometimes reach the original source.

The crucifixion of Christ continues incessantly. Instead of Christ himself, it is his teaching, his ideas, that are crucified; and the crowd which has faith in its leaders cries: " Crucify him! "

The two great religions which came into being one shortly after the other, namely, Christianity and Buddhism, have never been studied together *as completing one another*; they have usually been regarded as opposed to one another in their most fundamental points.

The life of Prince Gautama, who became the Buddha, i.e. the Enlightened One, is not a drama in the same sense as the life of Christ, or at least, as the three last years of the life of Christ; though in Buddhism the life of Buddha has become a myth from which also no single feature can be omitted and no word left out.

Buddha lived long and created a large monastic order, which after his death spread its influence far and wide and which has in fact never distorted the teaching of Buddha to the extent to which the teaching of Christ has been distorted by his followers. Of course the life of Buddha is also a conscious rôle through which many actors can pass and the playing of which is certainly not easy, though it belongs to the natural rôles. Christ's rôle was specially created.

The later Buddhism in its inner circles is also a school, preparing actors for the rôles of Prince Gautama and his nearest disciples and followers. But of course, like Christianity, it is not a school in its entirety. Just as in Christianity, only very rare and hidden currents in it can be connected with the school idea.

In connection with the question of the relation of ideas of eternal recurrence and " reincarnation in the past " to ideas of evolution, it is interesting to see whether any social theories exist in esotericism, that is, whether esoteric teachings conceive any possibility of an organisation of human groups or communities which would help the given culture to attain the greatest results and which generally would help the evolution of humanity.

This is particularly interesting in our times when such great importance is attached to social theories of every kind, and when the most fantastic speculations in this domain are elevated to the rank of sciences, or dogmatised directly as a kind of rationalistic religion.

An answer to these questions exists. The esoteric idea of the ideal organisation of humanity is division into castes according to the laws of Manu.

In the code of the Laws of Manu,[10] as it is known and has come down to us, division into castes is put as the corner-stone of the whole social structure. And the very essence of the nature of man is regarded as being the cause of this division, on the basis of which man was created.

LAWS OF MANU

Chapter I.

31. For the prosperity of the worlds he created from his mouth, his arms, his thighs and his feet the Brahman, the Kshatriya, the Vaisya and the Sudra.

88. To Brahmans he assigned teaching of the Veda and studying, sacrificing for their own benefit and for others, giving and accepting alms.

89. Kshatriya he commanded to protect the people, to bestow gifts, to offer sacrifices, to study the Veda and to refrain from attachment to sensual pleasures.

90. Vaisya he commanded to breed cattle, to bestow gifts, to offer sacrifices, to study the Veda, to trade, to lend money and to cultivate land.

91. One occupation only did the Lord prescribe to the Sudra — to serve uncomplainingly these other three castes.

And further:

98. The very birth of a Brahman is an eternal incarnation of the sacred law; for he is born for the fulfilment of the sacred law and is identified with Brahma.

99. Coming into the world, the Brahman occupies the highest place on earth, as the lord of all created beings, for the protection of the treasuries of the law.

---

[10] The following quotations are translated from the Russian text. *Laws of Manu.* Translation from the Sanscrit, by S. D. Elmanovitch. Published by the Society of Russian Orientalists, St. Petersburg, 1913. There is an English translation. *The collection of the Sacred Books of the East;* edited by Max Müller, translated by G. Buhler and published by the Oxford University Press in 1885.

100. All that exists on earth is the property of the Brahman; owing to the excellence of his origin the Brahman has in truth the right to it all.

101. The Brahman eats only his own food, wears only his own clothes, gives only his own property as alms; other mortals exist only through the benevolence of the Brahman.

102. In order clearly to establish his own duties and the duties of other castes, according to their order, the wise Manu, who originated from the Self-existent, composed these Institutes of the sacred law.

103. A wise Brahman must carefully study them, and he must properly instruct his pupils in them, but no one else must do so.

104. A Brahman who studies these Institutes and faithfully fulfils the duties prescribed in them is never defiled by sinful thoughts, words or deeds.

105. He sanctifies every assemblage which he may enter, seven ancestors and seven descendants, and he alone deserves to possess the whole of this earth.

Chapter IX.
322. Kshatriyas do not prosper without Brahmans, Brahmans do not prosper without Kshatriyas; Brahmans and Kshatriyas, being closely united, prosper in this world and in the next.

Chapter II.
135. Know that a Brahman of ten years and a Kshatriya of a hundred years stand to each other in the relation of father and son; but of the two the Brahman is the father.

Chapter IX.
329. A Vaisya must know the relative price of precious stones, pearls, coral, metals, clothes made of woven fabric, perfumes and condiments.

300. He must know the manner of sowing seeds, good and bad properties of the soil, and he must have a perfect knowledge of all measures and weights.

331. Moreover, the merits and demerits of merchandise, the advantages and disadvantages of different countries, the probable profits and losses on merchandise and means of properly rearing the cattle.

332. He must know the proper wages of servants, the various languages of men, methods of preserving goods and rules of purchase and sale.

333. He must make the greatest efforts to increase his property in a legitimate manner and must zealously give food to all created beings.

335. A Sudra who is pure, obedient to the higher classes, meek in his speech, free from pride and always seeking refuge with Brahmans, attains (in his future life) a higher caste.

Chapter X.
1. The three twice-born castes, discharging their prescribed duties, must study the Veda; but of them only the Brahman must explain it, and not the other two; such is the established rule.

2. The Brahman must know the means of subsistence prescribed for all, instruct the others, and himself live according to the law.

3. Owing to his supremacy, the excellence of his origin, the observation of special restrictive rules and the distinction of his initiation, the Brahman is the lord of all castes.

5. In all castes only those children who are born in direct order, from wives

equal in caste and married as virgins, must be regarded as belonging to the same caste (as their parents).

9. From a Kshatriya and a Sudra woman a being is born, called Ugra, resembling both a Kshatriya and a Sudra, horrible in his ways and finding pleasure in cruelty.

12. From Sudras with Vaisya, Kshatriya and Brahman women are born an Ayogava, a Kshattri and a Kandala, the lowest of men, sons who owe their origin to a mixing of castes.

57. A man of impure origin who does not belong to any caste, Varna, but whose character is unknown and who, although not an Aryan, looks like an Aryan, may be recognised by his actions.

58. Behaviour unworthy of an Aryan, rudeness, cruelty and habitual neglect of prescribed duties betray in this world a man of impure origin.

61. But every kingdom in which these illegitimately born persons destroy the purity of castes immediately perishes together with its inhabitants.

63. Refraining from injuring others, truthfulness, abstention from unlawful appropriation of the property of others, purity and restraint of the organs, Manu has declared the essence of the law for the four castes.

71. Seed sown on barren soil perishes in it; a fertile field in which seed that is not good is sown, will remain barren.

75. Teaching, studying, sacrificing for himself, sacrificing for others, offering gifts and receiving them are the six actions prescribed for a Brahman.

76. But of the six actions prescribed for him three serve as means of his subsistence: sacrifice for others, teaching and accepting gifts from pure men.

77. Three actions incumbent on the Brahman are forbidden to the Kshatriya: teaching, sacrificing for others and, third, accepting gifts.

78. The same are equally forbidden to the Vaisya, such is the established rule; for Manu, the lord of creatures, did not prescribe them for men of these two castes.

79. To carry sword and arrow is prescribed for the Kshatriya as means of subsistence; trading, breeding of cattle and agriculture are prescribed for the Vaisya; but their duties are generosity, the study of the Veda and the performance of sacrifices.

80. Among the different occupations the most appropriate for the Brahman is the teaching of the Vedas, for the Kshatriya, protection of people, and for the Vaisya, trading.

81. But if a Brahman cannot exist by his special occupations just mentioned, he can live by carrying out the duties of a Kshatriya; for the latter follows immediately after him.

82. If it be asked: " How must it be, if he is not able to maintain himself by any of these occupations? " the answer is: " He may lead the life of a Vaisya, employing himself in agriculture and breeding cattle."

95. A Kshatriya, fallen into misfortune, may subsist by any of these (means); but he must never arrogantly lead the life prescribed for his superiors.

96. A man of lower caste, who through greed lives by the occupations of a higher caste, must be deprived by the king of his possessions and banished.

97. It is better to fulfil one's own prescribed duty (dharma) imperfectly than to fulfil perfectly the duty of another; for the man who lives according to the rule of another caste is immediately excluded from his own.

98. A Vaisya who is unable to subsist by the fulfilment of his duties may maintain himself even by occupations peculiar to the Sudra, avoiding, however, actions forbidden to him, and he must give it up when he is able to do so.

121. If a Sudra, unable to subsist through serving the Brahmans, seeks a livelihood, he may serve the Kshatriyas, or he may also procure means of subsistence by serving a rich Vaisya.

122. But he, a Sudra, must serve the Brahmans either for the sake of heaven or for the sake of a double aim (this life and the future); for whoever is called the servant of a Brahman thereby attains all his aims.

123. The service of Brahmans is considered the most important occupation for a Sudra; for everything else he may do besides this will not bear him any fruit.

99. But a Sudra unable to find service with the twice-born (men of three castes) and threatened by the loss of his sons and wife through hunger may maintain himself by handicrafts.

From the rules for a Snâtaka (householder):

61. He must not live in a country governed by Sudras, nor in one inhabited by impious men, nor in one conquered by heretics, nor in one abounding with men of lower castes.

79. He must not be in the company of outcastes, nor of Kandalas, nor of Pukkases, nor of idiots, nor of arrogant men, nor of men of low class, nor of Antyâvasâyins (grave-diggers).

Chapter VIII.

22. A kingdom peopled mostly by Sudras, filled with godless men and deprived of twice-born inhabitants, will soon wholly perish, stricken by hunger and disease.

The Laws of Manu are remarkable in many respects. They contain much that the people of our times seek for and cannot find, because they do not know even how to approach what they want. First of all, it is altogether beyond doubt that the form in which the Laws of Manu have reached us is not the original form. Almost the whole of it is a later " Brahmin " fabrication. Of the original text of the Laws of Manu there remain only the skeleton and about a hundred verses admitting of a double interpretation, and by reason of this harmless from the point of view of the ruling castes, and therefore left unchanged. The passages quoted from the Laws of Manu constitute almost all that has remained of what can be regarded as genuine. The rest is a falsification, with the exception of a few verses of cosmological meaning in the beginning of the book, and also rules of a secondary importance admitting of different interpretations.

In the original the Laws of Manu were much less a code, in the sense of a civil or criminal code, than a record of physical and biological laws. And Manu himself was less a " lawgiver " than a law-investigator, or a law-discoverer. His teaching on castes is not legislation, but a " record " of the laws of nature. The laws of the castes are for him the laws of the universe, the laws of nature.

The definitions of castes in the laws of Manu are interesting first of all owing to the exactitude with which they point out the fundamental types of men, and also to the astounding psychological accuracy of the description of these types.

Verse 31. Chapter I.

For the prosperity of the worlds he created from his mouth, his arms, his thighs and his feet the Brahman, the Kshatriya, the Vaisya and the Sudra.

This verse points out, first, that mankind, as it is, was created for some cosmic purpose and plays a certain part in the life of the worlds; and, second, points out an analogy between mankind and Brahma. The idea is the same as that contained in the Biblical story of the creation of man, where God created man *in his own image and likeness*.

The definitions of castes and their functions are also full of significance.

To Brahmans pertain the study of the Veda and the teaching of others, the offering of sacrifices (prayer) for themselves and for others, the giving and receiving of alms.

Thus no external struggle of any kind enters into the activities of a Brahman. A Brahman must not fight for anything material. He only accepts what is given to him. All external struggle belongs to Kshatriyas and Vaisyas. But to Kshatriyas struggle is permitted and enjoined only *for others*, whereas to Vaisyas struggle is permitted *for themselves*.

Further, Kshatriyas and Vaisyas may only study the Veda, but must not teach others; they may give, but must not accept alms; they may offer sacrifices for themselves only, but not for others.

The fundamental difference between Kshatriyas and Vaisyas is that the activity of a Kshatriya is for others, he must protect and govern the people while obeying Brahmans only; whereas activity for himself is permitted to a Vaisya: he may trade, lend money, cultivate the land and is obliged to obey Kshatriyas and Brahmans.

The *only* duty of a Sudra is to serve the three castes. This means that Sudras are people without initiative or with wrong initiative, who must obey the will of others.

It is quite possible that there was a time, probably not a very long period, when the teaching of Manu was rightly understood somewhere, when the ruling position in life was occupied by Brahmans; Kshatriyas obeyed them, Vaisyas in their turn were subordinate to Kshatriyas, and Sudras served the three castes. But at that period the castes were certainly not hereditary.

Probably Brahmans, who controlled education, determined the caste of children, who were afterwards brought up in accordance with their natural faculties and inclinations as either Brahmans, or Kshatriyas, or Vaisyas, or Sudras. There undoubtedly existed a thoroughly elaborate system of observation of the children for determining their caste, and an elaborate system of tests for the verification of the observations.

Moreover it was possible for a man to be transferred from a lower caste into a higher one, as verse 335 of Chapter IX shows:

A Sudra who is pure, obedient to all castes, meek in his speech, free from pride and always seeking refuge with Brahmans attains (in his future life) a higher caste.

It is remarkable that in the Russian text I possess, as also in the English, these words (*in his future life*) appear in brackets. This means that they are not in the original, that is in Sanscrit, and have been inserted by the translators, because in their opinion they are implied by the preceding words.

It is necessary to understand what this may mean. Translations from Sanscrit in general present very great difficulties, for in Sanscrit many things are " implied." Usually in translations the implied words are placed in brackets. This naturally permits of the most varied interpretations. Very often the idea of one or another action, situation or relation is regarded as being contained in the preceding words. Thus the word " attains " means in certain cases " attains in his future life." Naturally, however, these formal meanings changed at different periods and different epochs. And it would certainly be wrong to assert that a given word *always* implies other words which should follow it, but which are not in the text. In this particular case the Laws of Manu are much older than the idea that the verb " *to attain* " implies " in the future life."

But this is precisely where the chief misunderstanding lies. The meaning of Sanscrit words changed in different periods of history. To which period do the " Laws of Manu " belong? If we take that period at which they already existed in the form in which we know them, it is not the period during which they first appeared. And at the period during which they appeared, that is, in the prehistoric epoch, language was simpler and all later additions to verbs in the form of implied words were not yet in existence. " *To attain* " meant simply " to attain now," exactly as it does in modern languages. Therefore, the text quoted, instead of strengthening the bondage of the castes, establishes the possibility of elevation to a higher caste. This possibility exists even for a Sudra. And it is only the later " Brahmin " interpretation that has added the new words or their meaning and has made this verse legalise the bondage of castes, whereas in reality it had a directly opposite meaning.

Further, the Laws of Manu relating to marriage are full of deep significance and therefore probably they are completely distorted. In his teaching concerning marriage Manu undoubtedly speaks of what happens or may happen as the result of a wrong union of people of different castes, that is, people who are different in their inner nature. And he specially emphasises those negative effects which result from the union of men of a higher inner development, men of the " higher castes," with women of an inferior development, of the " lower castes," or similarly, from the union of women of the higher castes with men of the lower castes. A Brahman must marry a Brahman woman. That is the principle. There must be equality in marriage. In an unequal marriage the lower brings the higher down to his own level. This is especially disastrous for women and their posterity.

The idea is that the sex instinct, both in man and in woman, and especially in woman, is the instinct of selection, the instinct of search for the best. To seek the best is the task which nature has imposed on the sex instinct. A sex instinct which does not answer this requirement does not fulfil its purpose. Degeneration inevitably results if instead of looking for the best and the strongest, the sex instinct either becomes indifferent or is drawn towards the worst and the weakest.

It is to the woman, because of her special properties, that is, because of her "instinctivity" and emotionality, that the chief rôle in upholding the higher properties of the race belongs. On her instincts, on her choice, depends the protection of the quality of the race. If these instincts act, the race remains on a definite level; if the instincts do not act, the race inevitably declines and degenerates. A woman who could choose a stronger and better man, but gives herself to a weak or inferior man for some kind of external consideration, or because of an inner perversion or loss of a right valuation of her own feelings, commits the greatest crime against nature. The worst possibility is the marriage of a Brahman woman with a Sudra. A Kandala, the lowest kind of man, is born from such a union.

But a right understanding and a right application of the Laws of Manu demand a very high development in men. It is quite clear that the ordinary " human " understanding could not help establishing hereditary castes. Did right castes ever exist? Did the order which Manu teaches ever exist? How can we tell? Did true Christianity ever exist? We understand perfectly well that historical " Christianity," in any case the greater part of it, is nothing but a distortion of the ideas of Christ and the Gospels. And it is quite possible that the Laws of Manu also in their true form and in their totality were never carried out in life.

Division into castes represents an ideal social organisation in accordance with esoteric systems. The reason for this lies, of course, in the fact that it is a natural division. Whether people wish it or not, whether they recognise it or not, they are divided into four castes. There are Brahmans, there are Kshatriyas, there are Vaisyas, and there are Sudras. No human legislation, no philosophical intricacies, no pseudo-sciences and no forms of terror can abolish this fact. And the *normal* functioning and development of human societies are possible only if this fact is recognised and acted on. All theories and all attempts at forcible reform based either on the principle of hereditary castes, or on the principle of " equality," or on the principle of the supremacy of the proletariat and the struggle against hereditary castes, are equally useless, and all alike only make the situation of humanity worse. And at the same time actually, *historically*, humanity knows nothing else. There are only two ways for it — either hereditary castes and despotism, or struggle with hereditary castes and despotism. All the fluctuations of the history of humanity occur between these two ways. The third way, that is, the right division of castes, is shown, but humanity has never, to our knowledge, followed this way, and there are no grounds for thinking that it will ever turn into this way.

In modern life there are no tendencies leading towards a right division of castes. There is not even any idea of such a division, and there cannot be such an idea, because the understanding of the right division of castes was forgotten long before the beginning of our civilisation.

But even an accidental approach to a right division into castes immediately gives a result which lights up history for many centuries afterwards.

All the most brilliant periods of history, without exception, were periods in which the social order approached the caste system, but in which the principle of hereditary castes either was already weakening or had not yet become firm enough. Such were the brightest periods in the history of Greece and Rome, such was the epoch of the " Renaissance," such was the 18th century in France and such was the 19th century and the beginning of the 20th century in Russia. These approaches were accidental and imperfect, therefore they did not last long and ended in catastrophes; and usually, the higher the rise went, the deeper and more real was the fall. After such a fall people are not willing for a long time to believe that the epoch of rise has passed and will not return again; and they seldom wish to understand that the very evil of the preceding period, that is, division between the classes of society, was the cause of the rise and growth of the culture.

It is remarkable that an approach to a division into castes is almost always accompanied in history by one and the same phenomenon, namely, by the formation of an independent " intelligentsia." The formation of an " intelligentsia " is the beginning of the gathering together of people of higher castes, people who are not yet conscious of themselves and do not understand themselves, but who, nevertheless, act in accordance with the principles of their dimly felt caste. The characteristic features of the " intelligentsia " are always and everywhere the same. First there is a craving for *disinterested* activity, then a very impatient feeling of the indispensability of *personal freedom* for all and a very rebellious attitude towards everyone and everything standing in the way of freedom of thought, speech and individual manifestation. In the conditions of modern life, that is, amidst all the absurdities of the present order of things, the " intelligentsia " becomes naturally revolutionary. It is very difficult to imagine the conditions in which the " intelligentsia " could be peaceful and loyal or constructing anything outside the sphere of science and art. In the conditions of modern life the " intelligentsia " is a destructive element. But the vagueness of its caste feeling and the vagueness of its understanding of aims and means, of friends and enemies, create the fundamental errors of the " intelligentsia." It is carried away by utopian theories of the common good and often finds that it has itself to serve the lower castes and be guided by their desires. Renouncing in this way its birthright the "intelligentsia" falls into the power of the "outcastes" and, becoming an instrument in their hands, begins unintentionally to serve their interests. Acting in this way the "intelligentsia" loses the meaning of its existence and the elemental forces aroused by it turn against it. This is exactly what happened in Russia with the most tragic consequences not only for the "intelligentsia" itself but chiefly for the "people" whom the "intelligentsia" strove to "liberate."

These tragic results of the "liberating movement" to which the intelligentsia gave its leadership, sympathy and support, are explained by the appearance, immediately after the intelligentsia, of two new classes of contemporary society — the "pseudo-intelligentsia" and the "semi-intelligentsia." These two classes represent outcaste formations and are, so to speak, *refuse* from the process of the formation of the intelligentsia. Like all outcaste formations the "pseudo-intelligentsia" and the "semi-intelligentsia" contain a very large percentage of the criminal element and in general sympathise with the criminal, are interested in the criminal and are ready at any moment to become criminal themselves, especially (the pseudo-intelligentsia) if it does not offer much danger.

But having no value of any kind, either moral or intellectual, these two new classes are very strong in numbers in modern life and power naturally passes into their hands (that is, into the hands of the pseudo-intelligentsia) when it falls from the hands of the old governments. In order to preserve this power they are ready to sacrifice anything and first of all the very "people" in whose name the intelligentsia carried on its struggle.

The intelligentsia cannot foresee this and even does not understand it after it has already happened because it does not understand itself and does not understand its rôle and the weakness of its theories.

Theories have played and they still play an unusually big rôle in the life of modern society. People have believed and many believe till now that they will be able to alter and reconstruct the whole life of humanity with the help of theories or by following theories. At no time in history have theories played such a rôle as at the present time, or, to speak more correctly, during the period immediately preceding the present time. Its faith in theories is the cardinal sin of the "intelligentsia." The "pseudo-intelligentsia," outwardly imitating the "intelligentsia," also bases itself on theories but it does not idealise its theories, on the contrary it introduces a great deal of sophistry into them and makes them the means of personal adaptation of life.

But in putting their hopes whether sincerely or insincerely in theories people neither see nor understand that at the moment of their practical application theories inevitably encounter other theories, and that resistance from these theories, as well as natural opposition from previously created forces and inertiæ, *inevitably change the results of the introduction of the-*

ories into life. In other words they do not realise that theories applied to life give, not the results expected of them, but almost inevitably the opposite. They do not understand that *resistance* changes the results of the application of theories as compared with the results that would have been obtained had there been no resistance. Actually no theory which meets with resistance can be applied to life in its pure form, it must be adapted to existing conditions. And the result is that even if a theory contains within it a certain possibility of realisation or a certain strength this strength will be consumed in struggling against resistance and nothing will be left of the theory except an empty shell, that is, nothing but words, names and slogans which cover facts diametrically opposed to the theory itself. And this is not due either to accident or to failure but to a general law, immovable and unchangeable. It is based on the fact that no theory can count upon general recognition, there will inevitably be another theory contradicting the first. And in the struggle for recognition both theories will lose their most essential features and become their own opposites.

Such is the vicious circle in which humanity moves and from which apparently it cannot escape.

In studying the structure of modern society from the point of view of the laws of Manu the question naturally arises whether the laws of Manu do not give any practical indications of the solution of the problems hanging over contemporary humanity.

But no practical indications of the methods of achieving a better order of things can be derived from the laws of Manu.

The laws of Manu merely show the complete helplessness of all attempts to reconstruct life by violent means and the uselessness of attempts to act through the masses or by using the masses, because in both cases the results which are obtained are the opposite to what was expected.

The reorganisation of society according to the laws of Manu, when such reorganisation is possible, must begin from above with the Brahmins and the Kshatriyas. This needs, to begin with, the formation of sufficiently strong enough groups of Brahmins and Kshatriyas and a corresponding preparation of other castes who should be able to obey them and follow them.

None of the modern ideas of the organisation or the reorganisation of society leads to this either directly or indirectly. On the contrary, they all without exception lead in the opposite direction, upholding the mixing of castes or creating new caste divisions upon entirely false bases. This explains the astonishing similarity and the almost complete identity of the results attained by social theories diametrically opposed in their aims, principles and slogans. But to observe this identity of results (if it is possible to give the name " results " to what, in many cases, is the direct opposite of the aim) one must " have eyes to see."

The blind leaders of the blind cannot see this and, walking in a circle or moving in a direction opposite to the one they have chosen they continue to believe they are moving in their original direction.

Where is the way out of all this? And is there a way out?

We must recognise the fact that no one knows this. There is only one thing certain and this is that none of the ways offered to humanity by its friends and benefactors is in any sense a way out. Life is becoming more and more entangled and more and more complicated, but even in this entanglement and complication it does not assume any new forms but endlessly repeats the same old forms.

The only favourable solution we can hope for comes to this: that the multiplicity of *opposed* negative forces may lead to a positive result. Such things happen and, in reality, it is only thanks to them that we exist in this best of all worlds.

1912–1934

Chapter XII

SEX AND EVOLUTION

❧

THE ENIGMA of death is connected with the enigma of birth, the enigma of disappearance with the enigma of appearance. The enigma of birth or appearance is connected with the enigma of love, with the enigma of sex, i.e. of the division of the sexes and their attraction to one another.

A man dies, and the moments of his death agony, the moments of his last thoughts and realisations, his last sensations and last regrets, are connected with the sensations of love which create new birth. Which precedes and which follows the other? All this must be simultaneous. Then the soul sinks into sleep, and then awakes in the same world as before, in the same house, with the same parents.

What happens at the moment when, according to the old allegory, the serpent bites its own tail, and when the death agony of one life comes into contact with the sensations of love which begin another life?

In the idea of the interrelation of love and death may lie the explanation of many of the incomprehensible phenomena of our life. Many allegories in ancient teachings, which are obscure to us, may refer to the same idea: such are the relation between death and resurrection in the Mysteries, the idea of mystical death and mystical birth, and so on. In ancient teachings and cults the words " death " and " birth " contained some strange enigma. These words had not one but several meanings. Sometimes " birth " signified death, sometimes " death " signified birth.

The idea may have two meanings. The first is from the point of view of eternal recurrence: death, that is, the end of one life, is birth, the beginning of another life. And the second meaning, which is much more complex, is that death on our plane of being may be birth on some other, " superhuman," plane of being.

But here it is necessary to proceed very carefully in order to avoid the " spiritualistic " understanding of death as birth and birth as death, when physical death is regarded as birth on the " astral " plane, in the world of spirits, and death in the world of spirits is regarded as birth on our plane; while at the same time a " spirit " differs very little from man, or even does not differ at all in his inner characteristics.

The idea of the ancient Mysteries is certainly far from such a "two-dimensional" view. The essence of the idea of the Mysteries lies in the analogy of the incomprehensible *new birth* with the circumstances of man's physical birth on earth. Two sides are particularly emphasised here: first, the passing of one into a new life simultaneously with the death of many and, second, the enormous difference between that which dies and that which is born, that is, between the germ or the seed and the human being who is born from it and who in his turn is a germ or a seed of another, a higher being, differing from him as much as man differs from the seed. Death is death. Death is not birth. But death contains the possibility of birth. Moreover, birth, taking place on some different plane, cannot be visible or comprehensible on the plane on which death takes place. This was the content of the Mysteries concerning death and birth. People, as was pointed out earlier (see ch. IV), were regarded as "grains," as "seeds," in the most real sense. The whole of their life was nothing but the life of "seeds," that is, a life which has no meaning by itself and which contains only one important moment — *birth*, i.e. the death of the seed.

This was the secret which was revealed to the initiated. The idea was that having learned, that is, having fully understood and felt, this secret, the man could no longer remain as he was before. The new understanding began to work within by itself, to give new meaning to the whole of life and to guide his own life and activities along a new path.

If we could accept the idea of man as a seed and if we could find confirmation of it as a theory, this would radically change all our conceptions of man and humanity and would explain at once many things at which before we have only dimly guessed.

The life which we know, in itself contains no aim. This is the reason why there is so much that is strange, incomprehensible and inexplicable in it. And indeed it cannot be explained by itself. Neither its sufferings nor its joys, neither its beginning nor its end, nor its greatest achievements, have any meaning. All these are either a preparation for some other, future, life, or merely nothing. By itself life here, on our plane, has no value, no meaning and no point. It is too short, too unreal, too ephemeral, too illusory, for anything to be demanded of it, for anything to be built upon it, for anything to be created out of it. Its whole meaning lies in another, a new, a future, life, which follows upon "birth."

Does not this appear as the inner meaning of religious teachings of esoteric origin, particularly of Christianity? And does it not explain all that especially strikes us in life as incongruous and incompatible?

If we, that is humanity, are only seeds, only germs, there cannot, nor could there possibly be, any meaning in our life on this plane. The whole meaning lies in birth and in another, a *future*, life.

But "birth" on that plane, i.e. on the plane of an unknown new level of being, is neither accidental nor mechanical. This new birth cannot be the result of solely external causes and conditions, as birth on our plane of being seems to be. The new birth is a matter of *will*, a matter of the desire and efforts of the " grain " itself.

This was the basis of the idea of " initiation," which led to birth, and also of the idea of " salvation " and attainment to " eternal life." " Eternal life " is a term which has several meanings. And it seems to contain a contradiction: on the one hand " eternal life " belongs not only to all people but even to everything that exists, while on the other hand it is necessary to be born again in order to obtain it. This contradiction would be inexplicable, if the difference between the fifth and the sixth dimensions had not been previously established. Both the one and the other are *eternity*. But one is unalterable repetition, always with the same end, and the other is escape from this repetition.

Thus we see two ideas of *birth:* birth on the same plane, continuation of life; and birth on another plane, regeneration, transformation, escape from the first plane. This *escape* may imply so many new facts which are quite unknown and inconceivable on our plane that we can have no clear idea about the consequences of escape.

Birth, in the ordinary sense of the word, is connected with sex, i.e. with the division of the sexes and with their attraction to one another, with " love." This attraction of the sexes to one another constitutes one of the chief motive forces in life, and its intensity and the forms of its manifestation determine almost all other characteristics and qualities in man.

As a rule, the stronger a man or woman, the greater the attraction that draws them to the opposite sex. The richer a man or woman is intellectually and emotionally, the greater is their understanding and appreciation of sex and all that is connected with sex. If there are exceptions they are very rare, and therefore they only prove the rule.

But even the most general view of the rôle of sex in life reveals the fact that the original aim of sex — that is, the continuation of life, or birth — recedes and is lost amid the clamour, the flash and sparkle, of the emotions created by this eternal attraction and repulsion between the sexes.

From the ordinary point of view, in creating love, that is, in creating the division of the sexes and everything connected with it, nature has only one aim — the continuation of life. But even from the ordinary point of view it is perfectly clear, and there can be no doubt about it, that nature has created in man much more " love " than is actually necessary for the purpose of the continuation of life. All this surplus of love must be used up somehow. And under ordinary conditions it is used up by being transformed into other emotions and other kinds of energy, which often are contradictory, harmful from the point of view of evolution, pathological, incompatible with one another, and destructive.

If it were possible to calculate how small a proportion of sex energy is actually used for the continuation of life, we should understand the basic principle of many of the actions of nature. Nature creates an immense pressure, an immense tension, in order to attain a certain aim, but in actual fact uses for the attainment of this aim only an infinitesimal fraction of the energy created. And yet without this immense inflow of force the original aim would probably not be attained, and nature would be unable to make people serve her and continue their species to serve her. People would begin to bargain with nature, to make conditions, to demand concessions, to ask alleviations; and nature would have to yield. The guarantee against this is the surplus of energy which blinds a man, makes him a slave, forces him to serve the purposes of nature in the belief that he is serving himself, his own passions, his own desires; or, on the contrary, it makes man believe that he is serving the purposes of nature, while in reality he serves his own passions and desires.

Apart from the first and obvious aim, the continuation of life and the securing of this continuation, sex serves two more aims of nature. And the existence of these two aims explains why the energy of sex is created in much greater quantity than is necessary for the continuation of life.

One of these aims is the keeping up of the " breed," the preservation of the species at a definite level, that is, what is ordinarily called " evolution," though " evolution " is usually endowed with other properties which in reality it does not possess. But what is possible in the sense of " evolution " and what actually exists, exists at the expense of the energy of sex. If the energy of sex in the particular " breed " is lacking, degeneration begins.

The other, far more deeply hidden, aim of nature is evolution in the true meaning of the word, that is, the development of man in the direction of the acquisition by him of higher consciousness and the opening up of his latent forces and faculties. The explanation of this latter possibility in connection with the using of sex energy for this purpose forms the content and meaning of all esoteric teachings. Thus sex contains not only two but three aims, three possibilities.

Before we pass to the third aim, that is, to the possibility of real evolution, or the attainment of higher consciousness, we will examine the second, that is, the preservation of the species.

If we take man and try to determine, on the basis of all our biological knowledge, what in man is the indication of the " breed," that is, the indication of the preservation of species, we shall obtain an exact and very significant answer.

In a human being, both in man and in woman, there are definite anatomical and physiological traits of the " breed," and a high development of these traits points to a sound type, whereas a weak expression or a wrong expression of them definitely points to a *degenerating* type.

These traits are the so-called *secondary sex-characters*.

Secondary sex-characters is the name applied to features and qualities which though not indispensable for the normal existence of the sex functions, that is, for all the sensations and phenomena connected with these functions, are nevertheless closely connected with the primary characters. This is shown by the fact that secondary characters depend upon the primary, that is, they are immediately modified, become weaker or even disappear, in the case of the weakening of direct functions or injury to the sex organs, that is, in case of change of the primary characters.

Secondary characters are all those features, apart from the sex organs themselves, which make man and woman different from and unlike one another. These features are difference in the lines of the body (independently of the anatomical structure of the skeleton), a different distribution of muscles and fat on the body, difference in movements, different distribution of hair on the body, a different voice, difference in instincts, sensations, tastes, temperament, emotions, reaction to external stimuli, etc.; and further, a different mentality, all that makes up feminine psychology and masculine psychology.

Academic biology does not attach sufficient importance to the study of secondary characters, and there is a tendency to limit the application of this term to those characters only which are very closely connected with sex functions. But in medicine the study of secondary characters and of their alterations often serves as a basis for the right distinguishing of various pathological states and for right diagnosis. It has been established beyond doubt for both man and woman that a weakening or an anatomical change of the essential parts of the sex organs, or their injury, leads to a complete alteration of the external type and to a change in the secondary characters, different for men and women, but in both cases following a certain definite system. That is to say, in a man, an injury to his sex organs and the derangement of their functions cause him to resemble either a child or an old woman, and in a woman the same thing causes her to resemble a man.

This gives the possibility of the converse conclusion, namely, that a type differing from the normal type, that is, a man with the features, properties and characters of a woman, or a woman with the features, properties and characters of a man, indicates, firstly, degeneration and, secondly, wrong development (that is, usually under-development) of the primary characters.

Thus normal development of sex is a necessary condition of a rightly developing type, and abundance and richness of secondary characters points to an improving, an ascending type.

The decline of the type, the decline of the " breed," always means the weakening and alteration of secondary characters, that is, the appearance of masculine characters in a woman and feminine characters in a man. " Intermediate sex " is the most characteristic phenomenon of degeneration.

Normal development of sex is necessary for the preservation and improvement of the " breed."

The second aim of nature which is attained in this case is perfectly clear. And it is clear that the surplus of sex energy is used precisely for the improvement of the breed.

The third aim of nature connected with sex, that is the evolution of man towards superman, differs from the first two aims in that it requires conscious actions on the part of the man himself, and a definite orientation of his whole life, an idea of which is given by the systems of Yoga.

Almost all the occult teachings which recognise the possibility of the "evolution" or transformation of man see the basis of this possible transformation in the *transmutation*, that is, in the conversion of certain matters or energies into quite different matters or energies, *in this case in the transformation of sex energy into energy of a higher order.*

This is the inner meaning, sometimes deeply hidden, sometimes almost obvious, of many occult teachings, of theories of alchemy, of various forms of mysticism, of Yoga systems, and the like.

In all teachings that admit the possibility of the change and inner growth of an individual man, that is, evolution not in a biological or anthropological sense, but as applying to the individual, this evolution is always based on the transmutation of sex energy. The utilisation of this energy, which is wasted unproductively in ordinary life, creates in a man's soul the force which leads him to the superhuman. There is no other force in man which could replace sex energy. All other energies, intellect, will, feeling, feed on the surplus of sex energy, grow out of it and live by it. The mystical birth of man, of which many systems speak, is based on transmutation, that is, on the transmutation of sex energy.

There are many occult and religious systems which not only recognise this, but attempt to give practical directions as to how to curb the energy of sex and how to subject it to the interests of inner evolution. These directions are usually utterly fantastic and cannot give any results, because they omit something which is most vital and most necessary. Nevertheless, the study of such theories and methods presents a certain interest from the psychological and historical point of view.

But before coming to the study of the ideas of *transmutation*, both in their right form (from the very few existing sources) and in their wrong form (from the very numerous sources), it is necessary to elucidate certain aspects of the biology and functioning of sex when it fulfils the two first designs of nature. Namely, it is necessary to establish whether sex in itself evolves. Can forms of evolving sex be found in man? Does the evolution of sex exist, that is, the evolution of primary characters and evolution of sex functions, and what does the evolution of sex functions mean?

If evolution of sex exists, there should be forms lower than the form we consider normal, and there should be forms higher than the form we consider normal. What then is the lower form and what is the higher form?

The moment we ask ourselves this question we are confused and perplexed by the ordinary conceptions of naïve Darwinism and of the usual "evolutionary" theories, which tell us of "lower" forms of sex in "lower" organisms, in plants, etc., of the propagation of fungi and the like. But all this is quite outside the scope of the question we have set ourselves. We are dealing only with man, and we must think only of man.

In examining the question before us we must try to establish what constitutes normal sex in man, then determine the lower forms of the sex life of man, that is, the forms which correspond to a degenerating type or to a type arrested in its development, and then determine the higher, that is, evolving, forms, if such forms exist.

The difficulty of defining normal sex is created first of all by the indeterminateness of the characteristics and properties of " lower sex," also by the complete absence of any understanding of what " higher sex " may be, and, further, at times even by the confusing of the lower with the higher, of the degenerating with the evolving.

Taking all this into consideration, it is necessary, before attempting to define normal sex, to determine lower sex, or *infra-sex*. A beginning has to be made with infra-sex because an understanding of supra-sex can be arrived at only through the elimination of everything that is determined first as infra-sex, and second as normal sex.

It is comparatively easy to establish infra-sex, if we take as its chief characteristic arrested development or a degeneration which has begun or is beginning.

But the detection of infra-sex is impeded by the variety and contradictory character of the forms in which infra-sex is manifested, and especially by the fact that some of these forms, from the ordinary point of view, appear to be a *strengthening* and an exaggerated development of sex energy, sex desires and sex sensations.

Therefore from the very beginning infra-sex must be divided into two categories, obvious degeneration and hidden degeneration.

To the first category of infra-sex belong most declining forms of manifestation of sex such as all obvious sex abnormalities: that is underdeveloped sex, all perversions, in the sense of either abnormal sex desires or abnormal sex abstinence; disgust of sex, fear of sex, indifference to sex, interest in one's own sex, though the latter has quite a different meaning in men from what it has in women, and in women it is not necessarily a sign of infra-sex.

To the second category of infra-sex belong cases which are often connected with heightened intensity of sex life, which while externally appearing to be normal, though exaggerated, in reality also point to inner degeneration. This category of infra-sex will be dealt with later.

For all categories of infra-sex the fundamental characteristic is the absence of coordination between the idea of sex and the ideas of other normal functions of man. Sex always leads people of infra-sex either into " temptation," or " sin," or crime, or insanity, or debauchery.

For normal man or woman sex contains no danger. In a normal human being sex harmonises with all other functions, including the emotional and intellectual, and even with the desire for the miraculous, if such exists in the soul of a man. A man's thoughts, emotions, aspirations, none of them contradict sex, nor does sex contradict them. Sex inwardly is completely justified in normal man, and this justification is based solely on the full

458   SEX AND EVOLUTION

coordination of sex with the intellectual and emotional functions.

But if a man is born abnormal or becomes abnormal a negative attitude towards sex and condemnation of sex almost always grow within him.

Abnormalities may be very different. There may be total impotence, incapacity both for external function and for sensation. There may be capacity for sensation connected with incapacity for external function, that is, the presence of desires, but the impossibility of satisfying them. There may be capacity for external function connected with complete absence of sensation. There may be capacity for sensation only on the condition of abnormal external functions. In all these cases sex sensations are accompanied by a feeling of disharmony between sex and other sides of inner life, particularly with the higher, or those which are taken to be the higher; and as a result there arises a non-understanding of sex, terror of sex and disgust of sex.

Infra-sex which condemns sex and repels it as " offence " represents a very curious phenomenon in the life and in the history of humanity.

In this case sex and all that refers to sex is declared to be sin. Woman is the instrument of the devil, man is the devil, the tempter. The ideal of " purity " is sexual impotence, infantile, senile or pathological, which in this case is manifested either in " abstinence," taken for an act of will, or in " absence of interest " towards sex, which is explained by the prevalence of other, " spiritual," interests.

In people of infra-sex sex is sometimes more easily subordinated to intellectual and emotional tendencies (usually of a negative character) than in a normal man or woman. Sex has no independent existence in a being of infra-sex, or in any case it differs greatly from sex in a normal man or woman.

To a man of infra-sex, therefore, a normal man appears as a man possessed by some incomprehensible and hostile force. And a man of infra-sex considers it his duty to struggle with this force in other people, because he believes that he has conquered it in himself.

And this really explains the whole mechanism of the influence that infra-sex has on life.

Among other people the people of infra-sex appear the most moral, in religion the most saintly. It is easy for them to be moral and it is easy to be saintly. Of course it is pseudo-morality and pseudo-saintliness, but people generally live with pseudo-values, and only extremely few wish to find real values.

It is necessary to understand that almost all the morality which has been imposed upon the human race, almost all the laws controlling sex life, almost all the restrictions guiding people's choice and decision in these cases, all taboos, all fears: all these have come from infra-sex. Infra-sex, precisely in virtue of its difference from normal sex, in virtue of its inability to become normal and in virtue of its non-understanding of normal sex, began to regard itself as superior, began to dictate laws to normal sex.

This does not mean that all morals, all laws and all restrictions relating to sex were wrong. But, as always occurs in life when right ideas come from the wrong source, together with what is right they bear within them a great deal that is wrong, that contradicts their fundamental essence, that brings about new confusions and new complications.

In the whole history of mankind it is impossible to find a more striking example of pathological forms making laws for normal forms; unless we take a broader view and realise that in fact the whole history of mankind is nothing but the rule of pathological forms over normal. Moreover, it is very characteristic that while infra-sex continually holds in suspicion and mercilessly condemns normal sex and its manifestations, it shows much more tolerance towards pathological perverted forms.

Thus infra-sex always finds an excuse and a justification for people of "intermediate sex" and for their tendencies, as well as for various abnormal means of sexual satisfaction. Of course people of abnormal inclinations are by this very fact people of infra-sex. But they are not aware of this and often are definitely proud of their difference from people of normal sex which they regard as "coarse" and "animal," lacking the refinement they ascribe to themselves. There are even theories which regard "intermediate sex" as the result of evolution.

All that has been said until now refers only to one category of infra-sex, although in this category there can clearly be seen several forms, from impotence to homosexuality.

The other category of infra-sex does not include either impotence or unnatural inclinations. And, as was pointed out earlier, manifestations of this category, with the exception of extremes bordering on obvious insanity, are not usually taken as abnormal.

Phenomena of this category can be divided into two groups.

To the first group belong those manifestations of sex which are coloured with what may be called the psychology of the lupanar. And to the second group belong those manifestations of sex which are characterised by their close relation to oppressive and morbid emotions of a violent or despondent character.

Both groups can be explained by the fact that sex and all that relates to sex possesses the capacity to connect itself with the most contradictory sides of a human being.

In the first group sex is connected with what is lowest in man. For such a man sex is surrounded with an atmosphere of uncleanness. A man speaks and thinks of sex with unclean words and unclean thoughts. At the same time he is a slave to sex and is aware of his slavery, and it appears to him that all other people are slaves, just as he is. He mentally throws dirt on sex and on everything connected with sex, invents indecent anecdotes or likes to listen to them. His whole life is full of obscene language; everything is as unclean to him as he is himself. If he does not degrade sex he derides it, takes it as a joke, *tries to find something comic in sex.*

This looking for the comic in sex, the introduction of laughter into sex, gives rise to a special kind of pseudo-art — *pornography*, which is characterised precisely by derision of sex.

Without this derision erotic art, even in its very extreme forms, may be quite normal and legitimate, as it was, for instance, in the Greek and Roman worlds, in ancient India, in Persia at the period of the flourishing of Sufism, etc. The absence of erotic art, or wrong forms of it, points, on the contrary, to the very low moral level of the particular culture and to the preponderance of infra-sex.

Infra-sex in all its manifestations of course tries to confuse erotic art with pornography. For infra-sex there is no difference between these two phenomena.

With regard to normal sex, it is necessary to point out that there is no laughter in it. The function of sex cannot be *comic*, it cannot be an *object of joke*. This is one of the characteristics of normal sex.

To continue the enumeration of the features of that form of infra-sex which is characterised by the psychology of the lupanar, it may be said that this form is determined by the separation of sex from other functions, and by the antagonism of sex to all other functions. For the intellectual and for the emotional life, even merely for physical activity (in the case of the people of this form of infra-sex), sex is only an impediment, an obstacle, a waste of force, a waste of energy. This waste of energy in sex functions and the realisation of this waste is one of the distinctive traits of the form of infra-sex in question.

In normal sex this waste does not exist, since energy is immediately renewed because of the richness and positive character of the sensations, thoughts and emotions connected with sex.

The form of infra-sex in question is often very active in its manifestations in life, and is widespread. Owing to many peculiarities in our life, especially owing to the power of the abnormal over the normal and of the "lower" over the "higher," many people who do not in fact belong to infra-sex learn about sex only from people of this form of infra-sex, in words and expressions belonging to this form of infra-sex, and they at once receive a shock from sex as from something unclean. They are repelled by the psychology of the lupanar, but they cannot throw off the impression they have received, they begin to believe that there is nothing else, and the whole of their own mentality in relation to sex becomes coloured and impregnated with distrust, suspicion, fear and repugnance.

And their fears and their repugnance in relation to this form of the manifestations of sex would be very well grounded if only they knew that the abnormal cannot be taken as the law for the normal and that in avoiding the abnormal it is important not to sacrifice the normal.

Sex in this form is very closely related to crime, and actually in life a criminal character, criminal tendencies, are scarcely ever met with apart

from this form of infra-sex. Even in ordinary scientific psychology this form
of sex manifestation, which is devoid of any connection with moral feeling,
is defined as the lower or the animal. And it is the prredominance of this
form of infra-sex in life which above all shows the level on which humanity
stands.

In the second group of manifestations of this category of infra-sex, that
is, in the group in which sex functions are not decreased but on the contrary are even increased in comparison with the normal, sex is connected
with all that is violent and cruel in a man.

A man of this form of infra-sex seems continually to be walking on the
edge of a precipice. Sex and all emotions belonging to sex become in him
inevitably connected with irritation, suspicion and jealousy; at any moment
he may find himself completely in the power of a sense of injury, insulted
pride, a frightened sense of ownership; and there are no forms of cruelty and
violence of which he is not capable in order to avenge his " outraged honour " or " injured feelings."

All kinds of crimes of passion without exception belong to this form of
infra-sex.

In Chapter X were quoted the words of Prof. Chwolson, who wrote that
" many efforts and prolonged work on oneself are necessary " in order to
become accustomed to the teaching of relativity. But a much greater mental effort is needed in order to see " infra-sex " and nothing else in all the
crimes and murders that are committed from jealousy, from suspicion, from
desire for revenge, etc.

But if we make this effort, and realise that in the figure of Othello for
instance, there is nothing but pathology, that is, abnormal and perverted
emotions, then the lies by which humanity has lived and lives become clear
to us.

The difficulty of understanding the nature of this particular category of
infra-sex is created by the continual embellishment of, and the desire to en-
noble and justify, all manifestations of violence and degenerate emotions
connected with sex and with crimes of passion. All the power of the hypnosis
of art and literature is directed towards the glorification of these emotions
and these crimes. It is this hypnosis which above all stands in the way of
the right understanding of things and makes people who do not belong to
infra-sex at all consider themselves obliged to think, feel and act like people of infra-sex.

All that has been said about infra-sex can be summarised in the following propositions:

The first category of infra-sex, from impotence to perversions, borders
on manias and phobias, that is, on pathological proclivities and pathological
fears; the second category, in its first, animal, form, is nearer to idiocy, to
absence of moral feeling; and in its second, more violent, form it has resem-

blance to delusional insanity or homicidal mania, and even in its milder manifestations is full of fixed ideas and fixed mental images, which are accompanied or evoked by tormenting and violent emotions.

So far I have spoken chiefly of infra-sex, but I have incidentally pointed out certain features of normal sex.

Normal sex, being the complete opposite of infra-sex, is first of all entirely coordinated with other sides of man's life and with his highest manifestations. It does not stand in their way and does not take energy from them; the energy used in the functioning of normal sex is immediately replaced owing to the richness of the sensations and impressions which are received by the intellect, the consciousness and the feeling. Further, in normal sex there is nothing that can be the subject of laughter, or that can be connected with anything that may be negative in man. On the contrary it repels, as it were, everything that is negative, and this in spite of the very great intensity of sensations and feelings connected with it.

It does not follow that a man of normal sex is free from sufferings or disappointments connected with sex life. So far from that, these sufferings may be very intense and acute, but they are never caused by the inner discord between sex and other functions, especially intellectual or higher emotional functions, as is the case in infra-sex. Normal sex is coordinated and harmonious, but life is not coordinated and is not harmonious; therefore normal sex may often bring much suffering. But a man of normal sex does not blame other people for his sufferings and does not try to make others suffer.

In his feeling there is a great understanding of the inevitability and fatality of everything connected with sex, and it is this understanding of inevitability that helps him to find a way through the maze of contradictory emotions.

The contradictory and uncoordinated nature of many emotions connected with sex, apart from the influence of life in general and of various kinds of infra-sex, is often due, in people of normal sex, to a different cause. This cause has hardly been touched upon by European psychology, though at the same time it is perfectly clear to ordinary observation. This cause is the difference between types. Science has approached and is approaching from different sides the idea of the difference of types, but the fundamental principles of this difference are as yet unknown. Until quite recently the old division into " four temperaments " with certain modifications was admitted. Some time ago there were established different " types of memory " such as " auditory," " visual," " narrative," and so on; at present there are established four *types of blood*; in endocrinology there are attempts to divide men into types according to their " formulæ " or according to their " constellations," that is, according to the combination of inner secretions working in them. But all this is as yet very far from the recognition of the radical and essential difference between various types of people, and from the actual establishing of these types. Exact and complete knowledge of types exists only in esoteric doctrines and therefore does not enter into the scope of the present subject. All that can be established by means of ordinary observation is confined to the fact that in relation to the life of sex both men and women are divided into a certain number, and not a very large number, of fundamental types. For every type of one sex there is one or several positive types of the opposite sex, which arouse desire, then several indifferent, and several definitely negative, that is repellent, types. In connection with this, complicated combinations are possible, when, for instance, a certain type of woman is positive for a certain type of man, but the given type of man is either negative or indifferent for the given type of woman, and vice versa. In this case a union between two wrongly assorted types produces both external and internal manifestations of infra-sex of one of the categories enumerated above. This means that for the normal manifestation of sex there is necessary not only a normal state in both man and woman, but the union of two corresponding types.

For a right understanding of esoteric theories concerning sex it is necessary to have at least a general conception of the rôle and significance of "types" in the life of sex.

From the ordinary point of view people, both men and women, are considered to be much more alike than they really are and much freer in their decisions and in their choice, which seems to be unrestricted except by general conditions of life, division of classes, and so on. In reality, even with the help of generally known psychological material it is possible to understand how the division of types is manifested in life and how people depend on this division.

The "strangeness of love" has always occupied men's imagination. Why does this man love this woman, and not that one? And why does the woman love another man and not this, and so on?

> " Ein Jüngling liebt ein Mädchen,
>   Die hat einen Andern erwählt;
>   Der Andre liebt eine Andre." . . .

Where is the end and where the beginning in this strange game of attractions, feelings, moods, sensations, vanities and disappointments? The answer is: only in the division of types.

In order to understand the principle of this division it is necessary to realise that for every man all the women in the world are divided into several categories, according to the degree of their potential physical and emotional influence upon him and quite independently of his or their expressed tastes, sympathies and inclinations.

Women of the first category, of whom there are very few for each man, arouse in him the maximum of feeling, desire, imagination and dreaming. They attract him irresistibly, regardless of any barriers and obstacles, often to his great astonishment and, in the case of mutual love, arouse in him the maximum of sensation. Such women remain ever new and ever unknown. A man's curiosity about them never weakens, and their love never becomes for him ordinary, possible or explicable. There always remains in it an element of the miraculous and the impossible. And there is no fading of his own feeling.

Women of the second category, of whom there are many more for a man, also attract him, but in these cases his feelings are more easily controlled by reason or by external conditions. It is a calmer love, which is more easily fitted into conventional forms, both inner and outer, may pass more easily into a feeling of friendship or sympathy and can fade and disappear, but always leaving a warm memory behind it.

Women of the third category leave a man indifferent. If they are young and attractive they can affect his imagination, not directly, however, but through some other life interest, such as pride, vanity, material considerations, community of interests, sympathy, friendship. But this feeling, having come from without, does not endure long and fades. The sensations are weak and colourless. The first satisfactions usually exhaust all interest. Sometimes, if the first sensations were sufficiently vivid, they can change into their opposites, antipathy, hostility and the like.

Women of the fourth category interest a man still less. They also can attract him in certain cases, or he may deceive himself and think that they attract him. But physical relations with them contain a tragic element. A *man does not feel them at all.* The continuation of intimacy with them is a mechanical violation of self and may bear heavily upon the nerves, produce impotence and various other phenomena of infra-sex.

It must of course be understood that a woman belonging to one category for one man may belong to a quite different category for another man, and that the number of categories may be larger or smaller for different people.

Women are in exactly the same position; for them also there are different categories of men; and just as little depends on their own intellectual or emotional decision and choice. Both the choice and the decision are made for them. No moral principles, no feeling of duty, affection, gratitude, friendship, sympathy, pity, no community of ideas and no community of interests, can create a *sensation* when it is not there, or stand in its way when it is there; that is, nothing can change anything in this truly iron law of types.

In ordinary life, owing to the many external influences which control people's lives, the law of the attraction and repulsion of types becomes partly modified, but in one direction only. This means that even the right and corresponding types may be repelled by one another and not feel one another under the influence of emotional conflicts and difference in tastes and understanding. But wrong and non-corresponding types cannot ever or in any circumstances feel one another. Moreover, even the slightest element of infra-sex either in the man or in the woman brings their relations, their feelings and their sensation of one another down to a lower category, or even completely destroys all that was positive in them.

If any escape from the law of the action of types is at all possible, it is possible only through following the principles of Karma-Yoga and with the condition of a full understanding of the nature of the difference between types. But this relates to the life of those who see or are beginning to see.

In ordinary life in general the leading principle is blindness. But this blindness is particularly striking in relation to questions of sex. Thus in ordinary understanding the idea is not admitted, and is even entirely unknown, that in the case of wrong combination of types one of them or both *will not feel the other at all*. Further, it is not taken into consideration that there is nothing more painful and more immoral than sex relations *without sensations;* also that the degree and the quality of the sensations can be very different. The fact of the possible absence of sex sensations in sex relations is of course known, but it is not regarded as dependent upon types. This is not taken into consideration at all, undoubtedly owing to the influence of infra-sex upon life.

Nevertheless, people realise the danger of a wrong choice. And the intention to avoid the consequences of a wrong choice and entrust the choice to one who knows more lies at the basis of the esoteric idea of the " marriage sacrament " which has to be performed by the " initiate."

The true rôle of the " initiate " certainly did not consist in performing a mechanical ceremony which allowed people to have sex relations. And people came to the initiate not for this ceremony, but for advice, for the final decision. The initiate determined their types, determined whether they were suited to one another or not, gave advice and decided whether the particular marriage could take place or not. Such was or such may have been " the marriage sacrament." But of course all this was forgotten long ago together with the teaching on types and the idea of esoteric knowledge.

Poets have always been aware of the other side of the idea and have sung of the irresistible force which attracts inwardly related types to one another, types whom nothing can part and nothing can prevent from striving towards each other. When such types meet the result is a case of ideal and eternal love which gives material to poets for thousands of years.

This idea of the mutual gravitation of inwardly related types constitutes the inner meaning of the allegory in Plato's " Symposium " about people's severed halves seeking one another.

But in actual life the dreams of poets and philosophers are very seldom realised, and in the conditions of our discordant existence the meeting of the most suitable types is, on the contrary, a very dangerous event, because of the accumulation of stormy emotions, and almost invariably ends in tragedy, and in Plato's *halves* again losing one another.

The teaching on types is of the highest importance because normal sex can manifest itself rightly, and in a certain sense " evolve," only with a successful combination of types. It is also necessary to understand that the division of types, in itself, is the result of " evolution," because among more primitive people the types are divided less markedly and completely, so that strongly expressed type is a kind of secondary character.

We must now try to establish what higher sex may be and whether any forms actually exist which can be considered as belonging to supra-sex.

But it is not an easy task to define supra-sex. To be more precise, the scientific material at our disposal contains no data for such a definition. And for material bearing on this question it is necessary to turn to esoteric doctrines. All that it is possible to do, using the ordinary and generally accessible material, is to determine *what is not* supra-sex, because, though ordinary thought does not contain the notions of infra-sex and supra-sex, the idea of them is very near to it, and, as it were, continually rises up behind ordinary conceptions. And very often in thinking of sex functions, people divide them, for instance, into purely " animal " or " physical " manifestations, which they look upon as infra-sex, as it were, and " spiritualised " manifestations, which for them take the place of supra-sex; or they introduce the idea of " love " as opposed to " sex feeling " or " sex instinct."

In other words, the ideas of infra-sex and supra-sex are not so far from our thought as might at first appear. In fact people always use these ideas in thinking about sex, but very often associate them with totally wrong images and conceptions.

Moreover, and this is particularly important, certain forms of infra-sex are often taken for supra-sex. This happens because people, dimly realising the difference in manifestations of sex but actually encountering besides normal sex only infra-sex, have taken the degeneration of sex for the evolution of sex.

In this case they have followed the line of least resistance, submitting to the influence of infra-sex. And having taken infra-sex for supra-sex, they have begun to regard normal sex from the standpoint of infra-sex, as something anomalous, unclean, hindering the salvation or the liberation of man.

It is only in those esoteric doctrines which have not passed through ecclesiastical and scholastic forms or have been preserved in their pure sense beneath the layers of ecclesiastical and scholastic forms, that traces of teaching on sex can be found which are worth attention. In order to discover these traces it is necessary to re-examine what is to be found on this subject in the doctrines of esoteric origin that are known to us.

From the standpoint of esoteric doctrines the outward aim of sex, that is, the continuation of life, and also the perfecting of breed by the development of secondary characters, is regarded as mechanically assured, and the whole attention of these doctrines is turned towards the hidden aim, that is, the possibility of a *new birth*, which on the contrary is not assured at all.

To return to the idea of transmutation of the intentional using of sex energy for the purposes of inner evolution, it must be noted that all the systems that recognise transmutation and the rôle of sex in transmutation may be divided into two categories.

To the first belong those systems which admit the possibility of the transmutation of sex energy in conditions of normal sex life and normal expenditure of sex energy.

To the second belong those systems which admit the possibility of transmutation only on the condition of complete sex abstinence and asceticism.

Whether or not we agree with the fundamental propositions of the theory of transmutation itself, the systems of the second category, that is, those which admit the possibility of transmutation on the condition of asceticism only, are historically more familiar to us and more comprehensible.

The reason for this lies in the fact that the principal religions of cultured humanity of the more recent epoch, Buddhism and Christianity, held and still hold this point of view, that is, that sex life is a hindrance to the salvation of man, or in any case something that can be admitted only as a sad necessity, as a concession to the weakness of man. Judaism also is nearer this point of view than the opposite one, and so is Mahomedanism, which after all is nothing but reformed Judaism liberated only from a spirit of depression and despondency, but preserving almost the whole ethics of Judaism and a rather scornful attitude towards sex.

Buddhism in its essence was a monastic order, and the teachings of Gautama the Buddha were always addressed to monks and contained the exposition of the principles and rules of the shortest way to *Nirvana* as he understood it. Laymen were admitted to Buddhism only later, and only as disciples preparing to become monks. Special rules were made for them, which represented a mitigated monastic discipline. These are the so-called " five precepts," the acceptance of which signifies the embracing of Buddhism. Sex is still admitted here. The third of these precepts reads: " I observe the precept to abstain from unlawful sexual intercourse." This means that there are still certain forms which are considered lawful.

But the next grade of Buddhism — eight precepts — includes a complete renunciation of sex life.

The precept concerning sex reads: " I observe the precept to abstain from sexual intercourse."

That is, the word " unlawful " is omitted or, in other words, all forms of sex life, both abnormal and normal, are regarded as unlawful. Those who have accepted the eight precepts do not necessarily live in monasteries, but they live like monks.

Thus Buddha and his nearest disciples considered the first condition of the transmutation of sex energy — the idea of which must have been clear to them — to be complete abstinence.

Christianity stands very near to Buddhism in this respect, and it is quite possible that this side of Christian teaching developed under the influence of Buddhist preachers. The rôle of the Apostle Paul and the influence of

Judaism in creating the Christian view of sex have been pointed out earlier.

Great significance for the establishing of the Christian view of sex was contained in Christ's enigmatic words:

For there are some eunuchs, which were so born from their mother's womb: and there are some eunuchs, which were made eunuchs of men: and there be eunuchs, which have made themselves eunuchs for the kingdom of heaven's sake. He that is able to receive it, let him receive it (Matt. 19. 12).

With this passage are generally connected the following passages:

And if thy right eye offend thee, pluck it out, and cast it from thee: for it is profitable for thee that one of thy members should perish, and not that thy whole body should be cast into hell.

And if thy right hand offend thee, cut it off, and cast it from thee: for it is profitable for thee that one of thy members should perish, and not that thy whole body should be cast into hell (Matt. 5. 29, 30).

These passages together have given material for many fantastic interpretations, beginning with a condemnation of sex life in general, as something unclean by nature, and ending with the teaching of the castrates and fanatical voluntary castration for the salvation of the soul.

These Gospel passages gave an enormous impulse to infra-sex in the idea of struggle against normal sex.

The true meaning of the above words of Christ cannot be understood without understanding the idea of supra-sex, since Christ spoke of supra-sex.

But, before passing to the examination of what we can know of supra-sex, it is necessary to establish a right view of other teachings on sex which are or were in existence, besides Buddhism and Christianity, that is, it is necessary to understand that the Buddhistic-Christian view on love and sex is by no means the only possible or the only existing view.

There are other forms of religious understanding of sex, in which sex, far from being condemned, is on the contrary regarded as the expression of the Deity in man and is an object of worship.

This is apparent even in modern Indian religions with their rows of lingams in the temples, with the ceremonial dances of an erotic character, and with the erotic images in the temples. I say *even* in modern Indian religions because they are undoubtedly degenerating in this respect and are more and more losing ground as regards their deification of sex. But there is no doubt that till quite recently several cults consisted entirely of the worship of sex and its manifestations.

This view on sex is for us utterly foreign, incomprehensible and strange. For us it is "paganism." We are too much accustomed to the Judaistic-Christian or Buddhist view of sex.

But the religions of Greece and Rome and the still more ancient cults of Crete, Asia and Egypt, also deified sex, and their esoteric doctrines and Mysteries saw the way to transmutation not in opposition to sex, but through sex. Which is the more correct it is impossible to say. We know too little of transmutation, of its possible results. If there are people who attain it, by that very fact they almost immediately leave our field of vision and disappear for us. But one thing can be said without any hesitation: if transmutation is possible, it is possible only for normal sex. None of the forms of infrasex can evolve. Only a grain that is sound can put forth a green shoot. A grain that is rotten within dies but is not born.

However strange it may appear at first sight, the esoteric idea of the dual rôle of sex, and also the idea of transmutation, is much nearer to scientific thought than might be supposed, that is, nearer to *modern* scientific thought than to the scientific thought of, let us say, the 19th century.

A new branch of scientific physiology, which is already developing into a separate science and throwing an entirely new light on other sciences, chiefly on psychology, namely *endocrinology,* or the study of the glands of internal secretion, promises a great deal in the direction of studying and establishing the properties and causes of man's various functions, among them the functions of sex and their relation to other functions.

The starting-point of the doctrine of internal secretions was the work of Claude Bernard on the glycogenic function (1848–57) and Addison's account, in 1849, of the suprarenal capsules. This led to experiments by Brown-Séquard, who, in 1891, introduced the notion of " specific substances " secreted into the blood by the various organs, and also the concept of functional humoral correlation. Two theories were advanced to explain the mechanism of correlation. The first was the theory of " hormones," the presence of which was established experimentally in 1902. The second was the theory connecting the endocrine secretions with the autonomic nervous system. Experiments, both surgical and by injection of gland extracts, were carried out on the adrenals, thyroid, parathyroid, and other glands, although, in the last thirty years, attention has been centred more on the pituitary body, which was visualised as leader of the endocrine system. That the internal secretions control the configuration of the body and are the activators of emotion, is emphasised by many writers. The psychological aspect of endocrinology, from the point of view of the psychological make-up of the individual, appeared later. It should be noted that, at present, opinion is divided as to whether endocrinology should include all parts of the body, on the ground that all organs give off chemical substances to the blood and lymph, or whether it should include only the ductless glands together with certain other glands of internal as well as external secretion.

In what follows, *endocrinology* is taken as the study of the *glands* of internal secretion (and also of the glands of internal and external secretion), that is, as a part of a wider science, *hormonology,* which studies the internal secretions of *all organs.*

According to the data of endocrinology all the physical properties and functions of man: growth, nourishment, structure of the body, functioning of different organs, and also all the psychic life, intellectual and emotional, the whole psychic make-up of a man, his activity, his energy, his strength — all these depend on the properties and on the character of the activity of the glands of internal secretion, which produce motive-power for the working of the organs, the nervous system, the brain, and so on.

All the external characteristics, everything we can see in a man, his height, the structure of the skeleton, the quality of the skin, eyes, ears, hair, voice, respiration, way of thinking, quickness of perception, character, emotionality, will-power, energy, activity, initiative — all these depend on the action of the glands of internal secretion, and, so to speak, reflect their state. Endocrinology has made an enormous stride in the study of man, a stride the true significance of which is as yet far from being appreciated and understood.

Scientific psychology, the development of which came to a complete stop about the end of the 19th century and which in the first decades of the 20th century did not produce *a single* work worthy of attention, is beginning to acquire new force and to revise all its theories from the standpoint of the ideas of endocrinology.

In the works on endocrinology which have already appeared there are some interesting attempts at the interpretation of the fate of historical personages from the point of view of the study of their endocrinological type, that is, of the combination of their internal secretions at different periods of their life.

As an example of such attempts I will refer to two books by Dr. Berman of New York.

In the first of these books, *The Glands Regulating Personality*, Dr. Berman, having indicated the principles of the endocrinological study of man which he follows, takes several historical personages with regard to whom there exist more or less definite data. The first of these is Napoleon, as known by his portraits, by the memoirs of his physicians, and by the data of the autopsy on his body in the island of St. Helena. On the basis of these data Dr. Berman gives, so to speak, an endocrinological history of Napoleon, that is to say, he explains, from his point of view, under the influence of which glands of internal secretion the different periods of Napoleon's life passed. Thus Dr. Berman explains all the failures of Napoleon's last campaigns, ending in the catastrophe of Waterloo, by the weakening of the secretions of the pituitary gland, which became even more accentuated on the island of St. Helena and completely changed his personality.

Later, Dr. Berman takes Nietzsche, Charles Darwin, Oscar Wilde, Florence Nightingale and others.

In his second book, *The Personal Equation*, he examines types which result from a predominance of one or another gland, and considers man as a marionette controlled by glandular secretions.

Dr. Berman's books cannot be called scientific. They are rather fantasies on endocrinological themes. But Dr. Berman's fantasies come very near to the real facts, which are not yet dreamt of in philosophy. From a strictly scientific point of view almost every separate conclusion of Dr. Berman can be refuted or regarded as unproved. And it is quite possible that each *separate* conclusion of Dr. Berman will be refuted, sooner or later. But what will not be refuted, but will on the contrary be established and proved, are the *principles* upon which he bases his reasonings. These principles will remain and will form the foundation for a new understanding of man, that is, new for modern thought, but in reality approaching the esoteric more and more nearly.

In connection with the problem of infra-sex and supra-sex, what is of particular interest is the meaning and rôle of the internal secretion of the *sex glands*, and the effect of this secretion upon all the functions of man and also upon other secretions.

As was established by physiology before the appearance of endocrinology as a separate science, the sex glands are at the same time glands of external and of internal secretion; and the internal secretion of the sex glands is the chief factor in creating and regulating the development of secondary sex-characters. To such an extent is this so that in the case of injured sex glands or in the case of castration, when internal secretion ceases or is impaired, secondary characters disappear or become modified, and a man becomes a degenerate type of infra-sex.

Thus modern science not only admits the dual rôle of sex, but bases a great deal on it, recognising in the internal secretion of the sex glands the necessary factor for the right functioning of the whole organism, and in the change or in the weakening of this secretion the cause of the weakening and deterioration of all other functions.

The internal secretion of the sex glands is the *transmutation* already recognised by science. The normal life of the organism and the conservation of secondary characters depend on this transmutation. Every weakening of the secondary characters points to the weakening of the transmutation; a considerable weakening or a cessation of transmutation produces *infra-sex*. The esoteric idea differs from the modern scientific view only in the admission of the possibility of the transmutation being increased and brought to a degree of totally incomprehensible and unknown intensity, which creates a new type of man.

If this new type of man belongs to *supra-sex*, what then does supra-sex mean?

Attempts at the endocrinological study of historical personages, as well as clinical investigations, establish quite clearly the facts of infra-sex, their origin, causes and effects. But they say nothing about supra-sex.

Where then can material for the judging of supra-sex be looked for?

On the horizon of our history we see two superhuman figures — Gautama the Buddha and Christ. Whether we take them as real men who actually existed, or as myths, as creations of popular fancy or esoteric thought, we find in them common features.

The story of the life of Gautama the Buddha tells us that in his youth Prince Gautama was surrounded by a brilliant court, full of beautiful young women, that he was married and had a son. He abandoned all this when he retired into the desert, and in his later life sex had no part. Except for several apocryphal legends, history has not preserved for us any description of temptations or struggle connected with sex.

Jesus is even more definite from this point of view. We know nothing of his sex life. So far as we know there was no woman in his life. Even in the temptation in the wilderness the devil does not try to seduce him with a woman; the devil shows him the kingdoms of the world in all their glory, promises a miracle, but does not offer love. Evidently by the design, by the idea, of the author who created the drama of Christ, Christ was already beyond these temptations and these possibilities.

We may now ask ourselves whether Christ and the Buddha were not men of supra-sex. There are no grounds which would permit us to classify them as belonging to infra-sex. And at the same time both undoubtedly differed from ordinary men.

Unfortunately we have no information concerning the structure of the body of Jesus and his external characters. All the representations of him of the first centuries are quite arbitrary.

But with regard to the Buddha the position is different, because there exists a very exact and detailed description of the structure of his body and of all his external features and characters.

I mean by this the so-called "thirty-two signs of Buddhahood" and the "eighty minor marks."

Concerning these signs there exists a legend which was in part adopted by the writers of the Gospels in relation to Christ.[1] When the Buddha was born, Asita, the old hermit, came down from the Himalayas to Kapilavastu. When he entered the palace, he offered the Argha sacrifice at the feet of the babe. Then Asita walked three times round the child, took him in his arms and "read" on his body the thirty-two signs of Buddhahood and the eighty minor marks that were visible to his inner sight.

Modern Buddhologists, on the basis of philological and historical researches, consider the "thirty-two signs" to be a later invention. And certainly there can be no doubt that the "thirty-two signs" contain much that is conventional, much mythology, much naïve allegory, and much that has been corrupted in oral transmission, in transcription and in translation.

But in spite of all this an endocrinological study of the thirty-two signs of Buddha would be of enormous interest, and it is not impossible that it would lift for us the veil covering the enigma of supra-sex.

There are several variants of the list of the "thirty-two signs of Buddha-

---

[1] See Chapter IV, p. 139.

hood " or the " thirty-two signs of perfection," as also of the " eighty minor marks." In all cases the translation is very doubtful and there are many different interpretations of different signs.[2]

I will give here only the variant which is accepted in modern popular Buddhist literature. In transcriptions, translations and interpretations many " signs " have completely lost their meaning and significance. But I think that, first, a philological and, second, a psychological, analysis of the more reliable variants may furnish texts, the endocrinological study of which may reveal much that is new and unexpected.

THE THIRTY-TWO SIGNS OF BUDDHAHOOD

1. A well-formed head and forehead.
2. The hair is blue-black and shining. Each curl grows from left to right.
3. Forehead is broad and straight.
4. Has a hair between the two eyebrows, turned to the right; it is as white as snow.
5. The eyelashes are like those of a newly-born calf.
6. Has shining blue-black eyes.
7. Has forty teeth, all even.
8. The teeth are close together.
9. The teeth are pure white.
10. His voice is like that of Maha-Brahma.
11. He has exquisite taste.
12. His tongue is soft and long.
13. His jaws are like those of a lion.
14. Shoulders and arms are beautifully moulded.
15. Seven parts of the body are round and full.
16. The space between the shoulders is well filled out.
17. His skin has a golden colour.
18. His arms are long, so that when he stands without bending his hands can touch his knees.
19. The upper part of his body is like that of a lion.
20. His body is straight like that of Maha-Brahma.
21. From each hair-sac a single hair grows.
22. These hairs bend to the right at the top.
23. The organs of sex are hidden by nature.
24. The calves of his legs are full and round.
25. His legs are like those of a deer.
26. His fingers and toes are slender and of equal length.
27. His heels are long.
28. The instep of his foot is high.

---

[2] *The Thirty-two Signs of Buddhahood.* " Jatakamala," by M. M. Higgins, Colombo (1914).

The Thirty-two Lakshana, Suddharma Pundarika. *Le Lotus de la Bonne Loi* (pp. 553–630), Burnouf.

The Thirty-two Signs of Perfection, Dharma Samgraha (p. 53), Kinjiu Kasawara and Prof. Max Müller.

29. Feet and hands are delicate and long.
30. Fingers and toes are covered with an epidermis.
31. His feet are flat and he stands firmly.
32. Under the soles of his feet two shining wheels appear with a thousand spokes.

What deductions from the point of view of endocrinological theories can be made from a study of the thirty-two signs of Buddhahood? And can any deductions be made? I think this is a matter for specialists. One thing however is undoubted, which is that if we take the thirty-two signs as a real description of a living man, we shall be compelled to say that *such men do not exist*. Buddha combines in himself contradictory features. He has features which seem to point to " femininity," others to " infantilism," and side by side with these there are features which point to an exceptionally strong development of the masculine type. Speaking generally, Buddha's secondary characters are intermixed, and in such combinations they are not met with in life. Buddha is a strange and a *new* type of man. And as it can already be regarded as established that all external features and characters depend upon one or another form of the development of the glands of internal secretion, the picture of the development of Buddha's internal secretions must be something utterly improbable and *new*. Moreover, the internal secretion of the sex glands in his case appears to be not weakened (as it should have been, judging by several characters), but on the contrary intensified to an extreme degree.

If this is transmutation, if this is supra-sex, does it not indicate the course our thought must take in endeavouring to understand the enigma of the evolution of man? And does it not mean that in the process of evolution sex energy, as it were, turns inward within the organism and creates in it a new life, capable of ever new, of *eternal* regeneration?

If this is the way of the transformation (evolution) of man, it means that man is a strange biological type, whose sex period, the period of propagation, belongs to the lower (or middle) phase of transformation. If we imagine a butterfly whose function of propagation, instead of belonging to the butterfly, belonged to the caterpillar, then the butterfly in relation to the caterpillar would be supra-sex. This means that the function of propagation and consequently the function of sex would be unnecessary in the butterfly and would cease to act. This would be the biological scheme of man's stages in evolution. Is this possible? Is this probable? These questions cannot be answered with the material at present available.

But the psychological picture of man's approach to supra-sex is a little clearer for us. There are in life strange emotions and strange sensations, inexplicable from an ordinary point of view, and in love and all sex sensations there is a strange melancholy and a strange sadness. The more a man feels, the stronger in him is this sensation of farewell, this sensation of parting.

This sensation of parting arises from the fact that in a man (or woman) of strong feeling sex sensations awaken certain new states of consciousness, new emotions. And these new emotions change emotions of sex, cause them to fade and disappear.

In this lies the secret of the deep melancholy of the most vivid sex sensations; there is a certain autumnal taste in them, the taste of something that must pass, must die, must cede its place to something else.

This " something else " is the *new consciousness*, for the definition and description of which there are no words, but which, of all we know, only sex sensations approach.

Mystical states possible to men show a very strange relationship between mystical experiences and experiences of sex.

Mystical sensations undoubtedly and incontestably have a taste of sex. To put it more correctly, of all ordinary human experiences only sex sensations approach those which we may call " mystical."

Of all we know in life, only in love is there a taste of the mystical, a taste of ecstasy. Nothing else in our life brings us so near to the limit of human possibilities, beyond which begins the unknown. And in this lies without doubt the chief cause of the terrible power of sex over human souls.

But at the same time sex sensations disappear in the light of mystical experiences.

The first sensations of mystical experiences intensify sex sensations, but the further waves of the light that a man begins to see completely absorb and cause to disappear those small sparks of sensations which before seemed to him a blaze of love and passion.

Consequently, in true mysticism there is no sacrifice of feeling. Mystical sensations are sensations of the same category as the sensations of love, only infinitely higher and more complex. Love, " sex," these are but a foretaste of mystical sensations. It is clear that the *foretaste* must disappear when there comes that which has been anticipated. But it is equally clear that struggle with the foretaste, the sacrifice of the foretaste, the giving up of the foretaste, cannot bring nearer or hasten anything.

Whether the struggle with normal sex is necessary for the attainment of supra-sex, or whether, on the contrary, supra-sex can be attained in the conditions of a normal functioning of sex, is a point on which the ideas of esoteric systems, as has been indicated before, differ very strongly. And as any contradiction between systems of esoteric origin is essentially impossible, this difference can have only one meaning. And this meaning is that there are types of people for whom the attainment of supra-sex is possible only through a struggle against sex, for their sex is not sufficiently coordinated with the other functions and does not evolve by itself; and there are other types of people for whom the attainment of supra-sex is possible without the struggle against sex, because their sex is transformed gradually in accordance with the transformation of the other functions.

Ordinary knowledge has not sufficient material for determining the course of this transformation, nor for determining the essential nature of supra-sex. And only an entirely new study of man, started and conducted on the condition of the abandonment of all petrified theories and principles, can discover the ways to the understanding of true evolution.

1912–1929

INDEX